ADVANCES IN MARINE STRUCTURES

ADVANCES IN MARINE STRUCTURES

Proceedings of an International Conference
held at the Admiralty Research Establishment,
Dunfermline, 20–23 May 1986

Edited by

C. S. SMITH and J. D. CLARKE

Admiralty Research Establishment, Dunfermline, Scotland, UK

ELSEVIER APPLIED SCIENCE
LONDON and NEW YORK

ELSEVIER APPLIED SCIENCE PUBLISHERS LTD
Crown House, Linton Road, Barking, Essex IG11 8JU, England

Sole Distributor in the USA and Canada
ELSEVIER SCIENCE PUBLISHING CO., INC.
52 Vanderbilt Avenue, New York, NY 10017, USA

WITH 57 TABLES AND 364 ILLUSTRATIONS

© ELSEVIER APPLIED SCIENCE PUBLISHERS LTD 1986

© CONTROLLER, HMSO, LONDON 1986—Papers 1, 9, 15, 18,
20, 24, 25, 27, 28, 29 and 30

British Library Cataloguing in Publication Data

Advances in marine structures: proceedings
of an international conference held at the
Admiralty Research Establishment, Dunfermline
20th–23rd May 1986.
1. Offshore structures—Dynamics
I. Title II. Smith, C. S. III. Clarke, J. D.
620'.4162   TC1665

Advances in marine structures.

Papers presented at the International Conference on
Advances in Marine Structures.
  Bibliography: p.
  Includes indexes.
  1. Naval architecture—Congresses. 2. Submarine boats
—Design and construction—Congresses. 3. Offshore
structures—Design and construction—Congresses.
I. Smith, C. S. II. Clarke, J. D. III. International
Conference on Advances in Marine Structures (1986:
Dunfermline, Fife)
VM5.A38 1986   623.8'1   86-24054

ISBN 1-85166-065-8

Printed in Great Britain at the University Press, Cambridge

Preface

The thirty-one papers contained in this volume were presented at an International Conference on Advances in Marine Structures held at the Admiralty Research Establishment, Dunfermline, Scotland, in May 1986. The purpose of the Conference, which attracted a full house of over 150 delegates from 15 nations, was to assemble international experts in the field of marine structures and to provide a forum for exchange of ideas and information, with cross-fertilisation between the naval and non-military fields and the disciplines of ship, submarine and offshore structures. An important aim of the Conference was also to mark the approaching retirement of Bill Kendrick, Head of the Structures Division, ARE, who is widely known as one of the world's leading experts on submarine pressure hull design. Appropriately, the Proceedings include a paper by Bill Kendrick on design of submarine structures.

Papers presented at the Conference covered a wide range of topics including:

   (i) statistical definition of wave action and other forms of load on ships and compliant offshore platforms;
  (ii) vibration analysis;
 (iii) linear and nonlinear finite element methods and their role in design;
 (iv) buckling behaviour and ductile collapse of ships' hulls, cylindrical shells and domes;
  (v) analysis of damage effects and damage tolerance in ships, offshore platforms and pipelines;
 (vi) design against fatigue and fracture in welded structures;
(vii) mechanics of underwater explosions and structural response of ships and submarines;
(viii) unconventional ships including SWATHs and corrugated hulls;
 (ix) developments in welding technology;
  (x) design methodology including probabilistic methods, optimisation techniques, cost minimisation and computer-aided design.

As well as describing the state of the art in most of these problem areas, papers contained in the Proceedings unveil a number of significant new technological developments.

The Conference on Advances in Marine Structures was judged by most participants to have been a lively, technically stimulating and socially enjoyable occasion. Acknowledgements are due to all members of staff at ARE Dunfermline who helped the programme to run smoothly. Thanks, too, are due to all authors, speakers and delegates, with a special tribute to visitors from overseas for whom the Conference provided, we hope, a favourable glimpse of Scotland and a sample of its peculiar sights, sounds and flavours.

C. S. SMITH
J. D. CLARKE

Contents

Shock and Explosion Effects

Design of Marine Structures

Optimisation and Computer Aided Design

Biographical Note

Dr S. B. Kendrick, OBE, DSc, C Eng, FRINA

Bill Kendrick graduated from Nottingham University in 1949 with 1st Class Honours in Mathematics. In 1950, after a year as a stress analyst with the Bristol Aeroplane Company, he joined the Admiralty Research Establishment, Dunfermline, known at that time as the Naval Construction Research Establishment (NCRE) and later as the Admiralty Marine Technology Establishment (AMTE).

Bill's early research was in the analysis of stiffened plates and shells and he soon established an international reputation with pioneering work on general instability of externally pressurised ring-stiffened cylinders. His efforts over the next three decades in building up a systematic approach to the design of submarine structures have established him as one of the world's leading experts in this field and have borne further fruit in a substantial contribution to the new British Standard (BS 5500) for pressure vessels. Bill's name is also well known for his research into explosion mechanics and contributions to the development of finite element analysis.

In 1970, Bill's troubleshooting work on supertanker design on behalf of the Department of Trade and Industry was acknowledged by the award of an OBE and a RINA Gold Medal and in 1986 his accomplishments over the years were recognised in the award of an honorary DSc by Glasgow University.

Bill Kendrick's retirement from ARE in July 1986 brings to an end one phase in a remarkably productive career. He will be missed by his Dunfermline colleagues not only for the achievements which did much to establish ARE's reputation as a centre of excellence, but also for his forceful managerial style, faculty for constructive criticism and irrepressible capacity for innovation. We wish him well in his new role as a consultant and also in his continuing activity as a notable yachtsman, skier and choral performer.

WAVE LOADING IN WARSHIPS

J D Clarke
Admiralty Research Establishment
Dunfermline, Fife, Scotland

ABSTRACT

The factors affecting vertical hull girder bending loads in warships
are considered and results of long term measurements of deck strains are
compared with theoretical predictions. Allowances for non-linear response
and bow slamming in deriving design values for extreme and fatigue loads
are discussed.

INTRODUCTION

The most important loading exerted by the sea on the usually slender
hull of a warship is vertical bending of the hull girder. This results in
alternating compressive and tensile stresses in the decks and bottom structure which must be limited to avoid buckling, fracture or fatigue failure.
Traditionally a design bending moment has been derived by calculating the
value arising from balancing the ship on a wave with length (λ) equal to
that of the ship (L) and height equal to L/20 (or $1.1 \sqrt{L(ft)}$, ie $0.6 \sqrt{L(m)}$,
in the USA). The stresses derived from this bending moment have then been
compared with suitably conservative allowable values. This approach has
been developed on a 'trial and error' basis from ship operation over many
years and has proved acceptably safe. However, it is only directly
applicable to future ships of the same type and operational history. When
different construction materials are used, eg glass reinforced plastic, or
different operation, eg high speed in rough seas involving increased slamming loading it is necessary to assess the real loading on the ship and
compare this with realistic stress criteria. To this end ARE, Dunfermline
has been measuring hull stresses in warships for many years and has
accumulated data on a number of ship classes. Maximum measured stresses
have exceeded the L/20 values by nearly a factor of two in some cases.

The derivation of realistic loading histories is also important in the assessment of fatigue damage, and in establishing wave induced hull deformation for predicting weapon and sensor alignment accuracy. The calculation of local impact pressures caused by slamming is also necessary for assessing the strength of the bottom structure.

Results obtained from long term measurements of extreme deck stresses in warships, and short term analogue recordings during trials are presented below and compared with theoretical predictions. The accuracy of the theoretical methods in the light of these comparisons and model test data is discussed and the factors to be taken into account in deriving design values for extreme and fatigue loading are considered. The paper concentrates on vertical loading since this is of major importance. Extreme horizontal bending moments are typically half the vertical values and are not generally limiting. Torsional moments are also not normally significant for the closed section of a warship hull.

MEASUREMENTS AT SEA

Long Term Measurement of Extreme Stresses

Maximum compressive and tensile deck stresses in periods of four hours are recorded using an automatic mechanical gauge developed at ARE, Dunfermline [1]. This measures the deflection between points on the structure 250 mm apart and magnifies it using a lever system to give a trace on a strip chart. The chart is stepped forward every four hours giving a series of vertical lines. These are subsequently measured by hand and the hogging (tensile) and sagging (compressive) components are separated by estimating the point on the line where the pen has spent most of the time, resulting in a noticeable thickening of the trace. Tests in the laboratory have shown that the gauges can respond to frequencies up to at least 3 Hz without significant change in the calibration. This is sufficient to cover the first two hull whipping modes for the ships of interest. The gauges are mounted on the webs of the main longitudinals as near the neutral axis of the stiffener/plate combination as possible to minimise local bending effects. Normally six gauges are attached to each ship instrumented, four across the strength deck and two in the superstructure. The gauges operate unattended for periods up to six months.

The accuracy of the mechanical gauges and the separation of the hogging and sagging components has recently been checked using a new electrical recording system which is being developed to replace the mechanical system. This uses a novel compensation for changes in the signal level due to temperature effects and drift in the electronic circuitry [2]. As the hogging and sagging components are unequal it is not possible to use a direct averaging technique to determine the mean. Instead the signal is automatically adjusted until equal time is spent above and below a value which is considered to be the true calm water level. Results to date suggest that the mechanical gauge may slightly underread the sagging component but the general agreement has been good.

The gauge readings together with information on ship speed, location and sea conditions from the ship's log are transferred to computer files for analysis. Figure 1 shows the cumulative probability distribution of stress for the Narrow Beam LEANDER class plotted on a Gumbel scale [3] which has been shown to give a good representation of extreme events. The Gumbel scale is derived from a linear plot of the 'reduced variate' (y) given by:

$$y(x) = -\ln(-\ln(1 - P(x))) \qquad (1)$$

where $P(x)$ is the probability of exceeding a value x. Since $-\ln(1 - P(x))$ tends to $P(x)$ for $P(x)$ small, for probabilities less than about 10^{-2} the scale is virtually indistinguishable from a log scale.

Measurements for the Narrow Beam LEANDER class now cover a period of 9 years at sea which represents more than a ship life since UK warships are at sea for typically one third of their lives. A design life of 20 years corresponds to about 1.5×10^{4} four hour periods at sea. The expected maximum bending moment in the ship life therefore corresponds to a probability of exceedance in a four hour period (P_E) of 6.7×10^{-5} (or 3.3×10^{-8} per wave encounter assuming typically 2000 wave encounters per four hour period). Current practice is to use a design value with a probability of exceedance in a ship life equal to 1% ($P_{.01}$). This corresponds to a probability of exceedance of 6.7×10^{-7} in a four hour period. If linear extrapolation is used it can be seen from Figure 1 that the design value would be a factor 1.42 above the expected maximum value. A linear

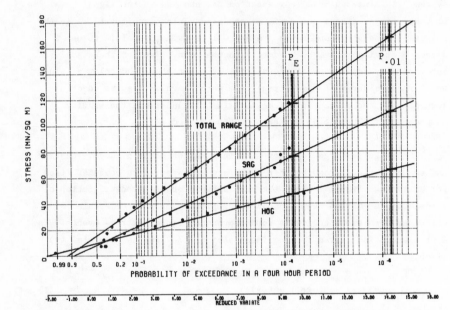

FIGURE 1. Gumbel Plot of Deck Stress Measurements in Narrow Beam LEANDER
Class.

extrapolation is likely to be conservative since the slope is expected to
decrease as the bending moment tends towards a limiting value. Linear
extrapolation of data for other ship classes gives similar ratios (1.39 –
1.45) between the expected maximum and the 1% design value, although the
measurements suggest that this extrapolation is more conservative for some
ships, eg COUNTY class where the Gumbel plot of the measurements is more
non-linear.

Figure 2 shows the probability density distribution of the maximum
bending moment in a ship life assuming that the linear extrapolation is
valid. The distribution is skewed because of the log scale, but if, as
expected, the extrapolation should really be concave downwards the true
distribution would be more symmetric and closer to a normal Gaussian
distribution.

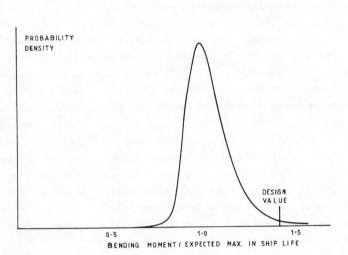

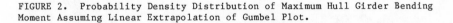

FIGURE 2. Probability Density Distribution of Maximum Hull Girder Bending Moment Assuming Linear Extrapolation of Gumbel Plot.

In order to relate the measured deck strains to vertical bending moment it is necessary to derive effective section moduli for the gauge positions. This is subject to some uncertainty because of the effect of openings in the deck, longitudinal bulkheads, superstructure effectiveness, etc. Where available, use has been made of finite element analyses, eg Ref [4] or detailed measurements of the stress distribution around the hull section, but there is still a significant uncertainty in the relationship between the measured stresses and the bending moment, and this must also be taken into account in assessing the accuracy of load predictions. Design values obtained from the long term measurements such as those shown in Figure 1 are applicable to typical operating histories with regard to ship speed and sea areas. Any marked change in the mode of operation of the ship can lead to higher values as discussed later.

Analogue Recordings During Short Term Trials

The mechanical gauges do not give any indication of the variation of stress with time and so do not show the significance of slamming, and also cannot be used directly to predicct fatigue loading. Recordings have now been made on a number of warships using electrical resistance gauges distributed round the hull during short term trials. One particularly useful trial was that involving LEANDER and TRIBAL class frigates [5, 6] where the ships were operated in close company so that comparisons could be made in the same sea conditions, which were accurately determined using wave buoys. It was also fortunate that severe seas were encountered with significant wave heights up to 8 metres. Figure 3a and 3b show transients measured on the TRIBAL during a large slam. The slam impact at the bow excites the hull girder whipping modes. At midships the two node mode predominates and it can be seen that the slam transient increases the sagging moment much more than the hogging moment. Further forward the higher modes are more evident and there is a significant tensile stress in the deck as the ship hogs over the region of impact. The whipping oscillations are damped out fairly rapidly in frigates, but can persist for much longer in some vessels. Figure 3c for example shows stresses measured in a flat bottomed landing craft. In this case the whipping made a major contribution to the fatigue induced cracking experienced on these ships.

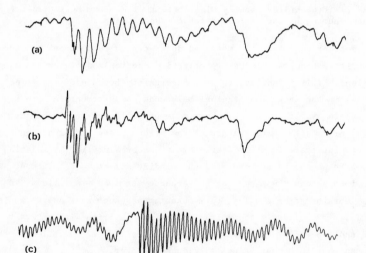

FIGURE 3. Slam Induced Deck Strains
(a) TRIBAL midships   (b) TRIBAL 0.2L from FP   (c) Landing craft midships.
(Sagging downwards)

The slam induced stresses tend to coincide with large waves so the probability distribution of sagging stress diverges from the normal Rayleigh distribution at higher stresses when slamming occurs as can be seen in Figure 4. This shows the probability distribution of deck stress measured in a LEANDER class frigate during a 30 min. run at 22 kts into head seas with $H_{1/3}$ = 6.0 m and T_1 = 10.8 s. The slam induced whipping component of the total stress approximately follows an exponential distribution as discussed further below.

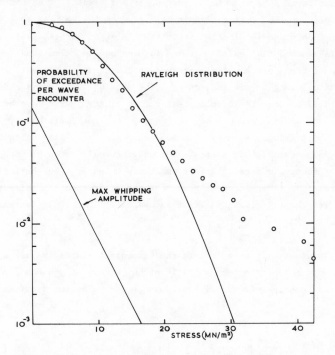

FIGURE 4. Cumulative Probability Distribution of Sagging Stress, LEANDER, 22 knots, Head Seas.

THEORETICAL PREDICTION OF HULL GIRDER BENDING MOMENTS

Long Term Predictions based on Ship Theory

Linear strip theory has the advantage that it can easily be coupled with wave spectral representations to give probability distributions of ship response at a given speed, heading and sea state. Summation of a number of such distributions covering the anticipated speeds, headings and sea states then gives a probability distribution for the whole ship life. The method has been detailed many times in the literature (eg Ref 7) so will only be described briefly here.

The first step is to calculate the 'Response Amplitude Operator', ie the response (eg vertical bending moment) in regular waves of unit height as a function of wave frequency, ship speed and heading. The computer program used at ARE, Dunfermline is derived from the US program SCORES [8]. The ship is divided longitudinally into a number of strips, typically 20 and it is assumed that added mass and damping can be calculated from two dimensional flow only, ie it is assumed that each strip is really part of an infinitely long prismatic section. The section is also assumed to be "wall sided" so that the displacement varies linearly with wave height. This is a major limitation since the method does not differentiate between hogging and sagging response. The bending moment responses so calculated are not very dependent on ship's speed and for small waves are not greatly different from values calculated from static balance. The vertical bending moment response is greatest in head seas and at frequencies corresponding to wave lengths (λ) slightly less than the ship length (L) (typically at $\lambda/L = 0.8$).

The next step is to calculate the response variance (m_o) in a given sea state by integrating the multiple of the square of the RAO and the chosen wave spectrum ($\phi(w)$) with allowances for directional spreading giving

$$m_o(v,\theta) = \int_o^\infty \int_{-\pi}^{\pi} R\,(w, \theta - \mu, v)^2\, \phi(w) S(\mu)\, d\mu dw \qquad (2)$$

Cosine square spreading is usually assumed, ie

$$S(\mu) = \frac{2}{\pi} \cos^2\mu \qquad\qquad -\pi/2 < \mu < \pi/2 \qquad (3)$$

$$= 0 \qquad\qquad\qquad \text{elsewhere}$$

An ISSC spectrum has been used in the calculations reported below, ie

$$\phi(w) = 173 \frac{H_{1/3}^2}{T_1^4 w^5} \quad \exp \quad - \frac{691}{T_1^4 w^4} \quad (4)$$

where T_1 is the chracteristic wave period, and w is the wave frequency.

Since the wave height distribution in a given sea state is assumed to follow a Rayleigh distribution, so also is the response. The probability of exceedance averaged over the ship life is thus given by

$$P(M) = \iiint P_v(v,H_{1/3}) \; P_\theta(\theta,H_{1/3}) \; P_s(H_{1/3},T_1)$$
$$- \frac{M^2}{2 \, m_o \, H_{1/3}^2} \quad (5)$$
$$e \qquad\qquad d\,\theta dv dT dH_{1/3}$$

where P_v is the probability of ship speed, which is also a function of wave height since the speed will be reduced in heavy seas.

P_θ is the probability of heading with respect to the waves. Again this is a function of wave height since there is a tendency to maintain a predominantly head seas course in severe seas.

P_s is the probability of a given sea state in terms of significant wave height and characteristic period.

Although shown as a continuous integral equation (5) is normally evaluated by summing over a limited number of combinations, typically 2 speeds, 7 headings, 16 periods and 24 wave heights giving 5376 combinations.

P_v and P_θ are obtained from an analysis of ships logs and P_s is obtained from published data based on visual observations and recordings. Wave height and period data from visual observations over a large number of sea areas was published in 1967 by Hogben and Lumb [9]. Comparison with the limited instrumental data available at the time suggested that the visually observed wave height was close to the significant value $(H_{1/3})$ and the visually observed period (T_v) was approximately related to the modal period (T_m) by $T_m = 1.12\ T_v$. Since for an ISSC spectrum $T_m = 1.296\ T_1$ the characteristic period can be approximated by $T_1 = 0.86\ T_v$. This is the assumption adopted in the calculations reported below. Since Ref 9 was published extensive measurements have been made using recording instruments in many parts of the world. Hogben and co-workers have reassessed the visually observed period and have concluded that better agreement with measurements can be obtained by deriving the period distribution from the visually observed wave height distribution. This is the approach which is adopted in the NMIMET wave climate synthesis program [10] which gives smoothed distributions by fitting the visually observed data to empirical expressions. The use of smoothed data is preferred in long term ship response calculations since it gives a better representation of the extremes of the wave height distributions where only a few visual obser- vations are reported. Calculations using the NMIMET data are being carried out at ARE, but the values reported in this paper have been derived from the data of Ref 9 for the North Atlantic with the probability values for all periods at each wave height factored to be consistent with the wave height distributions derived from warship logs.

For comparison with the mechanical gauge results the predicted maximum value in a four hour period is required. Assuming a typical wave encounter period of 7 secs the ship will encounter approximately 2000 waves in this time. Since the sea conditions will be fairly constant during a four hour period these wave encounters cannot be considered as statistically indepen- dent. The probability of exceeding a value M in N encounters at constant conditions is given by

$$P_N(M) = \iiiint P_v(v, H_{1/3})\ P_\theta(\theta, H_{1/3})\ P_s(H_{1/3}, T_1)$$
$$\left[1 - \exp \left\{ -N \exp \frac{-M^2}{2\ m_o\ H_{1/3}^2} \right\} \right]\ d\theta dv dT dH \tag{6}$$

It is unrealistic to assume that the speed and heading remains con- stant for the whole period. The choice of period over which conditions are assumed constant is somewhat arbitrary since it will be subject to vari- ation, and some parameters, eg speed and heading may change more quickly than the sea state. Fortunately the choice of this period has most effect at high probabilities of exceedance, ie low bending moments. A constant

period of one hour (500 encounters) has been assumed, and the probability
of exceedance in a four hour period has been calculated assuming that four
such periods are statistically independent.

A comparison between probabilities of exceedance calculated in this
way and measurements in a number of warship classes is shown in Figure 5.
There are some small differences between the agreement for different
classes, probably due to the errors in the effective section modulus
assumed and differences in mission profiles, but they all show the same
trend, ie the theoretical curve is in reasonable agreement with the sagging
measurement at low stresses but at higher stress the theoretical curve
becomes progressively higher despite the fact that slam induced stresses
have not been included in the theoretical predictions.

The main reason for the over-prediction is that strip theory is being
applied well into the non-linear region as discussed below.

Significance of Non-Linearities

The validity of the "wall-sided" assumption in the strip theory calculation can be assessed by considering the associated ship motions, for
example the relative motion between the bow and the sea surface. At a
probability corresponding to the maximum in a ship life, ie 3.3×10^{-8} per
wave encounter, the calculated value for the narrow beam LEANDER is
approximately 2.6 times the freeboard at the bow. It is not surprising
therefore that the theory over-estimates the bending moment under this
situation. An approximate estimate of the effect can be obtained by
limiting the cases summed in the long term statistics to those in which the
relative motion is less than the freeboard or some multiple of it. For
example the calculated expected maximum midships vertical bending moment in
a ship life for the narrow beam LEANDER is reduced by 47% if the contributions are limited to those in which the relative bow motion is less than
the freeboard, and by 34% if the limit is 1.5 times the freeboard.

Alternatively an estimate of the significance of the non-linearity can
be obtained from static balance calculations and model tests in regular
waves. Although a large number of combinations of sea conditions and
headings have been included in the long term statistics, investigation of

12

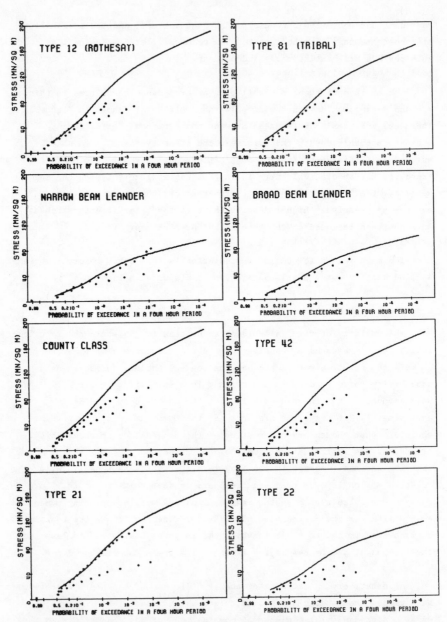

FIGURE 5. Comparison of Measured Stresses and Theoretical Estimates based on Strip Theory. Solid line is theoretical estimate, upper points are measured sagging values, lower points measured hogging values.

the individual contributions shows that only a relatively small number are
significant. These are the high wave height, head seas groups with characteristic periods corresponding to wave lengths near the ship length. A
good indication of non-linear effects can thus be obtained from the
response in regular waves of length close to that of the ship. Static
balance calculations give some indication of this although they do not
allow for the effects of the severe hull motions which occur in high waves.
Figures 6a and 6b show comparisons between strip theory and static balance
calculations for the COUNTY and Type 21 classes. Results from model tests
for these classes are also shown. If the Smith correction, which allows
for wave pressures due to orbital water particle velocities, is included
the static balance calculation is in good agreement with strip theory at
low wave heights. As wave height increases the static balance values fall
below the strip theory line, the reduction being greater for the hogging
case.

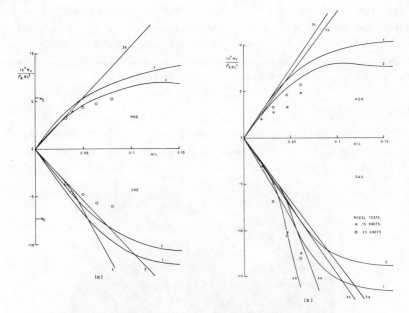

FIGURE 6. Non-Linearity of Midships Bending Moment in Regular Waves
(a) COUNTY (b) Type 21   (Curves: 1. Static balance λ = L without
Smith correction, 2. Static balance λ = L with Smith correction,
3. Strip theory, 4. Strip theory plus calculated slamming.
In Figure (b) a = 15 knots, b = 20 knots.)

The model test results in Figure 6a are for a segmented model run at
zero speed and $\lambda = 0.9L$ [11]. This model was not intended to measure
slamming loads so these results illustrate the non-linearity of the quasi-
static loading. Tests have recently been carried out by British Shipbuilders [12] on models of Type 21 and LEANDER frigates with flexible
joints giving correctly scaled vertical hull girder bending frequencies so
that slam induced whipping can be measured. Results for the Type 21 model
in regular waves with $\lambda = L$ and at scaled speeds of 15 and 20 knots are
included in Figure 6b. The hogging values are again just below the static
balance calculation but the sagging values are above the strip theory
prediction. The LEANDER model gave similar results.

Borresen and Tellsgard [13] have developed a non-linear theory for
regular wave response and show good agreement with midship bending moment
measurements on a destroyer model previously reported by Dalzell [14]. The
sagging moment (including slamming) is about 30% above the strip theory
prediction at $H/\lambda = 0.1$, whereas the hogging moment is only about half the
strip theory value. Non-linear calculations showing similar effects in
commercial ships have also been published by Yamamoto et al [15, 16] and
for a fast patrol boat by Meyerhoff and Schlachter [17].

Slam Induced Whipping

At high speeds in rough seas a substantial length of the bow can
emerge (Figure 7). The subsequent impact can cause failure due to hull
girder bending [18] or local damage [19].

FIGURE 7. Example of Bow Emergence, TRIBAL Class Frigate, 20 knots, Head
Seas.

The impact force can be considered to consist of two components,
'bottom impact' which covers the initial short duration (~ 0.01 secs) high
pressure transient, and 'momentum transfer' slamming which covers the
longer time (~ 1 sec) low pressure generated as water is thrown up either
side of the ship. Bishop, Price et al [20-23] have developed computer
programs to determine the effect of these impact forces on a flexible ship
using motions calculated by strip theory. Figure 8 shows a typical
calculated bending moment response.

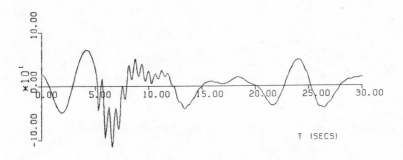

FIGURE 8. Calculated Midship Bending Moment, TRIBAL Class Frigate,
18 knots, Head Seas, $H_{1/3}$ = 5.9 m, T_1 = 9.7 s.

Since the exact sea surface profile during trials is not known, any
comparison with measurements has to be on a statistical basis. Calculations for the LEANDER/TRIBAL trial [24] show reasonable agreement if
momentum transfer slamming is ignored.[*] Figure 9 shows an example of the
theoretical and measured distribution of whipping amplitude. The variation
of slamming rate with ship speed was also well predicted.

The computer program has an option to calculate bottom impact slamming
either by the Ochi-Motter method [25] or the Stavovy-Chuang method [26].
The agreement is better with the Stavovy-Chuang method but this may be
fortuitous since momentum transfer slamming was not taken into account.

---

* An error has recently been found in one of the routines used by these
  programs (30). Correction of this only slightly affected the impact
  slamming response (see Table 1) but greatly reduced the momentum transfer
  component.

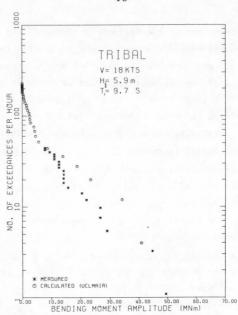

FIGURE 9. Comparison of Calculated and Measured Slam Induced Whipping
Amplitude at Midships.

The Stavovy-Chuang method is based on calculation of the local peak impact
pressure from the expression

$$p(\beta,V) = K(\beta)V^2$$

where V is the relative velocity at impact between the ship and the sea
surface. K is a function of the deadrise angle (β). Allowance is made for
the speed of the ship and the angle of the sea surface. In the program
this pressure is integrated over a number of slamming sections to give the
total slamming force. It is assumed that the time variation can be

approximated by multiplying the peak force by $\frac{t}{T_o}\left[\exp\left(1-\frac{t}{T_o}\right)\right]$, where T_o
has been assumed to be 0.01 s. The choice of T_o is another possible source
of error and may be too high thus overestimating the total impulse produced
by impact slamming. However, the same assumptions have also given reasonable agreement with the Type 21 and LEANDER model tests referred to

earlier, and so can be used to give some indication of the effect of slamming in design calculations.

DESIGN CRITERIA

Extreme Loads

Any attempt to incorporate slam induced loading into a design procedure for maximum bending moment is faced by two main problems. Firstly the statistical nature of the process, and secondly the influence that the Captain of the ship will have in taking avoiding action to limit the incidence of slamming. The fact that slamming does not occur with every wave encounter and does not have a well established probability distribution means that very long simulations of the ship in irregular waves are needed to obtain good statistical estimates of extreme values. This has been investigated using the programs described above [27] by repeating runs for the same significant wave height and characteristic period but different initial phase angles between the regular wave components of the spectra. It was shown that large differences can occur in the extreme values. The same conclusion is true of model tests and full scale trials. Whereas 200 wave encounters are sufficient to give a good fit to a Rayleigh distribution for the normal (ie in the absence of slamming) ship response they may only include 10 slams which is insufficient to give a reasonable statistical definition of the slamming loads. It is not possible at present therefore to include slamming in a long term statistics calculation because of limitations on computer time. There is also inadequate information available on the significance of the avoiding action taken by the Captain. Unlike normal wave induced bending the incidence of slamming is very speed dependent so an accurate speed profile would also be required. Any allowance for slamming therefore has to be very approximate at present.

To give some ideas of the relative magnitude of slamming bending moments calculations have been carried out for current class UK warships in regular and irregular seas. Results of some of the calculations are summarised in Table 1.

Although there are some variations in the relative positions of each ship class in the "slamming league" depending on the sea conditions, the

TABLE 1
Calculated Fractional Increase in Midships Bending Moment Caused by
Slamming.

CLASS	LBP (m)	Beam (m)	Regular Waves λ = L 20 knots				Irregular Waves (c) 20 knots Head Seas T_1 = 10 s $H_{1/3}$ = 8 m
			H = 5 m		H = 0.6 $\sqrt{L}$		
			(a)	(b)	(a)	(b)	
ROTHESAY	109.7	12.5	0.39	0.34	0.57	0.58	0.45
TRIBAL	106.7	12.9	0.95	0.83	1.02	0.90	0.95
NB LEANDER	109.7	12.5	0.45	0.44	0.64	0.51	0.47
BB LEANDER	109.7	13.1	0.63	0.55	0.85	0.65	0.69
COUNTY	153.9	16.5	0.05	0.01	0.17	0.23	0.21
TYPE 21	109.7	12.7	0.25	0.25	0.42	0.42	0.36
TYPE 42	119.5	14.0	0.27	0.26	0.57	0.54	0.35
TYPE 22	125.0	14.7	0.35	0.23	0.66	0.51	0.40

(a) Original programs, as used in References 20-24
(b) Revised programs
(c) From maximum values in a one hour period using original programs.

TRIBAL is always highest because of its fuller hull form and the COUNTY is
always the lowest, partly because it was the longest ship considered.

These differences are not fully reflected in the measurements at sea
because the Captain will adjust speed to minimise the sensation of slamming
at the bridge and so the TRIBAL will be limited to lower speeds in heavy
weather. This has been confirmed by questionnaires to Captains on relative
speeds of different classes, by analysis of ships logs, and in the case of
the LEANDER and TRIBAL by comparative measurements at sea [5, 6].

An approximation for the effect of non-linearity neglecting slamming
can be made by deriving the height of regular waves (trochoidal, λ = L)
which by strip theory would give the same bending moment as predicted by
the long term statistics, and then using this wave height in a static
balance calculation (with Smith correction). The rationale for this is, as
explained above, that the major contribution to the long term statistics is
from wave lengths near the ship length. Comparison with the limited test
data available (Figure 6, and Ref 13) suggests that this correction should
be fairly accurate for hogging but would tend to over-estimate the sagging
value. Expected maximum bending moments in a ship life derived in this way
are compared with values extrapolated from measurements at sea in Table 2.
The variation in the agreement for different classes is likely to be due
mainly to errors in estimating the effective section modulus and the
mission profile. It can be seen in Figure 5 that for the Type 42 and

Type 22 the calculated value is above the measurements even at low values.
The linear extrapolation of the measurements to the expected value in a
ship life is also more conservative for some ships, eg COUNTY class.
Despite this variation the sag/hog ratio is well predicted by this method
even though slamming is not included. Since slamming is expected to
increase sagging values more than hogging values in warships of this size
this suggests that the overestimation of the sagging value by the static
balance correction is approximately balanced by the increase due to
slamming. Secondly it appears that the action taken by the Captains to
limit slamming tends to reduce differences between ship classes. The
TRIBAL which has the largest calculated slam component in a given sea does
have the largest difference between the sag and hog measurement/theory
ratios, but it is only 15%.

TABLE 2

Comparison of Calculated and Measured Expected Maximum Midships Bending
Moment in Ship Life.

| CLASS | Midships Bending Moment (MNm) | | | | | Ratio Meas./Theory | |
| | Expected max. value from strip theory | Factored by static balance/ strip theory | | Extrapolated from measurements | | | |
		HOG	SAG	HOG	SAG	HOG	SAG
ROTHESAY	212	117	188	124	174	1.06	0.92
TRIBAL	196	111	161	109	182	0.98	1.13
NB LEANDER	218	118	187	138	207	1.17	1.11
BB LEANDER	234	122	209	123	215	1.01	1.03
COUNTY	586	373	545	325	445	0.87	0.82
TYPE 21	245	133	218	150	245	1.13	1.12
TYPE 42	320	176	320	134	238	0.76	0.74
TYPE 22	372	180	335	169	273	0.94	0.81
					AVERAGE	0.99 ± 0.13	0.96 ± 0.16

Although the static balance correction gives a good approximation to
the midships value, the bending moments further forward are higher than
predicted by the $\lambda = L$ static balance calculation because the slamming
component is relatively more important. Figure 10 shows the distribution
of bending moment measured on a TRIBAL class frigate at 20 knots in sea
state 6 compared with current design limits which are determined from the
static balance distribution for $\lambda = L$ plus an increase over the forward

region to allow for slamming. Also shown are relative bending moments in
regular waves of λ = L and height L/15 from the Type 21 and LEANDER model
trials referred to earlier. These limited comparisons suggest that the
currently assumed distribution is reasonable.

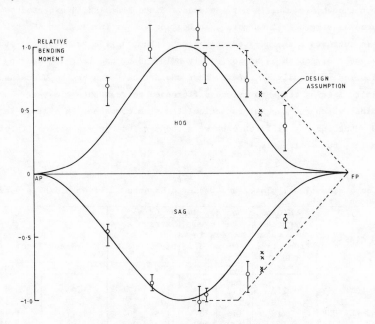

FIGURE 10. Relative Distribution of Bending Moment along Ship Length –
Comparison of Measurements with Current Design Assumption.

The discussion above relates to the wave induced bending moment which
is the dominant consideration. The still water bending moment must be
added to give the total design value but this is usually only about 10% of
the 1% probability of exceedance value (expected value times 1.4).

Fatigue Loads

The fatigue loading resulting from vertical hull bending can be
divided into two components. Firstly the distribution associated with the
maximum stress in each wave encounter, ie the probability distribution per
wave encounter multiplied by the number of wave encounters in a ship life
(assumed to be 3×10^7), and secondly the additional small cycles arising
from slam induced whipping.

The majority of fatigue cracking in warships occurs at welds for which the important design parameter is stress range since the weld induced residual stress tends to eliminate mean stress effects. Design fatigue curves for different structural features have been developed by a number of workers. Ref 28 gives a good summary and shows how fatigue life can be calculated assuming a Weibull distribution of stress range. Analysis of the ARE strain measurements using the methods discussed above to extrapolate from probability in a four hour period to probability per wave encounter shows that an exponential distribution (ie Weibull shape parameter = 1.0) is a good approximation to this data. The fatigue damage in a ship life due to these cycles is then given by

$$D_w = \frac{N_L \, b!}{A} \, S^b \qquad\qquad (7)$$

where the fatigue curve is represented by

$$N_f = A \, (\Delta\sigma)^{-b} \qquad\qquad (8)$$

the cumulative probability distribution of stress range $(\Delta\sigma)$ (per wave encounter) is given by

$$P \, (\Delta\sigma) = e^{-\,\Delta\sigma/S} \qquad\qquad (9)$$

and N_L is the number of wave encounters in a ship life (assumed to be 3×10^7.

This includes the effect of the enhancement of the maximum stress per wave encounter caused by slamming, but not the subsequent whipping. In cases where the whipping is of large amplitude, eg for the landing craft transient shown in Figure 3c an effective number of cycles per slam can be derived.

If the stress range for the nth whipping cycle is given by

$$\Delta\sigma_n = \Delta\sigma_1 \, e^{-\,(n\,-\,1)\delta} \qquad\qquad (10)$$

where $\Delta\sigma_1$ is the stress range for the first cycle and δ is the logarithmic

decrement (equal to 0.05 for the record in Figure 3c), then the fatigue
damage from whipping cycles is given by

$$D_s = \frac{1}{A} \left[(\Delta\sigma_1)^b + (\Delta\sigma_1 e^{-\delta})^b + (\Delta\sigma_1 e^{-2\delta})^b + \ldots \right]$$

$$= \frac{\Delta\sigma_1^{\;b}}{A} \left(\frac{1}{1 - e^{-\delta b}} \right)$$

(11)

putting $\delta = 0.05$ and $b = 3$ (typical value for steel welds) gives
$1/(1 - e^{-\delta b}) = 7.2$, ie the whipping following the slam transient produces
as much fatigue damage as approximately 7 cycles with a stress range equal
to the first.

In this case it was shown that the slam induced whipping was a major
factor in fatigue, and produced about 5 times the fatigue damage due to
normal wave action. In frigates and destroyers the damping coefficients
are higher so the effective number of fatigue cycles per slam is less, and
the relative impact forces are lower giving $D_s < 0.25 \, D_w$ at midships under
normal operation, but D_s is relatively more important further forward.

CONCLUSIONS

The statistical distribution of extreme midship vertical bending
moments in warship hulls can be reasonably represented by strip theory
derivations for the mission profile with corrections for non-linearity
based on static balance. The agreement with measurements at sea, which are
known to include a significant slamming contribution to the sagging moment
suggests that this method over-estimates the sagging moment by an amount
approximately equal to the slamming contribution.

Calculated slamming responses for different ship classes in a given
sea state show considerable variation but these differences are reduced by
speed and heading restrictions imposed by the ships Captains. The most
useful applications of slamming prediction methods are therefore to
maximise permissible speeds in likely sea states, and to predict the effect
of unusual features, eg bow sonar domes.

23

It is considered that a factor 1.4 on the expected maximum bending moment in a ship life is a sufficient design margin. This should give a conservative estimate of the 1% probability of exceedance value based on extrapolation of measured values, although it should be borne in mind that there can be 'rogue' waves which do not fit into the normal statistical distribution as discussed by Buckley [29].

The calculation methods described also enable estimates of fatigue loading to be derived which can be used to assess the crack initiation life from standard fatigue curves. Since fatigue occurs at local stress concentrations a detailed stress analysis is required to relate the bending moment to local stress. This generally involves a large finite element analysis.

REFERENCES

1. Smith, C.S., Measurement of service stresses in warships, Conf. on Stresses in Service. Inst. of Civil Engineers, London, March 1966.

2. Brown, J.C., Drift compensation of oscillatory signals, IEEE Transactions on Instrumentation and Measurement, to be published.

3. Gumbel, E.J., Statistics of Extremes, Columbia Univ. Press, New York, 1966.

4. McVee, J.D., A finite element study of hull-deckhouse interaction, Computers and Structures, Vol 12, 371-393, 1980.

5. Andrew, R.N. and Lloyd, A.R.J.M., Full scale comparative measurements of the behaviour of two frigates in severe head seas, Trans. RINA 123, 1981, 1-31.

6. Clarke, J.D., Measurement of hull stresses in two frigates during a severe weather trial, Trans. RINA 124, 1982, 63-83.

7. Bishop, R.E.D. and Price, W.G., Probabilistic Theory of Ship Dynamics, Chapman and Hall, London, 1974.

8. Raff, A.I., Program SCORES - ship structural response in waves, Ship Structures Committee publication, SSC 230, 1972.

9. Hogben, N. and Lumb, F.E., Ocean Wave Statistics, HMSO, 1967.

10. Dacunha, N.M.C., Hogben, N. and Andrews, K.S., Wave climate synthesis worldwide, RINA Symposium on Wave and Wind Climate Worldwide, London, April 1984.

11. Lloyd, A.R.J.M., Brown, J.C. and Anslow, J.F.W., Motion and loads of ship models in regular oblique seas, Trans RINA 122, 1980.

24

12. Suhrbier, K.R., Private communication.

13. Borresen, R. and Tellsgard, F., Time history simulation of vertical motions and loads on ships in regular head waves of large amplitude, Norwegian Maritime Research, Vol 8, No 2, 1980, p2.

14. Dalzell, J.F., An investigation of midship bending moment experienced in extreme regular waves by models of the Mariner type ship and three variants, Ship Structures Committee Report, SSC 155, 1964.

15. Yamamoto, Y., Fujino, M. and Fukasawa, T., Motion and longitudinal strength of a ship in head seas and the effects of non-linearities, Naval Architecture and Ocean Engineering, Vol 18, Society of Naval Architects of Japan, 1980.

16. Yamamoto, Y., Fujino, M. and Fukasawa, T., Longitudinal strength of ships in rough seas, NK Tech Bulletin, 1983, p1.

17. Meyerhoff, W.K. and Schlachter, G., An approach for the determinatio of hull girder loads in a seaway including hydrodynamic impacts, Ocean Engineering, Vol 7, 1980, 305-326.

18. Yamamoto, Y., Fujino, M., Ohtsubo, H., Fukasawa, T., Iwai, Y., Aoki, G., Watanabe, I., Ikeda, H., Kumano, A., and Kuroiwa,T., Disastrous damage of a bulk carrier due to slamming, Naval Architecture and Ocean Engineering, Vol 22, 1984, 159-169.

19. Yamamoto, Y., Iida, K., Fukasawa, T., Murakami, T., Arai, M. and Ando, A., Structural damage of a fast ship due to bow flare slamming, Int. Shipbuilding Progress, Vol 32, No 369, May 1985, 124-136.

20. Bishop, R.E.D., Price, W.G. and Tam, P.K.Y., On the dynamics of slamming, Trans RINA 120, 1978, 259-280.

21. Belik, O., Bishop, R.E.D. and Price, W.G., On the slamming response of ships to regular head waves, Trans RINA 122, 1980, 325-337.

22. Belik, O., Bishop, R.E.D. and Price, W.G., A simulation of ship responses due to slamming in irregular head waves. Trans RINA 125, 1983, 237-253.

23. Belik, O. and Price, W.G., Comparison of slamming theories in the time simulation of ship responses in irregular waves, Int. Shipbuilding Progress, Vol 29, July 1982, 173-187.

24. Bishop, R.E.D., Clarke, J.D. and Price, W.G., Comparison of full scale and predicted responses of two frigates in a severe weather trial, RINA Supplementary Papers, Vol 126, 1984, p153.

25. Ochi, M.K. and Motter, L.E., Predictions of slamming experiments and hull response for ship design, Trans SNAME 81, 1973, 144-190.

26. Stavovy, A.B. and Chuang, S.L., Analytical determination of slamming pressures for high speed vehicles in waves, J.Ship Research 20, 1976, 190-198.

27. Clarke, J.D., Price, W.G. and Temarel, P., The influence of seaway
     description on ship responses calculated from computer time simu-
     lations, Symposium on Description and Modelling of Directional Seas,
     Technical University, Denmark, June 1984.

28. Munse, W.H., Wilbur, T.W., Tellalian, M.L., Nicoll, K. and Wilson, K.,
     Fatigue characterisation of fabricated ship details for design, Ship
     Structure Committee Report, SSC-318, 1983.

29. Buckley, W.H., A study of extreme waves and their effects on ship
     structure, Ship Structure Committee Report, SSC-320, 1983.

30. Price, W.G. Private communication.

WAVE LOADS AND RESPONSE OF SHIPS AND OFFSHORE STRUCTURES
FROM THE VIEWPOINT OF HYDROELASTICITY

Y. Yamamoto
Tokyo Denki University
Hatoyama, Saitama 350-03 Japan

K. Sugai, H. Inoue
Ship Research Institute
6-38-1 Shinkawa, Mitaka 181 Japan

K.Yoshida, M. Fujino and H. Ohtsubo
Department of Naval Architecture, University of Tokyo
Hongo, Bunkyo-ku, Tokyo 113 Japan

ABSTRACT

Ships and offshore structures may suffer serious structural damage among waves, and stresses in such damage conditions can be determined with the aid of hydroelasticity. In Japan, disastrous structural damage of ships among rough waves have been investigated extensively, and investigations for new types of offshore structures have concentrated on huge semisubmersibles used for airports and tension leg platforms for deep waters; they will be discussed from the view-point of hydroelasticity in the present paper.

INTRODUCTION

Within eight days from Dec. 27, 1980, to Jan. 3, 1981 six large ships were lost in rough seas in the North Pacific Ocean off the South-East Coast of Japan. One of them was a bulk carrier under Japanese flag, and it was suggested by a theory that the disaster of the ship was caused by slamming impact. In 1982, a five year program started for the investigation of the safety of ships in rough seas, paying special attention to slamming. The program includes the following items;

1) investigations of waves in winter of the sea area,
2) theoretical and experimental investigations of structural response of ships against high waves,
3) structural experiments with the use of large scale models, and
4) development of an onboard system for safe navigation among rough seas.

The first part of the present paper contains results of item 2 of the program, and preliminary results of item 3 are shown in Appendix.

Compliant offshore structures will be used widely in near future because the oil and gas exploitation will proceed to deep waters and hazardous seas and also because multiple subjects of ocean exploitation, such as ocean space utilization, will be realized. Studies on compliant offshore structures recently carried out will be outlined briefly in the second part.

SHIP STRUCTURAL BEHAVIOR IN ROUGH SEAS
Fundamentals of a nonlinear strip theory

The vertical ship motions and the vertical wave loads will be treated from the viewpoint of longitudinal strength of ships in rough seas taking account of the effect of the impact loads due to slamming. It is assumed, for the sake of simplicity, that a train of regular waves of wave height H_w and wave length λ comes toward a ship travelling with a constant advancing speed U at an angle χ to the direction of the wave propagation. For the mathematical formulation for the dynamic behavior of the ship, the coordinate systems shown in Fig. 1 will be introduced. It is also assumed that in calm water the x_o, y_o-plane fixed to the ship coincides with the X, Y-plane or the surface of calm water.

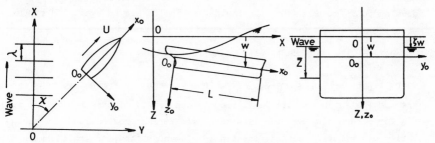

Fig. 1 Coordinate systems

The vertical displacement w of the ship hull, which includes the elastic deformation of the hull as well as the rigid-body displacement, is described by [1]

$$\mu\frac{\partial^2 w}{\partial t^2} + \frac{\partial^2}{\partial x^2}\left[EI\left(\frac{\partial^2 w}{\partial x^2} + \eta\frac{\partial^3 w}{\partial t\partial x^2}\right)\right] = f_z + \mu g \qquad (1)$$

where g is the acceleration of gravity, and μ, EI, η and f_z are the mass per unit length, the flexural rigidity for vertical bending, the structural damping coefficient, and the hydrodynamic vertical force, defined at each section of the ship. The hydrodynamic force f_z consists of the forces due to hydrodynamic inertia, impact and damping, and the Froude-Krylov force:

$$f_z = -\frac{D}{Dt}\left[M_H\left(\frac{Dw}{Dt} - v_z\right)\right] - N_H\left(\frac{Dw}{Dt} - v_z\right) + \int_s (-p)\, n\, ds \qquad (2)$$

where $\frac{D}{Dt} = \frac{\partial}{\partial t} - U\frac{\partial}{\partial x}$, M_H and N_H represent the sectional added mass and damping coefficients for heave, n is the z-component of the unit vector to the hull section, v_z stands for the vertical component of orbital velocity of wave particles, and the pressure p includes the static pressure increase due to ship motions and the water pressure of the incident wave. The first term of the right-hand side of Eq. (2) is resolved into three components:

$$- \frac{D}{Dt}[M_H(\frac{Dw}{Dt} - v_z)] = -M_H\frac{D}{Dt}(\frac{Dw}{Dt} - v_z) + U\frac{\partial M_H}{\partial x}(\frac{Dw}{Dt} - v_z) - \frac{\partial M_H}{\partial t}(\frac{Dw}{Dt} - v_z) \quad (3)$$

The first two components in this expression appear in the conventional linear theory of ships motions among waves. The third one, however, is not included in the linear theory; it is the hydrodynamic impact force due to the rate of change of the sectional added mass, and plays an important role in the theory of structural response of ship hull among high waves.

Since they are frequency dependent, the sectional hydrodynamic coefficients M_H and N_H should be determined appropriately. For the rigid-body motions, they are determined for the encounter frequency, and for vibratory motions, the high frequency approximation can be employed. The sectional damping coefficient N_H for the rigid-body motion can be evaluated approximately by

$$N_H = \frac{\rho g^2}{\omega_e{}^3}[2 \sin(\xi_b) \exp(- \xi_d)]^2 \quad (4)$$

where $\xi_b = \frac{\omega_e{}^2}{g} \frac{\bar{b}}{2}$, $\xi_d = \frac{\omega_e{}^2}{g} \bar{z}$, ω_e is the encounter frequency, and $\bar{b}$ and $\bar{z}$ are the instantaneous sectional breadth and draft. There are various methods for determining M_H; they are the Lewis form approximation, the singularity distribution method, the finite element method, the half-immersed circular cylinder approximation. In the case of the last method, the sectional added mass at infinite frequency is given by

$$M_H = \frac{1}{2}\rho\pi(\frac{\bar{b}}{2})^2 \quad (5)$$

where ρ is the mass density of water. For the hydrodynamic impact f_{imp}, or the third term of the right-hand side of Eq. (3), it is assumed on physical considerations that

$$f_{imp} = \begin{cases} - \frac{\partial M_H}{\partial t} (\frac{Dw}{Dt} - v_z) , & \text{if } \frac{Dw}{Dt} - v_z > 0 \\ \\ 0 , & \text{if } \frac{Dw}{Dt} - v_z < 0 \end{cases} \quad (6)$$

It should be noticed that M_H in Eq. (6) is frequency independent according to the theory of water impact.

There are two methods of approach for solving Eq. (1) or the equivalent one; they are the Galerkin method and the finite element method. In case of the latter approach, time integration can be performed either by the direct integration method or by the modal analysis with the use of the normal modes obtained by the finite element method. The vertical displacement w can be expressed by a linear combination of N coordinate functions W_j ;

$$w(x,t) = \sum_{j=1}^{N} W_j(x)\, q_j(t) \qquad (7)$$

where q_j's are the generalized coordinates. For the Galerkin method, the normal functions for a free-free uniform beam can be conveniently used for W_j's. In case of the finite element method, q_j's correspond to the nodal displacements. Substituting w from Eq. (7) into Eq. (1) and applying the Galerkin method to the resulting equation yield the matrix equation given by

$$[M_{ij}]\{\ddot{q}_j\} + [C_{ij}]\{\dot{q}_j\} + [K_{ij}]\{q_j\} = \{f_i\} \qquad (8)$$

The expressions for $[M_{ij}]$, $[C_{ij}]$, $[K_{ij}]$, $\{f_i\}$ can easily be obtained. It should be noticed that f_i's are expressed in terms of q_j's. The damping matrix is given in the form of the Rayleigh damping:

$$[C_{ij}] = \eta\,[K_{ij}] \qquad (9)$$

The logarithmic decrement δ_j for vibration modes is assumed to be in proportion to the corresponding natural frequency ω_j, and it is given by

$$\delta_j = \eta\pi\omega_j \qquad (j \geqq 3) \qquad (10)$$

The structural damping coefficient η used for calculations is obtained from actual data for δ_3 and ω_3. For time integration of Eq. (8), the Newmark β-method with $\beta = 1/4$ can be used conveniently.

Vertical bending moment and shearing force are obtained either by the integrating the expression $f_z + \mu g - \mu\dfrac{\partial^2 w}{\partial t^2}$ or by evaluating the formulas for respective quantities given in terms of w ; the former method gives better results. Among high waves, the effect of axial forces becomes significant, and the axial force gives an additional bending moment [3, 4].

Recent reports on structural damage of ships indicate that their fore bodies were vulnerable. Certainly the Galerkin method with the use of four coordinate functions, two for rigid body motion and two for vibration, gives sufficiently accurate results for structural response of the mid-bodies, but it may be insufficient to investigate response of the fore bodies because effects of higher mode vibrations including shear deformations become

significant [2]. For the analysis of a ship as a Timoshenko beam, the finite element method can be conveniently applied, and in the present paper
it will be performed by employing the Timoshenko beam element with 3 nodes
which can express pure bending in the limit case as shear rigidity tends to
infinity. For the sake of simplicity, Eq. (9) will be employed for structural damping with η determined for the two node vibration (j = 3). In
the following, numerical results obtained by this method will be mainly
discussed [2].

Calculations are carried out for a bulk carrier [3], whose particulars
are as follows;

$L \times B \times D \times d_a \times d_f = 216.4m \times 31.7m \times 17.3m \times 10.17m \times 8.94m$
$DW = 55,000t$

Her structural response among waves is obtained under the condition that

$Fn = 0.1, \quad \lambda/L = 1.0, \quad H_W = 12m, \quad \chi = 180°, \quad \eta = 0.00231sec$

Her weight, sectional moment of inertia and shear area are assumed to form
trapezoids.

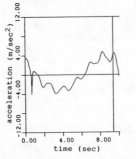 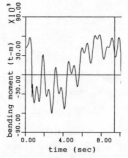

a. Modal analysis with 4 coordinate functions

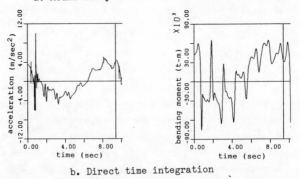

b. Direct time integration

Fig. 2   Time histories of acceleration (left) and
bending moment at S.S. 8 1/2

Fig. 2 shows time histories of acceleration and bending moment at S.S. 8 1/2 calculated according to the two procedures for time integration. Coordinate functions used for modal analysis correspond to two rigid body motions and 2- and 3-node vibration. Fig. 3 shows instantaneous bending moment diagrams obtained by the two procedures at the instant when sagging

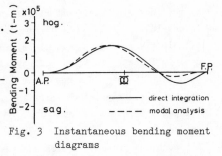

Fig. 3 Instantaneous bending moment diagrams

moment at S.S. 9 1/2 takes on maximum. Significant difference can be observed in the fore body, which suggests that modal analysis with 4 coordinate functions may be insufficient for analyzing local response of the fore body.

Effects of shear deformations can be observed by comparing Figs. 2 and 4; the latter is obtained by direct time integration with the Euler beam element which corresponds to the limit case as shear rigidity tends to infinity. Although the tendency of generalized coordinates for both models is almost the same, the response in time domain obtained by superposing all the modes results in different shape for the two idealizations.

Axial force is caused by the longitudinal component of pressure, and its most important part can be obtained on the basis of the Froude-Krylov hypothesis [3]. Additional bending moment on the ship hull may be caused by axial force. Axial force and bending moment can be calculated by considering the relative configuration of the ship and waves. Fig. 5 shows peak values of longitudinal deck strain at S.S. 8 1/2 obtained by theory and model experiments; it can be observed that better agreement can be attained

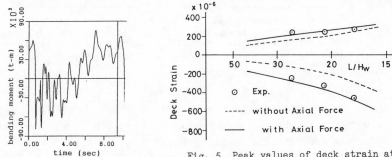

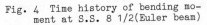

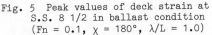

Fig. 4 Time history of bending moment at S.S. 8 1/2 (Euler beam)

Fig. 5 Peak values of deck strain at S.S. 8 1/2 in ballast condition (Fn = 0.1, χ = 180°, λ/L = 1.0)

by considering the effects of axial forces [4].

In the present paper, the hydro-dynamic force f_z in Eq. (1) is evaluated with the aid of a nonlinear version of the strip method which is developed with the two-dimensional hydrodynamic coefficients M_H and N_H. Although the present version has the same weakness for this point as the original linear version, accuracy of hydrodynamic coefficients may have a significant influence for the results. Hydrodynamic coefficients can be determined accurately with the aid of the singularity distribution method, and approximate values can be estimated by Eqs. (4) and (5). Calculations are performed for the model ship of an ore

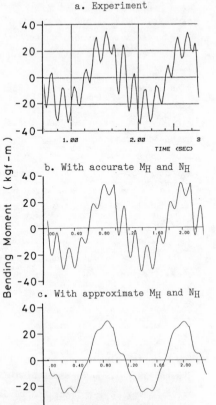

a. Experiment

b. With accurate M_H and N_H

c. With approximate M_H and N_H

1 sec.

Fig. 6 Time histories of bending moment at midship, experiments and calculations.

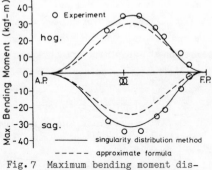
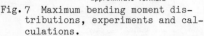

——— singularity distribution method

– – – – approximate formula

Fig. 7 Maximum bending moment distributions, experiments and calculations.

carrier used for experiments with structural damping coefficient $\eta = 0.001$ sec obtained by hammering tests of the model, and results are compared in Figs. 6 and 7, which show that computations with accurate coefficients result in better agreement with experiments. In connection to these results, it should be noted that the approximation given by Eq. (4) has a tendency to overestimate the damping coefficient N_H.

Experiments on Ships and Models

In order to confirm the validity of the theoretical investigation described in the previous section, various kinds of experiments on ships and
models have been conducted in real seas or in test basins. Most of ship
models used are so-called elastic models, and experimental technique with
them is established through the experiments. The structural models are
made of elastic materials,such as styrol form, for their hull so as to satisfy the similarity conditions for flexural rigidity and frequency of flexural vibration as well as geometrical form [5]. Fig. 8 shows an example of

ship model and arrangement
of sensors used. Fig. 9
shows a model of ore car-
rier advancing in a regu-
lar wave train at the
Ship Research Institute.
Characteristics of models
manufactured were obtained
by bending test and ham-
mering or vibration test.
If the law of similitude
holds exactly, the model

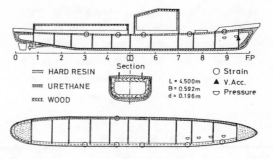

HARD RESIN
URETHANE
WOOD

Section

L = 4.500m
B = 0.592m
d = 0.196m

○ Strain
▲ V.Acc.
▽ Pressure

Fig. 8 Structural ship model

Fig. 9 Experiment in a seakeeping basin

acts as an analogue computer for estimating dynamic response even in slamming condition; that is, it connects external hydrodynamic forces with ship
structural response.

As part of the present investigation,experiments on eight elastic models,

34

one segmented and one wooden model were carried out for wide variation in ship types, loading conditions and encounter waves [6]. A characteristic pattern in time history of bending moments due to slamming impacts is shown in Fig. 10; vertical vibrations induced by bow slamming is laid over a component with the encounter wave period [7]. Some of experimental results are shown in the previous section. Comparison between theory and experiments shows the validity of the present theoretical prediction for the deck strain in head seas.

There is, however, a difficulty for a ship among oblique waves; vertical, horizontal and torsional vibrations as well as six components of the rigid body motions appear, and their interactions may become significant. For the sake of simplicity, it will be assumed that interactions among the rigid body motions is so small in oblique waves that each component of motions can be dealt with independently. Along this line of thought, calculations are performed, and results obtained are compared with experiments in Fig. 11, which shows good agreement.

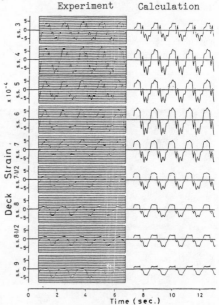

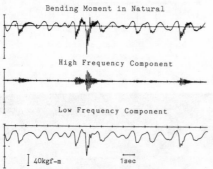

Fig. 10 Charchteristic pattern of bending moment at S.S. 5 1/2 measured in irregular waves

Distributions of impulsive pressure on the forward bottom of a large bulk carrier model were measured in irregular waves. Results obtained show that impulsive pressure is almost uniform in the transverse direction, while it

Fig. 11 Experiments and calculations of deck strains in oblique waves

takes a peak value at S.S. 9 1/2 in the
longitudinal distribution. The peak
value drops significantly as the ship
heading changes from right head to
bow direction. Experiments in two-
directional waves have a tendency to
cause severe slamming in comparison
to those in uni-directional waves.

A series of experiments on ships
in actual conditions at sea have been
planned. First, a patrol boat of
  L × B × D = 77.8m × 9.6m × 5.3m
  W = 1,344t, max. speed = 19.8kts
was used for this purpose; she
suffered frequent impacts on the
bottom forward in sea state 5.
Measured items were impact pressure

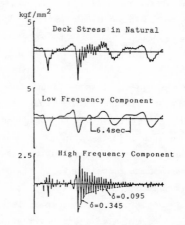

Fig. 12 Deck stress near midship
on a patrol boat in service.

on the flare part and the forward bottom, strains on upper deck and side
shell, ship motions and accelerations. As an example, Fig. 12 shows deck
stresses derived from strains measured on deck at midship, which shows good
agreement with results obtained by experiments on the corresponding elastic
model ship in a seakeeping basin [8]. As the second of the series, a container ship was employed, and analysis of data obtained is progressing.
As the third, an ore carrier is scheduled to be tested; since little slamming is expected on such a full-bodied ship, an automatic measuring apparatus is to be employed during winter season.

COMPLIANT OFFSHORE STRUCTURES

Huge Semisubmersible Type of Floating Airport

The Association of Shipbuilding Industries of Japan presented a conceptual design of a floating airport, which is a huge semisubmersible with
deck of 5,000m long and 840m wide. A series of tank tests were conducted
at the Ship Research Institute to investigate its performance [9]. The model
has a deck of 20.4m long, 3.3m wide and 0.2m deep, and the deck is supported
by 294 columns with footing arranged as 7 rows by 42 columns. The mass and
flexural rigidity of the deck were determined to satisfy the law of similitude for the conceptual design. In these tests, the model was moored by the

apparatus simulating a dolphin mooring system at five points along a longer
side and three points along a shorter side. As an extension of the studies,
huge semisubmersibles as offshore terminals are planned to be investigated.

As for prediction of response of semisubmersibles among waves, linear
analysis methods have been proposed. In the following, a method of analysis
for frequency response functions of floating framed structures among waves
will be discussed [10, 11]. For such huge semisubmersibles, the assumption
of pseudo rigid body motions does not hold, because their motions are influenced to a great extent by elastic deformations of structural members. In
this case, therefore, motions as a whole and deformations of the respective
structural members have to be analyzed simultaneously under the following
assumptions;

1) mooring apparatus is replaced by linear springs, and superstructure is
   regarded as a three-dimensional elastic frame structure;
2) incident wave is Airy wave whose length is long enough in comparison to
   sectional dimensions of structural members;
3) response is expressed as harmonic oscillation of small amplitude around
   the equilibrium configuration; and
4) hydrodynamic interactions between neighboring members are disregarded.

The superstructure is discretized into finite number of elements for
easy estimation of hydrodynamic forces and structural characteristics.
Elements are classified into two types according to their functions; one

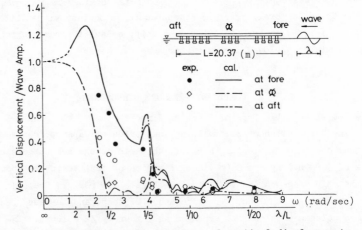

Fig. 13 Frequency response functions of vertical displacements
of floating airport model

is referred as hull element for estimating external and inertia forces, and the other is referred as beam element for estimating elastic rigidity as a structural member. Hull and beam elements are connected through rigid links to nodes, where the dynamic equilibrium condition and the condition of compatibility of the two types of elements are both satisfied.

In addition to the conventional space-fixed coordinate system, an element-fixed coordinate system is introduced for systematic estimation of restoring forces and moments due to the gravity force and the static buoyancy of hull elements even in the case of linear problems.

In Fig. 13 vertical displacement amplitudes calculated by the present method are compared with those measured in the tank test [9] , which shows good agreement except data for the aft end where theoretical values are much higher than experimental ones; wave exiting forces in experiments may be gradually attenuated with the increase of the distance from the fore end.

Tension Leg Platform

The subsea oil and gas exploitation is expected to proceed to deep waters of depth of 300m to 1,000m in near future, and eager attentions have been paid to tension leg platform or TLP because it is one of most promising types of production platform installed in such deep waters. Under these circumstances, behavior of TLP subjected to waves, wind, earthquake etc. has been studied.

Frequency response functions of motions and member forces can be analyzed by a slightly modified version of the method described in the previous section. As to nonlinear phenomena of TLP subjected to waves, subharmonic resonance, super-harmonic resonance and snap loading can be observed in the small scale model tests.

Effects of wind loads on behavior of TLP were studied by using an open type wind generating system shown in Fig. 14 [12], which is installed on the sea-keeping basin at the University of Tokyo. Although complete uniformity of wind velocity cannot be expected in this system, general features of TLP subjected to wave and wind loads can be observed.

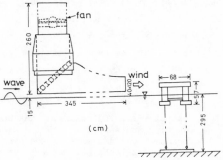

Fig. 14 Test system for TLP subjected
to wave and wind loads

38

In a series of tests, unexpected oscillations of TLP in a vertical plane were observed, and subsequent tension fluctuations in legs were measured; the RMS values of the tension fluctuations are shown in Fig. 15 against the mean wind velocity. From time histories measured, it is concluded that the frequency of oscillations is equal to the natural frequency of heave or pitch for the mean wind velocity in lower or higher range respectively; a critical wind velocity for the transition of mode of motion may exist. However, further studies are necessary to clarify this phenomenon.

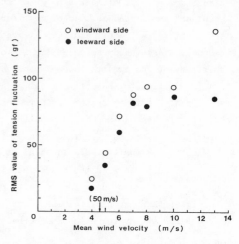

Fig. 15 RMS values of tension fluctuations of TLP model subjected to wind loads

CONCLUSIONS

The present paper deals with hydroelasticity of ships and offshore structures, and these fields have a close relation with serious damages or disasters. In the first part of the paper, a theory for predicting ships' structural response in steep waves is proposed, and its validity is confirmed by experiments with the use of elastic ship models. It will be helpful for ships' safety among rough seas. In the second part, compliant offshore structures are discussed from the viewpoint of hydroelasticity. Mooring systems have a vital influence on the safety of moored offshore structures. In the case of tension leg platforms, tension fluctuation discussed herein may be one of the key points of their design.

REFERENCES

1. Yamamoto, Y., Fujino, M., Fukasawa, T. and Ohtsubo, H.,
    Slamming and whipping of ships among rough seas.
    In: *Numerical Analysis of the Dynamics of Ship Structures*,
    Association Technique Maritime et Aeronautique (1978) 19–33.

2. Ohtsubo, H., Kuroiwa, T. and Yamamoto, Y.,
    Structural response of ships among rough seas.
    J. Soc. Naval Arch. Japan, **157** (1985) 391–402. (in Japanese)

3. Yamamoto, Y., Fujino, M., Ohtsubo, H., Fukasawa, T., Aoki, G., Ikeda,
    H. and Kumano, A.,
    Analysis of disastrous structural damage of a bulk carrier.
    In: *PRADS 83 - Proc. of 2nd Symp. on Practical Design in Shipbdg*,
    (1983) 11-18.

4. Fukasawa, T., Fujino, M., Koyanagi, M. and Kawamura, T.,
    Effects of axial force on deck stress in case of slamming of large
    bulk carriers,
    J. Soc. Naval Arch. Japan, 155 (1984) 257-265. (in Japanese)

5. Fukasawa, T., Yamamoto, Y., Fujino, M. and Motora, S.,
    Motion and longitudinal strength of a ship in head sea and the effects
    of nonlinearity - experiment.
    J. Soc. Naval Arch. Japan, 150 (1981) 308-314.

6. *Research on Ships' Response among Waves*.
    Report of SR 194, 380, Shipbdg. Res. Ass. of Japan (1985).(in Japanese)

7. Watanabe, I. and Sawada, H.,
    Relation between vertical acceleration and relative water elevation at
    a ship's bow.
    In: *Papers of Ship Research Institute* (to be published).

8. Hashizume, Y., Takemoto, H. and Oka, S.,
    Wave loads and ship response of a patrol boat among waves.
    In: *Abstract Note of 45th Annual Meeting*,
    Ship Research Institute (1985) 18-21. (in Japanese)

9. *Investigation Reports for Assessment of Floating Structure Type on the
    Kansai Airport Plan*,
    Ship Research Institute (1979). (in Japanese)

10. Yoshida, K. and Ishikawa, K. and Iida, K.,
    Periodic response analysis of floating framed structures
    J. Soc. Naval Arch. Japan, 136 (1974) 355-364. (in Japanese)

11. Yoshida, K. and Ishikawa, K.,
    Structural response characteristics of semisubmersibles for wave
    loading.
    J. Faculty of Engng., Univ. of Tokyo, B 35 (1980) 407-432.

12. Yoshida, K. and Oka, N.,
    Considerations on evaluation of wind loads on tension leg platforms.
    In: *Proc. of 7th Ocean Engng. Symp.*,
    Soc. Naval Arch. Japan (1984) 33-42. (in Japanese)

APPENDIX: STRUCTURAL MODEL TESTS OF FORE BODY OF A BULK CARRIER

Structural tests of three 1/6-scale models of the same form for the
fore body of a bulk carrier [3] were carried out by the multi-jack loading
system at the Ship Research Institute.Each model was fixed to rigid wall A
at the aft end (Fr. 228), and a loading block B was attached at the fore
end (Fr. 260)(cf. Fig. 16). The model was subjected to sagging moment
caused by 18 jacks, which was increased step-by-step in proportion to designated distribution patterns. Since there were no special differences

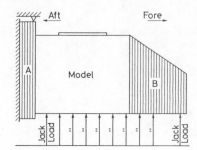

a. General arrangement

b. Deck structure

Fig. 16 1/6-scale structural model

a. Upper deck (look forward)

b. Inside of No. 1 Hold

Fig. 17 A tested model

between the respective distribution patterns, process of deformations were almost the same; buckling occurred in hatch coaming, deck plating, deck stiffeners, and side shell successively, and the model was collapsed finally as shown in Fig. 17 near the cross section at the mid-length of No.1 Hatch, where a discontinuity of structure exists as shown in Fig. 16. The nominal compressive stresses at the section in collapse conditions are given for the respective cases by

$$6.53 \text{ kgf/mm}^2, \quad 8.42 \text{ kgf/mm}^2, \quad 8.23 \text{ kgf/mm}^2$$

which are around one half of the theoretical value obtained by the finite element method. There might be unexpected amount of initial deflections caused by staggered weld for the attachment of deck stiffeners. This anomaly will be resolved by further investigations.

LOADING AND DYNAMICS OF COMPLIANT STRUCTURES

J A Mercier, Conoco (U.K.) Limited
Park House, 116 Park Street,
London W1Y 4NN, England
and
D J H Peters, Conoco, Inc.
P O Box 2197
Houston, Texas 77252, USA

Environmental parameters affecting the performance of offshore structures are random variables whose estimation for design purposes involves some amount of uncertainty. The influence of uncertainty of inputs on the responses estimated for a particular kind of compliant structure, a tension leg platform (TLP), are presented. Compliant structures are an important class of offshore structure whose design and performance characteristics are sensitive to multiple environmental inputs, including waves, wind, current and water level. The design problem, illustrating the effect of variations in design levels of the various inputs on principal design characteristics for the TLP, is also discussed. Lessons concerning the use of multiple-input environmental design criteria, taking account of simultaneous probability of occurrence, are drawn.

INTRODUCTION

The design of compliant structures for deepwater offshore oil and gas field development has to account for the effects of a number of environmental parameters. An important distinction between compliant structures, which move significantly due to the action of wind, waves and current loads, and conventional bottom-founded fixed structures is that for the compliant structures the multiplicity of environmental parameters tend to have greater influence on the design of the overall configuration as well as some of the component parts.

The most prominent characteristic of most environmental parameters is randomness, which needs to be represented in models of the environmental phenomena which are used to establish design-level inputs to the design-analysis process. Measured data, which is the chief basis for setting-up environmental models, usually has some associated scatter which manifests itself in the models as uncertainty. Further, design is usually concerned with extreme, or rare, occurence events, which by definition are infrequently observed, and the same uncertainty holds for the few large events which must be used to characterize the extremes, or tails, of the distributions of the environmental parameters.

Models for environmental parameter estimation are mostly incomplete in that they typically represent only one part of the environment at a time, for instance, wave height, wind speed, current or water level. Since compliant structures are significantly influenced by several environmental parameters some knowledge of the probability of simultaneous occurence of the several inputs would seem appropriate for rational analysis of such structures. Current work to improve environmental modelling includes a lot of effort on the subject of joint-probabilities of occurence of environmental phenomena that are more or less correlated.

How important are the issues of environmental parameter uncertainty and probability of simultaneous occurence of environmental inputs for system design? A full probabalistic design methodology would, in principle, provide the designer with some insights into these matters. In this paper a more elementary, quasi-deterministic, method is employed to demonstrate how the designer can assess the significance of variability of environmental parameters on characteristic responses for a basis design. The logic is carried one step further, to show how variability would affect changes to the basis design assuming equivalent acceptability criteria for responses. The method will be demonstrated for a Tension Leg Platform (TLP) and the characteristic responses considered will be platform offset in surge, water level elevation on the columns and tension leg loads. The world's first

Figure 1
Hutton Field TLP

commercial TLP, for the Hutton Field in the U.K. North Sea, is shown in Figure 1.

This paper may be considered to be an extension of previous papers by one of the authors, on aspects of tension leg platform design [1,2] and on environmental response evaluation [3,4].

A brief discussion of environmental conditions and combinations will be presented and methods for evaluating responses reviewed, so that the relevance of the example evaluations can be recognized. Design considerations for tension leg platforms, relating to weight, buoyancy and tension balance, tow-out stability and tension leg dynamic loading will also be summarized.

The effects of variability of environmental parameters on the responses of a basis design TLP will be presented and discussed first. This case corresponds to evaluations for an existing design where, possibly, estimated environmental parameters for performance prediction may change because of new or more complete data becoming available or better interpretation of data and models. Alternatively, it might apply to moving an existing installation from one location to another. Evaluating the effects of variability of environmental inputs on desired design features is an activity which is appropriate to the design stage for a new or revised design. It will give the designer insight into which aspects of his design are sensitive to which particular environmental inputs.

ENVIRONMENTAL CONDITIONS

The motions, loadings and stresses in offshore structures are importantly influenced by several environmental parameters and their characteristics:

Waves   –   intensity (height)
              periodicity
              directionality (including spreading)

```
Winds      -    intensity
                direction
                gustiness

Currents   -    intensity
                direction

Water      -    tidal
Level           meteorological surge

Earthquakes
```

The characterization of these parameters and the choice of appropriate levels for use in design is an important part of the art and science of offshore platform design.

The basis of environmental characterizations is measured data and the interpretation of the data requires models of the several random phenomena. Reports from the International Ship Structures Congress (ISSC) Committee I.1 on Environmental Conditions [5,6], which are published every three years, give valuable summary information on advances in models for describing the ocean environment and an additions to the data base. A number of authors have discussed ways to apply the data and models for design [7,8,9].

Authoritative recommendations for the design of ocean structures [10,11,12] acknowledge that the designer can take account of the probability of simultaneous occurence of events in design-analysis. In practice, there are only a few models which have been developed to relate joint probability of occurence of phonenema, and most of those are for related aspects of the same parameter, such as wave height and period described by the Longuet-Higgins model [13].

Another example of deriving a combined event which is significant for some offshore structure responses is for water level variations due to tide and storm surge. By recognizing that these components of water level are quite independent of one another, Pugh and Vassie [14] developed a rational way to predict long return period (low probability) extremes of water level from relatively few years of acquired data. Figure 2 shows an example of the combined probability distribution of water level for a typical offshore site.

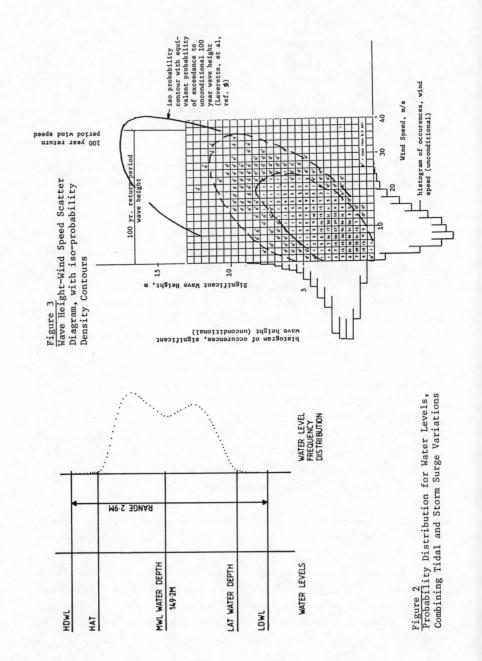

Figure 3
Wave Height-Wind Speed Scatter
Diagram, with iso-probability
Density Contours

Figure 2
Probability Distribution for Water Levels,
Combining Tidal and Storm Surge Variations

Leverette, et al, [9] have presented some examples of treating joint probability characteristics of several combinations of environmental phenomena. The basic objectives of such joint criteria estimation are to establish combinations of similar likelihood of exceedance, to quantitatively establish the probabilities of exceedance, and to compare the environmental "demand" with the system response "capability" (strength, or limiting excursion, for instance). Figure 3 shows a "scatter diagram" of wave height and wind speed, with histograms of the unconditional wave heights and wind speeds constructed along the axes. Iso-probability density contours can be drawn on the diagram and a "design" iso-probability-density curve may be chosen to have a prescribed probability of exceedance.

Further combinations of multiple events could be constructed if appropriate models, which account for the correlations between the several parameters, were available. Hindcasting models, which relate measured meteorological data to waves, currents and water level surge, offer some promise of providing a relatively complete representations of most of the key environmental parameters.

RESPONSE EVALUATIONS

Methods for calculating the behaviour of offshore structures in response to environmental effects have advanced rapidly in the past two decades as shown by rapidly expanding professional literature on the subject. Better methods for modelling, accounting for more features of inputs and responses, better numerical methods and better interpretations, for instance, for non-linear random response, have been developed.

When analysis methods become more complete and accurate it is generally appropriate for the designer to reconsider the related elements of the design process: i.e., selection of input parameter design levels and acceptance criteria, or partial safety factors. Introduction of more accurate three-dimensional potential theory computational models (discussed by Newman [15]), and accounting for more detailed information about the environment (such as wind gustiness, discussed by Kareem and Dalton [16] and by Simiu and Leigh [17]) should afford the designer more confidence in the reliability of his derived load estimates. Prudence requires retaining caution, however, because some uncertainty will remain due to the recognized variability of the inputs and because there will probably continue to be unknown-unknowns. A paper by Heaf, Henrywood and Wootton in 1975 [18] presented an assessment of the accuracy of the design process for offshore structures: they estimated the likely total error in platform strength, with 95% confidence limits, to be between 40 and 60 per cent, depending upon the amount of correlation between the several sources of error. It would be instructive to up-date this kind of assessment every ten years or so.

ENVIRONMENTAL DESIGN CONSIDERATIONS FOR TLP'S

Some characteristic responses for a tension leg platform will be discussed, so that the influence of variations in input environmental parameters can be reviewed further. Three modes of response will be considered as they have the greatest influence on design, when taken together with mission requirements, weight, space and arrangements and general structural configuration. These are: platform offset in surge, water level elevation on the columns and tension leg loads.

The schematic diagram of Fig. 4 illustrates a key feature of TLP's: steady (time-average) horizontal forces, $\overline{X}$, due to wind, current and wave-drift produce mean offsets, $\overline{x}$ in the horizontal direction. There is a set-down, or increase in draft, $\overline{z}$, associated with the offset. The mean horizontal offset is related to the mean horizontal force, the tension leg length, L, the excess buoyancy, and the effects of platform set-down, as follows:

$$\frac{\overline{x}}{L} = \frac{\overline{X} \cos \overline{\theta}}{\overline{T}} \tag{1}$$

$$\overline{X} = \overline{X} \text{ wind} + \overline{X} \text{ current} + \overline{X} \text{ waves} \tag{2}$$

$$\overline{T} = \overline{T} \text{ pres} + \Delta T_{wt} + \Delta T_{wl} + \Delta T \text{ set-down} \tag{3}$$

$$\Delta T \text{ set-down} = \gamma A_{wp} \overline{z} \tag{4}$$

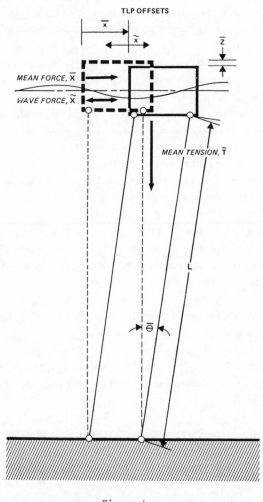

Figure 4

Schematic Representation of Forces and Movements of a TLP

$$\bar{z} = L(1-\cos\bar{\theta}) \simeq \frac{L}{2}\left(\frac{\bar{x}}{L}\right)^2 \tag{5}$$

where the meanings of most of the terms are evident from Fig. 4, and : $\triangle T_{wt}$ = change in total tension due to change in on-board weights (due, for instance, to consumption, resupply and/or ballasting); $\triangle T_{wl}$ = change in total tension due to varying water level (tide and storm surge); A_{wp} = cross-section area of the columns (water plane).

The set-down effect must be compensated in design by increasing deck elevation above still water level. Equations (2)-(5) provide a way to estimate the required increase in deck height to satisfy "air-gap" requirements. In addition, water level variations due to tide and meteorologically-induced surge, TLP slow-drift offsets and wave profile modifications should be accounted for; scale model tests are needed to pinpoint the latter influence. Designers may wish to "hedge their bets" on air gap assessment by designing underdeck structure to resist rare wave "slap" effects.

Tension leg loads must be estimated so that required strength can be provided and to assure that adverse effects of tendon slackness do not occur. The two chief purposes of tension leg pretension, or the excess of platform buoyancy over weight, are:

o   to provide horizontal restoring force to resist steady forces due to wind, current and waves

o   to prevent "snap" loads in case an extreme wave causes a large downward force which might cause the tension leg to go slack.

The second purpose usually controls the requirement for the amount of pretension used in design. It should be noted that this pretension will represent a significant portion of platform displacement, perhaps 15 to 30 per cent, and it should be recognized that this corresponds to a reduction of load-carrying capacity of the platform.

Efficient design of the TLP flotation structure calls for appropriate proportioning of the underwater hull form, that is, the displacement of columns and of pontoons, the draft, column spacing, and other details for a configuration like the Hutton TLP. Horton, et al [19] describe the optimization process for slender-cylinder configurations. The principles are discussed further by Gie and de Boom [20] and by Mercier, et al [4], among others.

A key lesson is that the amount of tension reduction due to wave action is greater for higher vertical centre-of-gravity because of surge-induced pitching moments. Therefore, increasing design weights high on the platform (on deck or above) requires buoyancy to be provided by the hull both to support its own weight, and a relatively larger amount of incremental pretension.

How "efficiently" can a TLP be with respect to environmental response? There are, of course, constraints due to preferred configurations and some responses, for instance due to winds, are not easily amenable to optimization. An indication of the "efficiency" of hull design for wave-induced tension leg forces is shown in Figure 5. The representation of the Tension leg force transfer function as a fraction of the hydrostatic buoyancy change due to water level variations gives an indication of the relative effectiveness of hull design for wave-induced tension leg force cancellation. The figure also illustrates the comparison of experimental results with results of two computer programs, DIFRAC described by Gie and de Boom [20] and TERICA described by Faltinsen, et al [21] from the model tests. Both programs use advanced velocity potential methods but even for the fundamental linear transfer function calculation it is evident that precise agreement is elusive. This kind of response is a consequence of hydrodynamic force cancellation effects which depend on hull form design and results are sensitive to calculate small differences.

Designers must have computational methods available for estimating a variety of hydrodynamic effects and the new analysis methods are filling these needs. However, scale model tests will continue to play

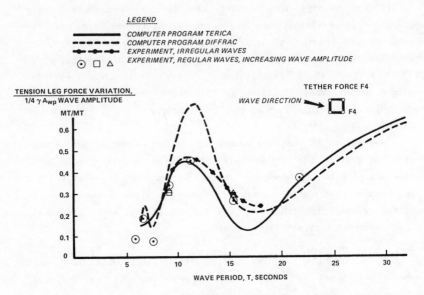

Figure 5
Comparison of Calculated and Experimentally Measured Tension Leg Forces.
Efficiency of wave-force attenuation is illustrated by force amplitude
being expressed as a fraction of hydrostatic buoyancy change.

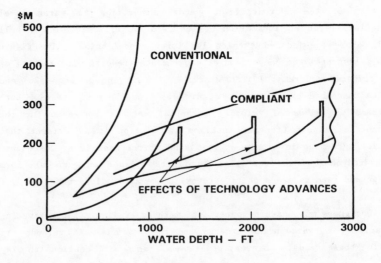

Figure 6
Effects of Technology Advances on Cost Trends for Platforms

a vital role in the development and design of marine structures in general and TLP's in particular.

Correlative design criteria for TLP's, which affect and are affected by hydrodynamic considerations, include the fundamental vertical force balance and Naval Architectural Stability during tow-out before installation. The vertical force balance, for calm weather, may be written.

$$\text{Weight + riser tension + pretension = displacement} \qquad (6)$$

Weight, in turn, is composed of some elements which are not very sensitive to hydrodynamic (and hydrostatic) design considerations, such as plant weight and added weights, and some which are, such as hull and deck structure.

The following discussion of the stability requirement is taken directly from Ref. 2:

"During construction and tow-out, up to the time of installation of tension legs, a TLP may spend considerable time as a column-stabilized mobile unit. Naval Architectural Stability considerations for this class of unit naturally apply to TLP's in this condition and can importantly affect design. Stability is dependent on weight distribution and hydrostatic characteristics of the hull form. Stability at small angles is measured by metacentric height (GM) which may be expressed by the following approximation, which shows the influence of column spacing:

$$GM = CDR \left(\frac{B^2}{4T} + \frac{T}{2} \right) + (1-CDR) \ \frac{T_{LH}}{2} - \overline{KG} \qquad (7)$$

where: B is the transverse spacing (centre-to-gravity) between rows of columns of the hull. T is the column draft. CDR is the ratio of column displacement (equal draft times columns cross-section area of all columns) to total hull displacement. T_{LH} is the depth of the lower hull (i.e., the depth of the pontoons). $\overline{KG}$ is the height of the CG.

"GM must be positive, preferably about 2 or 3 m. Stability can be significantly increased by increasing column spacing. For a given design, stability may be increased by reducing $\overline{KG}$, which can be affected by adding ballast water in compartments in the lower hull.

"TLP stability while afloat is a temporary requirement, up until installation is accomplished and the use of removable temporary flotation/stability chambers has been proposed. In this way column spacing may be chosen strictly to satisfy deck area requirements and some economics may accrue. For the present discussion, however, such temporary devices will not be considered.

"The premise of tow-out stability tends to produce designs having large plan form areas. Consequently, space allocation will generally not be a serious constraint for TLP designs."

The relationships discussed above are the bases for the following discussion on the influences of uncertainties.

INFLUENCE OF UNCERTAINTIES ON DESIGN

In order to illustrate the influence of uncertainties and variabilities in the response of, or alternatively, the design characteristics of a TLP a basis design will be chosen. Ref 2 describes some of the approximate characteristics for the design of a TLP for 600m water depth for service in the North Sea. Design parameters which are significant to principal TLP dimensions are given in Table 1.

TABLE I

BASIS TLP DESIGN REQUIREMENTS

o   Number of wells = 20 (11 producers, 9 injectors)

o   Oil production rate = 100,000 BOPD

o   240-man living quarters

o   Water depth 600 m

o   Seabed soil competent for piled or gravity foundations

o   Environmental conditions similar to Northern North Sea, e.g.

Design wave height: 16 m significant
Characteristic periods T_z: 13.0–14.6 s
Design wind (1 hr. mean): 37.5 m/s
Tide/surge water level variation: 1.5m
Current speed (average): 0.5 m/s

o   Drilling rig, equipment and stores for 20,000 ft. well depth

Weight estimates are given in Table II.

TABLE II

ESTIMATED WEIGHTS FOR POSTULATED 600m WATER DEPTH TLP

All weights in metric tons

Plant weight	6500
Riser tensions	4500
Deck structure	9000
Hull structure	20,600
Tension leg system support	400
Added weights	4500
Total	45,000

Principal Dimensions of the basis design are presented in Table III.

TABLE III

PRINCIPAL DIMENSIONS OF BASIS TLP DESIGN

Dimensions
Deck

Length	76 m
Breadth	76 m
Depth	12 m

Hull

Length overall	92 m
Breadth overall	92 m
Draft of MWL	35 m
Main deck elevation above baseline at MWL 6 columns	25.5m
Water plane area	1254m^2

Weights
    Design weight (from Table 1)   45,000 MT
    Mooring pretension, at MWL   15,000 MT

    Total displacement   60,000 MT

These characteristics are approximate, obtained from a conceptual design study only, and are not represented to be optimum in any way. They will suffice, however, to investigate the effects of variations in environmental parameters on platform response and on preferred design characteristics.

First, the effects on response of the basis design to variations in environmental parameters, expressing a plausible range of uncertainty in the basis conditions listed in Table I, will be shown. The assumed ranges are listed in Table IV:

TABLE IV

ENVIRONMENTAL PARAMETER UNCERTAINTIES

Parameter	Basis Value	Range
Wave ht	16 m signif.	14.4 m, 17.6 m (± 10%)
Design Wind (1 hr mean)	37.5 mls	33.75 m/s, 41.25 m/s (±10%)
Water Level Variation	± 1.5 m	−0.5 m and 0.5 m
Current Speed	0.5 m/s	0.3 m/s − 0.7 m/s

The effects of these variations in inputs on three modes of response are illustrated in Table V. The calculation methods used to derive these estimates of response are similar to those described in published literature, especially refs [4.19 and 20], and as recently codified in draft form in a recommended practice document for the design of TLP's, prepared by a group of specialists for the American Petroleum Institute [22].

TABLE V

INFLUENCE OF ENVIRONMENTAL PARAMETER
VARIATION ON RESPONSE OF BASIS TLP DESIGN

Parameter	Variation	Steady Offset (m)	Response W.L. Elev on Column (m)	Tension (per corner) Max (MT)	Tension (per corner) Min (MT)
Wave Ht	Basis (16m)	58	24.3	8700	200
	14.4m	56.5	22.15	8450	400
	17.6m	59.6	26.5	8950	(0)
Design Wind	Basis	58	24.3	8700	200
	33.75 m/s	50.7	23.6	8360	310
	41.25 m/s	66	25.2	9110	90
Water Level	Basis	58	24.3	8700	200
	−0.5	58	23.8	−	360
	+0.5	58	24.8	8360	−
Current Speed	Basis	58	24.3	8700	200
	0.3 m/s	50.5	23.6	8470	200
	0.7 m/s	69.0	25.6	9105	200

These results require some comment. First, wave height variation
has the greatest effect on the water level elevation on the column, due
mostly to wave crest height (which is assumed to be augmented about 10
per cent due to wave profile modification and run-up effects), and is
slightly influenced by set-down due to offset. There is significant
uncertainty associated with wave elevation estimates, and the design of
the underside of the deck should allow for possible wave impacts, so
the fact that wave elevation estimates exceed column height may be
marginally acceptable. Wave height also has greatest influence on
minimum tension, where no allowance is made for variations of platform
offset or setdown. Wind speed has, somewhat surprisingly, the greatest
effect on maximum tension, owing to a combined effect on overturning
moment and on platform offset and setdown. The relative importance of
water level and current speed is less clear inasmuch as the amounts of
variation considered are proportionately greater than for waves and
wind. The variations are, however, reasonable as expressions of
uncertainties of the design level estimates.

This approach to describing effects of uncertainty of design parameters on response is, perhaps, less elegant than the probabilistic method as expressed, for instance, by Nolte [23], but the exercise gives the designer a clear picture of the importance of the several variables.

How would the basis design be changed if the basis environmental parameters were modified by the amounts expressed in Table IV? Changes in column heights would affect tow-out stability requirements (column spacing), platform weight and tension leg loading. Correction of insufficient minimum tension requires additional pretension and displacement. Some simple approximate design estimates, based on equations (6) and (7) and crude weight formulations have been used to illustrate the probable effects on the basis design's principal dimensions, and other modes of response, for the changes in environmental inputs: results are shown in Table VI (see next page).

These results exhibited in Table VI are based on adjusting the original basis design so that it has essentially the same "clearance" between column top and calculated water level on the column and the same KG for tow out and/or the same estimated minimum tensions. The wave height variations assumed lead to the most significant adjustments from the basis design in terms of structural steel weight variation and principal dimensions of column spacing and deck elevation.

The effects of changes to more than one environmental parameter will produce cumulative changes to the design. For instance, reducing wave height by 10 per cent and increasing minimum design water level by 0.5m should enable the designer to reduce structural steel weight by around 1700 MT (about 6 per cent). For large variations of parameters the cumulative effects will not, of course, be simply linearly additive.

This type of ancillary design investigation allows the designer to better appreciate the influence of changes to design environmental parameters on the principal features of a TLP design. Other design considerations, including hydrodynamic and structural design/analysis

TABLE VI

INFLUENCE OF ENVIRONMENTAL PARAMETER VARIATION
ON PRINCIPAL DIMENSIONS OF REVISED DESIGN

Parameter	Variation	Displ (MT)	Weight (MT)	Dimensions Pretn's (MT)	Dk Elev (m)	Col Spcg (m)
Wave Ht	Basis	60,000	45,000	15,000	25.5	76
	14.4m	57,970	43,770	14,200	23.35	75.1
	17.6m	62,050	46,250	15,800	27.7	76.9
Design Wind	Basis	60,000	45,000	15,000	25.5	76
	33.75 m/s	59,095	44,445	14,560	24.8	75.7
	41.25 m/s	61,000	45,560	15,440	26.4	76.4
Water Level	Basis	60,000	45,000	15,000	25.5	76
	-0.5m	58,890	44,530	14,360	25.0	75.8
	+0.5m	60,230	45,230	15,000	26.0	76.2
Current Speed	Basis	60,000	45,000	15,000	25.5	76
	0.3 m/s	59,685	44,685	15,000	24.8	75.7
	0.7 m/s	60,570	45,570	15,000	26.8	76.5

procedures, general structural and hydrodynamic configuration, detailed structural features, construction sequences, etc., also influence the overall design quality and efficiency. It is important to try to maintain a fair balance of the different aspects of design: as improved methods are adapted for one element of design other elements should be reconsidered.

DISCUSSION

The objectives of advancing designs and design methods is to improve the system being considered in respect of performance capability, cost or some other measure. The example of the sensitivity of the design of a particular kind of compliant offshore structure, a TLP, to environmental design parameters, is intended to illustrate the possible scope for improvements in design if more complete and detailed information on combined environmental inputs were available. There is some reason to believe that research which is underway and being planned will show that designers can safely reduce overall design environmental criteria and therefore reduce platform size requirements. This, together with other design improvements may make possible sufficient cost savings that further progress in deepwater offshore exploration and production can be advanced in spite of reduced prices available for crude oil production. Figure 6, from a recent paper on Compliant Structures by Curtis and Mercier [24] illustrates a hoped-for effect of the introduction of improvements in design and technology for deepwater systems: advances leading to cost reductions. The first generation of designs for novel advanced systems has to adapt design methods for analogous systems in a somewhat conservative fashion. It is the author's belief that such advanced systems offer considerable scope for improvements in capability and reductions in cost as a consequence of adapting advanced design methods.

REFERENCES

1. Mercier, J.A., Evolution of Tension Leg Platform Technology, paper presented to the Third International Conference on Behaviour of Offshore Structures, Boston, (1982).

2. Mercier, J.A. Van Hooff, R.W. and Faulker, D., Deep Water Tension Leg Platform, Proceedings, Eleventh World Petroleum Congress, London, (1983).

3. Mercier, J.A., Environmental Loadings for Design of Oceanic Structures, Proceedings, Ship Structures Symposium '84 SNAME, Arlington, (1984).

4. Mercier, J.A., Leverette, S.J. and Bliault, A.L., Evaluation of Hutton TLP Response to Environmental Loads, OTC 4429, Proceedings, 14th Offshore Technology Conference, Houston, (1982).

5. Hogben, N. (Chairman), Environmental Conditions, Report of Committee I.1, International Ship Structures Congress, Boston (1979).

6. Ochi, M.K. (Chairman), Environmental Conditions, Report of Committee I.1., International Ship Structures Congress, Paris (1982).

7. Ochi, M.K., Wave Statistics for the Design of Ships and Ocean Structures, Transactions, SNAME, 86, New York, (1978).

8. Bea, R.G., Hurricane Wave Height and Forces, 5 part article in Oil and Gas Journal, Sept/Oct/Nov. (1983).

9. Leverette, S.J., Bradley, M.D., and Bliault, A., An Integrated Approach to Setting Environmental Design Criteria for Floating Production Facilities, Proceedings, Third International Conference on Behaviour of Offshore Structures, Boston, (1982).

10. D. of En. (U.K.), Guidance on the Design and Construction of Offshore Installations, HMSO, London (1977).

11. Det Norske Veritas, Rules for the Design, Construction and Inspection of Offshore Structures, Oslo (1977).

12. American Bureau of Shipping, Rules for Building and Classing Mobile Offshore Drilling Units, New York (1980).

13. Longuet-Higgins, M.S., On the Joint Distribution of Wave Periods and Amplitudes in a Random Wave Field, Proceedings, Royal Society of London A389 (1983) 241-258.

14. Pugh, D.T. and Vassie, J.M., Applications of the Joint Probability Method for Extreme Sea Level Computations, Proceedings, Inst. of Civ. Eng. London, Part 2, (1980).

15. Newman, J.N., Three Dimensional Wave Interactions with Ships and Platforms, Proceedings International Workshop on Ship and Platform Motions, Berkely, (1983).

16. Kareem, A., and Dalton, C., Dynamic Effects of Wind on Tension Leg Platforms, OTC 4229, Proccedings Fourteenth Offshore Technology Conference, Houston, (1982).

17. Simiu, E.L. and Leigh, S.D., Turbulent Wind and Tension Leg Platform Surge, J. Struct Eng, Vol. 110, No. 4, April (1984).

18. Heaf, N.J., Henrywood, R.K. and Wootton, L.R., Assessment of the Accuracy of the Design Process for Off-shore Structures, Proceedings Offshore Structures Conf, Inst. Civ. Engr., London (1975) 145-150.

19. Horton, E.E., McCammon, L.B., Murtha, J.P., and Paulling, J.R. Optimization of Stable Platform Characteristics, OTC 1553, Proceedings Fourth Offshore Technology Conference, Houston (1972).

20. Gie., T.S. and de Boom, W.C., The Wave Induced Motions of a Tension Leg Platform in Deep Water, OTC 4074, Proceedings Thirteenth Offshore Technology Conference, Houston (1981).

21. Faltionsen, O., Fylling, I., van Hooff, R.W., and Teizen, P.S., Theoretical and Experimental Investigations of Tension Leg Behaviour, Proceedings, Third International Conference on Behaviour of Offshore Structures, Boston (1982).

22. American Petroleum Institute, (Draft) Recommended Practice for the Design of Tension Leg Platforms, API RP2T Dallas (1986).

23. Nolte, K.G., The Effects of Uncertainty in Wave Force Coefficients for Offshore Structures, OTC 3066, Proceedings, Tenth Offshore Technology Conference, Houston, (1978).

24. Curtis, L.B. and Mercier, J.A. Compliant Structures paper presented to the 1985 Annual Meeting of the American Petroleum Institute, Dallas (1985).

VIBRATION OF SHIP STRUCTURES
WITH PARTICULAR REFERENCE TO WARSHIPS

G Ward
British Maritime Technology (BMT)
Wallsend, UK

ABSTRACT

A review of vibration criteria and appropriate limits is given as they are currently applied to merchant ships and how they could be applied to warships. Comprehensive vibration trials in a Type 42 are summarised: these refer to environmental excitation (for main hull resonance frequencies) and propeller-shaft excitation (for response). The relative significance of shaft rate and its multiples is illustrated for a number of warships and the importance of vibration trials' data on the development of design guidance is emphasised.

INTRODUCTION

Vibration is a topic which has played an important part in the work of BMT, and BSRA before it; vibration in warships has occasionally been part of that work. Most of the procedures and data previously reported by BMT [1] have been concerned with merchant ships but more recent work has been concerned with extending these procedures and data to a range of warship types. Some warships, such as Fleet Auxiliaries, are generally sufficiently similar to merchant ships for the existing BMT "Ship Design Manual - Vibration" to be applied directly; other types, such as the modern Aircraft Carrier or Mine Hunters constructed of GRP, have properties which would need particular consideration.

Slow speed diesel main engines with four or five cylinders are probably the main concern for vibration in merchant ships with hull surface forces in way of the propeller no longer a major problem. The topic of propeller induced vibration has been well studied and reported to the point that we have now reached a state where enough is known to avoid problems in service, provided there is time and a commitment to treat the subject at the design stage. Such studies have primarily been carried out on single screw ships but much of this work is relevant to twin screw ships, as indicated later, and therefore has direct application to many warships; this is true of both the detailed analysis of hull surface and propeller-shaft forces and the model test procedures. Propeller blade rate excitation and its harmonics are relevant to local vibration, especially in the aft region; auxiliary diesel machinery is also a source of local vibration. For warships, particularly of the Frigate type, in the absence of main propulsion diesels, it would seem that the interaction between the propeller-shaft and its bearings and supports is of particular concern for main hull vibration.

The objective of BMT's vibration work for merchant ships has been, broadly speaking, twofold. The first is concerned with the provision of design procedures and guidance, which has been consolidated into the Ship Design Manual-Vibration; this has provided formalised technological support which allows the naval architect to avoid vibration problems in service by good design work. The second, is the build up of experience which supports a trouble-shooting service which BMT has performed world wide, over the last 30 years or so; this has resulted in many ship trials the purpose of which has been to measure and analyse vibration and make recommendations on how to alleviate the problems. It needs to be emphasised that in both types of work there is a need to have criteria, with which to assess the results, and also limits of acceptability for each criterion.

Criteria which could be used to assess warship vibration should encompass requirements related to a suitable environment for continuous and efficient working of the equipment. Also, with regard to the crew and their exposure to vibration, the vibration environment at normal cruising speeds should be no worse than that in merchant ships (although there are of course special circumstances associated with emergency operations); indeed, the possibly longer voyage times and intense concentration required

for many tasks, imply that every attempt should be made to achieve
even lower levels.

2.   VIBRATION RESPONSE CRITERIA AND ACCEPTABLE LIMITS

Much has been written on vibration criteria for application in
merchant shipping practice and the limits that should be applied in
various circumstances, but [2] and [3] of the International
Organisation for Standardisation (ISO) are the only two appropriate
international documents. Limits presented in these documents, have
been the subject of much international debate and, as one would
expect, are increasingly being quoted in contractual dealings. The
guidelines for the overall evaluation of vibration in merchant
ships, [2], has gone from a draft proposal (D.P.1979), through the
stages of a Draft International Standard (DIS), to a full
International Standard (1984); even now the ISO document is open
to different interpretations and can be the cause of protracted
discussions between builder and owner. However, the two ISO
documents reflect current technology and general opinion and do
provide valuable guidance, in the form of criteria and limits, for
evaluation of the shipboard vibration environment.

Although the limits are defined explicitly in numerical terms
(to encourage precise measurements) it is important to take into
account the variability in the procedures used for taking and
analysing the measurements and the restrictions in their
application. Reference [2] provides guidelines for the overall
evaluation of ship vibration where experience related to structural
stress, effects on equipment and human performance and discomfort
have been applied. That is, a general assessment of acceptability
has been linked with a general measurement and definition of the
ship's vibration environment. More specific consideration of
equipment and machinery is covered by Defence Standards and
Classification Society requirements. Reference [3] is specifically
concerned with human safety, performance capability and comfort.

Considering [2] and [3] further, with respect to their application to warships, the former specifies severities of vibration (for both turbine and diesel ships) which may be applied to:-

    a) the assessment of hull and superstructure vibration in normally occupied spaces;

    b) the updating and improvement of hull reference amplitudes;

whereas [3] provides guidelines for the evaluation of human exposure to vibration, according to three general criteria :-

    a) comfort;

    b) working efficiency;

    c) safety and health.

Fig. 1, which is used in [2], shows the ISO limit curves on a grid of vibration displacement, velocity and acceleration against frequency. A response (peak amplitude), falls in one of three regions:-

    a) Adverse comments not probable;

    b) Adverse comments probable;

    c) A hatched zone which lies between a) and b) and which

represents a shipboard vibration environment commonly experienced and accepted.

It is the author's view that, because of the general nature of the data used to define these limit lines, they could be used for warship purposes (other than specific operational requirements), where the lower line could be taken as the design limit and the upper line could be taken as a contractual limit. The ISO document restricts its application to a frequency range of 1 to 100 Hz but it should be recognised that experience and related vibration data are limited at the lower end of this frequency range and the higher end is concerned with local vibration, for which additional criteria could apply. Also, Fig.1 has been derived from data taken on larger ships and therefore ISO has restricted its application to ships greater than 100m.

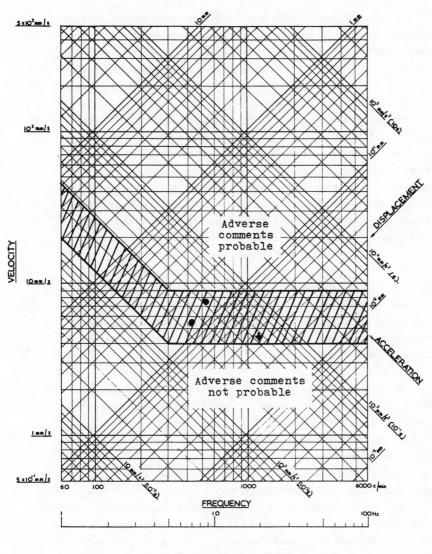

● Data from Figure 2   ✚ Data from Figure 3

FIGURE 1

Guidelines for the evaluation of vertical and horizontal
vibration in merchant ships (peak values).

Reference 3, which is a discussion document relating to human exposure on seagoing ships, and its source document ISO 2631/1, are specifically related to the effects of vibration on personnel and are based on laboratory measurements leading to limits defined by "reduced comfort boundary", "fatigue decreased deficiency boundary" and "exposure limit". Unfortunately, much confusion has arisen in attempting to relate these to Fig.1 which is used in [2]; both refer to analysed values at particular frequencies but the former uses rms values of vibration response and the latter uses maximum repetitive peak values. Where relevant detailed measurements have been taken then appropriate analysis can be carried out for both methods of presentation (Figs 2 and 3 give examples), but the suggested crest factors in [2] for conversion of rms and peak values do not consistently conform to experience at BMT.

There is an ISO working group currently attempting to reconcile the difficulties of having two guidance notes which use different terms and different criteria; at this time the writer would propose using [2] for design targets and as a basis for contracts, as stated above, with [3] used for assessing fatigue decreased proficiency at specific work stations.

There are, however, still further interpretation anomalies. These are related to vibration at a point which, when analysed displays:-

a) significant amplitudes at two or more frequencies close to each other (in one direction);

b) significant amplitudes in two directions perpendicular to each other (with the same frequency).

The components of a) and b) are currently assessed individually on the ISO diagrams and their combined effect on human reactions are not considered. As an example, Fig. 1 shows data from Fig. 2; each component is in the hatched zone and therefore acceptable but the combined effect could be expected to be unacceptable, as was actually the case for the ship referred to in

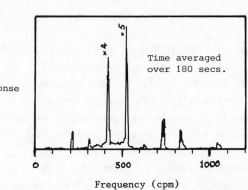

Response

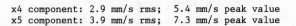

Frequency (cpm)

x4 component: 2.9 mm/s rms; 5.4 mm/s peak value
x5 component: 3.9 mm/s rms; 7.3 mm/s peak value

FIGURE 2   rms Spectrum of Wheel House Top Longitudinal Vibration
on a 45,000 TDW Bulk Carrier at 105 rpm

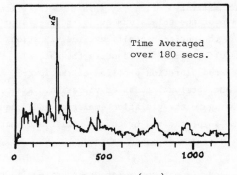

Response

Frequency (cpm)

x5 component: 1.8 mm/s rms; 4.3 mm/s peak value

FIGURE 3   rms Spectrum of Vertical Vibration in Crews Mess
(above propellers) in a Warship at 240 rpm

Fig. 2.

Another interpretation difficulty which appears to be related to warships is the presence of a broad band response with superimposed resonances, as shown in Fig. 3. The resonance amplitude when plotted on Fig. 1 is in the hatched zone and therefore could be expected to be acceptable but in this particular case the combination of a single resonance and the broad band response was considered subjectively to be unacceptable. Measurements on other warships display the same broad band characteristic, probably due to the lighter scantlings; therefore it would seem that warships could well have an extra factor to be taken into account when using the ISO criteria and limits. Fig. 2, which is typical of merchant ships, does not display the same characteristic.

3.   REVIEW OF SOME WARSHIP VIBRATION MEASUREMENTS
3.1 Type 42 Vibration Trials.
The main objective of the trials summarised below was to acquire information on the environmentally excited vibration response of the main hull in order to identify the natural frequencies and associated vibration profiles of the lower vertical, horizontal and torsional modes of vibration. A second objective was to investigate the vibration amplitude and frequency characteristics of the ship, excited by the propeller and shaft system and machinery, over a wide speed range.

The trials formed only a part of a larger investigation that BMT undertook for MoD(PE) in 1984, which involved full-scale measurements on twelve surface warships ranging from small patrol craft to the largest ships in the fleet. The results of the overall investigation will be used to extend and improve existing design prediction methods for estimating the main hull vibration characteristics.

3.1.1 <u>Ship and Trial Details</u>

The main details of the ship are:-

      Length O.A.   141m

      Breadth   14.9m

      Standard Displacement 3500 tonnes

The main propulsion plant comprises two sets of gas turbines, each set driving a 5-bladed controllable pitch propeller. The vibration tests were carried out in a depth of water greater than five times the mean draught, to avoid bottom effects. Measurements were taken in good weather, estimated to be Beaufort Force 1 with a slight swell.

3.1.2 <u>Measurement Programme</u>

For the measurements, a set of vibration velocity pick-ups and propeller shaft rotational speed pulses were recorded simultaneously on magnetic tape for laboratory processing on a FFT Modal Analyser.

To provide information on the natural frequencies and modal profiles of the lower hull modes, measurements were taken at various times, without interfering with the ship's normal operational duties. Responses were taken at each end of the hull and along the deck edge of the main deck, together with a few measurements on the centreline to aid identification of the torsional modes. Generally 5 minute recordings were taken.

To provide information on the vibration response of the ship's structure to excitation forces from the propeller and machinery it was necessary to carry out a second set of measurements. This involved recording the vibration at a number of positions such as the extreme ends of the main deck, bridge top, signal mast and machinery spaces as the propeller shaft speed was increased slowly (at a nominal rate of 1 rev/min/min) from 60 rev/min to a maximum

speed. Rudder movements during this period (about 3 hours) were
restricted.

3.1.3 Method of Analyses

The environmentally excited vibration levels were low, for the
conditions encountered during the tests. However, using the FFT
analyser and performing a large number of spectral analyses of the
records, it was possible to reject the background noise and enhance
the environmentally excited vibration. Using this technique
several of the lower resonant frequencies of the main hull
vertical, horizontal and torsional modes were detected from the
vibration measurements taken at the extreme ends of the hull.
Carrying out a similar spectral analysis for all the measurement
positions and by dividing each in turn by the reference aft end
vibration spectrum, the lower main hull modes were positively
identified by profile. This measurement and analysis technique has
the great advantage that the natural frequencies and hull modes can
be rapidly determined without the need for special trial conditions
related to ship speed or even weather.

For the propeller and machinery excited vibration three types
of analysis were carried out on the recordings:

.   A spectral analysis taken at nominally full power in order to
    assess the responses in terms of their constituent
    components and to establish the major components present
    at any one position.
.   An 'order' tracking analysis over the whole speed range
    (velocity amplitude versus propeller rev/min) for each of the
    major components in order to establish the amplitude-frequency
    characteristics of the structure.
.   A polar plot analysis of the records taken over a limited
    speed range, in order to determine accurate modal damping
    values of the lower hull modes of vibration.

3.1.4 Results

All the results are presented in terms of vibration velocity
mm/s (peak).

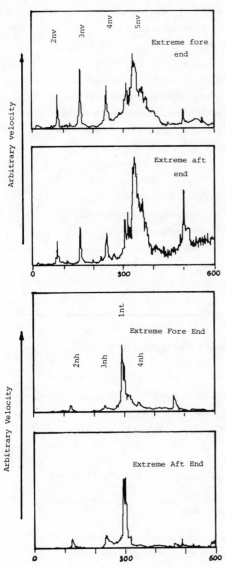

FIGURE 4

Environmentally Excited Vibration;
Vertical Hull Modes;
Type 42.

FIGURE 5

Environmentally Excited Vibration;
Horizontal and Torsional Hull Modes;
Type 42.

Environmental Excitation of Main Hull Vibration

The frequencies of the lower hull vertical modes can be
identified from the results given in Fig. 4 which show the vertical
vibration spectra measured at the extreme ends of the ship.
Additional plots of phase and coherence relationships helped
establish the modes. The minor peaks are generally associated with
multiples of the propeller shaft speed. A similar set of results
for the transverse measurements are given in Fig. 5 and these show
a number of clear resonance frequencies which are associated with
the lower hull horizontal and torsional modes of vibration.

Propulsion System Excited Vibration

Figs. 6 to 10 show selected spectra of vertical and transverse
vibration, measured at several positions on the ship for a
propeller shaft rotational speed of 240 rev/min.

The main features of the spectra are:

. The constituent components of vibration, with the exception of
  positions above the propeller, are generally associated with
  distinct multiples of the propeller shaft rotational speed.

. The dominant components of excitation at the aft end are seen
  to occur at all multiples of propeller speed from 1 to 5; the
  highest amplitudes are generally associated with the 1st and
  5th multiples at most locations. (The 5th is the propeller
  blade rate component).

. The higher frequency vibration attenuates with distance from
  the propeller; at the forward end only components in the
  range 0 to 15 Hz are evident (not reproduced).

. Above the propellers, the vibration is essentially broadband
  with the excitation of a large number of frequencies.

Figs. 11 and 12 present the vibration response characteristics

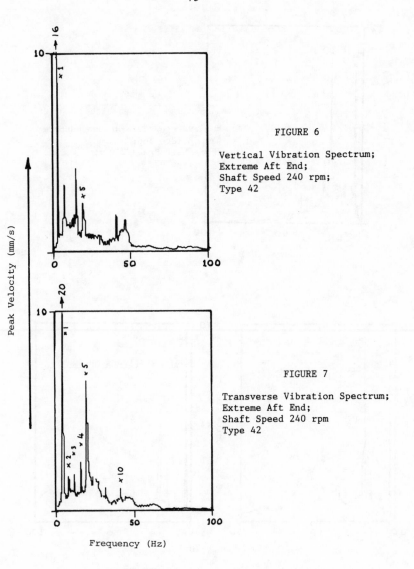

FIGURE 6

Vertical Vibration Spectrum;
Extreme Aft End;
Shaft Speed 240 rpm;
Type 42

FIGURE 7

Transverse Vibration Spectrum;
Extreme Aft End;
Shaft Speed 240 rpm
Type 42

Peak Velocity (mm/s)

Frequency (Hz)

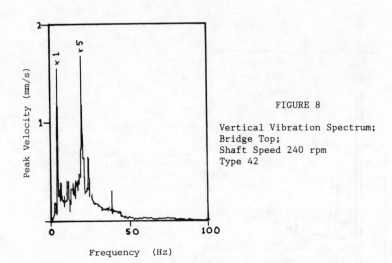

FIGURE 8

Vertical Vibration Spectrum;
Bridge Top;
Shaft Speed 240 rpm
Type 42

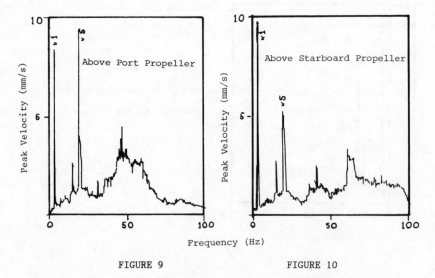

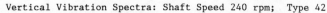

FIGURE 9   FIGURE 10

Vertical Vibration Spectra: Shaft Speed 240 rpm;   Type 42

measured at selected positions for propeller speeds between 50 and
240 rev/min.   The vibration responses shown are those excited by
the two major components of excitation namely the 1st and 5th
multiples of shaft speed respectively.

The results for vertical and longitudinal vibration excited by
1st order forces are shown in Fig. 11; they exhibit at each
location three distinct resonances, with frequencies corresponding
to the 2-, 3- and 4-node vertical modes as identified from the
environmental results.   The levels of vibration at resonance are
seen to be high.   At the extreme ends of the hull, these are in
excess of the acceptable amplitudes generally used for merchant
ships.

Comparable plots for the 5th order response in Fig. 12 show
the highest vibration levels occurring closest to the source of
excitation at the aft end.   The minor resonant peaks at low
propeller speeds are associated with the higher hull modes (for
example the 5-node).   The peaks in the upper speed range (e.g.
those at the extreme aft end) are associated with what are
essentially local vibration modes of the structure.

A similar set of results for the transverse measurements (not
reproduced) showed two distinct resonant frequencies which
correspond to the 2- and 3-node horizontal modes of vibration.
There was also a large 5th order component at the aft end.

<u>Damping</u>
Most damping values were derived directly from the response
curves, but the accuracy of this method depends on how well the
resonance peaks are defined.   Because propeller speed normally

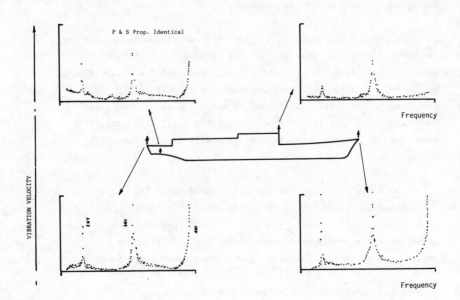

FIGURE 11   1st Order Vertical Vibration;   Main Hull & Superstructure

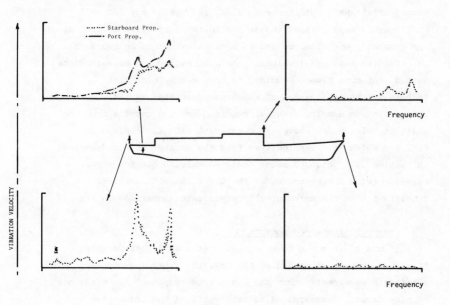

FIGURE 12   5th Order Vertical Vibration;   Main Hall and Superstructure

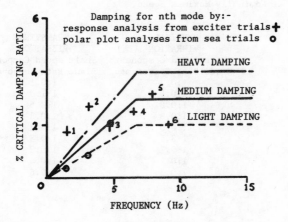

FIGURE 13.   Comparison of Modal Damping Values

shows variations about its mean value, such peaks may not be sufficiently well defined and errors in the derivation of damping are generally unavoidable, and in some cases it may be impossible to establish meaningful values. An alternative and more accurate method (but more time consuming) is to use the Polar Plot technique, the application of which was described in [4]. More information on damping is still required but the results from the analyses referred to above are consistent with those given in Fig. 13, which have been derived from the exciter trials described in section 3.3. Also, damping analyses carried out for other warships (with the exception of the G.R.P. mine hunter) are consistent with the merchant ship experience summarised in Fig. 13.

3.2   Major Vibration Components

It was of interest to note that over a series of warship trials, mainly Frigates and Destroyers, the vibration component at shaft rate was greater than the blade rate component for eight out of nine cases; this applied to both vertical and transverse vibration in a generally consistent manner. Table 1 shows these results expressed as a ratio with shaft rate response set to 1.

TABLE 1

Ratios of Vibration Components at Aft End for Shaft and Blade Rate Frequencies at Nominally Maximum Speed.

SHIP	VERTICAL VIBRATION Shaft Speed Component: Blade Rate Component	TRANSVERSE VIBRATION Shaft speed Component: Blade Rate Component
A	1:0.3	1:0.1
B	1:0.5	1:1.3
C	1:0.8	1:0.6
D	1:0.3	1:0.3
E	1:0.5	1:0.2
F	1:3.5	1:0.8
G	1:0.2	1:0.3
H	1:0.2	1:0.4
I	1:0.3	1:0.6

3.3   Exciter Trials and Comparisons with Calculation.

The sea trials summarised in the previous section provided
data on the general vibration characteristics of the ship and, with
similar sets of data for other ships, allow methods to be developed
for application in design. Such methods are both empirical and
analytical. For the latter, because of the lack of information on
the exciting forces, it is reasonable only to establish resonance
frequencies. However, the use of an exciter, where the forces are
known, allows one to derive the response per unit of exciting force
(mobility) which is then readily compared with analysis; this
provides a check on the modelling of all the modal properties.

There have been many papers presented on the applicability, or
otherwise, of the various modelling approaches to the calculation
of ship vibration characteristics; [5] summarises some of the work
done by BMT for 1, 2 and 3-D structural models and [6] is a
relevant recent thesis. Briefly, 1-D beam element models can be
used quite successfully for vertical, lateral and torsional lower
hull modes to identify resonance frequencies ([7] and [8]) but they
are not so suitable for the calculation of responses. 3-D finite
element methods (FEM) can be sufficiently accurate for the whole
range of frequencies of relevance, for both the calculation of
resonance frequencies and for responses, but the detailed
information required and the effort involved tends to restrict
their use to research exercises. Certainly for merchant ships, the
time requirements for such analyses is not consistent with the time
scales for design, but they should be of more relevance to warships
where the design period is more extended. A compromise is to use
2-D FEM, where not only the lower hull mode resonances can be
derived but also the mobilities (and responses, where the exciting
forces can be estimated). However, it needs to be emphasised that
for successful application of any of the three methods, experience
is required of modelling approaches which have been checked against
full scale measurements. In particular, the 2-D FEM model needs

correlation data and is probably best used in association with the 1-D model.

The applicability of various finite element models for the calculation of the dynamic behaviour of the Type 42 Destroyer has been investigated by BMT with calculations carried out of the lower hull vibration modes and of the vertical mobilities, at various positions, for a unit force acting on the quarter deck (the exciter position). These have been compared with full scale trials, some of which used a 30kN vibration exciter. The vibration exciter was of the counter rotating mass type and gave a unidirectional force proportional to the square of its rotational speed. It was mounted on a stiff seating, welded to the quarter deck at the centreline. Vibration velocity transducers were placed along the main deck and tests were carried out over a total frequency range of 1.5 - 10Hz. Figs. 14 and 15 show generally good agreement between the measured and calculated mobilities. The resonance frequencies of the first five measured modal peaks line up well with the calculated values using a 2-D FEM membrane-bar model, although there is some splitting of the third measured resonance.

The experimental damping ratios derived for each mode are shown in Fig. 13, and are compared with BMT's normally assumed values (based on merchant ships). The first two modes are seen to be more heavily damped than the medium damping which was assumed for the model. However, the values used for the calculations are seen to be a reasonable mean of the measured damping and hence merchant ship values can generally be applied.

3.4 Local Vibration

Local vibration problems are numerous and varied. The methods developed for merchant ships [9] could be applied for the prediction of panel response amplitudes in Fleet Auxiliaries, which may have large open deck areas. These methods are based on empirical data to predict the transfer of response from exciting

83

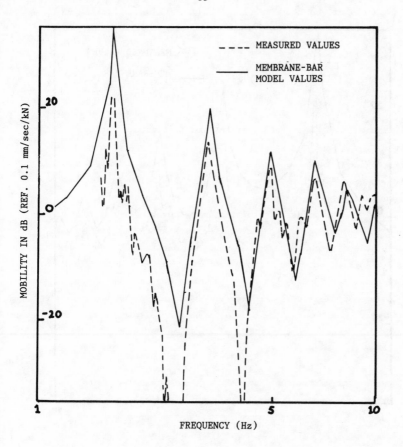

FIGURE 14

Comparison of Calculated and Measured Mobility
(Excitation at Quarter Deck and Response at
Extreme Aft End)
Type 42

84

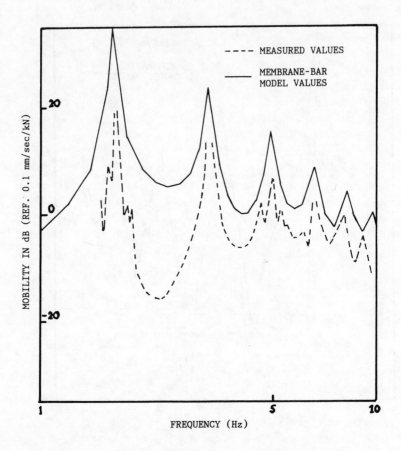

FIGURE 15

Comparison of Calculated and Measured Mobility
(Excitation at Quarter Deck and Response at Extreme
Fore End)
Type 42

source to the boundary of the stiffened panel under consideration,
and also to predict the response ratio between the centre region of
the panel and its boundary. Such methods are particularly useful
in the neighbourhood of diesel engines. For smaller panels,
between stiffeners, resonance is not usually a problem, but where
there is broad band excitation, such as in the vicinity of
propellers, problems may arise as demonstrated by the cracking of
plates in this region.

Local mounting of equipment, which has generally to withstand
shock, needs careful design (and probably laboratory
experimentation) if the various exciting components are not to
introduce excessive equipment vibration. Section 3.2 highlighted
the fact that considerable excitation is transmitted into the hull
structure at shaft speed and multiples of this up to blade rate.

4.   DESIGN CODES

As mentioned in the Introduction, BMT's Ship Design Manual for
Vibration (which contains various design procedures as reported in
[1]) can be applied directly to Fleet Auxiliaries and, with the
additional full scale data and related experience, to warships in
general. Resonance frequencies for about 30 warships of various
kinds have been tabulated against a number of ship parameters, in
the same way as was done for merchant ships. The mean frequencies
for warships were generally lower, for the same size parameter than
those for merchant ships for all modes. The particular properties
used to represent the ship size and the procedures (e.g.
statistical, similar ship etc.) are being reviewed currently by BMT
with the objective of improving the accuracy of empirical methods
of estimating main hull resonance frequencies.

Empirical methods for the prediction of response amplitudes
for propeller excited vibration were developed for merchant ships
and used quite successfully in preliminary design codes, but the
excitation and response characteristics for warships need more
detailed assessment. The results given in Table 1 indicate that
the shaft rate responses should be considered in association with

the propeller-shaft system calculation where the interaction with
the structure of the ship is taken into consideration. No doubt
the dynamic effects of the long shaft and the relatively flexible
ship make the shaft rate responses potentially large. For the
propeller exciting forces and associated responses there are
procedures and programs available, which were initially developed
for single screw ships, but which have been applied to the
calculation of propeller-hull surface forces for twin-screw
arrangements; these in turn can be used on one of the simplified
1-D or 2-D models (for example that used for the results in Figs.
14 and 15) for the hull vibration responses. Such programs for the
calculation wake, propeller forces, propeller cavitation and hull
surface pressures are reviewed in [10].

Some areas of local vibration, such as radar masts, can be
readily assessed for potential problems in service, by local
excitation of the structure during the building stage. Although
the economics of doing such work are governed by the contract
arrangements it is the experience of BMT that some of the more
critical local structures could be assessed this way with some
benefit to all parties.

5.   CONCLUSIONS
     It has been proposed that the guidelines for the overall
evaluation of merchant ships [2] should be applied to warships.
The criteria, and their limits, given in the ISO documents seem
appropriate both for the assessment of calculated values and
measured ship values.

Comprehensive vibration trials for a Type 42 warship have been
presented in a summary form; these have been concerned with
vibration set up by the sea environment, by the propeller and shaft
system and by an exciter. It was shown that resonance frequencies
for the main hull could readily be established by modal analysis of
very small amplitudes of vibration excited by the sea. The levels
of vibration excited by the propeller and shaft system was on

occasions well above the ISO limit values, with excitation of shaft
rate being a major component as well as that for blade rate.

Main hull vibration responses for 9 warships were summarised
in terms of the vibration at blade rate relative to vibration at
shaft rate and in 8 cases the shaft rate vibration was the larger.

Codes for design procedures and guidance to minimise vibration
in service could follow those developed for merchant ships,
provided that sufficient full scale experience and data are
available, both to provide empirical methods and to check the
analytical procedures.

6.   ACKNOWLEDGEMENTS
The author would like to thank British Maritime Technology
Ltd.'s directors and the MOD(PE) for permission to publish the
paper. The views expressed were those of the author.

REFERENCES

1.   WARD, G., The Application of Current Vibration Technology to
     Routine Ship Design Work. RINA, 1982.

2.   Mechanical Vibration and Shock - Guidelines for the overall
     Evaluation of Vibration in Merchant Ships. ISO, 6954-1984(E).

3.   Guide for the Evaluation of Human Exposure and Whole Body
     Vibration; Part 4: Evaluationn of Crew Exposure to Vibration
     on board Sea-going Ships. ISO, DIS. 2631/4-1978.

4.   WARD, G. and WILLSHARE, G.T., Propeller-Excited Vibration with
     Particular Reference to Full-Scale Measurements. RINA, 1975.

5.   CAMISETTI, C. and CATLEY, D., Cooperative Research into
     Mathematical Models for Ship Vibration. PRADS, Tokyo,
     October, 1983.

6.   HAKALA, M.K., Numerical Modelling of Fluid-Structure and
     Structure - Structure Interaction in Ship Vibration.
     Technical Research Centre of Finland, Publication No. 22,
     1985.

7.   SUNNERSJO, C.S.,BRANNSTROM, K.G. and JANSON, C.E., Model Hull
     Properties for a Small Ship. A Comparison of Vlassov -
     Timoshenko Beam Theory and Two-Dimensional FEM Modelling with
     Full-Scale Measurements. Int. Symp. on Ship Vibration,
     CETENA, Genova, 1984.

8.   JENSEN, J.J., and PEDERSEN, P.T., Recent Advances in Beam
     Models used for Ship Hull Vibration Analysis. Int. Symp. on
     Ship Vibration, CETENA, Genova, 1984.

9.   WARD, G., NORRIS, C., CATLEY, D. and CREXIS. A., Local
     Vibration in Ships' Structures. Trans. NECIES, 1981.

10. ODABASI, A.Y., FITZSIMMONS, P.A. and B.D.W. WRIGHT, SHADES: A
     Ship Hydrodynamic Assessment and Design System for Single
     Screw Ship Forms. PRADS, Tokyo, October 1983.

ON THE HYDROELASTIC RESPONSE OF A SWATH TO REGULAR OBLIQUE WAVES.

R.E.D. Bishop, W.G. Price and P. Temarel,
Brunel University,
Uxbridge, Middlesex, UB8 3PH, U.K.

ABSTRACT

The dynamics of a flexible SWATH (i.e. small water plane **area twin hull**) structure are discussed from the viewpoint of a three dimensional hydroelasticity theory which accounts for bodily and distortion responses as the SWATH travels with forward speed in regular oblique sinusoidal waves. A selection of results is presented which illustrates the versatility of the analytical approach. In particular, the influence of standing waves between the struts on the generalised hydrodynamic coefficients and on the generalised wave excitation is examined. Bending moment, shearing force and twisting moment are described as functions of frequency and position within the SWATH. Some typical principal stress values are also investigated.

INTRODUCTION

Although many prototype SWATH have been built [1] during the past twenty years it is only recently that a 3500t ocean going vessel has been constructed in Japan [2]. During this period the offshore industry has introduced many semi-submersible structures into exploration activities. The SWATH, semi-submersibles, catamarans, and so forth, are multi-hull structures involving many common design concepts although their roles of operation are diverse.

The SWATH was originally perceived as a high speed stable seagoing vessel able to out-perform an 'equivalent' mono-hull vessel in rough seas. (The idea has its origins in military thinking, though its validity has often been questioned.) By contrast, the offshore multi-hull structure remains at rest in a seaway, though it may be expected to travel from one exploration site to another at low forward speed.

Research into the behaviour of multi-hull vessels in a seaway has been sustained over the years, often in parallel with the construction and development of the prototype structures and with model tank experiments. The main purpose of this research has usually been the description of fluid loading on the structure (which is usually assumed rigid). Structural analysis has not received the same degree of attention although it is very easy to conceive of a SWATH structure as a large 'tuning fork' with low natural frequencies and resonance frequencies.

This paper presents a unified dynamic analysis of the responses (i.e. displacements, distortions, bending moments, shearing forces, torsional moments, stresses) at any arbitrary position in an idealised flexible SWATH structure travelling in regular sinusoidal waves at prescribed heading angles. The theoretical approach adopted is based on a general linear hydroelasticity theory [3-5], allowing the flexible SWATH to be represented as a three dimensional structure which, unlike a conventional ship, is not 'beamlike'; the fluid loadings are described by a three dimensional hydro-dynamic theory which allows for the influence of forward speed.

The general hydroelastic approach relies on the formulation of a 'dry' and a 'wet' analysis [6]. In the former, the dynamic characteristics of the SWATH are determined in the absence of internal damping and external forces whereas in the latter, allowance is made for the water in which the dry SWATH structure floats by representing structural damping and fluid actions as generalised external forces. Much of the underlying theory and philosophy of the hydroelasticity approach has been presented and discussed elsewhere and will only be briefly described here [3-9].

DRY SWATH ANALYSIS

In a finite element analysis, the continuous dry SWATH structure shown
in figure 1(a) may be idealised so as to have M degrees of freedom with m
nodes (M$\leqslant$6m) and the (mx1) column nodal displacement vector $\underset{\sim}{U}=\{\underset{\sim}{U}_1,\underset{\sim}{U}_2,\ldots,\underset{\sim}{U}_m\}$
satisfies the matrix equation

$$\underset{\sim}{M}\underset{\sim}{\ddot{U}} + \underset{\sim}{C}\underset{\sim}{\dot{U}} + \underset{\sim}{K}\underset{\sim}{U} = \underset{\sim}{P} \tag{1}$$

where the (mxm) partitioned square matrices $\underset{\sim}{M}$, $\underset{\sim}{C}$ and $\underset{\sim}{K}$ describe the system
mass, damping and stiffness properties respectively. The (mx1) column
matrix $\underset{\sim}{P}$ represents a generalised external loading applied to the structure
and, for free motion of the dry structure, $\underset{\sim}{P}=\underset{\sim}{0}=\underset{\sim}{C}$. At a natural frequency ω_r
of the dry structure, we assume that the general solution

$$\underset{\sim}{U} = \underset{\sim}{V}e^{i\omega t}$$

acquires the form $\qquad \underset{\sim}{U}_r = \underset{\sim}{V}_r e^{i\omega_r t}$.

Here, $\underset{\sim}{U} = \underset{\sim}{U}_r = \{\underset{\sim}{U}_1,\underset{\sim}{U}_2,\ldots,\underset{\sim}{U}_m\}$ while $\underset{\sim}{V} = \underset{\sim}{V}_r = \{\underset{\sim}{V}_1,\underset{\sim}{V}_2,\ldots,\underset{\sim}{V}_m\}_r$ contains
elements $\underset{\sim}{V}_{rj} = \{u_r,v_r,w_r,\theta_{xr},\theta_{yr},\theta_{zr}\}_j$ which represent the displacement
vector of the rth mode shape at the jth node. The translations u_r,v_r,w_r
and rotations θ_{xr}, θ_{yr}, θ_{zr} are defined with respect to an equilibrium (or
global) coordinate system of axes Oxyz which moves with the forward speed U
of the SWATH in water.

By defining suitable transformations [2-4] relating the local coordinate
system defined within the finite element and the equilibrium axis system, it
may be shown that the deflection in the rth principal mode at any arbitrary
point within the element may be expressed as

$$\underset{\sim}{u}_r = \{u_r,v_r,w_r\} = \underset{\sim}{\ell}^T\underset{\sim}{N}\underset{\sim}{\ell}g_r$$

where g_r denotes a submatrix of $\underset{\sim}{V}_r$, $\underset{\sim}{N}$ is the appropriate shape function
adopted in the finite element representation and the matrix $\underset{\sim}{\ell}^T\underset{\sim}{N}\underset{\sim}{\ell}$ describes
the transformation between the axis systems.

If it is decided to restrict attention to the lowest n principal modes and natural frequencies, then r=1,2,...,n. In a forced motion $P \neq 0 \neq C$, the nodal displacement at any one point within the SWATH structure may be written as

$$\underset{\sim}{U} = \sum_{r=1}^{n} V_r p_r(t) = \underset{\sim}{V} \underset{\sim}{p}(t) \; , \tag{2}$$

and displacement

$$\underset{\sim}{u} = \{u, v, w\} = \sum_{r=1}^{n} \underset{\sim}{u}_r p_r(t) = \sum_{r=1}^{n} \{u_r, v_r, w_r\} p_r(t)$$

where the n principal coordinates are associated with generalised displacements at the n principal modes of the dry SWATH structure.

The bending moment, M, shearing force V, torsional moment, T, stress, σ, etc. at any point (x,y,z) can be expressed in a similar form. Thus

$$M(x,y,z,t) = \sum_{r=7}^{n} M_r(x,y,z) \; p_r(t)$$

etc. where M_r (or equivalently V_r, T_r, σ_r, etc.) represents the relevant rth characteristic modal parameter of the dry structure. It will be noted that these characteristic parameters are such that $M_r = 0 = V_r = T_r = \sigma_r$ for the bodily responses of surge (r=1), sway (r=2), heave (r=3), roll (r=4), pitch (r=5) and yaw (r=6); each has the natural frequency $\omega_r = 0$.

When the principal coordinates $p_r(t)$ are known, all the responses may be evaluated. On substituting equation (2) into equation (1) and premultiplying by the transpose matrix $\underset{\sim}{V}^T$, it will be seen that the principal coordinate satisfies the matrix equation

$$\underset{\sim}{V}^T \underset{\sim}{M} \underset{\sim}{V} \ddot{\underset{\sim}{p}}(t) + \underset{\sim}{V}^T \underset{\sim}{C} \underset{\sim}{V} \dot{\underset{\sim}{p}}(t) + \underset{\sim}{V}^T \underset{\sim}{K} \underset{\sim}{V} \underset{\sim}{p}(t) = \underset{\sim}{V}^T \underset{\sim}{P} = \underset{\sim}{Z}(t)$$

or

$$\underset{\sim}{a} \ddot{\underset{\sim}{p}}(t) + \underset{\sim}{b} \dot{\underset{\sim}{p}}(t) + \underset{\sim}{c} \underset{\sim}{p}(t) = \underset{\sim}{Z}(t) \tag{3}$$

where the (nx1) column matrix $\underset{\sim}{Z}(t)$ represents the generalised external force arising from fluid actions. The stiffness matrix $\underset{\sim}{c}$ with element

$c_{ss} = \omega_s^2 a_{ss}$ is diagonal; the structural matrix $\underset{\sim}{b}$ is usually assumed diagonal because of the lack of any better information and the elements are given by [6].

$$b_{ss} = 2\nu_s \omega_s a_{ss}$$

where ν_s is the sth modal damping factor associated with the dry SWATH structure. The generalised mass matrix $\underset{\sim}{a}$ is not entirely diagonal because of contributions arising from the rigid body modes.

DYNAMIC CHARACTERISTICS OF SWATH

Although the geometric details of the chosen SWATH shown [4,5,9] in figure 1(a) are similar to a SWATH-6a the same cannot be said with any confidence of the structural properties illustrated in figure 1(b). This is because no detailed information is available on the 6a-configuration. The broken lines in figure 1(a) represent decks and bulkheads, while lumped masses placed in the bridging structure and submerged hulls represent the engines, equipment, etc.

The finite element mesh adopted to idealise this SWATH structure is shown in figure 1(c). It consists of 32 quadrilateral facet shell (plate) elements, 10 eight noded plate elements, 12 eight noded thick plate elements in the bridging structure and the submerged hulls (i.e. pontoons) were discretised by 32 beam elements with the offsets equal to the radius of the circular cross sections. To describe the dynamic characteristics of this SWATH the idealisation consisted of 166 nodes with 705 degrees of freedom.

An extensive investigation of the dynamic characteristics of the dry structure has been reported previously [9]. For this reason this data will not be presented here except for the first four principal modes of distortion (with modal indices such that $7 \leqslant r \leqslant 10$); these modes are illustrated in figure 2 and they form part of the set extending to r=16. For consistency

94

and for the purposes of illustration, the mode shapes are usually normalised to unity at the stern [9] but this is not a necessary requirement for the evaluation of the responses, which are naturally independent of the normalisation.

It will be noticed that the modes shown in figure 2 may be divided into those with symmetric (S) and those with antisymmetric (A-S) shapes depending on the general pattern of the overall distortion. For example, if the nodal displacements at transversely opposite positions in the port hull and starboard hull are the same in magnitude and direction then the mode is referred to as symmetric, etc.

The dry hull dynamic characteristics of the SWATH are presented in Table 1. The vessel is of displacement $V=2730m^3$, length $L=73.2m$ and has a metacentric height $GM=2.851m$.

TABLE 1. Dynamic characteristics of the dry and wet SWATH structure.

Modal index r	Mode shape S	A-S	ω_r (rad/s)	a_{rr} (kgm²)x10⁵	$c_{rr}=\omega_r^2 a_{rr}$ (kgm²/s²)x10⁸	$b_{rr}=2\nu_r\omega_r a_{rr}$ (kgm²/s)x10⁴	$(\omega_e)_r$ rad/s	$(\omega_e)_r$x √(L/g)
7		✓	9.52	8.63	0.78	8.55	7.54	20.60
8	✓		9.67	8.31	0.78	8.68	5.06	13.82
9	✓		12.28	3.17	0.48	4.29	6.70	18.30
10		✓	16.72	1.90	0.53	3.74	10.72	29.28
11	✓		19.64	0.92	0.36	2.32	11.44	31.25
12		✓	19.75	4.58	1.79	12.12	14.72	40.21
13		✓	21.45	1.57	0.72	4.72	15.32	41.85
14	✓		35.26	2.01	2.50	11.34	20.12	54.96
15		✓	36.06	2.25	2.92	16.22	21.00	57.36
16	✓		58.37	2.68	0.91	5.94	47.80	130.57

WET ANALYSIS

The wet analysis allows the fluid loadings on the flexible SWATH to be specified and the underlying theory is based on a velocity potential [3-5]

$$\Phi(x,y,z,t) \equiv U\overline{\phi}(x,y,z) + [\phi_o(x,y,z) + \phi_D(x,y,z) + \sum_{r=1}^{n} p_r\phi_r(x,y,z)]e^{i\omega_e t}.$$

In this expression the linear potential [10,11] amplitudes $\overline{\phi}$, ϕ_o, ϕ_D, ϕ_r respectively describe the steady motion of the SWATH travelling with forward speed U in calm water, the incident wave, the diffracted wave and the radiation wave caused by the responses corresponding to each of the principal modes of the dry structure. It therefore follows that these also relate to the principal coordinates

$$p_r(t) = p_r e^{i\omega_e t}$$

where p_r denotes an amplitude which may be complex in form. The frequency of encounter

$$\omega_e = \omega - \frac{U\omega^2}{g} \cos\chi$$

is associated with an incident wave of amplitude a and absolute frequency ω approaching the SWATH at a heading angle χ ($=180^\circ$ for head waves).

Assuming that the steady flow due to the presence of the SWATH is negligible, the remaining velocity potentials satisfy the boundary conditions [3-5]:

(i) $U^2\phi_{xx} - 2i\omega_e\phi_x - \omega_e^2\phi + g\phi_z = 0$ on z=0, ϕ representing ϕ_o, ϕ_D or ϕ_r (r=1,2,...,n), where $\phi_x = \partial\phi/\partial x$ etc;

(ii) On the mean wetted surface $\overline{S}$ of the SWATH $\partial\phi_o/\partial n = -\partial\phi_D/\partial n$ where

$$\phi_o = \frac{iga}{\omega} \exp\{kz - ik(x\cos\chi - y\sin\chi)\}$$

and $\underset{\sim}{n}$ denotes an outward unit vector normal to the wetted surface, with components (n_1,n_2,n_3) and transpose $\underset{\sim}{n}^T$;

(iii) Suitable bottom and radiation conditions at infinite distance from the oscillating, translating SWATH;

(iv) The generalised Timman-Newman relationships for the radiation potentials may be expressed as

$$\frac{\partial\phi_r}{\partial n} = [i\omega_e\underset{\sim}{u}_r + \tfrac{1}{2} \text{ curl } \underset{\sim}{u}_r x\underset{\sim}{W}] \cdot \underset{\sim}{n}$$

on $\overline{S}$ for each r=1,2,...,n and $\underset{\sim}{W} = -(U,0,0)$.

The unsteady pressure component on the instantaneous wetted surface S derived from Bernoulli's equation may be approximated to

$$p = - \rho \left(\frac{\partial \phi}{\partial t} - U \frac{\partial \phi}{\partial x} + gw \right)$$

and, since the rth component of the generalised external force Z may be written in the form

$$Z_r(t) = - \iint_S n^T \cdot u_r \, p \, dS \quad ,$$

it follows that

$$Z_r(t) = Z_r e^{i\omega_e t} = (\Xi_r + H_r + R_r) e^{i\omega_e t} \tag{4}$$

for $r = 1, 2, \ldots, n$.

In this last expression, the terms on the right hand side depend on the <u>mode shape of the dry structure</u>. Their significance is as follows.

(a) The rth generalised wave exciting force is defined as

$$\Xi_r = \Xi_{Or} + \Xi_{Dr} = \rho \iint_S n^T \cdot u_r \left(i\omega_e - U \frac{\partial}{\partial x} \right) (\phi_0 + \phi_D) dS \tag{5}$$

where Ξ_{Or} (associated with the incident wave potential ϕ_0) denotes the rth generalised Froude-Krylov contribution and Ξ_{Dr} (associated with ϕ_D) is the rth generalised diffraction force accounting for the scattering of the incoming wave.

(b) The rth generalised radiation force is

$$H_r = \rho \iint_S n^T \cdot u_r \left(i\omega_e - U \frac{\partial}{\partial x} \right) \sum_{k=1}^{n} p_k \phi_k dS = \sum_{k=1}^{n} p_k T_{rk} = \sum_{k=1}^{n} p_k (\omega_e^2 A_{rk} - i\omega_e B_{rk}) \tag{6}$$

for $r = 1, 2, \ldots, n$. The added mass or inertia coefficient which is in phase with the acceleration or displacement is given by

$$A_{rk} = \left(\frac{\rho}{\omega_e^2} \right) \text{Re} \left\{ \iint_{\overline{S}} n^T \cdot u_r \left(i\omega_e - U \frac{\partial}{\partial x} \right) \phi_k dS \right\} \tag{7}$$

whereas the damping coefficient which is in phase with the velocity is given by

$$B_{rk} = \left(-\frac{\rho}{\omega_e} \right) \text{Im} \left\{ \iint_S n^T \cdot u_r \left(i\omega_e - U \frac{\partial}{\partial x} \right) \phi_k dS \right\}, \tag{8}$$

Re{ }, Im{ } denoting the real and imaginary components respectively.

(c) The rth generalised restoring coefficient is

$$R_r = \rho \iint\limits_{S} \underset{\sim}{n}^T . \underset{\sim}{u}_r \sum_{k=1}^{n} p_k w_k dS = - \sum_{k=1}^{n} C_{rk} p_k \tag{9}$$

where $C_{rk} = - \rho \iint\limits_{S} \underset{\sim}{n}^T . \underset{\sim}{u}_r w_k dS$ for $r=1,2,\ldots,n$ and $k=1,2,\ldots,n$.

Substitution of equations (5)-(9) into equation (4) and of the resultant expression into equation (3) produces an equation of motion governing the principal coordinates. This may be cast into the matrix form

$$(\underset{\sim}{a} + \underset{\sim}{A})\ddot{\underset{\sim}{p}}(t) + (\underset{\sim}{b} + \underset{\sim}{B})\dot{\underset{\sim}{p}}(t) + (\underset{\sim}{c} + \underset{\sim}{C})\underset{\sim}{p}(t) = \underset{\sim}{\Xi}e^{i\omega_e t} ,$$

from which $\underset{\sim}{p}(t)$ and hence $p_r(t)$ may be determined.

COMPUTATIONS FOR THE SWATH IN WAVES

Details of the method used to derive solutions of the principal coordinates $p_r(t)$ are described elsewhere and are therefore omitted from this paper [3-5,9-11]. The evaluation of the fluid actions is based on a three dimensional source distribution panel method and, as can be seen from the theoretical model, it depends on the mode shapes of the dry SWATH structure, the forward speed, the frequency of encounter, the wave amplitude and so forth. The results to be presented are based on the assumption that the SWATH travels at forward speed $U = 12$ knots (Froude number $F_n = 0.22$) in sinusoidal oblique waves ($\chi = 135^{\circ}; 90^{\circ}$) of unit amplitude.

GENERALISED HYDRODYNAMIC COEFFICIENTS

Figure 3 presents a selection [9] of the calculated generalised hydro-dynamic coefficients A_{rr}, B_{rr} for $r=2,4,7,10$; these relate to antisymmetric dry modes. The major trends observed in all the generalised hydrodynamic coefficients (i.e. $r \leqslant 16$) for all values of r and k may be summarised as follows: (i) For $\omega_e\sqrt{(L/g)} < 1.5$, the coefficients A_{rk} vary significantly.

(ii) For $\omega_e\sqrt{(L/g)} > 10$, the coefficients A_{rk} assume constant values.

(iii) In these two regions the values of B_{rk} are small.

(iv) For $1.5 < \omega_e\sqrt{(L/g)} < 10$, the coefficients vary abruptly.

By way of illustrating this last feature, it will be seen from figure 3 (for the antisymmetric modes), that these variations are first observed in the hydrodynamic coefficients at $\omega_e\sqrt{(L/g)} = 3.3$. This correlates with an equivalent wavelength λ_e given by

$$\frac{\lambda_e}{B_i} = \frac{2\pi g}{\omega_e^2 B_i} \simeq 2$$

where B_i is the inner distance between the struts at the waterline. The phenomenon this suggests is the existence of a standing wave between the two struts with zero wave elevation at the centreline.

With the symmetric modes [9], a similar phenomenon first occurs at $\omega_e\sqrt{(L/g)} \approx 4.7$ or $\lambda_e/B_i \approx 1$, and so the standing wave has maximum waveheight at the centreline.

Ohkusu [12,13] and Wu and Price [14] observed similar trends when evaluating the hydrodynamic coefficients of multi-hulled rigid structures. The latter authors confirmed the existence of such standing waves and showed that they are a result of the mathematical model rather than a mathematical quirk inherent in the analysis.

GENERALISED WAVE EXCITATION

Figure 4 illustrates the real Ξ_r^R and imaginary Ξ_r^I components of the generalised wave excitation [9] for modes $2 \leqslant r \leqslant 9$. The ▢ indicate calculated values and the continuous line is drawn with the aid of a cubic spline interpolation.

All the components exhibit peaks and jumps in their values at the prescribed frequencies of the standing waves associated with the symmetric and antisymmetric modes. It is immediately seen that the magnitudes of the components greatly increase at these frequencies which are attributable to the standing wave phenomenon. It may therefore be concluded that the latter provides a mechanism which increases the vertical, horizontal and torsional loadings on the SWATH as it travels at the chosen operating condition in regular oblique waves.

PRINCIPAL COORDINATES

Figure 5 illustrates a selection [9] of the magnitudes of the principal coordinates $|p_r|$ relating to symmetric (r=3,5,8,9) and antisymmetric (r=2,4,7,10) modes respectively. These coordinates display resonances at the values quoted in Table 1. In addition to these resonances, the effects of the standing wave phenomenon may be observed in the principal coordinate curves at the prescribed frequencies discussed previously though the effect may be somewhat exaggerated by the cubic spline curve fitting to the wave excitation. The □ notation indicates predictions due to calculated wave excitation and this also applies in the response curves shown in figure 6.

RESPONSES

Figure 6 illustrates a selection of the major loading responses experienced in the SWATH as (i) a function of frequency $\omega_e \sqrt{(L/g)}$ at the position x=L/2 in the SWATH and (ii) as a function of position along the SWATH for fixed values of frequency $\omega_e \sqrt{(L/g)}$ corresponding to resonance frequencies in the modes $7 \leqslant r \leqslant 14$.

The amplitude of the bending moment in the horizontal plane about an axis parallel to Oz passing through the shear centre of the port pontoon hull is expressed as

$$|M_z(x,y,z,t)| = \left| \sum_{r=7}^{16} M_{zr}(x,y,z)p_r(t) \right|$$

This quantity is shown in figure 6(a,d).

The amplitude of the horizontal shearing force in the Oy direction at the shear centre of the port pontoon hull is given by

$$|V_y(x,y,z,t)| = \left| \sum_{r=7}^{16} V_{yr}(x,y,z)p_r(t) \right|$$

and this is shown in figure 6(b,e).

In a similar manner, the torsional moment about an axis parallel to Ox through the shear centre of the port hull takes the form

$$|T(x,y,z,t)| = \left| \sum_{r=7}^{16} T_r(x,y,z)p_r(t) \right|$$

and is illustrated in figure 6(c,f).

The effects of the resonances and the standing waves can be observed in figure 6a,b,c. Figure 7 illustrates the calculated maximum principal stress σ_{max}(MN/m^2) and direction ψ(degrees) on the outer surface of the port strut along the join with the port hull pontoon. This information is given as functions of frequency $\omega_e\sqrt{(L/g)}$ or position along the join. The data presented are based on the relationships existing [15] between the plane stress components and the principal (or maximum and minimum) stresses defined as

$$\sigma_{\substack{z \\ x}} = 0.5(\sigma_{max} + \sigma_{min}) \pm 0.5(\sigma_{max} - \sigma_{min}) \cos2\psi$$
$$\tau_{xy} = 0.5(\sigma_{max} - \sigma_{min}) \sin2\psi$$

where ψ is the angle between the Oz axis and the directions of the maximum direct stress measured from the Oz-axis,

$$\sigma_z = \sum_{r=7}^{16} \sigma_{zr} p_r \ , \quad \sigma_x = \sum_{r=7}^{16} \sigma_{xr} p_r \ , \quad \tau_{xz} = \sum_{r=7}^{16} \sigma_{xzr} p_r$$

where σ_{zr}, σ_{xr} and τ_{xzr} denote components of the modal stresses.

The amplitude of the maximum stress is given by [16]

$$|\sigma_{max}| = |0.5(\sigma_z + \sigma_x) + 0.5\{4\tau_{xz}^2 + (\sigma_x - \sigma_z)^2\}^{\frac{1}{2}}|$$

and its direction is defined as

$$\tan 2\psi = 2\tau_{xz}/(\sigma_z - \sigma_x) \ .$$

It is interesting to note that in general the responses of the SWATH travelling in oblique regular waves exceed those determined previously for the SWATH travelling at the same forward speed in regular head waves [9].

As an extension to this investigation, responses to beam ($\chi=90^{\circ}$) sinusoidal waves were evaluated. Figure 8 illustrates a typical set of responses namely bending moment $|M_z|$, shear force $|V_y|$ and torsional moment $|T|$ along the shear centre of the port pontoon for the resonance frequencies corresponding to the modes $7 \leqslant r \leqslant 14$.

CONCLUSIONS

The theoretical model developed is shown to be capable of analysing the responses of a flexible SWATH structure travelling in regular sinusoidal waves approaching the vessel at an arbitrary heading angle χ. An extension of the analysis to predict responses in irregular waves follows the traditional approach [17]. It is interesting and potentially important to note that, because the magnitudes of the responses predicted in regular sinusoidal waves at heading $\chi = 135^{\circ}$ tend to be larger than those for $\chi=180^{\circ}$, in irregular waves spreading seaways may be of greater significance than long crested head seaways. (This is in marked contrast to the predictions

for mono-hull structures.) Further investigation is needed both of this
feature and to determine the influence of transient loadings due to slamming
in irregular seaways. These are likely to be points of considerable
significance in the design of large SWATH structures.

ACKNOWLEDGEMENTS

We are grateful for discussions with, encouragement by and patience
of Mr. John Clarke and other members of staff of ARE (Dunfermline) in
the development of this study as well as for the financial assistance of
MOD(PE).

REFERENCES

1. International Conference on SWATH ships and Advanced Multi-hull Vessels.
    Royal Institution of Naval Architects, London, April 18, 19, (1985).

2. Hosoda, R. and Kunitake, Y.,
    Seakeeping evaluation in SWATH ship design.
    Reference 1 (1985) paper 4.

3. Price, W.G. and Wu Yousheng,
    Hydroelasticity of marine structures.
    XVIth International Congress of Theoretical and Applied Mechanics
    (ICTAM), Lyngby, Denmark (1984).
    Theoretical and Applied Mechanics (ed. F.I. Niordson and N. Olhoff),
    Elsevier (1985) 311-337.

4. Bishop, R.E.D., Price, W.G. and Wu Yousheng,
    A general linear hydroelasticity theory of floating structures moving
    in a seaway.
    Phil. Trans. Roy. Soc. London (1986) (To appear).

5. Wu Yousheng,
    Hydroelasticity of Floating Bodies.
    Ph.D. Thesis, Brunel University, (1984).

6. Bishop, R.E.D. and Price, W.G.,
    Hydroelasticity of Ships.
    Cambridge University Press (1979).

7. Price, W.G. and Wu Yousheng,
    Hydrodynamic coefficients and responses of semi-submersibles in waves.
    Second Int. Symposium on Ocean Eng. and Ship Handling, SSPA Gothenburg
    (1982) 393-416.

103

8. Price, W.G. and Wu Yousheng,
    Fluid interaction in multi-hull structures travelling in waves.
    Int. Symposium on the Practical Design of Ships (PRADS 83), Tokyo and
    Seoul (1983) 251-263.

9. Price, W.G., Temarel, P. and Wu Yousheng,
    Structural responses of a SWATH or multi-hull vessel travelling in
    waves.
    Reference 1 (1985) paper 13.

10. Inglis, R.B. and Price, W.G.,
    The hydrodynamic coefficients of an oscillating ellipsoid moving in
    the free surface.
    J. Hydronautics 14 (1980) 105-110.

11. Inglis, R.B. and Price, W.G.,
    Calculation of the velocity potential of a translating pulsating source.
    Trans. RINA 123 (1981) 163-175.

12. Ohkusu, M.,
    On the heaving motion of two circular cylinders on the surface of a
    fluid.
    Research Inst. of Applied Mech., Kyushu University 17 (1969) report 58.

13. Ohkusu, M.,
    On the motion of multi-hull ships in waves.
    Research Inst. of Applied Mech. Kyushu University 18 (1970) report 60;
    19 (1971) report 62.

14. Wu Xiong-Jian and Price, W.G.,
    A multiple Green's function expression for the hydrodynamic analysis
    of multi-hull structures.
    J. Applied Ocean Research (1986) (To appear).

15. Timoshenko, S.P. and Goodier, J.N.,
    Theory of Elasticity.
    McGrew-Hill, New York (1951).

16. Bishop, R.E.D., Price, W.G. and Temarel, P.,
    A hypothesis concerning the disastrous failure of the Onomichi-Maru.
    Trans. RINA 127 (1985) 169-186.

17. Price, W.G. and Bishop, R.E.D.,
    Probabilistic Theory of Ship Dynamics.
    Chapman and Hall, London (1979).

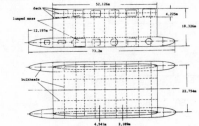

FIGURE 1(a)

104

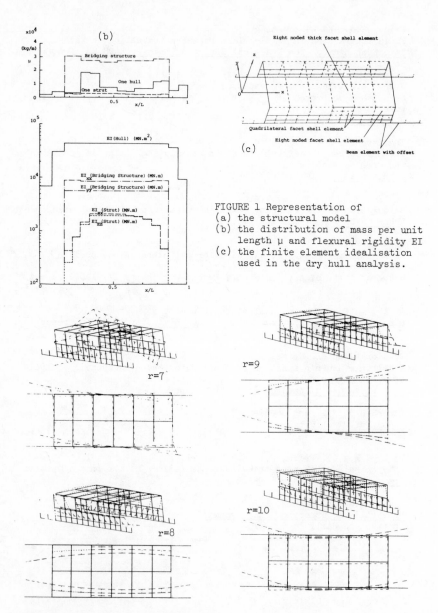

FIGURE 1 Representation of
(a) the structural model
(b) the distribution of mass per unit
    length μ and flexural rigidity EI
(c) the finite element idealisation
    used in the dry hull analysis.

FIGURE 2 The first four calculated principal mode shapes of distortion
of the dry SWATH r=7,8,9 and 10.

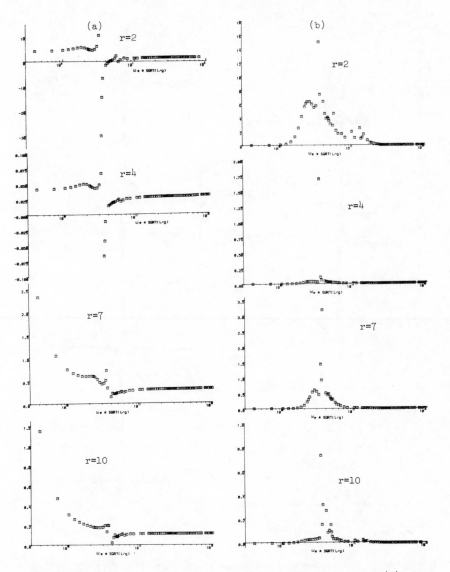

FIGURE 3 Non-dimensional generalised hydrodynamic coefficients of (a) added mass $A_{rr}/\rho\nabla\ell^2$ and (b) damping $B_{rr}/\rho\nabla\ell^2\sqrt{(g/L)}$, where $\ell=1$ m for r=2,7,10 and $\ell=L$ for r=4. The data relate to antisymmetric dry modes and complement the information given in reference[9] for symmetric dry modes.

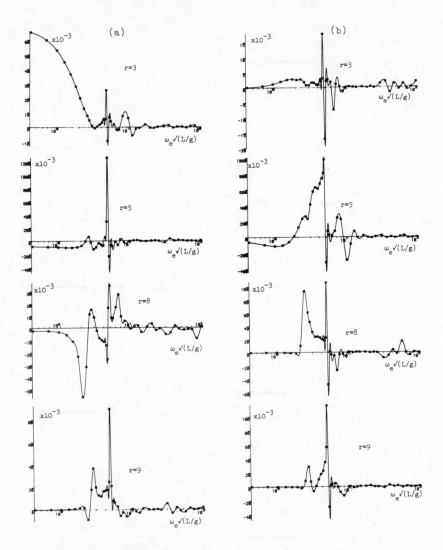

FIGURE 4 The amplitudes of the non-dimensional generalised wave force with
(a) real component $\Xi_r^R/a\rho g\nabla$ and (b) imaginary component $\Xi_r^I/a\rho g\nabla$ for the
SWATH travelling at Fn=0.223 in sinusoidal oblique waves (χ=135°) of
amplitude a(=1m). The subscripts r=3,5,8,9 refer to dry symmetric modes
and r=2,4,6,7 to dry antisymmetric modes.

107

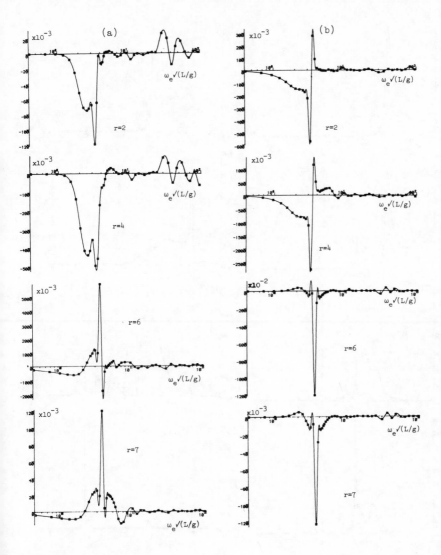

FIGURE 4 (cont.)

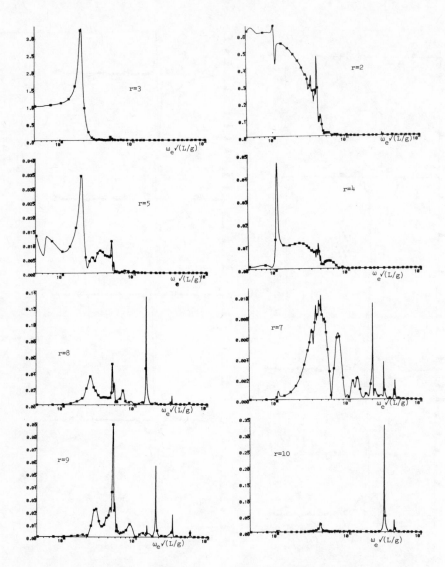

FIGURE 5 Comparisons of the amplitudes of the principal coordinates $|p_r|$ for the SWATH travelling at Froude number Fn=0.223 in oblique waves of unit amplitude with heading χ=135°. The modal indices r=3,5,8,9 relate to symmetric and r=2,4,7,10 to antisymmetric dry modes.

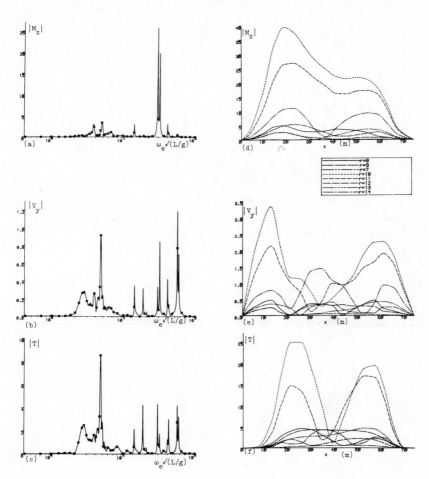

FIGURE 6 Illustrations (a),(b),(c) respectively show the amplitudes of bending moment $|M_z|$(MNm), shearing force $|V_y|$(MN), torsional moment $|T|$ (MNm) measured at $x=L/2$ in the port pontoon. The remaining diagrams (d), (e),(f) respectively show the same response amplitudes measured along the axis of the shear centre of the port pontoon at the quoted resonance frequencies $(\omega_e)_r$. The SWATH is travelling at Fn=0.223 in sinusoidal waves of unit amplitude (a=1m) approaching the bow at $\chi=135^\circ$.

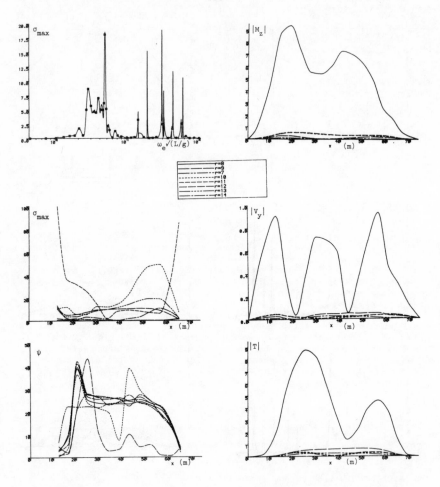

FIGURE 7   FIGURE 8

FIGURE 7 Estimated variations of maximum principal stress σ_{max} (MN/m^2) and principal direction ψ (degrees) with frequency, measured at x=38.3 m and with distance along the structure at the resonance frequencies $(\omega_e)_r$. The data relate to the outer surface of the port strut along the join with the port pontoon. The SWATH travels at Fn=0.223 in oblique waves of unit amplitude and heading χ=135°.

FIGURE 8 As for figure 6 (d),(e),(f) but with χ=90°, i.e. for regular beam waves of unit amplitude.

PROCESS OF DAMAGE IN THIN-WALLED CYLINDRICAL SHELLS

A C Walker and M K Kwok
Department of Mechanical Engineering
University of Surrey
Guildford, UK

ABSTRACT

The paper considers the mechanics of denting in thin-walled cylindrical shells. Results from tests on five nominally identical models, $R/t = 190$, are presented; the test results include relationships between the applied load and the consequent dent depth and the variation in strain on the shell surface.

An analytical approach is developed based on a plastic mechanism model which provides relationships between load, residual dent depth, etc. The correspondence between the analytical predictions and the test results are shown to be good. Hence the approach developed here, although requiring further validation, is a useful addition to the current techniques for the analysis of cylindrical shells used as components in offshore structures.

INTRODUCTION

Thin-walled cylindrical shells are used extensively as components in offshore structures; frequently they incorporate ring stiffeners. The shells are porportioned such that they can support the applied loads with an adequate margin of safety. It is now generally appreciated that the strength of such structural components is very dependent on their level of imperfection; such as, for example the degree to which they deviate from the nominal circular cylindrical shape. The analysis during the design phase therefore incorporates the effects of the deviations which would reasonably be expected to result from the fabrication process.

Another possible source of geometric imperfection is as a result of impact on the wall of the shell. This can, for example, occur during minor collision between vessels and the offshore structure.

Obviously impacts can occur in a very large number of ways, each having their own characteristic form of residual damage. However, it is important that the design engineer should be aware of the typical effect on the strength due to impacts of specified form and energy or force etc. There are two main aspects to this subject; one is related to the degree of damage which is likely to result from the specified impact. The other is that given the degree and form of damage, what is the residual strength of the structural components? The former is considered in this paper and some information on the latter will be presented in a subsequent paper[1].

The effect of impact damage on cylindrical members has roused the interest of many researchers and practising engineers during the past few years. Attention has been given particularly to tubular members with geometries relevant to jacket structure bracing members and to submarine pipelines. The energy absorption capacity of these structural components when subjected to local denting and overall bending due to impact[2-4], as well as the subsequent residual compressive strength[5-7] has been thoroughly studied.

However, for cylindrical members with relatively higher R/t ratios, which may be used as the main leg members of floating offshore structures, the published information is sparse. Some experimental and analytical studies have been carried out on typical ring- and orthogonally-stiffened cylinders[8-10] and a continuing programme of research in the general subject area of damage effects on shells is underway at several Universities in the UK. As part of this programme the present paper presents some of the results of work at the University of Surrey. The results considered here are restricted to tests on unstiffened cylinders; however, it has been found that the approaches developed can be extended to be applicable also to ring-stiffened cylinders[11].

The next section presents results from a series of tests on plain thin walled cylinder   A simple analytical approach to the relationship between dent depth and applied load is developed in a succeeding section and shown to provide good agreement with the test results.

TEST METHODOLOGY AND RESULTS

This section outlines the approaches used to impose specified damage to the test specimens. Since the complete test programme also included the determination of specimens' residual strength corresponding to a variety of loading conditions and degrees of damage, it was decided to restrict this initial programme to only one shell geometry, shown in Fig 1. One advantage of such an approach is that the results give a good indication of the variability of the process of damage within a population of nominally identical shells.

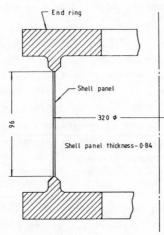

Fig.1 Nominal geometry of test model

The test specimens were subjected to localised denting damage at mid-height between the end support rings by the application of a radial load through a knife-edge indenter. The type of indenter used and the position of application were considered to simulate perhaps one of the more severe forms of damage which would occur in practice. Further investigation into the reduction in strength corresponding to other forms of damage is required to confirm this approach.

The denting process was essentially quasi-static. However, preliminary tests showed that for moderate rates of dynamic loading little effect was noted between the corresponding dent depths and applied loads.

Model Fabrication

The models were fabricated from cold-rolled low alloy medium strength steel sheet of 0.84mm thickness. The cylindrical cans of these models were generated by rolling and then clamped around a precisely machined mandrel and joined by longitudinal seam TIG welding. They were subsequently subjected to a normalising process.

Tensile tests showed[12] that the material had a well defined yield stress at 313 N/mm^2 with a maximum variation between tensile specimens of ±1%. The geometries of the shells, both before and during the denting process, were measured using a precise rotating table and radially fixed LVDT[13]. The maximum initial deviation from the nominal geometry in any of the shells was 0.64mm (0.76t) and generally the deviations were very small in comparison to the radius, or indeed to the dent magnitudes imposed.

Denting test

The specially designed denting rig is shown in Fig 2. It was arranged between the fixed crosshead and moving platen of a ±250kN Instron testing machine.

Displacement of the lower platen, corresponding to the dent depth generated on the model, was measured by a ±25mm LVDT relative to the lower platen. The corresponding denting load was measured by the load cell of the Instron machine above the cross-head of the indenting rig. The output from the LVDT and the load cell were recorded on a chart recorder so that the denting load, the loading dent depth and the residual dent depth were measured simultaneously.

Fig. 2   Experimental set-up

The denting process was carried out in such a way that both the dent depth under loading, dent depth when the load removed (residual dent depth) and the corresponding denting load could be recorded. This was accomplished by loading the models up to a certain depth followed by unloading until zero load was picked up by the load cell. It was then re-loaded to a larger dent depth and then unloaded again, forming a series of hysteresis loops of loading and unloading lines. The residual dent depth was measured as the distance between the point at where unloading line intersected with the zero load axis and the point of zero deflection. A typical output of the denting process is shown Fig 3. Tests were carried out in which the loading - unloading cycles were not included and identical load - dent depth curves were obtained thus indicating that the loading cycles did not incur extra strain-hardening effects.

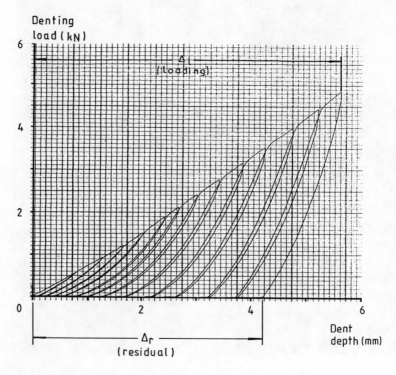

Fig. 3   Typical output of a denting test

Test Results

The photograph in Fig 4 gives a very good visual understanding of the deformations which occurred during the denting process. The model shown had a coating of brittle lacquer applied to it and the cracks indicate the regions of high surface strains. It can be seen that there were a series of semi-elliptic shaped zones of cracking on both sides of the dent line.

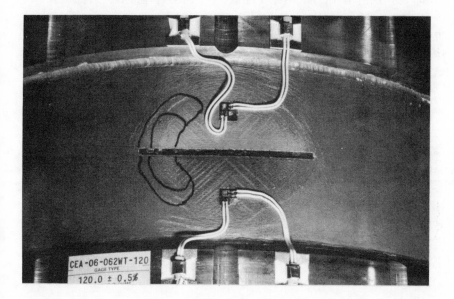

Fig. 4 Dented model with coating of brittle lacquer
($\Delta_r - 4.15\,mm$)

The cracks are different in nature from those which would be observed in lacquered material under uniform tension; these latter would be much finer in nature. Therefore it may be postulated that the observed cracks in the lacquer were generated due to large local rotations, ie slope discontinuities, on the shell surface and mark the boundaries of the dented regions at successively increased dent depths.

118

Cracks included at 45° to the dent line were also observed in the region bounded by the semi-ellipic cracking as seen in Fig 4. These result from high shear stress in the material and could indicate that the dented region was under a state of two dimensional stress.

Figure 5 shows the results for the relationship between applied load and dent depth for five nominally identical shells. There is evidently a general trend in this relationship, however, it is interesting to note that a fair degree of scatter of results exists. The same comments can be made with regard to the test results relating the applied load to the residual dent depth, Fig 6. This latter is a measure of the plastic action which has occurred during the denting process. As Fig 7 shows, the relationship between the full dent depth and the residual dent depth, ie the degree of elastic action, shows much less scatter. The causes for the various degree of scatter are not considered in this paper and may well be the subject of future research.

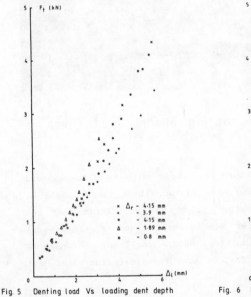

Fig. 5   Denting load Vs loading dent depth

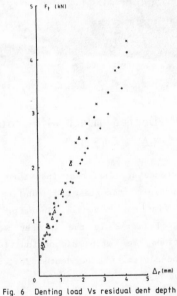

Fig. 6   Denting load Vs residual dent depth

Observations and measurement on the dented models showed that except for the immediate vicinity of the indenter contact zone, the shell remained essentially unaffected by the denting process. Close to the indentation the surface of the shell was flattened and this zone of flattening increased in area as the depth of dent was increased. It was also observed on the dented shells, that a series of yield lines remained on the shell surface and marked the boundaries between the dented region corresponding to each increment in dent depth.

Figure 8 shows a profile of the shell at the mid-height at the dent zone and it can be seen that the surface at the end of the flattened zone bulged outward very slightly. However, the extent of this area of bulging was very small and essentially the shell exhibited significant slope discontinuities at the boundaries of the flattened zone. Evidently since the bulge zone is so small in comparison with the flattened region there must be a change in circumference due to the denting process. The measurements of the deformed shell profiles were obtained in digital form and it was therefore a fairly simple task to integrate the readings to obtain the change in circumference. Typical results are shown in Fig 9 for three shells; one having a small dent depth of 0.8mm, the other two have approximately identical dent depths of 4mm. The computed values correspond to measurements taken circumferentially at intervals of 5mm along the length of the shell.

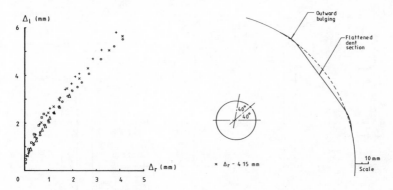

Fig. 7   Loading dent depth Vs residual dent depth   Fig. 8   Deformation profile of dent section

The change in length longitudinally in the dented zone was also obtained by an integration process of the deformation measurements. Some typical results are shown in Fig 10, which correspond to integration along generators at intervals of 2.9mm (1° interval) round the shell. Measurements and calculations on generators outside the zone of damage showed that no change in length had occurred.

As shown in Fig 4 one of the models had strain gauges attached to the inner and outer surfaces of the shell in order to determine the membrane strains during the denting process. The gauges were at the dented region and also at mid-length at 60°, 180° and 300° round the shell perimeter. These latter gauges recorded virtually zero strain during the whole of the denting process. Only those gauges in the dented zone indicated significant levels of strain, which confirmed that outside of the locality of the dent the shell was unaffected by the imposition of the dent.

As shown in Fig 11, residual membrane compressive strains in the hoop direction and tensile strains in the axial direction were recorded, with magnitudes well in excess of the material yield strains. It may also be seen in the figure that a distinct change of slope in the load-strain relationship occurred at a load of about 2.5kN.

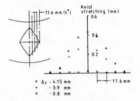

Fig. 10 Axial stretching around center line of damaged zone

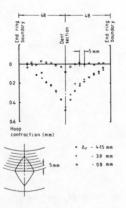

Fig. 9 Hoop contraction of damaged models

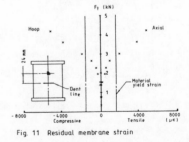

Fig. 11 Residual membrane strain

THEORETICAL ANALYSIS

This section presents a simplified form of analysis which seeks to use the test observations to develop a relationship between the applied load and the dent depth. The predictions of the analysis are compared to the salient test results with a view to proving the efficacy of the analysis. It is understood that the theory cannot be validated by comparison to results from only one shell geometry. Nevertheless, as is shown later, the agreement between the test results here and the theoretical prediction is encouraging.

Essentially, the analysis is based on a plastic mechanism approach which ignores any contribution to the denting process which will arise from elastic action. The resulting formulations, therefore, are more relevant to residual dent depth; that is, the damage which would exist after the vessel had impacted with the shell. Moreover, the method is applicable to situations in which significant damage has occurred and the plastic mechanism is fully developed.

The crux of any plastic mechanism analysis is the choice of mechanism shape and the assumptions regarding the stress combinations which exist in, and on the boundaries of, the mechanism region. From the test observations reported in the previous section, it may be concluded that evidence of damage is limited to the dent zone and that the remainder of the shell is unaffected. Flattening of the models circumference would generally require an expansion of the surface of the shell outside the dent zone in the hoop direction to maintain a constant perimeter length. However, because of the short length of the shell and its rigid boundaries the strength of the shell to resist the circumferential expansion is very large. Any change in shape away from the dent zone is resisted and the only manner in which the dent can develop is by shortening of the perimeter by plastic action in the material due to high membrane compressive stresses. Similarly, due to the high rigidity of the end rings and the considerable membrane rigidity of the shell, inward deflection of longitudinal generators will imply a material stretching in the axial direction. Hence, it is assumed in the analysis model that the region associated with the denting will be in a state of biaxial stress which is of such a magnitude as to cause plastic flow in the material. A rigid elastic — perfectly plastic model of material behaviour is assumed and factors such as elastic deformations and strain hardening are not included in the analysis. Further, it is assumed that the shell in the dent region is flat and that at each successive value of dent depth the shape of the boundary is similar. The plane of the dented region is assumed to be parallel at each successive state of dent amplitude and that rotation occurs only at the boundaries between the dent region and the remainder of the shell and that the rotation will occur plastically.

The assumption of parallel planes in the dented region is valuable in simplifying the analysis, but is indeed supported by the test measurements. As Fig 12 shows, the assumed straight and parallel faces of the dented region correspond well for most of the region with the results of measurements on the models. This assumption is, moreover, equivalent to assuming that the profile of the dented region is that obtained by cutting a cylinder with an inclined plane which, as shown in Fig 13 is in good agreement with the test observations.

In the following section the assumed deflected shape, together with the quasi-static material characteristics are incorporated to develop the plastic work done in various forms and hence evaluate the load-dent depth relationship.

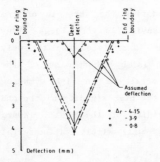

Fig. 12 Deflection at center line of damaged zone

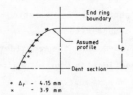

Fig. 13 Damaged zone boundary profile

PLASTIC WORK DUE TO AXIAL STRETCHING

With reference to Fig 14, consider a strip width dy at a distance y from the longitudinal centre line of the damaged zone. The strip is assumed to be subject to a stress σ_a parallel to the centre line and undergoes an extension $d\Delta'_s$ corresponding to a change in dent depth, $d\Delta_r$.

The plastic work done is

$$dw_1 = 4\sigma_a \, t \, L_u \, d\overline{\Delta}_s \tag{1}$$

where $d\overline{\Delta}_s$ is the mean change of extension of all such strips across the damaged zone, defined by

$$d\overline{\Delta}_s = \frac{1}{L_u} \int_o^{L_u} d\Delta'_s \, dy \tag{2}$$

The corresponding change in longitudinal strain averaged across the half width of the damaged zone is

$$d\overline{\varepsilon}_a = \frac{1}{L_u} \int_o^{L_u} \frac{d\Delta'_s}{L'_s} \, dy \tag{3}$$

which can be approximated by

$$d\overline{\varepsilon}_a = \frac{2(1 - \cos\,\alpha)}{\Delta_r} \, d\Delta_r \quad \text{where} \quad \cos\,\alpha = \frac{L_p}{L_s} \,, \quad \text{see Fig 15} \tag{4}$$

Now, we have also

$$d\overline{\varepsilon}_a = d\overline{\Delta}_s / \overline{L}_s \tag{5}$$

Where $\overline{L}_s$ is the average length of the damaged zone, hence, combining equations (4), (5) and (1) the plastic work done can be written

$$dw_1 = \frac{8\sigma_a t L_u \, (1 - \cos\,\alpha)}{\Delta_r} \, \overline{L}_s \, d\Delta_r \tag{6}$$

From the assumption that the damaged zone is formed by two flat planes, we have

$$\overline{L}_s = \frac{2}{3} L_s \quad \text{and} \quad L_s^2 = (\Delta_r^2 + L_p^2) \tag{7}$$

Hence the plastic work can be related to the change in dent depth, from equation (6) and (7).

$$dw_1 = \frac{16\sigma_a t L_u(1 - \cos \alpha)(\Delta_r^2 + L_p^2)^{\frac{1}{2}} d\Delta_r}{3\Delta_r} \tag{8}$$

PLASTIC WORK DUE TO HOOP COMPRESSION

Consider at strip width dx as shown in Fig 14, which is assumed to be subject to a stress σ_c acting normal to the longitudinal axis of the shell. The strip undergoes a change of length $d\Delta_c'$ corresponding to a change of dent depth $d\Delta_r$.

The plastic work done during this change of geometry is

$$dw_2 = 4\sigma_c t L_p d\overline{\Delta}_c \tag{9}$$

where $d\overline{\Delta}_c$ is half the average change of length in the y direction of the damaged zone, defined by

$$d\overline{\Delta}_c = \frac{1}{L_p} \int_0^{L_p} d\Delta'_c \, dx \tag{10}$$

The corresponding change in compressive strain in the hoop direction is

$$d\overline{\epsilon}_c = \frac{1}{L_p} \int_0^{L_p} \frac{d\Delta'_c}{L_u'} \, dx \tag{11}$$

which can be approximated by

$$d\overline{\varepsilon}_c = \frac{1}{2R} d\Delta_r \qquad (12)$$

Following the assumption of the geometry of the boundary of the damaged zone, we have

$$\overline{L}_u = \frac{2}{3}L_u \qquad (13)$$

and from equations (13), (12) and (9) the plastic work done can be related to the change in dent depth by

$$dw_2 = \frac{4\sigma_c t\, L_p L_u}{3R}\, d\Delta_r \qquad (14)$$

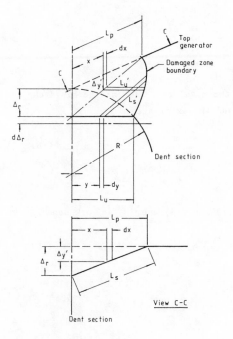

View C-C

Fig. 14   Plastic analysis model

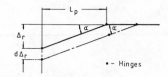

Fig. 15   Axial rotation model

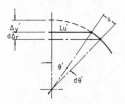

Fig. 16   Hoop direction deformation model

PLASTIC WORK DUE TO PLASTIC BENDING IN AXIAL DIRECTION

In this section we consider the axial component of the plastic bending at the boundaries of the damaged zone. Following the assumption that the planes of the damaged zone will always be parallel as the dent depth increases, there is no component of plastic bending work at the position of application of the indentor.

The work done due to rotation at the plastic hinges assumed to exist at the end of the strip, width dy, see Fig 15, is

$$dw_3 = 4 \int_o^{L_u} 2M_a \; \alpha \; dy \tag{15}$$

where

$$\alpha = \tan^{-1} \left(\frac{\Delta_r}{L_p} \right) \tag{16}$$

From equation (16)

$$d\alpha = \frac{L_p}{L_s^{\,2}} \; d\Delta_r \tag{17}$$

The moment of resistance in the axial direction at the hinge can be related to the plastic moment and the axial stress by

$$M_a = \frac{2}{\sqrt{3}} M_p \; (1 - \bar{\sigma}_a^{\,2}) \tag{18}$$

where $\quad M_p = \dfrac{\sigma_o t^2}{4} \quad$ and $\quad \bar{\sigma}_a = \dfrac{\sigma_a}{\sigma_o}$

Hence from equations (15), (17) and (18) the plastic work done is

$$dw_3 = \frac{16 L_u L_p}{\sqrt{3}_\Delta L_s^{\,2}} \; M_p \; (1 - \bar{\sigma}_a^{\,2}) \; d\Delta_r \tag{19}$$

PLASTIC WORK DONE DUE TO PLASTIC BENDING IN HOOP DIRECTION

The boundary of the damaged region are considered as plastic hinges, and as shown in Fig 16, they will undergo rotation corresponding to an incremental change in dent depth. Negecting the contribution to the plastic work due to the material subtended by $d\theta'$, the plastic work done is

$$dw_4 = 8 \int_0^{L_p} M_c \theta' dx \qquad (20)$$

where

$$\theta' = \tan^{-1} \left(\frac{L_u'}{R - \Delta_y'} \right)$$

Now,

$$\int_0^{L_p} \tan^{-1} \left(\frac{L_u'}{R - \Delta_y'} \right) dx = \frac{L_p}{3R^2 \Delta_r} (2R\Delta_r)^{3/2} \qquad (21)$$

Hence equation (20) can be written as

$$dw_4 = 3.76 \frac{M_c L_p}{R} \left(\frac{R}{\Delta_r} \right)^{\frac{1}{2}} d\Delta_r \qquad (22)$$

The moment of resistance of the hinge in the hoop direction can be related to the plastic moment and the applied stress by,

$$M_c = \frac{2}{\sqrt{3}} M_p (1 - \overline{\sigma}_c^2) \text{ where } \overline{\sigma}_c = \frac{\sigma_c}{\sigma_o} \qquad (23)$$

Hence the plastic work done is obtained from equations (22) and (23) as

$$dw_4 = 4.34 \frac{M_p L_p}{R} \left(\frac{R}{\Delta_r} \right)^{\frac{1}{2}} (1 - \overline{\sigma}_c^2) d\Delta_r \qquad (24)$$

PLASTIC WORK DUE TO FLATTENING IN THE HOOP DIRECTION

With reference to Fig 16, we now consider the segment of shell circumference subtended by the angle $d\theta'$. This segment changes from being curved to being flat during a change of dent depth. The corresponding plastic work done, assuming that the change of geometry takes place subject to the hoop stress σ_c, is

$$dw_5 = 4 \int_o^{L_p} \int_o^S \frac{M_c}{R} \, ds \, dx \qquad (25)$$

From the geometry shown in Fig 15

$$S = Rd\theta' = \frac{d\Delta_r}{\sin\theta} \qquad (26)$$

It can be shown that using equations (25) and (26) the expression for the plastic work can be developed and written as

$$dw_5 = \frac{4M_c L_p \left[(2R\Delta_r)^{\frac{1}{2}} - \Delta_r\right]}{(R\Delta_r - \Delta_r^2)} \, d\Delta_r \qquad (27)$$

where M_c is as given in equation (23).

EXTERNAL WORK DONE

The work done by the external load during an incremental change in dent depth is

$$dw_6 = F_t d\Delta_r \qquad (28)$$

The sum of the plastic work components in equations (8), (14), (19), (24) and (27) can be equated to the external work done, equation (28), to obtain a relationship linking the applied force to a corresponding value of dent depth. That is

$$F_t = \frac{dw_1}{d\Delta_r} + \frac{dw_2}{d\Delta_r} + \frac{dw_3}{d\Delta_r} + \frac{dw_4}{d\Delta_r} + \frac{dw_5}{d\Delta_r} \qquad (29)$$

Since the material within the dented regions is deformed plastically under a state of two dimensional stress, the unknown factors, σ_a, σ_c, M_a, and M_c can be evaluated by employing a plastic flow rule in conjunction with Mises yield criteria that is,

$$f = \overline{\sigma}_a{}^2 - \overline{\sigma}_a\overline{\sigma}_c + \overline{\sigma}_c{}^2 - 1 = 0 \tag{30}$$

$$\overline{\sigma}_c = \tfrac{1}{2} [\ \overline{\sigma}_a - (4 - 3\ \overline{\sigma}_a{}^2)^{\tfrac{1}{2}}] \tag{31}$$

For compatibility of strain in the axial and hoop direction

$$d\varepsilon_a = \eta \ \frac{df}{d\overline{\sigma}_a} = \eta(2\overline{\sigma}_a - \overline{\sigma}_c) \ \text{(tensile +ve)} \tag{32}$$

$$d\varepsilon_c = \eta\frac{df}{d\overline{\sigma}_c} = \eta(2\overline{\sigma}_c - \overline{\sigma}_a) \ \text{(compressive −ve)} \tag{33}$$

From equations (32) and (33) we can define a parameter β, as

$$\beta = \frac{d\varepsilon_a}{d\varepsilon_c} = \frac{2\overline{\sigma}_a - \overline{\sigma}_c}{2\overline{\sigma}_c - \overline{\sigma}_a} \tag{34}$$

Hence, considering the change $d\overline{\varepsilon}_a$ and $d\overline{\varepsilon}_c$ in the axial and hoop direction over the dented region we can use the following relationship,

$$\frac{d\overline{\varepsilon}_a}{d\overline{\varepsilon}_c} = \beta = - \ \frac{4R \ (1-\cos \ \alpha)}{\Delta_r} \tag{35}$$

and, therefore

$$\overline{\sigma}_a = [\ \frac{(4\beta^2 + 4\beta + 1)}{3 \ (\beta^2 + \beta + 1)}]^{\tfrac{1}{2}}$$

and $\overline{\sigma}_c$ can be evaluated from equation (31).

Now all constants and variables in equation (29) except L_p, the length of the mechanism in the axial direction, have been expressed in terms of the dent depth Δ_r . It is assumed that this length will vary with the deformation Δ_r and the hence applied load, F_t, in such a manner that the load required for each deformation increment is minimised. This can be incorporated theoretically by minimising equation (29) with respect to L_p, and using the resulting value of L_p to evaluate the corresponding load. Due to the complex nature of the equation, minimisation is not possible analytically. A numerical approach was, therefore, used to obtain a solution for the applied load corresponding to each residual dent depth.

The results of the analysis are shown compared to the corresponding test results in Figs 17-19. Figure 17 shows that the correlation is good with the test results providing a scatter band lying below the theoretical predictions. This is probably due to the slight over-estimation of the plastic work formulations which are consequent on the assumptions made.

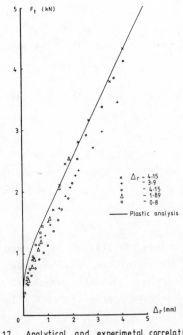

Fig. 17 Analytical and experimetal correlation

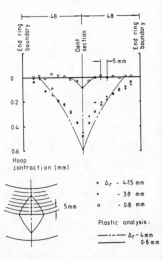

Fig. 18 Analytical and experimental correlc

The assumption of a rigid dented region boundary is of course a simplification, as shown by the slight bulging of the shell circumference measured in the test specimens. This perhaps resulted in the overestimation in the analysis of the hoop contraction and the underestimation of the axial stretching as shown in Figs 18 and 19 respectively. The magnitudes of these variations between test and theory are quite small and in fact their effects on the energy evaluation probably compensated each other. It should be noted, however, that these effects will become more significant for the denting of cylindrical members with high L/t and low R/t ratios and, therefore, this analysis method is not directly applicable to tubular components of structures.

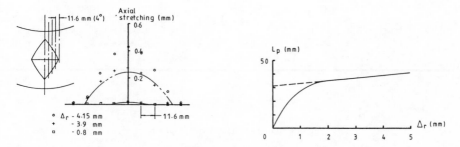

Fig. 19   Analytical and experimental correlation   Fig. 20   Length of mechanism from analysis

Figure 20 shows the length of the mechanism, L_p, derived from the analysis and corresponding to various depths of residual dent. The basic assumption in the analysis is that the damage zone is formed by the planes intersecting with the cylinder. The planes are assumed to remain parallel as the damage increases. Strictly then the mechanism length should increase proportionally with the residual dent depth. It may be seen in Figure 20 that for dent depths greater than approximately 2mm this in fact is the case. This depth corresponds to the development of the full membrane plasticity. However, in the minimisation process, the mechanism length was not constrained to be proportional to the dent depth and hence for low value of dent depth the basic assumption is violated and the load corresponding to dent depth may be somewhat over-estimated.

A parametric study on shells with the same material properties of the models but different R/t ratio is shown in Fig 21. It is hoped that this can provide some information for future experimental validation.

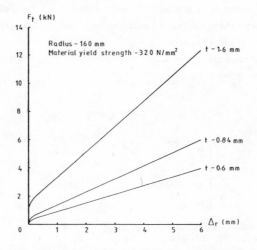

Fig. 21   Load - residual dent depth relationship

CONCLUSIONS

A simple plastic analysis method has been developed which provides a method for predicting the depth of dent corresponding to the load applied to the indentor. The results of the analysis agree fairly well with observations in test carried out on a number of shells having nominally identical geometries. However, it is obvious that much wider validation of the analytical approach is required, specially to determine the ranges of geometric parameters to which the analysis could be applied in practice.

ACKNOWLEDGEMENTS

The authors would like to acknowledge the support of the Science and Engineering Research Council's Directorate of Marine Technology. We would like also to thank Mr S McCall for his extremely valuable advice on the conduct of the tests.

NOTATION

F_t	denting load
L_p	length of mechanism in axial direction
L_s, L_s', L_u, L_u'	(see Fig 14)
M_a	bending moment per unit length in axial direction
M_c	bending moment per unit length in hoop direction
M_p	yield moment per unit length
R	radius of cylinder
t	thickness of shell
ε_a	strain in axial direction
ε_c	strain in hoop direction
σ_a	stress in axial direction
σ_c	stress in hoop direction
σ_o	yield stress in tension
$\bar{\sigma}_a$	ratio σ_a/σ_o
$\bar{\sigma}_c$	ratio σ_c/σ_o
α	angle of mechanism in axial direction
θ'	angle of mechanism in hoop direction
$dw_1 \ldots dw_6$	plastic work
Δ_c	hoop contraction of mechanism
Δ_ℓ	total (loading) dent depth
Δ_r	residual dent depth
Δ_s	axial stretching of mechanism
Δ_y'	deflection of section at distance x from dent section (Fig 14)

Other symbols will be defined as they appear.

134

REFERENCES

1. Kwok M K and Walker A C
   Effect of damage on the strength of thin walled cylinders.
   (To be published)

2. Furnes O and Amdahl J
   Ship collisions with offshore platforms.
   Intermaritec, Hamburg, 1980.

3. Petterson E and Johnsen K R
   New non-linear methods for estimation of collison resistance of mobile offshore units.
   Proceedings of the 13th Offshore Technology Conference, Houston, Texas, 1981, Paper no OTC 4135.

4. De Oliveria J G
   The behaviour of steel offshore structures under accidental collisons.
   Proceedings of the 13th Offshore Technology Conference, Houston, Texas, 1981, Paper No 4136.

5. Ellinas C P and Walker A C
   Ship Collision with bridges and offshore structures.
   IABSE Colloquium, Copenhagen, 1983.

6. Taby J and Moan T
   Theoretical and experimental study of the behaviour of damaged tubular members in offshore structures.
   Norwegian Maritime Research, No 2/1981, p26-33.

7. Smith C S, Kirkwood W and Swan J W
   Buckling strength and post-collapse behaviour of tubular bracing members including damage effects.
   BOSS '79, Imperial College, London, England, p303-326.

8. Onoufriou A and Harding J E
   Residual strength of damaged ring-stiffened cylinders.
   Proc 4th Int Symp Offshore Mechanics & Arctic Engineering, Texas, 1985.

9. Ronalds B F and Dowling P J
   Damage of orthogonally stiffened shells.
   Imperial College, University of London, 1985.

10. Frieze P A and Sachinis A
    Compressive strength of stress-relieved ring-stiffened cylinders including local damage.
    Proc. of Marine and Offshore Safety Conference, University of Glasgow, September 7 - 9, 1983.

11.   Walker A C, McCall S and Kwok M K
         Report to Department of Energy, 1986.

12.   McCall S and Walker A C
         Buckling test on stringer stiffened cylinder models
         subjected to load combination.
         Report to DnV, December 1981.

13.   Walker A C, Segal Y and McCall S
         The buckling of thin-walled ring-stiffened shells.
         Proceedings of a State-of-the-Art Colloquium, University
         Stuttgart, May 6 - 7, 1982.

ADVANCED STRENGTH AND STRUCTURAL RELIABILITY ASSESSMENT OF THE SHIP'S HULL GIRDER

Anil Thayamballi, Lembit Kutt and Y.N. Chen
American Bureau of Shipping, USA
Research & Development Division
45 Eisenhower Drive
Paramus, NJ 07652

ABSTRACT

This paper combines nonlinear finite element techniques with an Advanced First Order Second Moment method of reliability assessment in estimating the structural safety of the ship's hull girder under vertical bending. The methodology is used to evaluate the effect of evolution in hull framing systems from transverse to predominantly longitudinal, using three general cargo vessels. The ultimate strengths of the vessels are calculated through a dynamic nonlinear finite element technique. The sea-loads on the structure are obtained using shipmotion analyses. Both deterministic factors of safety with respect to the maximum expected load and probabilistic safety indices that explicitly account for the variability in loads and strength are obtained for the ultimate strength limit state.

INTRODUCTION

The structural integrity and safety of a ship's hull girder depends on various design, material, workmanship and operation related factors. Today's classification Rules [1] address both longitudinal strength of the hull girder and the transverse and local strengths of hull structures. The physical and mechanical properties required of hull structural materials are specified. The Rules also control, to varying degrees, the design of details and end connections, buckling, and the prevention of sub-yield strength fractures and crack propagation. Workmanship in hull construction is controlled through surveys. The Rules also require operational control on loads for most types of vessels. In addition, surveys assure the maintenance of the as-built qualities of the hull during its life.

There are various correlated failure modes possible for the ship hull girder, the primary failure mechanisms being plastification, buckling, fatigue and fracture. The interplay of factors affecting intact hull girder safety is outlined in Figure 1. This paper focuses on hull longitudinal vertical bending strength and safety considering plastification and buckling alone. Thus there is the assumption that the reliability of local elements of the hull girder in the failure modes not explicitly treated has been otherwise controlled.

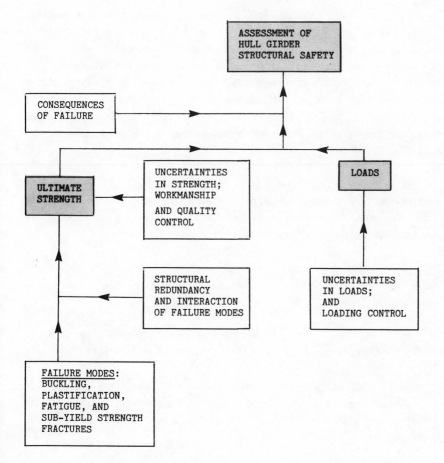

FIGURE 1: Factors Influencing Hull Girder Safety

Both deterministic and probabilistic measures of safety are outlined in this work. The deterministic treatment of safety aims at obtaining the nominal multiplicative safety factor that separates the hull girder longitudinal strength from the expected lifetime maximum total bending moment. The probabilistic treatment, i.e. the reliability analysis, results in safety indices, which can, in principle, be mathematically related [2] to the probability that the hull girder will not fail to carry the imposed loads, i.e. its "reliability".

In practice, because of imperfect knowledge and associated confounding factors, both deterministic safety factors and probabilistic safety indices are but comparative and notional measures of safety. Both are condensed descriptions of uncertainty in load and strength. An advantage of a reliability procedure, in comparison to a deterministic calculation of the factor of safety, is that the former facilitates a detailed and explicit treatment of all variabilities in strength and load, and thus provides a better framework for safety evaluation of the hull girder.

This work illustrates the safety assessment methodology by application to evaluating the effect of evolution of hull framing systems from transverse to predominantly longitudinal. For this purpose three general cargo vessels are considered:

Ship 1:   A 475 ft. general cargo ship typical of the late 1950's and early 1960's. The vessel has machinery amidships, and is completely transversely framed.

Ship 2:   The same as Ship 1, but with its double bottom longitudinally framed, reflecting the design practice in the late 60s and early 70s.

Ship 3:   A 492 ft "all-hatch" vessel representative of the 1965 to 1976 time period. The vessel has machinery 3/4 of length aft, longitudinally framed strength deck and bottom, and transversely framed sides and tween decks.

SHIPS 1 AND 2 - GENERAL CARGO VESSEL

SHIP 3 - GENERAL CARGO VESSEL

SHIP	L (m)	B (m)	D (m)	d (m)	Δ (tons)	DWT (tons)
1	145	19.4	12.5	9.2	17500	12000
2	145	19.4	12.5	9.2	17500	12000
3	150	22.9	13.2	9.7	19000	12000

FIGURE 2: Principal Particulars of Vessels Considered

Ship 1 was a 1959 design, while Ships 2 and 3 were 1970 designs. The sizes and structural and general arrangements of the vessels were based on statistics in the ABS data files and records. The principal particulars of the vessels are shown in Figure 2. Their midship sections may be found in Figure 3.

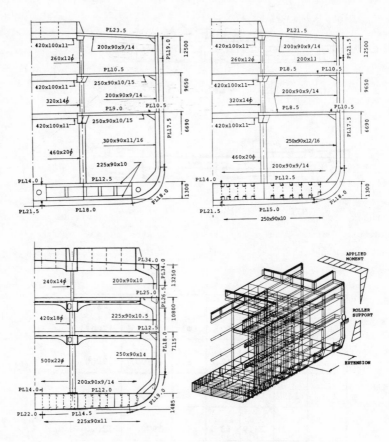

FIGURE 3: Midship Sections of Vessels Considered, and
Typical Finite Element Model (Ship 3)

Both loads and strength and related variabilities need to be
determined for purposes of safety assessment. The estimation of the
relevant variabilities is subsequently discussed. A variability may be
inherent (e.g. in yield strength), may pertain to the inexactitude in
theory as it relates to (an often unknown) reality, or may relate to the
precision of a measurement or estimation procedure.

FINITE ELEMENT CALCULATION OF STRENGTH

In this study, the longitudinal ultimate vertical bending strength of the ship hull is obtained by elasto-plastic, nonlinear finite element analysis using the computer program **ABS/USAS** (an acronym for Ultimate Strength Analysis of Structures) [3], [4]. With proper modelling procedures [5], the nonlinear finite element approach being used accounts for the interaction of the various local and global failure modes and the interaction of material elasto-plasticity and buckling and post-buckling effects in a unified and rigorous manner.

The USAS computer program solves the dynamic equations of motion through the explicit central difference method. However, it is the static ultimate strength which is being evaluated, and this is done by loading up the ship hull with a slow, quasi-static loading rate. Among the reasons for this approach are the numerical difficulties associated with static, Newton-Raphson type schemes for the solution of the finite element equations [3], [4]. Perhaps more important, however, is that structural behavior in the post-buckling range is oftentimes unstable, as in the snap-through buckling of arch or shell structures, meaning that dynamic effects are inherently a part of the process. In the case of a ship, not only can the collapse of the hull be preceded by a series of local failures, but the overall collapse of the hull girder can itself be an unstable, dynamic phenomenon. Thus, by solving the equations of motion with a quasi-static loading rate throughout the entire analysis, the response obtained on the stable paths of the structure is very close to the static states of deformation, as it should be, and when the structure becomes unstable, either locally or overall, the inertial forces are automatically included in the analysis to obtain the most realistic description of structural behavior.

Creation of optimal finite element models for the three ships in this study was a challenging task, due to the complexity of the deformation patterns in the nonlinear ranges of behavior, and due to the large computational effort involved. Reference [5] contains details of the finite element models used for the three vessels of this paper and also provides considerable physical insight into their plastification and buckling behavior.

In the finite element analysis of the three vessels, lateral pressure was excluded. The models contained uniformly distributed initial imperfections in the form of nodal perturbations, but did not include residual stress effects. Time histories of the resisting moment were obtained, from which their ultimate strengths were determined as the maximum possible resisting moment. Table 1 indicates the ultimate vertical moments in the hogging and/or sagging conditions. As it is unlikely that the general cargo vessels considered will ever sag in a stillwater condition, it is their hogging ultimate strength that usually is of interest.

TABLE 1: **ABS/USAS** Computed Ultimate Vertical Bending Strength

	SHIP 1	SHIP 2	SHIP 3
M_p (MNm) Fully Plastic Moment	1882	1816	2250
$M_{u,sag}$ (MNm) Sagging Ultimate Moment	1323	–	2068
$M_{u,hog}$ (MNm) Hogging, Ultimate Moment	1164	1780	2224
$M_{u,sag}/M_p$	0.703	–	0.919
$M_{u,hog}/M_p$	0.619	0.980	0.988

Note: Yield Strength = 220.6 MPa (32 ksi)

VARIABILITY IN STRENGTH

An underlying premise in the present work is that structural safety is assessed using today's technology and that all three vessels are built to today's practice. Thus the effect of any improvements that may have occurred over time in fabrication procedures, load and strength prediction techniques, materials technology, the Rules themselves, or by changes in structural efficiency (other than from buckling performance) due to improved detail design, control of material toughness and susceptibility to cracking, containment of the effects of cracking, or by the use of increasingly refined inspection procedures are not considered in the safety assessment.

The following sources of strength related variability are discussed herein: (a) inherent strength uncertainty, (b) uncertainties in the design process, (c) corrosion and wastage effects, (d) initial deformation and residual stresses, and (e) the accuracy of the strength assessment procedure used.

(a) Inherent Strength Variability

This source of variability in ultimate strength is related to component variabilities in yield strength (σ_y), modulus of elasticity (E) and plate thickness (t). The component COVs, estimated using available material test data, are as follows: yield strength-- 9%, modulus of elasticity-- 4%, and plate thickness-- 4%. The overall strength mean, $\overline{M}_u$, and COV, δ, can be shown [6], using linear theory of uncorrelated errors, to be given in terms of the component means and COVs, by

$$\overline{M}_u \simeq f(\overline{\alpha_i})$$

and

$$\delta^2 \simeq \sum_i (\frac{\partial f}{\partial \alpha_i} \frac{\overline{\alpha_i}}{\overline{M}u})^2 \delta\alpha_i{}^2$$

where α_i are the components σ_y, E and t, and $\delta\alpha_i$ are the component COVs, assumed small. The overbars denote the mean, and the partial derivatives are estimated at the mean. For purposes of applying this approach, we in essence calculate the limit state strength (and its derivatives) using a finite set of points, each obtained on the basis of a separate nonlinear finite element analysis. This is a noteworthy feature of the methodology presented here, and can be readily applied to cases other than inherent strength variability provided the appropriate component COVs and mean values can be quantified. The total inherent strength COV was thus estimated to be 7.2% for Ship 1 and 9.6% for the other two vessels.

The sensitivity study made for purposes of the above COV synthesis considered an all transversely framed vessel (Ship 1) and an all longitudinally framed vessel (a 233m tanker). The results of the sensitivity study for Ship 1 are shown in Figure 4, and those for the tanker may be found in [5]. Based on the study, Ships 2 and 3 under hogging were judged to behave similarly to Ship 1, except for a reduced imperfection sensitivity and a near-direct proportionality to yield strength. The results showed the ultimate strength to exhibit near-direct proportionality to plate thickness in all cases including Ship 1, which exhibits buckling prior to first yield. Also, compared to Ship 3, variability in yield strength is somewhat less important for Ship 1, due to buckling prior to first yield. This reduced sensitivity of ultimate strength to the yield strength in the case of Ship 1 is reflected in its reduced inherent strength COV. The effect of variability in the modulus of elasticity is found to be small in all cases.

For purposes of reliability assessment, one also needs to estimate the mean value of strength. The values of ultimate strength given in Table 1 are based on pre-1974 Rule minimum yield strengths of 220.6 MPa (32 ksi) and thus need to be appropriately magnified. In the case of Ship 1, which fails by buckling prior to first yield, the necessary magnification factor (viz. 1.05) was found from the sensitivity study whose results were noted above. The failure mode for Ships 2 and 3 was predicted to be predominantly plastification, and the appropriate magnification factor (1.1) was determined by the ratio of the mean to Rule minimum yield strength for pre-1974 ABS grade steels as evidenced by limited material test data.

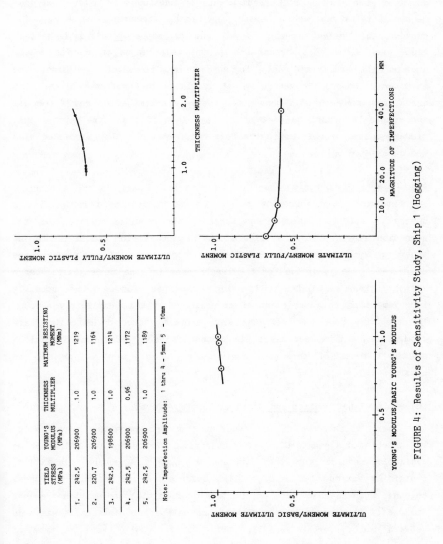

FIGURE 4: Results of Sensitivity Study, Ship 1 (Hogging)

(b) Design Process Uncertainties

This aspect relates to the ability of the designer to obtain a design that meets the Rule requirements of section moduli (or deck area requirement in the early period) and local strength precisely. The conventional design process is not one of mathematical optimization. Also, even simple procedures such as the calculation of section moduli are normally performed only to a certain degree of precision, and structural members are generally not available in fractional sizes. The associated strength COVs were conservatively estimated to be 3% for all three vessels, based in part on a comparison of their as-designed hull girder section properties to the Rule requirements. The associated bias was considered unity.

(c) Effects of Corrosion

In explicitly assessing safety on a probabilistic basis, it is desirable not to include any strength contribution related to the corrosion margin. Using available data [7] on section moduli before and after a 2mm corrosion correction, strength reduction factors were estimated to be about 0.9 for the length range of the three general cargo vessels, the associated COV being taken as zero. One possible improvement on this treatment of corrosion may be to explicitly account for the time dependence of corrosion effects, based on corrosion rate data. Such a treatment may be indicated if issues related to inspection or the effects of corrosion control (e.g. in tankers) are to be considered.

(d) Initial Deformation and Residual Stress Effects

These effects relate to manufacturing processes and workmanship. The associated strength COVs were subjectively estimated based in part on available results for the ultimate strength of square plates [8] containing various levels of initial deformation and residual stresses, together with an assumption on the levels of initial deformation present. Because of the approximate nature of our method, no distinction was made between the different vessels, particularly on the basis of type of framing. The resulting strength COVs were 3% in all cases. The associated strength biases were estimated to be about 0.96, but were not applied, in part because the original USAS calculations employed uniformly distributed initial nodal perturbations.

(e) <u>Strength Assessment Procedures</u>

The assessment of the reliability of any structure depends on a knowledge of the failure modes likely to occur, and the ability to determine the capacity of the structure considering those various failure modes. In this regard, when compared to past simplified strength analysis procedures, the present nonlinear finite element treatment is more complete. There is, however, uncertainty in the USAS calculated ultimate strength- uncertainty that arises from factors such as finite element discretization, inaccuracies in boundary conditions and the loading rate used. Generally, larger than ideal mesh sizes and loading rates appear to overestimate the strength of the structures considered, although in the present case, this possibility was minimized through numerical experimentation. The COVs related to strength prediction capability were estimated to be 8% for Ship 1 and 6% in the other two cases. The associated bias was assumed unity.

LOADS AND THEIR VARIABILITY

The total load on the hull girder is taken to comprise the sum of a stillwater bending moment (SWBM) and a wave bending moment (WBM). The safety indices for the designs are obtained for an assumed mean SWBM of 70% of the design value (see Table 2), reflecting the fact that in the long term, the average SWBM is less than the design SWBM due to the variety of loading conditions met in service [6]. Using subjective estimates based in part on available data, the SWBM was assumed to have a standard deviation of 30% of the design value. The effect of control on SWBM or the lack of it has a bearing on the upper limit of variability of SWBM, and thus on hull girder reliability. For the general cargo vessels considered, this effect is not treated.

Assessing safety also requires an estimate of the average magnitude and the COV of the extreme value of the wave bending moment that can occur in the lifetime of the vessel. For any given wave environment, this WBM is typically determined based on shipmotion analysis. The WBM in the present case was obtained for a 20 year nominal life using the ABS H-family of North Atlantic long term wave environment. Calculations assumed equiprobable headings, a realistic speed and sea exposure, and a loading condition that was somewhat conservative in its WBM. The most probable extreme (WBM) values so obtained are also shown in Table 2.

Even though the WBM so calculated is said to be the largest value
that is likely to occur in the lifetime of the vessel, this statement
should not be taken literally. The WBM is based on a particular set of
environmental conditions that imply a relatively severe wave climatology,
and is obtained using a particular (linear) response analysis procedure.
No allowance is made for factors such as varied areas of
operation, vessel routing, bad weather avoidance or the skill and
judgement of the operating personnel. Thus the WBM is really in the
nature of a criterion, and again, the safety measures so calculated are
useful mainly for comparative purposes.

The COV of the shipmotion calculated WBM arising from component
uncertainties related to inherent variability in the extreme value, and
uncertainties in wave environmental representation and response
amplitude operator calculation as they relate to reality, was estimated
to be a total of 20%, the associated bias being considered unity.

TABLE 2: Design Stillwater and Calculated Extreme Wave Bending Moments

SHIPS	SWBM (MNm)	WBM (MNm)	SWBM + WBM (MNm)
1,2	434	449	883
3	500	512	1012

SWBM = Design Stillwater Bending Moment
WBM = Most Probable Extreme Wave Bending Moment

MEASURES OF SAFETY

The strength and load related uncertainties having been determined,
Advanced First Order Second Moment probabilistic safety measures (safety
indices) were obtained using Wu-Wirsching algorithm [9]. The safety
indices are indicated in Figure 5, which also shows the deterministic
factors of safety on the expected total extreme load. The factors of
safety were obtained for the "as-built" hull.

149

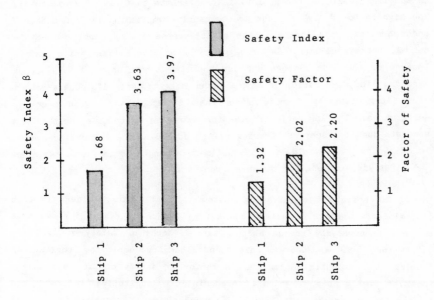

FIGURE 5: Safety Factors and Safety Indices

For purposes of ascertaining the safety indices, a linear limit
state expression equating strength to the sum of SWBM and WBM was used.
The total strength coefficient of variation was obtained by "adding" the
various individual COVs in a mean square sense, thus assuming the
different sources of uncertainty to be uncorrelated and of equal
importance. The resulting total COVs were: strength- 11.6% for Ship 1,
12.1% for Ships 2 and 3; SWBM- 43% and WBM- 20%, for all three ships.
The strength and SWBM were considered normally distributed, while the WBM
was assumed Gumbel distributed.

DISCUSSION AND RESULTS
The results of Table 1 show an increase of about 50% in ultimate
hogging moment between Ships 1 and 2, even though the scantlings of Ship
1 are nominally higher. This marked improvement in ultimate strength is
due primarily to the change in design practice related to double bottom
framing from transverse to longitudinal, which tends to considerably
enhance buckling performance under hogging.

150

Also shown in Table 1 is a measure of resistance of the hull girder to buckling, viz. the ratio of ultimate strength to fully plastic moment. The high ratio of 0.99 for the predominantly longitudinally framed Ship 3 under hogging again indicates the effectiveness of its cross section in the absence of buckling. Under sagging the same vessel is less effective because of the wide hatches and low buckling strengths of the deck box girders. The 0.98 ratio for Ship 2 under hogging, with its double bottom alone longitudinally framed, shows that it also has a good buckling performance. The low ratio of 0.62 for Ship 1 indicates its low buckling strength due to transverse framing of the double bottom. Buckling occurs in Ship 1 prior to yield, and its ultimate strength is in fact lower than the first yield moment for the cross section.

The effect of the framing system is also clearly evident in both deterministic factors of safety and safety indices. Figure 5 shows that the all transversely framed Ship 1 has a factor of safety of 1.32 and safety index of 1.68, whereas Ship 2 under hogging, employing longitudinal framing in the double bottom, has a factor of safety of 2.02 and safety index of 3.63. Ship 3, which is predominantly longitudinally framed, and is similar in arrangement to today's general cargo vessels, also shows similar levels of safety. The relatively low notional safety index for the all transversely framed Ship 1 is not surprising, see for example Faulkner [10]. The levels of safety of Ships 2 and 3 being significantly higher when compared to Ship 1, which is not dissimilar to the many transversely framed vessels that were built prior to the mid sixties and saw years of satisfactory service experience, is a fact that is in itself significant.

In closing, we note that the structural safety assessment methodology used, which effectively combines an elasto-plastic nonlinear dynamic finite element technique and an Advanced First Order Second Moment method of reliability analysis, holds promise for the evaluation of complex marine structures on a sound basis.

ACKNOWLEDGEMENTS
This paper reflects part of a continuing study by the American Bureau of Shipping into the strength and safety of marine structures. The authors wish to thank Dr. Y.K. Chen, Mr. R. Curry, Mr. J.T. Liu, Mr. R. Ng, Dr. C.M. Piaszczyk and Mr. D.P. Unger. The efforts of these

colleagues have either directly or indirectly contributed to the material in this paper. In addition, the valuable comments of Dr. H.Y. Jan, Dr. D. Liu and Mr. S.G. Stiansen of the American Bureau of Shipping, Prof. M.P. Bieniek of Columbia University in the City of New York, and Prof. A.E. Mansour of the University of California at Berkeley are gratefully acknowledged. Thanks are due to Mrs. P.B. Shelley for preparation of this manuscript.

REFERENCES

1. American Bureau of Shipping (1985). Rules for Building and Classing Steel Vessels.

2. Mansour, A.E., Jan, H.Y., Zigelman, C.I., Chen, Y.N. and Harding, S.J. (1984). Implementation of Reliability Methods to Marine Structures. Trans. SNAME, Vol. 92, pp. 353-382.

3. Chen, Y.K., Kutt, L.M., Piaszczyk, C.M., and Bieniek, M.P. (1983). "Ultimate Strength of Ship Structures", Trans. SNAME, Vol. 91, pp. 149-168.

4. Bieniek, M.P., Kutt, L.M., and Piaszczyk, C.M. (1985). "Some Problems of Analysis of Nonlinear Elasto-Plastic Structures", Numerical Methods in Engineering: Theory and Applications, Proceedings of NUMETA 1985, Vol. 2, Swansea, U.K., pp. 635-644.

5. Kutt, L.M., Piaszczyk, C.M., Chen, Y.K. and Liu, D. (1985). Evaluation of the Longitudinal Ultimate Strength of Various Ship Hull Configurations. Trans. SNAME, Vol. 93.

6. Stiansen, S.G., Mansour, A.E., Jan, H.Y., and Thayamballi, A. (1980). Reliability Methods in Ship Structures. Trans. RINA, Vol. 122, pp. 381-406.

7. Akita, Y. (1982). Lessons Learnt from Failure and Damage of Ships. Joint Session I, 8-th International Ship Structures Congress, Paris.

8. Dow, R.W., Hugill, R.C., Clarke, J.D. and Smith, C.S. (1981). Evaluation of Ship Hull Ultimate Strength. Proc. SSC-SNAME Extreme Loads Response Symposium, Arlington, VA, October 1981, pp. 133-148.

9. Wu, Y.T. and Wirsching, P.H. (1985). "A New Algorithm for Structural Reliability Estimation". Submitted to the Journal of Engineering Mechanics, ASCE.

10. Faulkner, D. (1981). "Semi-Probabilistic Approach to the Design of Marine Structures". Proc. SSC-SNAME Extreme Loads Response Symposium, Arlington, VA, October 1981, pp. 213-230.

DEVELOPMENT OF SHIP STRENGTH FORMULATIONS

A C Viner
Ship Research and Rule Development Department
Hull New Construction Division
Lloyd's Register of Shipping
71 Fenchurch Street, London EC3M 4BS

ABSTRACT

Behind the ship strength requirements of a classification society lies much detailed development work. To ensure that merchant ship structures possess a sufficient margin of safety at their design loads, increasing use is made of both structural reliability techniques and non-linear structural analysis. This paper describes some of the recent development work concerning ship structures carried out at Lloyd's Register of Shipping.

INTRODUCTION

The ship strength requirements of Lloyd's Register of Shipping are expressed partly as Rules and partly as direct calculation procedures. In addition, designers are free to use their own calculation methods and programs, providing these are acceptable to the Society.

A very important function of a classification society is to establish the structural criteria which the designer must meet. Considerable background development work is needed to provide the most up-to-date information for formulating such criteria and for maintaining and expanding the Rules and direct calculation procedures. Increasing use is made of both structural reliability techniques and non-linear structural analysis. Recent work on structural reliability has been reported in references [1] and [2]. This paper gives an outline of some of the developments concerning the ductile strength of ship structures.

The main aim of the R & D in non-linear structural analysis is to provide the capability to assess the margin of safety of any ship structure under any realistic combination of loads. The approach has been to make use of the numerical methods incorporated in a number of non-linear finite element programs, correlate with test results where these are available and then develop analytical solutions for use on desk-top computers. In the following sections, results are presented for stiffened panels under in-plane loading, hull girder strength, plates subjected to lateral pressure and plating under vehicle loads.

STIFFENED PANELS

Uniaxial Strength

Stiffened panels in ship structures are frequently subjected primarily to axial load and for this reason the subject of uniaxial compressive strength has received detailed attention. Several analytical procedures have been investigated and a beam-column approach, which has been shown to correlate well with test data, has been adopted for use within the Society. Moderate magnitudes of lateral pressure may be combined with the axial compression. This procedure, which is described briefly in reference [1] and in detail in reference [3], forms the basis of LR.PASS desk-top computer Program No 20202.

This program can be used to generate stress-strain curves (ie. load-end shortening curves) for plates stiffened by flat bars, bulb flats, angles and tees. The beam-column theory provides the ultimate stress value while one of four unloading procedures provides the post-ultimate strength characteristics. The unloading procedure is selected on the basis of the predicted failure mode, two being provided for plate-induced failure and two for stiffener-induced failure. In each case one procedure allows for buckling while the other assumes unloading to occur by yield alone.

Biaxial Strength

At some locations of the ship structure, for example the bottom shell, the biaxial compressive strength of a stiffened panel may be a limiting failure mode. Several investigations into this problem have been reported, eg. [4,5], but many of these consider an isolated plate with assumed boundary

154

conditions. In order to obtain some understanding of the behaviour of a stiffened panel subjected to this loading, a 3D finite element model of a typical longitudinal structure was constructed. The panel comprised plating of slenderness b/t = 60 and an inverted angle stiffener of l/r = 30 supported by a transverse frame. The area of analysis extended over four adjacent quarter panels, and computations were performed using the finite element program MARC. The model was composed of a total of 168 bi-linear 4-node thick shell elements. This element is very effective in comparison with other higher order elements, both in terms of its inherent ability to handle non-linear structural behaviour and utilization of computer resources. Because of the highly non-linear nature of the problem, the full Newton-Raphson technique with the Crisfield load correction algorithm in conjunction with the updated Lagrangian procedure coupled with an automatic load-stepping scheme was utilised to solve the system of equilibrium equations.

Symmetrical boundary conditions along the panel centre-lines were assumed for rotations, and all four edges were constrained to remain straight during loading, which was by displacement control. The constitutive relationship for the steel material was taken to be elastic-perfectly-plastic with a yield stress, σ_o, of 245 N/mm^2. Initial imperfections caused by

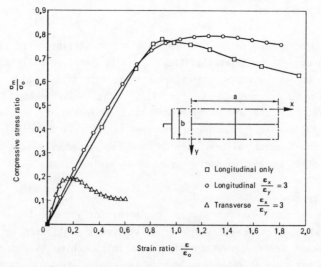

Figure 1   Load-end Shortening Curves for a Panel Uniaxially and Biaxially Loaded

production were modelled in the form of Fourier series and in addition small values of the buckling mode shapes were included to ensure that the lowest failure mode was triggered. A residual stress distribution caused by fillet welding of the stiffener and the frame to the plate was included in the model. The magnitude in the compression zones of the panel amounted to 10% of the yield stress in the longitudinal direction, and 4% transversely. In-plane loads were applied in the form of incremental displacements, such that the transverse increment was taken as a pre-determined fixed ratio of the longitudinal one, ie. $\varepsilon_x / \varepsilon_y = 3$, 5/6, 1/3 and 1/6, where $\varepsilon_x / \varepsilon_y$ is the longitudinal to transverse strain ratio. Results were also computed for pure longitudinal and transverse loading.

Examples of the load-shortening curves are shown in Figure 1, where it may be seen that the addition of a low to moderate transverse strain produces a much 'softer' response in the vicinity of the ultimate longitudinal strength and a marginal increase in this value. However, the maximum transverse strength is quite low and, in common with the lower ratios of $\varepsilon_x / \varepsilon_y$, occurs prior to attaining the longitudinal maximum. The failure mode for this example was predominantly three half-waves along the panel length, whereas for the lower strain ratios a single half wave was the most noticeable characteristic. An interaction diagram summarising these results is given in Figure 2. This illustrates two curves (1 and 2) plotted on the

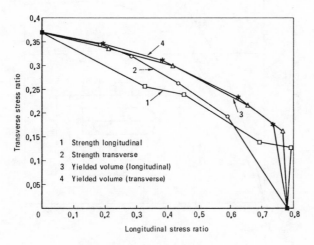

Figure 2   Interaction Curves

basis of maximum longitudinal strength with its associated transverse strength, and vice versa. The characteristics of these curves are quite different due principally to the transverse post-buckling behaviour. If the limiting strength under biaxial loading is taken at the point where the volume of yielded material under biaxial loading equals the volume of yielded material at failure under either longitudinal or transverse uniaxial loading, more regular interaction curves (3 and 4) result. It is interesting to observe that the character of the latter curves is rather similar to that derived from an analysis of an isolated panel [4].

Panel Cut-outs

Cut-outs are a necessary feature in structural design whether for reasons of weight control or for access. To maintain economy of production, it is usual in merchant ship design for these to be unstiffened. The most usual loading to which cut-outs are subjected is that of shear, and some papers, eg. [6], on this topic have been published. However, in some instances, for example in longitudinal girder webs, the response of cut-outs to compressive loading can be of interest. Numerical analysis of a panel including a cut-out and loaded in compression is now a relatively simple,

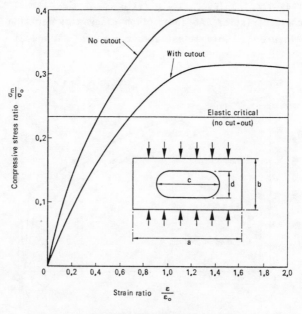

Figure 3   Panel with Cutout

albeit uneconomical task.   An example of this type of analysis is shown in Figure 3, where a simply supported panel with parameters a/b = 2.125, β = 2.40 and an initial imperfection of b/200 is subjected to a uniform transverse compressive displacement. The load-axial displacement curves show that for a large cut-out of c/a = 0.59 and d/b = 0.50, the ultimate compressive strength relative to the panel with no cut-out is much greater than the ratio (1- c/a).   This trend is predictable since a major contribution to the panel strength is contained within the plate area adjacent to the short sides.

HULL GIRDER STRENGTH

The Hull Bending Strength Program

A computer program was developed by the Society in 1979 to assess the ultimate strength of ships' hulls.   This program is based on an approach presented by Smith [7] for vertical bending, and has been extended to cover bending about both axes.

The procedure involves a subdivision of the structure into discrete elements for which stress-strain curves can be defined as above . The strain arising from a given hull curvature can then be used in conjunction with the curves, to obtain element stresses.

Figure 4 shows a hull cross-section subjected to curvatures C_x and C_y about the x and y axes respectively.   This system is equivalent to a

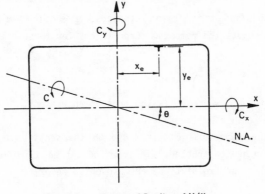

Figure 4   Combined Bending of Hull

combined curvature C acting at an angle θ to the x axis, where:

$$C = \pm \sqrt{(C_x^2 + C_y^2)}$$

and:

$$\cos \theta = C_x/C$$

On the assumption that plane sections remain plane, the strain in an element e, positioned at distances x_e and y_e from the neutral axis, can be obtained from the following expression:

$$\varepsilon_e = C(x_e \sin \theta + y_e \cos \theta)$$

This value of strain is then used to determine the corresponding value of stress, σ_e, from the stress-strain curves.

To maintain overall equilibrium of the structure beyond the proportional limit, it is necessary to re-define the position of the neutral axis. The required correction is obtained from the following expression which defines the movement necessary to achieve a net axial force of zero.

$$SHIFT = \frac{\Sigma(A_e \cdot \sigma_e)}{C \Sigma(E_e \cdot A_e)}$$

This correction is applied iteratively in conjunction with updated stresses and strains until equilibrium is achieved.

Having obtained the element stresses, a simple summation process is required to calculate the moments. Expressions for these components are:

$$M_x = \Sigma \sigma_e \cdot A_e \cdot y_e$$

and similarly for M_y, where A_e is the area of an element.

By applying increments of curvature to the section, a moment-curvature relationship can be constructed. This method has been applied to a number of ships and results for two of these are presented below.

Analysis of a Tanker

The first ship to be considered is an eleven year old tanker, 247m in length, which suffered a midship section failure. The ship was longitudinally stiffened throughout with longitudinal bulkheads positioned at 0.26B from the side shell. The deck structure was stiffened principally by inverted angle sections, these being interspersed by deeper girder members. Two such girders were provided in each of the wing tanks, and five in the centre tank region. The ship failed in a sagging mode close to amidships while on a final voyage to the breakers. The still water bending moment was far in excess of the design value and this, combined with an estimated wave height of between 6 and 8 metres, resulted in a total applied moment within the range 5.7×10^{12} Nmm to 6.1×10^{12} Nmm.

Corrosion levels reported for the ship indicated an average loss of thickness on the deck structure of 3mm. A more detailed inspection showed that corrosion of the stiffener webs was more pronounced close to the plating than it was near the stiffener flange. Two analyses were therefore carried out, one with a uniform reduction of 3mm assumed, and the other with stiffener webs tapered in accordance with measured values. Diagrams showing typical deck stiffeners and girders are given in Figure 5.

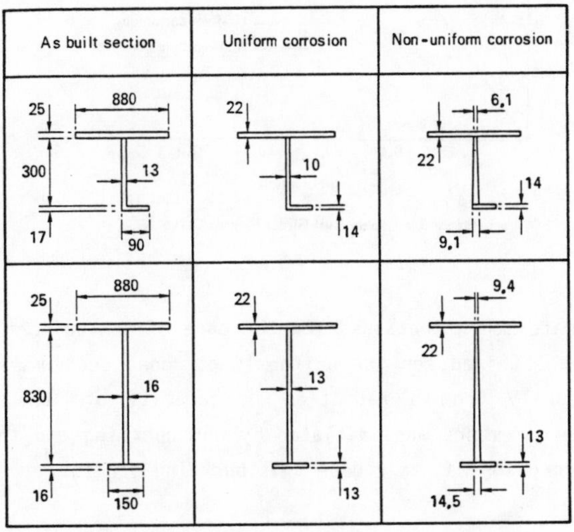

Figure 5   Typical Deck Stiffener and Girder Members

The yield strength of the material was obtained from samples taken from the deck structure after failure. This was reported to be 226 N/mm^2 for the deck plating and girders, and 262 N/mm^2 for the deck stiffeners.

Stress-strain curves were obtained for the elements shown in Figure 5 from a non-linear finite element program. Other sections were assessed using Program No 20202 (see above). These curves were provided as data in the hull bending strength program to obtain the moment- curvature relations shown in Figure 6. As may be seen, these results compare favourably with conditions believed to exist at the time of failure.

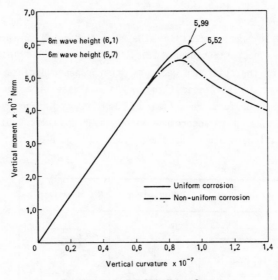

Figure 6   Tanker Hull Girder Moment Curve

The ultimate moment obtained for the case of non-uniform corrosion is 9% less than that obtained for the uniformly corroded section. This difference arises principally from a reduction in capacity of the girder members. Failure of these members was initiated by web buckling and the effect of the non-uniform corrosion was to reduce this buckling stress.

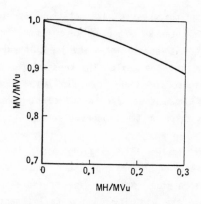

Figure 7 Interaction between Vertical
and Horizontal Moment

Figure 7 illustrates the effect of applying a horizontal curvature in addition to the vertical curvature component. This curve has been non-dimensionalized with respect to the vertical moment capacity, MVu, and indicates a strength reduction of 11% when the horizontal moment, MH, reaches 0.3 times the vertical moment.

Analysis of a VLCC

The second case to be discussed is a ten-year old VLCC, 327m in length, which broke her back while discharging oil. The hogging failure occurred close to amidships and resulted in considerable buckling damage of the bottom plating and associated stiffeners. Since the loading condition on this ship at failure is known, the case is particularly suitable for comparison with theoretical predictions.

The ship was longitudinally stiffened throughout with longitudinal bulkheads located at 0.25B from the side shell. Flat bar stiffeners were used for the deck longitudinals and fabricated tees were used in the bottom structure.

The deck and bottom structure were constructed from higher tensile steel while the bulkheads and side shell were of mild steel. As tensile test measurements were not available, calculations were based on nominal values of yield stress, these being 315 N/mm^2 and 235 N/mm^2.

162

Although corroded thicknesses have not been reported, it was stated that all cargo and ballast tanks inspected were generally found to be in good order. In view of the uncertainty involved, however, calculations were carried out both for the 'as built' thicknesses and for a nominal level of corrosion to investigate the significance of this parameter. In the latter case, a reduction of 1mm was applied to the plating and stiffener webs and a reduction of 2mm was taken on the flanges.

Since the ship failed in a hogging mode, it was necessary to take account of the effect of lateral pressure and transverse stress on the strength of the compression members. The pressure was known to be purely external as tanks in the vicinity of the failed section had been emptied. Two sets of calculations were carried out to investigate the sensitivity to lateral pressure, one of these being for a draught of 11.9 metres and the other being for zero pressure.

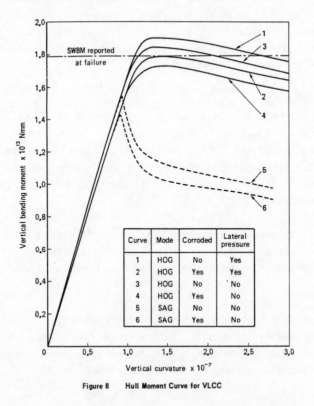

Figure 8   Hull Moment Curve for VLCC

Results of the analyses are shown in Figure 8 together with the still water bending moment reported to exist at the time of failure. For this ship, the application of lateral pressure has given rise to an increase in strength, the additional load component having delayed the onset of failure by stiffener compression. The effect of introducing corrosion on the structure has been to reduce the strength by 6%.

Also shown in Figure 8 are results obtained for the same ship in a sagging condition where, as expected, a lower failure stress is predicted.

Effect of General Corrosion on Hull Bending Strength

Hull ultimate sagging bending moments have been computed for several tankers, progressively reducing the topside scantlings (ie deck structure and upper 10 per cent of side shell and longitudinal bulkhead) to represent the effect of general corrosion. The results are summarised in Figure 9 where the factor by which hull ultimate bending moments are reduced is plotted against percentage corrosion of the deck plating. The reduction in hull modulus at deck is also shown for comparison. The upper parts of the shaded bands correspond to corrosion of longitudinals at the same percentage as the deck plating and the lower parts to corrosion of longitudinals at twice this amount.

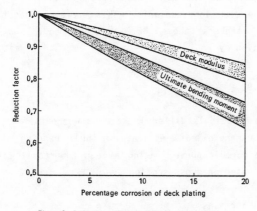

Figure 9   Reduction in Hull Bending Strength due to
Corrosion of Topsides

164

It may be observed that for 15 per cent corrosion of the deck plating, where the deck modulus is reduced by 12-16 per cent, the ultimate bending moment may be reduced by as much as 27 per cent.

Similar calculations for corrosion of the whole hull section indicated a reduction in ultimate bending moment of up to 31 per cent for 15 per cent corrosion.

Approximate Estimate of Hull Bending Strength

For a tanker, having all deck longitudinals in the midship region of the same scantlings, an initial estimate of hull sagging bending strength may be made by assuming that elastic behaviour occurs up to the point where the first deck longitudinal reaches its failure load and that this brings about immediate collapse. The ultimate hull sagging moment may be expressed as:

$$Mu = \alpha \cdot \sigma_u \cdot Z_D$$

where σ_u is the ultimate compressive stress of a deck longitudinal with associated plating and α is a coefficient normally in the range 0.92 - 1.05. It is convenient to use the deck modulus at side, Z_D, rather than the modulus at the highest longitudinal.

It may be shown that the value of α varies with the initial unloading modulus, E_u, of the deck longitudinals. This variation has been determined for a number of tankers above 80,000 tonnes dwt and a reasonable approximation is given by

$$\alpha = 0.92 - \frac{0.02}{E_u/E - 0.15}$$

Where deck longitudinals differ in size or where differential corrosion has taken place, an approximate estimate of hull bending strength may be found by using the formula above, taking a mean compressive strength of the deck longitudinals based on cross-section area.

Hull Girder Thermal Stresses

The carriage of heated cargoes in tankers and OBO ships is a frequent occurrence and for moderate temperatures is permitted without evaluation of the consequent thermal stresses. At temperatures above these defined limits, which are dependent upon ship configuration and cargo type, calculations of longitudinal thermal strains are required. Often a simple linear calculation is sufficient, but for higher temperatures thermal strains may cause the growth of out-of-plane panel deflections due to compression, in which case a non-linear calculation is more applicable. An example of this is the carriage of bitumen at temperatures around $180^{\circ}C$. This problem has been addressed in [8], where both longitudinal and transverse thermal stresses are considered. Based on this reference LR.PASS DTC Program 20201 has been developed to analyse hull girder longitudinal thermal strains.

PLATES SUBJECTED TO LATERAL PRESSURE

Many solutions have been developed for the analysis of unstiffened plates loaded by a uniform pressure, and several expressions in the ship Rules are derived from the 'classical' plastic collapse formulae. Most of the available solutions assume that the membrane restraint conditions are either free or fixed [eg 9,10,11], and few allow for any flexibility in the supporting structure. Of the latter solutions one by Jones [11] is more suitable to permanent sets of the order of, or greater than one half the plate thickness. A solution developed by Kamtekar [12] for beams or long plates is, however, applicable for both low and high values of permanent set. This solution is based on the following assumption for the deflected shape of a transverse plate strip of unit width

$$y = \sum_{i=0}^{4} a_i . z^i$$

where z is the distance along the strip, and the equation for strip extension,

$$\int_0^{b/2} \left(\frac{dy}{dz}\right)^2 dz + 2 \int_0^{b/2} \left(\frac{dy}{dz}\right) \left(\frac{dyo}{dz}\right) dz + \Delta = \frac{Sb}{tE'} + \sum_i e_{pi}$$

where yo = initial imperfection shape = $w_o \sin (\pi z/b)$
         S = the membrane force
   b, t = span, plate thickness
     e_{pi} = the plastic extension of hinge i
     $\Delta/2$ = in-plane movement of the support point.
      $E' = E/(1-\nu^2)$

The term $\Delta/2$ may be used to include the influence of a transverse displacement applied to the plate strip, and to include the movement due to the in-plane stiffness expressed as

$$\frac{\Delta}{2} = - \frac{Sb}{tE} \cdot \frac{K_b}{K}$$

where K_b/K is the ratio of the in-plane stiffness of the strip to that of the surrounding structure. The effect of this can be seen in Figure 10, where the results of this solution for a panel of aspect ratio 3 and b/t = 40 are compared with those of [9], [10], and [11] and also a non-linear finite element analysis with full membrane restraint. The solution assumes that no hinge rotation occurs until the local moment becomes equal to the plastic moment, and consequently a slight kink is introduced into the response curves.

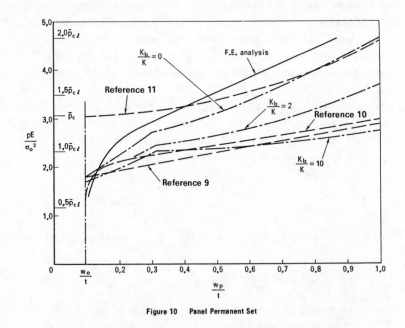

Figure 10   Panel Permanent Set

These equations are solved in four stages, from the elastic plate strip through to the plastic membrane, and at each stage the coefficients a_i are determined using boundary conditions and equilibrium at mid-span. Details of the solution to determine the total deflection y at each stage are given in [12]. A simple expression may then be used to approximate the permanent set at mid-span:-

$$w_p = b/4(\ \theta_e + \theta_c\ )$$

where θ_e and $2\,\theta_c$ are the plastic rotations of the end and centre-span hinges.

These equations are strictly applicable to beams or panels of infinite aspect ratio. An approximate and simple extension to panels of finite aspect ratio may be accomplished by noting that for values of 3 or larger, expressions for permanent set tend to become asymptotic, and therefore using the upper and lower bound equations of [11] a simple correction factor may be derived for application to panels of lower aspect ratio. In the extreme case of a square panel, a comparison of this approach with experimental results given by Clarkson [13] shows that this approach is slightly conservative with an error of between 5% and 10% in the range $0.05 < W_p/t < 1.0$. Inclusion of in-plane stress components other than transverse direct stress may easily be accomplished by using a modified value for yield. The methods described above form the basis of the panel capacity computed in the LR.PASS DTC Program 10604.

PLATING UNDER VEHICLE LOADS

An excellent use of non-linear numerical methods is to correlate with test data and then use this as a basis for the development of a simple design method. A good example of this is the analysis of deck plating subjected to wheel or patch loads. Earlier investigators had tended to use experimental or modified elastic methods to analyse this problem, for example references [14,15] and work carried out at the Glengarnock Structures Laboratory. More recently a paper by Jackson and Frieze [16] correlated a number of numerical analyses with experimental results and developed a series of design curves permitting different levels of acceptable permanent set to be selected. However, for the design of Ro-Ro decks for example, other criteria such as total deflection, stress range and wear-down should be considered, in addition to permanent set.

168

Initially a number of analyses were performed using differing models with various numerical methods and programs, and some comparisons with experimental results were made. Attention was given to the number of panels required to idealise the problem, boundary conditions, the flexibility of stiffeners, and the influence of in-plane direct and shear stresses on membrane stresses and local yielding within the panel. The problem of idealising a tyre load was investigated and it was found that the pattern of plastic yielding was sensitive to the way in which the tyre load was applied. Two simple idealisations were investigated, ie two line loads and a uniform patch pressure. The two line load model was considered to be more appropriate for jackfeet loading, and although local bearing stresses were not investigated, it was found that with regard to overall panel criteria, this representation was less onerous than that of a uniform patch pressure. Since the latter adequately represents a conventional pneumatic tyre, this case was used for all subsequent analyses. The results obtained were correlated against available experimental data, and the methods assessed for accuracy, cost and ease of use, and most of the further numerical analyses were run using the general purpose non-linear program MARC.

Unserviceability in the case of decks subjected to wheel loading is not limited by the onset of yielding, but by the total deflection under load, the permanent set remaining in the panel on unloading and the necessity to avoid fatigue cracking. The total (elasto-plastic) deflection, including some allowance for initial imperfection, is essentially limited by the safe control and operation of wheeled vehicles, particularly fork lift trucks. It is important that excessive permanent set is not caused by service loads although the limiting factors may frequently be non-structural, such as appearance, the collection of oil or water on decks etc. To provide a measure of protection against fatigue damage two simple criteria were adopted,

(i)   the stress range must not exceed twice the yield stress at any position in the plate (this is also needed to avoid alternating plasticity and the incremental growth of permanent set),

and (ii)   a maximum stress range perpendicular to the fillet welds that reflects satisfactory experience from existing designs.

In order to keep the design method simple, design curves have been developed reflecting the above criteria.

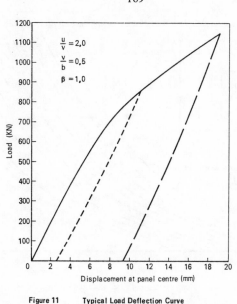

Figure 11   Typical Load Deflection Curve

After considering various options it was considered that a single design chart based on a print of aspect ratio = 2, acting on a long panel, with simple corrections to account for differing configurations, would give good results in a readily usable format. A number of numerical analyses were therefore made for this configuration with varying values of patch/panel width ratios and plate parameter, β, as defined in Figure 12. A typical load-deflection curve is given in Figure 11. From the data it was found that the curves satisfying the permanent set criterion were steeper than those determined by the total deflection criterion, the latter being the governing factor for thinner plates. A design chart , suitable for steel decks, has been produced which satisfies all the limiting criteria and incorporates the transition from deflection to permanent set limit, see Figure 12.

Although the design chart has been developed for the above configuration, a method applicable to any patch aspect or panel ratio is clearly required. To account for the effect of patch aspect ratio a number of simple expressions were developed based on idealised plastic hinge mechanisms. These formulations were then compared with numerical results for a variety of ratios and the one displaying the best correlation was adopted.

170

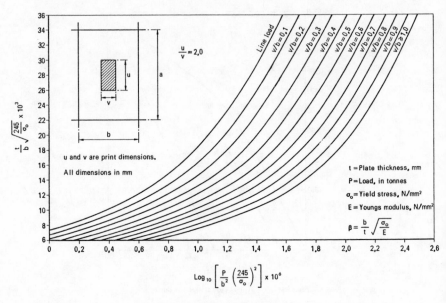

Figure 12   Design Chart for Steel Decks

The equation used was up to 5% conservative when compared with the numerical data. Results indicate that the panel aspect ratio has a much reduced effect on permanent set when compared to that for a uniformly loaded panel. The numerical analyses for the design chart were made on long panels where the support due to the short side is negligible. However, as the patch boundary approaches the short side it is evident that this will become increasingly effective in reacting the patch load. Some further numerical work was carried out to enable a simple formulation, quantifying this effect, to be developed. The case of a similar load on an adjacent panel was also considered as stresses normal to the longitudinals were expected to be higher. Although these stresses did increase, the permanent set criterion was found to be the limiting factor. Significantly, it was found that this load configuration was more severe than a patch load on one panel alone and therefore where adjacent panels can be loaded a reduction in the allowable load is required if the design criteria are not to be exceeded.

The load applied to the plate has been considered static throughout the study but in practice may be enhanced by accelerations due to wheels rolling on an uneven deck, changes in deck gradient, the effect of lifting or handling loads and ship motions. For the case of accelerations due to vehicle operations a simple inertia factor is recommended. A number of empirical expressions have been developed which may be used to estimate the vertical accelerations for a ship at sea and these can be used to modify the design load. Finally, consideration must be given to an allowance for wear and wastage of the plate when determining deck thicknesses.

By using the analyses outlined above, a quick and easy design method for determining the thickness of steel decks subjected to wheel loading has been developed, which may be applied to a large number of patch and panel configurations typically found on ships.

CONCLUSION

The use of non-linear structural analysis methods has enabled progress to be made on a number of topics concerning the ductile strength of ship structures, including the strength of stiffened panels under in-plane loading, the effect of cut-outs on plate compressive strength and the strength of plating subjected to uniform pressure and vehicle loads.

The hull bending strength of tankers may now be calculated with some confidence, as demonstrated by comparisons with two failure cases, and it is shown that corrosion may lead to a considerable reduction in hull strength.

The results of the development work on plating and stiffened panels, together with parallel studies on hydrodynamic loading and structural reliability, are being used to form the basis of revised classification requirements and direct calculation procedures.

ACKNOWLEDGEMENTS

This paper has been compiled from the work of several colleagues and the author wishes particularly to thank Mr G H Sole, Dr S E Rutherford, Mr Y F Cheng and Mr J C Hudson for their assistance.

REFERENCES

1. Hart, D.K., Rutherford, S.E., Wickham, A.H.S.
   Structural reliability analysis of stiffened panels.
   RINA,(1985).

2. Wickham, A.H.S.,
   Reliability analysis techniques for structures with time-dependent
   strength parameters.
   ICOSSAR '85, 4th International Conference on Structural Safety and
   Reliability.

3. Rutherford, S.E.
   Stiffened compression panels. The analytical approach.
   Lloyd's Register of Shipping, Hull Structures Report No 82/26/R2
   April 1984.

4. Dowling, P.J., Dier, A.F.
   Strength of ships plating. Plates under combined lateral pressure
   and biaxial compression.
   CESLIC Rep SP6, Engineering Structures Laboratories,
   Civil Engineering Department, Imperial College, London (1979).

5. Valsgard, S.
   Numerical design prediction of the capacity of plates in biaxial
   in-plane compression.
   Computers and Structures 12 (1980) pp 729-739.

6. Redwood, R.G., Uenoya, M.
   Critical loads for webs with holes.
   J Struct Div, ASCE, Vol 105, St10, (1979).

7. Smith, C.S.
   Influence of local compressive failure on ultimate longitudinal
   strength of ship's hull.
   PRADS - International Symposium on Practical Design in Shipbuilding,
   Tokyo (1977).

8. Sole, G.H.
   Non-linear thermal stresses in ship structures.
   PRADS (1983).

9. Faulkner, D., Adamchak, J.C., Snyder, G.J., Vetter, M.F. Synthesis
   of welded grillages to withstand compression and normal loads.
   Computers and Structures, Vol 3. (1973).

10. Hughes, O.F.
    Design of laterally loaded plating - uniform pressure loads.
    J of Ship Research, June 1981.

11. Jones, N.
    Plastic behaviour of ship structures.
    SNAME (1976).

12.   Kamtekar, A.G.
       An approximate analysis of the behaviour of laterally loaded, fully
       fixed beams and plates.
       Int J Mech Sci, Vol 23, No 7 (1981).

13.   Clarkson, J.
       A new approach to the design of plates to withstand lateral pressure
       Trans I N A, Vol 98 (1956).

14.   Haslum, K.
       Design of a deck subject to large wheel loads.
       European Shipbuilding, Vol 19,2 (1970).

15.   Sandvik, P.C.
       Deck plates subject to large wheel loads.
       Norwegian Inst of Tech, Div of Ship Structures,
       Report SK/M 28 (1974).

16.   Jackson, R.I., Frieze, P.A.
       Design of deck structures under wheel loads.
       RINA (1980).

THE APPLICATION OF NONLINEAR ANALYSIS
TO SHIP AND SUBMARINE STRUCTURES

D J Creswell and R S Dow
Admiralty Research Establishment
Dunfermline, Fife, Scotland

ABSTRACT

A review is given of the application of nonlinear structural analysis at ARE to the solution of design and post-design problems of Naval Ships and Submarines, emphasising areas where advances have been made.

INTRODUCTION

In recent years extensive use has been made at ARE, Dunfermline of nonlinear, elastoplastic structural analysis techniques [1-4]. The object of this paper is to show how nonlinear methods have been applied to Naval ship and submarine design problems, highlighting areas where: the design process has been rendered more accurate; non-conservativeness or redundancy have been identified; existing design methods have been validated in situations not readily open to experimental investigation. It will also be shown how nonlinear methods have contributed to the solution of post-design and post-construction problems, such as the assessment of structural damage and the granting of concessions on material and geometric tolerances.

Nonlinear Analysis of Surface Ship Structures

A typical warship structure is an assembly of flat, or nearly flat, thin-shell, orthogonally-stiffened panels (Figure 1). The dominant load is inplane-uniaxial but there are also shear, biaxial and lateral-pressure loading effects, the relative magnitudes being obtainable from wave-loading programs. Although some work has been carried out on combined load effects most applications of nonlinear analysis have been aimed at the dominant inplane loading situation.

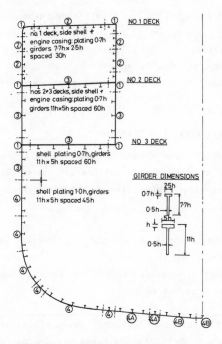

FIGURE 1. Typical Hull Section

The nature of the structure and its loading leads to a problem with the following characteristics: a sensitivity to geometric and material imperfections resulting from fabrication, welding, or damage, which may affect pre-collapse stiffness and collapse load; an unloading characteristic following collapse, giving panels post-collapse load carrying capacity considerably less than the collapse strength, which will shed load onto surrounding structure and affect the overall structural stiffness; a degree of structural redundancy such that local panel failure will not necessarily cause overall structural collapse.

Geometric complexity and the need for inelastic post-buckling behaviour precludes full three-dimensional analysis of the entire structure with present computing resources. Instead, an ELEMENTAL approach has been developed in which individual panels and stiffened sections are studied with an appropriate nonlinear analysis method under various forms of loading. Load-displacement curves for individual panels may then be used as effective stress-strain curves for the elements of a hull girder cross-section [5, 6], allowing the global failure characteristics and maximum bending moment to be examined.

Evaluation of the ELEMENTAL stress-strain curves requires incremental nonlinear, inelastic methods, with rather sophisticated elements and solution algorithms displaying good large-deflection capability, including facilities for pursuing unstable post-collapse behaviour. The final stage, evaluation of bending moment, although an incremental one, is a relatively straightforward problem with one degree of freedom, subject to the assumption that plane sections remain plane.

The ELEMENTAL approach makes full use of the one simplifying factor in the surface ship problem, namely the quasi-uniaxial nature of the dominant loading. It is particularly efficient for Naval surface ship design, because the overall complex geometry is usually an assembly of a small number of different types of section, minimising the number of detailed nonlinear analyses.

Nonlinear Structural Analysis of Submarines

The two main structural features of the submarine pressure hull are the torispherical dome and the ring-stiffened cylinder. Dominant in-service load is hydrostatic pressure, giving rise to biaxial stress fields in dome and cylindrical shell.

Dome collapse is highly sensitive to shape imperfections. Although in principle nonlinear, inelastic methods may be used to predict collapse pressure, if precise shapes and material characteristics are known, such methods have had relatively little real impact to date.

The collapse modes of the ring-stiffened cylinder may be broadly classified as interframe failure, where shell plate deforms between rings with relatively little in-plane frame displacement, and overall failure where rings plus contiguous plating deform radially commonly in the n = 2 ovalization mode [7, 9]. In practice some interaction will occur between these two types of collapse. Characteristics of the problem are: a sensitivity to shape and material imperfections; a load applied directly to hull plating, such that local failure will, via interaction mechanisms, precipitate total hull collapse; and, in the case of n = 2 overall and interactive collapse, an extreme sensitivity to both shell length and variations in frame spacing. Collapse pressures may be quite accurately predicted from a state of moderate deformation prior to collapse, obviating the need to pursue post-collapse behaviour, and simplifying the analysis. Full three-dimensional structural representation is however required for accurate representation of n = 2 stiffness, a severe complication. Although techniques used in surface ship analysis were used in the early days of nonlinear analysis of submarines [8], the tendency recently has been to use a GLOBAL approach, representing the entire hull, while using less sophisticated, cheaper, flat-shell elements, with the simplifications and computational economy accruing from the restriction to only moderate rotations.

NONLINEAR STRUCTURAL ANALYSIS CAPABILITIES

The computer programs regularly used at ARE to perform nonlinear structural analysis of stiffened plate and shell structures vary considerably in their: structural capability, element sophistication, ability to handle geometric nonlinearity and unstable post-collapse behaviour, and representation of material nonlinearity and residual stress (Table 1).

TABLE 1
ARE Capability for Nonlinear Structural Analysis.

Computer Program	Source	Structural Capability	Shell Elements
ADINA	Adina Eng [10]	General 3D	Curved Isoparametric
ASAS	Atkins [11]	General 3D	Curved Isoparametric
BOSOR	Lockheed [12,13]	Axisymmetric †	Finite Difference
FABSTRAN	ARE [14]	General 2D	Flat, Effective Breadth
LUSAS	FEA [15]	General 3D	Curved Isoparametric
N103	ARE [16,17]	2D Ring Frame, 3D Shell (approx)	
NS94	ARE [5]	Hull Ultimate Bending Strength	
STAGS	Lockheed [18]	General 3D	Flat Plate

Computer Program	Geometric Nonlinearity		Unstable Post Collapse	Material Nonlinearity			
	Large Deflection	Method		Yield Criteria	Hardening Theory	Sub-Increment	Residual Stress Input
ADINA	Large	TL/UL	Yes [19]	VM	I/K	No	Thermal
ASAS-NL	Large	UL	Yes [19-21]	VM/T	I/K/M	Yes	Direct
BOSOR	Large †	TL	No	VM	I	No	Thermal
FABSTRAN	Large	UL	Yes [14]	VM	I	No	Direct
LUSAS	Large	TL/UL	Yes [21]	VM	I	Yes	Direct
N103	Moderate	TL	No	U	None	No	Calculated
NS94 *	N/A		Yes [5]	N/A	N/A	N/A	N/A
STAGS (pre 1985)	Moderate	TL	No	VM	I/K/BW	Yes	Thermal

† also small deflection non-axisymmetric buckling.
* nonlinear properties handled implicitly.
TL Total Lagrangian: UL Updated Lagrangian.
VM Von-Mises: T Tresca: U Uniaxial.
I Isotropic: K Kinematic: M Mixed I, K: BW Besseling-White

In most programs quasi-Newton methods are used incrementally to solve the nonlinear equilibrium equation

$$\Delta\{\delta\} = -\left[K_T\right]_i^{-1} \{\psi\}^i$$

in which $\left[K_T\right]^i$ is the tangent stiffness matrix evaluated for displacement $\{\delta\}^i$ and the improved set of nodal displacements is given by

$$\{\delta\}^{i+1} = \{\delta\}^i + \Delta\{\delta\}$$

This procedure is carried out iteratively until the unbalanced force vector $\{\psi\}$ has converged to zero within some specified tolerance limit. The Newton-Raphson (NR) method requires that the tangent stiffness matrix be generated and reduced for equation solving in every iterative cycle. This is expensive. An alternative is Modified Newton-Raphson (MNR) iteration where the tangent stiffness matrix is used for a number of iterative cycles before being updated. This requires more iterative cycles to achieve convergence but because the tangent stiffness matrix is only formed and reduced once, it is much less expensive. These methods for solving the nonlinear equations work well unless the structure displays unstable post-collapse behaviour, then neither the NR nor the MNR techniques under either load or displacement control will converge to a solution. There are a number of techniques available [19-22] for solving this unstable post-collapse behaviour, the most popular appearing to be the Crisfield-Riks arc length procedure [21]. In the Crisfield-Riks arc length method the load P is no longer considered constant but is varied during the iterative process:

$$P = \Delta\lambda F.$$

In order to solve for $\Delta\lambda$ an additional constraint equation is required

$$\Delta\{\delta\}_i^T \ \Delta\{\delta\}_i - \Delta\ell^2 = 0$$

where $\Delta\{\delta\}_i$ is the incremental nodal displacement vector and $\Delta\ell$ is the

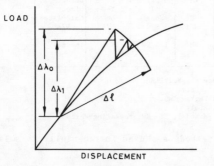

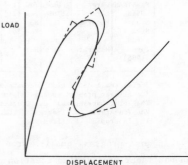

FIGURE 2.   Crisfield-Riks Arc Length Method.

FIGURE 3.   Crisfield-Riks Method Used to Track Unstable Post-Collapse Behaviour.

arc length. This technique is shown in Figure 2, with a practical example shown in Figure 3.

STRUCTURAL PROBLEMS REQUIRING NONLINEAR SOLUTION

This section is used to illustrate specific applications of nonlinear analyses, as outlined in the previous sections, to problems involving shape imperfections, residual stresses, post-collapse loss of strength and mode mixing effects.

In-Plane Loading of Flat Plates

Figure 4 shows the computed load-shortening curve of a simply supported flat plate for a variety of initial shape imperfections (Table 2). Calculations [1] were performed with ASAS-NL using eight-noded isoparametric shell elements (5 degrees of freedom per node, 2 x 2 Gauss quadrature inplane and 5-point Newton-Coates integration through the thickness). Elastic-perfectly plastic stress/strain curves were assumed with von Mises yield criterion and Prandtl-Reuss flow rule.

Figure 4a shows that the worst shape as regards first collapse is the $n = 5$ periodic one (case 3), which conforms most closely with the lowest buckling modeshape. However the localised dent produces an initial collapse stress only marginally higher but has a more rapid unloading characteristic. The overall sinusoidal imperfection gives a high collapse stress; the structure then snaps due to elastic buckling, into a quasi $n = 5$ mode accompanied by a sudden post-collapse loss of strength. The post-collapse load-carrying capacity of this case is very close to that of case 6.

Figure 4b shows the behaviour of the plate with a combination of overall and localised imperfection. The results of this study show:

(a)   that short wavelength imperfections (close to the critical buckling wavelength) are more significant than longer wavelength imperfections of the same amplitude.

(b)   that mode interaction effects are not linearly additive when determining collapse or post-collapse behaviour.

(c) that post-buckling load carrying capacity is determined principally by the character of the lowest buckling mode and relatively
insensitive to the magnitude or wavelength of the initial imperfection.

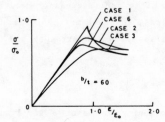

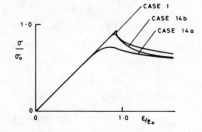

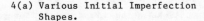

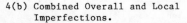

4(a) Various Initial Imperfection
     Shapes.

4(b) Combined Overall and Local
     Imperfections.

FIGURE 4. Computed Load-Shortening Curves for Simply Supported Flat Plates.

TABLE 2

Case No.	Definition of initial deformation	
1	$w_0 = \bar{w}_0 \sin\dfrac{\pi x}{a} \sin\dfrac{\pi y}{b}$, $\bar{w}_0 = 0 \cdot 008b$	
2	$w_0 = \bar{w}_0 \sin\dfrac{5\pi x}{a} \sin\dfrac{\pi y}{b}$, $\bar{w}_0 = 0 \cdot 008b(x/a < 0 \cdot 1, x/a > 0 \cdot 9)$ $w_0 = 0 \cdot 008b(0 \cdot 1 \le x/a \le 0 \cdot 9)$	
3	$w_0 = \bar{w}_0 \sin\dfrac{5\pi x}{a} \sin\dfrac{\pi y}{b}$,	(a) $\bar{w}_0 = 0 \cdot 008b$ (b) $\bar{w}_0 = 0 \cdot 0016b$ (c) $\bar{w}_0 = 0 \cdot 02b$
6	$w_0 = \bar{w}_0 \sin\dfrac{5\pi x}{a} \sin\dfrac{\pi y}{b}$, $(0 \cdot 4 \le x/a \le 0 \cdot 6)$	(a) $\bar{w}_0 = 0 \cdot 008b$ (b) $\bar{w}_0 = 0 \cdot 0016b$ (c) $\bar{w}_0 = 0 \cdot 02b$
14	(a) Case 1 + Case 6a (b) Case 1 + Case 6b	

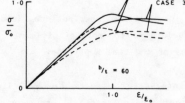

FIGURE 5.   Effect of Stiffeners on Plate Strength.

In-Plane Loading of Flat Stiffened Panels

Figure 5 shows the effect of stiffening on the collapse and post-collapse behaviour of a plate panel [1]. These small stiffeners produce an increase in collapse strength of approximately 20%, highlighting the fact that the interaction between the stiffener and the panel cannot be treated as independent characteristics.

The treatment of overall or column type buckling of longitudinally stiffened panels representative of a ship's side or deck structure could be carried out using a similar type of nonlinear analysis to that carried out for flat panels, and would have to be carried out if stiffener tripping,

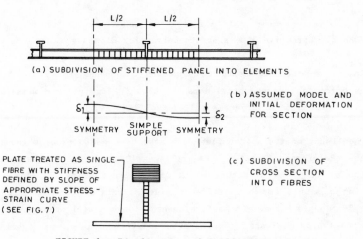

(a) SUBDIVISION OF STIFFENED PANEL INTO ELEMENTS

(b) ASSUMED MODEL AND INITIAL DEFORMATION FOR SECTION

δ_1 δ_2

SYMMETRY   SIMPLE SUPPORT   SYMMETRY

PLATE TREATED AS SINGLE FIBRE WITH STIFFNESS DEFINED BY SLOPE OF APPROPRIATE STRESS-STRAIN CURVE (SEE FIG. 7)

(c) SUBDIVISION OF CROSS SECTION INTO FIBRES

FIGURE 6. Idealisation of Stiffened Panel.

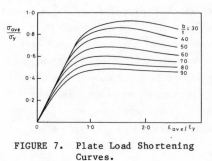

FIGURE 7. Plate Load Shortening Curves.

torsional or local buckling effects were important. The usual approximation is however to perform a nonlinear column analysis of one stiffener plus attached plating (Figure 6) and to assume effective plating properties derived from nonlinear studies on simply supported unstiffened plates (Figure 7). Some typical stiffened panel effective stress/

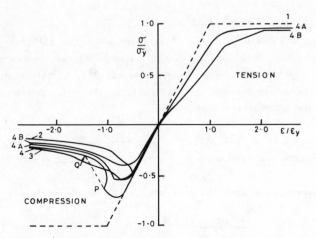

FIGURE 8. Effective Stress/Strain Curves for Elements of Hull Section.

strain curves obtained using the approach are shown in Figure 8, these curves correspond to the panel details shown in Figure 1 and were obtained using the ARE suite of programs called FABSTRAN [14].

Nonlinear analysis techniques can also be used to predict the failure of Glass Reinforced Plastic (GRP) grillages [2]. Figure 9 shows a typical section of GRP deck structure which was analysed using ASAS-NL, by considering a single top hat stiffener plus associated plating (Figure 10) using 8-noded isoparametric shell elements with material properties assumed to be anisotropic elastic. A two-span model was chosen, to highlight the interaction between overall and local buckling effects. Both local and overall imperfection shapes were represented in the analysis, the magnitudes of these imperfections being obtained from extensive experimental measurements of the model. Theoretical predictions and experimental results are compared in Figure 11, showing agreement within about 1 per cent on collapse load. The predicted failure mode shown in Figure 10, which agreed with experimental readings, showed the effect of mode interaction where in the upward deflecting half span the compressive stress in the plate is enhanced due to bending producing local buckling of the plating. This local buckling in turn reduces the overall column buckling strength of the stiffened panel.

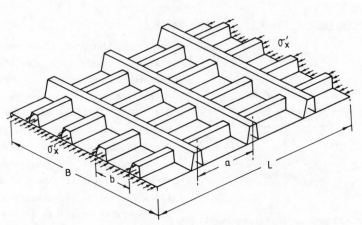

FIGURE 9.   Longitudinally Compressed GRP Panel.

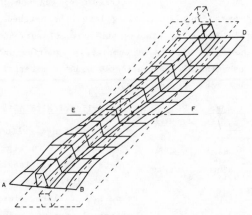

FIGURE 10.   Computed Deformation of Test Panel Just Before Collapse.

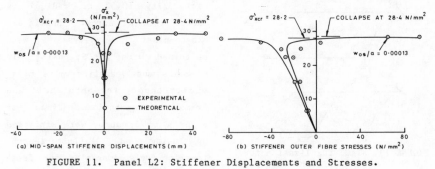

FIGURE 11.   Panel L2: Stiffener Displacements and Stresses.

Moment–Curvature of a Ship's Hull Girder

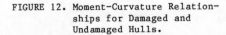

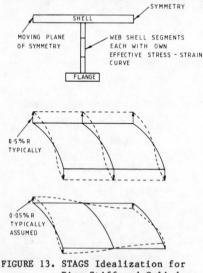

FIGURE 12. Moment–Curvature Relationships for Damaged and
Undamaged Hulls.

Once the effective strain curves of stiffened panels have been obtained (Figure 8), the moment curvature relationship of a complex hull girder (Figure 12) may be found using the incremental program NS94 [3, 5]. Curve C on Figure 12 shows the moment–curvature characteristic obtained for the structure of Figure 1. In evaluating the overall moment, the unstable–unloading sections of effective stress/strain curves (Figure 8) (eg the continuous curve PQ) are replaced by a dynamic unloading line (the hatched line PQ). The slope of PQ is related to the elastic stiffness of surrounding structure. Figure 12 also shows the effects of completely ignoring unloading effects (curve B) and of assuming elastic–perfectly plastic material properties for all elements of the cross-section (curve A).

Elasto-Plastic Collapse of Ring–Stiffened Cylindrical Shells

FIGURE 13. STAGS Idealization for
Ring Stiffened Cylinder
Collapse.

Ring-stiffened cylinder collapse is illustrated in Figures 13 to 15; data points are labelled i, o, io to denote interframe, overall or inter-active failure, respectively; a typical design value for out-of-circularity (0.5% of radius) is marked with an arrow. Nonlinear, elasto-plastic analyses were performed with STAGS, using 410 elements and Besseling-White plas-ticity theory for both shell and frame. Computational times, of order 4 to 5 hours, were minimised by using an 'infinite-length' idealization, comprising one frame plus one bay of plating with repeating symmetry boundary conditions (Figure 13), and with frame dimensions increased slightly by comparison with typical submarine geometries, to retain relative values of overall and interframe collapse representative of 'finite-length' submarine hulls. Three different values of shell thickness have been considered, one typical of submarine design, the others approximately 25% greater and 20% smaller than normal and, for each shell thickness case, three material idealizations have been examined (Figure 14); results have been normalised to the stress-relieved, submarine-thickness case in the shape-perfect limit (Figure 14a).

For the calculations shown in Figure 14a bilinear material properties of shell and frame were assumed, with a yield stress representative of high-grade submarine steel. The middle curve of Figure 14a shows the transition from interframe collapse, relatively independent of overall n = 2 amplitude, to overall collapse at high amplitudes (ϵ). Results have been plotted against $\epsilon^{\frac{1}{2}}$ to emphasise that the dependence of overall collapse pressure on n = 2 amplitude is less-than-linear; the predominantly overall results for the thicker shell show clearly the less-than-linear dependence. With a thin shell, interframe collapse occurs for all amplitudes up to 0.75%R. Interaction of interframe and overall collapse mechanisms for the midthickness case is indicated by the shaded area on Figure 14a. The sloping line has been drawn parallel to the overall collapse line for the thicker shell, which is linear to a good approximation when plotted against $\epsilon^{\frac{1}{2}}$. The maximum drop in collapse pressure due to interaction is about 5 to 6%.

The combined effect of cold bending residual stress and n = 2 overall shape is illustrated in Figures 14b and c. Reduced stiffness of shell and frame was allowed for in STAGS by means of effective stress-strain curves derived from a separate analysis, avoiding the need for thermal strains (Table 1). The cold bending process was simulated and thru-section integrations performed for prescribed strains, to give effective stress/strain curves for both shell and frames. Bauschinger effect was allowed for by reference to extensive tensile/compressive test data. Figure 14b shows results for a case where shell and frame flange were bent separately and the frame-web was initially stress free. In Figure 14c the frame was considered to be bent as a T-frame section and, in the STAGS idealization, the frame web was split up into three subsections (Figure 13) each with its own

186

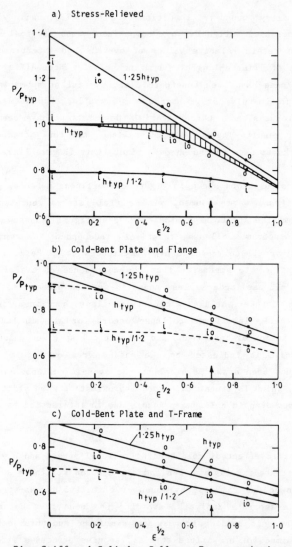

a) Stress-Relieved

b) Cold-Bent Plate and Flange

c) Cold-Bent Plate and T-Frame

FIGURE 14. Ring-Stiffened Cylinder Collapse Pressure Against Overall n = 2
Shape Amplitude for Three Shell Thicknesses (h_{typ} typical of
submarine design) and Three Material Idealizations.
$\epsilon = 100\ W_o/R$, where W_o is the n = 2 overall shape amplitude and
R the mid-shell radius.

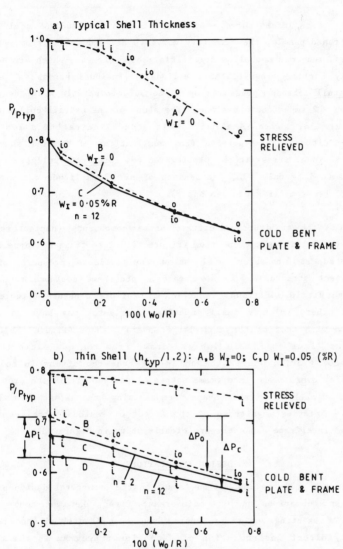

a) Typical Shell Thickness

b) Thin Shell ($h_{typ}/1.2$): A,B $W_I=0$; C,D $W_I=0.05$ (%R)

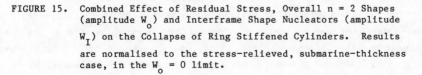

FIGURE 15. Combined Effect of Residual Stress, Overall n = 2 Shapes (amplitude W_o) and Interframe Shape Nucleators (amplitude W_I) on the Collapse of Ring Stiffened Cylinders. Results are normalised to the stress-relieved, submarine-thickness case, in the $W_o = 0$ limit.

effective stress/strain curve. By contrast with the FABSTRAN analysis of
flat stiffened panels, the effective curve is derived solely from material
properties, and does not allow for initial-shape effects, which are handled
explicitly for the ring-stiffened cylinder. Residual stress is seen to
lower overall collapse pressures by 20 to 30%, comparable with the effect
of 0.5%R n = 2 imperfections alone. The slope of the overall collapse line
becomes smaller as residual stress is added, indicating a less-than
linearly-additive effect arising from combinations of initial shape and
stress. Residual stress in the plating reduces interframe collapse for the
cases examined by only 10%, independent of n = 2 amplitude and state of
stress of the frame (Figures 14b and c).

When small amplitude interframe shape components (nucleators) are
added to the initial shape spectrum (Figure 13), interframe collapse can be
demonstrated at pressures well below the collapse pressure of the
shape-perfect structure. In some cases, interframe collapse tendencies
occur with little additional reduction in failure pressure (Figure 15a)
while in others, a very small interframe nucleator may have an effect
comparable with that of the much larger overall shape (Figure 15b). The
continuous lines on Figure 15b are drawn from the quadratic formula
$\Delta Pc^2 = \Delta Po^2 + \Delta Pi^2$, where ΔPo and ΔPi are the reductions in collapse
pressure for overall and interframe shapes alone, and ΔPc is the drop for a
combined overall/interframe shape, emphasising the less than linear
response. Relative magnitudes of the effect of residual stress, overall
shape, and interframe nucleator are clearly shown in Figure 15b.

DESIGN APPLICATIONS

Nonlinear analysis has had an impact on the structural design process
of ships and submarines in three main areas: first, where non-conservative
features of existing design procedures have been identified, and removed
either by direct incorporation of a nonlinear program in the design
procedure [14] or by generation of improved knock-down factors, safety
factors or effective plating stiffnesses; second, where empirical design
procedures have been validated or shown to be over-conservative by neglect
of post-buckling strength; and third, where modes of failure and weak
structural features have been identified, leading to recommendations for
improved design.

The Generation of Effective Breadth Data for Plates Loaded In-Plane

The flat-plate calculations (Figures 4 and 5) show that nonlinear analysis is required to identify the critical imperfection shapes which are not always those used in current design codes. Parametric studies may then be used to generate improved effective breadth data.

Mid Section Design of Surface Ships

Maximum sagging moment of a ship may be overestimated by 25% if post-collapse characteristics are ignored (Figure 12 curves B, C) and by 35% if elastic-perfectly plastic material properties are used (curves A, C).

Figure 16 compares the moment/curvature relation of a steel box-girder predicted by FABSTRAN and NS94 with the experimental results [6]. Two assumptions have been made concerning the spatial extent of 'hard spots' where decks and sides intersect. Curves A and B are seen to bracket the experimental result. Studies of this type have been used to make recommendations for appropriate modelling of 'hard spots'.

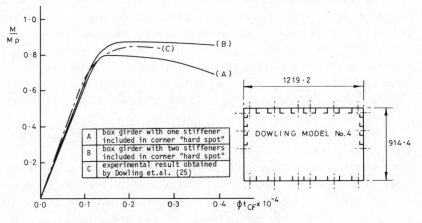

MID-SPAN MOMENT / CURVATURE RELATIONSHIP

FIGURE 16. Dowlings Box Girder Model No 4.

TABLE 3
Effect of a Design Change on Ultimate Sagging Moment.

Surface Ship Design	Fully Plastic Moment	% Improvement	Ultimate Moment Calculated Incrementally	% Improvement (Incremental Method
Original	1.0	-	0.765	-
Improved	1.004	0.4	0.833	9.0

Fully plastic moment of the original design is taken as datum.

Table 3 shows the ultimate bending moments of an actual ship design which was found by nonlinear analysis to have a weak, transversely stiffened midship section between the upper two decks. The side structure was redesigned with longitudinal stiffening, which demonstrated very little improvement as regards fully plastic moment (0.4%), but a 9% increase in maximum sagging moment determined by nonlinear methods.

The two-dimensional nonlinear program (FABSTRAN) is used directly in midship section design procedure.

Uniaxial Compression of a GRP Deck Grillage

Figure 17 shows the growth in out-of-plane mid-panel displacements of a GRP grillage tested under uniaxial compression loading. Unlike the earlier example, which failed as a column between transverse stiffeners (Figure 10), the present panel underwent severe deformation between longitudinal stiffeners followed by debonding of panel and longitudinal stiffener in one panel bay (Figure 18). Theoretical and experimental displacements (W_{op} = 0.001a, approximately the measured value) agree closely up to collapse, where a slight structural stiffening appears to be taking place.

Debonding of plates from stiffeners has been studied experimentally and the force required for this geometry is known. Figure 19 compares the experimental debonding load with the separation force between stiffener and plate calculated from the nonlinear analysis as a function of uniaxial applied stress. The debonding load is seen to be attained at a uniaxial stress corresponding to the failure stress in the grillage experiment, confirming the mechanism that precipitated collapse. Suggestions for

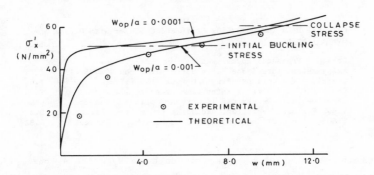

FIGURE 17. Maximum Buckling Displacements in Deck Laminate.

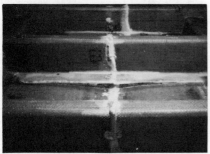

FIGURE 18. Test Panel Following Collapse.

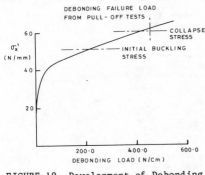
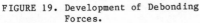

FIGURE 19. Development of Debonding Forces.

improvements in bonding techniques and recommendations for revision of safety factors have been made as a result of the studies [2].

Submarine Design

In the present submarine design procedure, interframe and overall collapse are treated as separate entities, interframe collapse predicted by an empirical method derived from an extensive series of experimental collapse tests on short models [7], and overall collapse allowed for with the inelastic frame-bending program N103 [17].

Interaction effects (Figure 14) may lower the interframe collapse pressure of a long shell below that derived from short model tests for which overall n = 2 deformations are precluded by the high shear stiffness of the shell, suggesting a possible non-conservativeness in the

TABLE 4
Collapse Data for Long Ring Stiffened Cylinder with 0.75%R n = 2
Overall Shape.

Collapse Pressures normalised to empirical value.	
Axisymmetric Interframe Failure Pressure from BOSOR5 [13]	1.11
Overall n = 2 Collapse Pressure from N103 [17]	1.04
Short-shell, Empirical Interframe Pressure [7]	1.00
Experimentally Determined Interframe Collapse Pressure	0.86
STAGS Failure Prediction, excluding Bauschinger Effect	0.89
STAGS Failure Prediction, including Bauschinger Effect	0.82

design procedure. Table 4 compares collapse data for a long uniformly framed submarine model with very large out of circularity (1.5 x permissible). Nonlinear analysis with STAGS explains both the anomalously low interframe collapse pressure and the failure in the central bays where n = 2 stresses were large.

In order to combat the sensitivity to cold bending idealization and to other uncertainties arising from: neglect of welding residual stress, simplified finite-elements, and limitation to only moderate rotations, a self-calibrating procedure is generally used, with effective stress/strain curves and interframe shape nucleators chosen to reflect the short shell empirical interframe collapse data and its scatter. Normalised results for an actual submarine are given in Table 5. A cold bending curve and 0.02%R axisymmetric interframe nucleator were used for the shell. Overall shapes were 0.5%R, n = 3 for the short shell and n = 2 for the actual structure. The interframe collapse pressure (P1) is only 3% lower than the empirical value. Even with a very conservative material idealization (10% below nominal), chosen to give short-shell collapse on the lower scatter band, collapse pressure (P2) is only 10% below the empirical value and well within existing safety factors.

TABLE 5
Normalised Collapse Pressures of a Submarine Compartment
and Short Test Section.

	Pi	P1	P2
Short (7 frame bays)	1.0	1.0	0.91
Long Compartment	1.0	0.97	0.90

Pi is the empirical interframe collapse pressure.
P1 and P2 are STAGS collapse predictions with nominal
and 10% reduced yield strengths, respectively.

On uniformly framed test model structures with 0.5%R (n = 2) shapes, larger interactive effects have been predicted and observed, with 8 or 9% drops below the empirical value quite common, even with nominal material properties. The different sensitivity to interaction effects shown by uniform and non-uniformly framed structures points clearly to the need to represent the entire submarine hull structure when performing nonlinear, inelastic collapse analyses. Investigations of this type have served to validate current submarine design procedures and safety factors.

POST-DESIGN APPLICATIONS

Nonlinear techniques have been applied successfully to the solutions of problems which arise during fabrication, launch and service. The granting of concessions and setting of tolerances on parameters such as shell thickness and weld metal strength are examples of fabrication problems. Damage resulting from collision, fire, grounding, berthing, docking and blast are examples of in-service problems.

Reduced Yield Stress in Submarines

Table 6 gives inelastic collapse prssures calculated with STAGS for a section of a ring-stiffened cylinder with 10% reduced yield strength material along the lines of circumferential and longitudinal plate welds (Figure 20). An infinite-length idealization has been used with repeating symmetry boundary conditions. The circumferential extent of the theoretical model was 60°, allowing representation of a 0.5%R n = 3 overall shape, for which the structure displays interframe/overall interactive behaviour. A small 0.02%R n = 0 interframe shape (Figure 13) was included to nucleate any interframe tendency. The 120° cyclic repetition of welds is representative of submarine fabrication practice. The spatial extent of the 'weld areas' was however three times the shell thickness, a limiting range of applicability for thin-shell theory, and clearly a crude representation of true weld properties.

Taking as datum the structural case $\emptyset$, with all areas treated as bilinear material of nominal yield stress, reductions in collapse pressure of several per cent are seen to occur with 10% yield strength reduction in the weld areas (Table 6). With a longitudinal 'weld' alone (Case 1), the reduction is 1.4%. Including both circumferential and longitudinal

194

TABLE 6
The Effect of Variable Yield Stress on Submarine Collapse Pressure.

		Material Curves		Weld Yield Stress	Interframe Amplitude %R	Collapse Pressure
		Parent Plate	Weld Area			
Case 0	No Weld	Bil	Bil	1.0	+0.02	1.00
1	L	Bil	Bil	0.9	+0.02	0.986
2	C + L	Bil	Bil	0.9	−0.02	0.979
3	C + L	Bil	Bil	0.9	+0.02	0.986
4	C + L	Res	Bil	1.0	−0.02	0.950
5	C + L	Res	Bil	0.9	−0.02	0.913

C, L   circumferential, longitudinal 'welds'.
Bil, Res   bilinear, cold-rolling stress-strain curves.
Yield stress normalised to parent plate value.

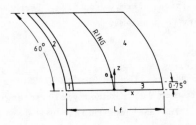

FIGURE 20. STAGS Idealization used for Variable Yield Stress and Plate Thinning Studies. Shape (as %R) 0.5 cos $3\theta \pm 0.02$ sin $\pi x/L_f$.

'welds', and with overall and interframe shapes in-phase along the weakened circumferential weld area, the drop is 2.1% (Case 2). When overall and interframe shapes are out of phase in the circumferential weld area, the weakening effect of the 'weld' is abated giving a collapse pressure reduction of only 1.4% (Case 3), as for the case with longitudinal 'weld' alone. Using cold bending material curves for areas remote from 'welds' and bilinear curves for 'welds' gives a

drop of 5% (Case 4), and a 10% reduction of bilinear yield stress in the weld areas, causes a further 3.7% drop.

Numerical studies of this type have proven useful in investigations of the relationship between yield stress variation, initial shape and residual stress in determining interframe collapse and the experimental scatter. They have allowed assessments to be made of the consequences and acceptability of yield-stress reduction along weld lines, although precise treatment requires three dimensional consideration of weld residual stresses.

Plate Thinning in Submarines

To meet existing tolerance specifications for variations in submarine plate thickness, it is often necessary to carry out extensive plate grinding, a time consuming process for the fabricator, and an expensive one for the customer. Nonlinear analyses with STAGS, using structural ideal-izations similar to that used for 'weld' analysis (Figure 20), have shown that small patches of slightly reduced thickness (small segment 1 on Figure 20) have a negligible effect (less than 1%) on collapse pressure, enabling more generous concessions to be given on the amount of thinning and the acceptable size of affected areas.

Assessment of Damage Effects in Flat Panels

Another important application of nonlinear analysis is the simulation of the damage process and subsequent evaluation of the residual strength of the damaged structure, subjected to its operational loading.

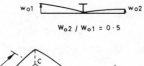

$W_{o2} / W_{o1} = 0 \cdot 5$

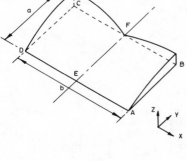

AB, BC } FIXED PLANE OF SYMMETRY

CD   MOVING PLANE OF SYMMETRY

DA, EF } SIMPLE SUPPORT

FIGURE 21.   Damaged Plate Model.

Figure 21 shows a typical longi-tudinal T-bar stiffener and its associated plating, this was mod-elled using 8-noded semi-loof shell elements in computer code LUSAS, assuming an elastic-perfectly plastic stress/strain relationship with associated flow rule for material properties. A two span model was chosen to represent the variation of imperfection in adjac-ent spans obtained from measurements of typical ship plating defor-mations. The damage process was simulated by applying lateral pressure loading to the model (ie to simulate bottom slamming) and then unloading to produce permanent plas-tic deformation levels of approxi-mately t, 3t and 6t in magnitude

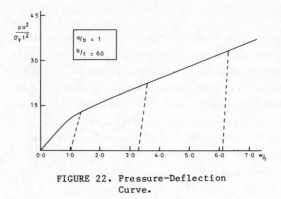

FIGURE 22. Pressure-Deflection
Curve.

(Figure 22). The residual strength of the panel, subjected to longitudinal axial compression, was then calculated for all three damaged conditions. The results for these and also for the undamaged plate are shown in Figure 23a showing clearly the loss of load carrying capacity due to increasing damage levels. Figure 23b presents results in a form which could be used by a designer to estimate reduction in strength due to damage.

This technique could be used to formulate design curves and empirical relationships to estimate the residual strength of damaged plate panels. It may also be applied to more complex structural problems such as overall buckling of damaged orthogonally stiffened panels, providing data for program NS94 to evaluate the ultimate bending strength of a damaged ship's hull.

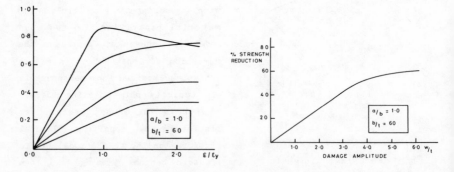

23(a) Load-Shortening Curves   23(b) Percentage Strength Reduction

FIGURE 23.   Residual Strength of Damaged Plate.

Ship Damage

Figure 12 (curve D) shows the midship bending moment curve for a surface ship which suffered damage, typically during launch. Calculations were performed in three stages. First, the damage process was simulated in FABSTRAN by applying point loads to the damaged area of the hull. Comparisons of the predicted residual deformation pattern can then be compared with actual ship damage enabling assessments to be made of both the magnitude of the forces necessary to create such damage and the level of residual stresses incurred. Second, load-shortening analyses for all damaged and undamaged stiffened panels were performed with FABSTRAN as discussed previously, with damage-induced shape and residual stress fields for the former, and normal design assumptions for the latter. Finally, the midship bending moment was calculated with program NS94. The effect of the damage on the overall strength (Figure 12) is seen to be quite small (15% in hogging and 3% in sagging). Nonlinear damage analysis, of this type, has been applied to actual ship damage situations allowing recommendations to be made of the structural significance of the damage and the need for repair.

RELATIONSHIP BETWEEN NONLINEAR ANALYSIS AND OTHER METHODS

Comparison with Analytic Methods

Access to sophisticated nonlinear finite-element codes has increased the possibility of tackling real engineering problems, without necessarily increasing the probability of obtaining reliable solutions. Because of their complexity, both skill and engineering judgement are required in the use of nonlinear programs. At ARE it has been found essential to use more than one nonlinear code for comparative purposes (Table 1) and also to use other, simpler methods to cross-check the predictions of more sophisticated approaches whenever possible.

Comparison with Experiment

Nonlinear analysis is used at ARE in a complementary way with experimental testing, the 'self-calibrating' submarine design approach being a prime example. The need for experiment has not been removed by new analytical capabilities although the number of costly experiments has been reduced and their quality improved by, for example, the use of pre-test analysis to determine favourable strain-gauge positioning. Uncertainties over boundary conditions and load eccentricities require both theoretical and experimental investigation. Some simulation of the fabrication process is required to determine the statistical distributions of shape and material imperfections, without which even a fully validated theoretical analysis will be of little value.

The nonlinear program may be best viewed as an additional 'experimental' tool, which in contrast to experiment, is highly reproducible, not subject to the statistical variations of experimental data. The reproducibility may be used to separate the important variables of a problem in a way impossible by experiment. For example, results of an experimental investigation into the effects of plate thinning, or locally reduced yield stress may be clouded by randomly different initial shapes in the models to be tested. The factors contributing to the experimental scatter may therefore be isolated in a controlled way with nonlinear inelastic collapse analysis, leading possibly to recommendations for changes in fabrication techniques. By making the maximum use of available experimental evidence, the significance of the present limitations of nonlinear inelastic analysis is considerably reduced, allowing practical advances to be made now.

FUTURE NEEDS/APPLICATIONS OF NONLINEAR ANALYSIS

Despite the sophistication of modern nonlinear analysis methods, developments are required: in element technology, in material idealization (such as the treatment of Bauschinger residual stress effect and fracture) and in solution techniques, particularly in the unstable post-collapse region where automatic load-step algorithms are not totally reliable and where dynamic effects may be significant.

The need for a variety of nonlinear analysis codes to tackle a given structural problem and the vast amount of output information generated requires a greater degree of interaction than currently exists between analysis codes and generalised pre- and post-processors.

Computer technology has considerably reduced the computational time of nonlinear analysis and by removing core-size limitations (eg by virtual memory), has allowed large-scale calculations to be attempted. Present size limitations are determined more by requirements of backing-store for restart and post-processing information. This constraint will lead to further development and increasing use of techniques such as the 'Idealised Structural Unit' [23] and the 'Boundary Element' [24] Methods, and also the greater use of substructuring in nonlinear finite element analysis.

Future applications of nonlinear analysis in the field of Naval ship and submarine structures are likely to be concentrated in two main areas: first, in the development of design curves and formulae for complex inter-active situations such as combined loading effects on orthogonally stiff-ened panels; and second, in the post design analysis of damaged structures and the granting of tolerance concessions.

REFERENCES

1. Dow, R.S. and Smith, C.S., Effects of Localized Imperfections on Compressive Strength of Long Rectangular Plates. Journal of Constructional Steel Research, Vol 4 (1984) pp 51-76.

2. Smith, C.S. and Dow, R.S., Compressive Strength of Longitudinally Stiffened GRP Panels. Proc. 3rd Int. Conference on Composite Structures, Paisley, September 1985.

3. Smith, C.S. and Dow, R.S., Residual Strength of Damaged Steel Ships and Offshore Structures. Journal of Constructional Steel Research, Vol 1, No 4, September 1981.

4. Creswell, D.J., Unpublished work.

5. Smith, C.S., Influence of Local Compressive Failure on Ultimate Longitudinal Strength of a Ship's Hull. Proc. Int. Sym. 'Practial Design in Shipbuilding' PRADS, Tokyo, 1977.

6. Dow, R.S., Hugill, R.C., Clarke, J.D. and Smith,C.S., Evaluation of Ultimate Ship Hull Strength. Extreme Loads Response Symposium, Arlington, VA, October 1981.

7. Kendrick, S.B., Externally Pressurized Vessels, Chapter 9 of 'The Stress Analysis of Pressure Vessels and Pressure Vessel Components', Ed. by S.S. Gill, Pergamon Press, London, 1970.

8. Smith, C.S. and Kirkwood, W., Influence of Initial Deformations and Residual Stresses on Inelastic Flexural Buckling of Stiffened Plates and Shells. Int. Conf. on Steel Plated Structures, Imp. College, London, July 1976.

9. Kendrick, S.B., Design of Submarine Structures, to be presented at Int. Conf. Advances in Marine Structures at ARE Dunfermline, May 1986.

10. ADINA 84 User Manual, Adina Eng. Report AE 84-1, Adina Eng. AB, Vasteras, Sweden, 1984.

200

11. ASAS-NL User Manual, Version 6, KINS Development Ltd, Epsom, UK, August 1982.

12. Bushnell, D., BOSOR4: Program for Stress, Buckling, and Vibration of Complex Shells of Revolution. Structural Mechanics Software Series - Vol 1, Edited by N Perrane and W Pilkey, September 1977.

13. Bushnell, D., BOSOR5: A Computer Program for Buckling of Elastic-Plastic Complex Shells of Revolution including Large Deflections and Creep, Vol 1, Users Manual. LMSC-D407166, Lockheed, California, USA.

14. Dow, R.S. and Smith, C.S., FABSTRAN - A Computer Program for Frame and Beam Static and Transient Response Analysis (Nonlinear), unpublished ARE Report 1985.

15. LUSAS User Manual, Finite Element Analysis Ltd, London, 1984.

16. Kendrick, S.B., The Influence of Shape Imperfections and Residual Stresses on the Collapse of Stiffened Cylinders, I.Mech.E Conf. Significance of Deviations from Design Shapes, March 1979.

17. Kendrick, S.B., The Elasto-Plastic Collapse of Ring-Stiffened Cylinders. Unpublished MOD(PE) Report.

18. STAGSC-1, User Instructions Volume II, Lockheed Palo Alto Research Laboratory, Palo Alto, California, 1980.

19. Bathe, K.J. and Dvorkin, E.N., On the Automatic Solution of Nonlinear Finite Element Equations. Computers and Structures, Vol 17 (1983), pp 871-879.

20. Powell, G. and Simons, J., Improved Iteration Strategy for Nonlinear Structures. Int. Journ. for Num. Methods in Eng., Vol 17 (1981) pp 1455-1467.

21. Crisfield, M.A., A Fast Incremental/Iterative Solution Procedure that Handles "Snap-Through". Computers and Structures, Vol 13 (1981), pp 55-62.

22. Bergan, Pal G., Automated Incremental-Iterative Solution Schemes. Int. Conf. on Num. Methods for Nonlinear Problems, Swansea, September 1980.

23. Ueda, Y., Rashed, S.M.H. and Katayama, M., Ultimate Strength Analysis of Double Bottom Structure by "Idealized Structural Unit Method", Trans. of JWRI, Vol 9, No 1, 1980.

24. Brebbia, C.A., The Boundary Element Method for Engineers, 1978, Halstead Press.

25. Dowling, P.J., Chatterjee, S., Frieze, P.A. and Moolani, F.M., Experimental and Predicted Collapse Behaviour of Rectangular Steel Box Girders. Int. Conf. on Steel Box Girder Bridges, London, 13-14 February 1973.

BUCKLING OF INTACT AND DAMAGED OFFSHORE SHELL STRUCTURES

B. F. Ronalds and P. J. Dowling
Department of Civil Engineering
Imperial College
London, SW7 2BU, U.K.

ABSTRACT

Compression tests are described on longitudinally stiffened cylindrical shells with denting damage. The behaviour is compared with that of similar intact shells to ascertain the stiffness and strength reductions in the presence of local damage. Modes of buckling are also discussed. The results suggest a simple analytical procedure which may be used in estimating the consequences of ship collision damage to buoyant offshore platforms.

NOTATION

A_1	stringer cross sectional area = $h_1 t_1$
A_r	intermediate ring frame cross sectional area = $h_r t_r$
ecc	eccentricity of load application from cylinder centre
E	Young's modulus
L	centre bay length
L_t	length of three bay cylinder between end rings
R	radius of cylinder
s	number of longitudinal stiffeners around circumference
t	shell thickness
δ_{Do}	central dent depth
Δ_A	central end shortening
σ_{YC}	compressive yield stress

INTRODUCTION

Considerable research has been undertaken into the resistance of offshore structures to ship collision. A loading situation frequently envisaged is the supply vessel berthing impact. The inclusion of this accidental loading as a design limit state in several Codes [1] has increased the need for greater understanding of the potential problem and prompted the development of corresponding analytical techniques. A substantial body of knowledge has been built up pertaining to the behaviour of thick-walled unstiffened tubes during collision and their residual strength afterwards [2], as these are a traditional component of steel platforms.

Attention has also been given to stiffened cylinders of the type forming the main legs of floating installations. Earlier phases of the research [3,4] concentrated on the behaviour of intact shells under axial and lateral pressure loadings. With the benefit of this experimental and theoretical work the present authors were able to examine the consequences of damage in the cylinders. A special problem for this type of structure is the lack of overall structural redundancy. Additionally the slender cross sections of the buoyancy columns have a relatively low resistance to denting and a small post-collapse strength.

In this paper a series of tests are described using small scale fabricated cylinders with either twenty or forty longitudinal stiffeners. A controlled dent was given to each model by slowly applying lateral load through a wedge. The indenter was located always at mid-depth and aligned at right angles to the longitudinal cylinder axis. Having a sixty degree included angle which was softened by a 3mm tip radius, the knife edge followed the set-up of Smith, Kirkwood and Swan's unstiffened tube tests [2] in both geometry and orientation.

Shells stiffened with ring frames have been investigated in a parallel programme of research. Intact models were tested by Tsang et al [5]. More recently Onoufriou and Harding [6] have examined the effects of damage.

MODELS

The models were fabricated from thin steel plate. Stiffener and shell elements cut from the plate were attached using a tungsten-inert gas welding procedure with no filler wire. The model was securely jigged during the process to keep the geometric distortions within the tolerance limits of the codes (Ref. [7] for example). However the residual stresses induced were unrealistically high and so the completed cylinders were heat treated. This was done with the model tightly sandwiched between a mandrel and an outer former. In the heat treatment process the temperature was increased at a rate of 100 degrees per hour to 650 degrees Celsius, which was maintained for about an hour before the oven was allowed to cool. This gave the steel mechanical properties representative of the thicker plate used in full scale construction.

Heavy steel rings were attached to the cylinder ends to provide full rotational and in-plane restraint. With the intact model tests this was achieved using a mixture of sand and epoxy resin. For the other models the end rings were welded into place to ensure that the high membrane tension forces generated during denting could be supported. In both cases the outer ends were made flat, parallel and smooth.

The geometries of all dented models are summarized in Table 1. In the labelling system the first digit is the number of bays. There are in fact three types of cylinder. The earlier models, including all the intact geometries, were stringer stiffened shells of single bay. Experience gained in the fabrication process later allowed three bay orthogonally stiffened models to be made. In series 3A the two intermediate ring frames were very sturdy. They did not deform when knife edge loading was applied mid-way between them and thus confined the dent to one bay. In contrast light ring frames were incorporated into the series 3B models. These satisfied the DnV requirements [7] for axial compression but could not support external pressure loading according to these rules. Line loading caused significant radial deflections of these rings and so the damage stretched over the entire model length. Due to the almost bi-linear profile of the dent the lateral deflection at the rings was about two-thirds of that in the dent centre. The mode of deformation during the denting process is described in greater detail elsewhere [8].

TABLE 1

Geometries of models

CYL NO.	MATERIAL	GEOMETRY								DENT
	E/σ_{YC}	$t=t_l$	R	L/R	s	h_l/t_l	L_t/L	t_r	h_r/t_r	δ_{Do}/R
1A2	580	0.84mm	160mm	0.416	20	8				0.047
1B1	609	0.63	160	1.08	40	6				0.104
1B2	609	0.63	160	1.08	20	6				0.104
3A2	580	0.84	160	0.331	40	8	2.83	3.0mm	8	0.038
3A3	580	0.84	160	0.331	40	8	2.89	3.0	8	0.051
3B1	618	0.60	160	0.60	40	8	3.0	0.82	8	0.046
3B2	618	0.60	160	0.60	40	8	3.0	0.82	8	0.078
3B3	618	0.60	160	0.60	20	8	3.0	0.82	8	0.081
3B4	618	0.60	160	0.60	20	8	3.0	0.82	8	0.107

COMPRESSION TEST RIG

The frame in which the models were crushed is shown schematically in Figure 1. The screw jack at the bottom was driven by a variable-speed electric motor through a low ratio gearbox. This allowed very slow loading rates to be achieved. Load was applied by reaction against a stiff cross-frame anchored to the laboratory strong floor, and was measured using three equilaterally arranged load cells. The cylinder was centrally located in the rig, with the dented region orientated on top of one of the load cells. Above the model lay a steel/PTFE spherical bearing to allow nonuniform compression. Lateral stability of the rig was ensured with the aid of three vertical columns.

INSTRUMENTATION

Transducers

To measure the end shortening three linear displacement transducers were placed inside the model, close to the end rings and on the same radial lines as the load cells.

A ring carrying forty radially aligned transducers was set up around the model, as photographed in Figure 2. The ring could be moved vertically

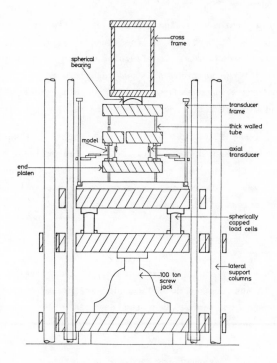

FIGURE 1   Rig for compression tests

FIGURE 2   Bank of transducers to monitor buckling deformations

by turning the four threaded columns which supported it simultaneously through a chain and gear mechanism. The transducers coincided with the stiffeners when the frame was in its "zero" position. However the frame could be rotated about the vertical axis and repositioned, using a location pin, at three successive angles of $\pi/80$. This enabled radial deformations at the quarter and mid-points of the panels to be read.

The same measuring frame was also used to obtain the shell surface readings before denting and compare them with a datum cylinder machined to a fine tolerance. The sum of the squares of the differences between readings was minimized to determine the best-fit perfect cylinder and thus the initial imperfections of the real model from it.

Strain Gauges

Strain gauges were used to enable details of the stress distribution to be observed. In the damaged models gauges were placed both in and near the dent zone, and also remote from the dent in order to monitor the overall section response.

EXPERIMENTAL BEHAVIOUR

Only two typical models are discussed in detail here; Refs. [8] and [9] contain similar information for the other geometries. The first model, Cylinder 1A2, has twenty stringers and a relatively short bay length. This contrasts with Cylinder 1B1 which has a very long bay length and forty small stringers.

Figure 3 shows the effect of a relatively small dent in Cylinder 1A2 by its comparison with the loading response of a similar intact model tested by Fahy [3,10]. The end shortening for the damaged model is defined as the nondimensionalized longitudinal displacement at the centre of the formerly circular section. The compression load is also nondimensionalized by dividing by the squash load of the cylinder. The consequences of a larger dent put into Cylinder 1B1 are seen in Figure 4. Here the behaviour of the "nearly perfect" model determined by Agelidis [4] is used as a datum.

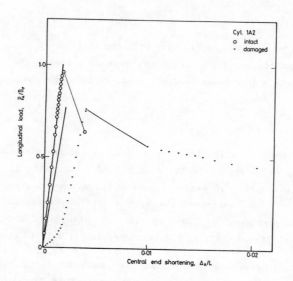

FIGURE 3   Cyl. 1A2 – Compression load versus end shortening responses

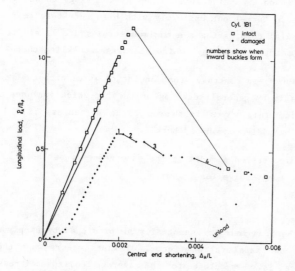

FIGURE 4   Cyl. 1B1 – Compression load versus end shortening responses

Intact Models

The undamaged models load linearly with the stiffness expected of stub columns and exhibit capacities close to the squash load. The very high strength in Figure 4 is noteworthy for a slender stringer geometry where

$$\frac{N_E}{N_P} = 0.59.$$

Here N_E is the Euler buckling load for a stringer and its associated shell having encastre ends, and N_P is its squash load. The ratio is of course four times smaller still if simple supports are assumed in computing the buckling load. This illustrates the high level of transverse restraint given to the stringers by the cylindrical skin, which makes the longitudinally stiffened shell an efficient structural unit in compression.

Rapid unloading occurs at collapse for both of the intact models illustrated. The buckling patterns are illustrated in Figures 5(a) and 6(a). The geometry of Cylinder 1A2 in Figure 5 buckles locally. The position of the panel buckles close to the end ring is observed quite frequently. Poisson expansion constrained at the rings causes most of the cylinder length to barrel out uniformly with high curvature near the ends. Combined with axial compression the maximum strains are likely to occur in the outer skin near this bending, which encourages buckling there.

Figure 6 shows, in contrast, that an intact model with the geometry of Cylinder 1B1 fails by general buckling of the bay which includes the light stringers. Nine full waves form around the circumference and each is clearly marked by a diamond-shaped buckle.

Fahy [3] also tested a model of the same geometry as those in Figure 3 under eccentric compressive loading with

$$ecc/R = 0.4.$$

In this case the behaviour is essentially as predicted by simply combining bending moment and axial force effects. Failure occurs when the maximum combined stress is very close to the average collapse stress of the concentrically loaded model. This is understandable as the slender panels have little capability of stress redistribution after first yield.

(a)   Intact model (Ref. [3])

(b)   Dented model

(c)   Inside view along dent centre-line

FIGURE 5   Cyl. 1A2 – Buckling deformations induced by compressive loading

Initially only the critical zone fails, but as postbuckling progresses
panel buckles gradually extend around approximately two-thirds of the
circumference.   For this reason unloading is more gradual than for the
concentrically loaded model.

(a) Intact model (Ref. [4])

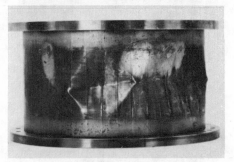

(b) Dented model

FIGURE 6   Cyl. 1B1 - Buckling deformations induced by compressive loading

Damaged Models

Figures 3 and 4 show that the dented cylinders respond very flexibly at the start of loading. This is due to convexity of the end rings, induced by residual strains present at the end of the denting process. Thus loading is nonuniform over the cross section for the first few load steps until the bulge is flattened out. Thereafter the behaviour is linear and remains so until just before peak load, when a very slight softening again becomes apparent.

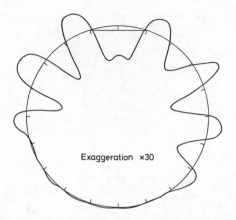

Exaggeration ×30

FIGURE 7   Cyl. 1A2 - Radial deflections immediately after peak load

The presence of the damage modifies the prebuckling deflections developing during loading.   All dented fibres try to bend inward, maintaining a relatively flat cross section in the dent.   This produces sharp circumferential curvature at the longitudinal edges of the dent with outward bulging in the adjacent undamaged material.   For geometries prone to panel buckling this encourages outward buckles next to the dent with further alternately inward and outward buckles spreading around the circumference (Figure 5(b)).   The stiffeners remain straight with no bowing, but twist in sympathy with the panels.   This is seen in Figure 5(c), a photograph taken inside Cylinder 1A2.   The mid-depth buckling pattern just after collapse is plotted in Figure 7.

Slightly different deflections are encouraged in Cylinder 1B1. Because the diamond-shaped buckles are essentially inward, the outward bulge next to the dent forms only a localized ridge with inward deflections immediately beyond.   Collapse is signalled by an audible bang and sudden growth of this bow-in on one side of the dent.   Figure 8(a) shows the distribution of radial deformations at mid-depth just after peak load.   The buckles extend around a small part of the surface only; outward barrelling is apparent elsewhere.

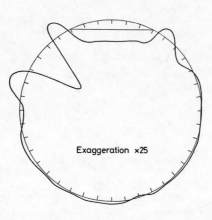

Exaggeration ×25

(a)   Immediately after peak load

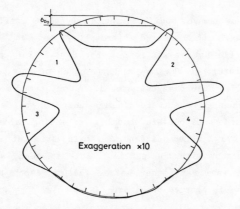

Exaggeration ×10

numbers give order of formation of inward buckles

(b)   Well beyond peak load

FIGURE 8   Cyl. 1B1 – Radial deflections at mid-depth

Unlike its undamaged counterpart, there is no dramatic unloading at failure. With further axial deformation the postbuckling curve continues to be relatively flat although several small jumps are discernible. The jumps correspond with the development of additional inward buckles, firstly on the other side of the dent and then further around the circumference. Numbers located on the post-collapse curve in Figure 4 tally with the labelling of the buckles in Figure 8(b). The final buckling pattern is photographed in Figure 6(b). It is interesting that both intact and dented models retain a very similar postbuckling strength.

In the three bay cylinders with light ring frames, approximately bi-linear deepening of the dent profile might be expected with the additional lateral deflection at the rings being about two-thirds of that at mid-depth. In fact the ring frames deflect very much less than this. Although previously deformed they retain sufficient rigidity to largely confine the dent growth to the centre bay under compressive loading.

ANALYSIS

An obvious approach towards analysing the axial response of dented cylinders is to simply ignore the damaged material. Dented fibres bend inwards as well as compressing longitudinally during loading, in a manner softened by the presence of residual stresses. This flexibility means that most of the applied load is distributed elsewhere around the circumference. A concentrically applied load acts at an eccentricity to the centroid of this effective section and so produces a nonuniform stress distribution, its maximum occurring adjacent to the dent. Thus it is these undamaged fibres that govern the strength of a damaged cylinder.

Although the dent is a large initial deviation from the ideal geometric shape, it does not primarily act out the role expected of an imperfection to instigate failure within its confines. Instead the adjacent undamaged material is forced to distort sharply to provide compatibility between the inward growth of the dent and the developing deflection pattern predisposed by the overall cylinder geometry. Collapse occurs when the stress carried by this formerly intact region reaches its modified capacity in the deformed state.

214

The simplest method of predicting the cylinder strength is to assume
that failure occurs when the stress next to the dent reaches the collapse
stress of an intact model with the same geometry. This provides an
adequate estimate for most of the cylinders tested because they have
sufficient stockiness to restrain the growth of prebuckling deflections in
the critical zone. Models may even be significantly stronger than
suggested by the analysis if they are able to redistribute stress
circumferentially after first yield. Cylinders 1B1 and 1B2, in contrast,
are weakened by the enforced deflections and an unconservative strength
estimate results from neglecting these deformations. However these latter
geometries are extremely slender and are unlikely to be employed in
platform construction. They are included mainly to ascertain the limits of
the analysis. The simple stiffness and strength predictions for Cylinders
1A2 and 1B1 are drawn in Figures 3 and 4 respectively.

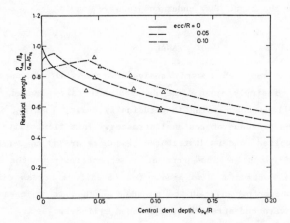

FIGURE 9   Effect of dent depth on the residual compressive strength

The theoretical variation of residual strength with dent depth is
plotted in Figure 9 for comparison with the test data. In this context
residual strength is represented as the load capacity of the damaged
cylinder as a fraction of the corresponding intact capacity. Due to
bending moments induced by the relocation of the centroid of the dented
section the strength erosion is significantly greater than that contributed
by loss in area alone.

Two additional curves are drawn for loading at small eccentricities from the cylinder centre, where positive eccentricity is defined as lying on the side away from the dent. Although it was the intention to load the models concentrically, the load cell readings indicated a small positive eccentricity for all tests, the range of values being

$$0.045 < ecc/R < 0.086.$$

This is attibutable to the end rings being aligned at a relative angle inwards toward the damage in the presence of the nonuniform stress distribution. Thus the point of contact with the spherical bearing is a little off-centre. A similar effect is indicated by Fahy's eccentrically loaded tests [3]. In his models the rotation resulting from the bending moment appears to cause the point of contact of the bearing to move "uphill" slightly and thus reduce the eccentricity.

The abrupt slope changes in Figure 9 are caused by an alternative failure criterion. At small dent depths first yield may occur diametrically opposite the dent centre.

Strain gauge results at the point of failure are correlated with the theoretical stress blocks in Figure 10. The upper diagram is for a stocky model which behaves as idealized. In the lower diagram Cylinder 1B1 exhibits a stress close to yield immediately adjacent to the dent, as predicted. However the next stringer away can support only half this stress. Its position coincides with the localized ridge of distortion seen in Figures 6(b) and 8. For equilibrium with the applied load there must be a similar reduction in stress on the opposite side of the model and a small stress increment at the cylinder centre. This results in a generally convex stress distribution and the weakened capacity of this model.

DISCUSSION

In applying the analysis to design, the problem remains of determining the strength of the intact cylinder. The approaches adopted by both Fahy and Adelidis consider the response of a single stringer and its associated shell. It is given an initial deflection corresponding to the largest imperfection measured on the cylinder. Fahy [3] developed a beam-column approach and Agelidis [4] modelled the unit with finite elements.

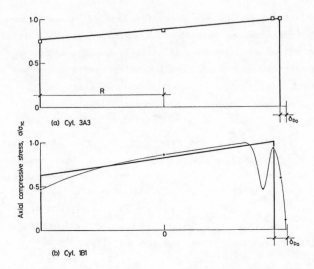

FIGURE 10 Axial stress distributions immediately before peak load

This points to an analytical difference between undamaged and damaged cylinders. Whereas the critical zone in an intact shell may be anywhere, depending on the distribution of imperfections, the location of failure is largely predetermined in a dented cylinder. Also the deflections that promote failure are unrelated to the initial imperfections existing in the critical zone adjacent to the dent and tend to be much larger. This implies that imperfections (other than the dent) may reasonably be ignored in any analysis of a damaged model. However, although the presence of significant damage modulates imperfection sensitivity, geometries which are imperfection sensitive under compressive loading will be more susceptible to the distortion generated near the dent and hence weakened to a greater degree. It is for this reason that the strength of an intact cylinder (including its imperfections) can be assumed to approximate the capacity of the critical zone in a corresponding damaged geometry.

It has been conjectured that the scatter of failure loads found in nominally identical intact cylinders, due to their different imperfections, bears little relation to their residual strengths in a dented state. The "intact" cylinder thus becomes a rather arbitrary datum. For design purposes an undamaged geometry containing the maximum imperfections permitted by the codes is perhaps the most relevant. Using this "worst" cylinder as the datum rather than the more perfect intact models tested by Fahy and Agelidis would then diminish the strength reduction caused by denting. Such an adjustment could readily by incorporated into the test results of this paper to give them more general applicability. Agelidis' extensive parametric study [4] using stringer units with the maximum DnV tolerances [7] would prove valuable here.

From the research aspect, the theoretical approaches of Fahy [3] or Agelidis [4] could only be adapted to the critical zone in a damaged cylinder if the growth of distortion caused by the dent was simulated. To do this it would probably be necessary to model a substantial portion of the cylinder and not just one stiffener. By completely neglecting this effect the very simple analysis of dented models suggested above gives quite reasonable estimates of the response and indicates when and why a more accurate analysis may be of benefit.

CONCLUSIONS

An understanding of the behaviour of nominally perfect stiffened cylinders acquired by previous researchers [3,4] enabled the effect of dents in these models to be studied. Tests showed firstly that the dent does not develop to precipitate a catastrophic collapse at low load. In fact the geometries are stocky enough to allow a very simple anlysis in which the damaged region is ignored but the intact material is assumed to remain fully effective.

This approach gives a very good estimate of the residual stiffness of the cylinder. Predictions of the reduced capacity are less accurate, being up to 13% conservative for stocky models with small dent depths due to their redistribution capability. The analysis overestimates the residual strength of very slender geometries by a similar margin due to deformations in the critical zone encouraged by the dent. Understanding the reasons for the discrepancies indicates how better predictions may be obtained if the additional accuracy is required. Bearing in mind the uncertain nature of actual collision damage, the simple method used here would seem to have value for the geometries currently in use offshore, facilitating rapid assessment of the possible consequences of accidental loading and being readily adjustable to suit other dent shapes.

ACKNOWLEDGEMENTS

The authors gratefully acknowledge the support given to this research by the U.K. Science and Engineering Research Council. Considerable additional funding was provided by the Department of Energy for the experimental work.

REFERENCES

1. Det norske Veritas, Rules for classification of mobile offshore units. Hovik, Norway (1981).

2. Smith, C.S., Kirkwood, W.C. and Swan, J.W., Buckling strength and post-collapse behaviour of tubular bracing members including damage effects. Boss' 79, London, p.303 (1979).

3. Fahy, W.G., Collapse of longitudinally stiffened cylinders subject to axial and pressure loading. Ph.D thesis, Imperial College, University of London (1985).

4. Agelidis, N., Collapse of stringer-stiffened cylinders. Ph.D thesis, Imperial College, University of London (1984).

5. Tsang, S.K., Harding, J.E., Walker, A.C. and Andronicou, A., Buckling of ring stiffened cylinders subjected to combined pressure and axial compressive loading. ASME 4th. Nat. Congress Pressure Vessels & Piping Technology, Portland, Oregon (1983).

6. Onoufriou, A. and Harding, J.E., Effect of impact damage on the residual strength of ring stiffened cylinders. Proc. 5th. Int. Symp. Offshore Mechanics & Arctic Engineering, Tokyo (1986).

7. Det norske Veritas, Classification notes - buckling strength analysis of mobile offshore units. Note No. 30.1, Hovik, Norway (1984).

8. Ronalds, B.F. and Dowling, P.J., Experimental investigation of the effects of damage on the compressive strength of orthogonally stiffened cylinders. CESLIC Report SS2, Imperial College (1986).

9. Ronalds, B.F., Mechanics of dented orthogonally stiffened cylinders. Ph.D thesis, Imperial College, University of London (1985).

10. Dowling, P.J. and Harding, J.E., Experimental behaviour of ring and stringer stiffened shells. Harding, J.E. et al eds. Buckling of shells in offshore structures. Granada p.73 (1982).

FINITE ELEMENT MODELING TECHNIQUES FOR BUCKLING ANALYSIS OF CYLINDRICAL SHELLS UNDER BENDING LOADS

Minos Moussouros
Naval Surface Weapons Center
10901 New Hampshire Avenue
Silver Spring, MD 20903-5000, U.S.A.

ABSTRACT

This paper presents a finite element based technique for predicting the bend buckling of a straight circular cylindrical shell subject to static end bending moments. The nonlinear finite element program ABAQUS is used in conjunction with schemes to accommodate "Brazier Ovalization" failure, "short wave length axial" buckling, material imperfection, and plastic response. To model the loading, an "end rotation" control technique is used which assumes plane sections remain plane at the ends. The technique predicts bending moment and work done on the structure as a function of mean curvature. Computational results are presented for several cylinder geometries and compare favorably with published experimental data.

INTRODUCTION

The problem of the deformation of a straight or curved cylinder, subject to end bending moments and possibly internal pressure, has been addressed in numerous articles.[1-39]

References [1], [2], [3], and [4] are essentially concerned with the linear bending of tubes subject to end bending moments. In modern terminology, they are referred to as "geometrically linear" analyses. The first "geometrically nonlinear" analyses are due to Brazier,[5] Chwalla,[6,7] Wood,[8] Reissner,[9,10] Reissner and Weinitschke,[11] and Weinitschke,[12] to mention a few.

Ades,[13] assuming that the cross-sections of a long cylinder remain elliptical after deformation, accounted for geometric and material nonlinearities. Afendik[14,15] presented an approximate analysis incorporating plasticity. References [16] and [17] allowed for geometrical and material nonlinearities, while Reference [18] extended an earlier analysis[19] to elastoplastic behavior of imperfect cylinders. References [20, 21, 22], and [34] are the only numerical papers (as applied to straight cylindrical shells) by the finite element method, of which the author is aware.

This paper addresses numerically the problem of a straight circular tube subject to end bending moments without internal pressure, allowing for geometric and material nonlinearities. The nonlinear finite element program ABAQUS[34] is used for the analysis. Results[33] are compared with experiment to validate the technique.

MODEL OF STRUCTURE

The cylinder is represented using ABAQUS[34] finite elements. To specify the elements and degrees of freedom, a global right-handed coordinate (x,y,z) system (Figures 1 and 2) is established with z as the longitudinal axis of the cylindrical shell, x the vertical, and y the transverse direction. Next, we discretize the structure by modeling only one-half the length and one-half the periphery, i.e., we employ a quarter model. It is assumed that the cylinder is perfectly circular (without imperfections due to fabrication and residual strains) and the end loads

221

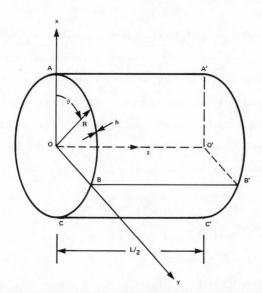

FIGURE 1. STRAIGHT CYLINDRICAL SHELL OF HALF LENGTH L/2, MEAN RADIUS R,
THICKNESS h, AND ASSOCIATED GLOBAL CARTESIAN COORDINATE SYSTEM (x, y, z)

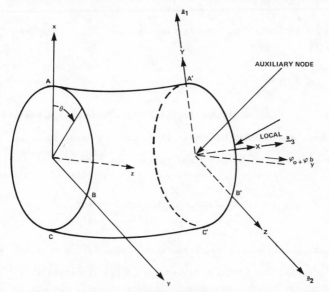

FIGURE 2. CYLINDRICAL SHELL WITH ASSOCIATED END SECTION A' B' C' AND AUXILIARY
NODE AFTER DEFORMATION, A LOCAL FRAME OF REFERENCE (X, Y, Z)

are symmetrical with respect to the x-z plane, with the bending couples
lying on the global y-axis. The cylindrical surface is replaced by ABAQUS
S8R shell elements with 3 integration points across the thickness.
Geometric and material nonlinearities are allowed. Perfect plasticity,
von Mises isotropic yield, and an associated normal flow rule are used by
ABAQUS. The employed mesh, including midside nodes, was 25 x 25 excluding
an auxiliary node. Figure 10 displays a 13 x 13 mesh which excludes all
midnodes.

All boundary conditions are given in the global Cartesian frame of
reference. Along both generators, AA' ($\theta = 0°$) and CC' ($\theta = 180°$),
owing to symmetry, we have

$$v = \varphi_x = \varphi_z = 0.$$

Along the half-circle ABC, symmetry implies that (half length analyzed
only)

$$w = \varphi_x = \varphi_y = 0.$$

Note that up to this point, the vertical rigid body motion has not yet
been removed, and it must be constrained prior to solution. This will be
done in conjunction with the method of exerting the external loading.

MODEL OF LOADING

A particularly attractive feature of ABAQUS is its nonlinear multiple
constraint capability (MPC). The loading on the structure is an overall
bending moment, set up by the action of longitudinal membrane stresses.

This will be modeled through a prescribed end rotation about the y-axis, applied incrementally. For small deformations, the vertical coordinate of the neutral axis from the center of the circular cross-section is extremely small. Consequently, the shift is approximately zero. However, for larger deformations this shift is substantial, necessitating an iteration if we are to assume that, initially, a linear distribution of forces produces a net applied moment. To avoid this iteration, the following approach is used.

First, three conditions or assumptions are considered to prevail.

1. Plane sections remain plane at A'B'C' arc (Figure 2) (at the end where the external loading would have been applied).

2. There will be no rotation of A'B'C' plane (Figure 2) about the local Y-axis.

3. An end rotation about the global y (or local Z) is incrementally applied. This third condition gives rise to a distribution of external longitudinal inplane forces along the local X-axis, which causes a bending moment.

In this approach, then, an auxiliary node is set up to coincide with the center of the original undeformed plane. The terminal couple is applied at this section. After deformation, it is assumed that plane sections remain plane. By St. Venant's Principle of "elastic equivalence of statically equipollent systems of load,"[40,41] we conclude that for lengths larger than the cylinder diameter, the stress distribution away from the load, due to a zero net axial force and a terminal bending moment, does not depend on the traction distribution, except perhaps locally in the neighborhood of the point of application of the load. This condition can be fulfilled if vector $\underline{a}_3$ (Figure 2) of the local frame of reference, located on the deformed plane, is orthogonal to any vector on that plane. A more detailed description of this approach can be found in Reference [34].

TEST CASES WITH COMPARISON TO EXPERIMENT

Four unstiffened circular cylinders[33] have been analyzed using the finite element program ABAQUS[34]: models 10A, 16A, 20A of Reference [33], and 20AI, which is an imperfect version of model 20A. Each of these cylinders is comparatively thick, so that premature collapse will not occur and so that plasticity effects will be exhibited, as the applied external moment increases past the yield moment. The above models fall in the range of "long cylinders." Their perfect discrete analogues would fail by ovalization or the "Brazier effect," or by plastic deformation. The experimentally imperfect models experienced buckling "failure"[33] as displayed on the moment-curvature curves.

Table 1 gives the geometrical and material properties of these models. The stress-strain curves can be obtained from Reference [33]. In this reference, external loading was applied by the use of a so-called

225

Table 1 Geometrical and Material Properties of Models [33]

MODEL No.	RADIUS R (IN)	THICKNESS h (IN)	YOUNG'S MODULUS E (ksi)	POISSON'S RATIO ν	YIELD STRESS σ_y (ksi)	HALF LENGTH USED IN COMPUTATION L/2 (IN)	R/h	L/R
10A	5.258	0.233	28,947.0	0.3	50.000	108.0	22.566	41.08
16A	7.870	0.260	30,000.0	0.3	45.272	162.0	30.629	41.17
20A	9.873	0.255	28,947.0	0.3	50.000	162.0	38.717	32.82

Table 2 Characteristic Parameters of Models

MODEL No.	(1) σ_{CR} (ksi)	(2) M_{CR} (k-in)	(3) k_{CR} (1/in)	(4) M_{BR} (k-in)	(5) M_o (k-in)	(6) F_y (k)	(7) I (in^4)
10A	776.35	15,711.0	0.510074×10^{-2}	8,552.0	1,288.33	384.88	106.40
16A	599.84	30,346.7	0.254063×10^{-2}	16,518.6	2,916.17	582.04	398.15
20A	452.49	35,334.7	0.158329×10^{-2}	19,233.8	4,971.28	790.93	770.97

NOTES:

(1) CRITICAL STRESS AT BIFURCATION $\sigma_{CR} = \dfrac{E}{\sqrt{3(1-\nu^2)}} \left(\dfrac{h}{R}\right)$

(2) CRITICAL MOMENT AT BIFURCATION $M_{CR} = \dfrac{\pi E}{\sqrt{3(1-\nu^2)}} Rh^2$

(3) CRITICAL CURVATURE AT BIFURCATION $k_{CR} = \dfrac{1}{\sqrt{3(1-\nu^2)}} \dfrac{h}{R^2}$

(4) CRITICAL BRAZIER MOMENT $M_{BR} = \dfrac{2\sqrt{2}}{9} \sqrt{(1-\nu^2)} \, \pi E \, Rh^2$

(5) PLASTIC MOMENT BASED ON YIELD STRESS $M_o = 4R^2 h \sigma_y$

(6) AXIAL FORCE BASED IN YIELD STRESS $F_o = 2Rh\sigma_y$

(7) MOMENT OF INERTIA OF UNDEFORMED CROSS-SECTION $I = \pi R^3 h$

"shear span" prior to the test section "bending span." To create the external moment in our research, we employed an additional span beyond the bending span, equal to the "shear" span, and then applied a fixed angle of rotation. Table 2 contains some parameters used in reducing the stresses, moments, curvatures, and forces into nondimensional form. These parameters can be used to determine relative magnitude for critical quantities such as yield moment.

Mean curvature k is defined as the ratio of the sum of the absolute values of direct longitudinal strains at 0° (top of cylinder, i.e. tension side) and 180° (bottom of cylinder, i.e. compression side) divided by the undeformed diameter of the shell. Figures 3 through 5 are the relevant M vs. k curves for models 10A, 16A, and 20A, together with the corresponding experimental results of Reference [33]. Agreement between experimental (dots) and computed results is good for all three cylinders. Imperfection sensitivity and the analysis of medium and short cylinders, where short-wave length buckling may control the collapse mechanism, will be addressed elsewhere.

Figure 6 displays the work done versus the moment parameter $\mu = M_{EXT}/M_0$, where $M_0 = 4R^2 h\sigma_y$, R = mean radius of cylinder, E = Young's Modulus, M_{EXT} = external bending moment, h = shell thickness, and σ_y = material yield stress.

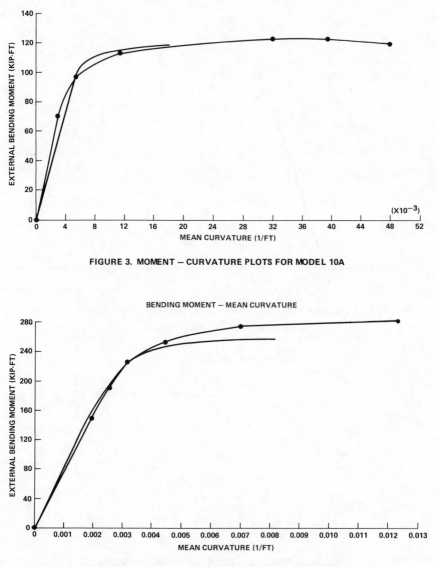

BENDING MOMENT – MEAN CURVATURE

FIGURE 3. MOMENT – CURVATURE PLOTS FOR MODEL 10A

BENDING MOMENT – MEAN CURVATURE

FIGURE 4. MOMENT – CURVATURE PLOTS FOR MODEL 16A

BENDING MOMENT – MEAN CURVATURE

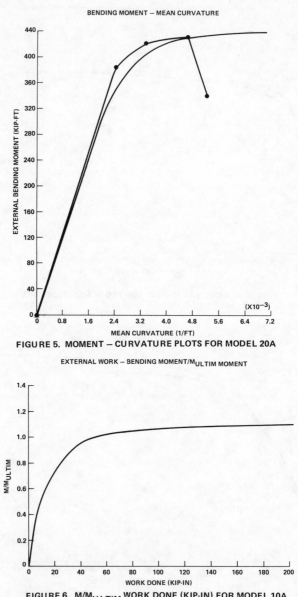

FIGURE 5. MOMENT – CURVATURE PLOTS FOR MODEL 20A

EXTERNAL WORK – BENDING MOMENT/M_{ULTIM} MOMENT

FIGURE 6. M/M_{ULTIM} WORK DONE (KIP-IN) FOR MODEL 10A

We define two ratios or parameters, longitudinal stress/stress at bifurcation and hoop stress/stress at bifurcation, where stress at bifurcation is

$$\sigma_{CR} = \frac{E}{\sqrt{3}\,(1-\nu^2)}\left(\frac{h}{R}\right).$$

Figure 7 represents plots of the longitudinal inplane stress parameter versus angular position. Additional local bending stresses across the shell thickness are not addressed. Note, however, that the longitudinal membrane stress distribution in Figure 7 does not follow simple beam theory. The stress distribution from the 0° and 180° points (top and bottom of the half-section) is reduced (tension zone) or increased (compression zone) slightly before it assumes a linear form.

Figure 8 displays the variation of the hoop stress parameter with angular location. The distribution of this stress over the half-section clearly indicates maximum compressive hoop stresses around the 90° location, with corresponding maximum tensile hoop stresses at 0° and 180°, respectively. These stresses, however, are smaller than the longitudinal membrane stresses by an order of magnitude. All stresses shown correspond to the final point of the moment-curvature plots.

Close examination of Figure 9 reveals that the M/M_{CR} vs. k/k_{CR} curves have a slope at the origin of approximately 1.0. This agrees fairly well with the initial slope predicted by Reissner's nonlinear theory[9] as well as Von Karman's linear analysis.[1] In the present

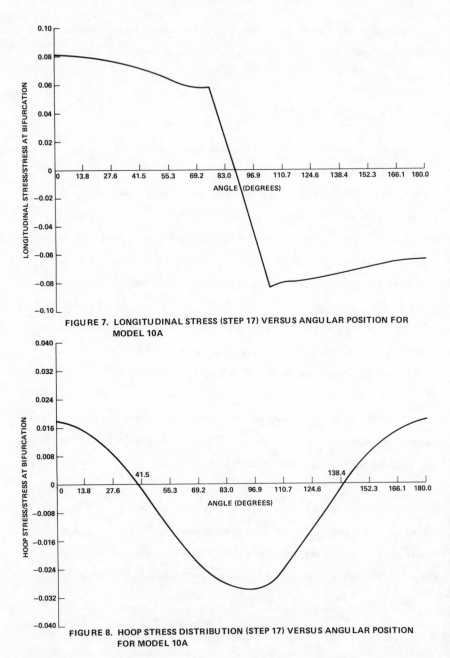

FIGURE 7. LONGITUDINAL STRESS (STEP 17) VERSUS ANGULAR POSITION FOR MODEL 10A

FIGURE 8. HOOP STRESS DISTRIBUTION (STEP 17) VERSUS ANGULAR POSITION FOR MODEL 10A

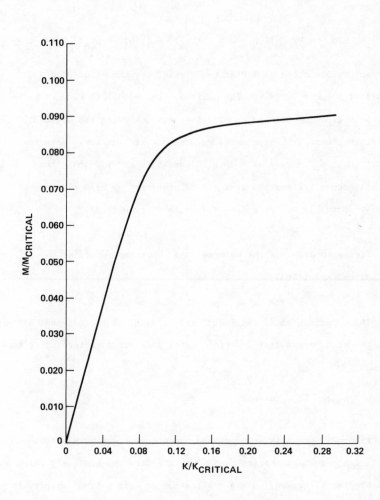

FIGURE 9. M/M$_{CRITICAL}$ VERSUS K/K$_{CRITICAL}$ FOR MODEL 10A

notation, Reissner's relationship between M/M_{CR} and k/k_{CR} can be written as

$$M/M_{CR} = k/k_{CR}[1.0 - 0.5 \ (k/k_{CR})^2 - (1/6) \ (k/k_{CR})^4 \ . \ . \ . \ ] \qquad (1)$$

with an obvious slope of 1.0 at the origin, maximum value of M/M_{CR} = 0.5011 at k/k_{CR} = 0.71954. The maximum value of 0.5011 is much higher than both experimental and numerical results, showing the effects of plasticity, which Reissner's theory does not account for. Note that plots of $\mu = (M_{EXT}/M_0)$ versus work done (Figure 6) clearly display that ultimate moment is reached at $\mu \approx 1$ as predicted by beam plastic theory. Actually, it exceeds $\mu = 1$ by about 10 percent.

Figure 10 displays the deformed and undeformed profiles of cylindrical model 20A.

The imperfection in the radial displacement of the original surface from the mean radius R of imperfect model 20AI varied according to the formula

$$h \sin \frac{\pi z}{L} \ \cos(10\theta) \ .$$

Figure 11 presents superimposed moment-curvature curves for both models 20A and 20AI. Notice that, since they are comparatively thick and fail by plastification, unlike ovalization or bifurcation failure, they are not imperfection sensitive. The response of the imperfect model 20AI is very similar to the perfect one.

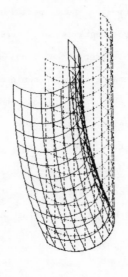

FIGURE 10. CYLINDRICAL SHELL (MODEL 20A) SUBJECT TO END BENDING MOMENT VIEWED FROM
100″,100″,500″ AT STEP 3, INCREMENT 55

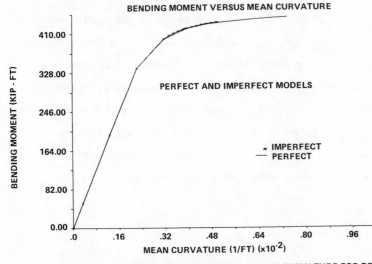

FIGURE 11. BENDING MOMENT DISTRIBUTION VERSUS MEAN CURVATURE FOR BOTH PERFECT
AND IMPERFECT VERSIONS OF MODEL 20A

Finally, an important point pertaining to the modeling issue must be addressed. The experimental set-up involved the analysis of a three-span beam (in all cases) subject to vertical self-equilibrating shear loads, to simulate overall bending over the two end spans. The middle span had no loads applied. In this analysis, one end span and half of the center span (symmetry) were modeled. A rotation was enforced through the "auxiliary node" concept and the MPC constraints. Subsequent computations without the "additional" end span gave a slightly different response. Consequently, what constitutes an adequate additional span to be included for proper response has not been determined, but is of major importance in this analysis.

SUMMARY

A modeling strategy is established to obtain the moment-curvature relation as well as the relation between work done and applied moment for circular cylindrical shells. This is achieved by using the nonlinear finite element program ABAQUS in conjunction with preprocessing and postprocessing computer programs. The results compare favorably with experimental data reported in the open literature. Such analysis is of potential use in predicting critical bending moments. Future studies on the bending and buckling of cylindrical shells should address "short" and "medium" length tubes with and without ring stiffeners.

REFERENCES

1. v.Karman, Th., Ueber die Formaenderung duennwandiger Rohre, insbesondere federnder Ausgleichrohren. Zeitschrift des Vereines Deutscher Ingenieure. 55 (1911) 1889-1895.

2. Lorenz, H., Die Biegung krummer Rohre. Physik. Zeitschrift. XIII (1912) 768-774.

3. Beskin, L., Bending of Curved Thin Tubes. J. Appl. Mech. A.S.M.E. 12 (1945) A-1 through A-7.

4. Clark, R. A., and Reissner, E., Bending of Curved Tubes. Advances in Applied Mechanics. II (1950) 93-122.

5. Brazier, L. G., On the Flexure of Thin Cylindrical Shells and other 'Thin' Sections. In: Proceedings of Royal Society of London, Series A. 116 (1927) 104-114.

6. Chwalla, E., Elastostatische Probleme schlanker, duennwandiger Rohre mit gerader Achse. Sitzungsberichte Akademie der Wissenschaften, Mathematische Nat. Klasse, Wien. 140 (1931) 163-198.

7. Chwalla, E., Reine Biegung schlanker duennwandiger Rohre mit gerader Achse. ZAMM. 13 (1933) 48-53.

8. Wood, J. D., The Flexure of a Uniformly Pressurized, Circular, Cylindrical Shell. J. Appl. Mech., A.S.M.E. 25 (1958) 453-458.

9. Reissner, E., On Finite Bending of Pressurized Tubes. J. Appl. Mech., A.S.M.E., 26 (1959) 386-392.

10. Reissner, E., On Finite Pure Bending of Cylindrical Tubes," Oesterreichisches Ingenieur Archiv. 15 (1961) 165-172.

11. Reissner, E., Weinitschke, H. J., Finite Pure Bending of Circular Cylindrical Tubes. Quarterly of Applied Mathematics. XX, (1963) 305-319. (Correction in Vol. XXIII (1965) 368).

12. Weinitschke, H. J., Die Stabilitaet elliptischer Zylinderschalen bei reiner Biegung. Zeitschrift fuer Angewandte Mathematik und Mechanik 50 (1970) 411-422.

13. Ades, C. S., Bending Strength of Tubing in the Plastic Range. Journal of Aeronautical Sciences. 24 (1957) 605-610.

14. Afendik, L. G., Bending of Thin-Walled Tubes with Considerable Curvature Beyond the Elastic Limit. Prikladnaia Mekhanika, Kiev, Naukova Dumka. IV (1968) (in Russian). (English Translation in Soviet Applied Mechanics by Plenum Press 27-30.)

15. Afendik, L. G., The Stability of a Circular Cylindrical Shell in Bending Beyond the Elastic Limit. Prikladnaia Mekhanika, Kiev, Naukova Dumka. VI (1970) 39-44 (in Russian). (English Translation in Soviet Applied Mechanics by Plenum Press, 951-955.)

16. Gellin, S., The Plastic Buckling of Long Cylindrical Shells under Pure Bending. Intl. J. Solids and Structures. 16 (1980) 397-407.

17. Kyriakides, S., and Shaw, P. K., Response and Stability of Elastoplastic Circular Pipes under Combined Bending and External Pressure. Intl. J. Solids and Structures. 18 (1982) 957-973.

18. Fabian, O., Elastic-Plastic Collapse of Long Tubes Under Combined Bending and Pressure Load. Ocean Engineering. 8 (1981) 295-330.

19. Fabian, O., Collapse of Cylindrical, Elastic Tubes under Combined Bending, Pressure and Axial Loads. Intl. J. Solids and Structures. 13 (1977) 1257-1270.

20. Almroth, B. O., Starnes, J. H. Jr., The Computer in Shell Stability Analysis. Presented at the 1973 ASCE National Structural Engineering Meeting, San Francisco, California, Apr 9-13, 1973. Also in ASCE J. Eng. Mech. 101 (1975) 873-888.

21. Stephens, W. B., Starnes, J. H. Jr., Almroth, B. O., Collapse of Long Cylindrical Shells Under Combined Bending and Pressure Loads. AIAA Journal. 13 (1975) 20-25.

22. Remseth, S. N., Holthe, K., Bergan, P. G., and Holand, I., Tube Buckling Analysis by the Finite Element Method. In: Proceedings of Finite Elements in Nonlinear Mechanics, International Conf., Geilo, Norway, Tapir, (1977) 671-694.

23. Caldwell, J. B., Ultimate Longitudinal Strength. Transactions of Royal Institution of Naval Architects. 107 (1965) 411-430.

24. Hovgaard, W., The Elastic Deformation of Pipe Bends. Journal of Mathematics & Physics. VI (1926-27) 69-118. Deformation of Plane Pipes. VII (1927-28) 198-238. Further Research on Pipe Bends. VII (1927-28) 239-297.

25. Wahl, A. M., Stresses and Reactions in Expansion Pipe Bends. Transactions ASME 49-50 (1927-28) 241-262.

26. Tueda, M., Mathematical Theories of Bourdon Pressure Tubes and Bending of Curved Pipes. Mem. Coll. Engineering Kyoto Imperial University. 8 (1934) 102-115. 9 (1936) 132-152.

27. Karl, H., Biegung gekruemmter, duennwandiger Rohre. ZAMM. 23 (1943) 331-345.

28. Vingness, I., Elastic Properties of Curved Tubes. Transactions A.S.M.E. 65 (Feb 1943) 105-120.

29. Reissner, E., On Bending of Curved Thin-Walled Tubes. In: Proceedings of National Academy of Sciences. 35 (1949) 204-208.

30. Huber, M. T., The Bending of the Curved Tube of Elliptic Section. In: Proceedings of the Seventh Congress of Applied Mechanics. 1 (1949) 322-328.

31. Clark, R. A., Gilroy, T. I., Reissner, E., Stresses and Deformations of Toroidal Shells of Elliptical Cross Section with Applications to Problems of Bending of Curved Tubes and of the Bourdon Gage. J. Appl. Mech. A.S.M.E. 19 (1952) 37-48. Discussion in 19 (1952) 565-566.

32. Kafka, P. G., Dunn, M. B., Stiffness of Curved Circular Tubes with Internal Pressure. J. Appl. Mech. A.S.M.E. 23 (1956) 247-254.

33. Jirsa, J. O., Lee, F. H., Wilhoit, J. C. Jr., Merwin, J. E., Ovaling of Pipelines under Pure Bending. OTC paper No. 1569, Fourth OTC Conference (1972) I-573 through I-578.

34. Hibbitt, Karlsson and Sorensen, ABAQUS User's Manual, Version 4 (1982). ABAQUS Example Problems (1982).

35. Axelrad, E. L., Flexible Shell-Theory and Buckling of Toroidal Shells and Tubes. Ingenieur Archiv, 47 (1978) 95-104.

36. Axelrad, E. L., Flexible Shells. IUTAM Proceedings 15th Congress, University of Toronto, (1980) 45-56.

37. Emmerling, F. A., Nichtlineare Biegung eines schach gekruemmten Rohres. ZAMM 61 (1981) T86 through T89.

38. Emmerling, F. A., Nichtlineare Biegung und Beulen von Zylindern und krummen Rohren. Ingenieur Archiv. 52 (1982) 1-16.

39. Seide, P., Weingarten, V. I., On the Buckling of Circular Cylindrical Shells Under Pure Bending. J. Appl. Mech. A.S.M.E. 28 (1961) 112-116.

40. Love, A. E., A Treatise on the Mathematical Theory of Elasticity, Fourth Edition, Dover Publications, Chapter V, Arts 87-89 (1944) 129-132.

41. Washizu, K., Variational Methods in Elasticity and Plasticity, Third Edition, Pergamon Press (1982) 8.

42. Wempner, G., Mechanics of Solids with Applications to Thin Bodies, Sijthoff & Noordhoff (1981) 62.

PLASTIC BUCKLING OF EXTERNALLY PRESSURISED DOME ENDS

G. D. Galletly, J. Blachut and J. Kruzelecki
Department of Mechanical Engineering,
University of Liverpool,
P.O. Box 147, Liverpool L69 3BX.

ABSTRACT

Theoretical plastic collapse pressures for clamped imperfect steel hemispherical shells are given in the paper for R/t = 100 and 200 and three values of σ_{yp}. The collapse pressures for some torispherical shells are also given. Two types of axisymmetric imperfection were considered in these calculations, viz. an increased-radius type and a Legendre polynomial.

The presentation of the collapse pressures in the form of curves of p_c/p_{yp} vs. $\bar{\lambda}$ (= $\sqrt{p_{yp}/p_{cr}}$) was also studied. Steel and aluminium shells having the same value of $\bar{\lambda}$ were examined and the p_c/p_{yp} values agreed well with each other when δ_o/t was the same for corresponding shells (δ_o = amplitude of initial imperfection).

Using the tolerances in shape allowed by the Codes, the collapse pressures of some imperfect hemispheres were determined numerically and compared with the lower-bound of the test results in the Codes. The agreement between the two was not very good.

The predicted buckling strengths of torispheres with sharp knuckles (i.e. r/D = 0.06) were, for the smaller amplitudes of initial imperfection, found to be significantly smaller than those of their hemispherical counterparts. Code-making bodies should be aware of this fact when formulating their buckling rules for torispheres.

NOMENCLATURE

m   number of waves in the circumferential direction

n   degree of Legendre polynomial (Eqs. (6) and (7))

p_c collapse pressure of imperfect hemispherical or torispherical shell

p_{cr} elastic buckling pressure of perfect sphere from linear theory
        (= $1.21 \ E(^t/R)^2$)

P_{cr}^* elastic, or plastic, bifurcation buckling pressure of perfect clamped hemisphere (from BOSOR 5)

P_{yp} yield pressure of spherical shell ($= 2(^t/R)\ \sigma_{yp}$)

r toroidal (or knuckle) radius of torisphere   - see Fig. 17

s_{imp} arc length over which radial imperfections, or radii of curvature, are measured

t thickness of shell

D diameter of cylindrical shell

E modulus of elasticity

K P_{cr}/P_{yp}

$P_n(\cos\varphi)$ Legendre polynomial of degree n

R radius of perfect hemispherical shell

R_{imp} radius of imperfect hemispherical shell

R_s radius of spherical portion of torisphere - see Fig. 17

α semi-angle of imperfection - see Figs. 1 and 3

δ_o amplitude (inwards) of radial imperfection at the pole ($\varphi = 0$)

λ $[12(1-\nu^2)]^{\frac{1}{4}}\alpha\sqrt{R/t}$

$\bar{\lambda}$ $\sqrt{P_{yp}/P_{cr}} = 1.285\sqrt{(R/t)(\sigma_{yp}/E)}$

λ_B $\lambda/\sqrt{R_{imp}/R}$

ν Poisson's ratio

φ co-latitude

σ_{yp} yield point of material

INTRODUCTION

Spherical shells subjected to external pressure are used in many industries and their buckling behaviour has been studied by numerous investigators. Elastic buckling has been the main subject of interest and reviews of the topic have been given by Kaplan [1], Newland [2], Tvergaard [3], Bushnell [4] and Kollár/Dulácska [5]. Plastic buckling of externally-pressurised spherical shells has not, so far, been studied to any great extent.

With reference to the elastic buckling of externally-pressurised spherical shells, it is known that initial geometric imperfections usually reduce their strength considerably. Some of the research workers who have been involved in past investigations of the subject are Koiter [6], Thompson [7], Hutchinson [8], Koga/Hoff [9], Bushnell [10],

Thurston/Penning [11] and Tong/Pian [12]. Hutchinson assumed imperfections
in the form of the elastic buckling modes given by linear shell theory;
some of the other authors assumed local axisymmetric imperfections, which
were either of the increased-radius (flat-spot) type or a smoothly-varying
dimple - see Fig. 1. The results of some calculations on elastic spherical
shells with axisymmetric imperfections are shown in Fig. 2 (p_c = collapse
pressure of an imperfect shell, δ_o = amplitude of initial (inwards)
imperfection at the pole). These calculations were made by the authors
using the BOSOR 5 shell buckling program [13]; the results agree, more-or-
less, with those already published in the literature [9,10,12].

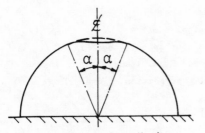

(a) Smoothly-varying dimple.

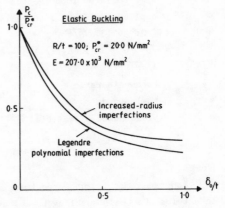

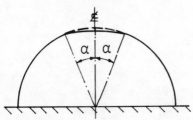

(b) Increased-radius flat-spot

FIGURE 1.   Two axisymmetric
localised imperfections.

FIGURE 2.   Elastic buckling of
clamped hemispherical shells.   A
comparison of increased-radius
and Legendre polynomial
imperfections.

From Fig. 2, it may be seen that the lower of the two p_c vs. δ_o curves
corresponds to imperfections which have the form of Legendre polynomials
(i.e. the buckling modes of linear elastic theory). However, there is not
a great deal of difference between the two curves. It is also not known,

at the present time, whether other shapes of axisymmetric imperfection would give lower p_c vs. δ_o curves. Hutchinson [8] considered non-axisymmetric shapes and one of these gave results slightly lower than the axisymmetric imperfections studied by him.

The imperfections in fabricated spherical shells will be distributed in a random manner and will normally consist of dimples and increased-radius flat spots of various sizes. The analysis is, of course, much easier if the imperfections can be assumed to be axisymmetric; if they are, the initial buckles will usually also be axisymmetric. Some experimental evidence that the initial buckles are axisymmetric in thin elastic spherical shells was provided by Hoff and his colleagues using a movie camera [14,15].

Hoff [14] also showed that the critical wavelengths of the localised axisymmetric imperfections studied by Koga and him were approximately the same as that of the classical elastic buckling mode of a perfect spherical shell.

Koiter [16] has recently discussed 'more-or-less localised' imperfections. He showed that they can be almost as effective as periodic imperfections in reducing the buckling strength of an elastic spherical shell.

With regard to hemispherical shells clamped at $\varphi = 90^{\circ}$, there does not appear to be any experimental evidence available on the shape of the initial buckles (the photographs in [17] show non-axisymmetric buckles but they are of shells which had failed and which had undergone considerable plastic deformation). Since the clamped boundaries are a considerable distance from the pole, it seems reasonable to assume that, near the pole, imperfect hemispheres behave like Hoff's imperfect complete spheres.

The actual localised initial imperfections may be at the pole (axisymmetric) or away from the pole. In the latter case, it still seems reasonable to assume local axisymmetric behaviour if the imperfection is not too near the clamped edges (say, $\varphi < 35^{\circ}$ for the centre of the imperfection). One can calculate the approximate angle, 2α, subtended by the first half-wave of a Legendre polynomial imperfection at the centre of the shell; from Ref. [14], one finds that $2\alpha = {}^{2.6}/\sqrt{R/t}$. For ${}^{R}/t = 1000$

and 100, it follows that $2\alpha \approx 5^{\circ}$ and 15°, respectively. For $\varphi = 35^{\circ}$, the localised imperfection will be more than three times its own arc length away from the clamped edge for $R/t = 100$ and more than ten times its own length for $R/t = 1000$.

With regard to the plastic buckling of externally-pressurised hemispherical or spherical shells, the situation is quite different from elastic buckling. Some tests on fabricated hemispherical shells were carried out about twenty years ago at the David Taylor Model Basin, U.S. Navy [17]. These tests have provided (in part, at least) the lower-bound curve used in most Codes for the design of spherical shells. On the theoretical side, Hutchinson discussed the general plastic buckling problem in [18] and the complete spherical shell in [19]. The plastic buckling of an imperfect hemisphere was considered by Marcal in [20] and some spherical caps were analysed in [21]. Two publications from Glasgow University on the buckling of imperfect hemispherical shells are [22] and the recent doctoral thesis by Shao [23]. In both of these references, it was suggested that there is a preferred location, about 11° from the pole, for buckling in spheres and hemispheres. However, there does not appear to be any experimental evidence in support of this suggestion.

References [22] and [24] also discuss design Codes and the initial imperfections in shape (i.e. manufacturing tolerances) permitted by them. For the stockier shells (i.e. those having low R/t-ratios) it was felt that some of the Code requirements were too stringent.

Scope of the Present Investigation

As shell buckling calculations are much faster when axisymmetric imperfections are used (and are also less expensive), such shapes were employed in the present study. Only single imperfections were considered; adjacent imperfections which might interact were left to a future date. As mentioned above, the behaviour of relatively small imperfections off the axis of symmetry should not be significantly different from those on the axis of symmetry. However, it is hoped to study non-axisymmetric imperfections in the future.

The shell buckling program used in the present numerical studies was

the finite-deflection, elastic-plastic BOSOR 5 [13]. The material studied
was mainly steel but some aluminium shells were also considered. The
stress-strain relations were either elastic or elastic, perfectly plastic
and the flow theory option in the program was used. Strain-hardening or
residual stresses were not taken into account in this study. The criterion
of collapse used in the study was that if no convergence was obtained with
that value of the pressure after ten iterations, then it was the collapse
pressure.

The specific problems considered in this paper are:

(a) Steel Imperfect Hemispherical Shells With Clamped Ends

    (i)   For increased-radius flat spots, curves of the plastic
        collapse pressures, p_c, versus the maximum imperfection
        amplitude at the pole δ_o, were obtained.

    (ii)   Using imperfections in the form of Legendre polynomials, the
        curves of p_c versus δ_o were again calculated.

    (iii) From (i) and (ii), one can find out how two axisymmetric
        imperfection shapes affect the collapse loads.

(b) Steel Imperfect Torispherical Shells With Clamped Ends

    Utilising imperfections in the form of Legendre polynomials in the
spherical portions of the torispheres, curves of p_c versus δ_o were obtained
for torispheres having knuckle radii of 6% and 20% of the cylinder diameter.
A comparison of these results with those found in (a) above illustrates the
difference in behaviour between hemispheres and torispheres.

(c) Results in the Form of p_c/p_{yp} Versus $\bar{\lambda}$ Curves

    A number of Codes give their allowable buckling design pressures as a
function of $\bar{\lambda}$, where

$$\bar{\lambda} = \sqrt{p_{yp}/p_{cr}} \qquad (1)$$

For a spherical shell, and $\nu = 0.3$, p_{cr} and p_{yp} are given by

$$p_{cr} = 1.21\ E(^{t}/R)^2 \qquad (2)$$

and

$$p_{yp} = 2\sigma_{yp}(^{t}/R) \qquad (3)$$

The parameter $\bar{\lambda}$ for a spherical shell is then found from

$$\bar{\lambda} = 1.285\sqrt{(R/t)(\sigma_{yp}/E)} \qquad (4)$$

Although the $\bar{\lambda}$ parameter is used in the design of columns, plates and cylindrical shells (sometimes with a reduction, or knock-down, factor included) its usefulness for general shells does not seem to have been explored to any great extent. For instance, it is not clear what one should use for p_{cr} and p_{yp} for torispherical shells. If the geometric ratios for the spherical portion only are adopted, then there is no distinction between torispheres which have different knuckle radii.

It is also not clear, with elastic-plastic buckling, if shells with the same $\bar{\lambda}$-value, but having different values of R/t and σ_{yp}/E, will have the same value of p_c/p_{yp}. How the magnitude of the imperfection amplitude should be varied in these plots is also uncertain (i.e. should δ_o/t or δ_o/R be constant, should δ_o/t vary as $\sqrt{R/t}$, etc.).

In order to acquire some information on the foregoing items, various heuristic studies (which will be described later) were carried out.

(d) Experimental Versus Theoretical Results

The lower bound of the experimental buckling results on hemispherical and torispherical shells, transformed into the p_c/p_{yp} vs. $\bar{\lambda}$ format, was compared with various numerical predictions. The intention here was to see if there was any relation between the maximum tolerances allowed by Codes and the minimum experimental buckling strengths.

NUMERICAL RESULTS

A. Clamped Hemispherical Shells

(i) Increased-Radius (Flat Spot) Axisymmetric Imperfections

The imperfection under consideration is shown in Fig. 3. Some authors measure the imperfection in terms of R_{imp}/R and others in terms of δ_o. A useful formula relating the two is, for small values of α [14]:

$$\delta_o/t \approx (\tfrac{1}{2})\alpha^2 [1 - {}^R/R_{imp}]({}^R/t) \qquad (5)$$

In the present study, the values of α varied from $3°$ to $15°$ by $2°$ intervals. The radius, R, of the shell was kept constant ($= 10.0$) and $^R/t$ was taken as either 100 or 200. R_{imp}/R varied from 1.0 to ∞ and the yield points studied were 207, 310 and 414 N/mm^2.

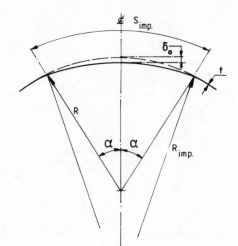

FIGURE 3. Geometry of increased-radius (flat-spot) imperfection.

As a check on the adequacy of the mesh distribution used in the further computations, it was decided to calculate the collapse pressures for elastic imperfect hemispherical shells. These are given in Fig. 2 and they are in reasonable agreement with the earlier results of Koga/Hoff and Bushnell (the present results are normalised with respect to p_{cr}^* and not p_{cr}. For $R/t = 100$, $p_{cr} = 25.0$ N/mm^2 and $p_{cr}^* = 20.0$ N/mm^2).

The plastic collapse pressures for clamped hemispherical shells having increased-radius type imperfections are shown in Fig. 4 for $R/t = 100$ and $\sigma_{yp} = 310$ N/mm^2. The end points of the curves for $\alpha = 3^\circ$, 5°, 7°, etc. correspond to flat imperfections (i.e. $R_{imp}/R = \infty$). By taking the envelope of these scalloped (or festooned) curves, one obtains the curves in Figs. 5 and 6. The curves in these Figures are the lower-bound envelopes for $\sigma_{yp} = 207$, 310 and 414 N/mm^2. For purposes of comparison, the elastic buckling results are also shown on Fig. 5 (for $R/t = 100$). As may be seen, the sensitivity of the collapse pressures to imperfections is not as high with plastic buckling as with elastic buckling. The strength reduction is also partly dependent on the value of σ_{yp}.

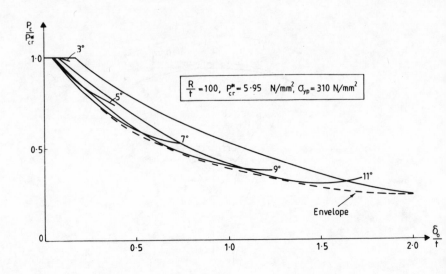

FIGURE 4. Plastic collapse pressures of clamped hemispherical shells
(R/t = 100). Increased-radius imperfections.

It should perhaps be mentioned that, with perfect clamped
hemispherical shells, the buckling mode consists of a buckle near the
clamped edge and m waves in the circumferential direction (some typical
values of m are given in parentheses on Figs. 5 and 6). However, with
imperfections of the size encountered in practice (say $\delta_o/t > 0.1$), the
buckling mode obtained for all the imperfect hemispherical shells
considered herein was an axisymmetric one (i.e. m = 0).

The plastic collapse pressures can also be plotted using the
representation employed by Bushnell [10] for elastic buckling. Due to
space limitations, only the results for $^R/t$ = 100, σ_{yp} = 310 N/mm² are
shown in Fig. 7. For elastic buckling, Bushnell was able to present all
the relevant information on a single plot. The authors hope to achieve
something similar with their plastic collapse results by including σ_{yp} or
p_{yp} in the definition of the pressure parameter.

(ii) Axisymmetric Imperfections in the Form of Legendre Polynomials
    The critical external pressure for the elastic buckling of a perfect
complete spherical shell is given by Eq. (2) (for ν = 0.3). Associated

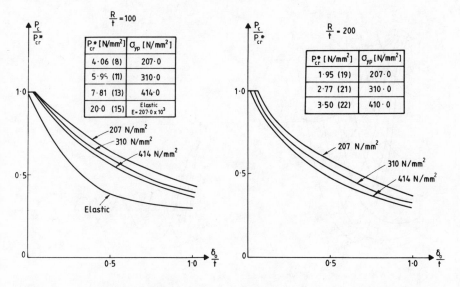

FIGURE 5. Lower bound envelopes of p_c/p_{cr}^* for hemispherical shells ($\bar{R}/t$ = 100). Increased-radius imperfections.

FIGURE 6. Lower bound envelopes of p_c/p_{cr}^* for hemispherical shells ($\bar{R}/t$ = 200). Increased-radius imperfections.

with this pressure are many linearly independent buckling modes involving spherical surface harmonics of degree n. The degree n is the integer which most nearly satisfies the relation

$$n(n+1) \approx [12(1-\nu^2)]^{\frac{1}{2}} \, R/t \qquad (6)$$

$$\text{i.e.} \quad n \approx 1.818 \sqrt{R/t} \qquad (7)$$

For axisymmetric buckling, the relevant spherical harmonic is the Legendre polynomial of degree n, i.e. $P_n(\cos\varphi)$. As indicated by Eqs. (6) and (7), n varies with R/t; an illustration of how the elastic buckling modes P_n vary with n is given in Fig. 8 for n = 9, 17 and 25.

The plastic collapse pressures were obtained for R/t = 100 (with σ_{yp} = 207, 310 and 414 N/mm²) and R/t = 200 (with σ_{yp} = 310 N/mm²) using imperfections in the form of Legendre polynomials and having the appropriate values of n. The results for R/t = 100, σ_{yp} = 207 and 414 N/mm² are shown on Fig. 9, together with the corresponding results for the

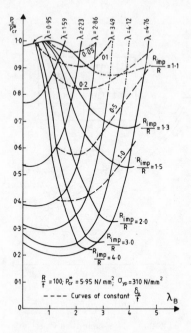

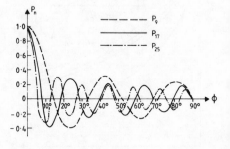

FIGURE 7. Plastic collapse
pressures for clamped hemispherical
shells (R/t = 100). Increased-
radius imperfections.
Bushnell's representation.

FIGURE 8. Legendre polynomials P_n
for n = 9, 17 and 25.

increased-radius imperfections. As may be seen, the imperfections in the
form of Legendre polynomials give the lower collapse pressures but there is
not a great deal of difference between them.

The presentation of the results in the form of $p_c/p_{cr}{}^*$ vs. δ_o/t curves
is fairly straightforward but more values of R/t and σ_{yp} still need to be
investigated. These curves may also give the impression that the collapse
pressure depends only on the amplitude of the imperfection. However, with
imperfections in the form of Legendre polynomials, the degree of the
polynomial, n, varies with R/t (see Eq. (7)) and the half-wavelength of the
central dimple is [14]:

$$s_{imp} = 2.6\sqrt{Rt} \qquad (8)$$

Thus, the extent of the imperfection comes into the calculations as well.

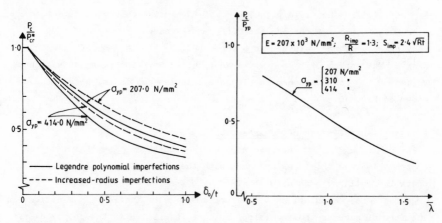

FIGURE 9. Lower bound envelopes of
p_c/p_{cr}^* for hemispherical shells
(R/t = 100). A comparison of
increased-radius and Legendre
polynomial imperfections.

FIGURE 10. p_c/p_{yp} vs. $\bar{\lambda}$ curve
for steel. Effect of varying σ_{yp}.
Increased-radius imperfections.

With increased-radius imperfections, one can show that their critical wavelengths are also proportional to $\sqrt{Rt}$.

B. Some Remarks on the Parameter $\bar{\lambda}$

Another way of presenting the results of the collapse pressure
calculations on imperfect shells is to use p_c/p_{yp} as the ordinates and $\bar{\lambda}(=$
$\sqrt{p_{yp}/p_{cr}}$) as the abscissae. The employment of these co-ordinates is
analogous to the use of similar parameters in the buckling of columns and
plates - see [25]. While the use of the parameter $\bar{\lambda}$ seems to simplify the
presentation of the results, one still needs different curves for the
different magnitudes of initial imperfection. In addition, the influence
that the extent of an imperfection has on the buckling strength, how
torispheres should be plotted on these curves, etc., needs to be
investigated.

(i) Effect of Different σ_{yp}'s

Calculations were made using imperfections of the increased-radius
type and having the BS 5500 [26] tolerances on local shape ($s_{imp} = 2.4\sqrt{Rt}$,

$R_{imp}/R = 1.3$). The yield point, σ_{yp}, of the steel was kept constant in each set of calculations and the different $\bar{\lambda}$-values were obtained by varying R/t. Three values of σ_{yp} were studied, viz. σ_{yp} = 207, 310 and 414 N/mm^2. The curves of p_c/p_{yp} vs. $\bar{\lambda}$ so obtained were the same for all three values of σ_{yp} and the results of these calculations is the single curve shown on Fig. 10.

(ii) Effect of Shape of Imperfection

The above BS 5500 local tolerances are equivalent (see Eq. (5)) to δ_o/t = 0.166 and this does not vary with the value of R/t. In order to check the collapse pressures obtained with the increased-radius imperfections, calculations were carried out using initial imperfections in the form of Legendre polynomials (having δ_o/t = 0.166 at the pole), σ_{yp} = 310 N/mm^2 and varying R/t. The collapse pressures so obtained were similar to those found with the increased-radius type imperfections - see curves A and B on Fig. 11. The largest difference occurred at $\bar{\lambda}$ = 1.5 (i.e. $R/t \approx 925$).

(iii) Varying R/t Versus Varying σ_{yp}/E

As shown by Eq. (4), the parameter $\bar{\lambda}$ for spherical shells involves both R/t and σ_{yp}/E. Theoretical p_c/p_{yp} vs. $\bar{\lambda}$ curves can, therefore, be generated numerically (e.g. with the BOSOR 5 program) by either keeping σ_{yp}/E constant and varying R/t, or vice versa. As it is not clear that the p_c/p_{yp} vs. $\bar{\lambda}$ curves obtained by the two methods will be exactly the same (particularly for plastic buckling), some calculations were made to explore this aspect of the problem.

The hemisphere in (ii) above (using Legendre polynomials) was selected again but this time the computations were carried out for R/t = 100, δ_o/t = 0.166 and varying σ_{yp}/E. The curves obtained are shown in Fig. 12. The dashed curve corresponds to the calculations in which R/t varied and the solid one to those in which σ_{yp}/E varied. As may be seen, the solid and the dashed curves are not the same. This shows that using the parameter $\bar{\lambda}$ in numerical buckling analyses of spherical shells does not always produce unique results. However, it should be noted that even though δ_o/t was held constant in this example, the value of δ_o/R varied with R/t (i.e. $\bar{\lambda}$) for the dashed curve. For example, at $\bar{\lambda}$ = 1.5 in Fig. 12, the value of δ_o/R for the solid curve is about nine times that for the dashed curve.

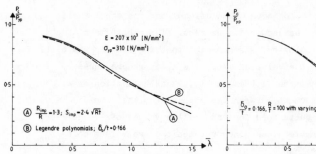
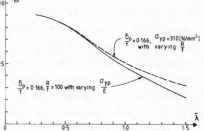
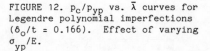

FIGURE 11. p_c/p_{yp} vs. $\bar{\lambda}$ curves for steel. Increased-radius vs. Legendre polynomial imperfections (δ_o/t = 0.166).

FIGURE 12. p_c/p_{yp} vs. $\bar{\lambda}$ curves for Legendre polynomial imperfections (δ_o/t = 0.166). Effect of varying σ_{yp}/E.

The above problem was repeated using increased-radius imperfections but this time there was no difference in the results for varying σ_{yp}/E and varying $^R/t$. At the moment, it is not known why the results for the two types of axisymmetric imperfection differ.

Additional calculations to study the effect of using different materials were undertaken on aluminium and steel hemispherical shells. These results are described in the next section.

C. Aluminium Versus Steel Hemispherical Shells

With elastic buckling, the collapse pressures of steel shells are usually considerably higher than those of similar aluminium shells. This is due to the three-fold difference in the value of the modulus of elasticity, E. However, with plastic buckling, the effect of σ_{yp} is usually more important than that of E and the collapse pressures of similar aluminium and steel shells are often quite close to each other. In this section, the collapse pressures of some externally-pressurised aluminium and steel imperfect clamped hemispheres will be compared.

(a) The first example is a shell similar to the one considered by Marcal in 1970 [20]. The shell has an increased-radius imperfection with R_{imp}/R = 1.15, R = 10.0 and the semi-angle α = 10°. The value of σ_{yp}

was taken as 310 N/mm² for both the aluminium and the steel shells and the strain-hardening was assumed to be zero. The amplitude of the imperfection at the pole, δ_o, was constant in this case (as was δ_o/R) but δ_o/t varied with the value of R/t. The collapse pressures, obtained from BOSOR 5, are plotted in Fig. 13 as a function of $\bar{\lambda}$; as may be seen, the agreement between the results for the aluminium and the steel shells is quite good for the smaller values of $\bar{\lambda}$. However, there was a considerable discrepancy between the two values of p_c/p_{yp} for $\bar{\lambda}$-values greater than 0.9.

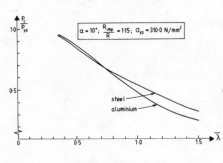

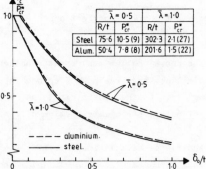

	$\bar{\lambda}=0.5$		$\bar{\lambda}=1.0$	
	R/t	P_{cr}^*	R/t	P_{cr}^*
Steel	75·6	10·5 (9)	302·3	2·1 (27)
Alum.	50·4	7·8 (8)	201·6	1·5 (22)

FIGURE 13. p_c/p_{yp} vs. $\bar{\lambda}$ curves for steel and aluminium hemispherical shells (δ_o/R is constant and = 0.002). Increased-radius imperfections.

FIGURE 14. Collapse pressure for steel and aluminium shells. Legendre polynomial imperfections.

(b) The second example is a hemispherical shell with imperfections in the form of Legendre polynomials. Two values of $\bar{\lambda}$ were selected (i.e. 0.5 and 1.0) and the p_c/p_{yp} vs. δ_o/t curves were found by varying δ_o/t. For this case σ_{yp} was taken as 414 N/mm² for the steel shells and 207 N/mm² for the aluminium ones. The collapse pressures for this case are shown in Fig. 14. The values of σ_{yp}/E for the steel and aluminium shells were in the ratio 2:3 in this example (i.e. not very different) and the two curves (for $\bar{\lambda}$ = 0.5 and 1) were fairly close to each other. Whether the agreement would be as good with a bigger difference in the σ_{yp}/E ratio is not known at this time.

(c) In the third example, increased-radius type imperfections were again used and they were the maximum size permitted by BS 5500 (i.e. s_{imp} =

$2.4\sqrt{Rt}$, R_{imp}/R = 1.3, δ_o/t = 0.166). The yield point of both the steel and aluminium was taken as 310 N/mm^2 and the $\bar{\lambda}$-values were obtained by varying $^R/t$. The agreement between the two sets of results was good for this example; the average curve obtained was very similar to the one given in Fig. 10.

Thus, from this limited number of cases, there does not appear to be much difference in the values of p_c/p_{yp} which are obtained for a given value of $\bar{\lambda}$ with aluminium and steel shells. At least, this seems to be the case when δ_o/t is the same for both shells and $\bar{\lambda}$ is not too large.

It is not known yet whether there would be better agreement between the collapse pressures of aluminium and steel shells if the DASt 013 [27] or DnV [28] imperfection parameter ($\delta_o/t \propto \sqrt{R/t}$) were to be used in the numerical analyses, instead of a constant δ_o/t.

D.   Lower-Bound Strength Curves and Tolerances in Codes

Several Codes use the lower-bound of buckling pressures obtained on tests of externally-pressurised hemispherical and torispherical shells as the basis of their design curves (there are, however, not very many test results available and more tests would be most useful in order to check the current lower-bound). The lower-bound curves are frequently plotted in terms of p_c/p_{yp} as ordinates and $\bar{\lambda}$ as abscissae (the BS 5500 curve uses K = $1/\bar{\lambda}^2$) and some Codes introduce safety factors into their design curves. However, the curve employed herein will be the lower-bound of the test results, without a safety factor, as given by Kendrick - see Fig. 6 of [29].

It is of interest to compare the above lower-bound strength curve with the predicted strengths obtained when using the maximum values of the tolerances on shape allowed by the Codes. To explore this topic, the BS 5500 and DASt 013 Codes were employed. Their maximum permitted local tolerances are as follows:

Code	s_{imp}	δ_o/t	R_{imp}/R
BS 5500	$2.4\sqrt{Rt}$	0.166 for increased-radius flat spots	1.3
DASt 013	$4.0\sqrt{Rt}$	$0.04\sqrt{Rt}$	-

With BS 5500, $\delta_o/t = 0.22$ for the increased-radius flat spots if $s_{imp} = 2.4\sqrt{R_{imp}t}$.

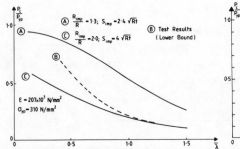

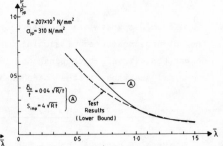

FIGURE 15. Lower bound of test results versus numerical predictions (BS 5500 tolerances). Increased-radius imperfections.

FIGURE 16. Lower bound of test results versus numerical predictions (DASt 013 tolerances). Increased-radius imperfections.

The previous collapse pressure results, obtained using increased-radius imperfections on hemispherical shells with $\delta_o/t = 0.166$, $\sigma_{yp} = 310$ N/mm² and varying R/t, are shown as curve A in Fig. 15. As noted before, the results of calculations made with imperfections in the form of Legendre polynomials agreed, more-or-less, with those given by curve A (see Fig. 11).

An additional set of calculations was made, again using increased-radius imperfections, but with $\delta_o/t = 1.0$, $s_{imp} = 4\sqrt{Rt}$, $R_{imp}/R = 2.0$. The yield point used in these calculations was $\sigma_{yp} = 310$ N/mm² and the different $\bar{\lambda}$-values were obtained by varying R/t. This curve is shown as curve C in Fig. 15 (note that for $R/t = 100$, $\bar{\lambda} = 0.49$ and $\delta_o/R = 0.01$; whereas for $R/t = 800$, $\bar{\lambda} = 1.39$ and $\delta_o/R = 0.00125$).

Also shown in Fig. 15 is the lower-bound curve of buckling test

results for spheres and torispheres (with no safety factor applied) i.e.
curve B. Comparing curves A and B, it appears that application of the
local tolerances in BS 5500 would produce considerably stronger shells than
those which gave rise to the lower-bound curve (see also [22]). On the
other hand, the tolerance $\delta_o/t = 1.0$ (over a distance of $s_{imp} = 4\sqrt{Rt}$) gives
numerical predictions which are lower than the test results in the plastic
buckling region but are reasonably close to them in the elastic buckling
region.

The corresponding calculations for the German DASt 013 Code are shown
in Fig. 16. In this case, curve A was obtained with $s_{imp} = 4\sqrt{Rt}$, $\delta_o/t =$
$0.04\sqrt{R/t}$, $\sigma_{yp} = 310$ N/mm² and by varying R/t (increased-radius
imperfections were again used). Comparing curve A with the lower-bound
curve of test results, it can be seen that they agree with each other
reasonably well over the range $0.9 < \bar{\lambda} < 1.5$ but the predictions are too
high for the smaller values of $\bar{\lambda}$ (for curve A, $\delta_o/t = 0.4$ for $\bar{\lambda} = 0.49$ and
equals 1.13 for $\bar{\lambda} = 1.39$).

The conclusion from this limited investigation into Code tolerances on
shape is that the correlation between them and the lower-bound strength
curve is only fair (residual stresses have, of course, not been
considered). Further study of this topic would seem to be warranted.

E.   Clamped Torispherical Shells Subjected to External Pressure

In this section, the effect of joining a toroidal transition piece to
a spherical cap, and producing a torisphere or dome end, is explored. The
axisymmetric imperfections used in the analyses were again Legendre
polynomials but they were only applied to the spherical portions of the
torispheres. This means that the spherical caps were imperfect (with 2-3
half-waves of the relevant Legendre polynomial) but the toroidal shells
were perfect. In view of other calculations carried out by the authors on
hemispherical shells, this approximation is not expected to affect the
results significantly. However, the matter will be investigated further in
the future.

(a) p_c/p_{cr}* vs. δ_o/t curves
      The R_s/D-ratio of the torispheres (see Fig. 17) was taken as 1.0 and

two values of r/D were investigated, namely $r/D = 0.06$ and 0.20. The
material of the heads was steel, σ_{yp} was taken as 310 N/mm² and the R/t-
ratio was 100. The results of the study are plotted in terms of p_c/p_{cr}*
and δ_o/t and they are shown in Fig. 18. The corresponding curve for
clamped hemispherical shells under external pressure is also given on this
Figure and it is apparent that, for δ_o/t-values greater than a certain
amount, imperfect torispherical shells behave like imperfect hemispherical
shells. However, for the smaller imperfection amplitudes (for this value
of R/t; $\delta_o/t < 0.6$ for $r/D = 0.06$ and $\delta_o/t < 0.3$ for $r/D = 0.20$), the
toroidal transition shells cause a significant reduction in the collapse
pressures. The latter then depend on the r/D-ratio and the reduction is
larger for the sharper knuckle radius, i.e. the smaller value of r/D.

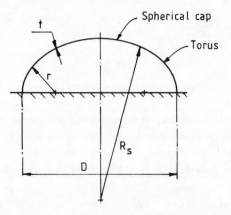

FIGURE 17. Geometry of a torispherical shell.

The mode of collapse in the above two regions is not the same. For
the larger values of δ_o/t, failure is by axisymmetric collapse near the
apex; for the smaller values (the nearly horizontal lines in Fig. 18)
failure is by bifurcation buckling, with the buckle occurring in the
toroidal shell near the clamped edge.

(b) $\underline{p_c/p_{yp}}$ vs. $\bar{\lambda}$ curves

As noted above, the collapse pressures of externally-pressurised
imperfect torispheres are, for the smaller values of δ_o/t, smaller than

their hemispherical counterparts. Thus, one would expect that the p_c/p_{yp} vs. $\bar{\lambda}$ curves obtained for torispherical shells with $\delta_o/t = 0.166$ would be different from that obtained for hemispherical shells.

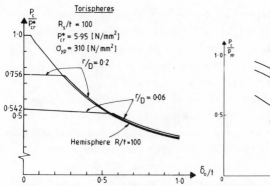
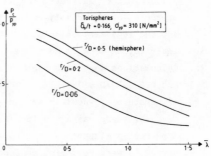

FIGURE 18. Plastic collapse pressures of hemispherical and torispherical shells versus δ_o/t (Legendre polynomial imperfections).

FIGURE 19. p_c/p_{yp} vs. $\bar{\lambda}$ curves steel hemispheres and torisphers: $\delta_o/t = 0.166$ (Legendre polynomial imperfections).

In order to verify this point, two steel torispherical shells with different knuckle radii were selected, i.e. $^r/D = 0.06$ and $^r/D = 0.20$ (both had $R_s/D = 1.0$). The yield point σ_{yp} was kept constant at 310 N/mm² and the different $\bar{\lambda}$-values were obtained by varying $^R/t$. The amplitude of the imperfection (a truncated Legendre polynomial) was kept constant at $\delta_o/t = 0.166$.

The relevant curves for the imperfect hemispherical and torispherical shells are shown in Fig. 19. As expected for this value of δ_o/t, the collapse pressures do vary with the ratio $^r/D$. The hemisphere is the strongest shell while the torisphere with the sharply-curved knuckle ($^r/D = 0.06$) is only two-thirds to one-half as strong as the hemisphere (it should be noted that, for the torispheres, the values used for p_{cr} and p_{yp} in determining $\bar{\lambda}$ were those appropriate to spherical shells, i.e. Eqs. (2) and (3)).

For the larger imperfection amplitudes (say, $\delta_o/t > 0.6$), the results illustrated in Fig. 18 show that the behaviour of imperfect hemispheres and imperfect torispheres are very similar. Calculations to verify this expected outcome in the p_c/p_{yp} vs. $\bar{\lambda}$ curve will be made in due course.

CONCLUSIONS

1. Using axisymmetric imperfections in the form of either Legendre polynomials or increased-radius flat spots, the plastic collapse pressures of externally-pressurised steel hemispherical shells (R/t = 100 and 200) were calculated. The results for both types of imperfection were found to be broadly similar.

2. Calculations were also carried out on torispherical shells (r/D = 0.06 and 0.20, R_s/D = 1.0, R/t = 100) using imperfections having the form of Legendre polynomials in the spherical caps. For the smaller values of δ_o/t, there was a considerable difference between the strengths of imperfect hemispherical and torispherical shells. However, the strengths were very similar for the larger values of δ_o/t.

3. The p_c/p_{yp} vs. $\bar{\lambda}$ ($= \sqrt{p_{yp}/p_{cr}}$) curves for some torispherical and hemi-spherical imperfect shells were also calculated and compared. Once again, there was a considerable difference in the respective curves for the smaller values of δ_o/t. However, for the larger values of δ_o/t the curves merged together.

4. The plastic collapse pressures of imperfect aluminium and steel hemi-spherical shells were compared on several problems. When the value of δ_o/t was the same for corresponding shells (δ_o = amplitude of the imperfection), the numerical values obtained for p_c/p_{yp} for the two materials were close. However, when δ_o/R (instead of δ_o/t) was kept constant there was sometimes a significant difference in the two sets of results. Further study of this problem is needed.

5. The p_c/p_{yp} vs. $\bar{\lambda}$ curve obtained numerically when the BS 5500 local tolerances on shape were used was compared with the BS 5500 lower bound of the buckling test results. The agreement was not very good, with the predicted values always being higher than the lower-bound curve. However, use of less stringent tolerances (i.e. δ_o/t = 1.0, s_{imp} = $4\sqrt{Rt}$), gave a predicted curve which was always below the lower bound curve (residual stresses and any strain-hardening effects were neglected in the foregoing comparison).

ACKNOWLEDGEMENT

The authors wish to acknowledge the assistance that one of them (JK)
has received from the Marine Technology Directorate, Science and
Engineering Research Council.

REFERENCES

1. Kaplan, A., Buckling of spherical shells. Thin-Shell Structures -
   Theory, Experiment and Design, (eds.) Y. C. Fung and E. E. Sechler,
   Prentice-Hall, New Jersey (1974) 247-288.

2. Newland, C. N., Collapse of domes under external pressure.
   I. Mech. E. Conference on Vessels under Buckling Conditions, London
   (Dec. 1972) 43-52.

3. Tvergaard, V., Buckling behaviour of plate and shell structures.
   Proc. 14th IUTAM Cong., (ed.) W. T. Koiter, North-Holland Publ. Co.,
   New York (1976) 273-247.

4. Bushnell, D., Buckling of shells - Pitfall for designers. AIAA J.,
   19 (1981) 1183-1226.

5. Kollár, L. and Dulácska, E. Buckling of Shells for Engineers,
   Akademia Kiadó, Budapest (1984).

6. Koiter, W. T., The nonlinear buckling problem of a complete spherical
   shell under uniform external pressure. Proc. Kon. Ned. Akad. Wet.,
   B72 (1969) 40-123.

7. Thompson, J. M. T., The elastic stability of a complete spherical
   shell. Aero. Quart., 13 (1962) 189-201.

8. Hutchinson, J. W., Imperfection-sensitivity of externally-pressurised
   spherical shells. J. Appl. Mech., 34 (1967) 49-55.

9. Koga, T. and Hoff, N. J., The axisymmetric buckling of initially
   imperfect complete spherical shells. Int. J. Solids and Structures,
   5 (1969) 679-697.

10. Bushnell, D., Nonlinear axisymmetric behaviour of shells of
    revolution. AIAA J., 5 (1967) 432-439.

11. Thurston, G. D. and Penning, F. A., Effect of axisymmetric
    imperfections on the buckling of spherical caps under uniform
    pressure. AIAA J., 4 (1966) 319-327.

12. Tong, P. and Pian, T. H., Postbuckling analysis of shells of
    revolution by the finite element method. Thin-Shell Structures:
    Theory, Experiment and Design, (eds.) Y. C. Fung and E. E. Sechler,
    Prentice-Hall, New Jersey (1974) 435-452.

13.   Bushnell, D., BOSOR 5 - Program for buckling of elastic-plastic
       complex shells of revolution including large deflections and creep.
       Comp. and Struct., 6, (1976) 221-239.

14.   Hoff, N. J., Some recent studies of the buckling of thin shells.
       The Aero. J., Roy. Aero. Soc., 23 (Dec. 1969) 1057-1070.

15.   Carlson, R. L., Senderbeck, R. L. and Hoff, N. J., An experimental
       study of the buckling of complete spherical shells. Expt. Mech., 7
       (July 1967) 281-288.

16.   Koiter, W. T., Amplitude modulation of short-wave buckling modes.
       Behaviour of Thin-Walled Structures, (eds.) J. Rhodes and J. Spence,
       Elsevier Appl. Sci. Publ., London (1984) 35-46.

17.   Kiernan, T. J. and Nishida, K., The buckling strength of fabricated
       HY80 steel spherical shells. U.S. Navy DTMB Rpt. 1721, Washington
       D.C. (July 1966).

18.   Hutchinson, J. W., Imperfection sensitivity in the plastic range.
       J. Mech. Phys. Solids, 21 (1973) 191-204.

19.   Hutchinson, J. W., On the postbuckling behaviour of imperfection-
       sensitive structures in the plastic range. J. Appl. Mech., 19 (1972)
       155-162.

20.   Marcal, P., Large deflection analysis of elastic-plastic shells of
       revolution. AIAA J., 8 (1970) 1627-1633.

21.   Kao, R., Large deformation elastic-plastic buckling analysis of
       spherical caps with initial imperfections. Comp. and Struct., 11
       (1981) 609-619.

22.   Papadimitriou, A. and Frieze, P. A., Numerical prediction of
       hemisphere strength. Buckling of Shells in Offshore Structures,
       (eds.) J. E. Harding, P. J. Dowling and N. Agelidis, Granada Publ.
       Co. (1982) 209-230.

23.   Shao, W. J., The Elastic Plastic Buckling Strength of Imperfect
       Hemispheres and their Reliability, Ph.D. Thesis, University of
       Glasgow (May 1985).

24.   Morton, J., Murray, P. R. and Ruiz, C., On the buckling design of
       spherical shells. Trans. ASME, J. Press. Vess. Tech., 103 (1981) 261-
       266.

25.   ECCS: European Recommendations for Steel Construction, Brussels,
       (Publ. No. 29 (1983) deals with the Buckling of Shells).

26.   BS 5500: Specification for Unfired Fusion Welded Pressure Vessels,
       British Standards Institution, London (1984).

27.   DASt (Deutscher Ausschuss für Stahlbau) Richtlinie 013 Beulsicher-
       heitsnachweise für Schalen, Cologne, Germany (July 1980).

28.   DnV (Det norske Veritas) Buckling Strength Analysis. Classification
       Note, No. 30.1, Høvik, Norway (July 1982).

29. Kendrick, S. B., The technical basis of the external pressure section of BS 5500. Trans. ASME, <u>J. Press. Vess. Tech.</u>, <u>106</u> (May 1984) 143-149.

BUCKLING OF FABRICATED RING-STIFFENED STEEL CYLINDERS UNDER AXIAL COMPRESSION

Y.Kawamoto and T.Yuhara
Nagasaki Technical Institute,
Mitsubishi Heavy Industries, Ltd.
Nagasaki, Japan

ABSTRACT

This paper deals with the axial buckling strength of fabricated cylinders which fail between ring-stiffeners. In recent years, over 30 buckling tests on large-scale fabricated steel cylinders with ring-stiffeners under axial compression have been performed in Japan, the U.S.A., the U.K., and Norway. Comparisons are made between these test results and the existing design criteria such as ASME and DnV and the discrepancies between them are indicated especially in the range of large radius to thickness ratio or high yield stress. The interactive effect of initial imperfection and yield stress on buckling which considers the stiffener spacing is investigated by the theoretical method. The elasto-plastic lower bounds by the reduced stiffness analysis give a good agreement with these test results. Based on a series of calculations by the reduced stiffness analysis, simple equations for predicting the inter-ring buckling are proposed over the radius to thickness range $150 < R/t < 650$, the ring-stiffener spacing range $1.5 < L/\sqrt{Rt} < 10$ and the yield stress range $24 \text{ kgf/mm}^2 < \sigma y < 60 \text{ kgf/mm}^2$.

INTRODUCTION

The buckling of cylindrical shells subjected to axial compression has been studied both theoretically and experimentally by many researchers. It has been commonly accepted that the wide experimental scatter and the poor correlation between classical theoretical values and experimental ones are mainly due to initial imperfections.

In practice, cylindrical shells are still designed in the traditional way by using an empirical "knockdown factor" which is determined from a lower bound to many experimental data. And the majority of experimental data for axially compressed cylinders are related to aircraft and aerospace structures.

But the buckling data of aircraft and aerospace structures are occasionally unsuitable for the design of marine structures. The following are the main reasons :

(1) The fabrication procedure -- Aerospace structures are riveted while marine structures are welded. Geometric imperfections and residual stresses are therefore different.

(2)   The failure mode -- Aerospace structures usually fail by general buckling while marine structures fail bylocal buckling of inter-ring shell elements. This difference is due to the ring-stiffener spacing and the ring-stiffener size.

(3)   The slenderness of structures -- The elastic buckling occurs mainly in aerospace structures while the elasto-plastic buckling occurs in marine structures. The effect of yield stress is very important for marine structures.

Recently, several test programs related to ring-stiffened fabricated steel cylinders have been carried out in the U.S.A. [1] [2], the U.K. [3], Norway [4] and Japan [5] [6]. The authors also carried out buckling tests on 14 large-scale fabricated steel cylinders under axial compression.

In this paper, the buckling strength of fabricated steel cylinders with ring-stiffeners under axial compression is discussed for marine structures which fail by local buckling of inter-ring shell elements.

First, some discussion of the relevant test results and comparisons with the existing design codes, such as ASME code case [7] and DnV classification note [8], is given regarding the following points :

(1)   Effects of ring-stiffener spacing.

(2)   Effects of yield stress.

(3)   Effects of geometric imperfection.

Secondly, taking into account the interaction between geometric imperfections and plasticity, the elasto-plastic lower bounds from the reduced stiffness analysis by J.G.A. Croll [9] are discussed. And comparisons with experimental results are made.

Finally, from these investigations, new simple equations for predicting the critical stress based on the reduced stiffness analysis are proposed.

TEST RESULTS

During the last decade, over 30 buckling tests on large-scale fabricated steel cylinders with ring-stiffeners under axial compression were performed in the U.S.A., the U.K., Norway and Japan to investigate the influence of ring-stiffeners on the critical axial compressive stress. These test results seem to be applicable to the design of marine structures.

These tests covered the following conditions :

(1)   The test models are fabricated from steel plates by cold bending and welding.

(2)   The radius to thickness ratios of models (R/t) are in the range of approximately 150 to 650.

(3)   The ring-stiffener spacings of models (L) are in the range of $1.5\sqrt{Rt}$ to $10\sqrt{Rt}$.

(4)   The test models buckle locally between ring-stiffeners.

Descriptions of Test Programs

The summary of test models, material properties and test results is shown in TABLE 1. Brief descriptions of test programs are given as follows :

ABS/CONOCO-MHI Tests [5] -- The test program was performed by Mitsubishi Heavy Industries, Ltd. (MHI) and prepared for ABS/CONOCO shell buckling test program. Eight fabricated ring-stiffened steel cylinders were tested under axial compression.

The models had a nominal inside radius of 1000 mm, and a nominal shell thickness of 3.2 mm. The nominal radius to thickness ratio was selected to be 312.5. The ring-stiffener spacing of models was varied from $2\sqrt{Rt}$ to $6\sqrt{Rt}$ to examine the influence of ring-stiffener spacing on the buckling strength. The models were made of steel plates with the two different nominal yield stresses of 33 kgf/mm^2 and 56 kgf/mm^2 to investigate the influence of plasticity on the critical stress. The initial imperfection of models was measured. The maximum values of imperfection between ring-stiffeners were in the range of 0.5 t to 1.0 t. The end parts of models were reinforced by ring-stiffeners with much smaller spacing.

Models MHI-3, MHI-4 and MHI-8 failed at the reinforced part near the ends of models. The test results of these models are referred to in TABLE 1 as the buckling strength of models with the objective specified ring-stiffener spacing ; the buckling strength will be nearly equal to, or above the failure loads of these tests.

ABS/CONOCO-CBI and UG Tests [1] -- The test program covered a total of 66 test models under various combinations of axial compression and external pressure. Six of these models were tested under only axial compression. One model was tested at Chicago Bridge and Iron Co. (CBI) in the U.S.A. and the others were tested at the University of Glasgow (UG) in the U.K.. The radius to thickness ratios were chosen to be 150 and 290. All models were fabricated from steel plates with a specified yield stress of 35 kgf/mm^2. The initial imperfection of models between ring-stiffeners was limited to 1/2 of the shell thickness. All models were stress-relieved except for model UG-4. Model CBI-1 failed in an end bay as did models MHI-3,4 and 8.

DOE-IC Tests [3] -- A series of buckling tests on small and large-scale models of stiffened cylinders was conducted for the Department of Energy of the U.K. (DOE). Three large-scale ring-stiffened models were tested under axial compression at Imperial College (IC) in the U.K.. Two models IC-1 and IC-2 had a nominal radius to thickness ratio R/t of 250 while model IC-3 had that of 150. Steel plates used for models had the specified yield stress of 25 kgf/mm^2.

CBI Large-Scale Tests [2] -- The test program was conducted by CBI. A total of 41 small-scale tests and 4 large-scale tests were performed under axial compression. Four large-scale tests were made on a large ring-stiffened cylinder. In each test the cylinder was loaded to failure and the permanent deformations after each failure were locally reinforced before the next test. The yield stresses of steel plates were in the range of 25.9 kgf/mm^2 to 32.2 kgf/mm^2. The ring-stiffener spacing was varied from $2\sqrt{Rt}$ to $6\sqrt{Rt}$.

TABLE 1
Summary of Buckling Tests of Fabricated Ring-Stiffened Steel Cylinders.

	Test No.	R (mm)	t (mm)	L (mm)	R/t	L/R	L/√Rt	σ_y	E	σ_{cr}	σ_{cr}/σ_y
ABS/CONOCO	MHI-1	1000	3.2	113	312.5	0.113	2.0	54.1	20600	28.4	0.525
	2	1000	3.2	113	312.5	0.113	2.0	33.2	20300	17.6	0.530
	3	1000	3.2	226	312.5	0.226	4.0	55.2	21300	24.8	0.449
	4	1000	3.2	226	312.5	0.226	4.0	55.7	21100	24.8	0.445
	5	1000	3.2	226	312.5	0.226	4.0	35.3	20800	17.5	0.496
	6	1000	3.2	340	312.5	0.340	6.0	54.7	21000	22.8	0.417
	7	1000	3.2	340	312.5	0.340	6.0	57.9	21600	24.8	0.428
	8	1000	3.2	340	312.5	0.340	6.0	33.0	20500	16.7	0.506
	CBI-1	571	1.97	114	289	0.200	3.40	42.5	20900	20.8	0.490
	UG-1	465	3.07	93.3	151	0.201	2.47	40.3	21900	37.7	0.935
	2	465	3.10	186	150	0.400	4.90	40.7	21500	39.1	0.960
	3	465	1.58	48.0	294	0.103	1.76	35.4	21000	26.0	0.734
	4	464	1.60	47.9	291	0.103	1.76	35.4	21000	26.4	0.744
	5	464	1.65	92.4	282	0.199	3.34	36.3	22200	21.1	0.582
DOE	IC-1	750	3.52	750	213	1.0	14.6	31.7	21000	18.1	0.569
	2	750	3.52	750	213	1.0	14.6	31.7	21000	18.4	0.579
	3	450	3.52	90	128	0.2	2.26	31.7	21000	25.6	0.807
CBI	CBI-1	3175	6.35	284.5	500	0.090	2.00	28.1	20400	14.1	0.500
	2	3175	6.35	569.0	500	0.179	4.01	28.1	20400	9.4	0.335
	3	3175	6.35	853.4	500	0.269	6.01	28.1	20400	10.0	0.354
	4	3175	6.35	853.4	500	0.269	6.01	28.1	20400	10.5	0.372
NTH	NTH-1	600	3.10	75	194	0.125	1.74	34.2	21000	27.8	0.815
	2	600	3.05	75	197	0.125	1.75	34.5	21000	27.5	0.798
	3	600	3.10	105	194	0.175	2.43	32.1	21000	23.9	0.744
	4	600	3.10	150	194	0.250	3.48	35.0	21000	23.1	0.661
	5	600	3.15	150	190	0.250	3.45	34.2	21000	23.2	0.679
	6	600	3.10	215	194	0.358	4.99	34.7	21000	23.5	0.677
	7	600	3.10	215	194	0.358	4.99	32.2	21000	23.0	0.715
	8	600	3.20	300	188	0.500	6.85	32.0	21000	23.4	0.731
	9	600	3.15	300	190	0.500	6.90	28.6	21000	20.2	0.707
PNC-MHI	AS-1	1304	2.0	178.7	651.8	0.137	3.50	32.2	20600	12.7	0.394
	2	1304	2.0	178.7	651.8	0.137	3.50	33.2	20600	13.1	0.395
	AM-1	1304	2.0	350.6	651.8	0.269	6.87	31.6	19600	10.7	0.339
	2	1304	2.0	350.6	651.8	0.269	6.87	31.9	20300	11.5	0.361
	AL-1	1304	2.0	510.6	651.8	0.392	10.0	32.4	20300	10.2	0.315
	2	1304	2.0	510.6	651.8	0.392	10.0	31.7	19600	10.1	0.319

note : The unit of σ_y and E is kgf/mm².

NTH Tests [4] -- The test program was performed at the Norwegian Institute of Technology (NTH) in Norway to develop the design criteria for marine structures. Nine fabricated steel cylinders with ring-stiffeners were tested under axial compression. The radius to thickness ratio of models was chosen to be approximately 195 and the specified yield stress was the grade of 33 kgf/mm². The ring-stiffener spacing of models was varied from $1.75\sqrt{Rt}$ to $7\sqrt{Rt}$. Five models had the horizontal butt welded joints in their center panels. Initial geometric imperfections and residual stresses in welded models were carefully measured. The maximum imperfections of models between ring-stiffeners were in the range of 0.3 t to 0.5 t.

PNC-MHI Tests [6] -- The test program was performed by MHI under contract with Power Reactor and Nuclear Fuel Development Corporation (PNC) in Japan to develop the design criteria for the steel containment vessels of nuclear plants. A series of buckling tests was made on 15 fabricated ring-stiffened steel cylinders. Six models were tested under axial compression. The nominal radius of models was 1303.6 mm and the nominal thickness was 2.0 mm. Then the nominal radius to thickness ratio was approximately 650. The steel plates used for models had a nominal yield stress of 32 kgf/mm². The ring-stiffener spacing was varied from $3.5\sqrt{Rt}$ to $10\sqrt{Rt}$. Initial geometric imperfections of models were carefully measured and the maximum imperfections of models between ring-stiffeners were in the range of 0.3 t to 0.5 t.

Comparisons with Code Recommendations

The test results gathered in the present investigation are compared with code recommendations of two available design codes of ASME code case [7] and DnV classification note [8]. And the problems of design codes are discussed.

For NTH tests, ABS/CONOCO-MHI tests and PNC-MHI tests, the relations between critical stresses and ring-stiffener spacing parameters $L/\sqrt{Rt}$ are respectively shown in FIGUREs 1,2 and 3. In each test program, the nominal radius to thickness ratio is constant while the ring-stiffener spacing is varied. The predicted values in the figures are calculated using the typical values of geometric parameters and material properties of each test program.

The following findings are clear from these figures :

(1)   The predicted values by both design codes give a good estimation for NTH tests with relative small radius to thickness ratio. But they are too conservative for tests with large radius to thickness ratio. The knockdown factors for the elastic buckling stress in design codes are conservative.

(2)   ABS/CONOCO-MHI tests indicate that an obvious difference of the critical stresses is caused by that of yield stress. It is interesting that the effect of yield stress is considerable in the range where buckling is estimated to occur elastically according to code recommendations.

(3)   In each test series, the critical stresses increase moderately in the range of the ring-stiffener spacing parameter $L/\sqrt{Rt}$ of 1.5 to 10 as the ring-stiffener spacing becomes short. Such a tendency is not found as DnV's recommendation in which the critical stress increases rapidly when the value of $L/\sqrt{Rt}$ becomes below 3.

(4)   The experimental scatter is not so wide in each test series. It seems that the buckling of fabricated cylinders is not essentially a wide-scattering phenomenon if the dimensions of a model

and the material properties are controlled. Therefore, the knockdown factor is not necessarily determined from a lower bound to all experimental data. The knockdown factor might be varied with the level of imperfection and yield stress.

Through this investigation, the existing design code for fabricated ring-stiffened steel cylinders might be improved for more efficient marine structures.

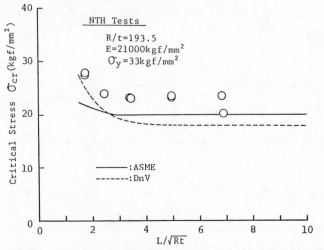

FIGURE 1. Critical stresses of NTH tests compared with code recommendations.

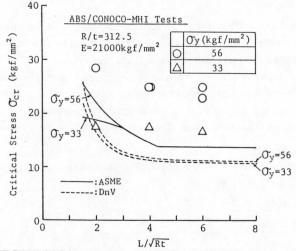

FIGURE 2. Critical stresses of ABS/CONOCO-MHI tests compared with code recommendations.

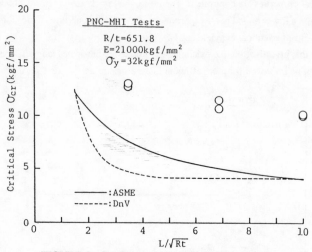

FIGURE 3. Critical stresses of PNC-MHI tests compared
with code recommendations.

THEORETICAL APPROACH

The discrepancy between the relevant test results and code recommendations for
fabricated ring-stiffened cylinders under axial compression indicates the need for improvement
of design criteria.

Now, a theoretical approach based on the reduced stiffness analysis has been tried.

First, the elastic buckling coefficient is determined from an elastic lower bound by the
reduced stiffness analysis. This coefficient is theoretical and purely elastic.

Secondly, taking into account the interaction between geometric imperfections and
plasticity, the plasticity reduction factor is shown as functions of the geometric imperfection
and the ring-stiffener spacing based on the elasto-plastic lower bound solution.

Finally, the predicted values by this method are compared with the relevant test results.

Lower Bound Elastic Buckling

According to reference [9] by Croll, the reduced stiffness critical stress by a cylinder
under axial compression σ_{er} is shown to be

$$\sigma_{er} = \frac{2E\left\{ \dfrac{(i^2+\lambda^2)^2}{12(1-\nu^2)} \left(\dfrac{t}{R}\right)^2 + \dfrac{\lambda^4}{(i^2+\lambda^2)^2} \right\}}{\left\{ \dfrac{(2-\nu^2)\lambda^2 + \nu i^2}{1-\nu^2} \right\}} \tag{1}$$

where E is the modulus of elasticity. ν is Poisson's ratio. And R, t and L are respectively the radius, the thickness and the ring-stiffener spacing of a cylinder. Consider a critical mode in which there are j axial half-waves and i circumferential waves. λ is defined as $j\pi R/L$.

Briefly, the reduced stiffness analysis ia s buckling analysis in which the non-linear circumferential membrane stiffness of a cylinder is eliminated.

The example of the elastic buckling coefficient obtained by equation (1), $\sigma_{er}=C_{er}\cdot Et/R$ is shown in FIGURE 4. The minimum elastic buckling coefficient occurs with the particular numbers of axial and circumferential waves, as in j=1 and i=13 in this example. Hereafter this minimum coefficient is called simply the reduced stiffness elastic buckling coefficient.

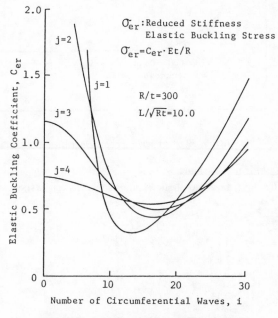

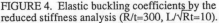

FIGURE 4. Elastic buckling coefficients by the reduced stiffness analysis (R/t=300, L/√Rt=10).

The comparison of elastic buckling coefficients by the reduced stiffness analysis with those by the classical theory and ASME code case is shown in FIGURE 5. The coefficient by the reduced stiffness analysis decreases gradually as the ring-stiffener spacing parameter L/√Rt increases. Because the level of instability increases as the slenderness of a cylinder increases. And the coefficient by ASME code case is below a theoretical elastic lower bound. The ASME code case is empirically determined by a lower bound of many experimental data in various conditions.

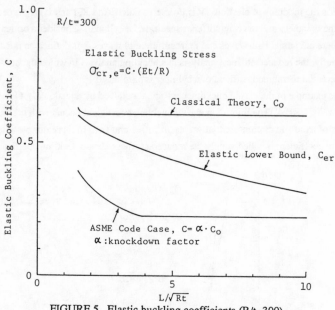

FIGURE 5. Elastic buckling coefficients (R/t=300).

Lower Bound Elasto-Plastic Buckling

Following Croll [9], the elasto-plastic buckling stress σ_{cr} can be shown as follows :

$$\frac{\sigma_{cr}}{\sigma_y} = N - \left(N^2 - \frac{\sigma_{er}}{\sigma_y}\right)^{1/2} \qquad (2)$$

where

$$N = 1/2 \cdot (1 + \sigma_{er}/\sigma_y + \rho) \qquad (3)$$

$$\rho = UE/2\sigma_y \qquad (4)$$

$$U = \frac{2i^2\lambda^2}{(i^2+\lambda^2)^2}\left(\frac{W_0}{R}\right) \qquad (5)$$

σ_y is the yield stress. σ_{er} is the reduced stiffness elastic buckling stress obtained from equation (1). And the initial imperfection of a cylinder is given to be $W = W_0\cos(i\Theta)\sin(j\pi\,x/L)$.

The expressions of equations (2) to (5) are the same forms as those used by Donnell and W̶a̶ [10] which are based on a first axial membrane yield criterion. The characteristic point of Croll's expression is the use of the reduced stiffness elastic buckling stress σ_{er} in place of the classical elastic buckling stress. These expressions might enable us to take into account the interaction between geometric imperfection and plasticity.

The relations between the elastic and elasto-plastic critical stresses by the reduced stiffness analysis are shown in FIGUREs 6 and 7. FIGURE 6 indicates the effect of ring-stiffener spacing at the imperfection parameter Wo/t=1.0. The relation at ring-stiffener spacing above $4\sqrt{Rt}$ is nearly equal to that at $L/\sqrt{Rt}$=4.0. FIGURE 7 indicates the effect of geometric imperfections at the ring-stiffener spacing parameter $L/\sqrt{Rt}$=4.0. The relation of plasticity reduction is not unique but varies with the geometric imperfection and the ring-stiffener spacing.

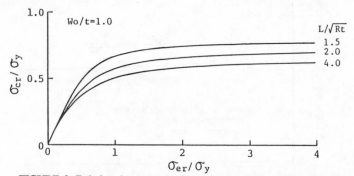

FIGURE 6. Relations between elastic and elasto-plastic critical stress by the reduced stiffness analysis. (The effect of ring-stiffener spacing.)

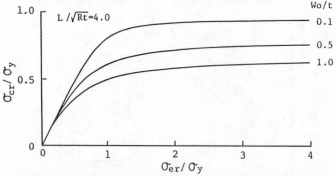

FIGURE 7. Relations between elastic and elasto-plastic critical stress by the reduced stiffness analysis. (The effect of geometric imperfection.)

Comparisons with Test Results

The comparisons between the predictions by the reduced stiffness analysis and the test results are shown in FIGUREs 8,9 and 10. The predicted values are calculated using the typical values of geometric parameters and material properties of each test series. The reduced stiffness analysis gives a good estimation in each test series. The tendency of the predicted critical stress with the ring-stiffener spacing is also consistent with that of test results. Considering the measured geometric imperfections, the effect of imperfections is properly expressed in the predictions.

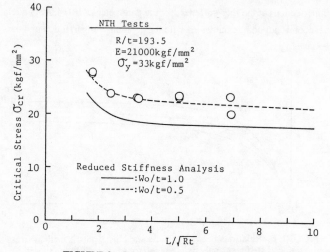

FIGURE 8. Critical stresses of NTH tests compared with the predictions by the reduced stiffness analysis.

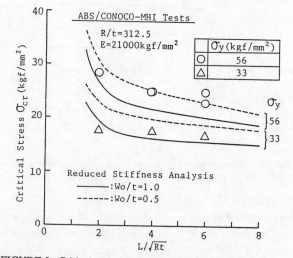

FIGURE 9. Critical stresses of ABS/CONOCO-MHI tests compared with the predictions by the reduced stiffness analysis.

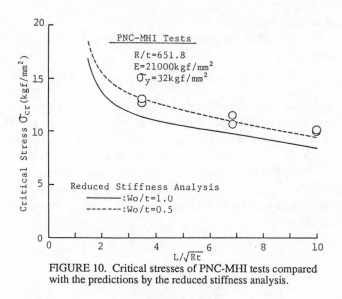

FIGURE 10. Critical stresses of PNC-MHI tests compared with the predictions by the reduced stiffness analysis.

PROPOSED FORMULA

Simple equations for estimating the buckling strength of fabricated ring-stiffened cylinders under axial compression are formulated. These cylinders have the radius to thickness ratio of 150 to 650, the ring-stiffener spacing of $1.5\sqrt{Rt}$ to $10\sqrt{Rt}$ and the yield stress of 24 kgf/mm² to 60 kgf/mm². This formulation is based on the calculations by the reduced stiffness analysis in the above ranges of geometric parameters and material properties.

Formulation of Elastic Buckling Stress

The elastic buckling stress can be shown to be

$$\sigma_{er} = C_{er} \cdot \frac{E \cdot t}{R} \qquad (6)$$

where E is the modulus of elasticity. R and t are respectively the radius and the thickness of a cylinder. C_{er} is the reduced stiffness elastic buckling coefficient which can be shown approximately as the function of the ring-stiffener spacing parameter $L/\sqrt{Rt}$.

$$C_{er} = \begin{cases} 0.649 - 0.292 \cdot \log(L/\sqrt{Rt}) & \text{if } 1.5 \leq L/\sqrt{Rt} \leq 4 \\ 0.703 - 0.383 \cdot \log(L/\sqrt{Rt}) & \text{if } 4 < L/\sqrt{Rt} \leq 10 \end{cases} \qquad (7)$$

where L is the ring-stiffener spacing, and Poisson's ratio is assumed to be $\nu = 0.3$.

The deviation of approximate equation (7) and the exact elastic lower bound by the reduced stiffness analysis is below 1%.

Formulation of Plastic Reduction

The relation of the elastic and elasto-plastic critical stress is given as the plasticity reduction of buckling strength.

$$\frac{1}{(\sigma_{cr}/\sigma_y)^n} = \frac{1}{(\sigma_{er}/\sigma_y)^n} + \frac{1}{(\sigma_o/\sigma_y)^n} \tag{8}$$

where σ_{cr} is the elasto-plastic critical stress and σ_{er} is the elastic buckling stress by equations (6) and (7). σ_o means the purely plastic strength of a shell with imperfections. Equation (8) is schematically illustrated in FIGURE 11. Equation (8) has the two asymptotic lines, σ_{cr}/σ_y $=\sigma_{er}/\sigma_y$ and $\sigma_{cr}/\sigma_y=\sigma_o/\sigma_y$. The line of $\sigma_{cr}/\sigma_y=\sigma_{er}/\sigma_y$ means the purely elastic relation while the line of $\sigma_{cr}/\sigma_y=\sigma_o/\sigma_y$ shows the purely plastic behavior. And the larger is the exponent n, the closer equation (7) comes to the two asymptotic lines. The value of σ_o/σ_y can be given approximately as the functions of the geometric imperfection parameter W_o/t and the ring-stiffener spacing parameter $L/\sqrt{Rt}$.

$$\frac{\sigma_o}{\sigma_y} = \begin{cases} \dfrac{1+0.017\cdot W_o/t \cdot (4-L/\sqrt{Rt})^{2.5}}{1+0.546\cdot W_o/t} & \text{if } 1.5 \leq L/\sqrt{Rt} \leq 4 \\[4mm] \dfrac{1}{1+0.546\cdot W_o/t} & \text{if } \quad 4 < L/\sqrt{Rt} \leq 10 \end{cases} \tag{9}$$

Equation (9) is schematically shown in FIGURE 12. And the exponent n is given in FIGURE 13.

These expressions enable us to estimate the buckling strength of a fabricated ring-stiffened cylinder depending on not only the geometric parameters of R/t and $L/\sqrt{Rt}$ but also the imperfection and the yield stress.

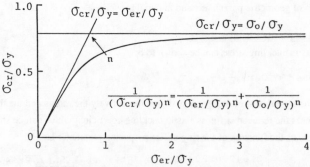

FIGURE 11. Estimative equation of the plasticity reduction.

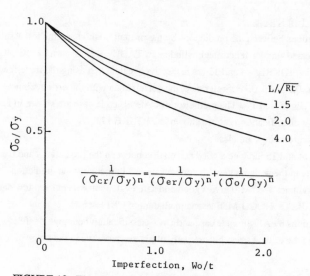

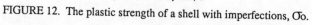

$$\frac{1}{(\sigma_{cr}/\sigma_y)^n} = \frac{1}{(\sigma_{er}/\sigma_y)^n} + \frac{1}{(\sigma_o/\sigma_y)^n}$$

FIGURE 12. The plastic strength of a shell with imperfections, σ_o.

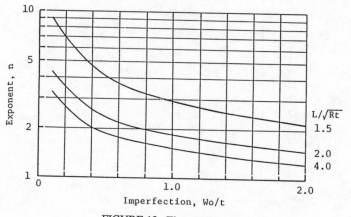

FIGURE 13. The exponent, n.

Correlation with Test Results

The correlations between the predictions by the present method and the test results for large-scale fabricated ring-stiffened steel cylinders in TABLE 1 are shown in FIGUREs 14 and 15. The predictions in FIGUREs 14 and 15 are respectively calculated using the imperfection parameters Wo/t=0.5 and 1.0. For reference, the correlations with the code recommendations are shown in FIGUREs 16 and 17. The predictions of ASME code case are shown in FIGURE 16 and those of DnV classification note are shown in FIGURE 17.

The following findings are clear :

(1)   FIGUREs 14 and 15 indicate a good correlation between the predictions and the experimental data in the wide range of the critical stress. Particularly the predictions using the imperfection parameter Wo/t=1.0 give a good and safe evaluation except for a few data which are a datum of ABS/CONOCO-MHI tests and all data of CBI tests.

(2)   The predictions by ASME code case and DnV classification note give a safe evaluation in the wide range of the critical stress but are particularly conservative in the range of low critical stresses.

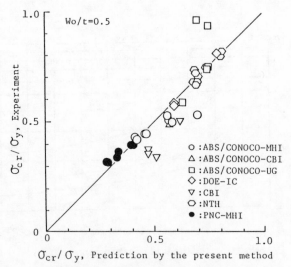

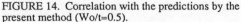

FIGURE 14. Correlation with the predictions by the present method (Wo/t=0.5).

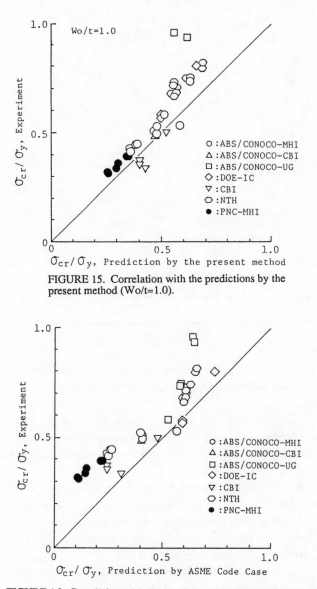

FIGURE 15. Correlation with the predictions by the present method (Wo/t=1.0).

FIGURE 16. Correlation with the predictions by the ASME Code Case.

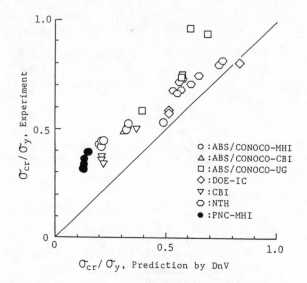

FIGURE 17. Correlation with the predictions by DnV classification note.

CONCLUSIONS

The investigations for the buckling of fabricated ring-stiffened steel cylinders under axial compression have been performed in over 30 large-scale buckling tests and the reduced stiffness analysis.

The main conclusions made from the present investigation are as follows :

(1)   The effect of yield stress is considerable even in the range where the buckle is predicted to occur elastically according to available design codes such as ASME code case and DnV classification note. (see FIGURE 2)

(2)   The experimental scatter is not so wide in each test series. It seems that the buckling strength of fabricated cylinders can be deterministically shown if the dimensions and imperfections of a cylinder and the material properties are given properly.

(3)   The discrepancies between the test results and the code recommendations are indicated in the range of high yield stress or large radius to thickness ratio.

(4)   The elasto-plastic lower bounds by the reduced stiffness analysis give a good estimation to the buckling strength of fabricated cylinders. And the tendency of the predicted critical stress with the ring-stiffener spacing is also consistent with test results. (see FIGUREs 8,9 and 10)

(5) The simple equations for estimating the buckling of fabricated cylinders under axial compression are formulated. These equations enable us to estimate the buckling strength depending on not only the geometric parameters of R/t and $L/\sqrt{Rt}$ but also the imperfection and the yield stress. (see equations (6) to (9)).

(6) Good correlation between the predictions by the present method and the experimental data is indicated over a wide range.

The authors expect that the present investigation will be useful for the advanced design of marine structures using lighter structural members and higher tensile strength steel.

REFERENCES

1. Chen, Y., Zimmer, R.A., de Oliveira, J.G. and Jan, H.Y.,
    Buckling and ultimate strength of stiffened cylinders : model experiments and strength formulations.
    OTC4853, Offshore Technology Conference [1985]

2. Miller, C.D.,
    Buckling of axially compressed cylinders.
    J.Struct. DiV., A.S.C.E., 103, ST3 [1977] 695-721

3. Dowling, P.J., and Harding, J.E.,
    Experimental behavior of ring and stringer stiffened shells.
    In : Buckling of Shells in Offshore Structures, Ed. by J.E.Harding, P.J.Dowling and N.Agelidis,
    Granada Publishing, London [1982] 73-107

4. Odland, J.,
    An experimental investigation of the buckling strength of ringstiffened cylindrical shells under axial compression.
    Norw. Marit. Res., 4 [1981] 22-39

5. Mitsubishi Heavy Industries, Ltd.,
    Buckling test data of 8 fabricated ring stiffened cylinders under axial compression.
    MHI Report [1982] prepared for ABS/CONOCO Shell Buckling Test Program.

6. Akiyama, H., Yuhara, T., Shimizu, S. and Takahashi, T.,
    Buckling of steel containment vessels under earthquake loadings. To be published in 1986 Fall Meeting of the Atomic Energy Society of Japan.

7. ASME, Boiler and Pressure Vessel Code Case N-284,
    Metal containment shell buckling design method.
    Section III, Division 1, Class MC, A.S.M.E., New York [1980]

8. Det norske Veritas,
    Buckling strength analysis of mobile offshore units.
    Classification Notes, No.30.1 [1984]

9. Croll, J.G.A.,
    Lower bound elasto-plastic buckling of cylinders.
    Proc. Instn Civ. Engrs, Part 2, 71 [1981] 235-261

10. Donnell, L.H. and Wan, C.C.,
Effect of imperfections on buckling of thin cylinders and columns under axial compression.
J. Appl. Mech.. A.S.M.E., 72 [1950] 73-83

FATIGUE PROBLEMS IN SHIP STRUCTURES

H. Petershagen
Institut für Schiffbau
Universität Hamburg
Hamburg
Federal Republic of Germany

ABSTRACT

Most cracks occurring in ship structures are likely to be fatigue cracks. Although fatigue cracking in ship hulls often does not cause serious safety problems, repair costs and possible damage due to water ingress may be high. Several methods for the fatigue life assessment of ship structures are briefly described and examples for their application are given. These methods are based on nominal stress or local strain and fatigue test data as well as conventional and finite element calculation models.

INTRODUCTION

As already stated in an earlier paper by Vedeler [1], most cracks occurring in ship structures are likely to be caused by service fatigue loads. This statement is made with certain reservation since the analysis of fracture surfaces is not successful in most cases due to the influence of the corrosive environment at sea. However, the appearance of such cracks points at fatigue loads as their reason.

Commission XIII of the International Institute of Welding (IIW) has collected and published cases of fatigue failures in welded structures and their interpretation [2]. Eight cases regarding ship and offshore structures are included. Conclusions from this collection are drawn in [3]. Most cracks initiated at details of classes F, F2 and G according to [4]. Details concerned are transverse and longitudinal fillet welded attachments, load carrying transverse fillet welds and butt welds with backing bars. Incorrect design dominates as a primary reason for cracking, but other reasons

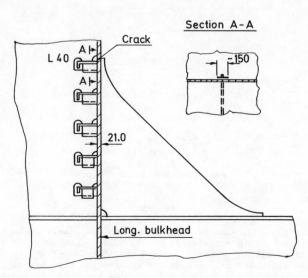

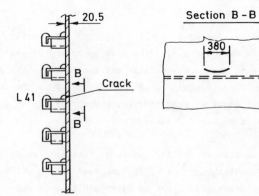

FIGURE 1.

such as bad workmanship and abnormal stresses may contribute to the failure. It should further be mentioned that only very few cases of fatigue cracks starting from planar internal weld defects are reported.

This statement is in accordance with the results of a study [5] on cracks found in the steel structure of VLCC's. No case was found, where a crack could be related to a planar internal weld defect, although a rather large number of such defects had been found by NDT. Most damages occur in the midship part. Cracks in brackets, at bulkheads and at other design notches dominate, examples being given in sketches (fig. 1).

Extensive work on the service performance of structural details in ships has been done by the US Ship Structure Committee. This work is summarized in [6]. Even if fatigue cracking in ship hulls is often not a serious safety problem, the cost of repair and possible damage due to water ingress or oil leakage may be high. But a few cases are also reported,where fatigue cracks developed into a brittle fracture and led to a major damage [7] or even to failure of the whole structure [8].

Summarizing it may be said that design for fatigue is a matter of detail design and especially a matter of design of welded connections.

Several concepts have been developed which may be used for the assessment of fatigue strength of ship structures. It is intended to give an outline of these methods and examples for their application in this paper.

NOMINAL STRESS CONCEPT

This concept is the most widely used one for welded connections. It is also incorporated in many codes and regulations. The brief description follows the recommendation developed in the International Institute of Welding (IIW) [9].

The concept is based on a conventional stress analysis, often a beam calculation, and data from fatigue tests with welded specimens.

It is an experimentally established fact that a common slope may be defined for the S-N-curves of welded connections. A grid of parallel

S-N-lines can then be defined and classes attributed to these lines
(fig. 2). The class number means the stress range at 2 million cycles. This
value is calculated as the mean value of available test results minus two
standard deviations, which corresponds to a survival probability of 97.7 %.

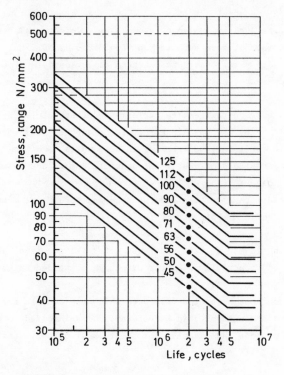

FIGURE 2.

Figure 3 shows examples of details related to classes. The recommendation
[9] is based on stress range only, while other codes consider a certain,
although not large influence of mean stress. Recent re-analyses of test results [10] support the stress-range concept (fig. 4). It is, however, also
argued that a certain influence of stress ratio will be present in large-
scale tests with spectrum load. Different approaches to the assessment of
fatigue strength under spectrum load are used in various codes and recom-
mandations. While in [9] the use of Miner's rule is recommended, test-based
transfer factors are used in other codes, for instance in [11]. The second-

mentioned approach is based on the observation that such transfer factors
mainly depend on the shape of the spectrum and common factors can be defined for all notch cases.

Joint configuration showing mode of fatigue cracking and stress considered	Description of Joint	Class
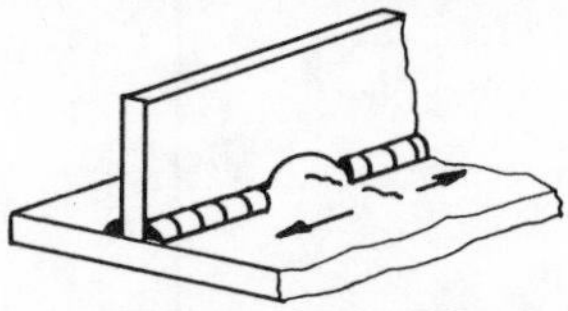	longitudinal fillet weld with cope holes (based on stress range in flange at weld ends)	71
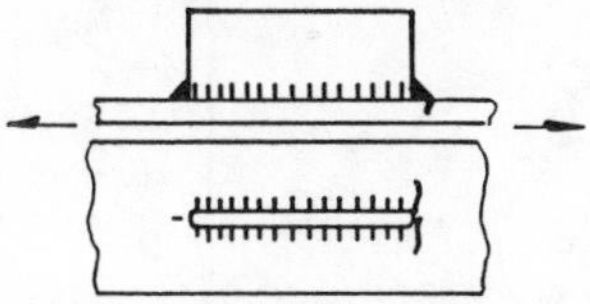	longitudinal fillet welded gusset shorter than 150 mm longer than 150 mm near the edge	71 63 50
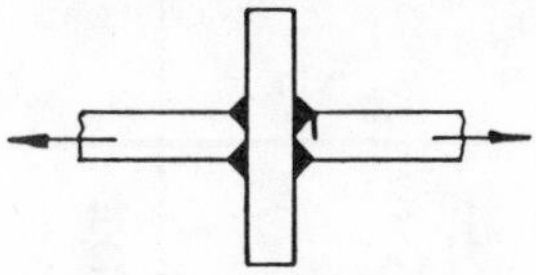	cruciform joint K-butt weld with fillet welded ends. Misalignment less than 15%	71
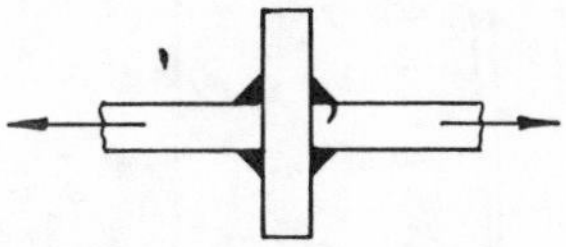	cruciform joint transverse fillet weld toe failure. Misalignment less than 15% plate thickness	63

FIGURE 3.

As an example for the application of the nominal stress concept, longitudinal strength of ship hulls is treated. In the common longitudinal
strength calculation, the hull is treated as a beam subjected to shear forces and bending moments due to unequal distribution of weight and displacement in still water and due to the action of waves. Class 71 details must
be expected in the design of longitudinal strength members. A typical
example are cope holes in stiffeners welded to the plating (fig. 3).

The permissible stress range is $71 \cdot \frac{3}{4} = 53$ N/mm², if a safety factor
of $\frac{4}{3}$ is assumed. This safety factor is for instance used in the fatigue

286

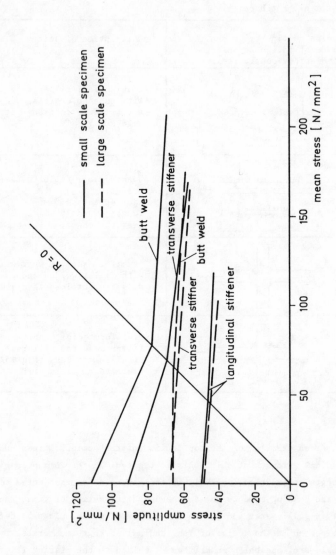

FIGURE 4.

design recommendations of Germanischer Lloyd [11].

This value for the permissible stress range must be transferred to the log-normal seaway spectrum (fig. 5). A transfer factor has been derived from test results in [12]. Due to the high number of cycles to fracture, test results for spectrum load were available from literature for longitudinal stiffeners only. Further tests with non-load carrying transverse stiffeners and with butt welds have been carried out in the Institut für Schiffbau der Universität Hamburg. Thus the test results cover the range of notch cases existing in ship structures. Figure 6 shows the test results.

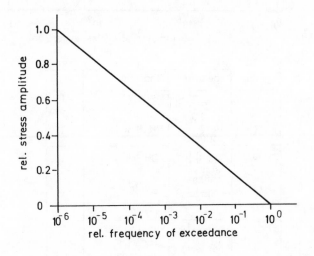

FIGURE 5.

The stress ranges are plotted over the number of cycles to fracture in a non-dimensional form based on the stress range for constant amplitude loading for 2 million cycles. A lower bound line parallel to the S-N-curve has been drawn.

From this, a transfer factor of 4 can be taken between stress range under constant amplitude load at 2 million cycles and stress range for spectrum load at 20 million cycles. The latter is considered appropriate for ocean-going merchant ships, taking average operation conditions and life time into consideration.

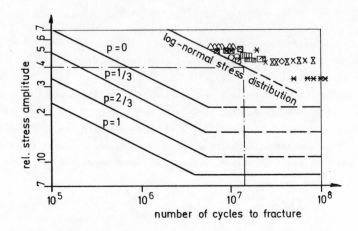

symbol	specimen	material	R
✳	⊢⊟⊣ 3.5	St 37	-1
×	a= 2.5	St 52	-1
⊠	long. stiffener	PN 18 502	-1
O	transv. stiffener	DH 36	-1
◇	a= 4	DH 36	-1
⊠ ◸ △	but weld	NF steel grade C Electrogas Electroslag submerged arc	 -0.5 -0.5 -0.5

FIGURE 6.

A permissible stress range of 4 x 53 = 212 N/mm² follows for the
class 71 detail. This figure may be compared with the well-known figures
for the permissible longitudinal bending stress, which is 150 - 160 N/mm²
for mild steel. This figure is increased to 192 N/mm² and 208 N/mm² respectively for higher strength steels HTS32 and HTS36. Since the fatigue
strength of welded structures does more or less not depend on the yield
point of the steels considered, it has to be checked whether the highest
permissible stress still meets the requirements of fatigue strength.

This is evidently not so for a stress ratio R = -1, which would mean a vessel with zero still water bending moment and seaway bending moment only.

However, this situation is not possible in merchant ships built according to minimum longitudinal strength standards. Using the formula for the maximum expected seaway bending moment as given in [11], it can be shown [13] that a ship built with minimum section modulus will always sail in the tension (or compression) stress range when the maximum permissible stress is reached. In other words, the maximum seaway bending moment will never exceed the permissible still water bending moment.

As the permissible stress range for a class 71 detail is slightly larger than the permissible stress for HTS36, it is shown that the latter covers the requirements of sufficient fatigue strength. This is not self-evident, since permissible longitudinal bending stresses have been established at a time when a fatigue assessment was not yet possible.

Further, it must be noted that for vessels built without minimum section modulus requirement, such as navy ships, a class 71 detail design may not be appropriate with respect to the fatigue strength of the structure.

FATIGUE STRENGTH AND STRESS ANALYSIS

In many cases, especially in the structural analysis of modern sophisticated ships, simple calculation models can no longer be used. In these cases, the finite element method has become a powerful tool for an adequate stress analysis. However, with the application of the method the problem arises that the results depend on the finite element mesh used. This is especially the case in way of structural details which, on the other hand, have a dominant influence on the fatigue strength of the structure.

One way to an engineering solution of this problem is the use of a relatively coarse finite element model together with the nominal stress concept.

An example, where this approach has been used, is shown in Figure 7. It concerns the end structure of a long superstructure above the main

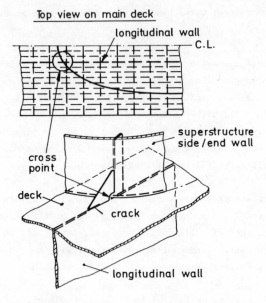

Top view on main deck

longitudinal wall

C.L.

cross point

superstructure side /end wall

deck

crack

longitudinal wall

FIGURE 7.

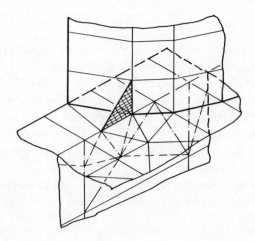

FIGURE 8.

strength deck. Long superstructures are effective with respect to longitudinal hull bending. Their ends form a discontinuity in the structure, where considerable stress concentrations may occur.

In the case considered here, the junction between superstructure side wall and longitudinal wall below the deck forms a "hard point". Although a bracket had been arranged, a crack occurred during the ship's service as shown in figure 7.

Starting from a given still water and wave bending moment distribution, a finite element analysis was carried out. The mesh in way of the damage is shown in figure 8. Evidently it is by far too coarse to permit an estimate of the local stress concentration. So the stress obtained in the bracket was used as the nominal stress for a fatigue assessment. In this, the fillet welded connection between bracket and deck was considered as a class 63 detail (see fig. 3) with a permissible stress range of $63 \cdot \frac{3}{4} \cdot 4 = 189$ N/mm² for a log-normal stress range distribution. The stress range obtained from the finite element calculation exceeded this value. The service behaviour of the structure was thus confirmed by the calculation.

For a reduction of the overall stress in the bracket modifications of the design would have been necessary, which were not compatible with the ship's service requirements. Instead of a design modification the fillet weld between bracket and deck was replaced by a full-penetration K-weld according to class 71. Further, the bracket was lengthened to a limited extent in way of the deck and the bracket end rounded. Although the formal classification of the detail was not raised, the last-mentioned measures were also expected to improve the fatigue strength. The further service experience has shown that the measures taken have been adequate to avoid further damage.

HOT SPOT STRAIN CONCEPT FOR WELDED STRUCTURES

This concept has been developed for the assessment of the fatigue strength of welded structures in cases where a nominal stress cannot be defined. The basic idea behind the method is that the fatigue life of a structure, or better the crack initiation life, depends on the strain at the critical point. This strain should include the effect of the design notch, but not the micro notch caused by the weld profile. A concise description of the method as well as available results and their use in pertinent codes is given in [14]. The application is strongly focussed on tubular joints in offshore structures. It seems to have been often overlooked, however, that the concept has been discussed in a more general way and investigations have been described already in a report published in 1968 [15].

An essential step in the method is the definition of the reference point, the "hot spot" to be used in connection with a fatigue design curve. Different definitions are used in existing codes. The design curves are generally based on stress ranges, where the stress is a fictitious elastic stress, that is the product of modulus of elasticity and strain. This terminology is a matter of convenience for designers, who are familiar with stress rather than with strain.

The use of the hot spot strain concept has been demonstrated in the interpretation of fatigue test results with butt welded specimens, fabricated by means of different welding processes [16].

The S-N curves obtained for the three processes investigated deviated significantly from each other. While no significant difference was found regarding weld shape, rather large differences existed in the angular distortion caused by the different weld processes.

When plotted against the strain at the critical point including axial and bending strain, nearly all results fell into one common scatter band (fig. 9). It may be noted that the hot spot strain could be calculated with sufficient accuracy by means of a simple beam model. Further it must be kept in mind that the effect of an angular distortion on the hot spot strain will be much smaller in longitudinally stiffened plates than in beam-like specimens.

Using the hot spot definition given in [15], a number of tests and comparative calculations for structural details has been carried out [17], [18]. They include longitudinal walls ending at a transverse wall with and without transition bracket, cope holes and ends of doubler plates. Ends of longitudinal walls are treated here as an example. The test specimens are shown in figure 10.

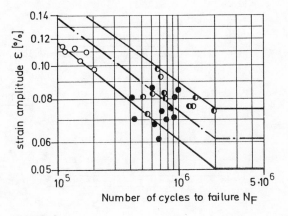

FIGURE 9.

According to [15] the strain 2 mm apart from the weld toe covers the influence of the structural notch without being influenced by the secondary notch caused by the weld shape.

The hot spot strain so defined has been measured by means of strain gauges and calculated using finite-element models. The model used consisted of plate elements. Figure 11 shows the idealisation in way of the weld, which has a large influence on the calculation results.

In figure 12 measured and calculated strain distributions in front of the weld are shown.

All test data are plotted in figure 13. With one exception for which an explanation could be given they fall into a common scatterband defined according to [15]. The upper strain for 2 million cycles at a stress ratio R = 0 and for 50% probability of survival is 0.1‰ in good accordance with the figure given in [15].

It should be noted that a linear load/strain behaviour was observed at the hot spot of form 1, while the forms 2 and 3 showed initial yielding during the first load cycle. However, the behaviour was quasi-elastic, too, after a shake-down period of only a few load cycles. From this it follows

294

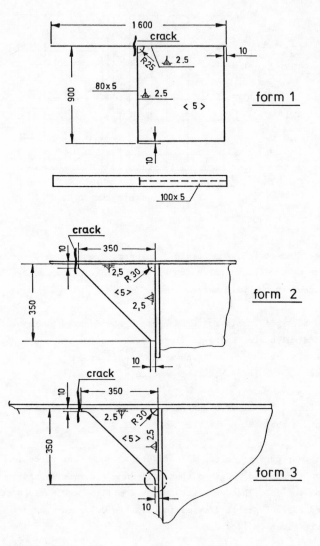

FIGURE 10.

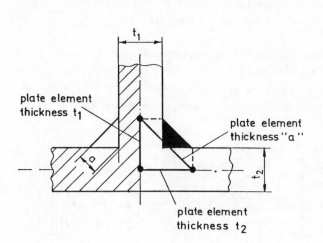

FIGURE 11.

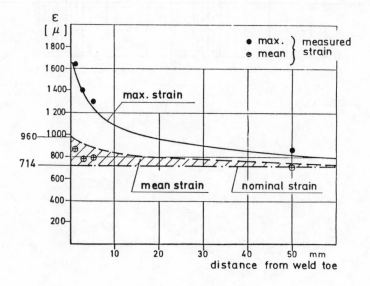

FIGURE 12.

that the fatigue strength assessment for welded structures can be based on the linear-elastic strain at the hot spot.

With regard to the detail design of ship structures it can be concluded that small transition brackets, even with rounded ends, do not improve the fatigue strength and should be avoided. This conclusion does of course not apply to large brackets necessary to keep the average stress sufficiently low.

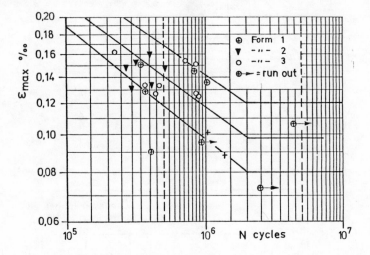

FIGURE 13.

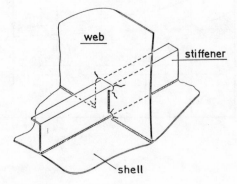

FIGURE 14.

LOCAL CYCLIC STRAIN CONCEPT

Contrary to what has been stated at the end of the preceding section for welded connections areas exist in the ship structure, where the relation between load and local strain is non-linear. A typical example is the penetration of a longitudinal stiffener through a transverse web (fig. 14). A rather large number of cracks has been found at this detail in the past and its load carrying behaviour has been the subject of several investigations.

These investigations have been extended in [19], [20] towards a fatigue life estimate based on elasto-plastic material behaviour. This approach is considered especially useful for a fatigue strength assessment in way of notches in the base material, where extended plastic zones are formed under service load.

An example from the bottom structure of a multi purpose bulk carrier is shown in Figure 15 [20]. The maximum linear-elastic stress range between the two loading conditions considered reaches nearly four times the yield stress.

It is obvious that under these circumstances a non-linear approach to fatigue strength becomes necessary.

The concept followed in [19], [20] is outlined in Figure 16. It is based on the assumption that the fatigue damage is caused by the stress / strain cycles acting on the element of the structure at the critical point. From this it can be concluded that this critical element of the structure should behave in a similar way as a small scale specimen of the same material subjected to the same sequence of stress / strain cycles. This is important as necessary data can be obtained from tests with small scale specimens.

From the load-time function closed cycles have to be derived by means of a suitable counting method. The rain-flow counting method is often advocated. It should be noted that for the detail considered here and for a

Ship in ballast on
wave crest

Ship loaded in wave
trough

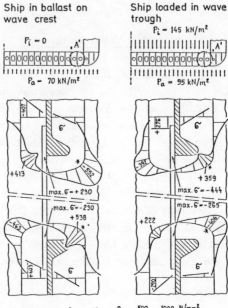

stresses in $[N/mm^2]$

0   500   1000 N/mm²

FIGURE 15.

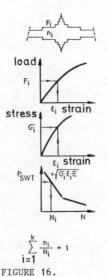

spectrum of load cycles

load - strain
relation

cyclic stress - strain
curve

relation
crack iniation life -
damage parameter

$$\sum_{i=1}^{k} \frac{n_i}{N_i} = 1$$

damage accumulation law

FIGURE 16.

ship travelling onehalf voyage in ballast and the second half voyage in
loaded condition, the effects of difference between the loading conditions
in still water and of the seaway are separated by the counting method. The
former causes a small number of cycles equal to the number of voyages during the ship's service life with high amplitudes. By the latter, a large
number of cycles with comparatively small amplitudes are caused with a
nearly exponential distribution.

Further, a relation between service load and strain, a cyclic stress-
strain curve for the material used, a relation between fatigue life and
damage parameter used and a damage accumulation law are required.

Non-linear finite-element calculations have been carried out [20] for
different notch configurations. The results have been compared with those
obtained from approximation formulae given in the literature. It was found
that the well-known Neuber equation

$$\sigma \cdot \varepsilon = \frac{\sigma_e^2}{E}$$

σ =   elasto-plastic notch stress

ε =   elasto-plastic notch strain

σ_e =   elastic notch stress

E =   modulus of elasticity

is most suitable for the purposes considered here.

Cyclic stress-strain curves have been derived from tests with small
scale specimens of mild steel grade A [19]. Polished specimens as well as
specimens with flame-cut edges have been included in the investigations.
As Figure 17 shows, cyclic softening at lower and cyclic hardening at higher strains has been found.

By means of Neuber formula and cyclic stress-strain curve the local
elasto-plastic stress and strain can be determined (fig. 18), if σ_e is
available from a linear-elastic finite element calculation.

The best fatigue life estimates were obtained using the damage parameter given by Smith, Watson and Topper [21]:

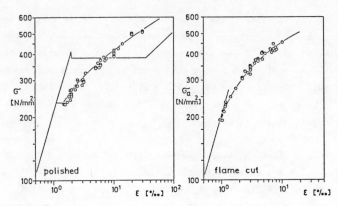

FIGURE 17.

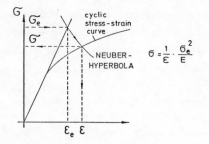

FIGURE 18.

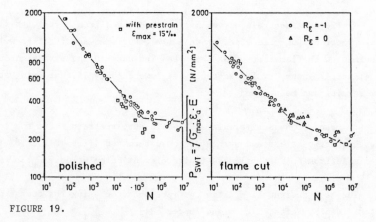

FIGURE 19.

$$P_{SWT} = \sqrt{\sigma_{max} \cdot \varepsilon_a \cdot E}$$

σ_{max} = max. elasto-plastic notch stress

ε_a = elasto-plastic notch strain amplitude

E = modulus of elasticity

This parameter includes the effect of mean load as well as of the load amplitude. It may be added that for reversed load (R = -1) the damage parameter becomes identical with the elastic stress σ_e if the Neuber equation is inserted into the expression for P_{SWT}. For the relation between damage parameter P_{SWT} and number of cycles to crack initiation curves similar to the well-known S-N-curves have been derived from small scale tests (fig.19). The curve for the flame-cut surface differs from that for the polished surface in that it is somewhat lower and shows a smaller slope in the lower and a larger slope in the higher cycle range.

Finally, as a damage accumulation law, the well-known Palmgren-Miner criterion has been used:

$$\sum_{i=1}^{K} \frac{n_i}{N_i} = 1$$

n_i = number of cycles at load level i
N_i = number of cycles to fracture at load level i
K = number of load levels

Results from tests and calculations with an exponential load distribution are given in Figure 20. Crack initiation lifes of models of longitudinal stiffener - transverse web penetrations and of small scale specimens subjected to the same strain sequence do not differ in a statistical sense. The predicted crack initiation curve is on the safe side for a blocked load sequence, but on the unsafe side for a random load distribution. This fact has to be met by applying appropriate safety factors. On the other hand, it is argued in [20] that for the bottom structure considered (fig. 15) the major part of the damage is caused by the loading / unloading cycle and not by the load variation caused by the seaway. Using data

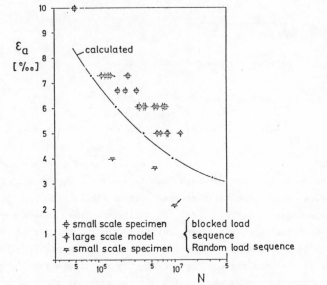

FIGURE 20.

from [19] it is shown in [20] that the number of loading / unloading cycles for a lifetime of the vessel of 20 years is in the range of the crack
initiation life.

The method briefly described thus appears suitable for a fatigue life
prediction in way of structural details in the base material. If a cyclic
stress - strain curve is available, the data from linear - elastic finite
element calculations are the imformations necessary to carry out the prediction calculation. Certainly the method is not a tool for everyday
design work. It has, however, already been used successfully in several
special cases.

REFERENCES

[1]   Vedeler, G.,
       To what extent do brittle fracture and fatigue interest
       shipbuilders today?
       Det Norske Veritas Publication No. 32 (1962)

[2]   Fatigue fractures in welded constructions-case studies
       collected by the International Institute of Welding
       Vol. I (1967) and Vol. II (1979)
       Publications de la Soudure Autogene, Paris

[3]   Harrison, J.D.,
        Lessons from service fatigue failures
        IIW-Document XIII-959-80 (1980)

[4]   Gurney, T.R.,
        Fatigue design rules
        Welding Institute Research Bulletin No. 17 (1976)

[5]   Kjellander, S. and Persson, B.,
        Hull damages - further investigation and significance
    /   of weld defects
        STU - report 76 - 3948 and 77 - 4205, March 1980 and
        IIW-Document XIII-984-80 (1980)

[6]   Jordan, C.R. and Krumpen jr. R.P.,
        Performance of ship structural details
        Welding Journal, January 1984

[7]   Lessons from "Kurdistan"
        The Motor Ship, January 1982

[8]   Yamamoto, Y., Fukasawa, T., Arai, T., Iida, M., Murakami, T.
        and Ando, T.,
        Analysis of structural damages of the fore body of a
        container ship due to slamming
        Journal of the Society of Naval Architects of Japan,
        Vol. 155 (1984)

[9]   Design recommendations for cyclic loaded welded steel
        structures
        Welding In The World Vol. 20 No. 7/8 (1982)

[10]   Olivier, R. and Ritter, W.,
        Catalogue of S-N-curves of welded joints in structural
        steels
        Deutscher Verband für Schweißtechnik Report No. 56

[11]   Germanischer Lloyd - Vorschriften für Konstruktion
        und Bau von stählernen Seeschiffen - Ausgabe 1982,
        Band I, Ergänzung No. 2, July 1984

[12]   Paetzold, H. and Petershagen, Ḧ,
        Untersuchungen zur Betriebsfestigkeit geschweißter
        Schiffbaukonstruktionen
        Schiff & Hafen No. 11 (1984)

[13]   Böckenhauer, M. and Petershagen, H.,
        zu "Untersuchungen zur Betriebsfestigkeit geschweißter
        Schiffbaukonstruktionen"
        Schiff & Hafen No. 6 (1985)

[14]   Iida, K.,
        Application of hot spot strain concept to fatigue
        life prediction
        IIW-Document XIII-1103-83 (1983)

[15] Haibach, E.,
Die Schwingfestigkeit von Schweißverbindungen aus der Sicht
einer örtlichen Beanspruchungsmessung
Laboratorium für Betriebsfestigkeit (LBF) Darmstadt,
Report No. FB-77 (1968)

[16] Petershagen, H. and Zwick, W.,
Fatigue strength of butt welds made by different welding
processes
IIW-Document XIII-1048-82 (1982)

[17] Petershagen, H. and Paetzold, H.,
Untersuchungen zur Bewertung schweißtechnischer Gestaltungs-
formen im Schiffbau
Forschungszentrum des Deutschen Schiffbaus (FDS),
Report No. 142 (1983)

[18] Paetzold, H.,
Schwingfestigkeitsverhalten ausgewählter Details aus der
Schiffskonstruktion
Forschungszentrum des Deutschen Schiffbaus (FDS)
Report No. 159 (1985)

[19] Paetzold, H.,
Beurteilung der Betriebsfestigkeit auf der Grundlage des
örtlichen Konzepts
Jahrbuch der Schiffbautechnischen Gesellschaft (1985)

[20] Fricke, W.,
Bestimmung der örtlichen Dehnung für schiffbauliche
Konstruktionsdetails
Jahrbuch der Schiffbautechnischen Gesellschaft (1985)

[21] Smith, K.N., Watson, P. and Topper, T.H.,
A stress - strain function for the fatigue of metals
Journal of Materials Vol. 5, No. 4 (1970)

THE FATIGUE CHARACTERISTICS OF SUBMARINE STRUCTURES
SUBJECTED TO EXTERNAL PRESSURE CYCLING

I M Kilpatrick
Admiralty Research Establishment
Dunfermline, Fife, Scotland

ABSTRACT

Fatigue is an important aspect of the submarine design process. The submarine is a large complicated welded structure subjected to compressive cyclic service loading. Current pressure vessel fatigue design codes lead to unacceptably short fatigue lives. It has thus been necessary to adopt an approach based on the testing of scaled submarine fatigue models.

This paper is concerned with the ARE, Dunfermline Submarine Fatigue Model Programme. An account is given of the model designs, pressure cycling facilities, test procedures and non-destructive examination (NDE) requirements for monitoring initiation and propagation. Results from typical models are presented together with a comparison with a fracture mechanics fatigue analysis.

INTRODUCTION

Submarine pressure hulls are subjected to fluctuating compressive loading. This would not normally be expected to cause fatigue problems. However, because the submarine pressure hull is fabricated by welding, local tensile residual stresses are set up at welded joints such as the structurally important frame to hull T-butt weld. This induces tensile restraint moments and forces, the magnitudes of which are dependent on the stiffness of the surrounding structure. Thus the applied compressive cyclic stresses superimposed on a tensile residual stress produces a net tension stress cycle under which fatigue cracks may initiate and propagate.

To study the fatigue behaviour of pressure hulls a fatigue model programme is underway at ARE, Dunfermline. The main aim is to detect initiation and establish propagation rates under given operational conditions, thus enabling the overall objective, which is 'to ensure the adequacy of current and future generation designs with respect to fatigue', to be met. A secondary, but no less important aim is to ensure that when defects are detected in a submarine pressure hull they be dealt with in a rational manner in relation to their significance to hull integrity so that sound advice may be given in maintenance and repair situations, taking account of operational requirements.

This paper briefly considers the current UK design code in relation to the submarine situation. This is followed by an outline of the ARE approach to submarine fatigue. The ARE Submarine Fatigue Model Programme is described including, types of model, pressure cycling facilities, test procedures and NDE requirements for crack initiation and propagation monitoring. A comparison of experimental and theoretical results for typical models is given.

THE CURRENT UK PRESSURE VESSEL DESIGN CODE AND THE SUBMARINE

BS 5500:1985 Appendix C, Recommended Practice for Assessment of Vessels Subject to Fatigue, is the current UK code. It covers internally and/or externally pressurised vessels with a single fatigue design curve. The curve is independent of steel type, being a lower bound to a large number of tests on steels with a large range of material properties and hence a wide scatter. Thus, only such a lower bound approach is justifiable. A stress concentration factor of at least 2.5 is recommended for the toe of as-welded butts or fillet welds. Application of the code to frame/ hull full penetration T-butt welds using the appropriate design stresses for submarines in Ql(N) steel gives an allowable fatigue life of the order of $\ll$ 1,000 cycles [1]. This is clearly unacceptable since during its operational life the submarine must be allowed to dive deep a considerably greater number of times than this. BS 5500:1985 recognises that it discriminates against high yield strength steels. Where the code gives unacceptable values fatigue tests may be carried out to demonstrate the adequacy of a structure.

The current submarine fatigue design stresses are limited to values derived from very limited data. Allowable stresses vary with detail geometry being highest at point stress concentrations such as penetrations and lowest at positions of axisymmetric stress concentrations such as the frame to hull intersections. This is based on consideration of the relative dangers of a through fatigue crack developing without detection.

It was clear that a programme of work on submarine fatigue was necessary to meet the stated aims and to examine the validity of current design criteria. Because it was recognised that small scale laboratory fatigue specimens were unlikely to adequately represent the behaviour of the complex welded submarine structure a Submarine Fatigue Model Programme was initiated.

THE FATIGUE MODEL PROGRAMME

The main reason for the model approach is the inability of small specimens to incorporate realistic welding residual and restraint stresses. These are the driving force for fatigue under external pressure loading. It is therefore necessary to resort to fatigue testing cylindrical models. Obviously full scale pressure hull models cannot be tested. Therefore, reduced diameter full thickness cylindrical models are tested at appropriate levels of external pressure to achieve stresses similar to those in an actual pressure hull. For the same thickness, reducing diameter increases fabrication restraint stresses. This will introduce a degree of pessimism into the observed crack growth rates. The extent of this can be assessed using restraint data in a fracture mechanics fatigue analysis. The programme assumes that if fatigue crack growth rate (life) can be related to the level of restraint stress and validated by fatigue tests at two model scale levels, (levels of restraint), then the use of the same fracture mechanics fatigue analysis incorporating measured submarine restraint stresses is justified for prediction of full scale hull behaviour.

Fatigue testing is carried out, depending on model size, in either the ARE Small or Large Fatigue Chambers, (SFC), (LFC). The SFC, Figure 1, is a welded laminated steel pressure chamber of approximately 1.5 m, (5'), internal diameter by 5 m, (16.5'), long. The maximum cyclic working pressure is 2,600 psi at a maximum rate of 4 cpm. The LFC, Figure 2, comprises an inner steel vessel with massive shrunk on steel rings housed in a prestressed concrete yoke 11 m, (36'), diameter overall and 25 m, (82'), high. Vertical forces exerted in the end plates are transferred to a reaction

308

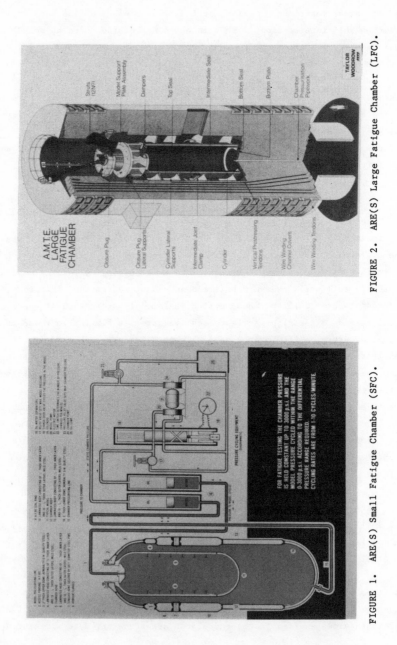

FIGURE 2. ARE(S) Large Fatigue Chamber (LFC).

FIGURE 1. ARE(S) Small Fatigue Chamber (SFC).

ring at the top of the yoke through a 110 ton cast steel closure plug and a
system of 12 Y-shaped struts. Loads on the bottom plate are transmitted
directly into the larger bottom cap of the 6,000 ton mass of the vessel.
The reaction ring is tied to the base by 180 vertical tendons, strung in
five concentric rings through the barrel section of the yoke. Wire winding
of the reaction ring and bottom cap resists the hoop bursting forces
imposed by the chamber pressure. The steel pressure chamber is 3 m, (10'),
internal diameter and 9 m (30') in length, (7.6 m (25') usable), with a
maximum cyclic working pressure of 4,000 psi and a rate of 1 cpm.

Both chambers operate on the soft cycling principle. Model and
chamber are filled with water and raised to the desired external pressure.
The model is then alternately depressurised and pressurised while maintaining the chamber pressure constant consequently subjecting it to cyclic
compressive loading. The great advantage of this is that the chamber does
not experience fatigue loading.

The programme involves models of approximately 1/6 and 1/3 full scale
diameter. The short term aim is to show that present design stresses and
fabrication procedures lead to acceptable fatigue behaviour. Plans also
include models in higher yield strength steels to assess their suitability
for hull construction.

FATIGUE TESTING OF SUBMARINE MODELS

Model Design

There are two basic model types. Figure 3 shows a typical S-series
model (SFC). This is a simple cylinder of external diameter up to 1.4 m,
(4.5'), containing a centrally located bulkhead. The bulkhead to hull
joint is a full penetration T-butt weld. The hull parallel length is
0.84 m, (2.75'), and is fabricated from two half shells joined by longitudinal seam welds at the port and starboard positions. The model thus
incorporates two crossing welds. The end closures are hemispherical domes,
the forward dome incorporating an access hatch.

Figure 4 illustrates a typical L-series model (LFC). This is a multi-
framed cylinder of 2.74 m, (9'), external diameter and parallel length
4.8 m, (15.75'), containing four longitudinal seam welds at crown, keel,

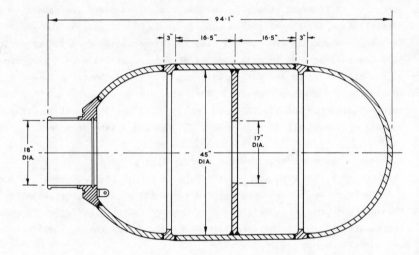

FIGURE 3. S-Series Fatigue Model.

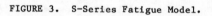

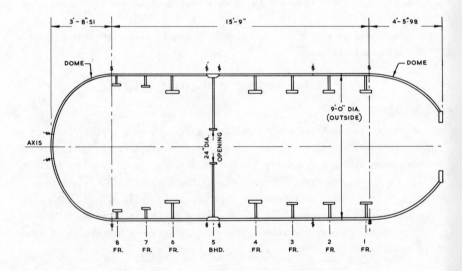

FIGURE 4. L-Series Fatigue Model.

port and starboard. The aft closure dome is torispherical and the forward hemispherical with an access hatch. A large bulkhead and seven frames of varying dimensions results in a wide range of applied stresses at the frame to hull full penetration T-butt welds. Many other variables have been built into this model to gain maximum information. These include different weld metals and processes, weld finishes, natural and artificial defects and hull plating mismatches.

To date only some of the S-series (SFC) models in the programme have been tested. The first L-series model tests is underway (at time of writing it has experienced some 2,000 cycles).

NON-DESTRUCTIVE EXAMINATION TECHNIQUES

Crack initiation and propagation data are obtained using a combination of NDE techniques.

Eddy Current

This technique [2] is used to detect the onset of cracking. An alternating current (AC) magnetic field induces eddy currents in the material at the position to be inspected. Changes in the impedance caused by surface breaking defects can be detected. Although changes in the geometry and material which occur at a weld can also give rise to changes, they are usually small enough to be neglected during crack detection. The technique is used purely as a means of detecting the onset of fatigue cracking. The measurements are of course made inside the model at the T-butt weld toe where cracking starts.

Alternating Current Potential Drop (ACPD)

Until fairly recently the most widely used PD method for crack sizing was the direct current (DC) technique. This is adequate on the laboratory scale where section sizes are small and consequently current requirements are not excessive. However, its use in large structures is impracticable since the much larger section sizes would necessitate the use of heavy currents to provide a measurable field strength. By using AC the current is restricted to a thin surface layer (the 'skin effect'), and consequently the current necessary to produce a given field strength at the surface is much less than with DC. The technique [3], [4], [5], relies on the change in resistance occurring when a crack is introduced into the structure. A constant AC is applied to the test area and the PD measured both across the crack and adjacent to it. The PD between the output probes is a measure of the current path, so that the ratio of the PD in the presence to that in the absence of a crack allows calculation of the crack length.

ACPD is being used extensively in the model programme. Fatigue cracks located by the eddy current technique are subsequently sized by ACPD. Both hand probe and continuous on-line [6] methods are in use. The measurements must again be made from the inside of the hull.

Ultrasonic Diffraction, or Time of Flight Technique (TOFT)

When a pulse of ultrasound is projected towards a crack the sound is diffracted (or scattered) at the crack tip. By placing transmitting and receiving transducers on either side of the crack and carefully measuring the pulse flight time, the crack depth can be calculated from transducer spacing, velocity, and flight time [7], [8], [9]. TOFT is one of the most accurate crack sizing techniques available.

It is used to establish crack depth profiles at intervals, and on completion of a test thus providing a good cross check on ACPD measurements. Although it may be used either inside or outside the model, it is much more convenient to work from the outside. This of course requires the model to be extracted from the pressure chamber.

EXPERIMENTAL AND THEORETICAL RESULTS FROM TESTS ON S-SERIES MODELS

Two S-series models (S8/1 and S8/2) in Q1(N) steel to the design in Figure 3 have been tested in the SFC as part of the overall programme. Both were built to the same welding fabrication specification. This duplication allowed reproducibility of fabrication procedures (in terms of induced restraint stress levels) and test results to be assessed. With regard to the first, the average restraint moment induced at the toe of the stiffener weld, in MNm/m, was 0.125 and 0.111 for S8/1 and S8/2 respectively [10]. These correspond to nominal bending stress to yield stress ratios of 0.80 and 0.79 indicating very consistent fabrication procedures.

The generalised fatigue test procedure is illustrated in Figure 5. Pressure cycling was carried out in approximately 2,000 cycle stages with a break for NDE (eddy current) at the end of each stage. As the test progressed cycling intervals were increased. Prior to cycling, a baseline NDE survey was carried out in which eddy current and ACPD measurements were taken at 5 degree intervals round the circumference of the model at both forward and aft toes of the frame to hull T-butt weld. These were repeated at the end of each cycling stage right up to final failure. In each model, fatigue cracking occurred at one weld toe only.

S8/1 failed after approximately 46,000 cycles sustaining a through crack at 270 degrees about 150 mm (6") long initiating from the forward T-butt weld toe. S8/2 failed at approximately 40,000 cycles with through cracks of about 250 mm (10") long at 270 degrees and 100 mm (4") at 90 degrees. Figure 6 shows the cracking in S8/2.

The ACPD measured crack depth (a) and eddy current readings were plotted against the number of fatigue cycles (N) for each of the 72 measurement stations on each model; Figures 7 and 8 show typical plots. The main difference between curves at each station were the number of cycles to initiation and the extent of the straight line portion and consequently the crack depth at which growth rate tailed off.

A study of the eddy current and ACPD curves for each model indicated that the earliest initiations for S8/1 and S8/2 were around 12,000 and 4,000 cycles respectively. The development of initiation sites at the toe of the T-butt weld is shown as a polar plot in Figure 9, for S8/2, and is typical of both models. The circumference represents the toe of the weld and the radius the shell thickness. The figure shows that multiple, non-simultaneous initiation occurs. These sites develop circumferentially and radially as cycling proceeds until a full circumferential crack is formed. This formed in approximately 20,000 cycles in S8/1 and 14,000 cycles in S8/2. Figure 10 illustrates the development of the full circumferential crack to final failure in S8/2. In both models through cracking occurred at or near to the positions of the longitudinal seam welds, ie where the circumferential T-butt crosses the longitudinal seam, Figure 11. The local stress strain approach (LSSA) to fatigue crack initiation prediction [11, 12] using the computer program in [13] gave reasonable agreement with

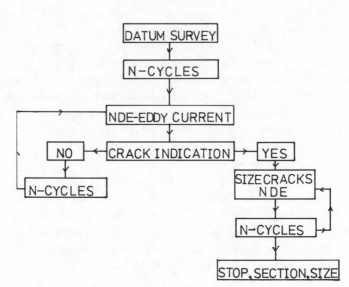

FIGURE 5. Fatigue Test Procedure for SFC and LFC Models.

FIGURE 6. Through Hull Fatigue Cracking in Model S8/2.

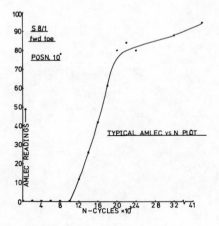

FIGURE 7.   Typical Eddy Current/Fatigue Cycles Plot.

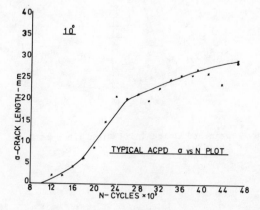

FIGURE 8.   Typical ACPD Crack Length/Fatigue Cycles Plot.

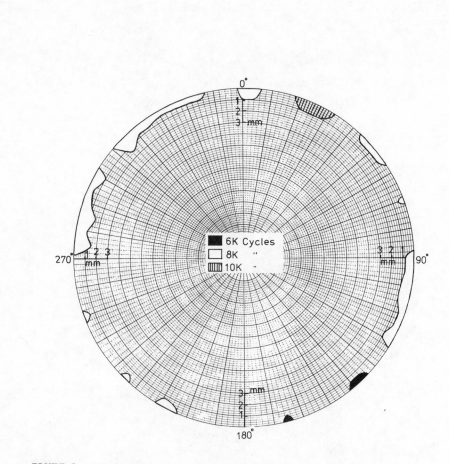

FIGURE 9. Development of Crack Initiation Sites in Model S8/2 (Crack Lengths Measured by ACPD).

317

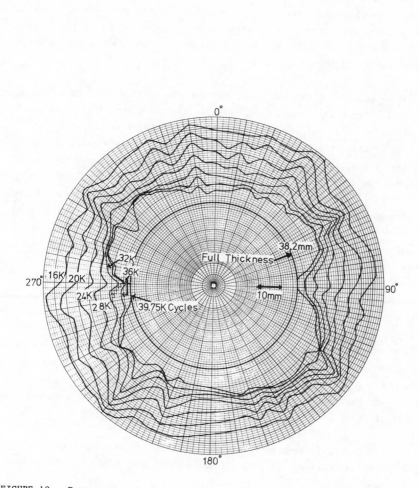

FIGURE 10.   Propagation from Full Circumferential Crack to Through Shell
Crack in Model S8/2.

lives to first initiation in the models. However, it is important to note that in neither model did final failure occur at the position of first initiation. Cycles to first initiation were approximately 10-12,000 in S8/1 and 4-6,000 in S8/2, whereas cycles to initiation at failure positions were roughly 12-14,000 for S8/1 and 10-14,000 for S8/2.

The quality of the NDE crack sizing techniques used on the models is given in Figure 12. This shows, in polar plot form, the final crack depth profile for model S8/2 as measured by ACPD and TOFT together with the actual profile obtained by sectioning and optical measurement. The ACPD is generally good although at certain positions it underestimates the crack depth. In S8/2 the maximum discrepancy is about 20%. The reasons for this are under investigation; possibilities include crack closure, non-metallic inclusions or crack branching etc. There is of course always the possibility of operator error in the cramped conditions under which these measurements were made inside a model only 1.2 m (4') ID. The TOFT was in very good agreement with the actual profile.

Figure 13 shows the measured crack depths versus number of cycles for all positions (S8/1 only). By defining initiation as a 2 mm deep crack the very long initiation lives of many of the positions is eliminated. This allows a direct comparison of growth rates from which it is seen that crack propagation rate is similar at all positions over the nearly linear part of the curves. The very wide spread from about 16,000 cycles on is due to the fact that most positions did not crack right through, and reflects the range of final crack depths.

A theoretical fracture mechanics prediction of crack propagation in the models was carried out [14, 15] using the linear elastic crack growth relationship,

$$da/dN = c(\Delta K)^n$$

The analysis required a knowledge of applied and residual/restraint stresses, material constants c and n, and the stress intensity factors (K) corresponding to the appropriate applied, (Ka), and residual, (Kr), stresses. The compressive applied stresses generated at the T-butt weld toe due to the external pressure loading were obtained using a finite

319

FIGURE 11. Through Crack at 270° in S8/1 - Also Shows Crossing Seam Weld.

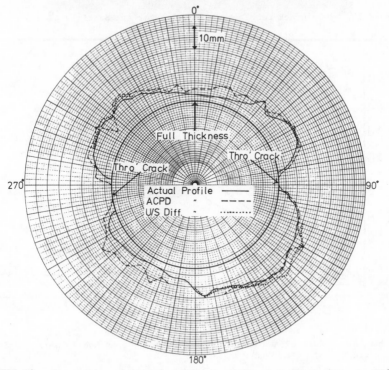

FIGURE 12. Comparison of Actual and Measured Final Crack Profile in S8/2.

320

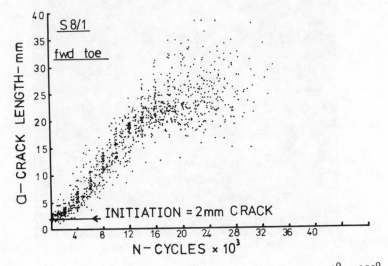

FIGURE 13. ACPD Crack Length versus Cycles for All Stations 0° – 355°.

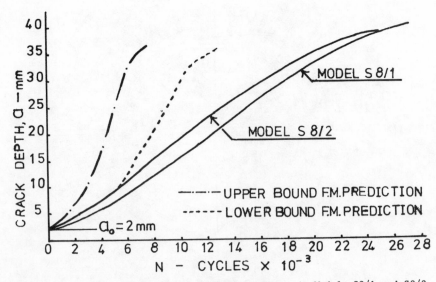

FIGURE 14. Predicted and Actual Propagation Lives in Models S8/1 and S8/2 at Similar Thro' Crack Positions.

element stress analysis programme [14, 15] while the through plate thickness residual stress distribution at the toe was deduced from the net
restraint moment obtained from strain gauge measurements made before and
after welding up the T-butt weld [10]. The crack propagation material
constants c and n used to give da/dN in mm/cycle for K in $MNm^{-3/2}$ were
taken from da/dN versus ΔK data on laboratory scale fatigue crack propagation tests in Q1(N) steel [16]. The values were:

$$\text{Upper Bound,} \quad c = 1.207 \quad x \ 10^{-6}, \quad n = 1.91$$
$$\text{Lower Bound,} \quad c = 6.90 \quad x \ 10^{-7}, \quad n = 1.91$$

Values for ΔK (the tensile component of the change in K during
cycling) were obtained by deriving the Kr and Ka relationships with crack
depth using the programme in [14]. The peak stress intensity during a
pressure cycle is that due to residual stresses acting alone in the unpres-
surised model (Kr). The application of external pressure reduces Kr to a
minimum value of (Kr + Ka), where Ka is the negative stress intensity
factor due to the compressive applied stress. If /Ka/ < Kr the net tensile
stress cycle is ΔK = /Ka/. If /Ka/ > Kr, ΔK = /Kr/.

Using this analysis procedure model propagation life predictions were
made in the form of crack depth (a) versus number of cycles (N) curves.
Upper and lower bound curves were derived using appropriate c and n values
for comparison with the experimentally derived curves. For this the
relevant ACPD a versus N results are those from the positions over which
the crack had fully penetrated the hull at similar positions (270/275 for
S8/1 and 260/270 for S8/2).

Figure 14 shows the relevant curves. It can be seen that there is
very good agreement between the models. The lower bound curve from the
fracture mechanics fatigue analysis shows the better agreement with the
experimental data while still providing a conservative estimate of crack
growth rate.

Table 1 gives the ratio of experimental to predicted propagation life
to a given crack depth for each model. It may be seen that the upper bound
predicted lives are out by a factor of two to three on the experimental
values. The lower bound curve gives better agreement, in this case the

TABLE 1

Predicted and Actual Fatigue Lives of Models S8/1 and S8/2

Crack Depth	N(exp)/N(pred)			
	S8/1		S8/2	
mm	UB	LB	UB	LB
5	2.57	1.5	1.71	1.00
10	2.33	1.30	1.80	1.00
15	2.51	1.44	2.00	1.15
20	2.69	1.55	2.26	1.39
25	2.92	1.65	2.58	1.50
30	3.13	1.78	2.86	1.63

factor lies between one and two. Viewed in these terms the theoretical model (lower bound) is reasonably satisfactory.

There are various factors which may have contributed to the prediction of shorter lives, eg biaxial loading in the models reducing crack tip stress intensity, crack closure, the assumption in the fatigue analysis of a circumferentially uniform crack depth during propagation, interruptions in cycling, relaxation of restraint stresses as the crack grows, uncertainty about residual stress patterns at crossing welds and the accuracy of restraint stress measurements. These aspects require attention if the theoretical prediction capability is to be improved.

CONCLUSIONS

Adherence to the current UK pressure vessel fatigue design code for the compressively loaded submarine situation leads to unacceptably low fatigue lives. This together with the inadequacy of small scale laboratory tests and the requirement to provide reassurance as to the fatigue resistance of pressure hulls led to the formulation of a fatigue model programme.

As part of the ARE Fatigue Model Programme the fatigue crack initiation and propagation characteristics of two identical S-series models under external pressure cycling has been determined using NDE crack detection and monitoring techniques.

The test results were in good agreement giving confidence in the scale model approach to the problem of fatigue in submarine pressure hulls.

Reproducibility of fabrication techniques has been demonstrated in that the induced restraint stresses at the bulkhead to hull T-butt weld were very similar.

In both models crack initiation occurred at the toe of the T-butt weld, with subsequent propagation proceeding from only one toe.

Non-simultaneous multiple site initiation was observed in both models these coalescing on further cycling to form a full circumferential crack. A wide spread of initiation lives was observed.

The local stress strain approach to initiation prediction appeared to give reasonable agreement with lives to first initiation; however, in neither model did final failure occur at the position of first initiation.

There was a preferred failure site in both models. Final failure in each model occurred at the position where the longitudinal seam weld crossed the circumferential T-butt weld. It would appear that the residual stress pattern at these positions exerts a strong influence.

Eddy current, ACPD and ultrasonic time of flight have been shown to be reliable NDE techniques for the detection and sizing of fatigue cracks in welded model structures.

A fracture mechanics fatigue analysis has been developed which allows a conservative estimate of crack growth in compressively cycled submarine models. The predictions based on lower bound growth constants were in fairly good agreement with the experimentally ACPD determined crack propagation at the through hull crack failure positions.

REFERENCES

1.   Kendrick, S.B., The AMTE fatigue programme philosophy. Unpublished MOD(PE) Report.

2.   Smith, T.P. and Beech, H.G., The application and use of eddy currents in non-destructive testing. Brit. J. Nondestructive Testing 18, (5), (1976) 137-173.

3. Dover, W.D., Charlesworth, F.D.W., Taylor, K.A., Collins, R. and
    Michael, D.H., The use of AC field measurements to determine the shape
    and size of a crack in a metal.
    In: Eddy Current Characterisation of Materials and Structures,
    Ed. by G. Birnam and G. Free, ASTM STP 722, (1981).

4. Dover, W.D., Charlesworth, F.D.W., Taylor, K.A., Collins, R. and
    Michael, D.H., AC field measurement-theory and practice.
    In: The Measurement of Crack Length and Shape During Fracture and
    Fatigue, Ed. by C.J. Beevers, Engineering Materials Advisory Service,
    Warley, (1980) 222-250.

5. Dover, W.D. and Collins, R., Recent advances in the detection and
    sizing of cracks using AC field measurements.
    Brit. J. of Nondestructive Testing, (1980) 291-295.

6. Livingstone, F., Cargill, J.M. and Kilpatrick. I.M., The alternating
    current potential drop (ACPD) 'on-line' method of fatigue crack
    sizing in submarine fatigue models. Unpublished MOD(PE) Report.

7. Silk, M.G. and Lidington, B.H., Defect sizing using the ultrasonic
    time delay approach. Brit. J. Nondestructive Testing (1975) 33-36.

8. Silk, M.G., Defect sizing using ultrasonic Diffraction.
    Brit. J. Nondestructive Testing (1979).

9. Cecco, V.S., Ultrasonic time-of-flight, B-scan presentation.
    AERE R10877, (1983).

10. Smith, W.J., Measurement of restraint stresses during building of
    models S8/1 and S8/2. Unpublished MOD(PE) Report.

11. Lawrence, F.V. Jr., Mattos, R.J., Higashida, Y. and Burk, J.D.,
    Estimating the fatigue crack initiation life of welds.
    In: Fatigue Testing of Weldments, Ed. by D.W. Hoepner,
    ASTM STP 648, (1978).

12. Rosenberg, T.D., The local stress-strain approach to fatigue analysis,
    Weld. Inst. Res. Bul. (1985) 10-17.

13. Ellingwood, B. and Martin, D., A computer program for simulating
    deformation response and crack initiation under cyclic loading.
    DTNSRDC 5602/39 (1976).

14. Hugill, P.N. and Sumpter, J.D.G., Stress intensities for crack growth
    prediction in S8 fatigue models. Unpublished MOD(PE) Report.

15. Hugill, P.N., NOCJS4 - Framed cylinder fatigue crack growth programme.
    Unpublished MOD(PE) Report.

16. Jones, B.F., High strength ferrous alloys for critical Naval
    applications. Unpublished MOD(PE) Report.

    N.B. MOD(PE) Reports quoted are not necessarily available to members
          of the public or to commercial organisations.

DESIGN AGAINST FRACTURE IN WELDED STRUCTURES

J D G Sumpter
Admiralty Research Establishment
Dunfermline, Fife, Scotland

ABSTRACT

Test and analysis methods used for predicting fracture safety are reviewed. Application of both empirical and fracture mechanics methods to high strength (550 to 750 MN/m^2) welded structures operating in their ductile to brittle transition temperature regime is considered. Tests near 0°C show that high strength weld metals typically exhibit low resistance to cleavage initiation, but good crack propagation resistance. The low resistance to cleavage initiation in deeply notched fracture mechanics test pieces may require designs to be validated by the testing of non-standard shallow notched specimens which are more structurally representative and give higher toughness. Alternatively, the adequacy of the weld's crack propagation resistance can be demonstrated by a large scale type-test such as the flawed bulge explosion test.

INTRODUCTION

In spite of intensive research over the past 40 years many problems still remain in predicting the fracture-safety of welded structures. This paper examines some of the approaches that are available, and highlights their advantages and shortcomings. Because of the complexity of the problem it is understandable that many of the methods used have been largely empirical in nature and angled towards one particular type of material or structure. Similarly, this review, although attempting to present a broad perspective on the subject, inevitably draws heavily on the author's own experience in assessing the defect tolerance of weld metals to be used in military submarine pressure hulls fabricated from steels in the 550 to 750 MN/m^2 strength range. For this application the service requirements are particularly severe, in that the welds must be capable of surviving high plastic deformation under explosive loads without pressure hull rupture. Many of the factors which must be taken into account when trying

to achieve this high level of performance are nevertheless inherent in the
nature of the welding process, and similar problems must be resolved,
albeit at a less onerous level, when assessing the fracture safety of any
welded structure.

TEST METHODS

Fracture research is notable for the very large number of different
tests which have achieved wide recognition in the literature, all nominally
measuring the same material property 'toughness'. In reality all of these
tests measure a slightly different aspect of material behaviour, and
attempts to find correlations between the toughness coefficients derived by
different test methods often prove impossible. The tests fall into three
main categories - type tests, empirical tests, and fracture mechanics
tests.

Type Tests (Wells Wide Plate, Robertson Crack Arrest, Pellini Bulge)

The aim here is to simulate, as far as is possible on a laboratory
scale, the characteristics of the structure (temperature, loading rate,
applied stress, defect type and location). In principle, therefore, the
results of these tests should be wholly unambiguous. The obvious drawback
is that the tests are difficult and expensive to perform. There is a considerable disincentive to carry out repeat tests. As a consequence it is
difficult to assess the potential scatter in structural performance, and
to conduct parametric surveys on, for instance, the effect which variations
in welding parameters may have on material behaviour.

Empirical Tests (Charpy, Dynamic Tear, Drop Weight Nil Ductility Transition)

Material development and quality control require a specimen which is
easy to manufacture and test. After eighty years of use the Charpy test
(Figure 1) remains firmly entrenched in this role. The shortcomings of the
Charpy specimen: its small size and blunt notch; its use of impact loading;
and the difficulty of interpreting its toughness index of absorbed energy
in terms of structurally meaningful parameters such as applied stress and
crack size have all been exhaustively documented. In spite of these shortcomings the Charpy specimen continues to be specified and used because of
its convenience and familiarity.

The Dynamic Tear test (Figure 1) is similar in concept to the Charpy test, but removes two obvious failings of the latter by using a larger specimen with a sharp crack. Unfortunately the energy required to break the specimen is typically ten times that for the Charpy, requiring a change from a simple pendulum machine to a drop tower assembly with attendant problems in energy measurement. For this reason there is little likelihood that the test will ever become as popular as the Charpy. Currently the main user is the US Navy, who employ it to assess weld and plate material for surface ships and submarines.

The Drop Weight Nil-ductility transition NDT test (Figure 1) employs a brittle weld bead deposited on one side of a small bend bar of the material under test. The specimen is subjected to a fixed angle of bend under drop weight loading. The suitability of the material for service is judged by the temperature at which it is able to arrest the running crack which emerges from the brittle weld bead. Above this temperature, termed the nil-ductility transition temperature (NDTT), the material can be said to have an increasing ability to tolerate small brittle areas and defects of the type which inevitably occur in welded structures.

Fracture Mechanics Tests (Plane Strain Fracture Toughness, Crack Tip Opening Displacement, J Integral)

The development of linear elastic fracture mechanics theory based on stress intensity factor, K, in the late 1950s, followed some ten years later by usable elastic-plastic methodologies based on crack tip opening displacement, CTOD or δ, and the J contour integral, has in principle made it possible to combine the virtues of the type test and quality control test in a single procedure. The fracture mechanics approach consists of testing a fatigue cracked specimen (typical examples are shown in Figure 2) at a controlled rate whilst monitoring both specimen load and displacement. The load and displacement at which fracture occurs are used to calculate a critical fracture toughness for the material. Fracture mechanics theory can then be used to predict the combinations of crack size and applied stress or strain which would result in this same critical toughness being exceeded in the structural application. In practice, the conditions under which currently proposed fracture mechanics criteria remain invariant with changes in crack size and loading geometry are still incompletely understood. In addition, the fracture mechanics methods currently standardised

FIGURE 1. Dynamic Tear (back), Drop Weight NDT (centre) and Charpy (front).

FIGURE 2. Crack Tip Opening Displacement specimens: through cracked (back), surface cracked (front).

are concerned with characterising the toughness at first fracture instability. Theories to quantify crack propagation and arrest are still in the
early stages of development.

FRACTURE SAFE DESIGN METHODS

Transition Temperature Approaches

Structural steels and their weld metals undergo a distinct change in
fracture mode with increasing temperature. At low temperatures fracture is
by cleavage. Once the threshold toughness for crack initiation has been
exceeded, the energy requirement for crack extension is so low that it can
usually be supplied by the release of stored elastic energy from the
system. Structural failure is consequently catastrophic unless fracture
initiation is avoided. At higher temperatures fracture initiation is by
growth and coalescence of voids, with subsequent crack extension being
sustained only by further increases in applied load or displacement. The
temperature marking the change in fracture mode is termed the ductile to
brittle transition temperature, and is a function of loading rate,
structural thickness, and notch acuity, as well as material microstructure.
Because of these complications fracture avoidance methods based on Charpy
energy or other transition temperature indices tend to rely for their
justification on correlation with a structurally relevant type test or
fracture mechanics test. Hence: BS5500 Appendix D [1] recommends Charpy
energy requirements to avoid fracture in Carbon-Manganese pressure vessels
based on correlation with the Wells Wide Plate test; and ASME III
Appendix G [2] specifies safe operating temperatures for nuclear reactor
pressure vessels based on correlation between Charpy energy, NDTT, and a
lower bound plane strain fracture toughness curve. Procedures such as
these usually work adequately for the restricted class of materials and
application for which they were derived. It is, however, virtually
impossible to construct an empirically based design approach which will
adequately cover all types of material and structure.

Fracture Mechanics Methods

Three approaches have attracted attention in the UK in recent years:
British Standard PD6493, based on CTOD, developed by the Welding Institute
[3]; the CEGB R6 method [4]; and a J based design curve, termed EnJ,

developed at Imperial College [5]. In the US a 'general engineering
scheme' for the estimation of J has been developed under the auspices of
EPRI [6]. Although these methods differ in detail, and their application
to the same problem can sometimes lead to different conclusions, the basic
concept is essentially the same in all cases. The severity of the structural flaw is estimated as a function of its size and applied stress or
strain by a crack tip parameter K, J, or δ. The structure is predicted to
be fracture-safe provided this estimated value is comfortably below that
found to be critical in a specimen tested at the loading rate and temperature appropriate to service conditions. Rules governing test piece dimensions are rather complex, but specimen sizes and crack depths are generally
much larger than those used in empirical tests. For a more sophisticated
structural analysis, any doubt over the accuracy of the estimation procedure embodied in a particular code can be removed by calculating K, J,
or δ directly using finite element analysis. 2D elastic analyses of this
type are now routine. Extension to three dimensions and to elastic-plastic
behaviour is becoming increasingly available with faster computers and more
efficient programs. The question remains - having made the best possible
estimate of K, J, or δ how closely will structural failure conditions be
predicted?

The present author would identify the major uncertainties as

(i)   the geometry dependence of presently postulated elastic-plastic
fracture criteria J_c and δ_c.

(ii) scatter in material toughness at a given test condition.

(iii) inadequate characterisation of residual stresses in as-welded
structures.

The importance of these various factors depends on the type of problem
being analysed. In ascending order of difficulty structural problems could
be categorised as follows

Category I   Brittle behaviour, elastic failure, homogeneous plate or
              stress relieved weld.

Category II   Ductile behaviour, elastic–plastic failure, material
               as I.

Category III   Transition temperature behaviour, elastic–plastic
               failure, material as I.

Category IV   As III but in un–stress relieved weld metal.

For category I where plasticity is limited to a very small region at the
crack tip, and elastic fracture theory is fully applicable, only material
scatter should affect the accuracy of the structural failure prediction.
Category II is an area where much effort has recently been expended in the
US in relation to failure avoidance for nuclear components. In general
such failures tend to be as much affected by a material's flow stress as
they are by its fracture properties. Geometry dependence and scatter do
play a role in ductile tearing failure, but their effects are less pro–
nounced than in the case of the cleavage failure mechanism which is
dominant in category III. Finally category IV combines all three uncer–
tainty factors in their extreme form. Scatter is especially severe in the
complex microstructure of as–deposited weld metals. If residual stresses
are known accurately their effect can be accounted for by appropriate
enhancement of the crack tip parameter. Unfortunately this is seldom the
case and some conservative estimate of residual stress magnitude and
distribution must be adopted. This can easily lead to an unrealistically
pessimistic prediction of failure conditions. On the other hand, complete
neglect of residual stresses in an as–welded structure will certainly
result in an overoptimistic appraisal unless the applied loading is well
above the yield stress.

Because the lower bound of the toughness scatter band is well below
the average in weld metals and weld heat affected zones, there is often a
requirement to show that cracks which are predicted to initiate will soon
arrest. This subject remains largely unquantified particularly with regard
to the role of shear lips and the propagation behaviour of surface breaking
semi–elliptical cracks. This and other topics reviewed in the introductory
sections will now be discussed with reference to ARE data on high strength
weld metals.

ARE DATA ON WELD METAL TOUGHNESS

Scatter in CTOD Testing

The following distribution of δ_c[†] values was obtained from one submerged arc weld for which sixteen surface notched CTOD specimens (Figure 2) were tested at a single temperature in the ductile to brittle transition region.

Toughness range Critical CTOD mm	Number of results
$\delta_c < 0.06$	6
$0.05 < \delta_c < 0.25$	4
$\delta_c > 0.25$	6

The average value was 0.17 mm with the minimum being 0.01 mm and the maximum 0.56 mm. Subsequent microstructural examination showed that the specimens divided into two groups. All specimens with δ_c less than 0.05 mm had their crack tips in as-deposited weld metal; that is, weld metal where the microstructure had not been refined by reheating from subsequent weld runs. In the remaining specimens, lowest toughness $\delta_c = 0.10$ mm, the crack tip was in the grain refined type of microstructure. The effect is illustrated in Figure 3. Although not all weld deposits have such clear delineation between as-deposited and grain refined regions, a complex multi-phase microstructure inevitably results from the differential heating and cooling rates experienced by different areas of the weld. Scatter in

---

[†] δ_c, J_c and K_{Jc} are used interchangeably in this report. The approximate equivalence is

$$K_{Jc} = \left[J_c E \right]^{1/2} = \left[2\delta_c \, \sigma_Y E \right]^{1/2}$$

where E is Young's modulus and σ_Y is yield stress. Any of these toughness parameters may be calculated from a static or dynamic test on fracture mechanics specimens of the type shown in Figure 2. This specimen is referred to as a CTOD (crack tip opening displacement) specimen throughout the text irrespective of the toughness parameter calculated from it.

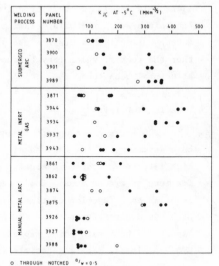

FIGURE 3. Fatigue crack tip in (top) as deposited, and (bottom) refined microstructure

FIGURE 4. Comparison between through and surface cracked δ_c

toughness will always be more extreme than it is in plate material, where care is taken to homogenise the microstructure through careful heat treatment.

The scatter in toughness experienced with surface notched weld metal CTOD specimens has led some investigators to adopt a through notched specimen (Figure 2) with the crack running along the weld. It is argued that a crack in this orientation will sample the whole range of microstructure, and will, by a weakest link principle, yield the minimum toughness appropriate to that particular welded joint. In the present author's experience this conclusion is not always substantiated. Figure 4 shows individual surface and through notched results at a given temperature for sixteen different weldments. It can be seen that the through notched results can lie almost anywhere in the scatter band of surface notched data. A drawback of the through notched specimen is that it requires precompression prior to fatigue cracking to equalise residual stresses across the weld

thickness. This is not required in the surface notched specimen. The surface notched specimen also closely resembles the structural geometry where
a crack is likely to start at a free surface and penetrate part way through
the thickness of the weld. Taking all these factors into account, the
author currently favours the use of surface notched specimens, accepting
that the scatter which they produce provides a realistic simulation of
structural behaviour.

Dynamic CTOD Testing

CTOD tests may be performed dynamically as well as statically. ARE
have investigated the rate sensitivity of a range of weld metals using a
high rate servo-hydraulic machine capable of reducing the event time to
fracture to around 5 ms. Load and displacement are recorded on a transient
recorder as a function of time. Results for sixteen different weldments
with yield strength in the range 550 to 750 MN/m^2 are presented in
Figure 5. Each data point represents the average of four surface notched
CTOD specimens. Plate materials in this strength range are normally
expected to show some decrease in toughness with increasing strain rate.
There is no consistent evidence of this trend in the present data. Indeed
when individual static and dynamic results are compared, as is done in
Figure 6 for MIG welds, it is tempting to conclude that any variations
between dynamic and static toughness are simply the result of scatter.

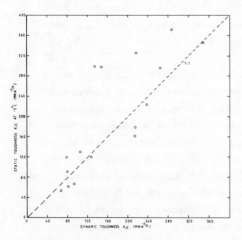

FIGURE 5. Comparison between dynamic and
static K$_{Jc}$ (averaged values)

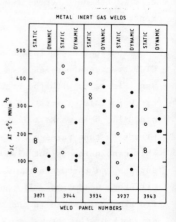

FIGURE 6. Comparison
between dynamic and static
K$_{Jc}$ (individual values)

Comparison with Empirically Based Toughness Design Curves

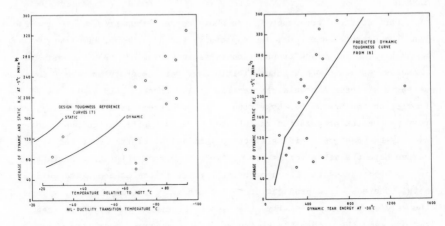

FIGURE 7. Comparison between
actual and predicted [7] K_{Jc}
values

FIGURE 8. Comparison between
actual and predicted [8] K_{Jc}
values

Figure 7 compares the CTOD data presented in the last section with
design reference static and dynamic fracture toughness curves based on NDTT
proposed recently by Pellini [7]. Drop weight NDTT for the welds tested
lay in the range $-30^{\circ}C$ to $-95^{\circ}C$. All CTOD tests were performed at $-5^{\circ}C$.
In line with the conclusions of the previous section the dynamic and static
CTOD data have been averaged together to give a single data point at some
variable distance above NDTT for each different weldment. It can be seen
that the design reference curves based on NDTT are highly overoptimistic
for the welds tested here.

A similar conclusion can be reached for design procedures based on
Dynamic Tear energy [8]. This approach requires that a temperature shift
for thickness be made, such that the 16 mm thick Dynamic Tear energy is
obtained at some fixed temperature below that at which the structural
toughness is required. Assuming the toughness is required at 50 mm thickness, corresponding to that used in the CTOD tests, the thickness shift is
$25^{\circ}C$. Figure 8 shows the resultant comparison between predicted and actual
toughness, the actual toughness data points being the same as those plotted
in Figure 7. Although not as unconservative as the NDTT correlation, there
are still many actual toughness data points lying well below the Dynamic
Tear based prediction line.

Crack Propagation Resistance. Comparison with Lower Strength Structural Steels

Part of the discrepancy in the above correlations arises from the fact that the Dynamic Tear test, and especially the Drop Weight NDT test, measure primarily crack propagation resistance, whilst the CTOD test measures resistance to fracture initiation. At temperatures near 0°C lower strength structural steels characteristically possess good static initiation toughness, but by virtue of their extreme rate sensitivity, have very poor crack propagation resistance. Fracture safe design must consequently be based on avoiding fracture initiation. In the weld metals tested here the situation is very different. Crack initiation resistance is poor because of the frequent brittle zones in the as-deposited weld metal, whereas crack propagation resistance is relatively high by virtue of the weld's rate insensitivity, the high toughness of the grain refined regions, and the propensity of the weld to form large shear lips which inhibit crack extension.

Figure 9 shows the heat tinted surface of Drop Weight NDT specimens for a typical manual weld. Break conditions (crack propagates completely along top surface) do not occur until the temperature drops to -65°C. At -5°C a small amount of crack propagation is still evident under the brittle weld bead, but there is no tendency for the crack to propagate along the surface of the specimen. A similar effect is evident from the heat tinted fracture surfaces of through notched CTOD specimens in Figure 10. There is a clear tendency for the weld to resist brittle fracture near a free surface. This has the advantage of constraining the crack to tunnel into a shape which is unfavourable for further extension. Significant further energy input is required to shear the uncracked surface ligaments. This behaviour is in complete contrast to structural steels, which, at the same initiation toughness exhibited by many of the weld metals at -5°C, show crack propagation by completely flat fracture with little evidence of shear lips. A typical example from a dynamic CTOD test on a BS1501-151-28A pressure vessel forging is shown in Figure 11. The initiation toughness for this specimen was K_{Jc} = 150 MN/m$^{3/2}$. This can be contrasted with the very large shear lips on the surface of the weld metal specimen in Figure 12 which exhibited an initiation toughness of only K_{Jc} = 75 MN/m$^{3/2}$. Specimen thickness was 50 mm in both cases.

337

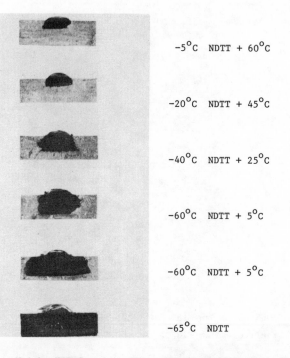

-5°C NDTT + 60°C

-20°C NDTT + 45°C

-40°C NDTT + 25°C

-60°C NDTT + 5°C

-60°C NDTT + 5°C

-65°C NDTT

FIGURE 9. Drop Weight NDT fracture faces. Heat tinting shows extent of crack propagation during test.

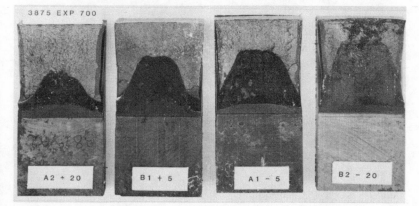

FIGURE 10. Through cracked CTOD fracture faces. Heat tinting shows extent of crack propagation during test. (Specimens have been deformed well beyond initial instability).

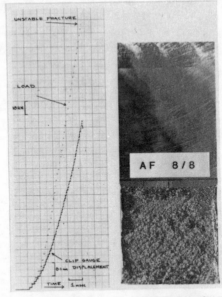

FIGURE 11. Dynamic CTOD trace fracture surface for mild steel tested at $+10^{\circ}C$. $K_{JC} = 150$ MN/m$^{3/2}$.

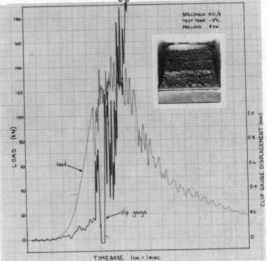

FIGURE 12. Dynamic CTOD trace and fracture surface for manual weld yield stress 700 MN/m^2 tested at $-5^{\circ}C$. $K_{Jc} = 75$ MN/M$^{3/2}$.

Crack Depth Effects on Initiation Toughness

The poor initiation toughness of many high strength weld metals apparently renders them unusable on the basis of conventional fracture mechanics analysis. The picture changes if notch depth effects are taken into account. Figure 13 shows dynamic CTOD data on a manual and a submerged arc weld at -5°C as a function of depth of surface crack. Suppose it is required that a structure fabricated from these two weldments be able to sustain a strain slightly in excess of yield at -5°C. Critical crack size predictions can be made using the EnJ relationship [5]

$$\frac{1}{Y^2 \pi a} \left[\frac{K_J}{\sigma_y}\right]^2 = 2.5 \left[\left(\frac{e}{e_Y}\right) - 0.2\right]$$

where Y is a linear elastic crack shape factor, a is crack depth, e is applied strain, σ_y is yield stress and e_Y is yield strain. For a long surface breaking crack Y = 1.12, thus for an applied strain of $e/e_Y = 1.2$

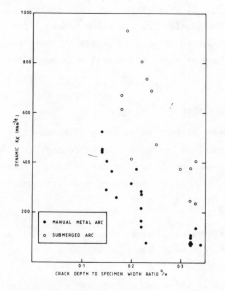

FIGURE 13. K_{Jc} as a function of crack depth. Dynamic CTOD tests on high strength weld metal at -5°C.

$$a_c \ (mm) \quad = \quad 100 \ \left(\frac{K_{Jc}}{\sigma_Y}\right)^2$$

where a_c is the critical crack depth. For a CTOD specimen with the standard depth of surface notch, a/W = 0.3, where W is specimen depth, minimum K_{Jc} values are 75 MN/m$^{3/2}$ for the manual weld and 225 MN/m$^{3/2}$ for the submerged arc weld. Yield stress is approximately 650 MN/m^2 for both welds so that predicted critical crack sizes become just over 1 mm for the manual weld and nearly 12 mm for the submerged arc weld. Clearly, on this evidence, the manual weld would have to be discarded as unsuitable for its structural application. Suppose, however, that the analysis is turned around, firstly by postulating that a particular crack depth, say a = 7.5 mm, is acceptable from an NDE viewpoint; and secondly by calculating the critical strain for this crack depth using the appropriate toughness from Figure 13. At a/W = 0.15, the minimum K_{Jc} for the manual weld becomes 275 MN/m$^{3/2}$. (Assumption of this toughness would be questionable in a structure subjected to pure tension, but most practical structures have a significant non-linear stress component peaking at the surface and encouraging stress relaxation for a shallow crack). The critical strain then becomes e/e_Y = 5, comfortably in excess of that required by most design codes. On this approach the manual weld would appear quite acceptable.

Type-testing for Submarine Hull Welds

As a final type-test for the adequacy of submarine hull welds, ARE use the flawed bulge explosion test. The basic concept is similar to that developed by Pellini and co-workers at the US Naval Research Laboratories is the early 1950s [9], but the following modifications have been made to make the test less empirical

(i) A semi-elliptical fatigue crack of known length and depth is introduced into the weld prior to the test.

(ii) The panel is tested at the applied strain level and temperature relevant to service application.

FIGURE 14a. General view of a flawed bulge explosion panel after test.
Overall panel dimensions 760 mm by 760 mm by 50 mm thick.

FIGURE 14b. Crack extension in a flawed bulge test shown by heat tinting.

Finally, to minimise charge weight and environmental noise nuisance, the test is performed underwater with sheet contact explosive at a small stand-off from the plate surface.

A view of a tested panel is shown in Figure 14a. After testing the panel is heat tinted and broken open to reveal the extent of crack propagation (Figure 14b). Strain level is determined by applying the same explosive charge weight applied to the flawed panel to a defect free panel containing a strain grid. Repeat tests can be conducted on panels with various initial defect sizes to determine the critical defect size to initiate fracture instability under dynamic loading. In cracks that do initiate the test can be used to study the extent of propagation under structurally realistic conditions.

Prediction of Critical Crack Depth in Flawed Bulge Panels

Figure 15 shows the results of a flawed bulge panel series for the two welds for which data were presented in Figure 13. The vertical axis represents applied strain normalised by Y^2 from equation (1). Thus a long shallow surface flaw would have a Y^2e value of 1.25e, and a semi-circular surface flaw with $a/t = 0.3$ would have a Y^2e value of 0.16e (pure bending deformation assumed) where e is the applied strain previously determined at that charge weight from a defect free panel. Each individual data point represents a different flawed bulge test. Crack depth is taken to be that at the deepest point of a semi-elliptical fatigue crack. The predicted critical crack depths are derived from equation (1), with toughness as a function of crack depth from Figure 13. Residual stresses need not be included in the analysis because of the high plastic strains involved. Line LL represents the bottom of the scatter band in Figure 13. At crack depth strain combinations below and to the left of this line no failures would be expected from the bulge panels. Line TT represents the top of the scatter band in Figure 13. Above and to the right of this line it is expected that all bulge tests will result in unstable crack extension. Between these two lines specimens lie within the toughness scatter band with an increasing probability of failure as TT is approached. It is seen that the bulge panel results are generally consistent with these predictions, although the manual weld behaves less consistently than the submerged arc weld.

343

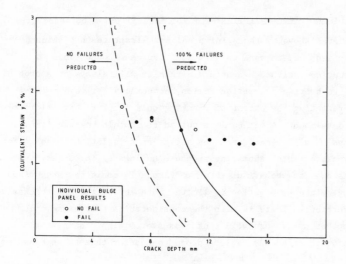

FIGURE 15a. Prediction of critical depth for crack extension in
flawed bulge panels (Manual Metal Arc).

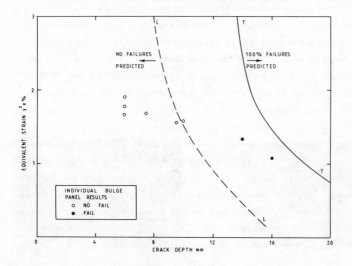

FIGURE 15b. Prediction of critical depth for crack extension in
flawed bulge panels (Submerged Arc).

Prediction of Crack Extension in Flawed Bulge Panels

As illustrated above, methods for predicting fracture initiation from laboratory specimens may be applied with some degree of confidence to structural situations, although scatter in results will always be a problem in the ductile to brittle transition region, especially for weld metals. Analyses for predicting the extent of cracking once fracture has initiated are less well developed. A method is required to explain why the crack in Figure 14b stops where it does, and does not go on to split the panel. For some applications, of which submarine pressure hull integrity under explosive loading is one, the behaviour shown in Figure 14 could be categorised as satisfactory, since propagation is limited both in the through thickness and length directions. There is also the consideration that since crack propagation depends on average weld toughness over a significant area, crack propagation theories may be less prone to scatter than those based on crack initiation.

Arguments in terms of crack shape factor can be advanced to explain why a crack of limited surface length will arrest once its depth significantly exceeds half the plating thickness in bending since its tip will then enter the zone of compressive stress beyond the plate neutral axis. Further through thickness extension can then be achieved only after shifting the neutral axis by lengthwise extension of the crack. As shown in Figure 14b, and as noted earlier in the context of DWNDT and CTOD tests, weld metals of the type tested here are very resistant to crack extension

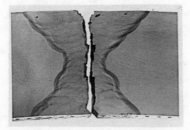 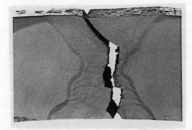

(a) at notch centre line   (b) away from notch centre line

FIGURE 16.   Sections through a fractured flawed bulge panel

at a free surface. Lengthwise extension at moderate applied strains can
occur only by tunnelling. At higher strain levels failure to the top
surface takes place along very large shear lips as shown in Figure 16.
Empirically a reasonable feel for the resistance to crack extension in
flawed bulge panels can be obtained from indices such as percentage
crystallinity in the Charpy test. Obviously, the higher the percentage
flat fracture seen in the laboratory specimen the less resistant the weld
is to crack extension at the free surface. More quantitative predictions
of the extent of cracking in a structure at various strain levels must
probably await the development of a theory capable of handling the complex
competing failure mechanisms which occur between the tunnelling crack and
the free surface. Development of such a theory will be considerably
hastened by the increasing availability of 3D elastic-plastic finite
element analysis.

CONCLUSIONS

Problems in predicting the fracture safety of welded structures have
been reviewed with particular reference to high strength welds in the yield
stress range 550 to 750 MN/m^2. Two types of method exist; those which rely
on an empirical test such as Charpy, Dynamic Tear, or Drop Weight NDT; and
those which employ fracture mechanics methods to calculate a critical
defect size at the intended operating conditions. Empirical methods may
work well for a restricted range of application but are liable to break
down when extended beyond their original data base. High strength weld
metals tend to have low cleavage initiation toughness, but reasonably good
crack propagation resistance. In this respect they differ considerably
from the rate sensitive structural steels from which most empirical
approaches were developed. Recent proposals based on NDTT and Dynamic Tear
energy are shown to lead to non-conservative predictions of cleavage
initiation toughness when applied to high strength weld metals. There are,
however, also problems in relying on conventional fracture mechanics when
assessing weldments. The heterogeneous microstructure in the weld leads to
considerable scatter in toughness as measured by J_c or δ_c. In addition,
these parameters are not geometry independent, higher values of J_c and δ_c
being recorded at structurally realistic shallow crack depths than in
standardised deeply cracked test specimens. The difficulty of characterising both crack initiation and crack propagation behaviour in a single

laboratory specimen means that type-testing is still required. ARE have adopted the underwater flawed bulge explosion test to fulfil this role when selecting suitable weld metals for submarine pressure hulls.

ACKNOWLEDGEMENT

The author gratefully acknowledges the invaluable collaboration of Mr A J Caudrey in acquiring the experimental data referenced in this report.

REFERENCES

1. British Standard specification for unfired fusion welded pressure vessels. Appendix D, Tentative recommended practice for carbon and carbon manganese steel vessels required to operate at low temperature. BS5500:1976.

2. ASME Boiler and Pressure Vessel code, Section III Nuclear power plant components. Appendix G, Protection against non-ductile failure, 1972.

3. British Standard published document, Guidance on some methods for the derivation of acceptance levels for defects in fusion welded joints. PD6493:1980.

4. Harrison, R.P., Loosemore, K., Milne, I. and Dowling, A.R., Assessment of the integrity of structures containing defects, CEGB Report R/H/R6 - Rev 2, 1980.

5. Turner, C.E., The J estimation curve, R curve, and tearing resistance concepts leading to proposals for a J based design curve against fracture. Welding Institute conference on Fitness for Purpose Validation of Welded Constructions, London November 1981.

6. Kumar, V., German, M.D. and Shih, C.F., An engineering approach for elastic-plastic fracture analysis. Electric Power Research Institute Report NP1931, 1981.

7. Pellini, W.S., Guidelines for Fracture-Safe and Fatigue-reliable Design of Steel Structures, 1983.

8. Lange, E.A., Dynamic fracture-resistance testing and methods for structural analysis, NRL Report 7979, 1976.

9. Hartbower, C.E. and Pellini, W.S., Explosion bulge test studies of the deformation of weldments. Welding Journal, June 1951, 307s-318s.

NUMERICAL ANALYSES OF THE LINEAR INTERACTION OF PRESSURE PULSES
WITH SUBMERGED STRUCTURES

H. Huang
Naval Surface Weapons Center
White Oak, Silver Spring, MD 20910,   U.S.A.

ABSTRACT

This paper discusses the dynamic response of submerged structures to the impingements of pressure pulses the strengths of which are such that their governing equations can be linearized. The range of validity of this linearization is assessed by comparing the linear and nonlinear solutions to a classical problem.

The numerical analysis technique for cases where the structure is surrounded by a noncavitating fluid utilizes the boundary element representation of the surrounding wave fields in conjunction with the finite element analysis of the structural response. The boundary element is formulated based upon the exact Kirchhoff Retarded Potential Integral solution to the linear wave equation. Therefrom a hierarchy of approximate boundary element formulations can also be obtained. The effectiveness of these formulations are examined by comparison of results to available classical solutions.

INTRODUCTION

To predict the dynamic response of a structure submerged in water and impinged upon by a pressure pulse, it is necessary to simultaneously solve the dynamic structural response and the pulse scattering problems due to the interaction amongst the incident pulse, the structure and its surrounding water medium. The scattered field includes the pressure field due to the submerged structure acting as an obstacle to the passage of the incident pulse and that due to the radiation by the vibratory structural response motion.

The general problem for arbitrary incident pulses is governed by the conservative principles of mass, momentum and energy of continuum mechanics and the constitutive equations of the materials involved. Due to the rapid expansion of computer technology in recent years, it appears feasible that the solution can be computed by modern nonlinear finite difference and/or finite element methods based on combined Lagrangian and Eulerian formulations. To this writer's knowledge, however, the state of the art of this approach is still in its infant stage as far as this interaction problem is concerned.

In the past four decades, the majority of the interaction problems attacked assumed linearized wave motions in the fluid medium. Most of the solutions were obtained based on the so called acoustic approximation [1-4] and some included the effect of cavitation, e.g., [5-8]. These solutions delineated many basic features of the problem. The extent of validity of the linearization, however, was seldom indicated.

The present paper aims to examine the criterion for linearization of the wave motion in the fluid, to appraise the validity of the linearized solution from a theoretical point of view and to discuss pertinent numerical techniques for solving practical problems.

FORMULATION OF
THE LINEAR INTERACTION PROBLEM

For short range propagation of pressure pulses in water, the heat conduction and the viscous effects are not significant and thus the propagation is governed by the Euler hydrodynamic equations of inviscid isentropic flows together with the equation of state of water [9].

$$\frac{\partial \rho}{\partial t} + \operatorname{div}(\rho \vec{v}) = 0 \tag{1}$$

$$\rho \frac{\partial \vec{v}}{\partial t} + \rho\,(\vec{v}.\mathrm{grad})\vec{v} = -\operatorname{grad} p \tag{2}$$

$$p = f(\rho) \tag{3}$$

where t represents time, v is the velocity of the fluid, its pressure and density are p and ρ respectively and an overhead arrow indicates vector quantities. Equation (1) is the continuity equation, equation (2) the momentum equation and equation (3) represents an isentropic equation of state which characterizes the material behavior of the propagating fluid medium. The isentropic equation of state is a relationship between the pressure and the density. For water, the most often used form for equation (3) is the Tait equation of state [9]

$$p - p_o = \frac{\rho_o c_o^2}{n} \left[\left(\frac{\rho}{\rho_o} \right)^n - 1 \right],$$ (4)

where

$$c_o^2 = \left(\frac{\partial p}{\partial \rho} \right)_{\rho_o}.$$ (5)

In the above two equations, the subscript o refers to the undisturbed water and n is equal to 7.15 in the case of sea water.

Applying Taylor expansions to equation (4) around the undisturbed state, the relationship between pressure and density can be written as

$$\frac{p - p_o}{\rho_o c_o^2} = \frac{\rho - \rho_o}{\rho_o} + \frac{n - 1}{2} \left(\frac{\rho - \rho_o}{\rho_o} \right)^2 + \frac{(n-1)(n-3)}{6} \left(\frac{\rho - \rho_o}{\rho_o} \right)^3 + \dots$$ (6)

or

$$\frac{\rho - \rho_o}{\rho_o} = \frac{p - p_o}{\rho_o c_o^2} + \frac{1 - n}{2} \left(\frac{p - p_o}{\rho_o c_o^2} \right)^2 + \frac{(1-n)(1-2n)}{6} \left(\frac{p - p_o}{\rho_o c_o^2} \right)^3 + \dots$$ (7)

If only the first term on the right hand side of either equation (6) or (7) is retained, they reduce to the linear acoustic pressure–density relationship which also implies constant propagation (sound) speed. The error of the linear acoustic pressure–density relationship for various overpressure magnitudes can be readily estimated by computing the corresponding changes of density in water and comparing results to those obtained by equation (4). The error percentage is tabulated in Table 1.

TABLE 1
Comparison of Acoustic and Tait's Equation of State for Water.

$(p-p_o)_{psi}$	$(p-p_o)/(\rho_o c_o^2)$	$(\rho-\rho_o)/\rho_o$		Error %
		Linear eqn	Tait eqn	
500	0.0014861	0.0014861	0.0014784	0.456
1,000	0.0029722	0.0029722	0.0029454	0.910
2.000	0.0059444	0.0059444	0.0058385	1.813
5,000	0.014861	0.014861	0.0142234	4.482
7,000	0.020805	0.020805	0.0195850	6.229
10,000	0.029722	0.029722	0.027317	8.805
12,000	0.035666	0.035666	0.032278	10.494
15,000	0.044583	0.044583	0.039457	12.989

It can be seen from the above table that for an over pressure of 5000 psi, which would be quite substantial for inducing structural responses, the error of using the linear relationship is below 5%. Even for an over pressure of 15,000 psi, the error is about 13%. Therefore, it appears quite justifiable, for overpressures in the range of thousands of psi, to use the linear relationship

$$\frac{p-p_o}{\rho_o c_o^2} = \frac{\rho-\rho_o}{\rho_o} \qquad (8)$$

as the equation of state neglecting the material nonlinearity in water. This linear equation can be likewise deduced from other equations of state for water such as the Gruneisen equation of state.

The particle velocity of the fluid behind a pressure discontinuity propagating with velocity U is [9]

$$v = \frac{\rho-\rho_o}{\rho} U. \qquad (9)$$

For small changes of density, it can be shown therefrom that

$$\frac{v}{U} = \left(\frac{\rho-\rho_o}{\rho_o}\right) - \left(\frac{\rho-\rho_o}{\rho_o}\right)^2 + \left(\frac{\rho-\rho_o}{\rho_o}\right)^3 - \ldots \qquad (10)$$

For pressure discontinuities in water, with magnitudes as those overpressures in Table 1, the induced particle velocities are only a small fraction of the corresponding propagation velocities. For instance, for a pressure discontinuity of 15,000 psi, the particle velocity is about 4% of the propagation velocity. Therefore, in this pressure range, the criterion [10] for dropping the convection terms $\vec{v}.\text{grad } \rho$ and $(\vec{v}.\text{grad})\ \vec{v}$ in equations (1) and (2) is also met and they are thus linearized. In other words, the "geometrical" nonlinearity is removed.

Equations (1), (2), and (3) linearized in this manner, can be combined to form the linear wave equation

$$\nabla^2 p = \frac{1}{c_o^2} \frac{\partial^2 p}{\partial t^2} \tag{11}$$

where ∇^2 is the Laplace operator. The mathematical theory and solution techniques for equation (11) have been firmly established and extensively documented since the last century.

For pulse–structure interaction problems, the boundary condition at the interface S between a structure and an inviscid fluid is that the component of the structural velocity normal to the interface is the same as the normal component of the fluid particle velocity. Due to equation (2), this boundary condition can be written for the linearized problem as

$$\rho \frac{\partial v_n}{\partial t} = - (\text{grad } p)_n \quad \text{on S,} \tag{12}$$

where subscript n refers to the normal component and $\frac{\partial v_n}{\partial t}$ is the structural normal acceleration at the fluid–structure interface.

The loading acting on the structure is the sum of the pressures due the incident and the scattered fields at the fluid–structure interface. The response of the structure is governed by appropriate equations of motion of structural dynamics. The structural behavior does not have to be confined to the linear regime even if the present linear fluid equations are used for the interaction problem.

This linearization for this class of problems is often termed the acoustic approximation. In view of equation (8), the criterion for linearization is not small pressure amplitudes but rather

$$\frac{p - p_o}{\rho_o c_o^2} \ll 1 . \tag{13}$$

To meet this criterion, the pressure amplitude could be many thousands of psi in water as previously calculated and only a few psi in air.

For the pulse-structure interaction problem, it is likely that the structural response motion in the direction away from the fluid could radiate a high amplitude tension wave into the surrounding fluid and that the combined field could be in tension. Since it is well known that water is unable to sustain much tension, cavitation could occur in the tension fluid region and the values for density and sound speed would be drastically different from those in the noncavitating region. The equation of state needs to be modified for the cavitated fluid or a two-phase fluid theory need be used for the interaction problem.

VALIDITY OF THE LINEAR
PULSE-STRUCTURE INTERACTIONS THEORY

Perhaps the first analytical solution obtained for this class of problems is for the response of a vacuo backed plate to an incident plane pressure wave as sketched in Figure 1. The uniform flat plate is of infinite extent with mass per unit area equal to m. Its right hand side is occupied

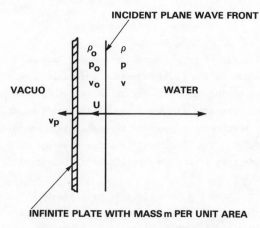

FIGURE 1. Interaction of an incident plane wave and
an infinite plate.

by water and its left hand side a vacuo. It is impinged upon by an incident
pressure pulse the wave front of which is parallel to the plate. The water
particle velocity and the response motion of the plate are in the x-direction
only. The problem is one-dimensional, i.e., any spatial variation is with
respect to x only. The equation of motion of the plate is simply

$$m \frac{dv_p}{dt} - (p_p - p_o) = 0 \tag{14}$$

where v_p is the plate velocity which is equal to the water particle
velocity at the plate and p_p is the resultant interaction pressure at the
plate. Prior to the arrival of the incident wave front, the plate and the
water are quiescent. The time when the incident wave front contacts the
plate is designated $t = 0$. The initial condition of the problem is the free
field pressure-time history of the incident wave at the point where the plate
is located. It is customarily represented by an exponentially decaying
function

$$p(t,x) - p_o = (\hat{p} - p_o)e^{-t/\theta} \tag{15}$$

where $\hat{p}$ is the peak pressure and θ the time constant of exponential decay.

To solve for the interaction pressure, equations (1), (2), and (3) are
needed. They form, for this problem, a one-dimensional hyperbolic system of
partial differential equations with the initial condition, equation (15) and
boundary condition, equation (14). If this system is linearized using the
acoustic approximation, an analytical solution is readily obtained and is
often referred to as Taylor's plate solution [11].

The solution to the nonlinear one-dimensional hyperbolic system can be
accurately computed by the well established method of characteristics. Snay
and Christian [12] performed such computations for incident waves of zero to
40 kilobars peak pressure and compared solutions to those obtained by the
acoustic approximation.

Typically, the time histories of the total pressure acting on the plate
are compared in Figure 2, where the conditions are that the incident wave
front pressure is 20 kilobars, a very high amplitude pressure wave, and that
$m/(\rho_o c_o \theta) = 1.0$. The pressure-time distribution appears to be quite
different for the nonlinear and the acoustic approximation results, since the
initial pressure is about 3.2 times the free-water pressure as indicated by
the rigorous nonlinear solution, whereas in the acoustic approximation, the

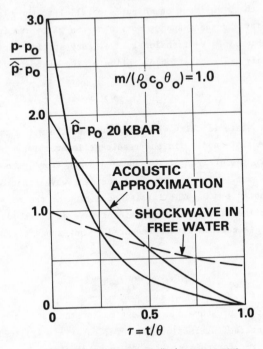

FIGURE 2. Effect of high-amplitude pressure wave
on plate pressure.

initial pressure is only twice that of the free-water pressure. Yet, the
areas under the two pressure-time curves (impulses) are comparable, the
acoustic approximation curve having somewhat higher impulse. The results
were computed up to the time when the resultant pressure acting on the plate
vanishes, since beyond that cavitation could occur, and the one-fluid theory
would not be valid.

The corresponding time histories of the plate velocity are compared in
Figure 3. The velocity is normalized with respect to the maximum free water
particle velocity [9]

$$\hat{v} = (\hat{p} - p_o)^{1/2} \left(\frac{1}{\rho_o} - \frac{1}{\rho} \right)^{1/2}. \tag{16}$$

The maximum plate velocity is reached at the time the resultant pressure
decays to zero as indicated by equation (14). The acoustic approximation

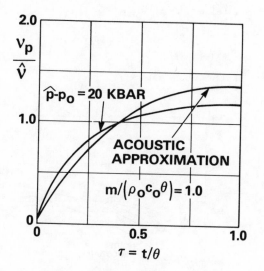

FIGURE 3. Effect of high-amplitude pressure
wave on plate velocity.

predicts the maximum plate velocity about 16% higher than the rigorous
theory. The agreement is better for the areas under the velocity–time curves
(displacements). The acoustic approximation still provides satisfactory
plate response results even for such a high-amplitude incident wave.

The energy flux of a high-amplitude wave in water is [9]

$$E = \int \rho \, v \, (\omega + v^2/2) dt \tag{17}$$

where v is the water particle velocity and

$$\omega = \int_{P_o}^{p} \frac{1}{\rho} \, dp. \tag{18}$$

In the acoustic approximation, the energy flux of a plane wave of exponential
decay calculated from equations (17) and (18) is

$$E = \frac{\theta}{2\rho_o c_o} (\hat{p} - p_o)^2. \tag{19}$$

356

The energy transmitted to the plate is

$$E_p = m v_M^2/2,$$ (20)

where v_M is the maximum plate velocity.

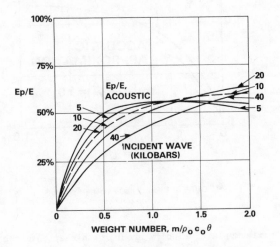

FIGURE 4. Plate energies in percent of the incident
wave energy.

The fraction of the energy that is transmitted to the plate relative to
the incident wave energy is plotted in Figure 4 for several different wave
amplitudes and for the acoustic approximation. Again, the Snay and Christian
results showed that the acoustic approximation for the energy transmitted to
the plate is quite satisfactory for moderately high amplitude incident
waves. This energy is of practical interest since it produces "damage" on
the target.

It would seem that the plate problem thus posed oversimplifies or
overidealizes any practical situation. On the contrary, the plate solution
has much practical significance as discussed in references [11-13]. Moreover, it has been analytically demonstrated [14-18] that the early time
transient response of single and double curvature shells to incident pressure
pulses reduces asymptotically to the plate response. The same validity of
the acoustic approximation can be inferred for the transient response of
arbitrary submerged structures.

NUMERICAL SOLUTION TECHNIQUES

As discussed previously, the acoustic approximation could provide satisfactory results for calculating dynamic response of submerged structures to incident pressure waves whose magnitudes are many thousands of psi provided that the cavitation effect is not significant. Therefore, it has many practical applications. For the partial differential system comprised of equations (11), (12), and the equations of motion of structural dynamics, classical solution methods only yield results for simple problems such as the response of plates, infinitely long circular cylindrical shells and uniform spherical shells [2–4]. For the response of arbitrary submerged structures, numerical techniques and modern electronic computers are needed.

For the present interaction problem, the solution of equations (11) and (12) can be expressed in terms of boundary values at the fluid-structure interface S by Kirchhoff's Retarded Potential integral equation [19]

$$p(r,t) = 2p^{inc}(r,t)$$

$$+ \frac{1}{2\pi} \int_S \left[p(r',t') + \frac{R}{c} \frac{\partial}{\partial t'} p(r',t') \right] \frac{1}{R^2} \frac{\partial R}{\partial n} \, dS \tag{21}$$

$$- \frac{\rho}{2\pi} \int_S \frac{1}{R} \frac{\partial}{\partial t'} v_n(r',t') dS$$

where r is the position vector of the observation point on S, r' the position vector of the integration point on S, $R = |r - r'|$, n is the unit normal on S into the scattering body, the subscript o for the fluid density ρ and sound speed c has been dropped, the retarded time

$$t' = t - R/c, \tag{22}$$

and p^{inc} and p are respectively the incident and the total pressure fields. The total pressure

$$p = p^{inc} + p^{sca} \tag{23}$$

where p^{sca} is the scattered pressure field. Equation (21) is two-dimensional, allows the use of the so-called boundary element method and avoids the mathematical modeling of the entire fluid domain. Thus, it has great advantages over those methods required to model the fluid domain. For numerical computation, equation (21) is replaced by an algebraic system through dividing S into a number of small surface elements and replacing the integrals on the right hand side by finite sums. This algebraic system is then solved simultaneously with the structural equations of motion for the pressure and the displacement distributions of S [20]. For instance, equation (21) has been interfaced with the finite element structural dynamic computer programs NASTRAN [21] and ADINA [22]. The effectiveness of this

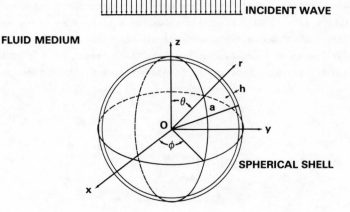

FIGURE 5. Interaction of an incident plane wave and a spherical elastic shell.

solution scheme has been demonstrated by comparing results to an analytical solution of the problem of the linear transient interaction of an incident plane wave and a submerged spherical elastic shell [23]. The geometry of this problem is illustrated in Figure 5. The incident wave is a step wave with a magnitude of

$$\hat{p}/(\rho_o c_o^2) = 1.0. \qquad (24$$

The material properties of water are

$$\rho_o = 999.6 \text{ kg/m}^3 \qquad (25$$

and

$$c_o = 1461.2 \text{ m/sec.} \qquad (26$$

359

The diameter to thickness ratio of the spherical shell is 100. The shell is
made of steel with mass density, Young's Modulus and Poisson's ratio of the
following values respectively

$$\rho_s = 7784.5 \text{ kg/m}^3, \tag{27}$$
$$E = 2.0684 \times 10^{11} \text{ Pa} \tag{28}$$

and

$$\nu = 0.3. \tag{29}$$

It is evident from Figure 5 that the problem is axisymmetric with respect to
the Z-axis.

Numerical results are obtained by the combined system of the Retarded
Potential integral equation and the ADINA code. The spherical shell is
represented by a gridwork of 20 ADINA 8-node axisymmetric continuum elements;
each subtends a polar angle of 9 degrees. A step by step time integration
procedure is used for solving the combined system. Figure 6 compares the

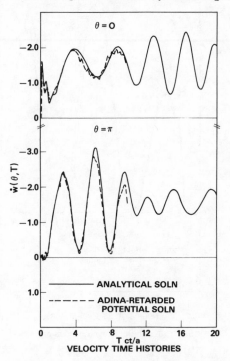

FIGURE 6. Time histories of radial velocity of the shell.

time histories of the radial velocity with those of the analytical solution normalized with respect to the particle velocity of the incident wave, at the two vertices of the shell. Figure 7 compares the hoop stress of the middle surface of the shell at the shadow side vertex. These comparisons indicate that the Retarded Potential ADINA solutions quite satisfactorily predict all important features of the transient response of the submerged shell. It is also obvious from the mathematical structure of equation (21) that the effect from an integration point takes a finite retarded time to arrive at the observation point. Therefore, in numerical computations, a substantial portion of the time histories of the normal acceleration and pressure distributions on S need be stored and operated on for each time step. This solution scheme requires a large core or a dynamic core storage facility. Modern computers should readily accommodate this requirement.

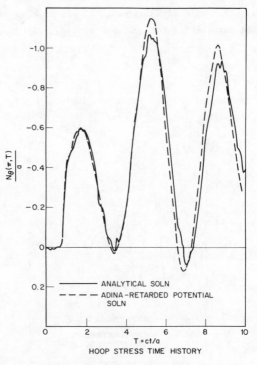

FIGURE 7. Time histories of hoop stress of the shell.

A family of early-time asymptotic formulas can be derived from Kirchhoff's Retarded Potential integral equation [24] including the plane wave approximation (PWA) [25] and the cylindrical wave approximation (CWA) [26]. Furthermore, using the method of matched asymptotic expansions, a hierarchy of doubly asymptotic approximations (DAA) formulae can also be derived from the Retarded Potential integral equation [27]. Doubly asymptotic approximations are differential expressions that approach exactness in the limit of early- and late-time and do not explicitly contain the retarded time terms. Therefore, they are particularly useful for obtaining approximate solutions to problems involving complex structures. They were first derived based on physical intuitions [28]. The first order doubly asymptotic approximation (DAA1) has been widely used [29,30]. The effectiveness of DAA1 has also been appraised using the problem depicted in Figure 5 as the test problem [28,31]. Figure 8 shows the time histories of the radial velocity of the shell similar to those of Figure 6. It can be seen from Figure 8 that DAA1 performs excellently for early-time much beyond the range of the plane wave approximation (PWA). It correctly approaches the mean value of the solution at late-time. However, this comparison also reveals that DAA1 overestimates the fluid damping force and the oscillations in the response are damped out prematurely. The second order doubly asymptotic approximation (DAA2) has alleviated this deficiency [28].

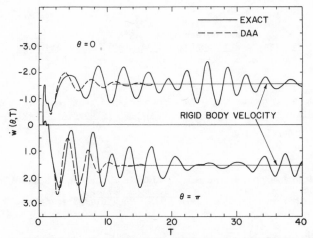

FIGURE 8. Appraisal of the first order doubly asymptotic approximation.

If the effect of cavitation needs to be included in the analysis, it no longer suffices to use the boundary element techniques previously discussed. A substantial region of the surrounding fluid must also be included in the mathematical model. Although cavitation is a microscopically heterogeneous phenomenon influenced by gas dilution concentration, yet it appears to be an effective practice to assume that the cavitating region is macroscopically homogeneous [32]. This leads to the representation of the fluid equation of state by a bilinear relationship between pressure and density [5,6,32]. For multi-dimensional problems, finite element representations of the bilinear fluid using the displacement formation [6] appear to be most promising. Recent results [6,32] show that for the interaction of an incident pressure pulse of the strength in the acoustic approximation range with a cylindrical shell, the cavitating region occurs at a considerable distance away from the shell. Under such circumstances, it could be expected that the use of the single fluid acoustic approximation techniques would still provide reasonably valid results.

REFERENCES

1. Bleich, H. H.,
   Dynamic interaction between structures and fluid. In: Structure Mechanics, Ed. by J. N. Goodier and N. J. Hoff, Pergamon Press, New York (1960) 263-284.

2. Grigolyuk, E. J. and Gorshkov, A. G.,
   Nestatsionarnaya Gidroupprugost Oblocheck, (Nonstationary Hydroelasticity of Shells), Sudostroenie Press, Lenigrad (1974).

3. Geers, T. L.,
   Transient response analysis of submerged structures. In: Finite Element Analysis of Transient Nonlinear Structural Behavior, Ed. by T. Belytschko, J. R. Osias and P. V. Marcel, AMD-Vol. 14, ASME, New York (1975) 59-84.

4. Ueberall, H. and Huang, H.,
   Acoustic response of submerged elastic structures obtained through integral transform. In: Physical Acoustics, 12, Ed. by N. P. Mason and R. N. Thurston, Academic Press, New York (1977) 217-275.

5. Bleich, H. G. and Sandler, I. S.,
   Interaction between structures and bilinear fluids. Int. J. Solids and Struct., 6 (1970) 617-638.

6. Newton, R. E.,
    Effects of cavitation on underwater shock loading--plane problem, final
    report. NPS-69-81-001, Naval Postgraduate School, Monterey, California
    (1981).

7. Driels, M. R.,
    The effect of a non-zero cavitation tension on the damage substained by
    a target plate subject to an underwater explosion. J. Sound Vib. $\underline{73}$
    (1980) 533-545.

8. Schauer, H. M.,
    The afterflow theory of the reloading of airbacked plates at underwater
    explosions. In: Proceedings of the First U.S. National Congress of
    Applied Mechanics, ASME (1951) 887-892.

9. Cole, R. H.,
    Hydrodynamic relations. In: Underwater Explosions, Princeton
    University Press, Princeton (1948) 14-66.

10. Landau, L. D. and Lifshitz, E. M.,
    Sound. In: Fluid Mechanics, Pergamon Press, New York (1959) 245-309.

11. Taylor, G. I.,
    The pressure and impulse of submarine explosion waves on plates. In:
    Underwater Explosion Research, $\underline{1}$, Office of Naval Research, Washington,
    D.C. (1950) 1175-1180.

12. Snay, H. G. and Christian, E. A.,
    The response of airbacked plates to high-amplitude underwater
    shockwaves. Navord Report 2462, Naval Ordnance Laboratory, White Oak,
    Maryland (1952).

13. Keil, A. H.,
    The response of ships to underwater explosion. Paper 7, The Annual
    Meeting of the Society of Naval Architects and Marine Engineering, New
    York (1961).

14. Payton, R. G.,
    Transient interaction of an acoustic wave with a circular cylindrical
    elastic shell. J. Acoust. Soc. Amer. $\underline{32}$ (1960) 722-729.

15. Huang, H. and Wang, Y. F.,
    Early-time interaction of spherical acoustic waves and a cylindrical
    elastic shell. J. Acoust. Soc. Amer. $\underline{48}$ (1970) 228-235.

16.   Peralta, L. A. and Raynor, S.,
      Initial response of a fluid-filled, elastic, circular, cylindrical shell
      to a shock wave in an acoustic medium.   J. Acoust. Soc. Amer. 36 (1964)
      476-488.

17.   Milenkovic, V. and Raynor, S.,
      Reflection of a plane acoustic step wave from an elastic spherical
      membrane.   J. Acoust. Soc. Amer. 39 (1966) 556-563.

18.   Tang, S. C. and Yen, D. H. Y.,
      Interaction of a plane acoustic wave with an elastic spherical shell.
      J. Acoust. Soc. Amer. 47 (1970) 1325-1333.

19.   Baker, B. B. and Copson, E. T.,
      The Mathematical Theory of Huygens Principle, Oxford Univeristy Press,
      London (1939).

20.   Huang, H., Everstine G. C., and Wang, Y. F.,
      Retarded potential techniques for the analysis of submerged structures
      impinged upon by weak shock waves.   In: Computational Methods for
      Fluid-Structure Interaction Analysis, Ed. by T. Belytschko and T. L.
      Geers, AMD-Vol. 26, ASME, New York (1977) 83-93.

21.   Butler, T. G. and Michel, D.,
      NASTRAN: A summary of functions and capabilities of the NASA structural
      analysis computer system.   NASA SP-260, Washington, D.C. (1971).

22.   Bathe, K. J.,
      ADINA - a finite element program for automatic dynamic incremental
      nonlinear analysis.   Report 82448-1, Acoustics and Vibration Laboratory,
      Massachusetts Institute of Technology (1978).

23.   Huang, H.,
      Transient interaction of plane acoustic waves with a spherical elastic
      shell.   J. Acoust. Soc. Amer. 45 (1969) 661-670.

24.   Felippa, C. A.,
      A family of early-time approximations for fluid-structure interaction.
      J. Appl. Mech. 47 (1980) 703-708.

25.   Mindlin, R. D. and Bleich, H. H.,
      Response of an elastic cylindrical shell to a transverse step shock
      wave.   J. Appl. Mech. 20 1953) 189-195.

26. Haywood, J. H.,
Response of an elastic cylindrical shell to a transverse shock wave.
Quart. J. Mech Appl. Math. <u>11</u> (1958) 129–141.

27. Felippa, C. A.,
Top down derivation of double asymptotic approximations for
structure–fluid interation analysis. In: <u>Innovative Numerical Analysis</u>
<u>for Engineering Science</u>, Ed. by R. P. Shaw, University Press of
Virginia, Charlottesville (1980) 79–88.

28. Geers, T. L.,
Doubly asymptotic approximations for transient motions of submerged
structures. J. Acoust. Soc. Amer. <u>64</u> (1978) 1500–1508.

29. Ranlet, D., DiMaggio, F. L., Bleich, H. H. and Baron, M. L.,
Elastic response of submerge shells with internally attached structures
to shock loading. <u>Compt. Struct.</u> <u>7</u> (1977) 355–364.

30. DeRuntz, J. A., Geers, T. L. and Felippa, C. A.,
The underwater shock analysis (USA) Code: A reference manual. Rep DNA
4524F, Lockheed Palo Alto Research Laboratory, Palo Alto, California
(1978).

31. Huang, H.,
A qualitative appraisal of the doubly asymptotic approximation for
transient analysis of submerged structures impinged by weak shock
waves. NRL Memorandum Report 3135, Naval Research Laboratory,
Washington, D.C. (1975).

32. Felippa, C. A. and DeKuntz, J. A.,
Finite element analysis of shock induced hull cavitation. <u>Comput.</u>
<u>Meths. Appl. Mech. Engrg.</u> <u>44</u> (1984) 297–337.

LINEAR ELASTIC RESPONSE OF A RING STIFFENED
CYLINDER TO UNDERWATER EXPLOSION LOADING

R S Haxton, B.Sc. Ph.D and J H Haywood, B.Sc, M.Sc
ARE Dunfermline

ABSTRACT

This paper describes a modal method of analysis for the rapid evaluation of the linear elastic response of a ring stiffened circular cylindrical shell subjected to underwater explosion loading. The cylindrical wave approximation is used to define the interactive behaviour of structure and fluid at the wet boundary. Two mathematical representations of the incident loading are assessed together with other factors which may influence the cylinder response such as stiffener design. The comparative behaviour of frames and plating is studied and an assessment is made of the merits of the method through a comparison with the response predictions obtained from more complex discrete element analyses in which the interaction process is treated using a doubly asymptotic approximation.

INTRODUCTION

During the last three decades a number of methods of increasing complexity have been developed to predict the elastic response of a submarine to the shock wave from an underwater explosion. One of the earliest approximation methods, known as the Cylindrical Wave Approximation (CWA)* was particularly suited for investigating the elastic response of a uniform cylindrical shell to a transverse exponentially decaying shock wave [1]. Subsequently Geers [2] has shown that the CWA approach gives a fairly close approximation to the exact solution at early or late times, at least for a plane step wave of constant amplitude. It has also been used to

---

*The CWA approximation was developed under the supervision of S B Kendrick in whose honour the Symposium is being held.

investigate the transient response of a periodically supported cylindrical shell to a suddenly applied hydrostatic pressure [3].

In this paper the modal method of [1] is extended to permit the study of the transient linear elastic response of an infinitely long <u>ring stiffened</u> cylinder to a transverse exponentially decaying shock wave. The number of modes required to obtain a fairly accurate representation of the incident shock waveform and the upper (early time) and lower (late time) bounds inherent in the formulation of the CWA are examined. The usual plane exponential shock wave loading is considered together with a modified form of loading to account for the peak pressure decaying inversely with distance from the explosion and diffraction effects in the shadow of the cylinder. A study is also made of the comparative motion of plating and frames and the sensitivity of the cylinder response to different frame scantlings.

Finally, the merits of this two-dimensional approximation method are assessed in terms of a comparison with response predictions obtained using the three-dimensional fluid-structure interaction computer codes ELSHOK [4] and USA-STAGS [5] which employ a doubly asymptotic approximation [6].

EQUATIONS OF MOTION FOR A RING STIFFENED CYLINDER

The equations of motion governing the behaviour of a ring stiffened circular cylinder subjected to a transverse shock wave may be derived using the Langrangian formulation,

$$\frac{d}{dt}\left(\frac{\partial T}{\partial \dot{q}_i}\right) - \frac{\partial T}{\partial q_i} + \frac{\partial V}{\partial q_i} = F_i \tag{1}$$

where $\dot{q}_i = \frac{\partial q_i}{\partial t}$, q_i are the generalised coordinates for the motion of the cylinder, F_i are the generalised forces acting on the cylinder and T, V are the kinetic and potental energy expressions.

Assuming the axial deflection u is small compared with the radial and circumferential deflections w, v of the cylinder and using the (x, θ, r) coordinate system defined in Figure 1, the kinetic and potential energy expressions derived from [7] are:

$$T = \frac{a}{2} \iiint \rho_s(\dot{v}^2+\dot{w}^2)\ dxd\theta dr$$

$$V = \frac{Ea}{2(1-\mu^2)} \iiint \left[\frac{(v_\theta-w)^2}{a^2} + \frac{(1-\mu)v_x^2}{2} \right] dxd\theta dr \quad +$$

$$+ \frac{Ea}{2(1-\mu^2)} \iiint \left[w_{xx}^2 + \frac{(w_{\theta\theta}+w)^2}{a^4} + \frac{2\mu w_{xx}}{a^2}(w_{\theta\theta}+v_\theta) \quad + \right.$$

$$\left. + \frac{(1-\mu)w_{x\theta}^2}{2a^2} + \frac{3(1-\mu)}{2a^2}(w_{x\theta}+v_x)^2 \right] (r-a)^2\ dxd\theta dr$$

(2)

where a is the mid-surface radius, E is Young's modulus, μ is Poissons ratio, ρ_s is the mass density of the cylinder material, and the integration extends over the volume of the cylinder.*

The radial and circumferential deflections w, v when confined to the dilatational, translational and inextensional flexural modes may be expressed in generalised coordinates in the form:

$$w = \sum_n Q_n \cos n\theta + \sum_m \sum_n q_{mn}(1-\cos\beta_m x) \cos n\theta \quad \text{for } n \geqslant 0,\ m \geqslant 1$$

(3)

$$v = \sum_n Q_n \frac{\sin n\theta}{n} + \sum_m \sum_n q_{mn}(1-\cos\beta_m x) \frac{\sin n\theta}{n} \quad \text{for } n \geqslant 1,\ m \geqslant 1$$

where m, n are the axial and circumferential modal indices and the Q_n, q_{mn} are functions of time only; Q_n being associated with the axially independent motion of the shell and stiffener and q_{mn} being associated with the axially dependent motion of the shell mid-surface relative to the stiffener. L, ℓ are the axial width of the shell plating and stiffeners, respectively, as illustrated in Figure 1, so that the Q_n are defined over the range $0 \leqslant x \leqslant L+\ell$ and the q_{mn} are restricted to the range $0 \leqslant x \leqslant L$. The axial modal wavelengths are given by the parameter $\beta_m = 2\Pi m/L$.

---

*Here dot notation denotes ⸱ temporal differentiation while suffix notation denotes differentiation with respect to the spacial coordinates.

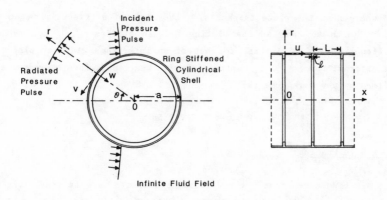

FIGURE 1.   Deflections (u, v, w) for Stiffened Cylinder

On substituting Eqn (3) in Eqn (2) and using Eqn (1) a set of coupled equations of motion for the ring stiffened cylinder is obtained in terms of the generalised coordinates:

$$\lambda_n \left[(1+\alpha)\, \ddot{Q}_n + \sum_m \ddot{q}_{mn}\right] + H_n \left[(1+\alpha)\, Q_n + \sum_m q_{mn}\right] +$$

$$+\, G_n \left[(1+\eta)\, Q_n + \sum_m q_{mn}\right] = F_n / \varepsilon_n \Pi a L \qquad \text{for } n \geqslant 0$$

$$\lambda_n \left[\ddot{q}_{mn} + 2 \ddot{Q}_n + \sum_k \ddot{q}_{kn}\, \varepsilon_{km}\right] + (H_n + G_n)\left[q_{mn} + 2Q_n + \sum_k q_{kn}\, \varepsilon_{km}\right] +$$

$$+\, \left[D_n\, (a\beta_m)^2 + G_o (a\beta_m)^4\right] q_{mn} = 2\, F_{mn} / \varepsilon_n \Pi a L \qquad \text{for } n \geqslant 0,\ m \geqslant 1$$

$$(4)$$

where

$$\varepsilon_n = \begin{cases} 2 & \text{for } n = 0 \\ 1 & \text{for } n \geqslant 1 \end{cases} \quad,\quad \lambda_n = \begin{cases} \rho_s h & \text{for } n = 0 \\ \rho_s h (1 + n^{-2}) & \text{for } n \geqslant 1 \end{cases}$$

$$\varepsilon_{km} = \begin{cases} 1 & \text{for } k \neq m \\ 2 & \text{for } k = m \end{cases} \quad,\quad H_n = \begin{cases} Eh/(1-\mu^2)a^2 & \text{for } n = 0 \\ 0 & \text{for } n \geqslant 1 \end{cases}$$

$$G_n = \begin{cases} Eh^3/12(1-\mu^2)a^4 & \text{for } n = 0 \\ Eh^3(1-n^2)^2/12(1-\mu^2)a^4 & \text{for } n \geqslant 1 \end{cases}$$

$$D_n = \begin{cases} 0 & \text{for } n = 0 \\ H_o(1-\mu)/2n^2 + G_o[2(n^2-1) + (1-\mu)(3-2n^2)/2n^2] & \text{for } n \geqslant 1 \end{cases}$$

and where h is the plate thickness, α the ratio of stiffener mass per unit axial length to that of the plating between stiffeners, η the ratio of stiffener moment of inertia to that of an interframe width of plate* and the external forces F_n, F_{mn} associated with the generalised coordinates are defined by the work done (W):

$$W = \sum_n F_n \delta Q_n + \sum_m \sum_n F_{mn} \delta q_{mn} \tag{5}$$

Shock Wave Loading

It is assumed that a given incident acoustic wave is travelling in a direction normal to the axis of the cylinder and strikes the cylinder initially at $\theta = 0^\circ$. It is also assumed that over a small axial length of the cylinder the radiated pressure pulse due to the response of the cylinder is a diverging cylindrical wave, that is the axial component is small compared with the radial and circumferential components of the radiated pulse. Accordingly for a diverging cylindrical wave a modal relationship between p_r and u_r has been obtained [1] of the form:

$$p_r = \rho \frac{\partial \phi}{\partial t} \ , \ u_r = -\frac{\partial \phi}{\partial r}$$

where $\phi = \sum_n \phi_n \cos n\theta$, $\phi_n = \int_0^\infty f_n(ct - r\cosh u)\cosh nu\, du$

This leads to the relationship:

$$\frac{\partial \phi_n}{\partial r} = -\frac{1}{c}\frac{\partial \phi_n}{\partial t} - \frac{1}{r}\int_0^\infty g_n f_n(ct - r\cosh u)\cosh nu\, du \tag{6}$$

where $g_n = (1 + n\sinh u\tanh nu)/(1 + \cosh u)$

Using Eqn (6) and the approximation made in [1] that the 'afterflow' coefficients g_n are constant gives the cylindrical wave approximation (CWA):

$$\frac{\partial \phi_n}{\partial r} = -\frac{1}{c}\frac{\partial \phi_n}{\partial t} - \frac{g_n \phi_n}{r} \tag{7}$$

---

* The formulation does not distinguish between internal and external stiffeners. The moment of inertia is evaluated relative to the shell mid-surface and not to the true neutral axis of the plating/stiffener combination. The effect of the neutral axis shift of the plating/stiffener may be studied to sufficient accuracy by variation of the mid-surface radius a.

At early time the $g_n = 0.5$ and at late time the $g_n = n$. In [1] mean values of g_n were adopted so that the CWA was not exact at either early or late time. In this paper the early, mean and late time values will be considered and their effect on the cylinder response examined.

Modal expansions for the incident $(p_i, u_i)*$ and radiated wave (p_r, u_r) are introduced of the form:

$$p_i = \sum_n p_{in} \cos n\theta \quad , \quad u_i = \sum_n u_{in} \cos n\theta$$

$$p_r = \sum_n p_{rn} \cos n\theta \quad , \quad u_r = \sum_n u_{rn} \cos n\theta$$

and Eqn (7) now becomes:

$$\frac{\partial u_{rn}}{\partial t} = \frac{1}{\rho c} \frac{\partial p_{rn}}{\partial t} + \frac{g_n}{r} p_{rn}$$

or

$$p_{rn} = \rho c \, e^{-cg_n t/a} \int e^{cg_n t/a} \dot{u}_{rn} \, dt \tag{8}$$

At the surface of the cylinder the condition that the radial velocity is continuous gives:

$$\dot{w}_n = u_{in} - u_{rn} \qquad \text{at } r = a \tag{9}$$

Therefore, eliminating u_{rn} from Eqn (8) using Eqn (9), the radiated pressure at the cylinder surface is obtained in terms of the radial component of the incident wave particle velocity and cylinder radial motion:

$$p_{rn} = \rho c \, e^{-cg_n t/a} \int e^{cg_n t/a} (\dot{u}_{in} - \ddot{w}_n) \, dt \quad \text{at } r = a \tag{10}$$

Two mathematical representations of the incident shock wave (p_i, u_i) are now considered. These are referred to as Loading Models 1 and 2.

---

* Note that u_i is the <u>radial</u> component of the incident wave particle velocity.

Loading Model 1 (LM1)

In this representation the incident wave is assumed to be a plane shock wave of constant peak pressure, p_o, and exponentially decaying profile with decay time constant Γ. The shape and directivity of this pulse are also assumed to be unaffected by the presence of the cylinder so that LM1 is reasonably representative of the loading conditions which prevail when the origin of the incident wave is at a standoff, R_o, which is large compared to the cylinder radius, that is when $(R_o/a) \gg 1$.

The incident pressure pulse may then be expressed as:

$$p_i = p_o \, e^{-[t-a(1-\cos\theta)/c]/\Gamma} \, H\,\{t-a(1-\cos\theta)/c\}$$

where H{ } is the Heavyside function.

It follows that:

$$P_{in} = \frac{2p_o}{\varepsilon_n} e^{-(t-a/c)/\Gamma} \, I_{n\theta}(-a/\Gamma c) \tag{11}$$

where $I_{n\theta}(z) = \dfrac{1}{\Pi} \displaystyle\int_0^\theta e^{z\,\cos\theta} \cos n\theta \, d\theta$ for $0 \leqslant \theta < \Pi$

is the incomplete modified Bessel function of the first order, and becomes the complete function $I_n(z)$ when $\theta = \Pi$ or $(ct/a) \geqslant 2$. Given that the radial component of the incident wave particle velocity is:

$$u_i = p_i \, \cos\theta$$

then
$$u_{in} = p_o e^{-(t-a/c)/\Gamma} \{I_{(n+1)\theta}(-a/\Gamma c) + K_n \, I_{(n-1)\theta}(-a/\Gamma c)\} \tag{12}$$

where $K_n = \begin{cases} 0 \text{ for } n = 0 \\ 1 \text{ for } n \geqslant 1 \end{cases}$

and again the incomplete Bessel functions become complete when $(ct/a) \geqslant 2$.

The complete modified Bessel functions may be generated using a standard scientific subroutine and the incomplete functions by the numerical integration of the first order differential equation:

$$\dot{I}_{n\theta}(-a/\Gamma c) = e^{-(t-a/c)/\Gamma} \, \frac{\cos n\theta}{\Pi \sin\theta} \tag{13}$$

Loading Model 2 (LM2)

For a more realistic representation of the loading when the origin
of the incident wave is close to the cylinder, that is, for $(R_o/a) \sim 1$, the
second loading model assumes that the peak overpressure varies inversely
with distance and that the radial component of the incident particle
velocity is negligible in the shadow of the cylinder. With reference to
the geometry given in Figure 2 the expression for p_{in} becomes:

$$p_{in} = \frac{2R_o}{\varepsilon_n \Pi} P_o e^{-(t+R_o/c)/\Gamma} \int_0^{\theta} \frac{e^{R/\Gamma c}}{R} \cos n\theta \, d\theta \qquad \text{for } 0 \leqslant \theta \leqslant \theta_t$$

$$\text{where } R = [a^2 + (R_o+a)^2 - 2a(R_o+a) \cos\theta]^{\frac{1}{2}} \qquad (14)$$

$$\text{and } p_{in} = \frac{2R_o}{\varepsilon_n \Pi} P_o e^{-(t+R_o/c)/\Gamma} \left[\int_0^{\theta_t} \frac{e^{R/\Gamma c}}{R} \cos n\theta \, d\theta + \int_{\theta}^{\theta} \frac{e^{R'/\Gamma c}}{R'} \cos n\theta \, d\theta \right]$$

$$\text{for } \theta_t < \theta \leqslant \Pi$$

where $R' = R_t + a(\theta - \theta_t)$ and R_t, θ_t defines the point of grazing
incidence beyond which the wave path length is measured around the surface
of the cylinder.

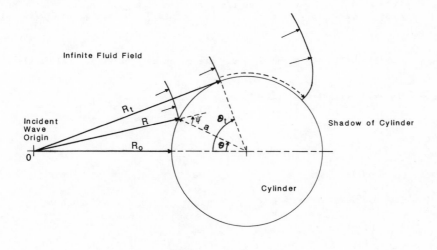

FIGURE 2.   Loading Model 2 Geometry

The equivalent expressions for u_{in} follow from the relationship $u_i = p_i \cos \psi$:

$$u_{in} = \frac{R_o}{\Pi} P_o e^{-(t+R_o/c)/\Gamma} \int_0^\theta \frac{e^{R/\Gamma c}}{R} \cos\psi \cos n\theta \, d\theta \qquad \text{for } 0 \leqslant \theta \leqslant \theta_t$$

and

$$u_{in} = 0 \qquad \text{for } \theta_t < \theta \leqslant \Pi$$

$$\text{where } \cos\psi = [(R_o + a)^2 - R^2 - a^2]/2aR$$

(15)

The integrals in Eqns (14) and (15) may be evaluated numerically by discretizing the angular interval between 0 and θ.

The work done by the external forces can now be expressed in terms of the pressure variables:

$$W = \sum_n F_n \, \delta Q_n + \sum_m \sum_n F_{mn} \, \delta q_{mn}$$

$$= \iint \sum_n (p_{in} + p_{rn}) \cos n\theta \left[\sum_s \delta Q_s + \sum_m \sum_s \delta q_{ms} (1-\cos\beta_m x) \right] \cos s\theta \, ad\theta dx$$

Substituting for p_{rn} using Eqn (10) and integrating θ over 0 to Π and x over 0 to L and L to L+ℓ leads to the following expressions for F_n and F_{mn}:

$$F_n = \Pi aL\gamma\epsilon_n \left[p_{in} + \rho c \, e^{-cg_n t/a} \int e^{cg_n t/a} (\dot{u}_{in} - \ddot{Q}_n - \sum_m \ddot{q}_{mn}/\gamma) dt \right]$$

$$F_{mn} = \Pi aL\epsilon_n \left[p_{in} + \rho c \, e^{-cg_n t/a} \int e^{cg_n t/a} (\dot{u}_{in} - \ddot{Q}_n - \sum_k \ddot{q}_{kn} - \ddot{q}_{mn}/2) \, dt \right]$$

(16)

where $\gamma = (L + \ell)/L$ and p_{in}, u_{in} are given by Eqns (11), (12) or (14),(15).

In velocity potential form:

$$F_n = \Pi aL\gamma\epsilon_n \left[p_{in} + \rho \frac{\partial\phi_n}{\partial t} \right]$$

$$F_{mn} = \Pi aL \, \epsilon_n \left[p_{in} + \rho \frac{\partial\phi_{mn}}{\partial t} \right]$$

where

(17)

$$\frac{\partial\phi_n}{\partial t} = u_{in} - \dot{Q}_n - \sum_m \dot{q}_{mn}/\gamma - g_n \phi_n \qquad \text{for } n \geqslant 0$$

$$\frac{\partial\phi_{mn}}{\partial t} = u_{in} - \dot{Q}_n - \sum_k \dot{q}_{kn} - \dot{q}_{mn}/2 - g_n\phi_{mn} \qquad \text{for } n \geqslant 0, \, m \geqslant 1$$

These expressions for F_n and F_{mn} may now be substituted in the RHS of Eqns (4). In final form the non-dimensional equations of motion become:

$$\lambda_n [(1+\alpha)\ddot{Q}_n + \sum_m \ddot{q}_{mn}] + H_n [(1+\alpha)Q_n + \sum_m q_{mn}] +$$

$$+ G_n[(1+\eta) Q_n + \sum_m q_{mn}] = \gamma \left[P_{in} + \frac{\partial \phi_n}{\partial \tau} \right] \qquad \text{for } n \geqslant 0$$

and $\qquad\qquad\qquad\qquad\qquad\qquad\qquad\qquad\qquad\qquad\qquad\qquad\qquad\qquad$ (18)

$$\lambda_n [\ddot{q}_{mn} + 2\ddot{Q}_n + \sum_k \ddot{q}_{kn} \varepsilon_{km}] + (H_n + G_n) [q_{mn} + 2Q_n + \sum_k q_{kn} \varepsilon_{km}] +$$

$$+ [D_n(a\beta)^2 + G_o(a\beta)^4]q_{mn} = 2 \left[P_{in} + \frac{\partial \phi_{mn}}{\partial \tau} \right] \qquad \text{for } n \geqslant 0,\ m \geqslant 1$$

where τ is the dimensionless time ct/a and the constants and dependent variables have been non-dimensionalised using appropriate scaling relationships.

SOLUTION OF EQUATIONS OF MOTION

Eqns (18) may be reduced to a set of first order differential equations through the introduction of two additional variables:

$$X_n = \dot{Q}_n \qquad , \qquad Y_{mn} = \dot{q}_{mn}$$

To arrive at a specific set of first order equations it is necessary to select an appropriate number of terms for the axial modal expansion. Given that the contribution to plate motion from modes greater than $m = 2$ is likely to be small, the resulting first order equations are:

$$\dot{Q}_n = X_n$$

$$\dot{q}_{1n} = Y_{1n}$$

$$\dot{q}_{2n} = Y_{2n}$$

$$\dot{X}_n = [4 \bar{P}_n - \bar{Q}_n - \bar{R}_n]/4\alpha$$

$$\dot{Y}_{1n} = [-4\bar{P}_n + (1+3\alpha)\bar{Q}_n + (1-\alpha)\bar{R}_n]/8\alpha \qquad\qquad (19)$$

$$\dot{Y}_{2n} = [-4\bar{P}_n + (1-\alpha)\bar{Q}_n + (1+3\alpha)\bar{R}_n]/8\alpha$$

$$\dot{\phi}_n = u_{in} - X_n - [Y_{1n} + Y_{2n}]/\gamma - g_n \phi_n$$

$$\dot{\phi}_{1n} = u_{in} - X_n - \frac{3}{2} Y_{1n} - Y_{2n} - g_n \phi_{1n}$$

$$\dot{\phi}_{2n} = u_{in} - X_n - Y_{1n} - \frac{3}{2} Y_{2n} - g_n \phi_{2n} \qquad\qquad \text{for } n \geqslant 0$$

where

$$\bar{P}_n = \gamma [p_{in} + u_{in} - X_n - Y_{1n}/\gamma - Y_{2n}/\gamma - g_n \phi_n]/\lambda_n -$$
$$- H_n [(1+\alpha) Q_n + q_{1n} + q_{2n}]/\lambda_n - G_n [(1+n)Q_n + q_{1n} + q_{2n}]/\lambda_n$$

$$\bar{Q}_n = 2 [p_{in} + u_{in} - X_n - \frac{3}{2}Y_{1n} - Y_{2n} - g_n\phi_{1n}]/\lambda_n -$$
$$- (H_n + G_n) [3q_{1n} + 2Q_n + q_{2n}]/\lambda_n - [D_n(a\beta_1)^2 + G_o(a\beta_1)^4]q_{1n}/\lambda_n$$

$$\bar{R}_n = 2 [p_{in} + u_{in} - X_n - Y_{1n} - \frac{3}{2}Y_{2n} - g_n \phi_{2n}]/\lambda_n -$$
$$- (H_n + G_n) [q_{1n} + 2Q_n + 3q_{2n}]/\lambda_n - [D_n(a\beta_2)^2 + G_o(a\beta_2)^4] q_{2n}/\lambda_n$$

Eqns (19) together with the incident wave loading Eqns (11) to (15) have been incorporated in a FORTRAN program implemented on a DEC VAX computer. This program solves the equations using a Runge–Kutta integration procedure and provides output in the form of radial response time histories of cylinder displacement, velocity and acceleration at selected angular and axial stations.

NUMERICAL STUDIES

In a series of numerical studies Eqns (19) are used to predict the radial velocity response of a ring stiffened circular cylinder which is loaded by an exponentially decaying pressure pulse from an underwater explosion. The studies serve not only to assess the validity of the assumptions inherent in the theory but also to examine the general response behaviour of a ring stiffened shell and the effects certain parameter variations have on that behaviour. Table 1 lists the physical constants, structural and loading parameters used in the studies.

Mode Selection

A prerequisite to the application of any modal method is the establishment of a criterion for modal selection/series truncation. In this study the measure of sufficient modal content is based on a comparison of the reconstituted incident pressure waveform with its analytic form. In this manner a truncated model series is established which has sufficient terms to represent adequately the incident loading and the resulting cylinder response.

TABLE 1

Values of Physical Constants (SI units)

Velocity of sound in water (c)	1500 m/s
Mass density of water (ρ)	1025 Kg/m^3
Mass density of cylinder (ρ_s)	7830 Kg/m^3
Youngs modulus (E)	21.0 10^4 MPa
Poissons ratio (μ)	0.3
Cylinder radius to wall thickness ratio (a/h)	100
Structural mass ratio (α)	0.75
Structural moment of inertia ratio (η)	340
Peak pressure of incident shock wave (p_o)	16 MPa
Decay time constant of incident shock wave (Γ)	86 µsec

Figure 3 shows a comparison between the incident pressure waveform used in this study and its reconstituted forms for increasing modal families of n = 12, 16 and 20. Such comparisons have indicated that a sufficiently accurate representation of the pulse profile may be obtained in this case using 16 circumferential modes.

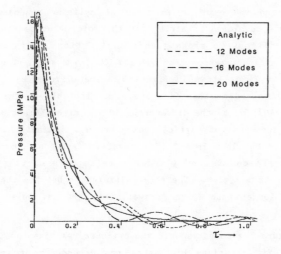

FIGURE 3.   Incident Pressure Pulse - Modal Representation

Selecting the Afterflow Coefficient Values

The sensitivity of the cylinder response to the choice of afterflow coefficient values may now be assessed. As previously discussed, three sets of g_n values are of interest, $g_n = 0.5$ (early time), $g_n = n$ (late time) and the mean values derived in [1].

The results of an evaluation using LM2 ($R_o/a = 2$) are shown in Figure 4 in terms of the radial velocity response comparisons at angular stations 0°, 90°, 180° for the frame and interframe ($x = L/2$) axial locations. At times less than the radius transit time the response is almost independent of g_n selection while at later times the increased 'added mass' contribution of the late time g_n values drives the cylinder in a slightly more oscillatory response. It is evident from these comparisons that the response behaviour is generally insensitive to the g_n coefficient variations considered here and in the following studies the late time g_n values are adopted.

Comparison of Loading Models LM1 and LM2

The features of the incident wave loading models LM1 and LM2 described earlier may now be examined in terms of cylinder response comparisons. Since LM2 was developed primarily for the more accurate representation of loading conditions in close standoff situations it is appropriate to compare the cylinder response to LM1 and LM2 for a small standoff to radius ratio ($R_o/a = 2$) as shown in Figure 5. The differences in the response amplitudes observed in this figure are attributable to the fall off with distance of LM2 and to the differences in the circumferential variation of the radial component of particle velocity, u_i, as indicated in Figure 6. In particular the lack in LM2 of a negative (suction) component of u_i in the shadow region of the cylinder permits more oscillatory response behaviour in that region. The phase differences between the responses are due to the longer path length travelled by the LM2 pulse in the shadow region.

In Figure 7 a comparison of the cylinder response to LM2 for long and short standoff situations highlights the dependence of the response to standoff. In this comparison the peak pressure at the 0° point is 16 MPa for both standoff cases.

379

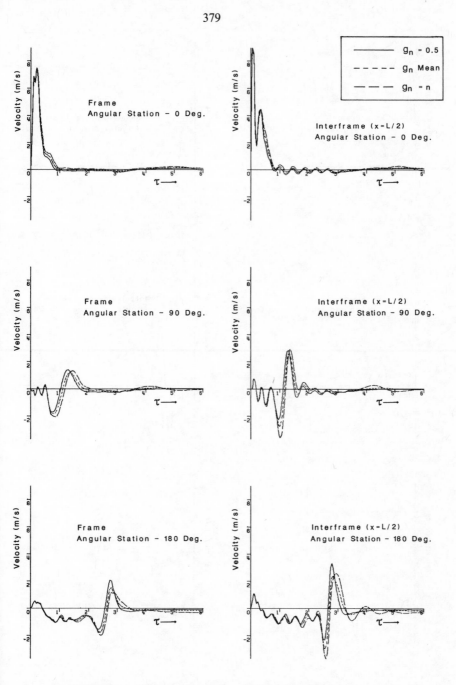

FIGURE 4.   Response Variation with g_n Coefficients

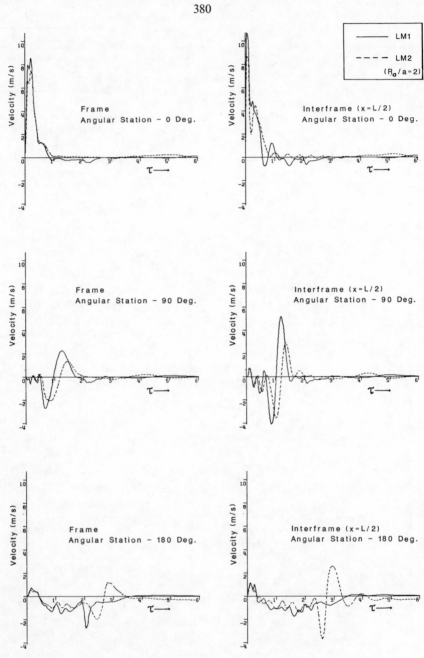

FIGURE 5.   Comparison of Loading Models 1 and 2 – Small Standoff

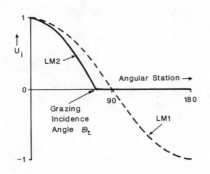

FIGURE 6.   Circumferential Variation of Radial Incident Velocity
             for LM1 and LM2

The choice of loading model is clearly problem dependent. For
situations where interest is confined to angular stations near 0° the
computationally more efficient (cheaper) LM1 is adequate irrespective of
standoff geometry. For the study of stations in the shadow region LM2 is
preferred particularly when the incident wave origin is in the vicinity of
the cylinder.

Frame/Interframe Response

The extension of the method described in [1] to permit the modelling
of discrete ring stiffened cylinders provides the opportunity to examine
the comparative behaviour of frame and interframe response. It is noted
that the Eqns (19) contain only the first two axial modes, $m = 1,2$. These
modal components are shown in Figure 8 at the interframe positions where
their individual contributions are at a maximum, that is at $x = L/2$ and $x =$
$L/4$ respectively. As expected the modal amplitude of $m = 2$ is smaller than
$m = 1$ and is damped out more rapidly.

Figure 9 shows a comparison between frame and interframe response
at $x = L/3$ where both axial modes contribute equal proportions of the

382

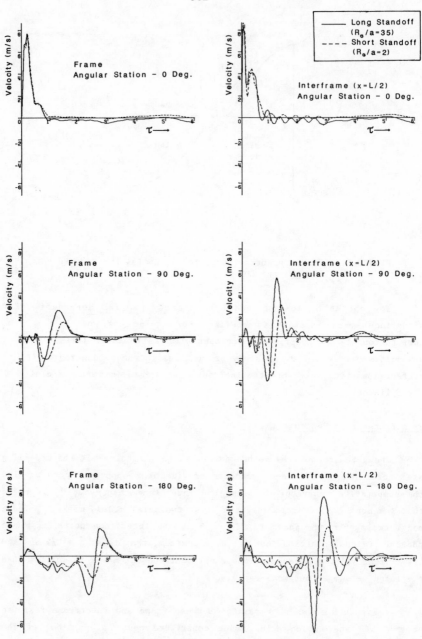

FIGURE 7.   Loading Model 2 – Response Variation with Attack Geometry

383

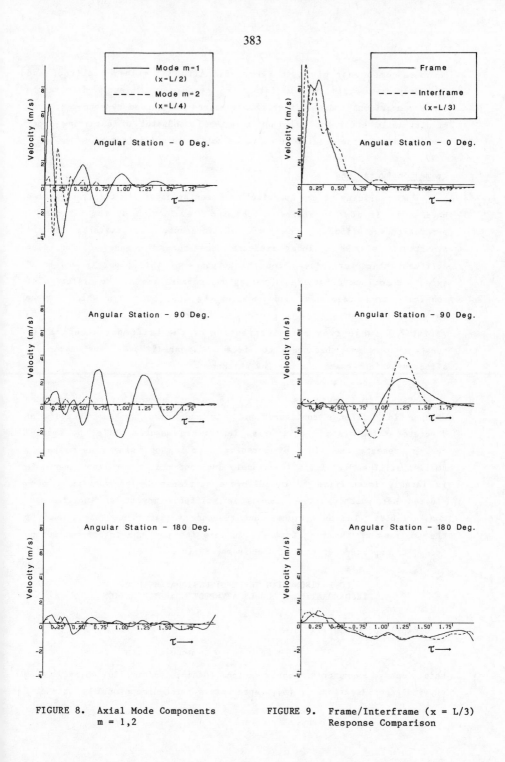

FIGURE 8.   Axial Mode Components
m = 1,2

FIGURE 9.   Frame/Interframe (x = L/3)
Response Comparison

response components given in Figure 8. Although higher amplitude and
frequency modulation of the interframe response is clearly discernable
these comparisons indicate that the frame and interframe responses are not
significantly different and that from the standpoint of assessing shock
severity levels the prediction of frame motion is sufficient.

Frame Configurations

The simplicity of the numerical implementation of the theory presented
here makes it ideally suited to the rapid evaluation of the effects of
parameter variations. One area of interest, for example, is the
sensitivity of the cylinder response behaviour to changes in the ring
stiffener characteristics. For the purposes of this paper it was found
expedient to look at stiffener variations constrained by the criterion of
constant structural mass, and consequently the parameters which may be
varied are related to the geometric distribution of material. The
variations range from a redistribution of the stiffener material for
constant plating thickness to frames 'smeared' over the cylinder,
effectively increasing the plating thickness.

Figure 10 illustrates the response variations which result from such
changes in stiffener configuration. In each case the same numbers of
discrete stiffeners per unit axial length are assumed while the smeared
case represents the limit of pursuing a policy of using closer spaced,
smaller stiffeners. It is immediately apparent that the cylinder response
is largely insensitive to the discrete stiffener design variations considered here although the changes in stiffener moment of inertia were
considerable. The only significant response variation is that caused by
the smearing of the ring frames. In this instance the interframe motion
tends, as expected, to that of the frame station.

COMPARISON WITH THREE-DIMENSIONAL METHODS
INCORPORATING A DOUBLY ASYMPTOTIC APPROXIMATION

Expressed in matrix form as:

$$\dot{\underline{p}}_r + \rho c \, \underset{\sim}{M}^{-1} \, \underset{\sim}{A} \, \underline{p}_r = \rho c \, \dot{\underline{u}}_r$$

this doubly asymptotic approximation (DAA1), originally derived from
physical considerations in [6], represents a three-dimensional relationship

385

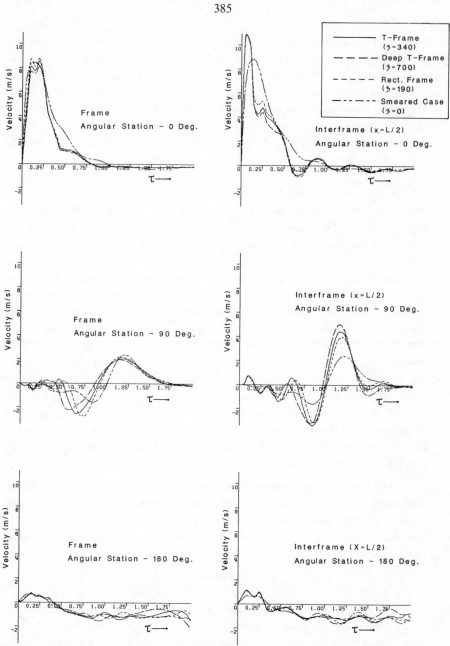

FIGURE 10. Effects of Stiffener Design Variations on Cylinder Response

between the radiated pressure vector, p_r, and the radiated particle velocity vector, u_r, which is similar in form to that of the two-dimensional CWA formulation of Eqn (8). In the last decade several computer programs incorporating this DAA1 formulation have been developed. These are based on a discrete element approach which permits the modelling of three-dimensional structures of 'arbitrary' interaction surface geometry. Two of these codes ELSHOK [4] and USA-STAGS [5] are used to assess the merits of the present theoretical method.

A three-way comparison of the radial velocity response predictions of the present CWA formulation using LM2 ($R_o/a = 2$), ELSHOK and USA-STAGS for a long ring stiffened cylinder is given in Figure 11. In broad terms these response predictions may be described as exhibiting similar trends although the USA-STAGS solution is distinctly more oscillatory for $\tau > 1$. At a more detailed level the following comments may be made regarding the frame response comparisons. At 0° the comparison is good both in terms of predicted peak amplitude and time to peak. At the 90° station the CWA predicts an outward peak response similar to that of ELSHOK and an inward peak response similar to that of USA-STAGS. However the outward peak response of USA-STAGS is twice that of either the CWA or ELSHOK. At 180° the peak outward and inward response predictions of the CWA are closer to those of USA-STAGS, bearing in mind the phase discrepancies caused by the line-of-sight loading used in USA-STAGS. With regard to the interframe response comparisons, the CWA result is again close in terms of peak motion, to that predicted by USA-STAGS while its late time behaviour is more akin to that of ELSHOK.

Although limited in application to circular cylindrical surface geometries, the reponse comparisons presented here indicated that the CWA formulation provides a viable alternative analysis method to the complex (costly) procedures generally available for the study of ring stiffened cylinders.

CONCLUSIONS

The viability of a simple modal method of analysis for the evaluation of the transient response of a ring stiffened circular cylinder to underwater shock loading has been demonstrated in terms of radial velocity response predictions which compare favourably with those derived using more complex analysis methods.

387

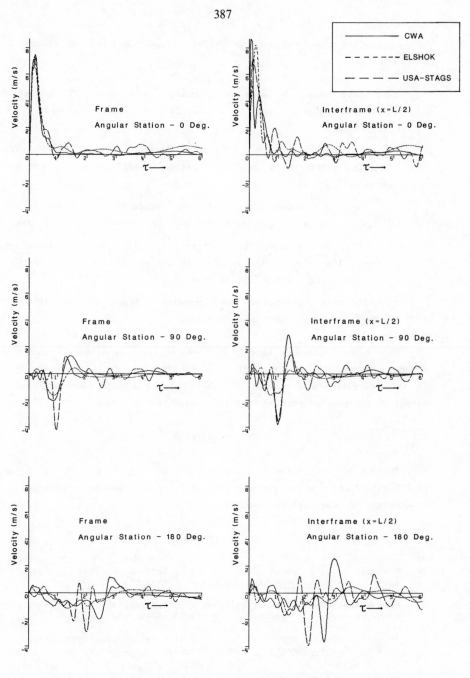

FIGURE 11.   Comparison of CWA, ELSHOK (DAA) and USA/STAGS (DAA)

From the numerical studies which have been carried out it may be concluded that:

a. When using the modal approach it is necessary to employ a sufficient number of modes to accurately represent the incident shock wave loading.

b. The selection of early, mean or late time values for the CWA afterflow coefficients has little noticeable effect on the cylinder response.

c. For close standoff geometries the incident wave loading model, LM2, gives a more oscillatory response in the shadow of the cylinder.

d. The study of comparative frame and plating response behaviour indicates that the prediction of frame motion alone is sufficient to assess the overall shock loading severity.

e. The ring stiffened cylinder response is generally insensitive to the frame design variations considered.

The method presented here is computationally more efficient than the discrete element analyses generally employed and as such it is considered to be a cost-effective method for the study of a wide range of fluid/structure interaction problems involving circular cylinders.

ACKNOWLEDGEMENTS

The authors are indebted to two of their colleagues, Miss D Bravin and Mr I Turnbull for their assistance in developing the computer program and conducting the numerical assessments.

REFERENCES

1. Haywood, J.H., Response of an elastic cylindrical shell to a pressure pulse. Quart. J. Mech. App. Math., 11 (1958) 129-141.

2. Geers, T.L., Excitation of an elastic cylindrical shell by a transient acoustic wave. J. App. Mechs, 36 (1969) 459-469.

3. Russell, J.E. and Herrmann, G., A modified cylindrical wave approximation. J. App. Mechs, 35 (1968) 819-822.

4. Vasudevan, R., and Ranlet, D., Submerged shock response of a linearly elastic shell of revolution containing internal structure - user's manual for the ELSHOK code. Defense Nuclear Agency, Washington DC, DNA-TR-81-184 (1982).

5. DeRuntz, J.A., and Brogan, F.A., Underwater shock analysis of non-linear structures, a reference manual for the USA-STAGS code (version 3). Defense Nuclear Agency, Washington DC, DNA 5545F (1980).

6. Geers, T.L., Residual potential and approximate methods for three-dimensional fluid-structure interaction problems. J. Acoust. Soc. Amer., 49 (1971) 1505-1510.

7. Haywood, J.H. and Wilson, L.B., The strain-energy expression for thin elastic shells. J. App. Mechs. 25 (1958) 546-552.

EXPLOSION INDUCED HULL WHIPPING

A. N. Hicks
Admiralty Research Establishment
Teddington, Middlesex
England, TW11 0LN

ABSTRACT

An easily implemented analysis is presented for the dynamic response of a ship to a nearby explosion. The paper shows clearly the essential features of the ship/explosion interaction, and calculated results are compared with experiment. The method is simple and accurate enough to be used during initial design for the prediction of hull girder stresses, enabling design against this type of loading.

INTRODUCTION

This paper is concerned with the effect of underwater explosions on ships. All navies have long been aware of shock effects from distant explosions, and protection against shock is standard practice everywhere. Similarly, for ships which are sufficiently large and important, side-protection systems against contact charges are fairly common. For charges at intermediate standoffs, while shock and hull rupture effects can both still be important, a new effect occurs; whipping. Although a well known weapon effect, it has been much less well publicised in the literature than the other two, and only relatively recently have naval architects started to consider how to design against the damage it can produce. Naturally, such consideration is only worthwhile for ships, like minesweepers, which are particularly likely to encounter severe explosion effects.

Whipping is the flexing motion of the whole hull of a ship, in its low frequency vertical vibration modes. For a close but non-contact

explosion such motion can easily be sufficiently severe that the hull
girder buckles and either breaks or loses all stiffness at the point of
failure (fig. 1). Protection against this form of damage consists of
designing the strength of the girder against whipping stresses rather than
against the more usual wave loadings. In order to follow such a design aim
of course it is necessary to be able to predict, at the design stage, the
magnitude of the loading from a given size and location of explosion. It
is the aim of this paper to present a relatively simple model of the
ship/explosion interaction in a form which is computationally
straightforward to apply yet provides fairly accurate predictions of hull
girder stresses.

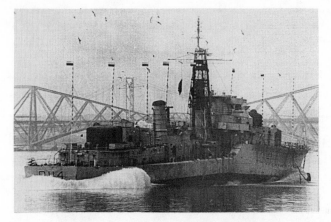

FIGURE 1. Effect of Severe Whipping

The work described here was in fact carried out over fifteen years
ago but it seems particularly appropriate for it to be presented now for
two reasons. Firstly, it was carried out at the instigation of Bill
Kendrick, in whose honour this symposium is being held, and with his
enthusiastic support. Secondly, although the basic principles of the
interaction were established and published over 30 years ago by George
Chertock in the USA [1], they seem since to have been forgotten or
overlooked. Two fairly recent papers [2] and [3] discuss the calculation
of whipping stresses. In both cases a natural but in fact mistaken
assumption has been made concerning the nature of the explosion loading.
In consequence, the magnitude and general character of the derived
predictions of ship response are questionable. It seems timely to provide
here a reminder of Chertock's early work, in a form more suitable for

computer implementation albeit lacking the elegance of the original derivation.

PHYSICAL PHENOMENA

The nature and characteristics of underwater explosions are still most comprehensively described in Cole's book [4], and most of the comments and equations used here can be found therein. The first and most immediately impressing feature of an underwater explosion is the shockwave. It carries outward with it almost one-third of the energy liberated by the explosion, and is responsible both for local hull splitting or deformation and for shock damage to internal equipment. At potentially damaging standoffs it is a very high intensity and short duration phenomenon with peak pressures typically around 100 to 400 bar and lasting some 300 – 600 μsec. This duration, together with the acoustic velocity for water of around 1500m/s, implies that the shockwave occupies a thin shell of water only about one metre thick. The short duration also implies that the loading it applies to the hull can, for whipping considerations, where the hull vibration frequencies are generally below 10Hz, be considered impulsive. In [2], various assumptions are made concerning the loading of the shockwave on the hull during the impulsive phase, leading essentially to a prescribed initial vertical velocity distribution along the hull girder, and the stresses in the hull then follow from the resulting free elastic motion of the hull.

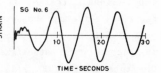

FIGURE 2. Whipping Deck Strain

The problem with this type of approach is illustrated in figure 2, which shows typical longitudinal strain records taken from the deck of a ship whipping fairly severely. The record shows that the motion of the ship is not just the free response of an elastic system to an initial impulse; the amplitude of the strain grows on each of the first three half cycles of the fundamental whipping mode. The explosion continues to excite the hull for around two seconds, long after the shockwave has passed. The record is typical in showing a distinct second 'kick' to the ship at around 0.65 seconds leading to a second cycle of the fundamental mode which is of substantially greater amplitude than the first cycle. The feature of the explosion which produces this extended interaction with the hull, and provides all the additional energy, is the bubble of gaseous explosion products.

The characteristics of the pulsating bubble are well established. Figure 3 shows photographs of the bubble from a very small explosion at various stages of its pulsation, and figure 4 shows a radius-time curve for a similar small explosion. The 'kick' in the ship strain record

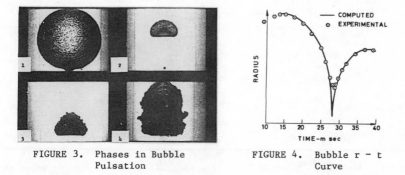

FIGURE 3. Phases in Bubble   FIGURE 4. Bubble r – t
          Pulsation   Curve

corresponds to a second pressure pulse as the bubble rebounds after collapse. Between the first two pulses, although pressure records suggest that there is no pressure acting, there is in fact a suction towards the bubble; much smaller in magnitude than the pressure pulses but lasting substantially longer; almost the entire period between the pulses, and capable of significantly affecting the ship motion. The amount of energy available in the bubble pulsation is large, being typically close to 50% of the original explosion energy. The period of the bubble motion is also fairly well matched to the fundamental frequency of smallish ships, being typically between 0.3 and 1.0 second. In consequence, the bubble is a very powerful and effective agent for inflicting whipping damage. Figure 5 summarises a few characteristics of the bubble for a particular charge size and depth. It is the interaction between the bubble and the ship which is modelled in this paper.

Surprisingly, even the early motion of a ship, the swing on the first half cycle, can be predicted well by the ship/bubble interaction, ignoring any direct effect from the shockwave. Physically this is readily explained however. Ships have fairly light hull plating against which the shockwave acts. G I Taylor [5] first described the nature of this early phase of shockwave loading on air-backed plating. Under the influence of the shockwave the plating accelerates rapidly. Due to the high acoustic impedance of the water, the inward motion of the plating then radiates a relief pressure wave back into the water. Very quickly the absolute

	METRIC	IMPERIAL
CHARGE WEIGHT	150 Kg	330 LB.
CHARGE DEPTH	10m	30 FT.
CHARGE DIAMETER	0·56 m	1·85 FT.
BUBBLE MAXIMUM DIAMETER	13·2 m	43·8 FT.
BUBBLE PERIOD	0·924 SEC.	0·954 SEC.

FIGURE 5. Typical Bubble Characteristics

pressure against the plate drops to zero and the water cavitates. Later loadings occur when the cavitation gap eventually closes as the water expanding around the gas bubble catches up again with the plating which is slowed by the elastic restraint of the hull frames, longitudinals and bulkheads. The main loading however is complete when cavitation occurs, which in a typical geometry happens in around 100 μsec. By the time of cavitation closure, the shockwave phase is long over and the subsequent loadings are controlled by bubble energy.

The energy absorbed by the plating in the pre-cavitation phase can be considerable, and can eventually cause severe local hull damage. At cavitation time however the plating has had no time to move appreciably; it has simply acquired a high velocity and the energy is stored as kinetic energy of the plating alone. The momentum of the plating motion subsequently transfers itself via the supporting frames and longitudinals into a bulk motion of the whole hull, which inevitably will mean some degree of whipping. However, such whipping is minor. The plating mass generally forms a relatively small part of the total mass of the ship; probably no more than 40 tons of bottom plating will be affected in a 2500 ton ship. Since the inertial mass of water around a ship in vertical motion is usually around $1\frac{1}{2}$ times the displacement of the ship, the shockwave induced momentum of the 40 tons of plating will be transferred eventually to around 6000 tons of ship and water. Such a momentum transfer from a high velocity on a small mass to a low velocity on a large mass is very wasteful of energy, and in the ship case substantially less than 1% of the shockwave energy will finally end up as a bulk whipping motion. The rest of the energy will be 'dissipated' as local hull damage or as higher frequency shock motions rattling around inside the hull. Ship whipping from direct shockwave effects is not a serious problem.

MATHEMATICAL MODEL

The mathematical model presented here is intended to show the physics of the ship/explosion interaction, and outline a practical computational scheme, rather than to delineate the 'state of the art'. Accordingly, the model has been broken into a set of distinct sub-models, and the simplest possible formulation used for each.

a) Hull Girder Model

As is usual for the low frequency modes of hull vibration, a simple beam model has been used to represent the elastic character of the hull. Since the stiffness and mass distributions vary widely and rapidly along the length, a lumped mass/weightless beam representation, as in figure 6 and based on about 20 lumped masses, is more appropriate than

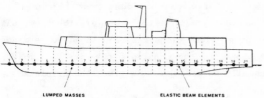

LUMPED MASSES   ELASTIC BEAM ELEMENTS

FIGURE 6. Hull Girder Model.

a consistent mass model. With this form of idealisation, the external forces $\underline{F}$ and moments $\underline{M}$ which have to be applied to maintain statically a given set of displacements $\underline{y}$ and bending rotations $\underline{\theta}$ are given by

$$\begin{bmatrix} \underline{F} \\ \underline{M} \end{bmatrix} = \begin{bmatrix} A & B \\ B^T & C \end{bmatrix} \cdot \begin{bmatrix} \underline{y} \\ \underline{\theta} \end{bmatrix}$$

where the elements of the sub-matrices A, B and C, which depend on the elastic beam characteristics of the hull girder, are defined in Appendix

A. They include the effect of shear deflections, which are important here.

In this application, the moments $\underline{M}$ during motion are largely provided by the rotary inertia of the ship and surrounding water and have been found in practice to affect the results little. Setting $\underline{M} = 0$, the equation becomes;-

$$\underline{F} = [A - BC^{-1}B^T] \underline{y} \qquad ; \qquad \underline{\theta} = -C^{-1}B^T\underline{y} \qquad (1)$$

b) Hull Hydrodynamics

As usual in ship applications, standard strip theory is quite adequate in most cases to represent the effect of the inertia of surrounding water. At any lumped mass, the added mass of water is assumed to be given by

$$m_w = \tfrac{1}{2}\pi\rho CJb^2 1$$

Here, C is a coefficient first defined by Lewis [6] which allows for the underwater shape of the hull. Values are readily available in the literature eg [6] - [11] to a variety of degrees of approximation. For a circular cylinder, C = 1. J is a factor which makes some allowance for the 3-D nature of the real flow, and reduces the added masses from the more constrained 2-D values. Values for J can be found from [6] or [7]. Strictly, a different value should be used for each mode of vibration, but in practice the error in whipping calculations has been found to be minor if the 2-node mode value is used in the equations covering all modes. Overall, the added mass is usually between 1 and $1\tfrac{1}{2}$ times the displacement of the ship.

For a ship vibrating in still water, the forces acting on it due to the pressures in the surrounding water will, with the above assumptions, be

$$\underline{F}_h = - M_w\ddot{\underline{y}} - K\underline{y} \qquad (2)$$

where M_w and K are the diagonal matrices (m_w) and $(2g\rho b1)$ and the latter matrix represents, approximately, the hydrostatic buoyancy force.

c) Bubble Hydrodynamics

Here too, the very simplest of models has been found to give usable answers. It is assumed that the flow around the explosion bubble is inviscid and incompressible, and that the bubble itself remains spherical and stationary. It is further assumed that the bubble motion is not modified by the presence of either the ship or the water surface. Finally, it is assumed that the gaseous explosion products obey the ideal gas law. Some of these assumptions are quite drastic, particularly that constraining the centre of the bubble to be stationary. In practice, bubbles can 'float' upwards very rapidly due to the huge buoyancy forces acting on them. Such movement modifies substantially the pressure pulse during the first bubble collapse, can bring the centre of that pulse upward, much nearer to the ship, and can modify the way the forces act on the ship. Nevertheless, although these effects can be included, quite reasonable answers are possible without complicating the analysis further.

The assumption of incompressibility is reasonable for most of the bubble pulsation except initially and, to a lesser extent, during the final stages of collapse. However, incompressibility at the start means the shockwave energy cannot be radiated away, so that part of the total energy must be excluded from the bubble at the outset. In consequence, a 'fictitious' initial radius must be used, substantially larger than the original charge size.

Under the above assumptions, the equation of motion governing pulsation of the gas bubble can be shown [4] to be, in non-dimensional form,

$$x^3 (\frac{dx}{d\tau})^2 + x^3 + kx^{-3(\gamma-1)} = 1 \qquad (3)$$

The length and time scales are given by

$$L = 3.63 W^{1/3} / z_0^{1/3} \text{ m}, \quad T = 1.422 W^{1/3} / z_0^{5/6} \text{ seconds,}$$

the adiabatic gas constant $\gamma = 1.25$, and k has the semi-empirical value $k = .0743 z_0^{(\gamma-1)}$. The constants in these equations were determined by Arons [12] to match equation (3) to TNT explosive.

The initial condition for (3) is that

$$x(0) \simeq k^{1/3(\gamma-1)} [1 + k^{1/(\gamma-1)} / 3(\gamma-1)]$$

The second term in the bracket is normally a very small correction, but can be vital for accurate integration of (3).

At a distance r metres from the centre of the bubble, the pressure is given by

$$pr = 8.10W^{1/3}z_o^{2/3}(\overset{..}{x^3}) \quad kPa.m \qquad (4)$$

and the fluid acceleration by

$$\overset{.}{u}r^2 = 7.88W^{1/3}z_o^{2/3}(\overset{..}{x^3}) \quad m^3s^{-2} \qquad (5)$$

In practice, rather than using (3) directly it has been found convenient instead, to avoid problems at the start and at the bubble collapse, to differentiate (3) and then integrate the resulting second order equation as a pair of first order equations. Thus (3) is replaced by

$$\overset{.}{x} = \sigma$$
$$\overset{.}{\sigma} = 3/2[(\gamma-1)kx^{-(3\gamma+1)}-(1+\sigma^2)/x] \qquad (6)$$

and then

$$\overset{..}{x^3} = 3x^2\overset{.}{\sigma} + 6x\sigma^2 = \frac{9}{2}x[(\gamma-1)kx^{-3\gamma}-(1-\sigma^2)] \qquad (7)$$

for use in (4) and (5).

Alternatively, equation (3) may be integrated much more efficiently by the method described in [13]. This uses a Tchebyscheff polynomial representation to integrate (3) between definite limits but may readily be extended to an indefinite upper limit.

d) Interaction Hydrodynamics

The interaction model is much less well established in the literature than the previous sub-models. Although the model used here is still very simple, it seems worth describing it more fully.

The interactive hydrodynamics is assumed to be incompressible and inviscid, consistently with the bubble hydrodynamics. In addition, it is assumed that the pressure field around the ship hull is dominated by the unsteady pressure term $\rho\overset{.}{\phi}$ rather than the steady stagnation pressure term $\frac{1}{2}\rho u^2$, which is neglected here. This assumption can be justified fairly easily, as shown in Appendix B.

For distant explosions there is a simple physical approximation which can provide the forces exerted on the ship by the bubble, and which is consistent with the strip theory used earlier for the general ship vertical vibration. The bubble on its own produces purely radial flow. The velocities it produces at the ship axis (the intersection line of the waterplane and the vertical centreline plane) define roughly the flow field which will interact with the ship. This velocity can be resolved, at each lumped mass, into three components, respectively parallel to the axis, vertical and perpendicular to the axis in the waterplane. The

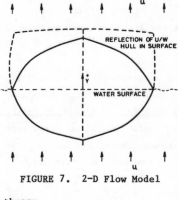

FIGURE 7.   2-D Flow Model

distant flow approximation assumes that only the latter two have any effect on the ship, and that at each lumped mass the transverse velocity around the whole section will be almost uniform in magnitude and direction. The hydrodynamic flow at each lumped mass is then approximated by a 2-D flow field, as in strip theory, instead of the full 3-D field. Clearly, for a distant explosion the accuracy of such an approximation should be very similar to that for strip theory.

The 2-D problem to be solved is that sketched in figure 7. It is identical to the standard strip theory one except that the surrounding fluid at a distance from the ship cross-section has a uniform acceleration $\dot{u}$. If the acceleration of the ship itself is $\ddot{y}$ then the relative acceleration between the water and the ship is $(\dot{u} - \ddot{y})$ and the resulting fluid force on the section will be

$$m_w(\dot{u} - \ddot{y})$$

where m_w is the strip theory added mass, as defined in section b. This force however is not the total fluid force acting on the ship. In order for the fluid away from the ship to have a uniform acceleration $\dot{u}$, there must be a uniform pressure gradient in the water of magnitude $\rho\dot{u}$. This pressure gradient is of course produced by the explosion gas bubble which is driving the fluid accelerations. So far as our approximation is concerned however it is directly equivalent to the pressure gradient which always exists in the water due to the acceleration of gravity, and like the latter gradient it induces a buoyancy force proportional to the displaced volume of water. In consequence, the total force induced on the section by the bubble is given by

$$f_b = m_w (\dot{u} - \ddot{y}) + \rho A l \dot{u}$$

where A is the submerged cross-sectional area of the hull. Setting $\bar{m}_w = \rho A l$, then

$$f_b = (m_w + \bar{m}_w)\dot{u} - m_w \ddot{y} \qquad (8)$$

and $\bar{m}_w$ is the displaced volume of water at the length of hull associated with the lumped mass concerned.

The above physical argument leading to equation (8) is essentially heuristic in nature. However, by setting up the idealised 2-D problem as a formal potential flow one, it may be shown that (8) is indeed the exact solution. Chertock, in [1], started with a more general and rigorous formulation of the problem than the approach above, but arrived at essentially the same result through a series of mathematical approximations.

Formula (8) can be expected to be reasonably accurate for distant explosions. For closer explosions, much of the flow will be directed more along the ship than across it, and for charges near the bow or stern, some flow will be "around the end". Even near the mid-ship section, the flow will actually be divergent around the section, rather than uniform as assumed here. Accordingly, it might be expected that the distant flow approximation would lose accuracy as the charge approached the ship, particularly near the bow and stern. To explore how quickly the approximation loses accuracy, it can be compared with the exact analytic solution for a point source near a prolate spheroid. Formulae for this case are given in Appendix C. Results

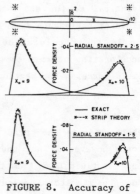

FIGURE 8. Accuracy of 2-D Model

for charges near the ends of the spheroid are shown in figure 8. Considering the very complex nature of the flow in such cases, and the closeness of the point source, the accuracy of the 'distant flow' approximation is extraordinary. Equally good results are obtained for point sources near the centre. In practical terms the results mean that the distant flow approximation is adequate at all normal standoffs. Charges which are so close that the approximation fails will be no better represented by most other approximations since at such standoffs the bubble will engulf the hull and local hull damage may also be expected, which will further distort the flow.

In all of the above discussion, it has been assumed that the ship is embedded in the water, rather than floating on it. The presence of the water surface will obviously have a substantial effect on the flow around the ship and hence on its motion. The free surface approximation adopted here is that the surface is one of constant pressure. Thus wave generation and Bernoulli pressure effects of the surface are neglected. In the case of wave effects this will lead to minor inaccuracies in the heave and pitch frequencies as calculated from the final form of the ship equations of motion, but, as shown by Ursell [14] and others, the whipping frequencies will still be fairly accurately represented.

To a partial extent the free surface effect is already included in the above equations, in the added masses m_w. The definition above, in section (b), includes a factor 1/2. The 2-D flow models whose solutions give the coefficient C in the definition of m_w assume a shape which is the underwater cross-section of the ship combined with its reflection in the water surface. The water surface is then one at zero potential. The factor 1/2 allows that the added mass in the ship case is only that which lies below the free-surface.

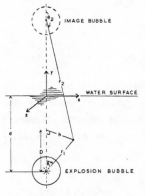

FIGURE 9. Bubble Geometry

To a similar level of approximation, the effect of the bubble acting on the ship in the presence of the free surface can be represented by the standard artifice of adding an

image bubble at the reflection point above the surface, as in figure
9. The original bubble is represented by a simple hydrodynamic
source and the image bubble by an equal strength sink. The fluid potential
at the water surface is then identically zero, so satisfying the constant
pressure criterion. At the water surface too, the combined effects of the
bubble and image reduce the horizontal velocities and accelerations to
zero while doubling them in the vertical direction. Since the distant flow
approximation only concerns itself with fluid accelerations at the
waterplane centreline, the whipping it predicts is always vertical, never
horizontal.

Allowing for the image bubble, the vertical acceleration for use in
(8) is

$$\dot{u}_v = \frac{cd}{r^3}(\ddot{x}^3) \tag{9}$$

where

$$c = 15.77 W^{1/3} z_o^{2/3}$$

e) Full Equations

The equations necessary to provide a full description of the ship
motion are now complete. The forces needed to maintain a given
displacement, as in (1), are provided by the inertial forces of the ship
motion and the fluid forces. Thus

$$[A - BC^{-1}B^T]\underline{y} = -M\ddot{\underline{y}} - M_w\ddot{\underline{y}} - K\underline{y} + (M_w + \bar{M}_w)\dot{\underline{u}}_v$$

whence

$$(M + M_w)\ddot{\underline{y}} + [A + K - BC^{-1}B^T]\underline{y} = (M_w + \bar{M}_w)\dot{\underline{u}}_v \tag{10}$$

where $\dot{\underline{u}}_v$ is a vector of the vertical accelerations given by (9) at the
lumped mass positions, and $\ddot{x}^3$ is given by integration of equations (6),
through equation (7). Equation (10) fully defines the dynamic response of
the hull as an elastic system acted on by forces due to the pulsating
explosion bubble.

f) Computational Details

The RHS of (10), although time dependent, is not dependent in any way
on the solution of the LHS and can be solved separately if necessary. This

can be advantageous since efficient numerical integration of the bubble equations requires a variable step length. Very small time steps are necessary at the start of the bubble motion and also later, around the time of bubble collapse. At intermediate times relatively large time increments suffice. For the integration of the LHS a constant time increment is most suitable.

As the LHS stands, it contains as many natural frequencies of vibration as lumped masses. Only the lowest few modes however will be accurately represented. It is sensible to use modal decomposition to decouple the equations and then to discard all but the lowest frequency modes. The equation is of the form

$$M_1 \ddot{\underline{y}} + S\underline{y} = \underline{g}(t) \tag{11}$$

where M_1 is diagonal and S symmetric. Since M_1 is diagonal, $M_1^{-1/2}$ has the obvious meaning $(1/m_k^{1/2})$ and equation (11) may be written

$$\ddot{\underline{z}} + (M_1^{-1/2} S M_1^{-1/2})\underline{z} = M_1^{-1/2} \underline{g}(t) \ ,$$

where

$$\underline{z} = M_1^{1/2} \underline{y}$$

The matrix $M_1^{-1/2} S M_1^{-1/2}$ is symmetric and positive definite, as S is, and so has eigen values ω_i^2 which are positive. If the corresponding normalised eigen vectors are $\underline{z}_i$, then

$$(M_1^{-1/2} S M_1^{-1/2})\underline{z}_i = \omega_i^2 \underline{z}_i \quad \text{and} \quad \underline{z}_i^T \cdot \underline{z}_j = \delta_{ij}$$

whence

$$S\underline{y}_i = \omega_i^2 M_1 \underline{y}_i \quad \text{and} \quad \underline{y}_i^T M_1 \underline{y}_j = \delta_{ij}$$

where the vectors $\underline{y}_i$, given by $\underline{y}_i = M_1^{-1/2}\underline{z}_i$, are the vertical vibration modes of the ship. The first two, $\underline{y}_o$ and $\underline{y}_1$, represent heave and pitch; only slightly coupled to bending, while the others represent true bending modes.

The general displacement $\underline{y}$ may now be represented in the form

$$\underline{y}(t) = \sum_o^N \alpha_i(t)\underline{y}_i$$

and equation (11) then decouples to (N+1) second order equations

$$\ddot{\alpha}_i + \omega_i^2 \alpha_i = h_i(t) \quad (i = 0, \ldots, N) \tag{12}$$

where $h_i(t) = \underline{y}_i^T \cdot \underline{g}(t)$. In practice, it has been found that only the first five or six modal equations need to be integrated to represent experimental results adequately.

The RHS of equation (12) is then given by

$$h_i(t) = \beta_i \cdot (\ddot{x}^3)$$

where

$$\beta_i = \underline{y}_i^T \cdot (M_w + \bar{M}_w) \cdot \underline{\mu}$$

and the vector $\underline{\mu}$ is $cd(1/r_1^3, 1/r_2^3, \ldots, 1/r_{20}^3)^T$. The RHS is therefore essentially the same for all modal equations, differing only in the constants β_i.

RESULTS

Data for a 2500 ton destroyer were prepared in a form suitable for the above equations and are given in table 1. The first few bending mode

Mass Number	Distance From bow feet x	Ship Mass tons m	Added mass tons m_w	Buoyancy tons $\bar{m}_w$	Immersion force tons/foot k	Section area in^2	Shear area in^2 A_s	Section inertia ft^2.in^2 I
1	8.8	34	3	14	2.50	333	111	37200
2	26.4	41	18	42	5.71	422	109	44000
3	44.0	62	47	68	8.97	510	107	52400
4	61.6	64	77	94	11.29	603	106	61500
5	79.2	120	113	117	13.50	693	108	71300
6	96.8	225	149	138	15.25	813	122	86000
7	114.4	241	184	156	16.78	1077	162	110100
8	132.0	103	218	172	18.04	845	136	69200
9	149.6	155	239	184	18.65	860	136	71600
10	167.2	136	248	193	18.83	875	137	73200
11	184.8	158	254	185	18.92	875	138	72800
12	202.4	191	252	185	18.90	863	138	71600
13	220.0	127	237	181	18.69	841	136	68400
14	237.6	137	221	173	18.38	783	129	62000
15	255.2	139	203	162	18.00	727	120	52800
16	272.8	238	176	145	17.25	654	108	42600
17	290.4	177	151	120	16.71	544	98	28800
18	308.0	60	137	92	15.40	478	82	19900
19	325.6	56	86	63	12.00	420	67	12000
20	343.2	54	60	35	9.90			
Total		2518	3073	2519				

TABLE 1. Elastic Beam and Mass Data for a Destroyer

shapes and frequencies, calculated as above, are compared with experimental results (crosses) in figure 10. The agreement is very reasonable. Numerical experiments with modified equations showed that inclusion of rotary inertias for the ship changed the lowest five bending mode frequencies by less than 1%, confirming their neglect above. Neglect of transverse shear however raised the lowest frequency by 9% and affected higher modes substantially more, confirming the importance of shear.

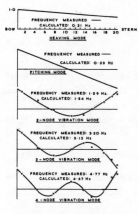

Figure 11 shows typical comparisons between experiment and theory. Figure 11a shows results for the ship in figure 1, for an earlier, elastic test. Figure 11b shows results for two tests against another ship, and shows the difference that the charge location can make in the dynamic response. The second test scarcely excited the lowest whipping mode and the strains measured are almost entirely due to the second and third bending modes.

DISCUSSION

FIGURE 10.   Vibration
                    Modes

Although only a few results have been shown, it is clear that the analysis presented contains the essential ingredients of the explosion/ship interaction. The data required are not extensive and can be estimated reasonably well early in the design process, which can then ensure that sufficient girder strength is provided to resist any particular severity of attack.

The analysis is the simplest form expected to give reasonable answers. A number of the approximations used may fairly easily be

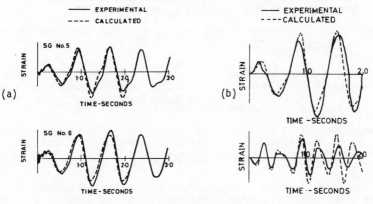

FIGURE 11.   Comparison of Theory with Experiment

improved, in most cases with relatively little increase in computational effort. Agreement with experiment can thereby be improved, but is already good so the improvements are somewhat marginal for most geometries.

REFERENCES

1. Chertock, G., The flexural response of a submerged solid to a pulsating gas bubble. J. Applied Physics 24 (1953) No 2.

2. Jinhua, M.A. and Qiyong, Z., The estimation of dynamic bending moment for a ship subjected to underwater noncontact explosions. Proc. Int. Symp. on Mine Warfare Vessels and Systems, RINA, London (June 1984).

3. Trimming C., Monocoque GRP minehunters. Proc. Inst. Symp. on Mine Warfare Vessels and Systems, RINA, London, (June 1984).

4. Cole, R.H., Underwater explosions Princeton University Press (1948).

5. Taylor, G.I., The pressure and impulse of submarine explosion waves on plates. Underwater Explosion Research, Vol 1 - The Shock Wave. Office of Naval Research (1950).

6. Lewis, F.M., The inertia of the water surrounding a vibrating ship, Trans. SNAME 37 (1929).

7. Taylor, J.L., Some hydrodynamical inertia coefficients. Phil Mag. 57, Vol 9, 55 (1930).

8. Prohaska, C.W., The vertical vibration of ships. The Shipbuilder and Marine Engine Builder (1947).

9. Wendel, K., Hydrodynamic masses and moments of inertia. Jahrbuch der Schiffbautechnische Gesellschaft 44 (1950).

10. Macagno, M., A comparison of three methods for computing the added masses of ship sections. J. Ship Research 12, 4 (1968).

11. Hoffman, D., Conformal mapping techniques in ship hydrodynamics. Webb Institute of Naval Architecture Report 41-1 (1969).

12. Arons, B., Secondary pressure pulses due to gas globe oscillation in underwater explosions- II selection of adiabatic parameters in the theory of oscillation. Underwater Explosion Research Vol II - The Gas Globe. Office of Naval Research (1950).

13. Shiffman, M. and Friedman,B., Studies on the gas globe resulting from underwater explosions: on the best location of a mine near the seabed. Underwater Explosion Research Vol II - The Gas Globe, Office of Naval Research (1950).

14. Ursell, F., On the heaving motion of a circular cylinder on the surface of a fluid. Quart J Mech and App Maths 2 (1949).

APPENDIX A

Stiffness Coefficients

The non-zero elements of the matrices A, B, and C of equation (1) are given by

$$a_{i,i-1} = -6\alpha_{i-1} \qquad\qquad b_{i,i-1} = -3\alpha_{i-1}l$$

$$a_{i,i} = 6(\alpha_{i-1} + \alpha_i) \qquad b_{i,i} = -3\alpha_{i-1}l + 3\alpha_i l$$

$$a_{i,i+1} = -6\alpha_i \qquad\qquad\quad b_{i,i+1} = 3\alpha_i l$$

$$c_{i,i-1} = \alpha_{i-1}l^2(1-\epsilon_{i-1}) \qquad c_{i,i+1} = \alpha_i l^2(1-\epsilon_i)$$

$$c_{i,i} = \alpha_{i-1}l^2(2+\epsilon_{i-1}) + \alpha_i l^2(2+\epsilon_i)$$

where

$$\epsilon = \frac{12(1+\nu)I_i}{A_{si}l^2} \quad, \qquad\qquad \alpha = \frac{2EI_i}{l^3(1+2\epsilon_i)}$$

and α_o and α_n are defined to be zero.

APPENDIX B

Neglect of Stagnation Pressures

The unsteady pressure p_u and stagnation pressure p_s are given by

$$p_u = \rho\dot\phi \sim \frac{\rho\ddot V}{4\pi r} \qquad\qquad p_s = \frac{1}{2}\rho u^2 = \frac{\rho\dot V^2}{32\pi^2 r^4}$$

whence

$$\left|\frac{p_s}{p_u}\right| = \frac{\dot V^2}{8\pi r^3 \ddot V} \sim \frac{L^3}{6r^3}\cdot\left[\frac{(\dot x^3)^2}{(\ddot x^3)}\right]$$

in the non-dimensional form of section (c). In general, the bubble maximum radius is in the range .9L to .95L so that

$$\left|\frac{p_s}{p_u}\right| \sim \frac{1}{8}\cdot\left[\frac{a_m}{r}\right]^3\cdot\left[\frac{(\dot x^3)^2}{(\ddot x^3)}\right]$$

This ratio can have any value from zero to infinity, since at different times during the bubble pulsation $\dot x^3$ and $\ddot x^3$ each becomes zero. However, the important features are the 'maximum' values of $\dot x^3$ and $\ddot x^3$ and their relative durations.

From the bubble equations of section (c),

$$\left(\overset{..}{x}^3\right)_{max} = \frac{9}{2}\cdot\frac{\gamma-1}{x_m^2}\cdot\left[1-\frac{\gamma}{\gamma-1}\cdot x_m^3\right]$$

so that, at the bubble minimum,

$$\left(\overset{..}{x}^3\right)_m \sim \frac{9}{2}\cdot\frac{(\gamma-1)}{k^{2/3(\gamma-1)}} \sim 150$$

at moderate depths, and at the bubble maximum,

$$\left(\overset{..}{x}^3\right)_m \sim -\frac{9}{2}\cdot\left[1-(\gamma-2/3)\right] \sim -4$$

For $\left(\overset{.}{x}^3\right)_{max}$, $\overset{..}{x}^3 = 0$, which occurs when $x^3 \sim 1/4$ and then

$$\left(\overset{.}{x}^3\right)_{max} \sim 1.75$$

Thus the maximum stagnation pressure is small even compared with the low suction values at the bubble maximum radius, as

$$\left|\frac{P_s}{P_u}\right| \sim .1\left[\frac{a_m}{r}\right]^3$$

and $P_s \ll P_u$ at the bubble surface, and decays far more rapidly at greater distances. The duration of the high stagnation pressures is also much less than that of the bubble suction. It seems then that $1/2\rho u^2$ stagnation pressures can be neglected down to standoffs at which the bubble touches the target at its maximum.

APPENDIX C

Prolate Spheroid Solution

The idealised problem of a point source near a prolate spheroid can be solved exactly since the Laplace equation for flow in an incompressible inviscid fluid is separable in ellipsoidal coordinates. The algebra is a little lengthy, but the transverse force $f(x)$ per unit length at a longitudinal position x can be reduced to

$$\frac{f(x)}{2\pi\rho\overset{.}{e}} = -\sum_{n=1}^{\infty}\frac{(2n+1)}{n(n+1)}\cdot T_n^1(\mu_1)[(1-\mu^2)^{1/2}\cdot T_n^1(\mu)]\cdot\frac{Q_n^1(\zeta_1)}{(\zeta_o^2-1)^{1/2}Q_n^{1\prime}(\zeta_o)}$$

where e is the strength of the source, a and b are the semi-major and semi-minor axes of the spheroid, and x_1 and c are the longitudinal and radial (cylindrical) coordinates of the point source. The ellipsoidal coordinates are given by

$$\mu = x/a, \quad \zeta_o = a/k, \quad \text{with} \quad k = (a^2 - b^2)^{1/2}$$

and ζ_1, μ_1 are derived from

$$c = k(\zeta_1^2-1)^{1/2}(1-\mu_1^2)^{1/2}$$

$$x_1 = k\zeta_1\mu_1$$

Unfortunately, the series is rather slowly convergent, and up to 150 terms were needed to achieve reasonable accuracy (.1%) for a 10:1 ellipsoid and a radial standoff c of $1\frac{1}{2}$ times the maximum transverse radius.

APPENDIX D

Notation

a_m	Bubble maximum radius
A^m	Shear area of ship girder cross-section
A^s, B, C	Stiffness matrices
b	Half-beam of ship section
C	'Lewis' coefficient for added mass
d	Depth of charge
E	Young's modulus
f	Force on a lumped mass
$\underline{F}$, $\underline{M}$	Force and moment vectors
g	Gravity
$\underline{g}(t)$	Forcing function vector
J	2-D to 3-D correction factor for added mass
k	Non-dimensional gas energy constant
K	Buoyancy matrix
l	Length of hull between adjacent lumped masses
L	Bubble length scale
m, m_w, $\bar{m}$	Ship, added and displacement masses
M, M_w^w, $\bar{M}_w^w$, M_1	Mass matrices (all diagonal)
p	Pressure in water
r	Radial coordinate (spherical)
S	Stiffness matrix
t	Time variable
$T_n^m(x)$, $Q_n^m(x)$	Associated Legendre functions of the first and second kinds
T	Bubble time scale
u, u_v	Water radial and vertical velocities
V	Bubble volume
W	Charge weight (kg of TNT)
x	Axial coordinate and non-dimensional bubble radius
y	Vertical ship displacement
$\underline{y}i$	Normal mode of ship (vertical vibration mode)
$\underline{z}_i$	Eigenvector
Z_o	Hydrostatic pressure at bubble centre

(d+ 10 m)

$\alpha_i(t)$ Mode coefficient

γ Gas adiabatic exponent

δ_{ij} Kroneker delta function

ζ, μ Spheroidal coordinates

θ Lumped mass rotation

ρ Water density

τ Non-dimensional time in bubble equation

σ Non-dimensional bubble surface radial velocity

ω_i Vibration mode radian frequency

ν Poisson's ratio

ϕ Velocity potential

DESIGN OF SUBMARINE STRUCTURES

S.B.Kendrick
Admiralty Research Establishment
Dunfermline, Fife, Scotland

ABSTRACT

A survey is given of methods for the analysis of submarine structure up to the point of collapse. It is shown that for many practical cases simple formulae are as accurate as the most advanced computer methods. Design criteria are discussed and a simple design optimisation technique is presented. Some problems requiring complex elasto-plastic analysis are described.

INTRODUCTION

The term submarine structure will be taken to mean one in which the dominant loading is external pressure with a small variation in the pressure magnitude over the structure. This is a considerable simplification since it excludes the many offshore structures which have to resist significant overall bending actions. In the absence of overall bending effects the use of longitudinal stiffening is inefficient and the primary structure is predominantly axisymmetric. Design is usually carried out assuming axial symmetry of structure and loads with subsequent detailed analysis of particular non-axisymmetric features such as openings and internal structure.

The predominant design need is to ensure an adequate static collapse pressure and for many civil purposes this is interpreted as ensuring that the risk of collapse at 1.5 times the maximum working pressure is acceptably small. This is the basis of the external pressure section of the British Pressure Vessel Standard BS5500 [1] where the intention is to provide a minimum safety factor of 1.5.

412

Ideally the safety factor of 1.5 should be partially verified by proof testing at about 1.25-1.30 times the working pressure but this is usually regarded as impracticable which puts a great premium on valid design procedures and fabrication control. For example, it is necessary to ensure that the strength of the material employed does not fall significantly below the design figure assumed. This is not easy since yield stresses can vary greatly for a given material even in one plate of a given material and there is no non-destructive method of evaluating yield stress. The guarantee on yield stress depends on all of the production checks being adhered to and not only on meeting the minimum strength requirement.

It is also necessary to ensure that shape tolerances are not exceeded since there can be a marked loss of strength for small departures from the design tolerance.

Valid design procedures are best checked by the use of model testing with the model fabrication method simulating that on full scale as far as possible. For example if cold bending procedures are employed on full scale, they should be employed on model scale. The model should also be manufactured with realistic shape tolerances especially those calculated to be the most critical. Scaling of welds is not usually possible but oversize model welds will usually produce a degree of conservatism in the model.

A secondary design requirement is to ensure an adequate fatigue life. Since the membrane forces and maximum stresses are compressive for externally pressurised structure a fatigue problem arises only because of the presence of high residual tensile stresses due to welding. If these can be eliminated by stress relieving, the fatigue problem will disappear. If not then fatigue cracking needs to be considered if repeated loadings occur. A simple but very conservative way of doing this is to consider the pressure to be internal and to use the criteria given by the major Pressure Vessel Codes such as BS5500 [1] or ASME VIII [2].

The paper will now consider the methods available for calculating the structural behaviour of externally pressurised vessels. This subject was treated by the author in [3] under the following headings:

a.   Stress Analysis
b.   Elastic Stability
c.   The Effect of Shape Imperfections
d.   Behaviour beyond the Elastic Limit
e.   Collapse Pressure Prediction
f.   Design.

Each subject heading will now be discussed briefly bringing out the advances made since [3] was published.

STRESS ANALYSIS

Axisymmetric

The derivation of the general differential equation governing the axisymmetric deformation of cylindrical shells is given in [4] where stress expressions are given for the case of equally spaced stiffeners neglecting the non-linear "beam-column" effect. This Reference shows that for one typical geometry the beam column effect rises from 3% to 6% as the yield stress is raised from 430 to 900 N/mm^2. For most designs the linearised expressions are adequate. Two of these formulae are used in the design code BS5500 [1]. A major advance has been the wide availability on mini-computers of the program BOSOR 4 [5] which uses a finite difference method of solution and can stress analyse any axisymmetric shell using linear or non-linear theory. It can also deal with a wide variety of materials and methods of construction, eg orthotropic and sandwich shell.

An alternative more specialised but better engineered program for stress analysis is described in [6]. Axisymmetric stress analysis is now quite straightforward and as will be shown later most vessels can be designed entirely using this type of analysis together with buckling analysis even when marked non-axisymmetric features are present. Lack of axial symmetry due to shape imperfections is a special case which will be dealt with later.

One particular use for general axisymmetric analysis is for avoiding premature collapse due to the end bay effect which is discussed in [4], Page 64.

Non-Axisymmetric Analysis

Some sophisticated vessels require non-axisymmetric stress analysis for reasons of keeping weight to a minimum or due to a need to use an unusual configuration or for fatigue analysis. This type of analysis is far more difficult and expensive and requires considerable experience to be meaningful. There are two main possible methods. Firstly the use of a general Finite Element program which involves much labour in terms of data preparation unless a specialised pre-processor is available. The choice of program will depend on availability and familiarity and upon whether or not linear analysis is adequate. In general, linear analysis is adequate for fatigue purposes and for verifying the adequacy of stiffening provided that premature collapse due to inadequate stiffening has been designed out.

When stiffener yielding can occur close to the design collapse pressure and before inter-stiffener shell collapse then nonlinear elasto-plastic analysis is needed. For such an analysis the use of nominal geometry will normally be inappropriate and non-conservative and possible departures from nominal shape will need to be included. In some cases where large deflection nonlinear analysis is required, the ability of the finite element program to allow for large deflection needs to be examined carefully.

An alternative for certain problems is to use a program for the linear analysis of axisymmetric structures under non-axisymmetric loading and to treat the interaction with non-axisymmetric structure by colocation methods. An example is illustrated in Figure 1 where the unknown reaction forces between the partial bulkhead and the stiffened shell are found by equating deflections at the boundary. A very suitable program for this type of analysis is BOSOR 4 [5] which has an excellent facility for analysing axisymmetric structure under non-axisymmetric loading.

The reinforcement around penetrations in cylinders can be analysed by assuming a fictitious axis of symmetry treating the shell as a flat plate with a 1:1 stress field on the boundary (Figure 2). The maximum stress concentration for the actual 2:1 stress field is usually similar to that for the 1:1 stress field.

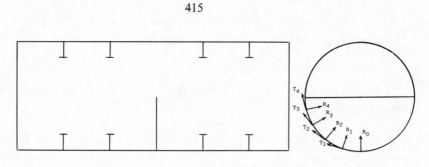

FIGURE 1.   Non Axisymmetric Structure

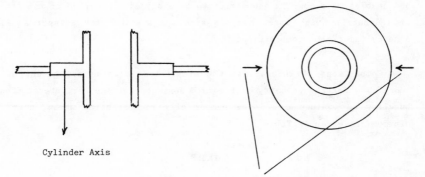

Cylinder Axis

Uniform Stress Field
at Large Radius

FIGURE 2.   Axisymmetric Analysis of a Penetration

ELASTIC STABILITY

The importance of the classical small deflection buckling pressure in pressure vessel design is discussed in [3] where methods of analysis suitable for micro-computers are given for the three cases of:

a.   Interstiffener buckling
b.   Overall buckling
c.   Local Instability

Simplified formulae suitable for hand calculators are also given for all three types of buckling.

An extension to the theory of local instability of [3] which treats shell-stiffener interaction correctly is given in [7].

The theories given in [3], [4], [7] are all idealised and use approximations based on physical thinking which enable simple formulae to be derived. The program BOSOR4 [5] now makes possible the calculation of small deflection buckling pressures for any axisymmetric structure without the need for approximations. This does not remove the need for the simplified formulae described earlier but enables their accuracy to be assessed and enables more complex geometries to be analysed. Examples of the latter are geometries with more than one size and spacing of stiffeners. Also cone/cylinder/dome combinations.

Comparisons of BOSOR4 with the simplified formulae are given in [4] and [7]. For the geometry of Figure 3 some comparisons for interstiffener buckling for values of n, the number of circumferential waves, near the minimum are given in Table 1.

TABLE 1

Elastic Buckling Pressures (N/mm^2) (Interstiffener Buckling)

n	N9E	P_m	BOSOR4
9	9.55	9.62	9.94
10	8.52	8.57	8.91
11	7.84	7.89	8.24
12	7.45	7.49	7.85
13	7.27	7.32	7.70
14	7.40	7.31	7.71
15	7.63	7.44	7.86

N9E refers to the ARE program written for combined shell and stiffener buckling theory of [7]; P_m is the interstiffener buckling pressure given

in [3]. The agreement is good and the simpler formulae are slightly conservative. Similar comparisons for local instability are given in Table 2.

TABLE 2

Elastic Buckling Pressures (N/mm^2)(Local Instability)

n	N9E	BOSOR4
2	16.6	15.7
3	16.4	15.4
4	16.6	15.5
5	16.9	16.0
6	19.5	18.6
7	21.2	19.9
8	23.6	22.0
9	26.5	24.5
10	29.9	27.3

The agreement is good but this time the simple formula is slightly non-
conservative.

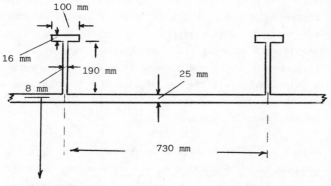

radius 2700 mm

FIGURE 3.   Shell & Stiffener Geometry

Comparisons for overall instability have been carried out for two overall lengths with the geometry of Figure 3 and are given in Table 3.

TABLE 3

Elastic Buckling Pressures (N/mm^2) (Overall Instability)

Overall Length 21,600 mm			Overall Length Infinite		
n	P_n	BOSOR4	P_n	BOSOR4
2	4.47	4.49	3.22	3.37
3	8.59	9.72	8.53	8.59
4	15.9	18.2	15.9	14.8

The P_n value is obtained from equation 3.18 of [4]. For the case of infinite length the agreement is excellent and in this case the BOSOR4 idealisation used branch shells throughout; ie no approximations except those of thin shell theory. For the shorter length the stiffeners were idealised as discrete rings so that engineering approximations are used in the formulation of stiffeners. This probably accounts for the BOSOR4 results being around 10% higher than p_n with the latter results from the simple formula being the more accurate. The formula p_n is a modified form of the Bryant formula allowing for reduced effective breadth. Dr Bryant was Chief Scientist of this Establishment in 1950 and this formula is one of the best illustrations of the use of intuitive physical thinking that was essential in the days when electrical powered mechanical calculations were the ultimate number crunchers.

P_n values for several overall lengths are given in Table 4. The results illustrate very clearly that p_2 is very sensitive to overall length L_c whereas p_3 and, even more so, p_4 rapidly become insensitive to increasing length.

It is also interesting to see what BOSOR4 gave for n = 14 for the above example with overall length = 21,600 mm. The results were 9.565,

9.582, 9.598 N/mm^2 for the first three buckling pressures. These compare with P_m = 7.31 N/mm^2 and 7.71 N/mm^2 from Table 1. It is clear that the BOSOR4 result for finite length is too high due mainly to excessive rotational restraint by the stiffeners arising from the use of discrete rings. Another factor may be the use of 10 integration points between stiffeners which may be too few for interstiffener buckling.

TABLE 4

Overall Elastic Buckling Pressure (N/mm^2)

L_c(mm)	3750	6750	8250	9750	11250	21600	Infinite
P2	112.0	43.7	27.0	17.6	12.2	4.07	3.22
P3	32.4	13.4	11.0	9.90	9.34	8.59	8.59
P4	22.3	16.9	16.3	16.1	16.0	15.9	15.9

The graphical output of mode shapes obtainable from BOSOR4 can be extremely informative. [4] shows several examples showing that the simple idealised shapes used in the simple analytical theories of [3] and illustrated in Figure 4 appear in BOSOR4 mode shapes. It is also shown in [4] that the mode shapes given can be spurious even when the buckling pressures are accurate. This is not due to any error in BOSOR4 but to the fact that mode shapes can be extremely sensitive to the number of integration points and to the way in which the stiffeners are idealised. An illustration is shown in Figure 5 which is taken from [4]. These mode shapes correspond to the three Eigenvalues for n = 14 given earlier. It is to be expected that completely different mode shapes would occur if for example one extra integration point was used in one shell section between adjacent stiffeners. They would differ again if one or some or all stiffeners were idealised as branch shells. The mode shapes are only meaningful if they are affected little by increasing the number of integration points.

BOSOR4 is also very valuable for calculating the buckling pressures for combinations of cones, cylinders and dome ends. The elastic buckling pressures for domes are of limited use, however, since the classical formula for a sphere applies to small wavelengths of buckle and therefore to most configurations of actual dome ends. The non-linear capabilities of

420

BOSOR4 are useful for examining the effects of areas where shape imperfections lead to areas of flattening on dome ends. However this is only useful in a research context.

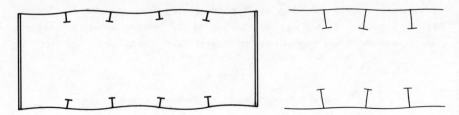

Interstiffener Buckling   Local Instability

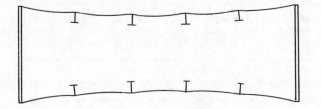

Overall Buckling

FIGURE 4. Idealised Buckling Shapes

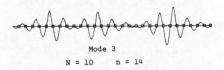

Mode 1

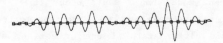

Mode 2

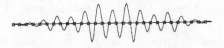

Mode 3

N = 10   n = 14

FIGURE 5. Mode Shapes from BOSOR4

THE EFFECT OF SHAPE IMPERFECTIONS

The previous section on buckling postulates a vessel with perfect axial symmetry so that pressures can be reached at which two equilibrium states are possible:

a.   An axisymmetric deformed state which may be nonlinear with pressure.

b.   A non-axisymmetric deformation of indeterminate magnitude.

At the buckling pressure the most minute disturbance to state 1 brings about state 2. Real vessels behave quite differently since the departures from perfect circularity grow steadily from their initial "as manufactured" values when external pressure is increased from zero. One definition of the small deflection buckling pressure is that at which these departures grow to indefinitely large values.

The calculation of the growth of initial shape imperfections is discussed in [3] where the stresses due to interstiffener shape imperfections are derived. For reasons discussed later this calculation is not useful in design but is the basis of Appendix M in BS5500.

Shape imperfections in stiffened cylinders and cones affect strength mainly due to the additional bending stresses induced in stiffeners. It will be shown later that collapse can be precipitated by yielding in the stiffeners at a pressure little higher than that at which the yielding first occurs. For this reason it is important to be able to calculate by simple methods the stiffener stress in the presence of shape imperfections. This can be done using the following equation, derived in [3].

$$f_b = (n^2-1)(Ee_f/a^2)[C_o \, P/P_n - p)]$$

where f_b is the bending stress at pressure p in the stiffener flange due to a shape imperfection of magnitude C_o in the shape of the buckling mode associated with overall buckling pressure P_n, e_f is the distance of the stiffener flange from the neutral axis, a is the shell radius and E is Youngs Modulus.

Adding this bending stress to the axisymmetric stress in the stiffener flange given in [4] gives the total stiffener stress. This total stress divided by the stiffener yield stress gives the quantity F_n used in BS5500 as the criterian for stiffener strength. It is evaluated for C_o = .005a and at pressures discussed in the section on design. The criterian used is that F_n must be less than or equal to unity for n = 2 to 6.

The influence of shape imperfection on the pressure causing yielding in the stiffeners is illustrated in Table 5 (taken from [4]) for the geometry of Figure 3 with stiffener yield stress − 400 N/mm_2.

TABLE 5

Pressures Causing Stiffener Yield (N/mm^2)

C_o/a	L_c(mm)	n	P_n	Yield Pressure (Py Stiffener)	P_c ZRS	P_c RS2
0	nr	nr	nr	5.28		
.0025	21600	2	4.07	2.66	2.64	2.32
.005	21600	2	4.07	2.15	2.21	2.03
.01	21600	2	4.07	1.61	1.73	1.66
0.0025	11250	2	12.25	4.48	4.42	4.56
0.0025	21600	3	8.594	3.14	3.14	2.80
0.005	21600	3	8.594	2.40	2.44	2.28
0.01	21600	3	8.594	1.68	1.70	1.62
0.0025	11250	3	9.342	3.28	3.33	3.12

nr not relevant

P_c values are from elastoplastic calculations discussed later

The pressure causing yield drops from 5.28N/mm_2 for perfect circularity to only 50% of that value for a shape imperfection of only 0.25% on radius and to only 30% for a shape imperfection of 1% on radius. This demonstrates clearly how important it is to keep within shape tolerance. The table also demonstrates that the most critical shape imperfection for long cylinder is ovality (n = 2) whereas for shorter cylinders, n = 3 can be more critical. For even shorter cylinders higher values of n can be critical.

To a good approximation the equation (1) can be used for more general shape imperfection W_o defined as Fourier series.

$$W_o = \sum_{n=2}^{N} \sum_{m=1}^{M} [C_{mn} \sin n\theta \sin(m\,x/L_c) + D_{mn} \cos n\theta \sin (m\,x/L_c)]$$

where x is the axial coordinate

This approach is of little use in design since the coefficients C_{mn}, D_{mm} cannot be known in advance. For design purposes, the shape impefection is assumed to be in a pure mode which is conservative except for the consideration discussed in [3] Page 454. This concerns the fact that the half sine wave longitudinal shape does not necessarily give the highest stresses for long stiffened cylinders. This error is small however and is swamped by the difference due to mixed modes in real fabrication.

BEHAVIOUR BEYOND THE ELASTIC LIMIT

For practical designs collapse always involves plasticity and the calculation of elasto-plastic collapse is always significantly more lengthy than elastic stress analysis or elastic buckling analysis. It will be shown later that collapse can usually be predicted with sufficient accuracy without recourse to elasto-plastic analysis provided that certain conditions are met. It is nevertheless useful to consider the capabilities of elasto-plastic analysis in order to:

a. examine the validity of partial safety factors when simpler methods are used in design.

b. Assess the ability of elasto-plastic methods to assess the adequacy of vessels which deliberately or accidentally do not meet the usual design tolerance.

As an example of b. above, the design criteria of [1] requires vessels to meet shape tolerances for various pure mode shapes. A vessel might well be fabricated outwith these tolerances but be adequately strong due to a favourable phasing of the shape departure components. The measurement of the full 3D shapes combined with elasto-plastic analysis would be a formidable task but could be justifiable in some circumstances. For example rebuilding the vessel could be unacceptable in terms of cost or timescale. Obviously it would be necessary to be fairly sure before carrying out such a calculation that the answer would be acceptable. This would require simpler methods of assessment.

A valid elasto-plastic calculation must take into account many complex factors including the effect of shape imperfection and the effect of residual stresses. Elasto-plastic analysis methods that are available involve either the numerical integration of differential equations or the solution of finite difference equations or the solution of equations produced by finite element methods. Differential equations methods are usually only useful for very specialised problems whereas finite element methods are of general application with finite difference methods somewhere between in terms of range of applicability.

A differential equation approach is used in the theory of [9] which calculates the overall collapse pressure of stiffened cylinders with initial shape imperfections. This theory incorporated in ARE Program N103 has given good agreement with experimental collapse pressures in the limited number of relevant tests. These require built-in shape imperfections that approximate to buckling modes. Results from this program are compared with yield pressures from elastic theory in Table 5 for the cases:
   a.   ZRS with zero initial residual stress.
   b.   RS2 with cold bent shell and stiffeners.

It can be seen that the plastic collapse pressures are very close to the yield pressures for Case a. This is in part due to the use of T-bar stiffeners for which flange yielding leads to a rapid loss of stiffness. The collapse pressures are seen to be reduced by the presence of cold bent stresses with the effect reducing as the out-of-roundness increases.

The program N103 referred to above is suitable for a micro-computer and is useful in design but has limitations because it cannot deal with the following factors:
   a.   interstiffener collapse
   b.   general intial shapes
   c.   variable stiffener size or spacing
   d.   Yield stress variation over the shell or stiffeners.

Several non-linear finite element programs claim to be capable of calculating the deformations in stiffened shells up to the collapse pressure and several (10), (11), (12) are maintained and have been tried out at ARE.

The STAGS program (11) has been used more extensively and successfully at ARE Dunfermline than ASAS(N/L) or LUSAS. Typical results from STAGS are as follows:

For overall collapse with 0.5% out-of-circularity
n = 2   STAGS collapse pressure   2% lower than N103
        STAGS collapse pressure   4% higher than P_y (Stiffener)
n = 3   STAGS collapse pressure   8% higher than N103
        STAGS collapse pressure   5% higher than P_y (Stiffener)

For interstiffener collapse
STAGS collapse pressure 2% higher than the empirical collapse curve
                with 0.5% n = 3 out-of-circularity
                0.6% higher with an additional .02% axi-
                symmetric inwards departure from the
                cylindrical

The agreement with P_y (Stiffener) was only as close because it was for a case with zero residual stress.

The few comparative calculations using ASAS(N/L) have shown extremely close agreement with STAGS.

The non-linear calculations discussed briefly above and treated in more detail in [13] show encouraging agreement with N103 and with the empirical design curve. It is likely that they are of similar rather than better accuracy compared to the simpler methods for the idealised problems for which the latter are suitable. The computer times required are considerable. The overall collapse n = 2 calculations referred to above with a small additional n = 3 component required 70 hours CPU on a VAX 782.

This makes clear that at the present time the main use of non-linear analysis is for research or for examining special problems for which simpler methods are not available. One typical research task is to examine the effect on collapse of variable yield strength material. This is relevant to the calculation of reliability since virtually all vessels will be fabricated from plate which is on average significantly stronger than the minimum specification. Overall collapse cannot be expected to correlate with the yield strength of the weakest part of the vessel. Taken together this means that the probability of the overall collapse pressure being as low as that for a vessel with uniform yield strength equal to the minimum specification is negligibly small. The probability of it being at least 10% higher is quite high since the average yield stress is likely to be at least 10% higher than the minimum.

A typical special problem for which Non Linear Analysis is required would be the calculation of the collapse strength of the structure of Figure 1. Simpler design methods would probably evolve from the results of such an analysis.

COLLAPSE PRESSURE PREDICTION

The prediction of collapse pressures was discussed in detail in [3] where it was concluded that the most reliable method is to use an empirical plot of the parameter p_c/p_y against p_e/p_y where

P_c = collapse pressure

P_y = yield pressure

P_e = classical buckling pressure relevant to the collapse mechanism.

This approach is only valid if premature overall collapse due to inadequate stiffening is avoided. For ring stiffened cylinders the yield pressure p_y is the pressure at which the maximum circumferential mean stress equals the 0.2% proof stress σ_y. The parameter p_e is the Von Mises pressure minimised with respect to n [3]. For hemispheres or the spherical part of torispheres

$$P_y = 2 \sigma h/a$$
$$p_e = 2Eh^2/a^2[3(1-\mu^2)]^{1/2}$$

The empirical plots for cylinders and spherical surfaces are given in Figures 6 and 7. Figure 6 shows the mean curve through published experi-

427

mental points and the lower bound curve for all results for which the yield
stress is known and the maximum shape imperfection is not greater than 0.5%
of the radius. Also shown is the design curve used in BS5500 which has
ordinates(1/1.75) times the mean curve. The experimental scatter is shown
in [3] and is within +10% of the mean curve for $P_e/P_y > 1.5$. For $p_e/P_y <$
1.5 the scatter is greater and reflects the fact that on the straight line
part of the mean curve, where $p_c = p_e/1.71$, cylinders with good shape and
small fabrication stresses can collapse close to p_e. However there is good
published experimental evidence that "as-welded" cylinders manufactured
with shape imperfections less than 0.5% on radius can collapse at $P_e/2$ for
$P_e/P_y < 1$.

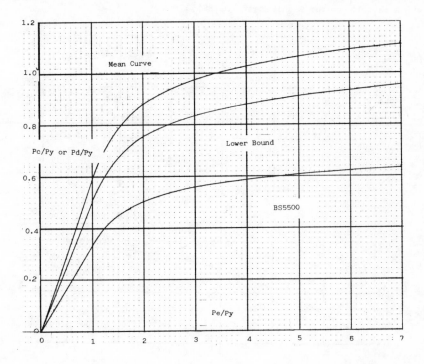

FIGURE 6.   Collapse Curve for Cylinders

It is worth noting that this collapse prediction method does not
require detailed stress analysis allowing for shape imperfections. This is

because it has been demonstrated that localised yielding due to bending actions have little effect on collapse. The only use of detailed stress analysis is for concession purposes when the shape is out-of-tolerance and the design pressure produces low mean stresses. This occurs commonly in internally pressurised vessels but very rarely for submarine structures.

Figure 7 shows the scatter band curves for spherical shells and the design curve used in BS5500. The mean curve is not given due to the large scatter and the fact that for an unknown reason large diameter spheres plot near the lower bound. Thus the lower bound curve must be used as a possible collapse curve. The scatter band for Figure 7 is for spheres which meet the shape requirements of BS5500.

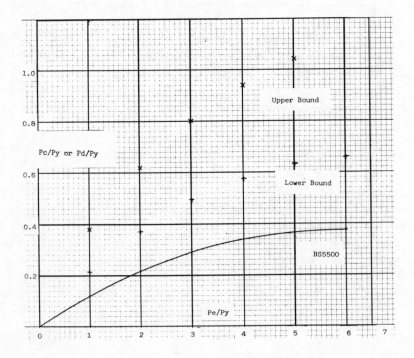

FIGURE 7.   Collapse Curves for Spherical Shells

The collapse curve of Figure 6 was obtained from tests on uniformly stiffened cylinders. A limited amount of experimental work has been carried out which shows that the curve has more general validity for general cone-cylinder combinations. This is discussed in [14] where a simple method of calculating p_e for complex geometries is described. [14] also describes how to assess the adequacy of stiffening for complex geometries using a general program such as BOSOR4. The same method should be applicable to non-developable surfaces using the curves of Figure 7 but this has not been checked experimentally.

The generalised collapse prediction method described above cannot be used unless the following criteria are satisfied:

    a.   There is a guaranteed minimum yield stress which applies to the whole vessel.

    b.   The shape is circular within 0.5% on radius.

    c.   The nominal structure is axisymmetric.

The last criterion can be ignored in the case of properly compensated penetrations in stiffened cylinders. There is considerable evidence that collapse pressures will not be affected by penetrations designed in accordance with (1) or (2) although the point of collapse initiation may be influenced by their presence.

When these criteria are not satisfied due to damage or poor fabrication it may still be necessary to estimate strength. Conservative estimates are usually possible using engineering judgement combined with elastic analysis. More accurate collapse estimates will require the elasto-plastic methods described earlier. These should be undertaken with extreme caution making certain in every case that the type of calculation has been proved against simpler geometries for which alternative collapse estimates are available.

DESIGN

The paper has so far discussed modes of collapse and methods of predicting some of them. The most certain prediction is for interstiffener collapse since this is relatively insensitive to shape imperfection. Overall collapse can be predicted simply provided that shape imperfections are in pure buckling modes. For more general shape imperfections, collapse prediction requires very lengthy calculations quite unsuited to design. This matters little since shape departures are unknown at the design stage for fabricated vessels. Collapse due to local instability cannot be predicted with certainty even with simple shape imperfections since there has been no experimental work in this area. It can however be avoided using simple criteria that are not onerous in design.

The above considerations lead naturally to a design process in which the aim is to achieve collapse initiated in an interstiffener mode with premature overall collapse avoided using adequate margins for nominal shape departures. Local instability is avoided by choosing a margin of elastic instability pressure over the design pressure which has been shown to be adequate. It must be noted that this procedure will not lead to designs which collapse interframe with the frames remaining circular. The additional load thrown onto the stiffeners due to interstiffener collapse will precipitate overall collapse and local instability unless unrealistic margins are used for overall collapse.

The code BS5500 [1] uses design curves which ensure that shell collapse will not occur at less than 1.5 times the design pressure provided that premature overall collapse is avoided. This is achieved by requiring the total applied stress in the presence of 0.5% shape imperfection to be less than or equal to the yield stress at twice the design pressure for cold bent stiffeners. For stress relieved stiffeners 1.8 times the design pressure is allowed. Numerical studies show that these factors allow for the weakening due to cold bending stresses and for mixed mode interaction between interstiffener and overall collapse.

Adequate stiffener proportions are achieved by requiring the small deflection elastic buckling pressure for local instability to be at least three times the design pressure. This is the same ratio as for inter-stiffener buckling where the design curve ensures that $p_e > 3p_d$. The use of this criterion leads to simple design equations and it is considered that little design advantage would be gained by reducing the pressure ratio. BS5500 [1] gives simple design criteria which are conservative but BOSOR4 [5] can be used to calculate the local instability stress using a model which is one stiffener plus one-half bay of shell on each side with appropriate boundary conditions. A simple preprocessor is used for this purpose at ARE [15]. Using this preprocessor there is a slight problem in avoiding the overall modes which are associated with low buckling pressures. This is overcome by plotting the mode shapes or examining the mode shape numerical output and eliminating the type 0 modes as described on Page 78 of [4]. The other mode shapes are not necessarily local instability but this is unimportant provided that the buckling pressure is high enough. The simplest method of identifying local instability is by examining the effect of increasing the flange dimension. Local instability pressures will increase much more rapidly than interstiffener pressures.

A simple but powerful program has been developed at ARE [16] which enables designs to be optimised with respect to minimum weight or to meet other criteria. The fixed parameters of this program are design pressure, radius, overall length, material properties of shell and stiffeners, maximum bending stress at a stiffener, pressure ratio for yielding in a stiffener, amplitude of out-of-roundness and stiffener proportions. The program calculates designs which meet the criteria for a range of stiffener spacings and sizes. There is an alternative option which calculates minimum weight solutions. The program runs happily on a micro.

A plot of the weight parameter W_p (weight/unit length divided by that of an unstiffened steel cylinder with thickness equal to 0.01 times the radius) for the stiffener proportions of Figure 3 is given in Figure 8. The corresponding shell thickness values are given in Figure 3.2.1 of [4]. For each pair of values of stiffener area A_s and spacing L_s there is a unique shell thickness which just enables the interstiffener and overall collapse criteria to be met. The use of a slightly smaller thickness would mean that one of the criteria would not be met. The curves at Figure 8 are labelled with the mode numbers that are critical. When $n = 0$, P_y (stiffener) is greater than 4 for all values of n. For any other value of n the shell thickness is determined by the need to achieve P_y (stiffener) = 4 for that value of n. It can be seen that for $A_f < 5000$ mm^2 the shell thickness is governed by overall collapse conditions ($n > 2$) Minimum weight is seen to be associated with A_s around 6000 mm^2 and is insensitive to stiffener spacing in this case. As an example of the output the results for $A_s = 5000$ mm^2, $L_5 = 700$ mm are given in Table 6.

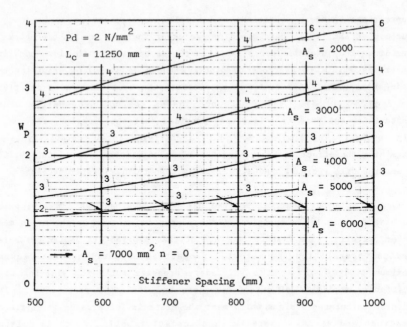

FIGURE 8. Iterated Design Solutions

TABLE 6

Value of n	Required Shell Thickness (mm)	P_y (Stiffener) $(N/mm)^2$	P_{n_2} N/mm^2)
0	24.0	5.84	
2	24.0	4.50	16.3
3	27.8	4.00	22.5
4	27.8	4.07	40.2
5	27.8	4.12	63.3
6	27.8	4.14	90.8

Table 6 shows that the thickness 24.0 which gave $P_d = 2.0$ exactly for interstiffener collapse was adequate for the shape imperfection in the form of ovality (n = 2). For n = 3 a greater thickness was required to give P_y (Stiffener) = 4.0 and this greater thickness was adequate for higher values

of n. It also shows that in order to avoid overall collapse it was
necessary to raise the overall instability pressure P_n for n = 3 to 16.3
N/mm^2, ie 8 times the design pressure. Thus the criterion $P_e > 3P_d$ used
for local instability does not hold for overall collapse. Several other
criteria are evaluated in the design iterations but for this particular
case they had no effect on the solution.

The above design program assumes an overall length between sections
which remain circular under pressure. For example stiffened diaphragms,
heavy rings or dome ends will produce suitable endings. In the latter case
an additional length equal to 1/3 of the dome height is assumed. In cases
of doubt about the efficiency of these "compartment splitters" the methods
of [14] can be used. When the "compartment splitter" is markedly not
axisymmetric (eg Figure 1) or operates in the post-buckling range, full
elasto-plastic analysis (large deflection in the latter case) is required.
This is a formidable undertaking. Alternatively a purely elastic design
can be used which is structurally inefficient. Such designs should be
avoided wherever possible by the use of heavy ring stiffeners.

REFERENCES

1. Unfired fusion welded pressure vessels. British Standards Institution
   BS5500.

2. ASME Boiler and Pressure Vessel Code ANSI/ASME BPV VIII.

3. Gill, S.S. (1970), The Stress Analysis of Pressure Vessels and
   Pressure Vessel Components, Pergamon Press, Oxford.

4. Shell Structures, Stability and Strength, Ed. by R.Narayanan, Elsevier
   Applied Science Publishers 1985.

5. Bushnell, D. (1974), Sress, Stability and Vibration of complex
   branched shells of revolution. Computers and Structures 4.

6. Monks, A.H., ASPREPA, An ASSSAI preprocessor for single skinned
   submarines. Unpublished MOD (PE) Report.

7. Developments in Pressure Vessel Technology - 4, Ed. by R.W.Nichols,
   Applied Science Publishers 1983.

8. Bushnell, D. (1976), Program for buckling of elastic-plastic complex
   shells of revolution including large deflections and creep, Computers
   and Structures, 6.

434

9. Kendrick, S. (1979), The influence of shape imperfections and residual stresses on the collapse of stiffened cylinders. I Mech E Conference on Significance of Deviations from Design Shape, March pp 261-267.

10. ASAS-NL Users Manual Version 6, August 1982, Atkins Rand D Ltd.

11. STAGS C-1 Users Manual, January 1980, Lockheed Palo Alto. California, USA.

12. LUSAS Users Manual, 1984, Finite Element Analysis Ltd, London.

13. Creswell, D.J., Dow, R.S., The Application of Nonlinear Analysis to Ship and Submarine Structures. International Conference on Advances in Marine Structures, May 1986, Dunfermline, UK.

14. Kendrick, S., Design for External Pressure Using General Criteria, Int. J. Mech. Sc., Vol 24 No 4 pp 209-218, 1982.

15. ARE Program SD008 Single Frame BOSOR4 Preprocessor.

16. ARE Program SD009A Design of Externally Pressurised Stiffened Cylinders and Cones.

AN OVERVIEW OF U. S. NAVAL SHIP DESIGN

Peter M. Palermo
Assistant Deputy Commander/Technical Director
for Ship Design and Engineering
Naval Sea Systems Command, Navy Department
Washington, D. C. 20362-5101, U. S. A.

ABSTRACT

The purpose of this paper is to broadly address the evolution of the design of a warship. Detailed technical expositions will not be included because they are amply addressed elsewhere in the literature. Nor will the paper deal with the excruciating detail of sizing and plating the hull during detail design and construction. Instead this paper will deal with that often frustrating, always interesting - never dull period from the germination of the concept until the birth of the design as represented by a set of specifications explaining in extensive detail a description of the ship.

Like commercial ships, warships must have a reason for being, but unlike commercial ships they are designed for 30, 45, or more years of service with full knowledge that as payloads change, the ship must be amenable to accepting such change. The often frustrating administrative (or bureaucratic) requirements are briefly alluded to, the role of and experiences from past designs, the application of existing technology and the often necessary extension of the state-of-the-art are put into context.

Foremost in the paper is the basic premise that the hull structure is designed to efficiently and effectively contain a payload. No matter how exotic the design, aesthetic the structure, or powerful the computation method and tools, the underlying fact remains that as unpleasant as it may be, the ships are designed as warships and the ruggedness to go into "harm's way" must be the first consideration.

INTRODUCTION

The design of a warship is one of the most difficult, perplexing, challenging and stimulating tasks that can confront a Naval architect. The thought of developing a ship that can sail into harm's way in meeting today's threat, and still be available and capable of meeting the threat

---

The opinions expressed herein are the author's own and do not necessarily represent the official views of the Navy Department nor of the Naval Service at large.

forty or more years from now is almost inconceivable. In addition, some of
the ships are the largest moving objects ever built, and in fact are
equivalent to small cities - others are small, quiet, and operate beneath
the ocean. From a structural standpoint they all pose one major problem in
that they must function at the air water interface, they must be efficient
in both environments, and they must be affordable.

This paper will discuss the general design requirements for warships,
with emphasis on the structural design. To concentrate solely on the
structural aspects of the design would deny the reader the necessary insight
concerning the requirements of, and therefore the constraints imposed by
other ship systems. In addition to the constraints imposed by other system
requirements, the structural designer is also heavily impacted by the
constraints inherent in any bureaucratic system and by time.

NAVAL SHIP DESIGN

The Navy ship design process consists of three major
segments - Exploratory Design, Acquisition Design and Service Life Design.

EXPLORATORY DESIGN. The exploratory design stage can last anywhere from one
year to fifteen or more years. It is during this stage that concepts
slightly beyond the current state-of-the-art capabilities are evaluated, and
if they look sufficiently promising, ship systems and combat systems R&D
programs are structured to support such long-range ship goals. During this
stage fundamental hull, mechanical, and electrical systems, as well as
electronics, weapons, launchers and sensors proceed through advanced
development, factory testing and operational testing.

ACQUISITION DESIGN. Figure 1 depicts the Naval ship acquisition process,
its major approval milestones, and the related document flow. Once the
intent to acquire a ship has been stated and a Tentative Operational
Requirement (TOR) has been promulgated, a series of Feasibility Studies are
initiated. These studies are focused toward a specific mission requirement
and are intended to aid the OPNAV decision makers in selecting the desired
balance between cost and capability. Various ship concepts are evaluated
and capabilities, costs, and major technical risks are examined. In some

FIGURE 1. Naval Ship Acquisition Process

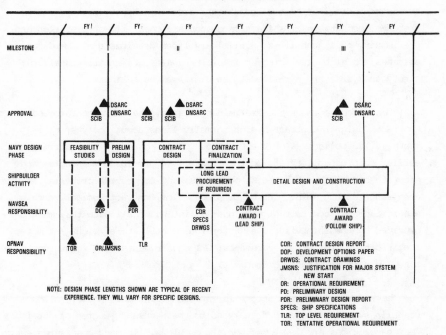

NOTE: DESIGN PHASE LENGTHS SHOWN ARE TYPICAL OF RECENT
EXPERIENCE. THEY WILL VARY FOR SPECIFIC DESIGNS.

CDR: CONTRACT DESIGN REPORT
DOP: DEVELOPMENT OPTIONS PAPER
DRWGS: CONTRACT DRAWINGS
JMSNS: JUSTIFICATION FOR MAJOR SYSTEM
       NEW START
OR: OPERATIONAL REQUIREMENT
PD: PRELIMINARY DESIGN
PDR: PRELIMINARY DESIGN REPORT
SPECS: SHIP SPECIFICATIONS
TLR: TOP LEVEL REQUIREMENT
TOR: TENTATIVE OPERATIONAL REQUIREMENT

cases R&D may be found to be still incomplete and a particular concept will
be shelved. Often a concept will be accepted for further development but
specific accelerated R&D efforts will be identified. At the completion of
the Feasibility Studies, the primary ship characteristics will have been
decided upon. A general concept of the ship will be available, including a
description of the principal features and mission critical subsystems; speed
and endurance estimates; overall arrangement sketches; a one-digit weight
estimate; a manning estimate; a technical risk assessment; and a Class F
cost estimate. Depending on the number of trade-off studies conducted, the
Feasibility Study phase can last from several weeks to several years.

Upon acceptance of the Feasibility Study, the Navy then embarks on an
intensive Preliminary Design that usually lasts approximately six months.
The purpose of the Preliminary Design phase is to refine the Feasibility
Study estimates; to quantify the ship's performance; to reduce or eliminate
major technical and schedule risks, and to develop a budget quality cost
estimate (Class C). A host of significant documentation is developed during

the Preliminary Design phase including a list of major equipments; general arrangement drawings to the compartment level; machinery arrangement sketches; combat system space arrangement sketches; mid-ship section and preliminary hull scantlings; preliminary lines drawings and appendage sketches; model test results; reliability and maintainability analyses; safety analyses; and a refined three-digit weight estimate.

Upon acceptance of the Preliminary Design, the Navy then proceeds into Contract Design. Contract Design normally lasts about one year to 18 months. The objectives of the Contract Design phase are to confirm the earlier ship capability and cost estimates; to provide a meaningful and accurate bid package for the shipbuilders; and to provide criteria for Navy acceptance of the ship. The major products of Contract Design are ship specifications; contractual drawings; a listing of all data that must be provided by the shipbuilder; a Master Equipment List; a weight estimate; specifications for GFE procurements; GFI requirements; T&E requirements; and a preliminary ship manning document.

The structural design effort is intense during this phase. All scantlings are developed and analyzed to the necessary degree of detail. Design solutions are developed for all problems. In many cases prospective shipbuilders assist the design team especially in the area of producibility. Again only a small portion of this effort is actually included in the contract package, but all of it is documented for future reference.

The next stage is to bid the ship detail design and construction, evaluate the bids and to award a contract for Detail Design and construction. During Detail Design the shipbuilder develops fabrication and assembly drawings requirements for and purchase of machinery and auxiliary components; tests various systems; installs GFE; and finally presents a ship to the Navy for acceptance trials.

At this point the structural design is turned over to the building yard under the general review of the local Supervisor of Shipbuilding, Conversion and Repair (SUPSHIP). NAVSEA only reviews or approves the most critical aspects of the design as identified by the Contractor Deliverables Requirements List (CDRL) which is part of the contract package.

During the various stages of acquisition design the work effort
escalates exponentially. For a typical frigate the number of drawing pages
increases approximately as follows: seven in Feasibility Study phase to 47
in Preliminary Design, to 280 in Contract Design, to almost 10,000 in Detail
Design. The manpower estimates follow a similar curve for a complex
warship, approximately as follows: 50,000 MD for Preliminary Design;
100,000 MD for Contract Design and 500,000 MD for Detail Design.

SERVICE LIFE DESIGN. The Service Life Design stage lasts from the time that
the ship is delivered until it is retired or stricken from the lists.
During this period complex designs for modernizations and conversions are
conducted. In many cases the designs are of such complexity that the entire
gamut of efforts from Feasibility Studies to Contract Design are conducted.
The major effort during this period is Ship Alteration Design to improve the
technical or the military capabilities of the ship. Very often ship
alterations during the life of the ship interface with other systems or with
other SHIPALTS. In such cases considerable design coordination is
necessary. The requirements for a SHIPALT may originate from a variety of
sources. Usually NAVSEA engineers develop the SHIPALT proposal, and the
Planning Yard for the specific ship develops the detailed engineering as a
SHIPALT record and associated drawings which NAVSEA reviews.

CHECKS AND BALANCES. U. S. Navy ship design is not conducted in a vacuum –
there are a number of approval and review points along the path to acquiring
a ship. In addition to the official reviews there is generally a continuing
dialogue between the operator and the designer. The principal reviews are
with the Ship Characteristics Improvement Board (SCIB). The SCIB reports
directly to the Chief of Naval Operations and it comprises seven permanent
members – the DCNO for Surface Warfare, DCNO Submarine Warfare, DCNO Air
Warfare, DCNO Logistics, COMNAVSEA, Director, Navy Program Planning, and
Director, Naval Warfare. The primary purpose of the SCIB is to establish
the characteristics of new Naval ships.

The Feasibility Study phase ends when the SCIB officially selects and
endorses a particular feasibility study and promulgates a set of preliminary
ship characteristics based on it. These characteristics are formally

documented in an Operational Requirement (OR). If no study is approved, the SCIB gives additional direction to the design team. The next formal session of the SCIB occurs at the end of the Preliminary Design phase when, if they approve the design, they then promulgate a set of approved ship characteristics formally documented in the Top Level Requirements (TLR) for the ship. Near the mid-point of the Contract Design phase another formal SCIB review is held after major subsystem tradeoffs are complete and cost estimates are more firm. This is Milestone II which provides approval for lead ship acquisition. In the course of the review the SCIB may revise the ship characteristics in the TLR to reflect changed priorities or other circumstances that may have occurred in the year or more since the characteristics were first approved. During the lead ship Detail Design and construction phase the SCIB will meet a fourth time to review and approve the design and TLR for the acquisition of follow ships.

SHIP DESIGN

Ship design by its very nature is an iterative process that is rigidly controlled by past experience and present day constraints. The Navy ship design process is the means to the end of developing a ship to meet specific mission requirements without compromising fundamental principles of naval architecture and marine engineering. Therefore, the process is technically directed by adherence to documented and approved design standards. These standards are clearly defined, specific and inviolate rules or principles for judging technical acceptability of achieving a specific requirement. At the next echelon below the technical standards are practices, procedures and specifications.

A technical practice is something normally done in ship design to implement a standard. However, a practice can be modified. A procedure is a particular analytical technique that is used to support the standard. Finally, a specification is a requirement placed on others to implement the standard.

An example of the above is a U. S. Navy design standard to provide camber on the weather decks of all ships. The practice is to normally use straight line camber because it is more producible and economical than parabolic camber. The procedure for determining the amount of slope for deck camber is given in a Design Data Sheet (DDS). The ship specifications specify deck camber developed in accordance with DDS 130-4. Table 1 is a listing of representative design standards for U. S. Navy ships.

TABLE 1.

Listing of Typical Ship Design Standards.

GENSPEC SECTION	TITLE	SDS 051-1
051	Resistance and Powering Assessment	051-1
070	Service Operation During Ship Motion in Seaway	070-1
070	Blist and Trim Limits	070-2
071	Passageway and Overhead clearance	071-1
073	Noise Standard	073-1
076	Reliability and Maintainability	076-1
079	Seakeeping Performance Assessment	079-1
079	Minimum Freeboard	079-2
085	Hull Lines and Offsets Drawings	085-1
096	Acquisition Mass and KG Margin Policy Value	096-1
096	Service Life Mass and KG Allowance Value	096-2
114	Underwater Appendages	114-1
116	Stem Shape Design	116-1
130	Deck Camber and Sheer	130-1
150	The Use of Aluminum in Ships	150-1
161	Propulsion Shaft Struts and Fairings	161-1
200	Endurance Fuel Calculation	200-1
322	Lighting	322-1
422	Anchor Lights (Navigation)	422-1
422	Ship Task Lights (Navigation)	422-2
512	Heating, Ventilation and Air Conditioning	512-1
517	Oil-Fired Ausiliary Boiler Selection	517-1
521	Fire Pump Selector	521-1
531	Distilling Plant Selection	531-1
532	Fresh Water	532-1
551	Low Pressure Air Compressor (LPAC) Selection	551-1
562	Control Surface	562-1
565	Motion Stabilization Systems	565-1
581	Anchor Handling Systems	581-1
588	Helicopter Fight Deck Survivabillity Standard	588-1
630	Treatments	630-1
640	Living Spaces	640-1
650	Personnel Services	650-1
660	Post Office	660-1
670	Stowage Space Requirements for New Construction and Major conversions of Ships	670-1
703	Magazine Placement	703-1

REQUIREMENTS. As in any other meaningful field of endeavor the first step in ship design is to set down the requirements. What must the ship do, where must it do it, how must it do it, are all questions that control the ship design. Sometimes the answer may be relatively simple in the conception but difficult in the implementation. For example, in the early 1940's when the U. S. realized that a ship to transport and rapidly off-load men and material on hostile shores would probably be required, the LST concept was born. In fact, the initial naval architectural sketches and calculations were performed on the "back of an envelope." In the early

1950's when the INCHON harbor was left virtually unprotected because of its shallow navigation draft, requirements were immediately drafted for a ship with sufficient range to cross the Pacific Ocean from the U. S. mainland, with certain specified fire power, and with a draft of less than seven feet - the Inshore Fire Support Ship.

In today's environment the free world's naval force levels are below those of the Communist bloc - so too are naval force defense budgets. Therefore our present day requirements are based on more capable, higher quality, more reliable ships. We are not in a contest to win on sheer numbers of assets - but rather on capability and quality of assets and our requirements reflect this thinking.

AFFORDABILITY. It has been stated that there are two fundamentals for ship design - the ship must float and the ship must float upright. To these must be added a third - the ship must be affordable. In today's environment, after all characteristics are reviewed and evaluated and priorities established - affordability must be addressed.

Too often when we talk affordability only initial acquisition cost is considered. This is false reasoning just as first of class cost is not considered representative. Because of the many non-recurring cost items usually associated with the first ship and inherent "learning curve" economies in the next two or three ships, average cost of a ship of a given class is usually based on the cost of an early but downstream hull. So too should operational costs play a major role in assessing the affordability of a given design.

Quality, reliability, maintainability, survivability, and safety must all be designed in right from the start since they are usually too expensive to "backfit" into a ship. Likewise when sizing and arranging the ship these factors must all be given serious attention. For example, the initial acquisition economies associated with zone outfitting and palletizing methods of construction can be offset if improper attention to maintenance/reliability concerns are not included in the initial design. Reduction of volume and ship size associated with initial acquisition optimism can result in large in-service cost penalties due to major ripouts if adequate accessibility for maintenance and replacement is not considered.

Conversely, overly pessimistic considerations that result in too large a ship can also lead to excessive life cycle costs. For example, a "few more feet" of hull length is often cited as not costing too much. From a steel and fabrication standpoint the cost may well be insignificant – but the secondary costs can be staggering. Additional lengths of run for all the distributive systems, possible upgrades (i.e., more or larger) systems for electrical power, heating, cooling, etc., as well as the extra fuel required for propelling the heavier ship must all be considered.

MARGINS. In order to ensure that the delivered ship meets the size, cost and performance goals that were established early in the design process, certain margins are employed. These margins are additional allowances above the normal performance, design characteristics, or capacities established for the ship; and should not be confused with safety factors. Safety factors represent an allowance for statistical distribution in properties, inadequacies in analytics, and operational variations. Margins on the other hand are intended to account for the unknown changes that may be necessary because of imprecisely defined requirements or overly optimistic estimates during early design stages and the cascading effects of such changes on other systems.

Ship design margins can be specified in three different categories; margins used during design and construction, margins used during the service life of the ship, and margins to assure adequate performance at off-design points.

Margins that are used during design and construction account for estimating technique inaccuracies; unknown items; and anticipated minor requirement changes during design development. In general these margins are in terms of weight, KG, electric power and HVAC. These margins are decreased with increasing refinement of a design and any unused portion of a given design phase margin allowance is not carried over to the next stage. These margins are normally expressed as percentages.

Margins provided in a ship at delivery to be used during the service life of the ship are intended to permit the later installation of new systems to improve capability during the life of the ship, and account for the predictable service life of weight growth associated with all ships, i.e., paint build-up, personnel belongings, etc., and the increasing load demands on ancillary subsystems as a result of class improvements, i.e., manning increases, electric plant, chilled water, and HVAC demand increases. When a ship's service life margins are depleted, compensation for new additions must be made by modifying the ship.

Assurance margins increase the probability that a specified level of performance can be achieved at any time during the life of the ship. They are not intended to be used up during the life of the ship. The most common of such margins is the speed-power margin. While the absolute margin decreases due to refinements during the early design stages, a certain percentage is carried over to account for such things as hull and appendage surface deterioration and propulsion plant deterioration.

U. S. Navy margins are based on historical data and the margins are regularly reviewed and changed as necessary to reflect statistical shifts in the available data. Margins must be scrupulously guarded by the designer because they are the prime target of cost cutting efforts by budgeteers only concerned with initial acquisition cost. Conversely, the designer must be scrupulously objective in the assignment of margins because of the costs associated with them.

PRODUCIBILITY. Enhancements in production capabilities, though most affected during the late stages of design, must be considered during all design stages. Uniformity of stiffeners, standardization of details, and elimination of minor changes in plating thickness all lead toward a more producible design. Fabrication considerations such as accessibility for automated welding equipment, accessibility for equipment installation, removal and maintenance, and the installation of, and possible interference between various distributive systems are usually resolved by use of mock-ups. Also, during the early design stages it is necessary to take a global view of producibility and the industrial base to determine any needed ancillary efforts for the industries supporting the fabrication.

The availability of unambiguous, up-to-date specifications that are tailored to the true requirements of the ship being designed is one of the biggest factors in improving productivity and producibility. In this same regard the advent of the micro-processors and the large storage capacity of today's mini-computers makes the development of a standard data base for a given design a reality. With this capability it is possible to produce component hull sections to identical tolerances at different locations, and to completely outfit each component hull section to close tolerances so that distributive systems will be properly aligned when the sections are joined. Considerations for this mode of production must start with the earliest design stages to ensure that structural, general, and machinery arrangements are all properly integrated.

DESIGN INTEGRATION. A ship is a floating city and needs utility and repair facilities. Design of systems for power generation and distribution, air conditioning and ventilation, main propulsion, life support, environmental pollution control, piping, life support, habitability, vibration, noise control, health services, equipment repair, aircraft support, communications, and many others are all part of the ship design. It is the role of the ship designer to meld and integrate all of these systems with their divergent requirements into a synergistic compromise called a warship.

As shown in Figure 2, the single biggest contributor to the displacement of a warship is the hull structure - it accounts for about 37 percent of the total displacement; fuel and loads about 20 percent; combat systems, 11 percent; auxiliary systems, 10 percent; propulsion systems, 9 percent; outfit and furnishing, 8 percent; and electrical systems, 5 percent. Even though the HM&E systems together represent 69 percent of the displacement compared to the combat systems 11 percent, development and design costs for HM&E represent only 32 percent of the total ship acquisition cost. Sail

446

away costs and peacetime operating and support costs represent 43 percent and 60 percent, respectively, compared to combat system costs. Therefore the designer must carefully integrate combat systems into his design while closely watching unnecessary or uncontrolled growth in the HM&E areas.

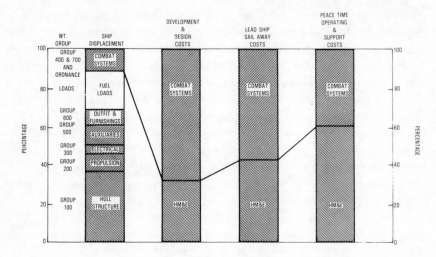

FIGURE 2. U.S. Naval Combatant Displacement and Cost Comparison

The early stage design effort is heavily influenced by available data on comparable type ships. Coefficients from earlier designs, lessons learned, and synthesis models are used to determine a first cut at characteristics. U. S. Navy synthesis models, in addition to providing ranges of technical characteristics, also contain a cost module to provide some concept of total cost. Starting with a generalized profile and arrangement concept, hull form coefficients can be estimated. The designer then moves into the famous design spiral (Figure 3) estimating powering characteristics, fuel and endurance, weights, stability, structure, manning, etc. As the ship starts to evolve, various disciplines are conducting in-depth trade-offs such as types of propulsion plants, auxiliary systems, powering profiles, structural arrangements and details, vibration analysis, etc., and the iterative nature of the design spiral inexorably moves toward an acceptable, technically feasible solution. As the broad first cut characteristics are being quantified in more and more detail during each iteration of the design, so too are other more detailed factors now being included. System configuration, cost effectiveness, specifications and technical data, ILS requirements, and life cycle costs are now being included in the design equation — and finally the spiral is stopped and a final design is accepted. The spiral may start up again at some later date when class improvements or modernizations are required — and when it does, it will follow a similar iterative path until it hones in on a technically acceptable, affordable solution that meets the requirements.

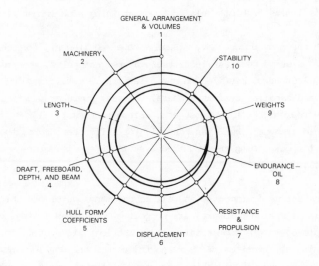

FIGURE 3. The Design Spiral

NAVY SPECIFICATIONS AND STANDARDS

Navy specifications and standards reflect the requirements of a unique owner. This owner has a wide range of ship types for which he is responsible. Many types have unique missions unrelated to any commercial operation. The system for supporting the many classes of ships has no commercial equivalent. The crews that man the Navy's ships are young and transient. The environment in which the ships are expected to operate and the ship operational profiles are significantly different from those of commercial ships. The expected operational life of the ships is longer than that expected by a commercial owner. There is no provision for insuring financially against loss of ship or life. The procurement process limits the ability to establish the "owner preference" flexibility that is available to the commercial ship owner.

With the wide range of Navy ship types there are incentives for standardization. These are most pronounced in such areas as crew training and logistic support. System design commonality allows greater flexibility in assignment of crew members, reduces training requirements, and at the same time limits problems related to maintaining wide ranges of spare parts.

With the many unique Navy missions come requirements for unique shipboard systems such as aircraft elevators, catapults, weapons handling systems, launchers, missile and gun directors, aircraft and helicopter landing and handling systems, radars, tactical computers, data links, underway replenishment systems, etc. Since no commercial requirements exist for such equipment other than possibly for helicopter decks, the appropriate vehicle for describing the required systems and performance is a Navy specification.

These unique equipments, as well as the many equipments which are more conventional marine hardware, are supported by a logistics system unlike that employed in the commercial world. The logistic system, in addition to maintaining an inventory of spare parts, covers the development of technical manuals to be used aboard ship, and provides for training of crew members as new systems are introduced.

The logistic support system is particularly important because of the types of crews on Navy ships and the way in which the ships are operated. Enlisted crew members are normally young and inexperienced when recruited. Progress through the ranks involves periods of off-ship training and reassignment to new stations or ships on a fairly regular basis. This transient mode of staffing requires that the logistic support system provide parts and documentation such that newly assigned personnel can quickly master the operation and maintenance of equipments at their new duty station. This station could well be on a ship to be deployed to the Indian Ocean for six months, or to one involved in amphibious exercises in the Norwegian Sea, or to one engaged in ASW exercises off the U. S. Coast.

While the commercial ships go to sea and face the same weather and sea environments as Navy ships, their mission profile differs substantially from that of the Navy ship. The commercial cargo ship or tanker transits from port to port and performs its principal function of loading or unloading in a relatively benign environment. In contrast, the majority of Navy ships and craft are designed to perform their principal functions at sea. Examples of such functions include launching and recovering aircraft, performing air and underwater surveillance, controlling and firing weapons, performing underway replenishment, performing blockade or barrier operations, and recovering from battle damage. Performing these functions at sea involves not only the operation of the system involved but also maintenance, alignment, and calibration as appropriate.

Trained personnel are required to perform these functions, but of equal importance is equipment designed to perform the function reliably. The equipment must be designed for a long service life which involves exposure to a wide range of environments covering factors such as ship motion, temperatures, humidity and varying operating profiles. Many ship systems, and especially the hull structure, are expected to function over a period of 30 years, and some hulls are currently being pushed through service life extension programs to an operating life of as much as 45 years.

These factors all enter into the rationale for military specifications from the perspective of system performance or operability. There are other factors relating to procurement requirements which further drive us to the use of military specifications. One is the problem of assuring performance requirements are met. This is presently accomplished through testing and quality assurance provisions contained in the specification. While the "warranty" process is being currently legislated into procurements, it is still highly desirable that system tests be performed to demonstrate acceptability of end items, both through factory testing and operational testing.

Procurement regulations make a specification approach to acquisition almost mandatory. All potential suppliers must be given the opportunity to bid on a given acquisition. This includes proven suppliers with an established record of performance, as well as a new small business trying to break into the field. Specifications and standards can enable such companies to learn what must be done to produce acceptable products, while at the same time protecting the procuring activity by requiring that suppliers use materials and processes that will result in a quality product.

One additional factor adds to the list of features which must be addressed in specifications for Navy ships. That is the requirement for these ships to operate in hostile environments. Included in this category are requirements for equipment to withstand loadings from underwater shock or air blast. Added to this are ship design features which provide for damage control and fire fighting; features designed to permit recovery from the effects of battle damage or accidents at sea. Redundancy is provided in many systems so that we have not only high system availability under normal operating conditions, but also backup capability in the event of loss of specific components due to damage from hostile or accidental events.

It is through specifications and standards that we manage to state requirements which are consistent with the planned use for our ships and their installed systems. These requirements include consideration of the people involved and the interaction of people and equipment from the standpoints of operability, maintainability and safety.

The core of Navy shipbuilding specifications is the GENSPECS. This is a document containing 198 sections. It forms the basis for the individual ship specification which is especially developed and tailored for a specific ship design. GENSPECS and the average ship spec reference approximately 2500 other documents. An individual comparison section by section with the composite of commercial specifications represented by Coast Guard Regulations, ABS Rules, MARAD specifications and various industry standards is a difficult task, due to differences in purposes of the various documents and the resulting differences in format and organization of requirements.

In fact, because GENSPECS is tailored to create each specific ship spec, there are differences in spec requirements across the spectrum of Navy ship types with combatants being largely based on MIL-SPECS and auxiliaries specifications being increasingly more commercialized as their missions became more like those of commercial ships. Certain elements covered in GENSPECS are eliminated in tailoring GENSPECS to suit an auxiliary ship acquisition, such as the elimination of sections covering shock, reliability and maintainability, system safety and integrated logistic support. In effect in the "commercialization" of a design, cost savings are accomplished in part by reducing survivability, and deemphasizing reliability.

Such omissions are perhaps acceptable for commercial operations and manning, particularly in a peacetime environment and where port to port operation provides access to commercial sources of parts and labor, and losses can be covered by warranties and insurance. However, the Navy scenario for an AO as compared to a commercial tanker involves delivering fuel in support of ships and aircraft engaged in military operations at sea, and failure to deliver can jeopardize a major fleet operation or action. This is the picture seen by the operating forces and which is held by the President of the Board of Inspection and Survey (PRESINSURV). Of course, all of this relates to risk and the price which must be paid to reduce it.

The reduction gear is another example of an area in which changing from commercial requirements was necessary to improve expected service life and at-sea maintenance capability. In order to meet Navy requirements for a long life reliable gear, the reduction gear must be custom designed and built to satisfy the particular power and RPM requirement. Changes involve a double helical design as opposed to the single helical in commercial practice, and use of journal bearings instead of rolling contact bearings. As for other items, the MIL SPEC requirements for testing, noise/vibration and quality assurance may be modified and shock requirements eliminated for "commercialized" Navy applications.

One significant area of difference between commercial and Navy design criteria is the design of the firemain system. This is an area in which Navy standards are more stringent than commercial standards, with the

exception of those for passenger ships. Navy design incorporates a
composite of vertical and horizontal flow paths for the firemain system.
Cutout valves are provided to permit segregation of the system for damage
control purposes and also to permit isolation of portions of the system and
provide sufficient physical separation of the pumps to minimize loss of
pumping capacity in the event of local damage.

The firemain in a Navy design is a "wet" system, with pressure available
at all discharge points at all times. This permits a trained crew to attack
fires with minimum delay. The firemain also supplies the topside washdown
system which is used in the event of nuclear, biological, or chemical
contamination. This feature of a "wet" system requires the use of more
costly materials throughout to protect against the corrosive effects of
seawater. The costs of redundancy and separation and of higher quality
materials are countered by the longer life, lower maintenance, and quick
response capability of the Navy design. The design provides greater safety
for the crew in dealing with accidental or warfare damage and significantly
reduces the risk of total loss of the ship due to fire.

Navy specifications and standards cannot be dismissed lightly and
replaced by "commercial marine equivalent." First, because commercial
marine specifications do not exist in many areas and second, because many of
the commercial marine specifications are not equivalent since they do not
provide the performance, supportability, and service life features required
by the Navy. Navy specifications reflect the lessons learned from operating
ships in both peacetime and wartime environments throughout the world. They
reflect the need to satisfy their most demanding mission requirements while
at sea, and to be ready for action when needed. All of these elements of
specifications, equipments, supplies and people combine to define a
significant attribute of military systems called readiness.

STRUCTURAL DESIGN

Because of its highly iterative nature, hull structural design is
difficult to differentiate from hull structural analysis. In both,
materials, loads, configurations, scantlings, and structural responses are
mathematically manipulated. In design the scantlings are the output, in

analysis the response is the output. The designer iterates between the two until he arrives at an acceptable solution. He rarely, if ever, arrives at the optimum solution but does arrive at an optimum structure within configuration constraints. His measure of effectiveness for optimization can be cost, weight, or producibility - unfortunately in many cases the three are mutually exclusive.

The primary hull material used today is steel. Navy combatants have steel hulls that range from as-rolled medium steel to quench and tempered high yield steels. Aluminum has been used in superstructures of Navy ships and in the hulls of some smaller ships and craft. Precipitation hardening stainless steels have been used for some special high performance ship applications. Glass Reinforced Plastic (GRP) and wood are used for the hulls of mine hunting ships.

Prior to using a new material in a hull application, it is characterized for its various properties under the expected environmental conditions. Of utmost importance in characterizing a material is evaluation of its fabricability and its fabricated properties. Material application in design is based on fabricated material properties. Material characterization tests include laboratory specimens, structural elements, scaled models and full scale evaluation. Large scale models and full scale evaluations also serve as fabrication test structures.

In selecting a material for a specific ship application, fracture performance is a major consideration. Whenever possible commercial specifications are used, but in those areas where high toughness is necessary, specific Navy requirements must be followed. For example, crack arrest strakes must have an NDT of at least $-60^{\circ}F$ or below, be on the upper toughness shelf at $0^{\circ}F$ and have a high energy shelf value.

During the design stages, details are optimized and these details are then subjected to analytical scrutiny to ensure that potential stress concentrations have been precluded. Obvious structural details have evolved over the years, and after demonstrating under service loadings their overall adequacy, they are accepted. Such requirements as continuity of primary strength stiffness, rounded corners, gradual taper in changing section sizes, reinforcement of openings, minimizing number of adjacent openings, etc., all fall into this category. When newer concepts are required, the designer usually evaluates the details analytically and experimentally before acceptance. Before final acceptance of a novel detail, the designer will usually consult with the fabricator to ensure feasibility of his design.

The following paragraphs provide a cursory review of the structural design. They provide an overview and therefore are not exhaustive in their coverage. However ample material on any of the following items can be found in the open literature.

SURFACE SHIPS. The ship system is subjected to a complex spectrum of external and internal forces. Wave loadings, sea slap, planning, vibration, thermal, cargo, buoyancy, aircraft landing, weapons and docking are some of the loadings that must be considered. Unfortunately the magnitude and distribution of these loads are in some cases handled in an imprecise, though totally adequate, manner. A generalized matrix of types of applied loadings to be considered for various structural elements is given in Table 2. The applied loadings are broadly classified into groupings, those that should be considered in combination and those that should be considered independently.

The Navy utilizes classical naval architectural theory to determine hull girder bending loads. The ship is considered to be statically balanced on a trochoidal wave having a length equal to the ship length and a height of 1.1 times the square root of the ship's length ($1.1\sqrt{L}$). This criteria was adopted in the late 1940's and has been recently re-evaluated in comparison with a sea spectra analysis. Even though the $1.1\sqrt{L}$ wave equates to a 10^{-8} chance of exceedence, it would appear somewhat conservative. From an engineering design standpoint, it is a reasonable criterion because it does ensure a degree of ruggedness for combat survivability. Sea spectra analysis are used for determining ship motion factors, hull distortion levels, and fatigue analysis. Torsional bending is seldom a problem in warships but it is evaluated when necessary. Shear too is always considered, however it is seldom controlling except around large openings in the side shell. The design standard for hull girder primary strength is mandatory for hull design.

TABLE 2. Load Matrix.

LOAD MATRIX / STRUCTURE	LOADS TO BE COMBINED							INDEPENDENT LOADS							
	PRIMARY (HULL GIRDER)	HYDROSTATIC (EXTERIOR)	TANK LOADS (TO TOP OF TANK)	DEAD LOAD	LIVE LOAD	WIND, ICE SNOW	STOWAGE (CARGO, HELO)	SEA SLAP SLAM	TANK LOADS (TO OVERFLOW)	FLOODING	GUN & MISSILE BLAST	INTERIOR OVER PRESSURE (MISSILE STOWAGE)	DRY DOCKING	OPERATING (UNREP BOATS, & ETC)	AIRCRAFT-HELO LANDING
I SHELL PL & FRAME															
A. MIDSHIPS	X	X	X	X	-	-	-	-	X	-	-	-	X	X	-
B. FWD	X	X	X	X	-	-	-	X	X	-	-	-	X	X	-
C. AFT	X	X	X	X	-	-	-	-	X	-	-	-	X	X	-
D. SPONSON SHELL	-	X	-	X	-	X	-	X	-	-	-	-	-	X	-
E. WEB FRAMES	-	X	X	X	-	X	X	X	X	X	X	-	X	X	-
II BULKHEADS															
A. LONG'L	X	-	X	X	-	-	-	-	X	X	-	X	-	-	-
B. TRANS	-	-	X	X	-	-	-	-	X	X	-	X	-	-	-
C. BENTS	-	-	-	X	X	-	X	-	-	-	-	-	-	-	X
D. MISC	-	-	-	X	X	-	-	-	X	X	-	X	-	-	-
III DECKS															
A. INTERIOR	X	-	X	X	X	-	X	-	X	X	-	X	-	X	-
B. WEATHER	X	X	-	X	X	X	X	X	X	-	X	X	-	X	X
C. PLATFORMS	-	-	X	X	X	-	X	-	X	X	-	X	-	-	-
IV STANCHIONS	-	X	X	X	X	X	X	-	X	X	X	X	-	X	X
V SUPERSTRUCTURES															
A. LONG	X	X	-	X	X	X	X				X	X	-	X	-
B. SHORT	-	X	-	X	X	X	X				X	X	-	X	-
VI APPENDAGES															
A. STRUTS	-	-	-	X	X	-	-	X	-	-	-	-	-	-	-
B. FOILS	-	-	-	X	X	-	-	X	-	-	-	-	-	-	-

Navy design combines stresses from hull bending (primary) with stresses from local loads (secondary). However in all cases a certain portion of the total stress, depending on hull material, is reserved solely for primary stresses. Historically this Design Primary Stress reservation has resulted in structurally sound hulls of adequate stiffness with acceptable margins against ultimate failure. The total allowable strength of the material is utilized but a certain portion is reserved for primary stress and only primary stress. Navy design practice provides for a primary bending stress equal to one-half of the Design Primary Stress at the neutral axis. This provides a degree of side shell plating ruggedness to account for ship motions, heading into oblique seas and for small craft or camel's bumping.

Plating thickness is based on local and hydrostatic loads. Navy criteria for design stresses in plating varies according to location and function of the plate - in some instances stresses in excess of the nominal yield strength are acceptable. The acceptance of permanent set due to high stress is based on low probability of occurrence, such as flooding heads, or helicopter landing pads under extreme landing gear loads. In most other cases, permanent set equivalent to acceptable welding distortion is allowed. Plating subjected to load reversal or in areas where smooth fair surfaces are required are designed to operate in the elastic range. In order to preclude the possibility of rapid crack growth, high toughness material is used in lieu of the design material at the sheer strake, stringer strake and turn of the bilge. The use of crack arrest strakes is another example of the mandatory design standards described earlier.

Navy design practice assumes that longitudinal stiffeners act as columns in resisting primary (axial) and secondary (lateral) loads. Tests have demonstrated that a slenderness ratio (ℓ/r) of 60 or less is adequate to resist buckling of the plate stiffener combination. We normally use longitudinal stiffeners on 18 to 30 inch centers with transverse frames every eight feet. We compensate for the wide spacing of transverse frames by the use of stanchions. Present Navy practice is to make transverses three to four times as stiff as the longitudinals. Stanchions are designed to develop full strength in tension as well as compression.

Superstructures are not considered to contribute to the strength of the hull girder. They are however designed to resist primary stresses. Hull girder primary stresses are transmitted into the superstructure and if proper attention is not given to superstructure details a myriad of maintenance problems will occur. In the early 1950's the Navy went to aluminum superstructures in order to conserve topside weight. A number of maintenance problems occurred - first the connection of the aluminum superstructure to the steel deck was a mechanically fastened connection that had a number of corrosion problems. This was overcome by going to a bimetallic welded joint. A problem also occurred at the superstructure ends where the bulkhead would tend to "lift-off" the steel deck. This was overcome by the use of diaphragm plates. Though the early aluminum superstructures were susceptible to exfoliation cracking until the alloy was changed, by far the biggest problem with aluminum superstructures has been the unforgiving nature of the material with resulting cracking at less than optimum details. As a result the Navy no longer uses aluminum in combatant ship structures.

Drydocking and associated loadings are another area considered by the structural designer. Recent designs have involved large overhangs and resultant high block loads. The ship, as well as the blocking system, must be designed to resist these high concentrated loads.

As indicated earlier, it is the structural details that make a good design. Attention to detail is mandatory if the ship is to successfully survive normal seaway much less combat loadings. Attention to structural arrangements is mandatory. In this regard Table 3 is a listing of U. S. Navy rules of thumb of Dos and Donts for structural arrangements.

TABLE 3.

Arrangement Guidelines for Structure.

Dos

1. Align stanchions and/or bulkheads vertically.
2. Arrange openings such that the maximum dimension is in the longitudinal direction.
3. Provide vertical continuity of transverse bulkheads into the superstructure to resist racking.
4. Provide sufficient clearance between structure and equipment for maintenance and repair of equipment or structure.
5. Openings shall have radiused corners of at least 1/8 of the opening dimension normal to the principle stress.
6. Openings shall be kept as far from the intersection of structural bulkheads as practicable.
7. Mast legs shall continue down for at least two levels for adequate structural support.
8. Locate openings to disrupt the least number of stiffeners.
9. Align deck stiffeners with bulkhead stiffeners.
10. Provide fixity at ends of stiffeners.

Don'ts

1. Do not align holes/openings transversely or vertically.
2. Do not locate openings in bulkheads directly below heavy loads or primary support structure.
3. Do not abruptly step housesides, decks or bulkheads. If a jog is necessary, a slope of approximately 4 to 1 should be provided between major support members.
4. Do not place openings in the sheer or stringer strakes.
5. Manholes shall not be cut in rider plates.
6. Access or lightening holes shall not be cut in center vertical keels.
7. Do not allow "knife edge" crossings of bulkheads above deck with girders below.
8. Do not allow long crossing of stiffeners with weld seams in the shell.

SUBMERSIBLES. Submersibles of one sort or another date back to 410 B.C. where they were used in the siege of Syracuse, and in 330 B.C. when used by Alexander the Great in his operations against Tyre. In the American Revolutionary War, Bushnell's turtle was used against British ships. However, the modern submersible was not developed until the 1890's. John

Holland, credited with the invention of the "modern submarine" and his
contemporaries such as Simon Lake, required proof testing of their designs
by submerging the unmanned craft to twice the rated operating depth. Such a
conservative approach was necessary because at the time there was very
little knowledge concerning the structural response of a ring-stiffened
cylinder to external hydrostatic pressure. Such an approach to establishing
safety factors severely penalized the craft with respect to size, volume,
speed, payload, etc. Thus it is easy to understand the multi-national
efforts that were mounted to increase the understanding of the response of
submarine structures under external hydrostatic pressure. In general the
early work was initiated in Europe with later developments coming from both
the UK and the U. S. U. S. Navy structural design, as well as the designs
of all nations, have benefitted from and have utilized the work of these
many researchers as published in the open literature.

Shell plating, stiffener, end closure and tank structure design have
evolved over the nine decades since Holland first demonstrated the
usefulness of the submarine. Initial plating design based on the Boiler
Formula gave way to more sophisticated analysis by people such as Von Mises,
Von Sander and Gunther, Windenberg and Trilling through to the inelastic
analysis capabilities of today. Frame strength studied in great detail by
Marbec, Hovgaard and Tokugawa has now been extended into the inelastic
range. The effects of framing on the overall instability mode of failure
has been extended over the last 30 years by the work of Kendrick and
Reynolds. The critical effects of even supposedly minor imperfections on
the strength of spherical shells has been demonstrated by Krenzke. All of
these efforts, heavily supported with experimental verification, have led to
the design approach utilized today.

The problems in submarine structural design are unique because the
submarine pressure hull is the only major engineering structure with a
thickness to diameter ratio less than 0.005 that is subjected to relatively
high external pressure. Other such pressure vessels are subjected to low
internal pressure and have rather generous factors of safety. The design of
a submarine pressure hull involves the selection of a minimum weight
structure to provide the required factor of safety at the design test depth.
In essence, such a design requires the correct distribution of material in

both the transverse framing and the pressure hull. Because of the obvious safety ramifications associated with adequacy of hull and framing, reduction of material thickness therein must be based on a sound analytical foundation verified by experimental results. Thus, safe submarine design practice requires a high degree of reliability in the analytical predictions and also in strain and deflection measurements on both model and prototype so as to permit a lower factor of safety than is commonly used in the design of steel structures.

Scaled model tests of various compartments of the submarines provide relatively inexpensive methods of verifying the collapse pressure of submarine hull structures, and these are the designers' only real method of obtaining advance proof of the adequacy of the structure. However, in most cases, they are not of sufficiently large enough scale for studying the detailed structural response. Determination of the detailed structural behavior to confirm analytical predictions and the empirical factors to be used in design can only be accomplished from measurements taken on deep submergence tests of submarines or on tests of very large-scale expensive models. In most instances, the use of large-scale models is too costly, and the only recourse is to take measurements on prototype submarines. Therefore, both model and full-scale testing are required to ensure adequacy of structures for present day and future submarines. This in no way implies that theoretical treatments are of secondary importance in the design of submarine hulls, nor is it implied that theoretical treatments are of primary importance. Theory is the basis for the initial design, but because of the complexity of the formulation, many of the theories must be simplified before they become attractive to the designer. Thus, theoretical analysis joins model and full scale testing to form the trinity for design and analysis of submarine hull structures. No single element of this trinity will by itself provide complete information for use by the designer of submarine hull structures.

By the techniques of scaled model tests, full-scale tests, and the comparison of these experimental results with theoretical predictions, the Navy continually reexamines the adequacy of design criteria and, where necessary, improves these criteria so that more efficient, more economical, lighter, stronger, and deeper diving submarines can be constructed.

U. S. Navy structural practice is to design for the most efficient mode of failure ensuring that other less efficient instability modes will not intervene by (a) establishing building specifications that preclude deleterious circularity and sphericity defects; and (b) by applying higher safety factors to more sensitive instability modes of failure. In this way optimum advantage is obtained from the hull material selected, thus submarine hull weights are minimized and hull size is lessened or payload is increased.

Inherent in submersible structural design is the need to reduce weight – this is generally accomplished through the use of higher strength hull materials. The higher strength materials are less tough than other materials and therefore much more attention must be placed on the design of details and on the fabrication process. As the material strength level increases, toughness decreases, usually to the point where the material can be "semi-brittle" with a very high sensitivity to minute flaws. In such cases details must be developed with smooth contours, minimized welds, castings and forgings – in other words, clean design that lends itself to mechanized welding.

STRUCTURAL INTEGRITY

THE CONCEPT. The U. S. Navy has utilized a Structural Integrity (SI) approach for many years. Modern computer capabilities and technology improvements have permitted a formalized and quantitative approach to and evaluation of what used to be called "good design and shipbuilding practice." In today's designs SI is the total integration of design, production and welding engineering in considering material properties, flaw sensitivity, design and analysis capability, fabrication and life cycle maintenance and economic considerations during all phases of the design and construction process. By its very nature SI encompasses structural soundness (strength or load carrying capability) and structural adequacy (rigidity, maintainability, availability, etc.).

The SI requirements result in a structural systems analysis approach to design and, as shown in Table 4, require consideration of the interplay of the following six primary items:

TABLE 4. Structural Integrity Requirements

ITEM \ MATERIAL	STEELS					TITANIUM	COMPOSITES	ALUMINUM
	ABS/MS	HTS	HY 80	HY 100	> HY 100			
LOADING SPECTRUM	X*	X	X	X	X	X	X	
MATERIAL CHARACTERISTICS	X	X	X	X	X	X	X	X
FLAW GROWTH ANALYSIS				R	S***	S	S	S
DESIGN & ANALYSIS	R**	R	R	R	S	S	S	R/S
FABRICATION CONTROLS			R	R	S	S	S	S
SPECIAL MAINTENANCE REQUIREMENTS						X	X	X	X

*X   NECESSARY
**R   ROUTINE, GENERALLY SIMPLIFIED REQUIREMENTS
***S   SOPHISTICATED TECHNIQUES

a. Basic Material Properties - characterizations of the material system as fabricated including full thickness mechanical and physical properties of base plate, product forms, and weld metal.

b. Flaw Sensitivity - crack initiation and growth rate data for fabricated base plate and product forms. Effects of built in stresses, cyclic rates, and hold times on fatigue life. Sensitivity of the material system to all environmental conditions must also be known.

c. Loading Spectrum - sea loads, cargo, vibration, aircraft landing, docking, groundings, weapon loadings and residual stresses must be evaluated and addressed.

d. Design and Analysis - availability and capability of analytical tools to properly size the structure and to predict stress distribution, failure modes and flaw initiation and growth, in order to preclude premature failures that could impair mission requirements.

e. Fabrication - fabrication constraints must be considered by the designer. Included are such items as standardizing structural details and spacings in order to minimize the numbers of special jigs and fixtures and maximize the potential for automating cutting and welding. In addition, the capabilities and criteria of the quality assurance program must also be considered.

f. Maintenance - life cycle requirements for inspections, reapplication of protective coatings and occasional repair of defects and removal of equipments should be addressed in the early stages of design. Use of lower strength, more forgiving material, in inaccessible areas, use of heavier plating in areas subject to severe corrosion or to regular in-service damage, as well as special weld dressings to preclude crack initiation in service must all be considered.

The above six items are mandatory first steps in any design - though it is not necessary to rigorously address them all in every design. The engineering designs which dictate the degrees to which SI requirements must be applied can be broadly bounded within the following limits:

o Elaborate - mission requirements dictate the use of high strength, exotic materials, therefore a high flaw sensitivity exists.

o Routine - mission requirements permit the use of the more conventional materials and therefore more tolerance to flaws is inherent.

From a SI standpoint, critical elements of the design are designated in the detail specifications, and in-service inspection requirements are promulgated. These critical elements are defined as a result of refined computer analysis, scaled model test results, and performance of comparable areas on earlier ships. The type periodicity and scope of in-service inspections are defined after a careful review of large-scale structural test data and/or operational experience at sea.

In those cases where a detail tends to develop flaws in service, immediate feedback to the designer will result in design improvements in an early follow ship. Graphic evidence of the advantages of the structural integrity approach in developing such improvements is shown in Figure 4 for three different classes of ships. All ships were subjected to basically the same routes, yet the improvements in the later designs are most dramatic. For the number of ship year's operation shown, the later designs clearly demonstrate performance improvements resulting from design changes and fabrication improvements alone.

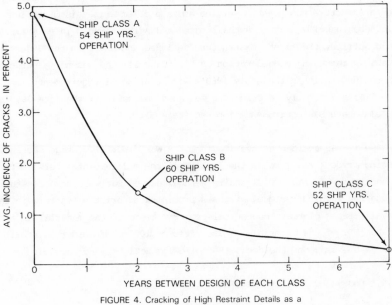

FIGURE 4. Cracking of High Restraint Details as a
Function of Learning Experience

Certain details can continue to be a source of problems regardless of the sophistication of analysis or extra care taken in fabrication. In such instances other somewhat obvious approaches are taken. For example, even though analytical methods indicate low stress levels at square deckhouse corners, these details have been a source of problems. The solution — replace them with rounded corners. Other problems can be solved by revising operational guidelines where feasible. For example, fuel tanks can be designed to accommodate any pressure during refueling, but the weight and

464

cost penalty associated with a design for a rare overloading case may not be warranted. The solution - either provide larger diameter overflow pipes or restrict the pumping rates during refuelings at sea. While this latter case at first glance may not seem to be an application of SI technology, on closer examination it fits within the definition since it is a cost effective means of ensuring undamaged structure by controlling the loadings.

IN-SERVICE APPLICATIONS OF SI. The SI concept in initial design stages where the designer has a clean sheet of paper and is somewhat less constrained is fairly straightforward and readily applied. Its application after a structure has been in service and a problem arises is often less obvious but usually much more challenging and stimulating. Three examples should suffice, the first, a structure designed and built in the 1940's, probably without any consideration of SI, (Case I); the second, a structure designed and built in the early 1960's with routine SI requirements imposed (Case II); and finally, a structure designed and built in the late 1950's with elaborate SI requirements imposed (Case III).

Case I - An accidental overloading of a World War II vintage sectional floating drydock resulted in the failure of the splice plates between two of the sections. Initial weld repairs were attempted but were unsuccessful because the welding residual stresses precipitated brittle fracture in the sidewall keeper plates. Mechanical property tests of the material indicated that the NDT of the material was in excess of 100°F. In order to repair and preserve the usage of the dock, the following actions were pursued:

a. Undamaged portions were left alone.

b. Preheaters were installed at the damaged sections, the temperature was raised to approximately 225°F, and weld repairs were accomplished.

c. All critical welds were contoured.

d. A special overload test was conducted.

The overload test was conducted by first installing preheaters on all splice plate welds between the dock sections and heating the welds to 225°F to

465

ensure ductile behavior. The various dock sections were then flooded
sequentially to induce hogging and sagging conditions 20 percent greater
than the maximum design condition for the dock. The rationale was that such
an overload would redistribute tensile residual stresses and would cause any
existing minute flaws to grow some small distance in the now "ductile"
material and then blunt themselves. Any such defects would then be left "as
is" but monitored during the life of the dock. Upon completion of the test,
the strip heaters were removed, and another loading test to a slightly
lesser hogging and sagging condition was conducted to verify the adequacy of
the dock. Upon completion of that test, ballasting procedures were
specified that would result in maximum stresses approximately 75 percent of
the maximum design condition. Even with these lower operating stresses the
dock can accommodate the largest ships that can physically fit in the dock.
The dock has been operating satisfactorily now for over seven years and the
existing flaws are being visually monitored.

In this case we were fortunate in that we could apply certain SI
principles after the fact. We were able to use strip heaters to put a
normally brittle material into a ductile regime for special crack blunting
purposes. We could prescribe ballasting schemes that controlled the
loadings and permitted a redistribution of harmful tensile residual stresses
as well as operational stresses within prescribed limits. Fortunately we
were able to demonstrate that we could apply modern technology to an old
design.

Case II - In this case a ship was found to have out of specification
butt welds joining stiffener sections. The approach to this case was to
apply more modern analytical techniques to assess the adequacy of the
structure. Laboratory fatigue data was obtained for the welded detail at
various stress levels, sufficient data were generated to develop a
statistical distribution of data at a number of stress levels. The sequence
of analysis is shown graphically in Figure 5. The steps in the procedure
were as follows:

a. Determine the expected ship lifetime loading. The ship was assumed
to spend 50 percent of the time in the North Atlantic and 50 percent of the

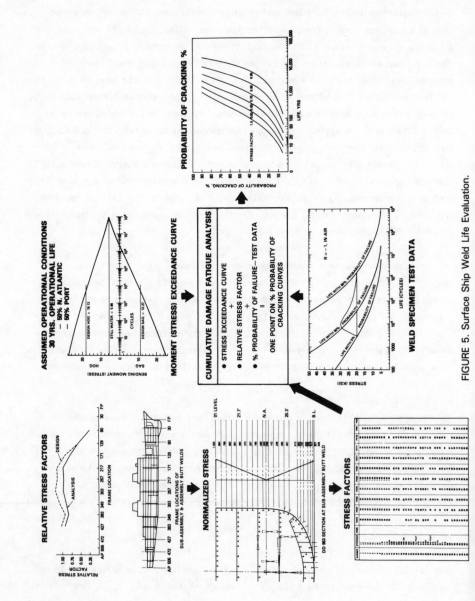

FIGURE 5. Surface Ship Weld Life Evaluation.

time in port. Longitudinal bending moments resulting from wave action and
dynamic response due to whipping were calculated based on North Atlantic sea
spectra.

b. For the ship in question, the design stress distribution (i.e.,
without deckhouse contribution) was developed and then modified to account
for the deckhouse. This permitted determination of actual longitudinal
stresses directly related to the Navy design moment. The stress values were
then divided by the moment values to determine stress sensitivities, these
values were then multiplied by the lifetime moment values (step (a) North
Atlantic) to determine lifetime stresses. All stress values were then
normalized to the maximum calculated stress for simplification.

c. Weld sections removed from the ship in question were then subjected
to fully reversed axial fatigue testing in air. Sufficient data were
generated to develop the statistical characteristics of the S-N curves, thus
various probabilities of occurrence.

d. Linear cumulative damage theory was then used to determine the
probability of cracking. Using the 30 year lifetime North Atlantic
distribution, an exceedence stress distribution for the highest stressed
detail was generated. This curve was normalized to one year by dividing by
30 to determine the number of cycles per year. Analysis is then performed
to determine how many of these one year spectrums have to be cycled for
failure to occur. The reference value is then multiplied by the normalized
stress factors resulting in an expected fatigue life for a given probability
at various normalized operating stresses. Since the S-N curves were
sufficiently detailed to permit statistical probabilities of cracking, the
process was repeated for different probabilities of failure. Curves
representing probability of failure versus ship life for varying stress
factors were then developed.

In this case we were able to demonstrate that in a 30 year lifetime 20
percent of the 50 highest stressed stiffeners and 40 percent of the 40
stiffeners stressed from 0.8 to 0.9 of design value could have surface
cracking. Thus in 30 years the probability was that about 26 stiffeners
would be cracked. The next step was to evaluate the dynamic response under

these conditions and the results indicated adequacy of structure. As a result the highest stressed stiffeners are visually inspected approximately every three years. Any visible cracks will be repaired.

Case III – In this case a ship was designed using elaborate SI procedures. The material was very tough and fully characterized and a number of specific details had been studied analytically and experimentally under all combinations of service loadings. In fact charts similar to Figure 6 had been developed to rapidly assess the effects of various types of defects. During a routine inspection of the 1960's a UT defect was noted in a specific detail. The indication was not a cause for concern but the location was noted and was routinely UT inspected. Things seemed dormant for about 15 years and then on another routine UT inspection the indication seemed to be twice as deep as on the previous inspection. There was no evidence of undue or excessive loadings between inspection cycles, but there was evidence that UT inspection capabilities had improved over the years. More sophisticated and refined inspection techniques had confirmed the larger size of the defect, but time and cost considerations precluded gouging out and repair at the time. Since considerable characterization data was available on the material, the weld metal, the specific detail, and the loading spectrum, the following analytical approach was utilized.

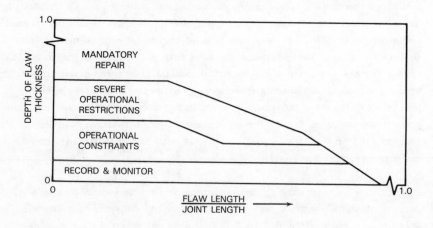

FIGURE 6. Typical Assessment Chart for a Flawed Deta.

469

A load/time – flaw growth curve was generated for three basic conditions, Figure 7.

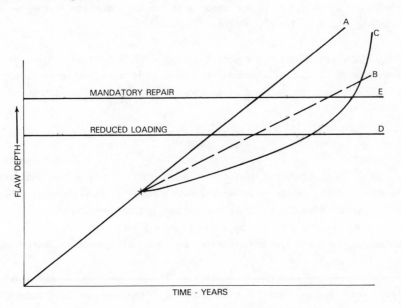

FIGURE 7. Assessment of Implications of an In-service Depth

a. Assuming the flaw grew from zero to present depth during the ship's lifetime – Curve A.

b. Utilizing existing flaw growth data from structural models of the detail, project the future growth – Curve B.

c. Utilizing existing computer programs with crack growth data from simple laboratory specimens, and the known loading history project the future growth. (Since the output of this computer code is nonlinear, many blocks of the loading spectrum were applied until the output predicted the existing flaw depth – the future growth was then predicted from that point) – Curve C.

d. Superimposed upon the curve were the criteria for reduced loading and mandatory repair similar to Figure 6 – Curves D and E.

Evaluation of the results indicated that considerable time in service could be accumulated before any repair was necessary, except for the most severe assumptions. Therefore it was recommended to leave matters as they were but to reinspect on a slightly shorter time schedule.

This latter situation is the more common type of in-service problem, and it demonstrates that if SI is considered right from the start, potentially serious problems can be handled in a relatively routine cost effective manner.

SUMMARY

Naval ship structural design, while outwardly appearing evolutionary, does reflect the impact of advancing technology. In fact the impact of technological advances in other disciplines has had meaningful effects on structural requirements for both soundness and adequacy. The structural-material system has had to keep pace with advances in such areas as:

HULL FORM - Though monohulls will probably be the dominant hull form for many years to come, rigorous sea kindliness requirements and special mission requirements make Small Waterplane Area Twin Hull (SWATH), air cushion or foilborne hulls a necessity. All of these high performance hulls require unique structural design - material application considerations.

MACHINERY SYSTEMS - Marine Gas Turbines with attendant requirements for large deck cutouts for intakes and exhausts will also be with us for many years. The promise of superconducting machinery, while attractive from a generator weight and size standpoint, should not materially affect the structural impact of gas turbines.

WEAPONS SYSTEMS - Vertical launch systems with their requirements for large cutouts in the strength deck require special consideration for hull girder strength and stiffness. Added to this complexity is the rigidity requirement for structure supporting phased array radars. Again, the use of lighter support systems (i.e., fiber optic in lieu of cable for signal transmission) while beneficial to the total ship design, may not offer the structural designer any real help when sizing specific elements of structure.

PAYLOAD - Because of the long service life expected of Naval ships, they must be adaptable for changes in payloads such as aircraft, vehicles, cargoes, etc. New types of aircraft may impose significantly different types of loads due to radical landing gear configurations or due to thermal effects. Cargo holds and magazines may be subjected to higher loads due to higher density packaging or configuration changes.

U. S. Navy structural design today is based on the use of proven analytical techniques, experimental data, and adherence to structural integrity requirements. The operational requirements dictate the need and often the approach to the design. To assure uniformity of technical considerations and confidence in the quality of the finished product, utilization of technical design standards and detailed technical specifications is implemented. The design is reviewed by the operating forces to ensure that it not only reflects the operational requirements but also the budgetary constraints. The structure is the containment system to carry and to protect the payload and the other systems such as propulsion, auxiliary, electrical communication, weapons, people, etc. While most other systems can be replaced or renewed during overhauls, the hull structure to any great extent cannot and must be adequate for the entire service life of the ship. Therefore, its design must incorporate the often conflicting requirements of these other systems. However the adequacy and soundness of the structural design is paramount, and even though it may be compromised to meet other system constraints, it must incorporate quality, reliability, maintainability and survivability. Otherwise it is an unacceptable design!!

ADVANCES IN THE DESIGN OF OFFSHORE STRUCTURES
FOR DAMAGE - TOLERANCE

Torgeir Moan
Division of Marine Structures
The Norwegian Institute of Technology
Trondheim, Norway

ABSTRACT

Introductory remarks about platform concepts for deep water are
followed by a review of requirements in current regulations and codes for
design of offshore structures for damage tolerance; with emphasis on the
specific requirements of the Norwegian Petroleum Directorate. Methods for
determining the ultimate strength of intact and damaged trusswork steel
platforms, and examples to illustrate the behaviour of such systems, are
presented. Future research needs in this area are highlighted.

1. INTRODUCTION

Various types of platforms may be employed in the exploration and
exploitation of hydrocarbons. They may for instance be characterized by
the support and station-keeping system.

Fixed or bottom-supported platforms are connected to the seafloor by
relatively stiff structural elements, allowing mainly horizontal motions
(deflections) of the order 0.1-1 m, and negligible vertical deflections.
The traditional fixed steel structure has been the jacket, see e.g. Fig.
1a. New types of fixed platforms such as tripods (see Fig. 1b), have been
developed to achieve a more effective load-transfer to the seafloor. The
load-carrying system can be made compliant (see Fig. 1c-d) to reduce the
wave load effects in the structure. Such platforms are designed with
eigenperiods for the rigid body motions which exceed the wave periods. The
wave forces then will be balanced by inertia forces, distributed along the
tower nearly in the same way as the extreme wave forces. The global shear-
forces and moments in the towers will therefore be significantly less than

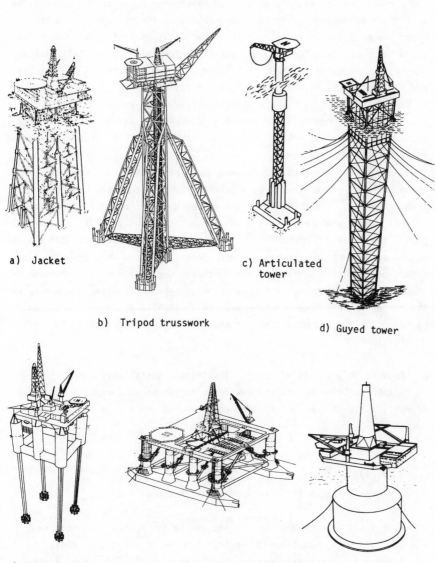

a) Jacket

c) Articulated tower

b) Tripod trusswork

d) Guyed tower

e) Tension leg platform (TLP)

f) Catenary anchored floater (CAF)

FIGURE 1. Types of Support and Station-keeping Systems

for a corresponding fixed platform. However, the joint of the ALP will be a critical element. The large area occupied by the mooring system of the guyed tower is inconvenient from an operational point of view. The first guyed tower was installed in the Gulf of Mexico in 1984. Installation and inspection and repair of deepwater fixed and compliant towers are complex and may contribute significantly to the total costs.

Future developments in deeper water (250-400 m) and smaller and hence more marginal fields, make floaters more competitive. The incentives may be a less expensive load-carrying structure and shorter installation, hook-up time, and ease of inspection/maintenance. The reduced wave (and earthquake) forces in the structure, and hence the reduced costs of floaters compared to e.g. fixed platforms are achieved at the expense of greater motions, which would represent a challenge in the design of risers and partly the process equipment etc. It may thus be necessary to shut down or disconnect risers on catenary anchored floaters in bad weather. The first floating production systems in the North Sea were based on converted semi-submersible drilling rigs. The first purpose-built floating production was the Hutton TLP which came into operation in 1984. A floating production platform for the Balmoral field is under construction and will start production in 1987.

Besides cost-effectiveness of fabrication, installation and inspection/maintenance, safety requirements represent important considerations in the design. Minimum requirements are set by authorities to avoid

- loss of human lives;
- significant pollution;
- economic losses of importance to the national economy.

Additional requirements may be imposed by the operating companies, especially from a cost-benefit consideration of investment in design to limit inspection/maintenance repair and ensure availability during operation.

The present paper outlines developments in the safety appraisal for offshore platforms, with emphasis on damage-tolerance.

2. SAFETY REQUIREMENTS

2.1 Background

Experiences (see e.g. [1]) show that accidents develop in event sequences, sometimes from initial incidents which have small consequences. These
incidents may be caused by maloperation, fabrication faults or even design
errors or omissions. Accidents do not seem to be realisation of the risk
implied by using too small safety margins to account for the uncertainties
in demand and capacity in e.g. structural design. This fact indicates that
the safety factors in the conventional design checks of components could be
reduced without noticeable effect on the frequency of accidents. On the
other hand, it is important to recognize the occurence of accidental
situations and all barriers to control the risk. Small initial damages
should especially be prevented from resulting in progressive failures with
catastrophic consequences. Such a progressive limit state check may, of
course, in the end result in an increase of the scantlings of some parts of
the structure. However, the benefit from this increase of material is
greater than just using higher safety factors (than necessary) in the whole
structure.

In principle, the most efficient measure against errors and omissions
involves motivation, education and training of individuals, use of an adequate management system (organization, responsibilities), implementing QA/QC
within the organization which designs, fabricates or operates the facility, or by third parties. It is, however, felt that other, more direct
measures should also be applied at least in the short-term range to control
the risk. These measures involve consideration of accidental conditions
and implementation of a progressive failure criterion in the design of the
platform system.

Progressive failure criteria have been generally applied in regulations
and codes for stability of ships and mobile units for a long time. Similar
requirements relating to structural integrity, were first recognized in the
NPD regulations for loading-carrying structures and DnV's rules for fixed
platforms in 1977, and for mobile units after the Alexander L. Kielland
accident. Many other regulations and codes, including model codes [2, 3],

contain general statements about "fail-safe" qualities of the structure or the mooring system. Damage-tolerance may especially be crucial for deep-water fixed platforms, where inspection and maintenance of the deeply submerged parts of the structure may be difficult, if not impossible. The application of the NPD approach to the structure and anchoring systems, is further described below.

2.2 Structural design criteria

The design of marine structures should preferably be made in distinct stages - at least a concept and an engineering stage, because it is advantageous to devote special efforts on the overall concept from a functional and safety point of view before large efforts are spent on detailed engineering. A procedure for conceptual safety evaluation has been devised by e.g. NPD [4]. Risk control is most effectively exercised in this concept stage, when the overall layout is chosen. The detailed engineering design should include requirements which refer to service-ability- (SLS), ultimate -(ULS), fatigue- (FLS), and progressive failure (PLS) limit states. The most important structural design criteria relating to loss of lives is concerned with system failure by (rapid) progressive collapse.

The criteria in present <u>regulations and codes for structural integrity</u> differ in various ways. Ship rules primarily contain a serviceability (SLS) and ultimate strength (ULS) check of components by an allowable stress format. Fatigue and progressive failure are not explicitly considered. The implicit safety factor of the component strength may be 20-40% smaller than those used for offshore structures. This is commonly explained by the inherent reserve strength in ships, which obviously will vary.

Ultimate strength requirements for mobile and fixed platforms also vary - due to different approaches to calculate load effects, the structural capacity and the safety factors applied.

Fatigue requirements vary among different codes for mobile units and fixed platforms. The UK Dep. of Energy (DoE), however, cover mobile and fixed platforms by the same guidance notes [6]. The NPD requirements [5] to production platforms and DnV requirement to mobile units are quite close, but have more restrictive fatigue requirements for welded joints which may lead to progressive failure, than the DoE.

The most significant difference between the NPD regulations [5] and other regulations and codes, including all rules for ships, is the quantitative progressive failure criterion applied in the former regulations.

Since ships and floating platforms are now being employed in all industrial activities offshore, there is a need to harmonize strength criteria so that the variation in implied safety level corresponds to a desired variation in target level. SLS, ULS and FLS criteria should then be calibrated on a probabilistic basis. The safety factors applied should reflect the uncertainties inherent in design data and analyses and the consequences of failure.

Codes for catenary mooring systems made of steel wires or chains have been developed for drilling rigs by authorities (NMD [7]; DoE's will appear shortly) and classification societies, see e.g. ref. [8], and include an explicit check of ultimate and progressive failure, and do not refer to fatigue, wear and other deterioration phenomena. The latter effects are supposed to be covered by inspection and repair/replacement during operation. Obviously requirements for mooring systems of production platforms should be developed based on the experiences with mobile units, with due regard to the differences in mode of operation, consequences of failure, etc.

Existing guidelines for tension-leg systems comprise ref. [9], which impose SLS, ULS and FLS requirements. API and DnV among others are developing such guidelines. No authorities have up to now issued specific information about such systems. However, the NPD regulations [5], in principle cover tension-legs and more specific guidelines are under development. The latter regulation and guidelines cover explicit PLS requirements.

The following sections deal with the progressive limit state check of the load carrying structure and mooring systems.

2.3 Progressive limit state check

Procedure

The NPD regulations [5] require that the progressive limit state be checked in the following two steps when a systems failure may lead to severe consequences:

1) Resistance against abnormal loads

It is to be demonstrated that the structure, when subjected to certain abnormal loads suffer no more than local damage, i.e. not progressive failure.

Abnormal loads are taken to be accidental loads (collisions, falling objects, fires/explosions, blowouts, differential pressures, ... etc.) as well as natural loads at an extremely low probability of occurence. For normal operations this probability level is 10^{-4} pr. year. For other temporary conditions the possible abnormal loads have to be specified in each case.

Load and resistance factors are normally set equal to 1.0 in this case.

2) Resistance in damaged condition

After possible local damage due to abnormal loads or other damage e.g. due to abnormal strength, as discussed below, the structure should resist functional and specified natural loads without progressive structural failure, flooding, capsizing or sinking.

In the check of a damaged platform in the normal operational phase, natural loads refer to an annual probability of 10^{-2}. For temporary conditions during operation, the design loads have to be specified in each case.

Analyses for demonstrating the damage - tolerance, may be based on elasto-plastic behaviour when the structure has adequate ductility and repeated plastic deformations do not occur.

Load and resistance factors are normally equal to 1.0 in this case.

Some accidental events occur quite suddenly and hence involve both a (dynamic) transient and a steady-state condition. When the the effect of the accidental events is combined with other conditions, e.g. environmental loads, the duration of the accidental event and the possible correlation between the accidental event and the other conditions, should be accounted for.

Damage condition - abnormal strength

Accidental structural damage may occur due to one or both of the following reasons:
- abnormal loads
- abnormal strength

The former aspect is treated in detail for instance in refs. [10-13]. Therefore, only a few remarks will be devoted to abnormal strength here.

Abnormal strength may be caused during fabrication (welding) of steel structures and mooring chains; and wear and tear and handling damages during operation of steel wire in mooring systems.

Clearly QA/QC activities, particularly inspections following fabrication and during operation, are devised to control such faults and set up actions to ameleriorate their effects. However, small damages such as cracks, occur frequently and their detection can not be made with high reliability. Based on an assessment of the occurrence of fabrication cracks, crack growth and reliability of detecting cracks, accidental cracks corresponding to an annual probability level of 10^{-4} may be defined, and used in the PLS check. It is noted that this target level corresponds to a probability of occurrence of $50 \cdot 10^{-4} = 5 \cdot 10^{-3}$ in a 50 year life time if the occurrences in every year are independent. Undetected cracks in braces of semi-submersibles and jacket platforms have led to failures of members.

A majority of the 81 breakages of chains on semi-submersibles in the North Sea during 1968-84, involving some 160 platform years, were initiated by fabrication defects (cracks, burnmarks, erronous heat treatment, ..). Also wear at fairleads, especially caused by local bending stresses due to inadequate fit between the chain and fairlead, contributed [14]. Wire failures seem often to be caused by general wear during handling or when subjected to high local stresses at fairleads and winches [15]. Obviously, inadequate of inspection/repair had an effect on the failures.

A reliable estimate of damage conditions corresponding to an annual probability of 10^{-4}, requires about 20.000 platform years of consistent data. Since the total accumulated experience basis worldwide amounts to about 50.000 platform years, over a period with changing technology, damage conditions cannot be based on experience only. In other words, deducing damage conditions for design from experiences are likely to underestimate them. Hence, a rational extrapolation of the damage size to low probabilities would be needed.

2.4 Structures

Analysis is necessary to determine
- the actual damage condition due to accidental loads;
- the residual strength.

The basic damage modes are
- dents, which mainly affect the ultimate compressive strength;
- reduction of cross-section area due to corrosion;
- cracks in or complete fracture of a member.

Depending on the source of the damage (fires, explosions, collisions, falling objects, ..) various kind of analyses would be necessary as reviewed e.g. in [10-13]. The damage condition for design may typically comprise complete failure of a (slender) brace or partial damage of a heavily stiffened, steel plated structural component.
Depending upon the fatigue design criteria and the inspection/maintenance procedures applied, fracture of simple joints due to the combined effect of fabrication defects and crack propagation may be considered as a damaged condition.

Dynamic effects may be of importance in the global behaviour depending upon the ratio of the eigenperiods and wave periods. Such effects are neglected here, but are of importance for e.g. deepwater fixed platforms.

Dynamic effects may also be caused when forces are redistributed following fast fracture. The magnitude of the dynamic load factor depends on the time of force redistribution relative to the eigenperiod of the associated behaviour mode. The unloading period by fracture in a steel tube etc., may be estimated by assuming a fracture velocity of 100 m/s. The maximum transient response occurs up to a few seconds after the fracture. This implies that the condition of external loads on the structure may be assumed to be that at the instant of fracture.

The dynamic magnification associated with the load redistribution after the failure of the brace in the "Alexander L. Kielland" was found to vary between 1.4-2.6 in the various members, [16], while the dynamic load factor for a single degree of freedom system will be 2.0 for instantaneous unloading.

Obviously, by neglecting the dynamic transient effect, the low frequency wave and wind load and possible line dynamics, the uncertainty increases and increased safety (correction) factors should be applied.

2.5 Tension-leg system

The PLS check [5] for the damaged tension-leg system may be formulated as:

$$S_o(P+W_s) + S(E^+) \leqslant R_c$$

where S_o is the stress due to pretension, permanent loads (P) and the weight of the actual submerged tether (W_s) at the mean water level. $S(E^+)$ is the stress due to environmental loads, appropriately combining the maximum water level, wave crest and "set-down". The characteristic capacity R_c is easily determined.

The above equation may be applied to all behaviour modes, even when slack occurs. Since a detailed analysis of slack is complex and uncertain, slack is commonly avoided by requiring:

$$S_o(P+W_s) - S(L) - S(E^-) > 0$$

where L represents live loads; and E⁻ environmental loads appropriately combining minimum water level and wave through.

The crucial point in connection with the PLS check is the determination of the actual accidental condition, due to accidental loads (dropped objects; a continuing fire in a column; abnormal tension due to faulty ballast/weight, flooding due to collision, or subsea gas blowout; ...); abnormal tether strength (due to fabrication-induced cracks, dents, corrosion, wear or tear combined with inadequate inspection/monitoring); or any relevant combination of the above events.

The most probable cause of tether fracture is a combination of existing defects (e.g. cracks in tubular tethers) and extreme environmental loads. Slack is most likely caused by an abnormal mean tension combined with extreme environmental loads. Slack is commonly the most critical event.

The step 1 in the procedure in Section 2.3 in this case must be accomplished for two conditions:
1. Overload during the transient dynamic response that will occur.
2. Steady-state damaged condition considering reduced tension capacity in one corner and unsymmetric stiffness.

The quasi-static redistribution of forces due to failure of one tether is easily determined by the condition of compatibility and equilibrium, assuming the hull to be rigid compared to the tethers. With n tethers in each of four corners the quasi-static increase in tension in the corner where the failure occurs, is found to be $300/(4n-3)$ %. The reduction in the opposite corner is $100/(4n-3)$ %. If the failure is by fracture, the unloading time of the failed tether will be very short compared to the pitch and heave periods. This implies a magnification factor of about 2.0 on the redistributed forces. The maximum transient response is attained so short time after the fracture that the average tension may be assumed to be the same as at the time of fracture. The correlation between tether failure and high tether tension suggests that a sea-state with relatively high intensity be considered in the design check.

The second check is straightforward.

In addition to these checks, other consequences of a possible tether fracture must be considered. The lower part of the fractured tether will be a "dropped object" and may cause damage on bottom installation, risers and other tethers.

2.6 Catenary mooring systems

In case of catenary mooring systems step 1 in the PLS check in Section 2.3 may be omitted, as the damage condition conveniently can be taken to be failure of one or more lines. Failure of one line is expected to be a mandatory damage condition, as used by NMD [7]. The historical frequency of multiple line failures is about 10^{-2}, [1]. However, the introduction of a PLS design criterion itself obviously would reduce the failure probability significantly. Assuming this to be the case, it is felt that failure of one line is a reasonable compromise. Depending upon the reliability of the thruster system, failure of one or more thrusters may be a damage condition analogous to failure of one or more anchor lines. Another possible damage condition occurs when the floater attains deeper draught or heeling due to an accidental buoyancy loss. This accidental floating condition may increase the environmental loads on the platform, and hence on the anchoring system. In both the latter examples of accidental conditions the anchoring system itself is intact, but the load condition will be abnormal.

The design check of the damaged system may be formulated as

$$T_P + T_E < R_C$$

where T_P and T_E are the pretension and the tension due to environmental loads, respectively. R_C is the characteristic breaking strength.

The design check should be performed for two conditions - a transient and a steady - state one - as for the tension-leg system. The determination of transient response is not trivial and is commented upon below.

The response of the damaged mooring system is governed by the hydrodynamic behaviour. The time duration from line failure to maximum transient

response is typically half the surge/sway period. For the intact system
the eigenperiod may be 50 s and higher; and will increase by line failure
due to the change of stiffness. Comparisons between full-scale tests and
calculations [17, 18] demonstrate that the transient can be well simulated.
The main problem consists in assessing the combined effect of the transient
and the "continuous" environmental loads due to current, first and second
order wave loads and steady and fluctuating wind loads. The failure can
occur at an "arbritrary point" in time, but will be correlated with a
high intensity of line tension. A complete time domain approach would in
principle allow for all stochastic and dynamic effects. However, extensive
simulations would be needed to limit the sampling uncertainty. Further
work would be needed to develop a realistic approximate approach.

3. ANALYSIS OF DAMAGED STRUCTURAL SYSTEMS

3.1 General remarks

The verification of damage tolerance e.g. according to the criteria in
Section 2.3 requires analyses of the residual strength of damaged structures. The behaviour of systems with damages such as dents and cracks,
depends upon the layout and load conditions. In trusswork systems, tether
and catenary mooring systems the components may fail due to ductile
collapse, fatigue or fracture - or even wear and tear. The progressive
failure of other components then would be by ultimate collapse. For single
hull or member structures such as monotowers and ships, total failure may
be a sequential ductile collapse or fatigue/fracture.

In the present section methods for analyzing damaged structural
systems will be considered, with the emphasis on systems composed of
slender components with ductile behaviour.

3.2 Trusswork steel platforms

General remarks

The advent of finite element and other computer based methods provides a basis for realistic non-linear analyses of offshore platforms made of tubular steel structures. In investigations of steel trusswork structures simplified methods have been particularly popular. Marshall et al. [19], Zayas et al. [20], applied phenomenological brace models based on a given relationship between axial force and displacement for a truss element in earthquake analyses of jackets. Rashed [21] later extended the Idealized Structural Unit method (ISUM) [22] to analyse tubular frame structures. Supplementing modifications of this work are due to Aanhold et al. [23]. The practical study by Lloyd and Clawson [24], applying the INTRA system [19] also provides valuable information.

Moan et al [25] considered two methods, FENRIS and USFOS, for calculating the ultimate strength based on beam theory; accounting for large displacements and elasto-plastic material behaviour. Both methods employ finite elements with 6 degrees of freedom in each node. A principal difference is the assumption of displacement fields. In the FENRIS model [25, 26] the members are subdivided in several elements, with a polynominal approximation to the displacements in each element. The USFOS model [25] employs shape functions which represent the exact solution of the 4th order differential equation of a beam subjected to a constant axial force within each member. Both methods are incremental; FENRIS includes iterative equilibrium corrections while the present version of USFOS does not. The models for pre- and post-ultimate strength behaviour of locally damaged elements presented in[27, 28], can be incorporated in the element methods.

Case-study - simple 3-D system

The aim of the present section is to present numerical results from analyses of 3-D X-braced systems, and illustrate factors that influence reserve and residual strength. Both intact and damaged systems will be considered, and the simplified procedure used in USFOS will be compared to the more accurate one in FENRIS.

Two systems with equal member arrangement (Fig. 2) and dimensions as shown in Table 1, will be considered. The vertical X-braces have different slenderness ratios. An elastic-perfectly-plastic material law with a yield stress of 330 MPa was used. The chosen type of system may be regarded as a subsystem of a four-legged jacket.

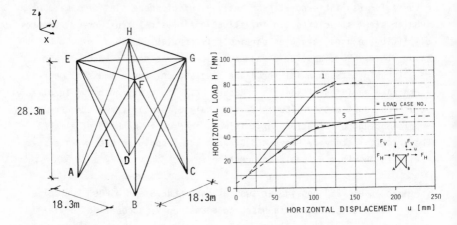

FIGURE 2. 3-D Systems analysed   FIGURE 3. Load-Displacement Curves for
          by FENRIS and USFOS   Load Cases 1 and 5
                                            (System S1)

Eleven load cases were analysed by FENRIS. These are summarized in Table 2. Various combinations of nodal point loads and direct member loads are thought to simulate different positions of the subassemblages S1 and S2 in the total structure. In addition to the horizontal loads a constant vertical load amounting to 120 MN is applied. This load is applied before the incrementation of the horizontal loads start. As also seen from Table 2, three different types of damage are considered. In the case of global damage to member EI, this damage was taken as an initial out-of-straightness $\delta_0/L=0.024$ (in negative y-direction). The two other damaged conditions considered total removal of the compression member EI and the tension member IF, respectively. As also seen from Table 2, the undamaged structure was analysed both with and without small initial imperfections, typically $\delta_0/L=0.0015$. Further details are given in [26].

The reference design load, H_d was determined from linear analyses, using the interaction equations recommended by API to perform the member checks.

TABLE 1
Dimensions for Members in 3-D X-Braced Systems
(Abbreviations are explained in footnote)

MEMBER TYPE	SYSTEM	D [m]	t [m]	L [m]	N_p[MN]	M_p[MNm]	D/t	L/r
Legs	S1, S2	2.0	0.060	28.53	120.67	74.54	33	41
Horizontals	S1, S2	1.0	0.040	18.29	39.80	12.17	25	54
Horizontal X-brace	S1, S2	1.0	0.040	25.86	39.80	12.17	25	76
Vertical	S1	1.016	0.038	33.66	38.53	12.00	26.7	97
X-braces	S2	0.508	0.019	33.66	9.63	1.50	26.7	195

N_p and M_p denote plastic axial force and moment, respectively

D=diameter; t=thickness; L=length; r=radius of gyration

Table 2 summarizes the results from the analyses. It is seen that relative simple structural systems may possess considerable strength reserves compared to estimates obtained by a simple design check. These systems also display the ability to tolerate quite serious damages to the structural members. All structures considered can easily carry the design load in the damaged condition considered, signified by a value of H_r/H_u larger than unity. The results seem also to indicate that structures having large slenderness ratios, possess larger reserve strength than structures having smaller slenderness ratios. However, they suffer larger strength reductions in cases involving damages to the members. This observation may be explained by the fact that slender members exhibit larger strength differences in tension and compression than more stocky members.

TABLE 2
Summary of Load Cases for the 3-D Systems analysed by FENRIS
(Abbreviations are explained in footnote)

CASE	TYPE OF LOADING	INITIAL DEFLECT	DAMAGE CONDITION (See Fig. 2)	H_u	$\dfrac{H_u}{H_d}$	$\dfrac{H_r}{H_u}$	$\dfrac{H_r}{H_d}$
SYSTEM S1: L/r = 97							
1	NPL	No	Intact	82.0	1.86	-	-
2	NPL	Yes	Intact	80.4	1.83	-	-
3	NPL	Yes	Member EI	76.0	-	0.95	1.7
4	NPL	Yes	Compression member EI removed	60.0	-	0.75	1.3
5	NPL	Yes	Tension member IF removed	55.8	-	0.69	1.2
6	NPL + EL	Yes	Intact	88.8	2.22	-	-
7	NPL + EL	Yes	Tension member IF removed	63.7	-	0.72	1.5
SYSTEM S2: L/r = 197							
8	NPL	Yes	Intact	16.9	2.11	-	-
9	NPL	Yes	Tension member IF removed	10.6	-	0.63	1.3
10	NPL + EL	Yes	Intact	18.9	2.36	-	-
11	NPL + EL	Yes	Tension member IF removed	12.1	-	0.64	1.5

NPL = Nodal Point Loads, EL = direct member loads
The horizontal load acts in the x-direction (see Fig. 2)
H_d = design load; H_u = collapse load; H_r = residual strength after damage
L = length of member; r = radius of gyration

Linear analyses are often used in practice to check the residual
strength of a platform in damaged condition. This method was used here to
recompute case no. 5, taking all safety factors equal to unity. By this
procedure the ultimate load becomes 29 MN compared to 55.8 MN from the
FENRIS-analyses (see Table 2). This shows that the use of linear elastic
methods for checking the residual strength of a damaged structure, may
yield overly conservative results. Therefore, non-linear analyses may
become especially useful for these types of analyses if excessively conservative designs are to be avoided.

The results from the analyses also show that non-structural members,
i.e. members that practically carry no load in a design condition, may play
an important role in the redistribution of forces. Consequently, these
members are of more importance to the damaged structure than to the intact
structure. This is documented in more detail in [26].

USFOS was also used to analyse the cases described above, and gave in general good agreement with the FENRIS-results regarding maximum load capacity. This is documented in Fig. 3, where load-displacement curves are shown for two of the cases. Similar results are obtained for the other cases. The required computer time for the FENRIS-runs was typically in the order of 1 hour CPU-time on a NORD-560 computer, and for USFOS less than two minutes. This shows that such simplified methods may have a great potential for analysing complex systems. The FENRIS-results were obtained by using an element model consisting of 108 beam elements and 93 nodal points.

Case-study-Jacket

Fig. 4 shows an eight-legged platform which will be used to further illustrate some aspects of reserve and residual strength. The platform geometry and X-bracing configuration are fairly typical of North Sea installations at about 70 m water depth. The members have been sized according to the API-RP2A design code. Foundation support is provided by insert piles in the legs and three skirt piles at each corner leg.

The deck is modelled by single beams that have about the same stiffnesses as typical deck structures of this size. The strength of the deck has not been explicitly studied but it may be important for redistribution of loads when damage occurs near the top of the jacket.

The conductor framing system is modelled in a very simplified manner. The loads from the conductors are distributed to the corners and midsection of the frames. Functional loads and environmental loads are considered. The total deck load is distributed as equal point loads on the top of the legs. The environmental loads consist of loads from waves, current and wind. Three load cases are considered:

- LC1: Waves 45^0 relative to longitudinal axis. Wave height = 26 m
- LC2: Waves along the longitudinal axis. Wave height = 27 m
- LC3: Waves perpendicular to the longitudinal axis. Wave height = 20.6 m

490

The wave heights correspond to design waves with a return period of 100
years for the considered directions. The current acts parallel with the
waves. The same profile is used in all directions with a maximum velocity
of 1.2 m/s at sea surface.

Fig. 4 shows the damage cases used in the residual strength analyses.
They may be considered to result from ship collision or dropped objects,
and possibly fatigue fracture. The ship collision damages consist of two
cases. In the first case, DC1, a complete X-bracing at sea level is considered ineffective. Secondly, a corner leg is assumed damaged at sea surface. The cross-section has been dented to a depth of 0.35 m (i.e. 22% of
the diameter) and the neutral axis has got a permanent off-set of 0.68 m
(i.e. 3.2% of leg span). This damage corresponds to an impact from a supply
vessel with a design energy equal to 14 MJ.

With respect to dropped objects members at the lower end of the
jacket will be more exposed. However, the potential impact energies may
not imply serious damages if the member behave in a ductile manner.
However, failure of the tubular joints may be induced by the relatively
large axial strains caused by impacts transverse to the members. Fatigue
fracture developing from fabrication defects may contribute to the failure.
The following cases are studied: DC3- end row X-bracing ineffective, DC4 -
X-bracing at front row end ineffective.

The analyses have been carried out with the program USFOS. The
environmental loads were monotonically increased until the stiffness of the
structure degraded to zero and the platform could not resist the next load
increment.

Examples of response curves for diagonal seas are given in Fig. 5.
The load is plotted versus the transverse displacement of a top corner node
of the jacket. The load is nondimensionalized against the load with a 100
year return period. The results of all calculations are also summarized in
Table 3.

Table 3 shows that the jacket possesses a tremendous reserve strength beyond the design load, similar to the results for the Gulf of Mexico jacket analysed in [24]. Considerable redistribution of forces takes place beyond first yield hinge which occurs at a load of about 50-70% of the ultimate strength. This illustrates clearly that using a linear program to assess the reserve strength will be far too conservative. The loads at first yield hinge also indicate the magnitude of safety factors (intended or unintended) used in the design. The relatively severe collision damages assumed at sea level have a minor influence on the residual strength of the platform. The largest strength loss is produced by removal of one x-bracing at end row in bottom storey for diagonal waves with a $H_r/H_u=0.72$. This is reasonable because these members are also the most stressed ones in the design condition.

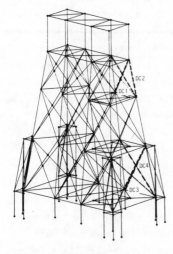

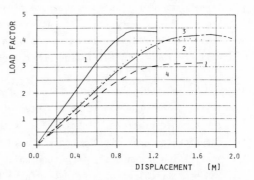

FIGURE 4 Example problem structure with damage cases indicated

FIGURE 5 Load versus transverse displacement of top corner node of jacket structure. (LC1-diagonal waves, case nos. refer to Table 3).

TABLE 3

Summary of Calculation Results. Load Factors are given with Reference to a Load with Return Period of 100 Years (H_d)

CASE	LOAD CASE	DAMAGE CASE (See Fig.4)	H_y	H_u	H_u/H_d	H_r/H_u
1	LC1-diag.waves	Intact	2.60	4.39	4.39	-
2	" " "	DC1-X-brac.sea lev.	2.64	4.10	-	0.93
3	" " "	DC2-dented leg	2.52	4.25	-	0.97
4	" " "	DC3-X-brac.end row bot.	2.00	3.15	-	0.72
5	LC2-long.waves	Intact	2.49	3.71	3.71	-
6	" " "	DC4-X-brac.front row bot.	1.82	3.38	-	0.91
7	LC3-transv.waves	Intact	2.99	4.32	4.32	-
8	" " "	DC3-X-brac.end row bot.	2.19	3.39	-	0.78

H_y = load when first yield hinge is formed; H_u = collapse load;
H_r = residual strength after damage

A typical failure sequence for diagonal and transverse sea is that the end row bracing at bottom fails initially. Additional forces are redistributed through the conductor frame system to the adjacent parallel row. After failure of this row additional forces are in turn being transferred to adjacent rows by the intermediate horizontal bracings which eventually fail. Beyond this load virtually no more forces can be carried because a large number of plastic hinges are created. These cases illustrate how members with a very low utilization in intact condition may play an important role in redistributing forces when damage has taken place, and hence will be crucial in fulfilling PLS criteria.

In the above case the ULS check of members and other requirements to installation etc. result in a system with significant reserve strength of the damaged platform. In other cases this might not necessarily be so. Therefore an explicit PLS check should be carried out (see Section 2.3). Application of an analysis method which accounts for nonlinear material and geometrical effects in determining the reserve strength then implies significant potential saving of scantlings and hence costs.

3.3 Framed platforms

The hull of semi-submersible drilling rigs are built-up of heavily stiffened pontoons, columns and deck girders, with light trusses in the transverse direction. In permanently located floating platforms, including tension-leg platforms, mobility is not a desirable feature, and heavy transverse pontoons may be used instead of the braces (see Fig. 1e).

The method described in the previous section has been applied in the analysis of a semi-submersible subjected to various kinds of damages in the trusses and deck [10, 29]. Further improvement in such methods is needed to cope with systems where the failure occurs in girders built of stiffened panels. Such framed structures consist of a few elements, and the representation of the element - behaviour will be crucial. In the limit this system consists of a single stiffened beam - a ship or a monotower. The simple method devised by Smith, see e.g. [30,31] may be a first step of modelling the longitudinally stiffened girders subjected to axial and bending forces. A further improvement may be obtained by using the structural unit method for panels [32,33].

4. CONCLUDING REMARKS

There is a potential for increased safety and cost saving in offshore structures by reducing the safety factors in ultimate strength design checks and including quantitative progressive limit state (PLS) requirements for structures. A rational PLS check involves determining the magnitude and location of damage (dents, cracks or failed members) and the behaviour of the damaged system.

In the present paper the focus is upon methods for analyzing the behaviour of ductile trusswork/-frame systems consisting of simple tubes up to global collapse. The non-linear material and geometrical behaviour accounted for in the actual methods allows an accurate representation of load distribution before system collapse, and hence of the significant extra capacity often present beyond the strength predictd by conventional design methods based on linear global analysis. Even if some progress has been made in analyzing stiffened, steel-plated structures, further work is needed in this area. Also, work is needed to develop methods for analyzing crack growth and fracture and the interaction between cracks and ductile behaviour.

Further work is also required to establish probabilistically based damage conditions; and load criteria for the damage condition.

5. REFERENCES

1. Moan, T.: "Safety of Offshore Structures", Proc. Fourth ICASP Conference, Firenze, Pitagora Editrice (1983).

2. EECS: "European Recommendations for Steel Construction" (1978).

3. CEB-FIP: "Model Code for Concrete Structures" (1978).

4. The Norwegian Petroleum Directorate: "Guidelines for Safety Evaluation of Platform Conceptual Design", Stavanger (1. September 1981).

5. The Norwegian Petroleum Directorate: "Regulations for Load-carrying Structures for Extraction or Exploitation of Petroleum", Stavanger (1984).

6. Department of Energy: "Offshore Installations. Guidance on Design and Construction", London (1977), with 8 amendments until 1984.

7. The Norwegian Maritime Directorate (NMD): "Regulations for mobile drilling platforms ..", Oslo (1973); with later amendments, e.g. about stability and mooring systems (3.February 1982).

8. Det norske Veritas: "Rules for Classification of Mobile Offshore Units", with "POSMOOR supplement", Oslo (January 1984).

9. Lloyds Register: "Preliminary Guidance Rules, Tension-leg Installations", London (Sept. 1983).

10. Bach-Gansmo, O. et al.: "Design Against Accidental Loads on Mobile Platforms", Project Summary Report, Veritec/Otter, January 1985.

11. Amdahl, J.: "Collisions and Falling Objects. Calculation of Probabilities and Consequences", Seminar on Loads and Safety for Marine Structures, the Norwegian Society of Chartered Engineers, NTH, Trondheim, 7.-9. January 1985.

12. Moan, T.: "Accidental Loads", Seminar on Loads and Safety for Marine Structures, The Norwegian Society of Chartered Engineers, NTH, Trondheim, 7.-9. January 1985.

13. Ellinas, C.P. and Valsgård, S.: "Collisions and Damage of Offshore Structures: A State-of-the Art", Proc. 4th OMAE Conf., Dallas (1985).

14. Taraldsen, A.: "Anchor Chain Fractures"; Proc. Offshore Technology Conference, Paper No. 5059, Houston (1985).

15. Dalväg, T.: An Operators Experience from Floatel Mooring", Offshore Gøteborg (1985).

16. Norwegian Public Reports: "The Alexander L. Kielland-accident", Report NOU 1981: 11, Oslo, March 1981.

17. Mørch, M. and Moan, T.: "Comparison between Measured and Calculated Behaviour of a Moored Semi-submersible Platform", Proc. BOSS '85 Conf., Elsevier, Amsterdam (1985).

18. Furuholt, E.: "Extra Loads from Non-Optimal Operation of Mooring System. Line Breakage", Seminar on Mooring of Floating Platforms, Norwegian Society of Chartered Engineers, Fagernes, Oct. 18.-20., 1982.

19. Marshall, P.W., Gates, W.E. and Anagnostopoulos, S.: "Inelastic Dynamic Analysis of Tubular Offshore Structures", Proc. Offshore Technology Conference, Paper No. 2908, Houston (1977).

20. Zayas, V.A., Mahin, S.A. and Popov, E.P.: "Ultimate Strength of Steel Offshore Structures", Proc. of the Third International Conference on the Behaviour of Offshore Structures (BOSS), Boston (1982).

21. Rashed, S.M.H.: "Behaviour to Ultimate Strength of Tubular Offshore Structures by the Idealized Structural Unit Method", Report No. SK/R51, Div. of Marine Structures, The Norwegian Institute of Technology, Trondheim, 1980.

22. Ueda, Y. and Rashed, S.M.H.: "An Ultimate Transverse Strength Analysis of Ship Structures", Journ. of the Soc. of Nav. Arch. of Japan 136 (1974).

23. Aanhold, J.V.: "Ultimate Strength Analysis of Framed Offshore Structures", OTTER-report STF 88-A83002, Trondheim, 1983.

24. Lloyd, J.R. and Clawson, W.C.: "Reserve and Residual Strength of Pile Founded, Offshore Platforms", Proc. Int. Symp. on the Role of Design, Inspection and Redundancy in Marine Structural Reliability, Williamsburg, Virginia (1983).

25. Moan, T., et al.: "Collapse Behaviour of Trusswork Steel Platforms", Proc. BOSS '85 Conf., Elsevier, Amsterdam (1985).

26. Engseth, Alf: "Finite Element Collapse Analysis of Tubular Steel Offshore Structures", Doctoral Thesis, Division of Marine Structures, The Norwegian Institute of Technology, Trondheim, December, 1984.

27. Ueda, Y. and Rashed, S.M.H.: "Behaviour of Damaged Tubular Structural Members", Proc. 4th OMAE Conf., Dallas (1985).

28. Yao, T.; Taby, J. and Moan, T.: "Ultimate Strength and Post-Ultimate Strength Behaviour of Damaged Tubular Members in Offshore Structures", Proc. 5th OMAE Conf., Tokyo (1986).

29. Kavlie, D. and Søreide, T.H.S.: "Progressive Collapse of Mobile Offshore Platforms", PRADS' 83, 2nd. Int. Symp. on Practical Design in Shipbuilding, Tokyo/Seoul (1983).

30. Smith, C.S.: "Influence of Local Compressive Failure on Ultimate Longitudinal Strength of a Ship's Hull," Proc. PRADS, Tokyo (1977).

31. Smith, C.S.: "Structural Redundancy and Damage Tolerance in Relation to Ultimate Ship-Hull Strength", Proc. Int. Symp. on the Role of Design, Inspection and Redundancy in Marine Structural Reliability, Williamsburg, Virginia (1983).

32. Ueda, Y., Rashed, S.M.H., and Katayama, M.: "Ultimate Strength Analysis of Double Bottom Structures by Idealized Structural Unit Method", Trans. Japan Weld. Research Inst., Vol. 9., No. 1 (1980).

33. Pettersen, E.: "Analysis and Design of Cellular Structures", Doctoral Thesis, Div. of Marine Structures, The Norwegian Institute of Technology, Trondheim, Report UR 79-02, 1979.

TECHNICAL INNOVATIONS FOR DESIGN
OF ADVANCED SHIPS

A. B. Stavovy
Ship Structures Division
David W. Taylor Naval Ship R&D Center
Bethesda, Maryland 20084-5000
U.S.A.

ABSTRACT

The change in operational needs and the emergence of new ship
performance requirements have placed greater demands on existing
technologies. Technical innovations developed at the David W. Taylor
Naval Ship Research and Development Center (DTNSRDC) have helped advance
structures technology used in the design of advanced ships. The computer
has become a major force in revolutionizing the design and analysis
processes. Centralized instrumentation and advanced data acquisition
systems have played a major roll in developing new design criteria.
Small and large scale modeling have proven useful in verifying analytical
results. All of this has led to improved fatigue analysis, structural
synthesis, load determination and weight/cost optimization. These topics
are discussed relative to the Center's contributions as they have evolved
over the past twenty years.

INTRODUCTION

Planning and implementing a surface ship structures technology development program for some twenty years has been a challenging and rewarding
experience. The impact of this technology in the design and construction
of naval ships has been gradual and, in itself, heavily influenced by other
technological innovations. The planning process included considerations
of short term and long term needs and how and when research milestones
should be achieved to assure suitable structural technology transfer into
design guidance. Although initial plans were ambitious, the process was
heavily influenced by near-term ship designs and acquisitions. Progress
appeared slow at first, but was rapidly changed with greater flexibility

introduced by other technological innovations and with the ever changing
ship operational requirements.

Naval ships must be designed for the needs of the future and designed
with vision and inspiration while maintaining the time honored tradition
of safety and reliability. The ever changing roles that naval ships must
perform included many different tasks. They ranged from rapid deployment
of personnel and materials to maintaining open sea lanes. To carry out
these missions and to meet the ever increasing demand for superior performance, new types of ships were envisioned. A whole spectrum of hull
configurations emerged that were quite different than the conventional
displacement ship.

The surface ship operates at the turbulent interface between air and
sea and must survive operations in each of these media and contend with
the added and difficult problems that the interface introduces. Therefore,
emphasis had to be placed on the need to develop rational predictive techniques for environmental loadings, to provide reliable analysis for resulting structural response, and to take maximum advantage of both conventional
and unconventional hull structural materials while overcoming the problems
in the area of reliability, cost, fabrication and maintenance. Operational
needs had to be translated into structural requirements, and technology
developed to meet them. This included greatly expanded utilization of computers in design, analysis, and fabrication, and in structural system and
material trade-off studies for new concepts.

This paper reviews the pacing parameters introduced by advanced ships
and the impact on generic technology as derived by new operational requirements. It describes the associated technological innovations that accelerated the application of generic technological developments. Finally it
addresses design and analysis methods derived from research and development
that are now essential for reliable structural performance.

THE INFLUENCE OF R&D ON HULL CONFIGURATION

Rational selection of any hull form, whether conventional or unconventional, requires that the designer have available methods to evaluate the
basis for the design to assure safe and reliable structures. Therefore, in

order to establish the direction for research to take and to achieve safe
and reliable structures, special attention was given to (1) technological
developments that would include data and methodology applicable to a large
number of ship types, and (2) knowledge which could unify and expand the
structural research for all advanced ships.

Table 1 illustrates the types of ships of interest and the variations
in hull configurations. It also identifies pacing technical problems that
are unique to particular hull configurations. The broad generic areas in
Table 2 were then identified as loads, strength, reliability, and weight/
cost.

LOAD TECHNOLOGY for advanced marine vehicles suffered from a lack of
sufficient operational experience to adequately bound the load parameters
for each type of vehicle. Prototype vehicles with defined performance
scenarios were needed to be instrumented for full scale evaluations to
acquired data in prescribed seas. This also meant that such data would be
correlatable with either model or analytical results as projected for the
ship in question.

Paradoxically, load problems associated with advanced ships arose,
in part, from the successful use of empirical load criteria in the design
of conventional displacement ships. The empirical method was adequate as
long as other loads did not overshadow primary loads; such was the case for
multihull ships. Experimental and analytical studies of the catamaran,
reported in reference [1], revealed that forces due to beam and quartering
seas were sufficiently large to create primary bending in the bridging
structure in the transverse direction.

"Frequency domain" analysis methods used for estimating maximum
loadings assume that wave heights in storm-driven seaways can be considered
Gaussian, and more often than not, that craft motions and wave loadings are
linear. These assumptions have not been adequately tested in random seas,
although one method for doing so has recently become available; see reference [2]. Considering the inherently nonlinear character of slamming loads
and the nonlinearity of craft response to large waves in general (especially
the occurrence of air cushion craft venting of the cushion and hydrofoil

TABLE 1
Pacing Parameters Leading to Establishing Valid Load-Response Envelopes

Ship Type	Pacing Parameters
Conventional	• Local and overall shear and bending moment due to slamming, whipping and vibration. • Superstructure interaction with hull girder.
Multihull	• Local and overall transverse bending and shear due to beam seas. • Hull interaction with cross structure. • Wet deck response to water impact.
Surface Effect Ship	• Local and overall shear and bending moments governed by high speed impact. • Riged sidewalls interaction with the hull. • Wet deck response due to water impact.
Air Cushion Vehicle	• Local and overall shear and bending moments governed by high speed impact. • Wet deck response due to water impact. • Skirt interaction with the hull.
Planning Craft	• Local and overall shear and bending moment due to slamming, whipping and vibration.
Hydrofoil	• Local and overall shear and bending moment governed by high speed impact. • Foils interacton with struts and struts interaction with hull.

TABLE 2
Impact of Associated Technologies on Generic Problem Areas

Technology Development Generic Areas	Computer Evaluation	Small Scale Evaluation	Large Scale Evaluation	Instrumented Prototype
Loads	High	Medium	Low	High
Strength	High	High	High	High
Reliability	High	High	High	High
Weight	High	Low	Medium	Low
Cost	High	Low	Medium	Low

broaching of the foils), the assumption of linearity appears to be most tenuous.

STRENGTH ANALYSIS is a more mature technical area than loads. However, the sizing of the ship structure depended upon loads experienced during lifetime performance. Basic analysis has heavily depended upon tried and proven methods. Frame tripping and performance of structural details received the initial consideration for high performance craft. Aluminum was the most commonly used light material; however, steel and glass reinforced plastics or some combination of these were specified for some applications.

A minimum of structural validation was performed because of the confidence in existing design criteria. However, it was soon recognized that the ultimate strength of the overall structure was needed. Knowing the ultimate strength of a structure relative to nominal operational levels of restraint, provided a better appraisal of safety, at least for static loading. Such an approach to predicting ultimate strength was recently published in reference [3].

RELIABILITY can be defined as the probabilistic measure of assurance of performance, and in the realm of structures it would be the probability of survival of a structure. Although absolute reliability is an unattainable goal, probability theory combined with first principles provide a framework for the development of criteria for design which will ensure that the probability of failure is acceptably small. Since the 1970's considerable work was performed in the marine field with methods being applied that were developed in other fields. Aircraft technology and construction influenced this special problem area; however, the work continued to remain marine in character.

WEIGHT-COST TRADEOFFS are required relative to mission performance. One particular characteristic of high performance advanced ships is the critical effect of excess weight on ship performance. Weight is correlatable to payload, range, and ship speed. With structures as the largest portion of fixed weight in ship hull systems, this area became a prime target for reduction. Structural weight reductions can be achieved by using higher strength-to-weight ratio materials and advanced design and fabrication techniques which allow for more efficient structures.

The need for any "exotic" material to meet structural performance requirements must be traded against increases in cost, even though structural systems are not necessarily the most expensive system in the total ship, and designers must consider potential savings in the life-cycle cost to offset the initial cost. Better designs and materials could contribute to lower life cycle costs through reduced maintenance and repair requirements.

These "generic" areas provide the basis for program development and the framework for assessment of the quality of design. The success of the R&D program depended on the successful transition of technology into design. The technical advances were greatly influenced by <u>associated technological developments</u>. As the computer has affected the speed with which computations can be accomplished, it has enabled the researcher to refine the analytical approach to reflect real performance.

ASSOCIATED TECHNOLOGICAL DEVELOPMENTS

Technology innovations that spurred the development of the "generic" areas included the computer, small scale structural modeling, large scale structural modeling, and instrumented sea trials. All have had a major impact on advancements in structural technology. However, experience has shown that this impact varied with certain factors; how urgent it was to obtain an R&D solution, how expensive it was to get the solution, and how critical it was to obtain the accuracy of the solution. The matrix shown in Table 2 illustrates the apparent degree of impact these associated technology developments have had on the "generic" problems.

COMPUTER-AIDED EVALUATION capabilities have enabled major advancements in the past decade through its applications to such areas as analysis, design, data acquisition, control of testing, and data comparison.

For analysis and design, computer technology has provided great savings in time and money. The ability of the engineer to quickly modify the designs and perform parametric studies using the modern computer has provided a flexibility that was unimaginable some twenty-five years ago. Small desk top computers are now capable of accomplishing tasks that previously took weeks, months, or even longer to perform.

Computers have allowed powerful automated data preprocessors (data generators) to be developed for structural analysis using the finite element method. These programs were developed primarily to remove the mechanical drudgery associated with preparing input data for the finite element analysis. Such programs make the development of large volumes of data relatively fast and easy. However, the potential for misuse and mis-interpretation is inherent if used by inexperienced personnel.

LARGE SCALE STRUCTURAL EVALUATIONS were emphasized in the early 1970's to develop lifecycle experimental techniques for naval applications and to provide a validated technology base for aluminum hulled, ocean going ships. As early as 1967, the use of large structural models in place of prototype structures to validate design predictions was explored so that a capability would be available and applicable to advanced surface ships. Until that time, numerous sea trials provided only the most basic of response data which were limited to a few strain gauges and accelerometers. For conventional ships the concern was not as great because experience had shown that their performance was reliable and that local problems could easily be monitored and corrected. However, the lack of experience in advanced hull forms with unconventional configurations and new manufacturing capabilities suggested that this capability would need further exploration.

It was realized early in the program that a need existed for (1) finding new and innovative methods of appling loads to the model, (2) controlling the test fixture, (3) acquiring the data, and (4) analyzing the data. These areas were addressed and resulted in a reliable test fixture in the Structural Evaluation Laboratory which simulated at-sea responses in the large scale model.

The unique test fixture for testing large structural models is shown in Figure 1 and is also described in reference [4]. The method of loading the 100-foot Aluminum Structural Evaluation Model (shown in Figure 1) during testing was performed through a series of 13 load frames which introduced vertical and lateral bending loads simultaneously. Fore and aft movement was restricted by the use of load frame guides. Loads were introduced as in-plane loads into the bulkheads and were reacted by rigid floor frames. The loads were introduced through rigid steel frames bearing on rubber pads. These pads, which work quite well, were carefully designed

504

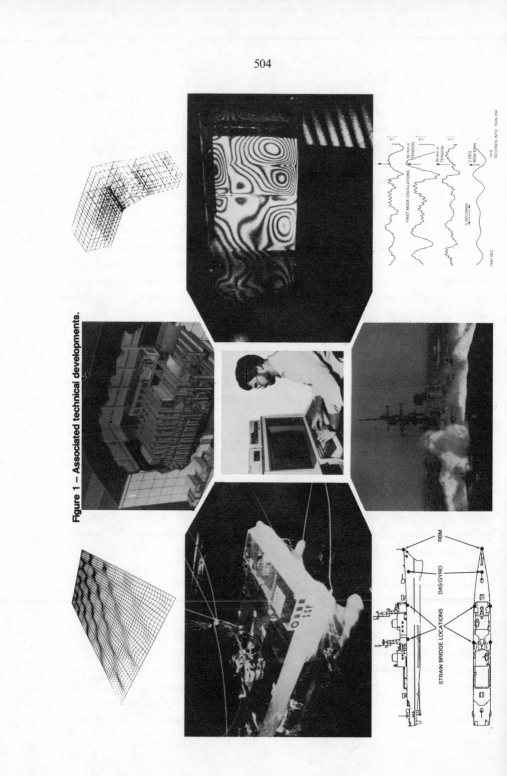

Figure 1 – Associated technical developments.

and installed to eliminate secondary and tertiary stresses.

The critical part of the Structural Evaluations Laboratory was the control and data acquisition system which was designed to (1) monitor tests in progress, (2) control hydraulic actuators in the application of loads to the model, and (3) collect and record data, both from load measuring equipment in the control loop and from strain gauges attached to the structure. A real time computer was used to perform the these functions.

Design load spectra were developed based on factors that influence a ship's response in a seaway. A ship's dimensions determine how it will respond in waves under the operating conditions defined by its mission. Predicting ship structural performance under lifetime loading is based primarily on empirical relationships derived from the results of full-scale trials and model tests on similar ships.

SMALL SCALE STRUCTURAL EVALUATIONS have been advanced via the aggressively exploited use of polyvinyl cloride (PVC), a clear plastic material used to model a structure.

The thermoplastic modeling approach enjoys a number of advantages that include: (1) reduced costs in materials, time, and manpower as compared to similar models in steel or aluminum; (2) reduced costs in forms and fabrication; (3) reduced load levels resulting in less expensive loading rigs; (4) easy modification; (5) easy instrumentation; and (6) abililty to model a structure in detail on a small scale. "Bakelite" rigid-vinyl PVC was selected for modeling application because of its ideal mechanical properties to satisfy both static and dynamic testing, and to simulate metallic structural performance. Although the material is somewhat sensitive to temperature changes, this was not a serious drawback.

Optical techniques have proven to be important experimental tools at the Center in the accurate measurement of structural responses. For half a century, photo-elasticity has been an established method for measuring stresses in structural models composed of birefringent materials. The development of lasers and the discovery of new holographic techniques have opened the field of holographic structural analysis through displacement, strain, stress, and vibration studies for applications in nondestructive testing, fatigue analysis, and fracture mechanics.

Photoelasticity is a common experimental technique used at the Center for measuring stress in birefringent materials. Photoelasticity lends itself directly to the analysis of two-dimensional models. Three-dimensional models composed of materials with properties that vary with temperature can also be analyzed by the stress freezing technique.

Holography is also used at the Center as a very effective and economical tool when applied to many problem areas of interest to the marine field. In particular, the inherent potential of holography for recording minute physical causes of the order of the wavelength of light makes it a powerful tool for analyzing a wide variety of engineering problems for which no other practical solutions exist.

FULL-SCALE DATA SEA TRIALS ACQUISITION AND ANALYSIS methods have undergone some drastic changes with the advent of reliable digital data handling systems. Although response test data can be acquired from many different sources, ranging from small scale model static, fatigue, and dyanmic structural tests, to full scale at-sea surface ship structural evaluations, the most demanding of these is the on-board measurement of wave-induced ship responses for full scale sea trials.

With present day minicomputers, this picture has improved considerably. One data system used on a recent at-sea trial allowed the recording of a total of 100 data channels by a system half the size of the analog system in use just five years earlier. Each of the 100 channels sampled data at a rate of 40 times per second for a frequency response of approximately 5 hertz. The maximum through-put rate was, therefore, 4000 samples per second. These data were stored on nine track digital tape. For these trials, a separate data analysis system was placed on board with the acquisition system to provide a dedicated on-board analysis capability as well as complete redundancy of all major computer hardware components. The types of analysis software available for use on-board the trials ship included a peak analysis to determine mean values, minimum and maximum values and their time of occurrence, as well as RMS values. This analysis may actually be performed in real time, i.e., as the data are being sampled. The peak values of each channel for every data run was, therefore, available as soon as the run was completed. These values were also stored in a separate data file which was accessed during later analyses to improve the timewise efficiency of the analyses program. The on-board data handling capability also included histograms of single amplitude distributions for any given key channels. Software also existed on-board to singularly determine and plot power spectral densities for specified channels. This last program also had the ability to determine and plot response amplitude operators (RAO's) for any one channel with respect to any other specified channel. This on-board capability provided the test with an excellent means of insuring the collection of highest possible quality data as well as providing the input for a preliminary report issued soon after the trials had been completed. A more detailed analysis was performed upon return of the equipment and personnel to the laboratory where more enhanced program software was available to efficiently handle large quantities of raw data rapidly.

Studies of structural responses are not really complete without some knowledge of the forcing function, in this case, sea state. Traditional methods employed to obtain wave height data include stationary weather buoys, deployed wave rider buoys, and the Tucker Sea State Meter. All these devices have been available for many years, but due to problems with reliability, sensor location, buoy deployment and retrieval, and correct interpretation of the data, none of these devices is currently used very extensively. One of the most pressing needs is the development of an accurate on-board system that would combine measurements of the ship relative bow motion with rigid body accelerations to determine the actual wave height. The sensors required for such a device are available with little modification necessary. The advent of reliable, portable sea-going minicomputers provides the processing capability necessary to perform the required data manipulations. Wave height data would then be processed either in real time or immediately following the data run, and presented as spectra and/or time histories.

IMPROVEMENTS OF DESIGN AND ANALYSIS METHODS

The advancement of structural technology in the Ship Structures Division is a blend of the application of structural mechanics and the utilization of technological innovations that enhance the development of

analytical and computational tools. As described earlier, breakthroughs
resulting from related technological achievements had a major impact on the
improvement of new structural analysis tools and design methods.

Structural design is directly driven by the performance requirements
of a total system of which the structure is a part. Structures must perform in a given environmental envelope; must be produced at minimum cost
with minimum weight; and must sustain strength, durability, and reliability
as specified. Successes and failures have threaded the way toward design
philosophy improvments and the development of the analytical tools needed
to assure reliable structural performance. A better understanding of
redundancies in structural design has resulted from a symposium, "Design –
Inspection Redundancy," held in Williamsburg, Virginia, in 1983. The loop
between design inspection and redundancy provides the feedback to improve
structural design and analysis methods and provides a procedure for developing highly reliable ship structures. What was done and how it affected the
total ship design process is best understood if the structural performance
is examined concurrently with the design of the total ship.

Papers published by DTNSRDC on ship structures discuss structures
technologies as discussed earlier, and some papers also tend to embody
these contributions into summary applications. For example, reference [5]
describes a method for estimating the lifetime loads and fatigue lives for
SWATH and conventional monohull ships. Reference 5 also provides information relative to the environmental conditions, the ship operational
profile, the ships' response characteristics, the lifetime fatigue load
spectrum, and the maximum longitudinal bending. Similarly, other papers
include summaries of structural strength, structural synthesis on special
studies associated with specific ship studies, and conceptual design work.

The following provides a limited description of consolidated technology applications which has lead to improvements in design and analysis
methods.

FATIGUE LOAD SPECTRUM AND MAXIMUM LONGITUDINAL BENDING is best
described by reference [5]. In this paper, a method to determine wave-
induced lifetime sea loads on ships was developed from accumulated monohull
data to produce a generalized RAO's for ships in various sea headings.

Speeds were included in the generalizations as well as probability of occurrence of sea state, heading, and speed to produce lifetime load spectrum for any desired time at sea. To set a standard lifetime vertical response for monohulls, bending moments were calculated for the midship section of eighteen hulls. The design allowable bending moment to maximum lifetime bending moment ratio was found to be 0.73.

The authors of reference [5] used this information to develop load criteria applicable to the small waterplane area twin hull (SWATH) ships based on the same rationale as monohull ships. However, the primary load design criteria to obtain strength equivalent to the monohull were derived through the use of model data and statistical analysis. Unit responses for combinations of speed and heading, together with the six-parameter spectra from reference [6], were used to predict lifetime fatigue spectra.

The fatigue load prediction method was also applied to obtain lifetime maximum primary load and stress predictions for several conventional ships. The load and stress levels obtained, together with the SWATH side load algorithm, provided a basis for designing SWATH's with static strength equivalent to current conventional displacement ships.

STRUCTURAL SYNTHESIS programs suitable for design or analysis of ship structural sections have been of interest for many years. A Structural Synthesis Design Program (SSDP), described in reference [7], was developed at DTNSRDC and has been used successfully to rapidly perform the repetitive, time consuming tasks involved in structural design. The SSDP was used to design (or to analyze) the longitudinal scantlings of a variety of ship cross sections consisting of any practical combinations of decks, platforms, bulkheads, and materials, i.e., various steel and aluminum alloys; providing that the bending moment and shear loads are known. The final hull section design will have the lowest practical weight for the chosen geometric configuration, structural arrangements, and imposed loadings. The SSDP was developed for preparing point designs and conducting parametric studies to determine weight sensitivity due to various design loads and material selections. Versions of the program have been put together to develop structural members for SWATH and surface effect ship (SES) structures.

ANALYTICAL METHODS continue to provide the basis from which strength assessments are made, stress limits are contained, and fitness for service is determined. To improve the finite element analysis process further, special purpose finite element generators have been developed so that detailed stress analysis of complex structures can be performed in days rather than months. This rapid modeling of surface ship structures has been applied to a variety of design and fleet support problems. The first program was developed specifically for the modeling of SWATH structures, allowing for a wide variety of both external and internal geometries but with a modest amount of input data. Studies of SWATH structures have shown that conventional analysis and design methods have serious shortcomings when applied to SWATH configurations and hence the need for numerical analysis techniques to reliably predict stress/strain magnitude and distributions. The second program was developed to allow for the systematic and comprehensive study of the hull/deckhouse interaction phenomenon for conventional surface ships. This program allows the user to rapidly and with a minimum of input data, model the hull and deckhouse structure of surface ships having deckhouses (or superstructures) with varying yet realistic geometries. Numerical analysis techniques are the only practical analytical approaches for describing the behavior of deckhouses possessing realistic features, such as abrupt changes in scantlings or geometries, cut-outs, etc.

In order to assess strength capabilities relative to extreme loads and to assure a more balanced design, an analytical method and a computer program were developed for predicting the collapse moment (in ductile failure) of a ship's hull under longitudinal bending; (see reference [3].) The most probable ductile failure modes corresponding to cross-section yielding, Euler beam-column collapse, and stiffener lateral-torsional instability (tripping) are incorporated into the program, as well as the effects on these failure modes of the presence of lateral pressure loading and fabrication induced distortion. The fundamental premise on which the program is based is that the collapse of the hull occurs due to a sequence of local component failures rather than a simultaneous general instability of the total cross section. On this basis, the maximum or ultimate moment is determined by successively imposing increments of overall curvature to the hull, computing the resulting increments of strain in each local structural component, and then integrating the corresponding stress values over the total cross section of the hull. The ultimate moment is defined (in essence) when the cumulative moment "peaks" out and then begins to drop with increasing curvature. The program is applicable in the early or preliminary stages of design when most of the major decisions regarding the structural configuration are made. As such, it is an approximate approach based on a mixture of both theoretically and empirically derived relationships developed over a period of years. It has value both for estimating the peak moment capacity of hulls in the intact condition, and for estimating the latent strength of structures in the damaged condition. While the current program must be viewed as a preliminary version with many potential improvements, it has already, while under development, been applied to a number of on-going projects.

IMPACT PRESSURE DISTRIBUTION AND LOADINGS in extreme seas or at high speeds can be of such a large magnitude as to cause severe bottom damage including plate dishing, longitudinal tripping, and bulkheads and transverse stiffener distortion. Local impact loads due to bow emergence cause increased hull girder bending and shear responses. Such responses can be determined provided a definition of impact loads is available. However, local loads and their applications to the hull girder remained an uncertainty until "two-dimensional model" studies were initiated in the early 60's which defined pressure distributions for flat bottom impact and pressure distributions for impact of bottoms with small deadrise angles. The results of this investigation led to a better understanding of air entrapment and air mixture with water particle flow just prior to bottom contact with the water.

The information from the "two-dimensional model" drop tests was used to design new tests of prismatic (wedge) shaped forms with varying structural rigidity and tested in still water and regular waves. Results of these tests were related to cone (shaped form) drop tests, to theory and to tests for both two and three-dimensional slamming. A state-of-the-art review of the structural response aspect of slamming and water impact is discussed in reference [8]. Data from these tests were used to calculate three-dimensional pressure distributions and loads that, in turn, allowed developing pressure versus area design curves used in the design of bottom structures subject to impact pressures. On the basis of the solid background of the theoretical and experimental data available, the work was

512

extended further at DTNSRDC to develop a simplified method to predict the
contours of slamming pressures on planing and other high performance craft
bottom structure; see reference [9].

COST/WEIGHT OPTIMIZATION led to the development of a Ship Structural
Cost Program (SSCP) for assessing relative costs and weights among variations of a baseline structure in order to perform efficient sensitivity and
optimization studies; see reference [10].

Cost/weight estimates are based on a three-phase sequence of construction operations where Phase 1 covers construction of single panels or grillages within the shop area, Phase 2 covers erection of modules from these
single units within the shop area, and Phase 3 covers installation of these
modules into the ship structure in the drydock. Cost estimates are based
on a tabulation of material costs and construction costs accounting for
lofting, layout, cutting, rolling, assembly, installation, and welding
operations. The SSCP provides a detailed breakdown of these various cost
factors for determining trends and critical operations. The SSCP is primarily intended for relative comparisons as opposed to absolute cost
estimation. Used in conjunction with automated design tools such as the
SSDP, rapid automated cost/weight studies may be efficiently performed.

CONCLUSION

Major improvements in structural technology as applied to ship design
have advanced quite rapidly as a result of advances in the computer-aided
design, small scale modeling evaluations, large scale structural modeling,
optical and laser systems, and data acquisition systems for full-scale sea
trials.

Now that we have the tools and methods that will allow us to examine
new structural concepts with greater confidence and perform design trade-
offs rapidly and routinely to produce sound, reliable, structural systems,
we have new capabilities. New tools are available to
° Perform structural designs of different hull configurations using
   uniform strength criteria
° Rapidly determine structural scantlings using SSDP
° Design for realistic loads

° Use materials to their greatest effectiveness

° Perform rapid analyses using finite element modeling

° Determine the ultimate strength and margin of safety between extreme
  loading and the limit of structural load carrying capability

° Perform weight-cost tradeoff studies

Are we through? By no means. We are now in a position to develop
more structural system options that can perform functions demanded of
advanced ships and craft. Flexibility in system options also provides the
owner with greater latitude for considering how to perform a given function.
The greater the number of ship hull forms and performance requirements, the
greater will be the demand on design tools and improvements in all technology areas, such as

° Ship structural behavior that is not fully understood, analyzed, or
  validated

° Ship response to extreme waves, impacts, collisions, and fire

° Structural response to nonlinear and three-dimensional effects, both
  static and dynamic

and for

° Computers and computer graphics to become natural contributors to
  the design process

This completes the loop that provides the feedback to improve structural
design, analysis methods, and highly reliable ship structures.

REFERENCES

1. Dinsenbacher, A. and Andrews, J.,
   Model test determination of sea loads on catamaran
   cross structure.
   DTNSRDC Report 2378 (May 1967).

2. Buckley, W.,
   Hull girder structural design –
   the case for new loading conditions for extreme waves.
   Naval Engineers Journal (Feb 1978).

3. Adamchack, J.C.,
   An approximate method for estimating the collapse
   of a ship's hull in preliminary design.
   Ship Structure Symposium 1984, Arlington, Va.
   (Oct 1984) 37-61.

4. Pohler, C.H., Stavovy, A.B., Beach, J.E. and Borriello, F.F.,
    A technology base for aluminum ship structures.
    Naval Engineers Journal, Vol 91, No. 5 (1979) 33-43.

5. Sikora, J., Dinsenbacher, A. and Beach, J.,
    A method for estimating lifetime loads and fatigue
    lives for SWATH and conventional monohull ships.
    Naval Engineers Journal (May 1983) 63-84.

6. Ochi, M.,
    Wave statistics for the design of ships and ocean structures.
    SNAME Transactions, Vol. 86 (1978) 47-76.

7. Wiernicki, C.J., Gooding, T. and Nappi, N.,
    The structural synthesis design program -
    its impact on the fleet.
    Naval Engineers Journal Vol. 95 (May 1983) 87-99.

8. Nagai, T. and Chuang, S.L.,
    Review of structural response aspects of slamming.
    SNAME Journal of Ship Research, Vol. 21
    (Sep 1977) 182-190.

9. Allen, R.G. and Jones, R.R.,
    A simplified method for determining structural design-limit
    pressures on high performance marine vehicles.
    AIAA/SNAME Conference, San Diego, Calif. (April 1978).

10. Furio, A.,
    Ship structural cost program.
    REAPS Technical Symposium, Baltimore, Maryland (Sept 1981).

STRUCTURAL DESIGN OF LONGITUDINALLY CORRUGATED
SHIP HULLS

C S Smith
Admiralty Research Establishment
Dunfermline, Fife, Scotland

ABSTRACT

An evaluation is made of the use of longitudinal shell corrugations in place of conventional stiffeners to provide strength and rigidity in ships' hulls. Particular reference is made to GRP ships, in which corrugated shells are readily constructed offering cost savings through elimination of most separately fabricated stiffeners and improvements in performance through reduced reliance on bonded connections. Theoretical and experimental studies are described referring to longitudinal strength (including buckling behaviour), transverse strength and explosion resistance of corrugated hulls. A comparison is made between some alternative MCMV hull configurations including corrugated and unstiffened "monocoque" designs.

INTRODUCTION

Efficient design of a ship's hull generally requires that the deck and bottom shell structure over most of the ship's length should be reinforced by closely spaced longitudinal stiffeners, providing strength and stability under conditions of longitudinal hull bending, together with relatively widely spaced transverse frames which give intermediate support to longitudinals and provide rigidity and strength under transverse loads. In the case of hulls fabricated in glass fibre reinforced plastic (GRP) this form of construction has two serious disadvantages:-

(i)   the high cost of fabricating large numbers of hat-section stiffeners and in particular of tailoring stiffener intersections;

(ii)   the difficulty of providing reliable, impact-resistant bonded connections between stiffeners and the shell, particularly in the case of mine-countermeasures vessels (MCMV) which must be designed to with-stand underwater explosions.

These difficulties have led, in the case of the prototype GRP minehunter HMS WILTON [1], to adoption of a relatively inefficient transversely framed form of hull construction in which frame to shell connections were rein-forced, effectively but at high cost, by a large number of metal bolts.

An alternative method of reinforcing shells against in-plane and lateral loads, which has been employed in high-performance structures such as aircraft fuselages and rocket motor casings and is widely used in civil engineering and building construction and in containers for road and marine transportation, is provision of shell corrugations aligned in the direction of dominant in-plane or bending stress. This form of construction is often adopted in the bulkheads of steel and GRP ships and has been used to a limited extent in the hulls of GRP fishing boats [2]. Corrugated construc-tion is particularly suitable for use in GRP ships where (unlike corrugated steel plating) it may be incorporated without difficulty into doubly curved as well as prismatic regions of a hull, offering the following significant advantages:-

(i)   substantial weight saving relative to transversely framed construc-tion by virtue of longitudinal stiffener orientation;

(ii) large cost savings resulting from reduction in the need for separ-separate fabrication of stiffeners;

(iii) improved robustness, particularly under explosive loading, resulting from elimination of most bonded stiffener attachments.

The purpose of the present paper is to examine the problems and merits of corrugated hull construction with reference to larger GRP ships including particularly MCMVs.

POSSIBLE FORMS OF HULL CORRUGATION

The shape, depth and spacing of longitudinal shell corrugations will depend on various factors including:-

(i)   the requirements of longitudinal and transverse stiffness and strength (which also control the size and spacing of transverse frames;

(ii) hull shape requirements in relation to hydrodynamic performance
      (resistance and seakeeping);

(iii) constraints of shipyard fabrication procedure.

Some alternative forms of shell corrugation are shown in Figure 1. These
include "inward-pointing" and "outward-pointing" unsymmetrical corrugations, which may be trapezoidal, rounded or triangular in shape as shown in
Figure 2, together with balanced corrugations in which equal proportions of
shell are disposed inwards and outwards. Triangular corrugations as shown
in Figure 2d are commonly incorporated in the bottom shells of fast planing
craft, primarily for flow-control reasons but also clearly serving a
structural purpose.

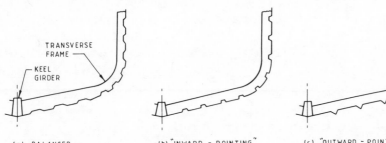

(a) BALANCED   (b) "INWARD - POINTING"   (c) "OUTWARD - POINTING"
    CORRUGATION   CORRUGATION   CORRUGATION

FIGURE 1.   Possible Corrugated Hull Configurations

     Fairing of the hull surface, if required, may be provided either:-

(i)   by filling the troughs of inward-pointing corrugations, eg with rigid
      foam strips serving as formers during hull lay-up, finished
      with sealing plugs (Figure 2e), or

(ii) by adopting a "quasi-corrugated" form of construction, as shown in
      Figure 2f, in which outer plies of the shell laminate are laid up in
      the normal way on a smooth mould while inner plies are diverted over
      formers to provide trapezoidal corrugations: the ratios b_1/t_1 and
      b_2/t_2 would usually be kept equal.

     In the case of open corrugations it will normally be desirable to
minimise as far as possible the trough angle Ψ (see Figure 2) in order:-

(i)   to reduce irregularity of hull sections and consequent hydrodynamic disturbances;

(ii) to minimise the ratio γ = developed girth/projected girth and hence the hull surface area;

(iii) to simplify the hull fabrication process, particularly at "overhangs" on the ship's sides.

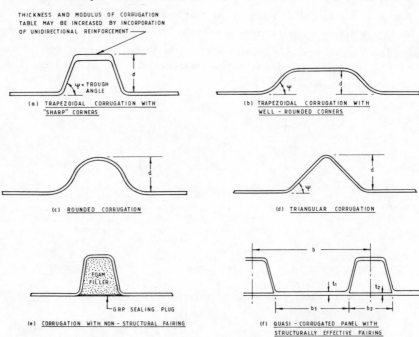

FIGURE 2.   Alternative Forms of Corrugation

Balanced corrugations offer, for a given trough depth, maximum flexural rigidity and are therefore normally preferable to unsymmetrical inward or outward-pointing corrugations.

STRESS ANALYSIS OF CORRUGATED SHELLS

Evaluation of stresses and deformations in a corrugated shell may be carried out by standard finite element methods, using shell elements to represent webs and tables of corrugations. Such analysis involves a large

number of degrees of freedom and is for most practical purposes prohibit-
ively expensive. It is generally preferable to evaluate the effective
orthotropic membrane and flexural rigidities of a corrugated shell and
hence to use orthotropic plate, grillage or orthotropic shell analysis to
examine the behaviour of corrugated panels or 3-dimensional shell
structure.

Direct and shear forces per unit width N_x, N_y, N_{xy} acting at the
mid-surface of an element of anisotropic shell, together with bending and
twisting moments M_x, M_y and M_{xy}, may be related to corresponding strains
and curvatures as follows:

$$
\begin{bmatrix} N_x \\ N_y \\ N_{xy} \\ M_x \\ M_y \\ M_{xy} \end{bmatrix} =
\begin{bmatrix}
A_{11} & A_{12} & A_{16} & B_{11} & B_{12} & B_{16} \\
A_{12} & A_{22} & A_{26} & B_{12} & B_{22} & B_{26} \\
A_{16} & A_{26} & A_{66} & B_{16} & B_{26} & B_{66} \\
B_{11} & B_{12} & B_{16} & D_{11} & D_{12} & D_{16} \\
B_{12} & B_{22} & B_{26} & D_{12} & D_{22} & D_{26} \\
B_{16} & B_{26} & B_{66} & D_{16} & D_{26} & D_{66}
\end{bmatrix}
\begin{bmatrix} \varepsilon_x \\ \varepsilon_y \\ \gamma_{xy} \\ -\dfrac{\partial^2 w}{\partial x^2} \\ -\dfrac{\partial^2 w}{\partial y^2} \\ -2\dfrac{\partial^2 w}{\partial x \partial y} \end{bmatrix}
\tag{1}
$$

or in abbreviated form

$$
\begin{bmatrix} N \\ M \end{bmatrix} =
\begin{bmatrix} A & B \\ B & D \end{bmatrix}
\begin{bmatrix} \varepsilon \\ \kappa \end{bmatrix}
\tag{2}
$$

where matrices A, B and D are symmetrical. For an orthotropic shell
representing an element of longitudinally corrugated hull structure,
assuming that reference x and y-axes are directed longitudinally and
transversely and that principal axes of elasticity are similarly oriented,
membrane direct and shear rigidities A_{ij} and flexural and twisting rigidities D_{ij} may be estimated as follows:

$A_{11} = \gamma E_x t$

$A_{12} = 0$ (for practical purposes, since $A_{11} \gg A_{22}$)

$A_{22} = A_{11} D_{11}/D_{22}$

$$A_{66} = G_{xy} t / \gamma$$

$$D_{11} = E_x I_x \tag{3}$$

$$D_{12} = 0 \text{ (since } D_{11} \gg D_{22})$$

$$D_{22} = E_y t^3 / [12\gamma(1 - \mu_x \mu_y)]$$

$$D_{66} = (1 + \gamma) G_{xy} t^3 / 24$$

where t is the shell thickness, E_x, E_y and G_{xy} are principal Young's moduli and shear modulus of the shell material and I_x is the moment of inertia per unit width of the corrugated section. The only expression which is not straightforward is that for A_{22}: this has been shown (3,4) to be an accurate approximation to the transverse membrane rigidity of isotropic corrugated plating and is equally applicable in the case of orthotropic materials. Coefficients A_{16}, A_{26}, D_{16} and D_{26} are zero since the x and y-axes are assumed to correspond to principal directions of elasticity, ie to the directions of reinforcing fibres in FRP laminate. Coupling between membrane and flexural rigidities (coefficients B_{ij}) may also be ignored in most practical cases. The terms given in eq. 3 will require slight modification where variations occur in laminate thickness and moduli, eg where unidirectional reinforcement is incorporated in corrugation tables.

A feature of corrugated plates and shells is the sharp imbalance between rigidities in the longitudinal and transverse direction (A_{11}/A_{22} and D_{11}/D_{22} typically in the range 100 to 1000). A possible consequence of this imbalance is loss of numerical accuracy in carrying out finite element or similar analysis of equivalent orthotropic shells (analogous with loss of accuracy caused by use of excessively elongated shell finite elements). It is always advisable to guard against such inaccuracy by carrying out a pilot analysis for a small representative panel which can be compared with exact orthotropic plate analysis or finite element or folded-plate solutions for models with discrete representation of corrugations.

In the case of a corrugated shell incorporating transverse hat-section frames effective transverse membrane and flexural rigidities, which are affected not only by the corrugated form of the shell but by "bites" taken out of frame webs in way of corrugation troughs, depend on a complex inter-action between bending and membrane deformations of strips of laminate forming the shell and transverse frames: finite element analysis offers the only practical means of examining such behaviour. Two illustrative arrangements, labelled Designs P and Q, are shown in Fig 3. In order to evaluate transverse membrane and flexural rigidities it is possible, by assuming that panels are long and wide, to confine finite element analysis to a representative segment ABCD of each structure, as shown in Fig 4, corresponding to half a transverse frame-space and half of a span between corrugations with appropriate boundary conditions at the edges; by considering unit transverse displacement and unit flexural rotation of section AB relative to section CD on each segment and evaluating the associated transverse force and bending moment, an estimate may be made of the effective transverse extensional and flexural rigidities. These may be related to the rigidities of a flat panel having the same transverse frames in order to obtain "efficiency" factors referring to each corrugated shell.

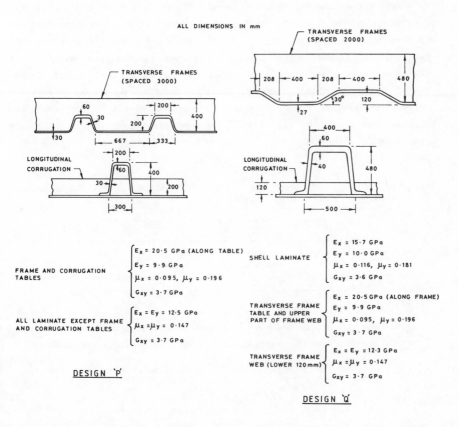

FIGURE 3. Corrugated Shell Designs

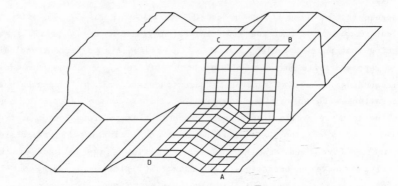

FIGURE 4.   Finite Element Idealization of Frame-Shell Segment

Some representative results computed for designs P and Q are indicated in Table 1 in the form of efficiencies η_m and η_f (= transverse membrane or flexural rigidity per unit length of corrugated panel/rigidity per unit length of corresponding flat panel). Corresponding distributions of direct transverse stress acting across sections AB and CD in Design Q are illustrated in Fig 5. Also included in Table 1 are ratios S_m and S_f relating maximum transverse stresses in the corrugated panels to corresponding stresses (estimated by beam theory) in equivalent transversely stiffened flat panels.

TABLE 1

Relative Transverse Membrane and Flexural Rigidities and Maximum Stresses in Transversely Stiffened Corrugated Panels

	η_m	η_f	S_m	S_f
DESIGN P	0.30	0.18	3.51	1.73
DESIGN Q	0.75	0.43	1.52	2.08

η_m = transverse membrane rigidity of corrugated panel/membrane rigidity of equivalent flat panel

η_f = transverse flexural rigidity of corrugated panel/flexural rigidity of equivalent flat panel

S_m = max. stress in frame of corrugated panel/max. stress in equivalent flat panel (under unit transverse strain)

S_f = Max. stress in frame of corrugated panel/max. stress in equivalent flat panel (under unit transverse curvature)

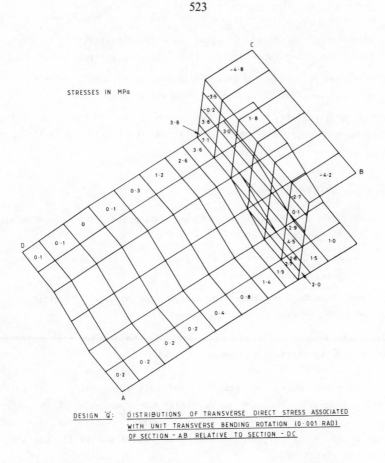

STRESSES IN MPa

DESIGN 'Q': DISTRIBUTIONS OF TRANSVERSE DIRECT STRESS ASSOCIATED
WITH UNIT TRANSVERSE BENDING ROTATION (0·001 RAD)
OF SECTION - AB RELATIVE TO SECTION - DC

FIGURE 5.   Stress Distribution Induced by Transverse Bending

LONGITUDINAL STRENGTH CONSIDERATIONS

Design of a ship's hull girder to withstand static, wave-induced and
possibly explosion-induced bending and shear involves:

(i)   provision of hull section moduli sufficient to confine bending and
shear stresses to acceptable levels relative to material failure
stresses, with due allowance for stress concentrations and fatigue
effects;

(ii)   provision of sufficient flexural rigidity to restrict hull girder deformations and raise natural frequencies to acceptable levels;

(iii) provision of adequate buckling strength, particularly under compressive loads in bottom and deck structures.

No particular difficulty arises in meeting the first two requirements for a corrugated hull section; some peculiarities do however occur in the buckling behaviour of corrugated structure.

Analysis of Buckling Behaviour

Instability of a corrugated shell under longitudinal compression might be expected to take the form of either

(i)   column-like buckling of the corrugations into a single half-wave between transverse frames, or

(ii)   "panel buckling" of the strips of laminate forming corrugations into several half-waves between transverse frames.

Consideration must also be given to overall buckling of shell structure contained between transverse bulkheads.

Accurate and economical evaluation of both local and overall initial buckling stresses may be made using folded-plate analysis [5] in which a corrugated shell is represented as a prismatic assembly of rectangular orthotropic plate strips. In-plane deformations of each strip satisfy the simultaneous equations

$$A_{11} \frac{\partial^2 u}{\partial x^2} + A_{12} \frac{\partial^2 v}{\partial x \partial y} + A_{66} \left(\frac{\partial^2 v}{\partial x \partial y} + \frac{\partial^2 u}{\partial y^2} \right) + N_y \frac{\partial^2 u}{\partial y^2} = 0 \tag{4}$$

$$A_{22} \frac{\partial^2 v}{\partial y^2} + A_{12} \frac{\partial^2 u}{\partial x \partial y} + A_{66} \left(\frac{\partial^2 v}{\partial x^2} + \frac{\partial^2 u}{\partial x \partial y} \right) + N_x \frac{\partial^2 v}{\partial x^2} = 0 \tag{5}$$

while out-of-plane displacements w satisfy the equation

$$D_{11} \frac{\partial^4 w}{\partial x^4} + 2 H \frac{\partial^4 w}{\partial x^2 \partial y^2} + D_{22} \frac{\partial^4 w}{\partial y^4} - N_x \frac{\partial^2 w}{\partial x^2} - N_y \frac{\partial^2 w}{\partial y^2} = 0 \tag{6}$$

Assuming conditions of simple support at the ends of the structure, solutions have the form

$$u = u_n \sin \alpha_n x$$

$$v = v_n \cos \alpha_n x \qquad\qquad (7)$$

$$w = w_n \sin \alpha_n x$$

in which $\alpha_n = n\pi/L$ and u_n, v_n and w_n are functions of y independent of x. In the case of local buckling L corresponds to the spacing (a) of transverse frames while rigidities $A_{11} = E_x t/(1-\mu_x\mu_y)$, $A_{22} = E_y t/(1-\mu_x\mu_y)$, $A_{12} = \mu_x A_{11}$ ($= \mu_y A_{22}$), $D_{11} = E_x t^3/[12(1-\mu_x\mu_y)]$, $D_{22} = E_y t^3/[12(1-\mu_x\mu_y)]$, $H = G_{xy} t^3/6 + \mu_x D_{11}$ are those of the shell plating or laminate. In the case of overall buckling L corresponds to the spacing of transverse bulkheads; A_{11}, A_{12}, A_{66}, D_{11} and D_{12} are as given by eq. 3, A_{22} and D_{22} may be estimated using computed factors η_m and η_f as illustrated in Table 1 and it may be assumed that $H = \frac{1}{2}GJ_y$, where GJ_y is the torsional rigidity per unit width of closed-section transverse frames, other components being negligible.

Finite element analysis, which offers an alternative means of evaluating local and overall buckling stresses, is generally less accurate and much more expensive than folded-plate analysis but may be the only effective means of examining a highly irregular shell, eg one containing penetrations or appendages. Nonlinear finite element analysis provides an effective means of investigating post-buckling and collapse behaviour of longitudinally [6] and transversely [7] stiffened FRP shells.

Approximate evaluation of interframe column – buckling stresses for a corrugated panel may be made using the Euler formula

$$\sigma_{xcr} = \frac{\pi^2 E_x I_x}{a^2 \gamma t} \Big/ \left(1 + \frac{\pi^2 E_x I_x}{a^2 G_{xy} A_s}\right) \qquad\qquad (8)$$

where GA_s is the effective shear rigidity per unit width. As discussed below, some care must be taken in applying this formula to shallow corrugations with small trough angle.

A lower-bound estimate of local buckling stresses for strips of laminate forming corrugations may be obtained using the formula for a long, simply-supported orthotropic strip

$$\sigma_{xcr} = \frac{2\pi^2}{b_1^2 t} \ (H + \sqrt{D_{11} \ D_{22}}) \tag{9}$$

where b_1 is the strip width. The corresponding upper-bound expression for a clamped orthotropic strip is [8]

$$\sigma_{xcr} = \frac{\pi^2}{b_1^2 t} \ (2.4 \ H + 4.6 \sqrt{D_{11} \ D_{22}} \ ) \tag{10}$$

Overall buckling of a rectangular longitudinally corrugated, transversely framed panel of length L and width B may be examined using the formula for a simply supported orthotropic plate

$$\sigma_{xcr} = \frac{n^2 \pi^2 D_{22}}{B^2 \gamma t} \ \Big(\frac{D_{11}}{D_{22}} \frac{B^2}{L^2} + \frac{2H}{n^2 D_{22}} + \frac{L^2}{n^4 B^2} \Big)$$

Overall buckling of a corrugated vee-bottom structure may be evaluated approximately using data curves given in [9].

Initial buckling stresses and mode shapes evaluated for three alternative corrugated shell configurations (Designs Q, R, S) using folded-plate analysis and the approximate formulae are summarized in Fig 6. In the case of Design R, which has deep corrugations with a large trough angle, the local forms of instability described above are clearly evident: Eq. 8 gives a slightly non-conservative estimate of the "column" mode while equations 9 and 10 give rather widely spaced bounds on the preferred "panel" mode. Where d and Ψ are reduced, the latter to 30° (Design Q), eq. 8 is found to overestimate the initial "column" buckling stress by a larger margin (19%) and "panel" buckling is preceded by an unfamiliar twisting form of instability. In the case of a very small trough angle (Design S) twisting instability is found to be the preferred mode and eq. 8 substantially overestimates the "column" buckling stress.

Approximate formulae clearly cannot be relied upon to identify initial buckling stresses accurately: folded-plate or equivalent analysis should therefore always be used for this purpose. Very small trough angles are

527

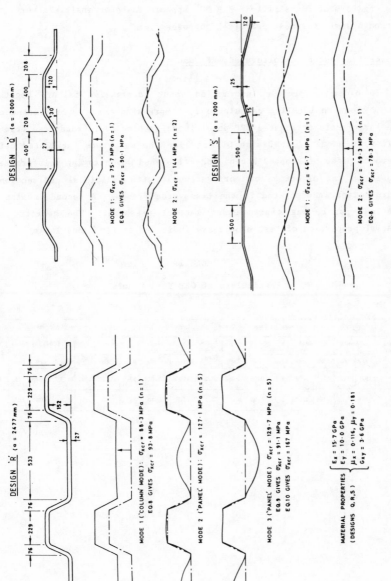

ALL DIMENSIONS IN mm

DESIGN 'Q' (a = 2000 mm)

MODE 1: σ_{xcr} = 75·7 MPa (n=1)
EQ.8 GIVES σ_{xcr} = 90·1 MPa

MODE 2: σ_{xcr} = 144 MPa (n=2)

DESIGN 'S' (a = 2000 mm)

MODE 1: σ_{xcr} = 46·7 MPa (n=1)

MODE 2: σ_{xcr} = 49·3 MPa (n=1)
EQ.8 GIVES σ_{xcr} = 78·3 MPa

DESIGN 'R' (a = 2477 mm)

MODE 1 ('COLUMN' MODE): σ_{xcr} = 88·3 MPa (n=1)
EQ.8 GIVES σ_{xcr} = 93·8 MPa

MODE 2 ('PANEL' MODE): σ_{xcr} = 127·1 MPa (n=5)

MODE 3 ('PANEL' MODE) σ_{xcr} = 129·7 MPa (n=5)
EQ.9 GIVES σ_{xcr} = 91·1 MPa
EQ.10 GIVES σ_{xcr} = 167 MPa

MATERIAL PROPERTIES $\begin{cases} E_x = 15·7 \text{ GPa} \\ E_y = 10·0 \text{ GPa} \\ \mu_x = 0·116, \mu_y = 0·181 \\ G_{xy} = 3·6 \text{ GPa} \end{cases}$
(DESIGNS Q, R, S)

FIGURE 6. Buckling Modes in Corrugated Panels

associated with loss of flexural efficiency and emergence of an unfamiliar, twisting form of instability: $\Psi \approx 30^{\circ}$ appears to be a sensible lower limit to trough angle for most practical purposes.

Compression Test on a Corrugated GRP Panel

In order to provide information about compressive failure together with a check on buckling calculations, compression tests were carried out on a large-scale corrugated GRP panel incorporating four transverse frames, similar in geometry to Design Q (Fig 3). The panel was fabricated using alternate plies of chopped-strand and 4/1 biased woven-roving reinforcement (biased in the direction of corrugations), with additional undirectional reinforcement incorporated in the transverse frames. A second, nominally identical panel, was tested under lateral pressure. The geometry and material properties of test panels are indicated in Fig 7 and Table 2.

TABLE 2

Particulars of GRP Test Panels

Panel No	Corrugated Panel Laminate										Transverse Frames						
	t_1 (mm)		E_x (GPa)		E_y (GPa)		μ_x*	$G_{xy}*$ (GPA)	Longl. Comp Strength (MPa)		t_2 (mm)		t_3	E_y (GPa)		Transv. UTS (MPa)	
	mean	cov	mean	cov	mean	cov			mean	cov	mean	cov		mean	cov	mean	cov
1	19.0	0.07	12.7	0.08	9.0	0.08	0.12	3.2	190	0.06	33.9	0.06	25.2	14.9	0.07	283	0.02
2	20.8	0.05	11.5	0.07	8.9	0.09	0.12	3.2	179	0.10	38.5	0.03	25.2	15.8	0.08	267	0.04

* calculated values

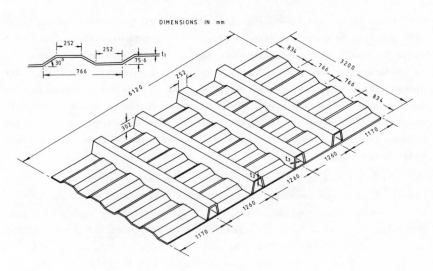

DIMENSIONS IN mm

FIGURE 7.   Geometry of Corrugated GRP Test Panels

Test Panel No 1 was mounted horizontally on a test rig previously developed for experiments on steel grillages [10], which has been used also in compression tests on longitudinally and transversely stiffened GRP grillages [6,7].   The ends of the panel and of transverse frames were reinforced by steel sandwich plates: conditions of simple support were simulated at the ends and sides, with longitudinal edges of the panel unrestrained against in-plane displacements.   Compressive load was applied by hydraulic jacks acting through load transducers at one end of the panel and was reacted through a passive set of jacks at the other end.   Strains were monitored at transverse cross-sections in order to check the uniformity of applied load.   Vertical displacements were recorded at transverse frame positions and at selected longitudinal sections between frames.

Laminate thicknesses were measured using an ultrasonic transducer: values indicated in Fig 7 are means derived from a large number of readings.   Material properties (moduli and strengths) were evaluated from coupons cut from the panel following tests.

Compressive load was applied progressively, with stops during which displacements and strains were recorded. No damage was observed at loads up to 95 MPa, when some cracking was heard. Collapse occurred suddenly at an average compressive stress of 101 MPa and was evidently associated with column-like buckling of the corrugations between transverse frames leading to compressive fracture across the full width of the laminate adjacent to one of the end frames. A substantially higher compressive strength was achieved than in any previous test on GRP panels with conventional hat-section stiffeners [6,7].

The preferred initial buckling mode indicated by folded-plate analysis was found to be column-like interframe buckling. Assuming simple support at transverse frame positions with an effective interframe span of 1260 mm, the computed initial buckling stress was 59.3 MPa, with a further critical stress, corresponding to a twisting mode as shown in Fig 6, of 145 MPa. It is evident from experimental observations that torsionally stiff hat section frames exert substantial rotational restraint at the ends of each interframe span and under these conditions it is clear that column buckling stresses estimated as described above will give a conservative estimate of compressive strength.

TRANSVERSE STIFFNESS AND STRENGTH

The behaviour of transversely stiffened corrugated panels or shells may be examined using grillage or orthotropic plate or shell analysis in which transverse flexural and membrane rigidities and maximum stresses are estimated using efficiency factors η_f and η_m and stress factors S_f and S_m based on local finite element analysis as described above. The validity of this approach has been evaluated by tests on a small-scale perspex model and a large-scale GRP panel.

A simply supported perspex panel, shown in Fig 8, with overall dimensions of 900 x 1090 mm and geometry similar to that of Design Q (Fig 3) was subjected to lateral air pressure of up to 0.07 bar. Maximum displacements and outer-fibre strains measured in transverse frames were found to differ by less than 15% from calculated values.

GRP test panel No 2, with geometry and material properties as defined in Fig 7 and Table 2, was mounted in the compression test rig and subjected to lateral pressure by means of a water-filled rubber bag. Various combinations of lateral and compressive load were also applied. Under a pressure of 1.03 bar, a maximum displacement of 43 mm and outer fibre strain of 0.0045 were recorded in transverse frames: the corresponding displacement and strain computed by grillage analysis using the approximations described above were respectively 47 mm and 0.0056. The panel was finally tested under lateral load alone until collapse occurred, somewhat prematurely, at a pressure of 1.7 bar, involving failure of the attachment at the end of one of the transverse frames.

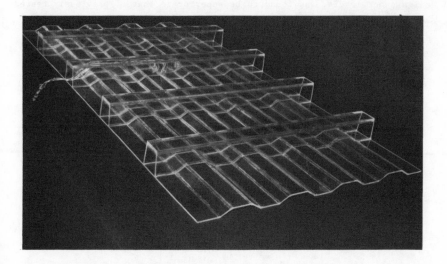

FIGURE 8.   Corrugated Perspex Test Panel

Results indicate that the approximate characterisation of flexural rigidity and section modulus described above should give reasonably accurate estimates of bending deformation and stresses in transversely framed corrugated shells.

STRENGTH UNDER EXPLOSIVE LOAD

In order to evaluate the performance of a corrugated structure under explosive loading, underwater explosion tests were carried out on an air-backed GRP panel, 3 m square, incorporating three longitudinal corrugations and two transverse hat-section frames. Geometry and material properties corresponded to Design Q (Fig 3) at about 2/3 scale.

A standard test procedure was employed, as illustrated schematically in Fig 9, which had been used extensively in previous tests on conventionally stiffened GRP structure. The corrugated panel was bolted at its edges, through rubber mountings and seals, to a steel box and was subjected to a series of underwater explosions of increasing severity [10]. Damage occurrence was monitored by careful visual inspection after each explosion. The performance of the corrugated panel, judged by the extent of damage at design shock levels, was found to be superior to that of previously tested panels with conventional hat-section stiffening.

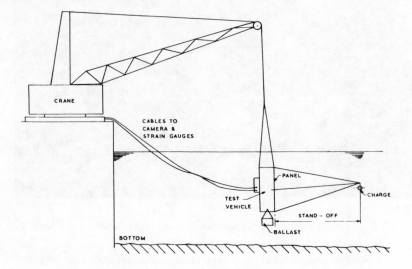

FIGURE 9.   Arrangement of Explosion Tests on GRP Panel

WEIGHT AND COST CONSIDERATIONS

Comparison of Alternative MCMV Hull Designs

As a basis for assessing the weight and cost characteristics of corrugated hull construction a comparison has been made between four alternative designs, intended to meet similar strength requirements, referring to a

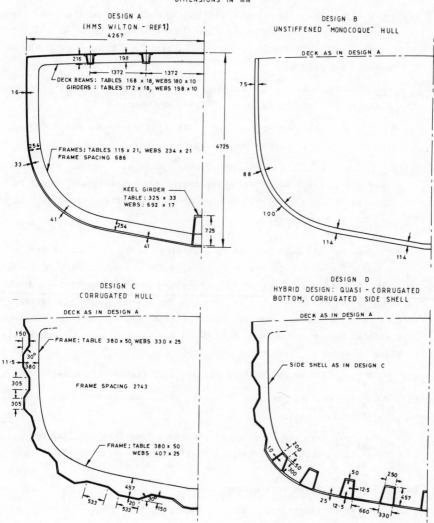

DIMENSIONS IN mm

DESIGN A
(HMS WILTON - REF 1)

DESIGN B
UNSTIFFENED "MONOCOQUE" HULL

DESIGN C
CORRUGATED HULL

DESIGN D
HYBRID DESIGN: QUASI - CORRUGATED
BOTTOM, CORRUGATED SIDE SHELL

FIGURE 10.   Alternative MCMV Hull Designs

long midships compartment in a GRP minehunter of 47 m overall length.

Design A, taken as a reference design, corresponds to the prototype, transversely framed GRP minehunter HMS WILTON, details of which are given in [1]. The hull compartment contains 11 transverse frames and a deep keel girder.

Design B, corresponds to an unstiffened, "monocoque" hull of the type employed in the Italian "Lerici" Class minehunter [11].

Design C, is a corrugated hull, broadly similar to Design Q (Fig 3), incorporating two transverse frames.

Design D, is a hybrid design with a quasi-corrugated bottom shell and a corrugated side shell. The quasi-corrugated geometry was judged to be unsuitable for the ship's side because of the difficulty of fabricating corrugation overhangs.

Laminate moduli were assumed throughout to be $E_x = E_y = 13.8$ GPa, $\mu_x = \mu_y = 0.13$, $G_{xy} = 3.4$ GPa in the shell, with a somewhat higher Young's Modulus (E = 18.6 GPa) in stiffener tables. In relation to material failure, permissible strains were taken to be $\varepsilon_p = 0.004$ in all cases. In accordance with the recommendations of Refs 6 and 7, the ratios between permissible (short duration) average stress σ_p and initial compressive buckling stresses σ_{cr} were taken to be:

(i) $\sigma_p/\sigma_{cr} = 1/1.8$ in the case of transversely framed structure;

(ii) $\sigma_p/\sigma_{cr} = 1/1.5$ in the case of local "panel" buckling of longitudinally stiffened structure;

(iii) $\sigma_p/\sigma_{cr} = 1/2$ in the cases of interframe column-like buckling or overall instability of longitudinally stiffened structure.

Design load conditions were assumed to be

(i)   A vertical/longitudinal bending moment of 17.9 MNm;

(ii) a uniform hydrostatic pressure of 0.5 bar extending from the keel to the deck edge, in accordance with current requirements for ships of this size.

Because of the complicating influence of minor bulkheads, superstructure and hatch openings on bending and buckling of the deck,

535

consideration was confined to behaviour of the shell structure and to variations in the shell design. For the purpose of estimating hull section moduli and weights the deck structure of Design A was retained throughout (it may be noted, however, that this structure is not very efficient and that weight and cost savings could be achieved by adopting a quasi-corrugated deck configuration). Bulkheads, superstructure, machinery and equipment were also assumed to have the same weight in each case.

Assessment of each design included

(i) evaluation of hull section modulus and associated stresses induced by hull bending (estimated by beam theory);

(ii) computation of local buckling behaviour using folded plate analysis as described above (see Fig 6 and Refs 6 and 7);

(iii) evaluation of overall buckling behaviour under a linearly varying distribution of stress corresponding to hull bending, using folded plate analysis as illustrated in Fig 11, with orthotropic rigidities of stiffened shells estimated as described above and assuming simple support at the ends of the compartment;

(iv) computation of overall displacements and strains induced by lateral pressure, assuming simple support at the compartment ends, again using folded plate analysis;

(v) calculation of weights, referring to the shell alone, to the complete hull structure and to total ship displacement, based on the following assumptions for Design A:

$$\text{total structural weight } (W_{st})/\text{displacement} = 0.25$$

$$\text{weight of shell} = 0.55 \ W_{st}$$

$$\text{weight of decks} = 0.22 \ W_{st}$$

$$\text{weight of bulkheads, superstructure and all secondary structure} = 0.23 \ W_{st}$$

Results of the study are summarized in Table 3, which compares hull rigidities, design stress levels σ_d (at the keel) induced by hull bending, local and overall buckling stresses, maximum displacements (Fig 12) and strains induced by lateral pressure and structural weights for the various designs, normalized where appropriate with respect to Design A values.

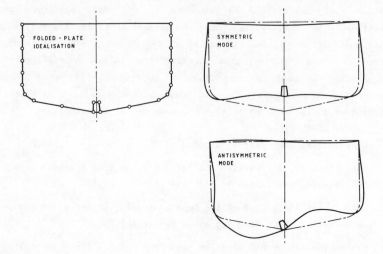

FIGURE 11.   Overall Buckling of Shell Structure under Hogging BM

Although the comparison is not entirely conclusive since none of the designs has been optimized by coaxing design stresses up to maximum permissible levels, it is clear that both the corrugated and hybrid designs (C and D) offer substantial weight savings relative to Design A.   It is also clear that the "monocoque" form of construction (Design B), which has the merits of high explosion resistance and suitability for economical, automated fabrication, carries a large weight penalty.

TABLE 3.

Comparison of Alternative MCMV Hull Designs

Design	Hull Rigidity $\frac{EI}{EI_A}$	Design Stress (at Keel) σ_d (MPa)	Lowest Buckling Stresses & Modes				Transverse Stiffness & Strength		Weight Estimates (W/W_A)		
			Local		Overall		w_{max} (mm) See Fig 12	ε max	Shell only	All Hull Structure	Ship Displacement
			σ_{cr} (MPa)	Mode	σ_{cr}^*(MPa)	Mode					
A	1.0	14.1	58.0	Type-3 (See Ref 7)	–	–	17	0.0016	1.0	1.0	1.0
B	1.72	7.0	–	–	67.5	Antisym (n=3)	35	0.0019	1.91	1.49	1.12
C	0.66	28.3	58.6	"Column" (n=1)	>200	–	33	0.0020	0.47	0.72	0.93
D	0.68	27.3	59.7	"Panel" (n=14)	89.5	Antisym (n=1)	64	0.0028	0.63	0.80	0.95

* Stress level at Keel

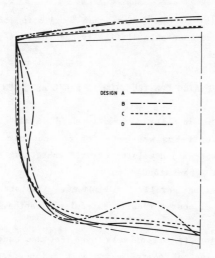

FIGURE 12.   Mid-Compartment Deformations under Lateral Pressure

Fabrication Feasibility and Cost Assessment

Practical experience of corrugated construction was provided by the fabrication of several GRP test panels. Some concern was felt initially about possible difficulty in fabricating corrugation "overhangs" in the side shell: this process was examined by constructing one of the GRP test panels in a vertical position and it was found that no problem arose provided that the trough angle was restricted to 30°.

One of the main objects of a corrugated hull design is to simplify the fabrication process and hence reduce costs by eliminating the need for separate fabrication of most stiffeners. In order to obtain an independent evaluation of fabrication feasibility and costs a leading UK boatbuilder, Halmatic Ltd, was contracted to carry out an assessment referring to

(i)   a light, commercially available, transversely framed GRP hull of 26 m length;

(ii) an equivalent corrugated hull designed by ARE with a 20% overall structural weight saving.

The findings of this study [12] were that fabrication of a corrugated hull would present no insurmountable difficulty and that a saving of 25% in hull cost could be expected.

USE OF CORRUGATED CONSTRUCTION IN STEEL AND ALUMINIUM HULLS

Corrugated steel plating is widely used in the bulkheads of large tankers and bulk carriers where it offers economic advantage through reduction of preparation and welding of stiffeners. It seems possible that this advantage could be extended to the external hull structure of large steel ships with long parallel mid-bodies. Resistance and seakeeping implications would of course require careful evaluation.

Aluminium alloy is extensively used in the construction of high-performance hulls (patrol boats, hydrofoils and hovercraft). Because of the susceptibility of welded light alloy structure to distortion and fatigue cracking, riveting is often employed or, alternatively, welding is kept to a minimim by use of sophisticated extrusions incorporating stiffeners [13]. A further alternative would appear to be use of a corrugated light alloy shell, possibly with "flying" transverse frames as shown in Fig 13 employing welded or riveted and/or bonded attachment to the shell. Hydrodynamic implications would again require evaluation although it may be noted that most of a hydrofoil or SES hull is out of the water during high-performance operation.

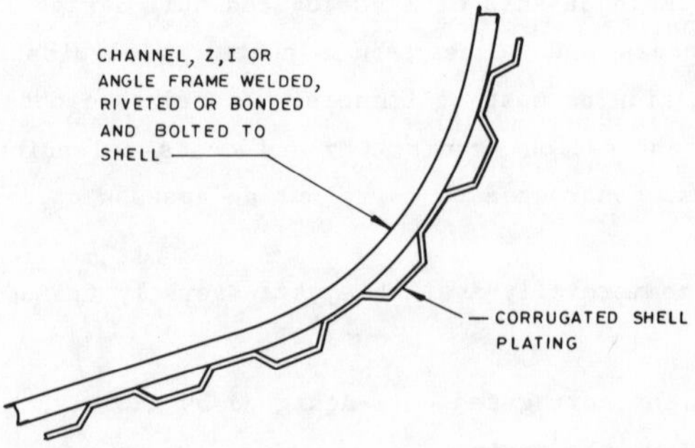

CHANNEL, Z,I OR ANGLE FRAME WELDED, RIVETED OR BONDED AND BOLTED TO SHELL

CORRUGATED SHELL PLATING

FIGURE 13.   Corrugated Light Alloy Shell

CONCLUSIONS

Analysis and tests have confirmed that corrugated construction offers an efficient means of meeting longitudinal strength requirements in a GRP hull. A corrugated shell will generally provide high compressive strength, although buckling of shallow corrugations with small trough angles requires careful assessment.

Transverse strength requirements may also be achieved in a corrugated shell reinforced by a small number of widely spaced transverse frames. It has been shown that the flexural rigidity of transversely stiffened corrugated panels may be characterized with reasonable accuracy using efficiency factors based on finite element analysis of a representative element.

The expectation that a corrugated shell would have better resistance to underwater explosions than a conventionally stiffened shell was borne out by tests on a GRP panel.

Comparison of alternative hull designs for a 47 m GRP minehunter indicated that corrugated or quasi-corrugated construction would offer substantial weight savings relative to conventional transversely framed or unstiffened "monocoque" construction. An independent assessment of the feasibility and economics of corrugated hull construction indicated that a corrugated GRP hull, designed to be 20% lighter than an equivalent, conventionally stiffened hull, would also give a cost saving of 25%. On the basis of these findings a decision was taken to procure and carry out proof tests on a prototype corrugated hull: details of this project are contained in a separate paper [14].

Use of corrugated construction in the parallel mid-bodies of large steel ships and in the light alloy hulls of certain high-performance craft appears to merit further consideration.

ACKNOWLEDGEMENTS

Acknowledgements are due to the author's colleagues Messrs W C Kirkwood, W L Somerville and J W Swan for assistance in carrying out tests and computation.

540

REFERENCES

1. Dixon R H, Ramsay B W, Usher P J : "Design and Build of the GRP Hull of HMS WILTON". Proc. of Sympos. on GRP Ship Construction, RINA, London, 1972.

2. Hallet H R, Simpson J H : "Fabrication of Large RP Trawlers" Reinforced Plastics, Vol 12, June 1968.

3. Yoshiki M, Fujita Y : "On the Ultimate Strength of Corrugated Plates Subjected to Compressive Load". J. Soc. Nav. Arch., Japan Vol 106, Jan 1960.

4. Basu A K, Chapman J C : "The Behaviour of Corrugated Plates under Uniform Pressure". BSRA Report NS 196, British Ship Research Association, 1966.

5. Smith C S : "Bending, Buckling and Vibration of Orthotropic Plate-Beam Structures". J. Ship Research, Vol 12, Dec 1968.

6. Smith C S, Dow R S : "Compressive Strength of Longitudinally Stiffened GRP Panels". Proc. 3rd Internat. Conf. on Composite Structures, Paisley, Sept 1985

7. Smith C S : "Compressive Strength of Transversely Stiffened FRP Panels", in "Aspects of the Analysis of Plate Structures" (D J Dawe et al eds), Clarendon Press, Oxford 1985.

8. Wittrick W H : Correlation between Some Stability Problems for Orthotropic and Isotropic Plates under Biaxial and Uniaxial Direct Stress". Aeronaut. Quarterly, Vol 4, No 1, 1952.

9. Smith C S : "Buckling and Vibration of a Ship's Vee Bottom Structure". Trans RINA, Vol 116, 1974.

10. Pattison D : Unpublished MOD (PE) report, 1978.

11. Trimming M : "Monocoque GRP Minehunters". Proc. Internat. Sympos. on Mine Warfare Vessels and Systems, RINA, London, June 1984.

12. Dove C : Unpublished Halmatic report, 1980.

13. Kaneko Y, Baba E : "Structural Design of Large Aluminium Alloy High-Speed Craft". Proc. 2nd Internat. Sympos. on Small Fast Warships and Security Vessels, RINA, London 1982

14. Gass W, Dove C, Chalmers D W, Smith C S : "Fabrication and Testing of a Prototype Corrugated GRP Hull". Proc. Internat. Conf. on Advances in Marine Structures, Dunfermline, May 1986.

FABRICATION AND TESTING OF A PROTOTYPE CORRUGATED GRP HULL

W Gass (ARE, Dunfermline)
C Dove (Halmatic Ltd, Havant, Hants)
D W Chalmers (CNA, Ministry of Defence, Bath)
C S Smith (ARE, Dunfermline)

ABSTRACT

An account is given of the fabrication and proof-testing of a 26 m prototype corrugated GRP hull. In addition to demonstrating the feasibility of corrugated construction and confirming favourable hull cost predictions, a satisfactory outcome was obtained from towing tests to evaluate hull resistance, hull bending tests under hogging and sagging load conditions and evaluation under a series of underwater explosions. Performance was compared in each case with that of a similar, conventional GRP hull.

INTRODUCTION

A preliminary study of the use of longitudinally corrugated shells in the external hull structure of GRP ships [1] has established a rationale for meeting the requirements of longitudinal and transverse stiffness and strength and has demonstrated that this form of construction offers significant improvements in performance and/or weight savings relative to conventional transversely framed GRP hulls with hat-section stiffeners. An independent study carried out by a leading UK boatbuilder [2] has indicated that corrugated hull construction would also provide substantial cost savings. On the basis of these findings a decision was taken to procure and carry out proof tests on a prototype corrugated GRP hull as a candidate for future use in mine-countermeasure vessels (MCMV). The aims of this project, summarized in the present paper, were as follows:

(i)   to demonstrate the feasibility of corrugated hull construction under shipyard conditions, identifying, and overcoming any problems which might arise during the fabrication process, and in particular to obtain confirmation of favourable hull cost predictions;

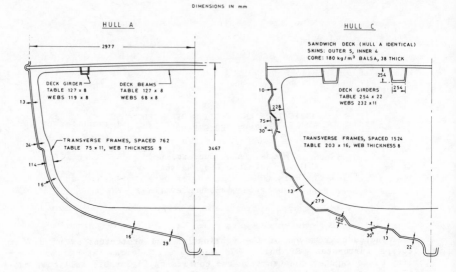

FIGURE 1. Conventional and Corrugated Hulls: Midship Sections.

(ii)   to evaluate the resistance characteristics of a corrugated
         hull by carrying out a comparative towing trial alongside a
         similar conventional hull;

(iii)   to check that longitudinal strength requirements would be met
         by carrying out hull bending tests under hogging and sagging
         load conditions;

(iv)   to evaluate explosion resistance, supplementing previous panel
         tests [1], by subjecting a complete corrugated hull to a
         series of underwater explosions.

HULL DESIGN

A commercially produced light, transversely framed GRP hull of 26 m
overall length, which had previously been evaluated for possible use in an
MCM role by carrying out static bending and explosion trials [3], was
adopted as a reference design (Hull A).   An equivalent corrugated hull
having the same overall dimensions (Hull C) was designed at ARE,
Dunfermline, following procedures developed in Ref 1.   Details of the two
designs, referring to a midships compartment of length 4.57 m, are shown in
Figure 1.

It was assumed that the orientation of corrugations should correspond as closely as possible with flow lines associated with forward motion of the hull in still water. Flow lines for the conventional design (Hull A), computed using a program developed by Gadd [4], were used to guide the alignment of corrugations in Hull C. A general view of each hull is shown in Figure 2.

In order to minimize hull surface area and disturbance of flow, shallow corrugations were adopted, similar in form to Design Q of Ref 1, with a maximum depth of 100 mm in the bottom shell reducing to 75 mm in the side and a trough angle of 30°. The 4.57 m compartment of Hull A contained 5 closely spaced transverse frame rings: these were replaced in Hull C by two relatively widely spaced transverse frames. The rather light, transversely stiffened sandwich deck structure of Hull A was replaced in Hull C by a stronger deck incorporating two longitudinal girders on each side.

The shell laminate in Hull A was formed by polyester resin reinforced mainly by 900 g/m^2 E-glass chopped-strand mat (CSM) together with 2 plies of 800 g/m^2 balanced woven rovings (WR) increased to 4 plies at the keel and side-shell chine. Frames were fabricated using 900 g/m^2 CSM with 600 g/m^2 unidirectional (UD) reinforcement incorporated in the tables. The shell laminate of Hull C was reinforced by 600 g/m^2 CSM with addition of 4 plies of 4:1 longitudinally biased 800 g/m^2 WR below the waterline and 4 further plies of WR in the keel region. Frames were constructed using 600 g/m^2 CSM with inclusion of 10 plies 600 g/m^2 UD in tables. Estimates of material moduli and strengths were based on properties of CSM, WR and UD laminates defined in [5] and in unpublished MOD specifications, assuming "rule of mixtures" in the case of CSM/WR and CSM/UD combinations.

Each hull was designed to withstand vertical/longitudinal hogging and sagging bending moments of 0.79 and 1.19 MNm respectively, together with a uniform hydrostatic pressure of 0.5 bar extending from the keel to the deck-edge. Hull girder rigidities EI, normalized with respect to that of Hull A, are indicated in Table 1, together with maximum keel and deck stresses σ_d associated with the design BM. Local and overall buckling of the shell structure under longitudinal compression was evaluated using methods discussed in [1]: the ratio of the design stress to the lowest

FIGURE 2. Comparative Views of Conventional and Corrugated Hulls.

TABLE 1
Design Features of Hull A and Hull C.

Hull	Hull Rigidity $\frac{EI}{EI_A}$	Design Stress σ_d (MPa)		Design Stress/ Lowest Buckling Stress σ_d/σ_{cr}	Relative Weight (W/W_A)		
		At keel	At deck		Shell (with frames)	Shell and Deck	Overall Hull Weight
Hull A	1.0	1.75	3.65	0.67	1.0	1.0	1.0
Hull C	0.90	3.94	2.37	0.08	0.65	0.82	0.85

buckling stress (σ_d/σ_{cr}), indicated in Table 1, was found to be well below the maximum permissible level of 0.5.

An efficiency factor η_f, relating the transverse flexural rigidity of a transversely framed corrugated panel to that of an equivalent flat panel (see Ref 1), was found, by finite element analysis of a representative element of the shell, to be 0.22; a corresponding factor S_f, relating maximum bending stress in the corrugated panel to that in the flat panel, was found similarly to be 1.91. On this basis transverse frames in Hull C were designed to have a somewhat higher effective flexural rigidity per unit length than those of Hull A.

A summary of weight estimates for the two hull designs, normalized with respect to those for Hull A, is included in Table 1. It is evident that the shell structure of Hull C, including transverse frames, is about 35% lighter than that of Hull A; assuming that the weight of bulkheads and secondary structure, comprising 23% of the total weight of Hull A, is the same in each design, the overall weight saving in Hull C is found to be 15%.

HULL FABRICATION

Mould Preparation

The production objective was straightforward: to create a longitudinally corrugated GRP hull utilizing an existing standard mould. A commercial constraint was that the mould should not suffer damage as a result of the necessary tooling adaptation.

The geometry of corrugations was defined on the screeve boards. Girth dimensions were then lifted at each section and transferred to the mould surface. Pre-formed sections of high-density (80 kg/m^3) polyurethane foam, profiled to the shape of the corrugations, were aligned and stuck on the mould surface using double-sided adhesive tape and masking tape. The surface of the foam was finally sealed with a thixotropic filler, special attention being paid to intersections with the mould to ensure a neat radius (approximately 50 mm) and a fair line. Minor modifications to the run of corrugations proved necessary and these were made by eye.

It is likely that somewhat different mould preparation would be employed for production of a batch of corrugated hulls. In this case a permanent corrugated GRP mould would be fabricated, probably using foam formers on a male plug to achieve the required shape.

Hull Lay-up

The mould was prepared for lay-up by applying several layers of wax in the normal way. Special care was taken to avoid disturbance of the corrugation formers during application of the first ply of CSM reinforcement. Hull fabrication was aided by experience gained from previous manufacture of corrugated test panels, including one laid up in a vertical position [1]. No serious difficulties were encountered. Fabrication of the shell structure proved straightforward and was accomplished easily within the target time. Hand lay-up followed normal Halmatic procedures. Resin was applied by brushing; plies of reinforcement, generally measuring 3 m x 1 m, were draped transversely in the case of CSM and longitudinally in the case of biased WR; consolidation was by brushing and rolling.

The supporting structure for the shell was unusual in GRP terms, a minimum number of transverse frames and bulkheads being employed. Frames were constructed as continuous members running from gunwale to gunwale. Frame formers, fabricated from 30 kg/m^3 polyurethane foam, were over-laminated using CSM with unidirectional reinforcement incorporated in the frame tables. An internal view of the hull during fabrication is shown in Figure 3.

FIGURE 3. Hull C During Fabrication.

Separately fabricated GRP double-bottom tanks were incorporated into the hull. Each unit was dry-fitted into position, notched to accommodate transverse frames and finally bonded to the shell using CSM boundary angles.

Bulkheads were fabricated from 25 mm plywood reinforced by vertical aluminium alloy angle stiffeners. The bottom of each bulkhead unit was notched to accommodate bottom shell corrugations and was attached to the shell in the usual way by double-sided CSM boundary angles. Side-shell corrugations were faired internally in way of bulkheads using polyurethane foam, overlaid by CSM laminate to complete the bulkhead/shell connection.

Deck Construction

The main deck was fabricated in two (forward and after) sections on a standard mould. Each section was of sandwich construction with inner and outer GRP skins and an end-grain balsa core as shown in Figure 1. The balsa core was replaced by hardwood blocks at positions of high concentrated load. The deck was stiffened by four substantial longitudinal girders, laid up over foam formers on the inner skin. This feature simplified the fabrication process considerably and reduced production times relative to those of Hull A.

Each deck section was dry-fitted at the ship and attached to the side shell and bulkheads by plies of CSM laminate. Continuity between forward and after deck sections was provided by a double-sided scarph joint in the midships region. The assembly was completed by continuing the side-shell transverse frames round the deck-edge as far as the outboard deck girders.

COMPARATIVE RESISTANCE TRIALS

Although shallow corrugations with small trough angles may be adopted, as in Hull C, in order to minimise flow disturbance, the hydrodynamic (resistance and seakeeping) implications of a corrugated hull form clearly require evaluation. It may be noted that an investigation by Haver and Telfer [6] led to the (somewhat controversial) conclusion that side-shell corrugations could have a beneficial influence on wavemaking resistance.

Resistance Evaluation

To investigate the effects of shell corrugations on resistance, it was decided that a simple towing trial involving comparison between a smooth and a corrugated hull would provide useful guidance. Two such hulls existed at ARE: Hulls A and C, apart from the corrugations, were of identical outer shape. The displacements of Hulls A and C, determined from draughts, were respectively 72.9 and 68.3 tonnes including water ballast in tanks and heavy steel blocks simulating machinery.

The smooth hull (Hull A) was removed from the Dockyard Basin at Rosyth and was thoroughly cleaned of marine growth. Descriptions of surface roughness prior to the towing trial were:

Hull A   (a)   forward 3 m, very clean, as new finish.
                    rms – 37 micron, standard deviation – 26 micron.
          (b)   aft 22 m, clean but not polished.
                    rms – 44 micron, standard deviation – 12 micron.

Hull C   (a)   corrugation trough:
                    rms – 10 microns, standard deviation – 26.6 micron.
          (b)   corrugation outer surface:
                    rms – 22 micron, standard deviation – 17.7 micron.

Two days of resistance towing trials were conducted over the measured mile at Burntisland on the North coast of the Firth of Forth. This mile is marked out by a pair of aligned white posts at each end and is 1851 m long. The chart datum depth along the course varies from 18 to 36 m.

Each hull was towed by a DOG Class tug; tugs were interchanged between Hulls A and C for the second day of trials in order to account for the effects of any dissimilarity between towing gear, wake effects etc. Each tow rope was 68 m long and of 150 mm nylon. A photograph of Hull C under tow is shown in Figure 4. Particulars of the hulls in the towed condition are given in Table 2.

It was intended to assess resistance at 5 different speeds, the lowest being that at which directional stability of the tug and hull tow could be maintained and the highest being determined by the maximum speed at which the tug could tow. In the event, assessments were only made at 4 speeds. This was due to a low lying mist falling and obscuring the marker posts. The time taken to traverse the mile was estimated by stop watch readings taken on passing the aligned marker posts.

For each nominal speed a tug's shaft rpm setting was estimated and four consecutive runs were made along the mile with each tug and hull tow running in parallel. Speeds were then assessed by the mean of means technique which cancels out tidal and current effects [7].

The tension in each tow line was measured by a hydraulic Statimeter. The Statimeter load cell was attached in series with the tow line at a point half a metre outboard of the bullring situated at the bow of each hull. The load indicator dial was sited just inboard on the open deck. The tow load was transmitted to the hull structure via a cleat fixed to 1 Deck above the forward bulkhead. Load readings were manually recorded, an attempt being made to record successive maxima and minima.

The results of the two days of towing trials are summarized in Figure 5. At the end of each speed run, a sample of water from mid draught was taken and the temperature and specific gravity were measured. These varied little over the trial and averaged 11.7°C and 1.026 respectively.

FIGURE 4. Hull C at Speed Under Tow.

TABLE 2
Towing Trial: Hull Particulars.

	Hull A	Hull C
Draught (m) Fwd	1.61	1.65
Aft	1.67	1.70
Displacement (tonnes)	72.9	68.3
KG (m)	1.13	1.20
GM (m)	2.243	2.21
Wetted Surface Area (m^2)	124.7	130.7
Waterplane Area (m^2)	97.7	89.8
Waterline Length (m)	23.20	23.29
Midship Section Area (including Skeg) (m^2)	4.96	4.77

It is apparent from the plots of resistance versus speed that there is no penalty incurred at equivalent draughts by adopting a corrugated form. When resistance is normalized with respect to displacement (Figure 5b) it is evident that curves for the corrugated hull fall slightly above those for the smooth hull: the reduction in displacement which may be achieved by

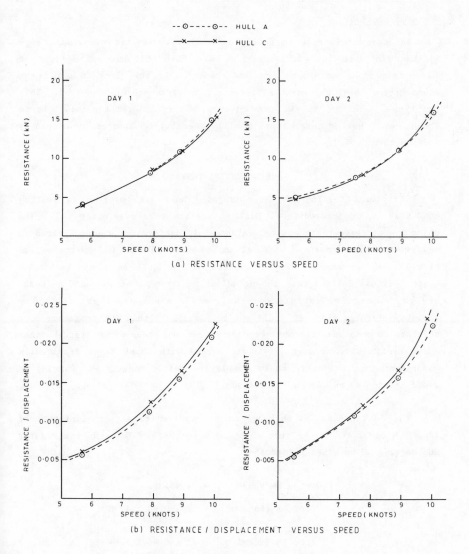

FIGURE 5. Results of Towing Trials.

use of corrugated construction should however be borne in mind. Further evaluation of corrugated hull performance should include resistance and seakeeping among waves, where it seems likely that the corrugated hull form will offer beneficial reductions of pitching, heaving and rolling motions.

Noise Generation

An attempt was made to determine whether corrugations caused a significant increase in hydrodynamic noise. Each hull was twice towed at 10 knots past a set of hydrophones suspended in the water 60 m off the towed track. No significant difference in performance was observed. This could have been due to the predominance of tug generated noise. It is thought that hull generated noise will generally be swamped by machinery and propulsor noises.

HULL BENDING TESTS

Structural testing of the corrugated hull was modelled on testing conducted on the conventional Hull A several years previously [3]. The objective of these tests was to evaluate hull performance when subjected to severe static longitudinal bending, and by means also of underwater explosive trials, to assess the suitability of the hull as a candidate MCM craft. It was decided that the principal requirement of the bending tests was to demonstrate satisfactory hull performance under proof bending moments amidships since it would not be possible within the programme constraints to model exactly hull bending moment and shear force distributions under design wave loading. It was agreed with Chief Naval Architect's Department that a midship BM of double the design hogging and sagging BM would be adopted as target proof loads.

The design midships BM range was determined for a trochoidal wave of length L equal to that of the ship and height L/9. The midships hogging and sagging BM were determined thus:

$$
\begin{array}{lll}
\text{Design BM Range} & = & 1.98 \text{ MNm} \\[6pt]
\text{Proof BM (Sagging)} & = & 2 \times 0.60 \times 1.98 \\
 & = & 2.38 \text{ MNm} \\[6pt]
\text{Proof BM (Hogging)} & = & 2 \times 0.40 \times 1.9 \\
 & = & 1.58 \text{ MNn}
\end{array}
$$

A ratio of 1.5 between peak sagging and hogging BM was assumed in accordance with current design practice.

In previous large scale proof tests conducted by ARE, considerable care was taken to devise a method of load application which would give a reasonable approximation to required BM and SF distributions without causing excessive local deformation and damage. For Hull A a four-point bending scheme was devised. Hull C was tested in a similar manner in the Large Test Frame at ARE. The loading configuration is shown in Figure 6. In each of the four-point bend tests, the loads were applied at bulkheads B, C, E and F and transmitted through specially designed steel loading boxes bolted port and starboard to the corrugated side-shell structure (see Figure 7).

In the sagging test, four loads were each applied through 2000 kN hydraulic jacks in series with load cells. They were positioned port and starboard under the steel jacking struts located at bulkheads B and F. The loading forces imposed on the hull were reacted at the other two pairs of loading positions at bulkheads C and E, through pinned ties anchored to the floor structure of the Large Test Frame. For the hogging tests, the jacking and reaction positions were reversed.

The response of the hull to the applied loading was recorded by numerous electrical resistance strain gauges and displacement transducers. Results were interpreted using simple beam theory and rule of mixtures techniques to determine section properties at the midships section. Calculated and measured peak strains under design bending moments are summarized in Table 3. Measured strains are evidently somewhat lower than calculated values, possibly because of omission of secondary structure (minor decks, bulkheads, tanks etc) from calculated section moduli.

Deformations of the hull, treated as a nonuniform beam, were computed using ARE's FABSTRAN finite element program [8]. Calculated and measured deformations are compared in Figure 8.

Both hogging and sagging tests had to be terminated slightly prematurely because of localized damage, including debonding of bulkheads from the shell, in the immediate region of loading points. A maximum hogging BM of 1.7 times the design load and a maximum sagging BM of 1.9 times the design load were however attained. It was apparent from deck and keel strains, which remained linearly proportional to applied loads and were far below material failure and calculated buckling levels, that overall hull strength substantially exceeded the peak applied loads.

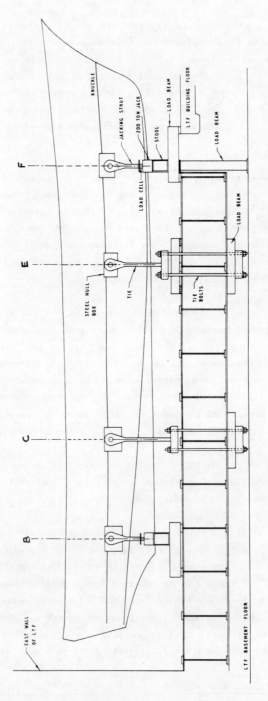

FIGURE 6. Hull Bending Test in Large Test Frame: Sagging Load

(a) Hull C in Large Test Frame

(b) Details of Loading Arrangement

FIGURE 7.

TABLE 3
Maximum Strains in Hull C under Design BM

Condition	Keel Strain (x 10^6)		Deck Strain (x 10^6)	
	Measured	Calculated	Measured	Calculated
Hogging	252	311	211	230
Sagging	374	466	311	345

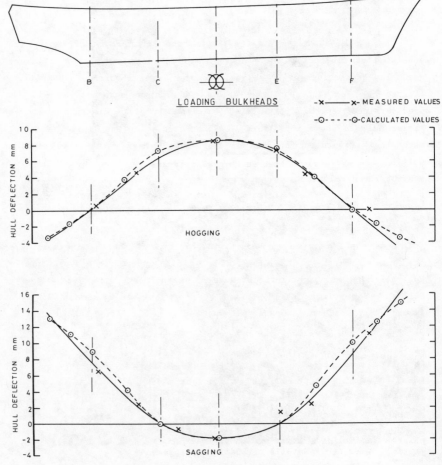

FIGURE 8. Hull C: Calculated and Measured Deflections.

557

EXPLOSION TESTS

Following the bending tests, a series of explosion tests was carried out on the corrugated hull. After minor repair work, which included sealing the holes in the hull at the loading box positions with watertight bolts, Hull C was ballasted to a displacement of 46 tonnes. This was achieved by a combination of water ballast in the centreline tanks and steel masses inside the hull and on the decks. The hull masses represented items of machinery and equipment and were bolted, to locally reinforced bottom longitudinals. Deck masses were held down by studs onto steel backing strips underneath the deck. This condition was based on that used for shock testing Hull A [3].

The shock trial was carried out in the River Forth off Rosyth and consisted of subjecting the hull to a series of underwater explosions of gradually increasing severity up to the peak level required in MCMV design (Figure 9). For each shot, the explosive charge was suspended on a wire of predetermined length from a buoy positioned a given distance abeam the target hull as shown in Figure 10. Instrumentation was limited to simple mechanical measurement of maximum displacements, as in previous tests on Hull A [3]. Careful visual inspection was carried out after each shot to monitor the development of any damage.

Response of a hull to underwater shock loading involves a complex interaction between structure and water. In particular, the dynamics of a stiffened shell tend to cause delamination of the shell and debonding of the frames from the shell. As was the case in the previous shock trial of Hull A, there was very little evidence of significant structural damage to Hull C. Some minor damage, in the form of laminate whitening and local debonding of seatings, was however observed in the region of concentrated masses.

From the evidence of incipient damage in Hulls A and C, supported by the results of explosion tests on 3 m square panels [1], it was concluded that the explosion resistance of the corrugated hull was at least as good as that of conventionally stiffened hulls.

FIGURE 9. Explosion Test on Hull C.

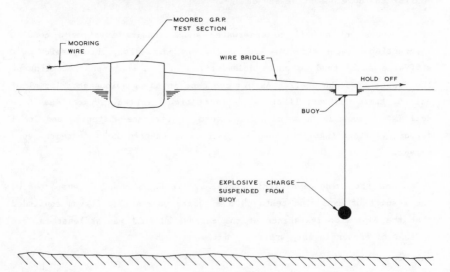

FIGURE 10. Schematic View of Explosion Test.

CONCLUSIONS

Fabrication of a prototype corrugated GRP hull has demonstrated the feasibility of this type of construction under practical shipyard conditions. No serious difficulty was encountered during the fabrication process. The total cost of hull production proved to be 76% of the cost of an equivalent conventionally stiffened hull (Hull A), confirming a predicted cost advantage for the corrugated form of construction.

Towing trials carried out simultaneously on a corrugated and an equivalent smooth hull at speeds of up to 10 knots ($V/\sqrt{gL} = 0.34$) showed negligible difference in performance under conditions of approximately equal draughts with a displacement advantage of 6.3% in favour of the corrugated hull. When resistances were normalized with respect to displacement, the performance of the smooth hull was found to be marginally superior: this difference would, however, usually be eliminated by the lower displacement of a corrugated ship.

Hull bending tests carried out under hogging and sagging load conditions confirmed that the corrugated shell structure had more than adequate longitudinal strength.

Underwater explosion tests demonstrated that the corrugated hull was able to meet the full MCMV design requirement without experiencing significant damage and that its performance was at least as good as that of a conventionally stiffened GRP hull.

Fabrication and proof-testing of a prototype corrugated GRP ship have provided confirmation of certain predicted cost, weight and performance advantages and appear to have established this form of construction as a strong candidate for future use in MCMV hulls.

ACKNOWLEDGEMENT

Acknowledgements are due to the authors' colleagues Messrs W L Somerville and J M Penman for assistance in carrying out experimental work. Thanks are due to the Captain of the Port, HM Dockyard, Rosyth, for support in carrying out towing and explosion trials. Procurement of Hulls A and C was funded by Director of Ship Design (now Chief Naval Architect), MOD, Bath.

REFERENCES

1. Smith, C.S., Structural Design of Longitudinally Corrugated Ship Hulls. Proc. Internat. Conf. on Advances in Marine Structures, ARE, Dunfermline, May 1986.

2. Dove, C., unpublished report, Halmatic Ltd, 1980.

3. Jackson, R.I. and Allison, D.M., Commercial Hulls for Low-Cost Mine-hunting. The Naval Architect, September 1982.

4. Gadd, G.E., A Method of Computing the Flow and Surface Wave Pattern around Full Forms. Trans. RINA, Vol 118, July 1976.

5. Johnson, A.F., Engineering Design Properties of GRP. British Plastics Federation, Publication No 215/1.

6. Haver, A.H. and Telfer, E.V., The Propulsive Performance of the Corrugated Ship. Trans. RINA, Vol 67, 1925.

7. Rawson, K.J. and Tupper, E.C., Basic Ship Theory (2nd Ed). Longman, London, 1976.

8. Dow, R.S. and Smith, C.S., FABSTRAN: a Computer Program for Frame and Beam Static and Transient Response Analysis (Nonlinear). Unpublished MOD report.

STRUCTURAL OPTIMISATION:
WHAT IS WRONG WITH IT?

J.B. Caldwell
Department of Naval Architecture and Shipbuilding
University of Newcastle upon Tyne
England

ABSTRACT

The results are reviewed of a large number of studies carried out in recent years by a research group at Newcastle University, which have had as their common theme the search for improved designs of ship structure. These range from simple stiffened panels, flat or pitched grillages, corrugated and sandwich structures to the transverse framing systems of large tankers and small warships. A variety of optimisation techniques has been explored, from elementary unconstrained minimisation to more elaborate schemes involving sequential linear programming or augmented Lagrangian methods. Various objective functions, such as weight or construction cost have been used; and recent work has investigated the potential of multiple-objective optimisation, and the inclusion of reliability criteria.

Evidently there is considerable scope for the practical application of optimisation in structural design work; but in reality rather little use appears to be made of it. Hence the title of the paper.

1. INTRODUCTION

The question mark in the title is important; because it is one objective of this paper to encourage discussion as to whether the very substantial volume of work on structural optimisation over the past 15-20 years has in fact had much noticeable or beneficial influence on the practical business of designing structures, particularly marine structures. And if not, why not?

To those (such as the author) at the more academic end of structural research, it is by no means clear that the growing power and efficiency of formal optimisation techniques is yet finding expression in significantly improved designs of actual structures, though there are some encouraging signs [1] here and there. Is this because these techniques do not yet adequately model the realities and constraints of practical design work; or do not address the correct objectives; or are perhaps mistrusted as too academic and abstruse? Should such work be now directed, not only to further developments in technique (especially in relation to optimisation of form) but also to the generation of design guidance, which would help point the way towards improved designs rather than identify some theoretical (and perhaps inapplicable) optimum?

It may be that, from among this distinguished gathering of structural experts, enough examples can be cited of the effective practical application of optimisation methods to be able to answer "Nothing" to the title question. But if this is not the case, then this conference could be a valuable opportunity to comment on the shortcomings, and suggest necessary changes, in the direction of current design-oriented structural research.

The author's views on the question are presented mainly by reference to the way in which the work of a small research group at Newcastle University has developed over the past 15 years. A series of studies, including some commissioned work, have had as their central theme the search for improvements in the synthesis - rather than analysis - of marine structures. From early work based on deterministic solutions for structures with single, simple measures of quality, more recent work has been exploring the applications of optimisation with multiple objectives and/or probabilistic aspects to the design. Various results from these studies are given to illustrate some of the general findings and opinions on optimisation work; and these are gathered together in a brief concluding section.

2. EDUCATIONAL ASPECTS

Before reviewing such research, however, it may be relevant first to touch briefly on the point that confidence in the practical use of optimisation should have its roots in the education of the structural designer. This is not simply a matter of introducing, as is now being done, formal courses on optimisation methodology; the need is rather to find a better balance in education programmes between structural analysis (to which the great majority of lectures and courses are devoted) and structural synthesis. The latter is more than just the inverse of the former; since the contrast between the multiple solutions of synthesis and the unique solutions of analysis require an intellectual jump which students sometimes find difficult.

This transition may best be effected by inviting students to address structural problems which, although at first sight rather trivial, can help to bring out some essential features of design and optimisation. Currently used examples include:

(a) pin-ended strut under specified load. The choice of optimal (prismatic) cross-section for minimum weight is not intuitively obvious, and the crucial importance of constraints on thickness and plate slenderness ratios, as well as the inadequacy of Euler's formula, are soon made apparent.

(b) structure to transmit central lateral load to two simple supports, subject to constraints on depth, for a range of different materials. The dramatic effects of the choice of structural form (beam, arch, truss, etc.) and of material strength/weight properties, on weights and costs, are very clear. Some results of this exercise were reviewed in [2].

(c) minimum cost design of a stiffened plate panel under hydrostatic pressure, with a range of labour cost parameters. This demonstrates the sensitivity of design to the ratio of material/labour costs, and to the form and layout of plate reinforcement selected.

For these undergraduate design exercises it would be possible to give students access via the computer to standard optimisation routines for use as "black boxes". But there are pedagogic arguments against this. Firstly, it is a major deficiency of optimisation theory that no method can yet handle satisfactorily the optimisation of _form_ (as distinct from lay-out and scantlings within a chosen form). Secondly there is a real learning value in having to perform hand-driven searches for realistic solutions within a multi-dimensional design space.

Indeed it sometimes happens that such a search can lead to useful insights and guidance of a more general kind. A recent example occurred in seeking a minimum cost design of a simply-supported p x 1 grillage (example (c) above) under uniform lateral pressure, Fig. 1. For such a redundant, multi-variable design structure, manual optimisation requires

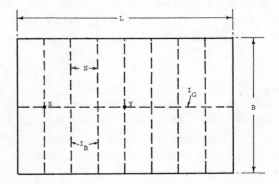

FIGURE 1.

time-consuming iterations and analyses, in which the ratio I_G/I_B of stiffnesses of the girder and the beams is a key parameter. A final year student, E. Kyratsous [3], suggesting intuitively that, for economy in design, the maximum stress in the beam set (which would probably occur at point X) should equal that in the girder (at point Y), and using distributed reaction theory for the latter, went on to derive a proposed optimal stiffness ratio:-

$$I_G/I_B = 2.64 \left(\frac{L}{B}\right)^3 \left(\frac{L}{S}\right)$$

which, even if not entirely rigorous in its justification, can provide useful guidance for deciding the initial value in a design search for optimal grillage structures.

Such exercises in synthesis can provide a foundation for the later appreciation and application of formal optimization procedures. They also demonstrate very clearly:-

- the need to identify at the outset all the design variables and especially those over which the designer has genuine control;

- the crucial importance of explicit identification of all constraints, geometric, behavioural and other;

- the role and selection of analysis models and methods in design synthesis;

- the need to define unambiguously the objective function, or measure of quality, by which the optimal design is identified.

3. DESIGNING FOR MINIMUM WEIGHT

The pioneering work of Moe [4] and others in the late 1960's, together with mathematical development of optimisation theory, encouraged the structures group at Newcastle to explore further the potential of such methods for a variety of problems. Woodhead [5] carried out a comprehensive state-of-the-art survey, and emphasized that the choice of optimisation method for a particular problem must take account of their efficiency, reliability and generality, which vary widely among the available methods.

3.1 Tanker Bottom Structure

To test the potential benefits of using formal optimisation in designing a representative component of ship structures, Chow [6] selected a panel of tanker bottom structure, 21.05m long and 10.40m wide under a uniform pressure head of 20m of water. Using constrained minimization with an exterior penalty function, elastic response analysis based on Clarkson's work [7] together with constraints on bending and shear stresses, plate slenderness ratios, plate thickness, flange widths and overall deflection, Chow first determined a minimum weight design using the original arrangement of three transverse and nine longitudinals; and then investigated the effects of varying the number and spacing of these reinforcing members.

TABLE 1

Optimisation of tanker bottom grillage L = 21.05m   B = 10.40m

	ORIGINAL	OPTIMAL 1	OPTIMAL 2	
No. of longitudinals	9	9	15	
No. of transverses	3	3	3	
Longitudinals - depth	839	771	656	mm
- width	203	209	273	
Transverses - depth	2745	2320	1980	
- width	356	382	549	
Plating thickness	27	23	16	
Weight of plating	46.3	40.0	26.8	tonnes
Weight of stiffening	44.7	41.0	44.2	
Total weight	91	81	71	

The summarised results are shown in Table 1. They confirm what other studies have shown:-

-   that a substantial weight reduction (from 91 to 81 tonnes) is possible even without any change in the stiffening arrangement.
-   that if there is freedom to optimise the stiffening arrangement, a further significant reduction (from 81 to 71 tonnes) is feasible by using 3 transverses and 15 longitudinals. This gives an overall 30% reduction from the original conventional design.
-   that amongst the side constraints, plate thickness limitation is nearly always active; plate slenderness ratio frequently so; and in this particular problem, flange width also, to ensure adequate access between longitudinals for welding.
-   that in minimum weight designs the ratio of weight of plating to weight of stiffening is much reduced from conventional values - in this case from 1.04 to 0.61. Further comments on this ratio are given in para 4.1 below.

3.2 Tanker Transverse Structure

A more substantial investigation, by Smith [8], was undertaken with support of a local shipyard and SRC, at a time when there was much debate about the relative merits of different forms and arrangements of the transverse framing structure of large tankers. The resulting development of a powerful design scheme, in which a finite element structural analysis model is linked to an optimisation process using sequential linear programming, has been reported elsewhere [9,10] and will not be further elaborated here. This work certainly demonstrated that even for complex three-dimensional blocks of ship structure involving many (in this case more than twenty) design variables and as many non-linear constraints, an efficient and rapidly converging optimisation procedure was feasible.

Less prominence was given, however, in refs. [8-10] to the practical design implications of the results obtained, and these are worthy of mention in the context of the present paper. In general the designer needs to know not only what is the maximum feasible value of some measure of quality (such as economy in weight) and the corresponding design, but also - and perhaps more importantly - how that objective function varies with changes in the key design variables, or in the constraints imposed on the design.

Ref. [8] contains a variety of charts which supply this kind of information. Fig. 2 is a typical example.

Although the objective function here was minimum weight, it was nevertheless of interest to investigate what weight penalties would be incurred if, for convenience of production, a degree of standardisation of the depths of the transverse frame members were to be introduced. For the "strutless" design of wing tank (one of three basic forms considered in the study) Fig. 2 shows, as expected, that minimum weight (55.4 tonnes) results from leaving these depths unconstrained; but that the additional weight resulting from various degrees of standardization of web depths is no more than a few percent. If depths are standardized in pairs, the minimum weight of a transverse increases only to 57.7 tonnes. In such ways can optimisation for minimum weight be used to assess the effects of different production strategies.

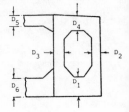

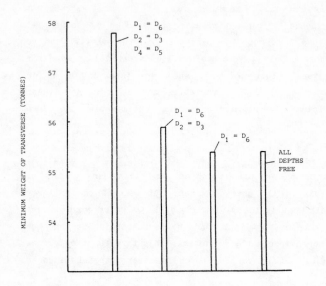

FIGURE 2.

3.3 Compartment of a Small Warship

For many years, economy in structure weight has been a more deliberate objective in warship design than in cargo ship design. Hence it was a logical step to extend the work at Newcastle to warship structures; and the award of an MOD contract led to a detailed study of the weight optimisation of the framing structure of small, single-deck warships. Given the shape of the hull cross-section, the required hull section modulus, deck structure and plate thickness, together with a variety of design loading conditions on the hull, what are the optimum arrangements and corresponding scantlings of the internal framing of the hull?

A full account of this work is given in [11]. In small warships with a pronounced rise of floor, shearing and in-plane forces are more significant than in full-bodied tanker structures; and it was found helpful, in formulating the elastic response analysis for a compartment bounded by two transverse bulkheads, to devise a new composite plate-beam finite element. This led to a fast and efficient analysis model, which when linked to a sequential linear programming optimisation procedure, again produced good convergence towards minimum weight designs.

With a large number of free design variables defining the number, positions and scantlings of main frames and major longitudinals (the minor longitudinals being incorporated into the plate-beam elements) it was necessary to "regionalize" these variables, so that within given regions the variables had constant values. By adopting also practical ratios of width to thickness of flange and web elements, the number of design variables was reduced to 21, comprising web depth(d), and thickness(t_w) and flange thickness(t_f) in shell longitudinals(L) and frames(F) in each of three regions:- near deck(D), around bilge(B) and near keel(K), together with those three dimensions for the keel itself.

Time precluded any extensive application of this scheme to the design of small warship structures; but a few runs were made, with results of the kind summarized in Table 2.

It can be seen that:-
- after only 5 iteration cycles the optimisation process has already converged to a result very little different from that after a further 4 cycles.

- the final scantlings can differ quite markedly from the initial values. In this respect the optimisation scheme appears quite "robust".

- plate thickness constraints are often active.

TABLE 2
Weight Optimisation of Longitudinals and Frames of a Single-Deck Warship

Zone	Member	Dimension	Scantlings (Inches)		
			Initial	5 Cycles	9 Cycles
DECK	L_D	t_w	0.125	0.117	0.122
		t_f	0.187	0.202	0.201
		d^f	6.000	3.279	3.000
	F_D	t_w	0.187	0.234	0.237
		t_f	0.250	0.219	0.219
		d^f	8.000	10.548	10.679
BILGE	L_B	t_w	0.187	0.100	0.100
		t_f	0.250	0.170	0.171
		d^f	8.000	4.000	4.000
	F_B	t_w	0.250	0.205	0.204
		t_f	0.250	0.291	0.294
		d^f	10.000	9.209	9.172
KEEL	L_K	t_w	0.250	0.125	0.125
		t_f	0.250	0.139	0.139
		d^f	10.000	5.625	5.625
	F_K	t_w	0.250	0.333	0.333
		t_f	0.375	0.187	0.187
		d^f	12.000	20.744	20.764
	KEEL	t_w	0.250	0.500	0.500
		t_f	0.375	0.328	0.327
		d^f	12.000	22.500	22.500
WEIGHT (lbs)			19,074	14,100	14,139

In general it appeared from these limited experiments that such a procedure might lead to arrangements and scantlings significantly different from those conventionally used, and with corresponding scope for weight saving.

It is not known to what extent this work has been followed up by its sponsors. Since it was completed (in 1977) other optimisation procedures, notably that due to Hughes et.al [1] have, it is believed, found application in warship design. It would be of great interest, in relation to the title of this paper, to know in what way the design of warship structures has been influenced thereby.

4. DESIGNING FOR MINIMUM PRODUCTION COST

Early work by Evans and others [12] had shown clearly that there was an incompatibility between the objectives of minimisation of weight and of cost when standard design-by-rule is applied to the structures of conventional cargo ships. As competition in ship construction and operation grew keener, it was inevitable that interest in structural optimisation would change its emphasis from weight to cost. From the first studies in this area about 15 years ago [13] work at Newcastle has continued at various levels.

4.1 Preliminary Unconstrained Optimisation

At the simplest level it is possible by fairly primitive analysis to show that designs for minimum weight and cost are likely to differ markedly. Thus for a flat rectangular panel under uniform lateral pressure, consisting of plating reinforced by a regular set of parallel, equal stiffeners, it is not difficult to relate the total production cost (material plus labour) to the free variables : plate thickness (t), size (sectional area A) and spacing of stiffeners (s). These variables must of course also be such that material stress limits in plating and stiffeners are not exceeded under the specified pressure. If the labour cost is proportional to the plate-to-stiffener weld length, then by a process of unconstrained optimisation it can easily be shown [14] that, to minimize the cost of production, the design should be such that:-

$$\frac{st}{A} = (1 - m) + \frac{C_w}{C_s}$$

in which

A is assumed proportional to Z^m, in which m is typically about 2/3;

Z   = section modulus of stiffener (including plating);

C_w = labour cost of unit length of welded joint;

C_s = material cost of unit length of stiffener.

Since st/A is in fact the ratio of plating weight to stiffener weight, the above result shows that the optimal value of this ratio would be around 1/3 for the theoretical minimum weight design (ie. by neglecting labour costs, $C_w = 0$); but around 4/3 if $C_w = C_s$, and higher as C_w/C_s increases. Thus the value of this latter ratio turns out to have a major effect on the arrangement and scantlings of cost-optimal designs.

4.2 Panel Design Optimisation Using The Lagrange Multiplier Method

Clearly it was important to substantiate these rather simplistic results both by studying more thoroughly the costing element of this approach to structural design, and developing more rigorously the optimisation procedures. These were the objectives of Hewitt's work [15], some of which was described in ref. [16].

Cost optimisation raises the basic problem of assigning realistic costs to the various unit operations involved in structural fabrication and assembly. Hewitt's very detailed study used data from shipyard workstations to relate work content, manhours and labour costs, and also proposed a method of overhead allocation in the resulting calculation of production costs. These could then be related to the structural design variables, so that weight, costs and structural response to load could all be expressed as functions of both free (X) and fixed (Y) design variables. Hewitt also explored the use of a mixed objective function [13] involving "weighted" functions of weight and cost ratios:-

$$U = f(X,Y) = F\left(\frac{W}{W_o}\right) + (1 - F) \frac{C}{C_o}$$

in which F is a factor ($0 \leqslant F \leqslant 1$) controlling the relative importance of weight and cost. Constraints $g_i(X,Y) \geqslant 0$ were imposed on stresses, thicknesses and dimensional ratios (for buckling or production reasons). Then this constrained optimisation requires the solution of

$$\frac{\partial U}{\partial x_j} = \sum_{i=1}^{n} \lambda_i \frac{\partial g_i(X,Y)}{\partial x_j} \quad , \quad j = 1,2,\ldots n$$

in which λ_i are Lagrange Multipliers, such that

$$\lambda_i g_i(X,Y) = 0$$

$$g_i(X,Y) \geqslant 0$$

$$\lambda_i \geqslant 0$$

and $\lambda_i = \dfrac{\partial U^*}{\partial \bar{g}_i}(X,Y)$

where the asterisk denotes an optimum value.

By this means it proved possible to solve exactly the optimisation problem for singly-stiffened (px0) panels, or (px1) grillages, for minimum weight, or production cost, or to minimize the mixed function defined above. Application to practical cases confirmed again that the resulting design may differ markedly depending on the objective function, and therefore that production costs should not be regarded as proportional to the weight of the structure. Fig. 3 shows the sections of two panels designed for the same lateral pressure loading - one to minimize weight, the other production cost. The message is clear.

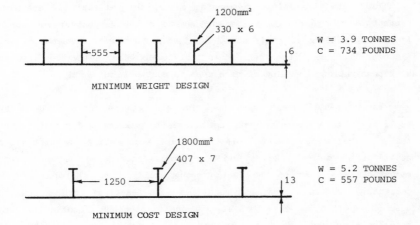

FIGURE 3.

4.3   Grillage Design

Despite the useful results obtained, Hewitt's work showed that searching for cost optimal designs by combining elastic stress analysis with the rigorous Lagrangian approach leads to extreme complexity if more than about six free design variables are involved. Work by Chowdhury [17] had shown that plastic or limit-state analysis appeared to offer a less cumbersome basis for the design of grillages under lateral loads; and this led into an extensive study [18] of strength analysis as an alternative basis for structural design and optimisation. A parallel objective was to examine the possibility of presenting for the designer more quantitative guidance as to the stiffening arrangements which would be attractive from the standpoint of reducing production costs.

It was necessary first to study very thoroughly, both theoretically and experimentally, the validity of strength analysis as applied to grids, and to find methods of identifying the appropriate collapse mechanism in any particular case. These procedures were then extended to grillages with orthogonal stiffening, with plating scantlings also derived from strength, rather than stress, analysis.

To determine grillage production costs, the material and overhead elements were treated in a similar way to ref. [15] but labour costs (including welding of stiffeners, fabricated girders, intersections and plate butts) were further refined to include auxiliary activities such as work preparation, handling of machines and post-welding work.

Having tested these procedures for strength and cost analysis by application to a pontoon deck, an oil-tight bulkhead and a watertight bulkhead, it was decided that rather than using sophisticated optimisation methods to identify optimal designs, a procedure of parametric searching of the design space would be more helpful to the designer in showing trends and penalties. In practical grillage design also it is often the case that for reasons of structural continuity with adjacent structure, the number or positions of girders are prescribed and should not be regarded as free variables.

So the eventual output of this approach to grillage design synthesis
has been a large number of "design charts" of which Fig. 4 is typical.
This shows, for a simply-supported grillage 18.8m x 25.0m under a 13m
pressure head with three cross-girders, how the total cost of production
will vary according to the number of stiffeners used, and the unit costs
involved. The results indicate that if material costs only are included
(hence the result is, for the materials selected, a minimum weight
design) the optimum design requires about 20 stiffeners. If labour costs
(stiffener welds S, girder welds G, intersection welds I) are included at
the "basic cost" rates shown, the optimum (least cost) design requires
14-16 stiffeners. But if these production cost rates are, say, 5 times
the basic rates shown, the optimum number of stiffeners reduces to only
8. Moreover the "sharpness" of the optimum increases rapidly with
production cost rates; so that the penalties for missing the optimum are
more severe. Such results confirm again the large differences which may

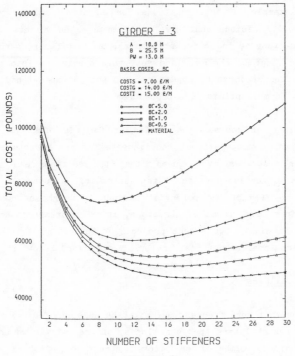

FIGURE 4.

exist between minimum weight and minimum cost designs, and this further underlines the importance of:

- a clear statement of design objectives.
- more reliable data on unit costs of production.
- the availability of design charts, such as Fig. 4, to guide designers towards more efficient designs.

5. THE CHOICE OF STRUCTURAL FORM

Of all the geometric design variables which influence the optimal design of structures, those concerned with the choice of form, or the overall configuration, are generally the most potent in their effect. Even in the elementary design exercises with students (Section 2 above), and in other early exploratory studies on the design of structural elements [2], it was very clear that the choice of structural form (as between, for example, a beam, a truss, or an arch) can be the most important of all decisions that have to be made. The variety of forms available, for example, in bridge structures, or in offshore structures, testify to the range of choice. And yet, this crucial decision between generically different forms of structure, has not yet been found capable of solution by formal optimisation procedures.

In practice, of course, the choice of form is often so heavily constrained either by operational requirements for the structure, or by the production processes to be used, that the designer can exercise rather little inventiveness in this aspect of structural design. Nevertheless, in view of the potential savings in weight or cost which might result from novel forms of structure, it is important to keep such possibilities in mind. Two recent projects, concerned with alternative forms for conventional structures, are briefly outlined below.

5.1 Pitched Grillages

The notion that more frequent use might be made, in designing marine structures to resist lateral pressure loads, of the well-known arch-like strength of hipped, cambered or pitched structures, instead of flat panels, was advanced in ref. [2]. This led to an extensive study [19], some results of which were reported in ref. [20]. Because of the essential three-dimensional nature of this form of structure and its response to load, and the key part played by in-plane compressive and shear stresses in the plating and stiffeners of pitched panels, it was first necessary to develop the general elastic analysis of such structures. This was then incorporated in a design procedure, together with explicit constraints on behaviour and dimensions, so that some possible practical applications of pitched panels could be investigated. In view of the exploratory nature, parametric search was felt to have more educational value in this study than use of formal optimisation techniques.

The results were very encouraging. For stiffened panels subject to lateral pressure, and having the overall dimensions, boundary conditions and stiffener configurations typical of, say, deep tank bulkheads in ships, it was found that by replacing conventional flat panels by optimally-designed pitched panels, weight savings of 25-45% could be achieved. Moreover, the optimum pitch angle, usually in the range 15°-25°, together with significant reductions in stiffener scantlings, resulted in pitched structures which do not appear incompatible either with space considerations, or with the need for economic and efficient production.

FLAT PANEL   PITCHED PANEL

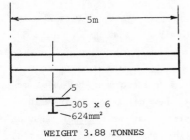

WEIGHT 3.88 TONNES   WEIGHT 2.62 TONNES

FIGURE 5.

Fig. 5 compares typical cross-sections of flat and pitched panels, 8m long and 5m high designed for a pressure head of 8m of fresh water above the base. Note that the superior efficiency of the pitched panel does not depend on the presence of restraint against transverse displacement at the ends of the stiffeners. Thus the concept appears worthy of further consideration where weight-saving is important. The underside of the cross-structure of twin-hulled vessels is one such possibility.

5.2 Corrugated or Sandwich Structures?

The conventional stiffened-plate element, whose use is so widespread in marine structures, represents an acceptable compromise between production convenience and tolerable (but not very good) structural efficiency. The alternative forms of this element, such as corrugated plating, have long been known [21] to offer improved efficiency through higher strength/weight ratios, but being considered less production-kindly, have not found such general adoption. It is well understood that the use of more "balanced" forms of stiffening elements would be desirable; and one possible form is the sandwich structure, as has been used to good effect in aircraft and other lightweight structures.

The potential benefits of sandwich structures for marine use were first studied at Newcastle by Guiton [22] in the early years of the development of glass-reinforced plastics. Guiton's experiments on structures comprising two laminated plates separated by a corrugated and foam-filled core confirmed their promising properties of strength and stiffness; but the concept has not been widely followed up in marine GRP work.

But more recently, interest in sandwich structures has been re-awakened by the discovery that, thanks to new developments in welding technology, it is now possible to contemplate the use of steel sandwich panels as a practical alternative to flat stiffened, or corrugated, plating. Although more work on production aspects needs to be done - and is in progress at Newcastle University - it is nevertheless of interest

now to explore further the comparative structural merits of these
alternative forms of steel structure.

This is being done by deriving, through formal optimisation (using
in this case an augmented Lagrangian Multiplier method), the minimum
weight designs for both corrugated and sandwich panels of various spans
between simple supports and loaded either by a uniform pressure head, or
by in-plane compressive stress. Both forms of structure have the
advantages, to the analyst, not only of symmetry, but also of being
completely defined by rather few (typically five) design variables.
Constraints have to be imposed on minimum plate thickness, and against
various modes of failure, including overall and local bending, buckling
and shearing.

The results can be expressed in the form of comprehensive charts, of
which Fig. 6 is typical. This shows, for corrugated plating, the minimum
achievable "effective thickness" (t_E) which, when multiplied by the
surface area (L x B) and the material weight density, gives the total
panel weight, over a wide range of spans (L) and pressure head loads (p).

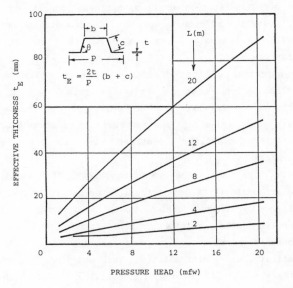

FIGURE 6.

Such results of optimisation analyses are valuable in showing designers what is achievable in overall weight terms, as well as detailed scantlings for specific cases. Charts similar to Fig. 6 are being prepared for steel sandwich structures, comprising two plates separated by a thin steel corrugated core. From preliminary results it is of interest to note two points:-

- whereas the optimum trough angle θ of corrugated plating is around 60°, in sandwich structures it is generally nearer 30°.

- the attainable efficiency (strength to weight ratio) of sandwich panels is critically dependent on the permissible minimum plate thickness. With present limitations, the sandwich structure is unlikely to offer any saving in weight, although it does have other very attractive and important attributes.

6. OTHER RECENT STUDIES IN BRIEF

During the past two years, work at Newcastle has continued [23] on both the theory and application of formal optimisation methods for marine structures. Limitation of space precludes full description here of this work which will be presented in a sequel paper. The main lines of development have been:-
- a re-appraisal of the efficiency and reliability of the many optimisation procedures now available, by testing them in various structural applications such as grillages and frameworks. It appears that some of the established methods suffer from numerical instability problems in handling non-linear constraints.
- investigation of the applicability of multi-objective optimisation to stiffened-plate structures. It is characteristic of marine structural design that the designer is frequently confronted with multiple, conflicting, and often non-commensurable objectives, such as weight, cost, space, reliability, or maintainability. This study has explored the use of "Pareto-optimal" solutions, involving a "weighting minimax

581

method" by which, for example, the "best" combination of low
weight and low risk of failure might be identified.

- application of reliability-based optimisation, by bringing
  together two lines of research (at Newcastle and elsewhere),
  namely, on structural reliability and design optimisation.

This latter work is exemplified in Fig. 7. For a 3 x 3 regular
simply-supported grillage under central point load P, if a limit state
design is used, the two design variables to be optimised are the fully
plastic bending moments (PBM) of the two sets of stiffeners. Using a
reliability-based optimisation method, the optimum (minimum weight W)
design points corresponding to a range of safety factors (SF) and the
associated probabilities of failure (PF) can be derived as shown in Fig.
7. Such studies can help not only to establish clear quantitative
indications of the sensitivity of structural weight (and material costs)
to the probability of failure, but also enable the designer to determine
the best combination of design variables for any prescribed risk of
failure.

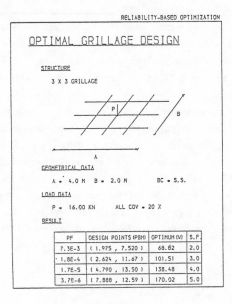

FIGURE 7.

7. CONCLUSIONS

The work of one research group has ranged from the design of simple elements to complex three-dimensional structures, using design and optimisation techniques likewise varying from the simple to the sophisticated. What conclusions can be drawn from these many man-years of effort which may help to answer the question posed in the title of the paper?

(i)   The science of optimisation has outstripped the practice. A wide range of applicable techniques is now available, though care is needed in selecting the best method for the job in hand.

(ii) Provided the designer can specify his objective, or can rank, or weight, a number of desirable properties of his design, then it is possible, in principle, to guide him towards the "best" design.

(iii) However, it is essential that continuing effort is made to quantify the factors involved, such as production costs, parameter variabilities, load statistics etc.

(iv) It is also essential to state, explicitly and logically, all constraints affecting design, since one or more will inevitably be active. Safety margins, and thickness or other dimensional limits, are especially critical in their effects on attainable quality.

(v)   There is still evidently much potential for improving the quality of design of marine structures. Investigation of alternative structural forms should be encouraged.

(vi) Until optimisation procedures and packages are more widely used, their chief value is in generating guidance for designers, for example through design charts and data sheets.

(vii) Educational programmes, including up-dating courses, should provide a better balance between structural design synthesis and analysis.

ACKNOWLEDGEMENTS

If this paper has appeared to pay scant regard to a great deal of pioneering work on structural optimisation elsewhere around the world, (and in UK, for example, currently at the Universities of Glasgow and Southampton) this is only because within the prescribed confines of the paper it has been difficult enough to do justice to 15 years' work of only one research group. Certainly the author, and his colleagues mentioned above, have been very conscious of the debt they owe to the ideas and methods of many other people too numerous to mention here, or list in the references. Just as structural optimisation has benefitted from their effort, so also has marine structures research and design benefitted in a more general way from many distinguished contributions from the Admiralty Research Establishment here in Dunfermline. It is a pleasure to have this opportunity to pay tribute in particular to the outstanding work of Bill Kendrick, whose work in the past 25 years has done so much to advance the science and practice of marine structures.

REFERENCES

1. Hughes, O.F. Ship structural design. Wiley Interscience, New York, 1983.

2. Caldwell, J.B. and Woodhead, R.G. Ship structures : some possibilities for improvement. Trans N.E.C.I.E.S. 89 (1974).

3. Kyratsous, E. Note on grillage design. University of Newcastle upon Tyne (1984). Unpublished.

4. Moe, J. Ship structure optimisation. Int. Symp. on Computers in Optimisation of Structural Design. Swansea (1972).

5. Woodhead, R.G. The application of optimisation methods to structural design. BSRA Tech. Memo 412. Wallsend (1972).

6. Chow, Y.T. Optimisation of grillages. B.Sc. thesis. University of Newcastle upon Tyne (1972).

7. Clarkson, J. The elastic analysis of flat grillages. Cambridge University Press (1965).

8. Smith, G.K. Design optimisation of mammoth oil tanker structures. Ph.D. thesis. University of Newcastle upon Tyne. (1973).

9. Smith, G.K. and Woodhead, R.G. A design scheme for ship structures. Trans. R.I.N.A. 115 (1973) 47-58.

10. Smith G.K. and Woodhead, R.G. An optimal design scheme with application to tanker transverse structure. Int. Symp. on Optimisation in Civil Engineering. Liverpool (1973).

11. Chowdhury, M. The optimal design of ship structures. Ph.D. thesis. University of Newcastle upon Tyne (1977).

12. Evans, J.H. Ship structural design concepts. Cornell Maritime Press. Cambridge (1975).

13. Caldwell, J.B. Design for production. De Ingenier 84 (1972).

14. Caldwell, J.B. Design for production. 1st WEGEMT School on Advanced Ship Design Techniques. Newcastle. (1978).

15. Hewitt, A.D. Production-oriented design of ship structures. Ph.D. thesis. University of Newcastle upon Tyne. (1976).

16. Caldwell, J.B. and Hewitt, A.D. Towards cost-effective design of ship structures. Paper 18. Int. Conf. on Structural Design and Fabrication in Shipbuilding. Welding Institute, London (1975).

17. Caldwell, J.B. and Chowdhury, M. Grids and grillages : strength analysis and design. Proc. Int. Symp. on Steel Plated Structures. Paper 30. London (1977).

18. Kim, K.S. Strength analysis as a basis for structural design and optimisation. Ph.D. thesis. University of Newcastle upon Tyne.

19. El Somokhly, S.Y. Pitched structures in ships : theory and design. Ph.D. thesis. University of Newcastle upon Tyne. (1981).

20. Caldwell, J.B. and El Somokhly, S.Y. Pitched structures in ships, analysis, design and applications. Trans. RINA 125 (1983).

21. Caldwell, J.B. The strength of corrugated plating for ships' bulkheads. Trans. RINA 98 (1955) 495.

22. Guiton, J. Glass-reinforced plastic ship construction. M.Sc. thesis. University of Newcastle upon Tyne (1968).

23. Yang, Y.S. Marine hazard assessment. Ph.D. thesis. University of Newcastle upon Tyne (1985).

DEVELOPMENTS IN FINITE ELEMENT ANALYSIS OF NAVAL STRUCTURES

J D McVee
Admiralty Research Establishment
Dunfermline, Fife, Scotland

ABSTRACT

The history of the application of linear finite element techniques to structural problems at ARE (Dunfermline) is briefly reviewed. Static elastic analyses of surface ships using SESAM-69C to investigate hull deckhouse interaction and more recently to provide fatigue design information are described. Case studies of the use of MSC/NASTRAN coupled with the interactive graphic pre and postprocessors FEMGEN and FEMVIEW to solve penetration and buckling problems arising in submarine design are presented.

Current difficulties in large scale detailed analysis of first of class designs are identified and interfaces with CAD systems discussed. Advantages to be gained by the use of suitably configured supercomputers are demonstrated.

INTRODUCTION

The development and application of linear elastic finite element techniques to naval structures at ARE (Dunfermline) dates back to the late nineteen fifties when Yuille and Wilson [1] produced a curved grillage analysis applicable to a complete ship section between bulkheads [2]. Concurrent work by Kendrick [3] concerning the elastic deformation of axisymmetric thin shells resulted in the early 1960s in a Pegasus autocode computer program [4, 5] for the axisymmetric stress analysis of submarine structures and ancillary programs were developed for the subsequent idealisation of structural components such as decks and bulkheads which, once the loading had been adequately determined, could be analysed as plane frames [6] or grillages [7]. The axisymmetric program, later adapted and rewritten in FORTRAN by Hurwitz and Cuthill [8] is still very much in use as a highly regarded design tool and has been incorporated, along with a variety of ARE (Dunfermline) structural programs, in the GODDESS ship design system [9].

As the 1960s progressed, the machine coded curved grillage program was superseded by the more general KDF9 autocoded ICSL structural analysis program [10] which contained quadrilateral and triangular membrane plate elements in addition to six degree of freedom beam elements. As a result of its three dimensional application, using relatively coarse meshes, to submarine structural problems and the analysis of supertankers [11] a special purpose suite of FORTRAN programs for tanker transverse strength analysis was developed [12] in which refined 2D analysis of areas of interest was facilitated by automatically extracting and redistributing loads obtained from the 3D analysis. Experience gained by this project [13] and others [14] demonstrated the practical advantages in modelling, datageneration, computation and reanalysis to be gained at that time from an efficient user-orientated implementation of the superelement technique and, subsequent to a comprehensive multi-level analysis of the first of class VSTOL carriers [15] influenced the use of SESAM-69C [16] by ARE (Dunfermline) throughout the 1970s. Major applications during this period included finite element models of a 2/3 scale MCMV test section [17] and several studies of hull deckhouse interaction [18, 19] which demonstrated correlation between computed and experimental stresses and deflections. Many other analyses, some of which used MSC/NASTRAN [20], relating to stress concentrations adjacent to deck penetrations [15, 21], the design of bulkhead stiffeners and hull longitudinals in glass reinforced plastic (GRP) materials [21], the elastic response of initialy deformed stiffened cylinders [22] and element accuracy [23] were also carried out.

During the 1980s, the acquisition of a medium power (1.8 Mip) in-house Digital VAX-11/782 tightly coupled asymmetric twin processing computer system with 8 Mbytes of shared memory and 3 Gbytes of on-line disk storage with VMS implementations of MSC/NASTRAN and SESAM-69C has significantly increased the number, size and scope of analyses undertaken at ARE. In particular extensive application of the MSC/NASTRAN linear buckling capability and the superelement capability [24], introduced as a standard solution sequence in the late 1970s, has been made to a variety of submarine structural problems via interfaces to the FEMGEN [25] and FEMVIEW [26] pre and postprocessing systems. SESAM-69C continues to be used, especially for surface ships, in parallel with the recently implemented SESAM'80 [27] which has a fully integrated graphics preprocessor incorporating interactive superelement assembly and a FEMVIEW based postprocessor.

The interactive graphic processors are driven from Tektronix 4128 and 4113 colour terminals and Tektronix 4014 and low resolution Digital VT240 monochrome terminals. Direct screen hard copy is available via a rasterized colour hard copy unit multiplexed to the 4128 and 4113 and a monochrome unit attached to the 4014. On-line plots can be obtained on either 11" or 22" Versatec plotters via the VAX.

SURFACE SHIPS

Within the last ten years, various linear elastic finite element analyses have been carried out of the hull with, and without, the superstructure of various types of surface ships subjected to a given longitudinal hull girder bending moment distribution based upon a static balance in a design wave.

Figure 1 illustrates the complexity and size of a typical 4844 degree of freedom (dof) late 1970s multi-level SESAM-69C superelement (SEL) model [18] judged necessary to provide adequate definition of the force interaction between the hull and deckhouse and to determine average stress

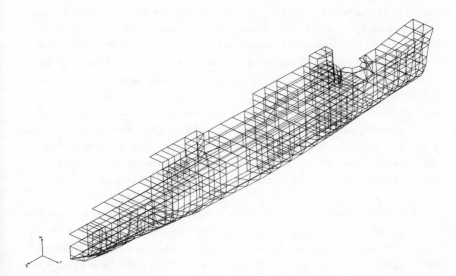

FIGURE 1. Symmetric Finite Element Idealisation of a Surface Ship with Typical Coarse Mesh Discretisation for Load Path Analysis.

distributions throughout the regions of obvious interest at the hull deck-house interface, particularly at the deckhouse ends. The model assumed a centreline plane of transverse symmetry, omitted minor hull bulkheads, the funnel and masts and incorporated the structurally weakest option where transverse symmetry does not exist in the ship. Hull structure fore and aft of the deckhouse was included in order to minimise errors induced by assumed boundary conditions. Continuous hull structure which comprised 1 and 2 decks and the curved side shell and bottom were idealised as stiffened thin faceted shell SELs with the discontinuous 3 and 4 decks and the transverse bulkheads idealised as 2D membrane SELs and the entire deckhouse by 3D membrane SELs. All the plated structure was modelled using lower order quadrilateral or, if necessary, triangular elements with constant thickness equal to the average thickness of the actual structural plating. The frames, longitudinals and girders which stiffen the plating were represented by grouping them together into lumped beams with equiv-alent cross sectional areas and, for the thin shell idealisations, in-plane inertias, out-of-plane inertias including the contributions of an effective breadth of associated plating and nominal torsional rigidities. In total the model consisted of 3419 elements of which 999 were quadrilaterals, 197 were triangles and 2223 were beams. It was composed of three levels of superelements and comprised 56 basic first level thin shell or membrane SELs distributed throughout seven second level assemblies each of which represented a complete longitudinal section of the ship. Strict geometric tolerances were specified at coincident supernodes and, where necessary, nodal linear dependence on adjacent nodes was used to accommodate unequal mesh gradings along SEL boundaries taking care not to adversely affect the SEL bandwidths which were minimised at each level. Response of the hull alone was readily achieved by deleting the first level deckhouse SELs from the relevant four second level assemblies and solving the resulting 4040 dof, 2783 element model on the fourth level.

Analysis of the results quantified the significant contribution of the deckhouse to the effective midship section modulus and for the particular configuration of deckhouse attachment considered, the relative increase in the longitudinal and shear stresses in the vicinity of the deckhouse ends and the vertical stresses in the hull bulkheads. In addition, hard spots where the deckhouse sides intersect with supporting hull bulkheads were identified, but owing to the relative coarseness of the idealisation the

589

attendant stress concentration factors could only be obtained by successive
mesh refinement or experimental testing. Comparison with full scale
measurements obtained from ships in service showed that the computed stress
distributions were consistent with available longitudinal bending strains
and excellent agreement was obtained with average ratios of 01 to 1 deck
longitudinal stresses. Moreover it was demonstrated that classical
solutions [28] to the perennial naval architectural problem of hull-
deckhouse interaction are inferior to solutions obtained by suitable finite
element discretisations in the detail and accuracy of design information
that can be obtained. However, even using a program with relatively powerful datageneration facilities, the application of finite element techniques
has proved to be extremely labour intensive when modelling complicated ship
structures from scantlings extracted from ship drawings.

In order to reduce the tedious, time-consuming and error-prone phase
of preparing data for such calculations, the experience gained from the
aforementioned analysis was used to develop and test a preprocessor [29]
for automatic coarse discretisation of the complete, or partial, length of
the ship's structure from minimum data input. The preprocessor computes
the topology of the primary components of the model from transverse section
offsets at various stations along the length of the ship and other given
data consists solely of plating thicknesses and stiffener cross sectional
areas and inertias. Encoded SESAM-69C data is written to a disk file in an
input format which automatically generates second level SELs, corresponding
to each predefined ship section, which have then to be manually assembled
on third or higher levels to form the complete model. A separate preprocessor [30] evaluates and discretises the net vertical loads and equili-
brating end bending moments and shear forces, if any, from given vertical
shear forces and longitudinal bending moments at the ship ordinates. With
the exception of the side shell and weather deck which are idealised as
stiffened thin shells, the remaining first level SELs are stiffened membranes. Succcessful and efficient application of this preprocessor was made
in the generation of a 4689 dof, 4464 element model of an as-built patrol
craft and the partial generation of the significantly more detailed 19617
dof, 9534 element model of another surface ship.

With the increasing importance being given to fatigue as a design
criterion [31, 32], much finer mesh density is mandatory in order to

provide adequate stress estimates in potentially susceptible regions of the
hull particularly between 2 deck and 01 deck. Figure 2 illustrates a four
level, 33353 dof, 13340 element model of the after end of a surface ship
directly generated for this purpose in which each stiffener in the side
shell and transverse hull bulkheads above 2 deck and in 1 and 01 decks are
separately idealised and the relatively finer mesh density around cut-outs
is continued in way of adjacent structural idealisations in order to avoid
any errors induced by linearly dependent mesh grading. For various reasons
FEMGEN did not prove to be particularly amenable to generation of this
SESAM-69C model and the topology preprocessor [29] was too rudimentary and
restrictive. Datageneration was aided by the development of a beam generation program [33] which automatically produced the relevant SESAM-69C
input including cross sectional areas and inertias incorporating effective
breadths of plating from given stiffener types, spacing and plating thicknesses. The hull consisted of five second level SELs assembled on the
third level and the deckhouse comprised two second level SELs which were
coupled to the third level hull assembly and solved on the fourth level

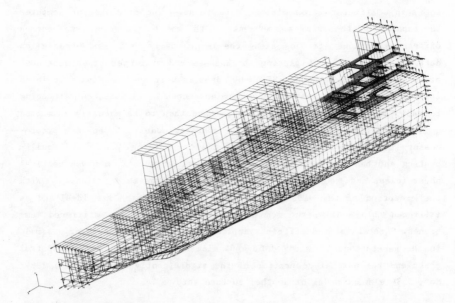

FIGURE 2. Symmetric Finite Element Idealisation of a Surface Ship with
Typical Mesh Grading for Identification of Stress Concentrations.

enabling variations in the deckhouse configurations to be readily investigated, if necessary. All the vertical loads were applied to the first level side shell SELs with the longitudinal forces corresponding to equivalent end bending moments applied to appropriately retained fourth level nodes by adaption of [30]. Error free VAX 11/782 computing cpu times used by this calculation amounted to 45 minutes for datageneration and 33 hours 40 minutes for solution of which 2 hours 40 minutes was devoted to complete retracking of element forces, stresses and nodal deflections throughout the model. Reanalysis with new load vectors and full retracking required 10 hours cpu time. The input data, basic restart file and solution output occupied 1 Mbyte, 75 Mbytes and 18 Mbytes of disk space respectively.

Initial validation of results consisted of ensuring that all the diagonal decomposition ratios and the computed Euclidean norms of the out of balance and applied nodal forces were satisfactory and that there was no obvious irregularities in the plotted displacements which were of the same magnitude as those obtained from an analogous simple beam calculation. Equilibrium was confirmed by examining vertical reaction forces and ensuring that the computed longitudinal bending moment at midships equalled the applied bending moment. These checks which were expedited using specially written postprocessors [34] revealed deficiencies in the original model and several corrective reruns were necessary before proceeding with some confidence to a more detailed examination, again utilising [34], of load paths and the most highly stressed regions of interest where further analyses and convergence studies were undertaken using separate refined models.

Although the recent dramatic decrease in computer and intelligent high resolution terminal hardware price/performance ratios and continuous, often user driven, improvements in proprietary software now makes large scale linear finite element analysis of entire surface ships possible on in-house supermini computers with adequate disk space, first of class calculations are still inevitably bedevilled by initial lack of detailed preliminary design information at the outset. In addition numerous significant scantling changes have to be continuously monitored and incorporated into the idealisation as the final design evolves during a still too extensive time scale, not only of model generation and modification but, notwithstanding the advantages of superelements, also for solution processing, reanalysis and presentation of validated results. Such calculations undoubtedly yield most useful research and development information for future vessels but are often of only belated use to the first of class designers and builders. Moreover further modifications to the final design finite element model are necessary to produce an as-built model which may require a change in emphasis in mesh density and scantling details in many regions of the structure in order to provide an analytical device for ready evaluation of necessary structural additions or modifications during the ship's life and to downstream members and future batches of the class.

It is envisaged that turn round time would be significantly reduced by utilising mature ship design systems which store the complete structural design, and related loads, in a database form that is regularly and reliably updated by the designers and builders in order that the current design scantlings could be readily retrieved in a standard easily portable format. Such a scheme would rely on the development of specialised expert preprocessors, necessarily interfacing with a number of finite element systems depending on the primary aim of the analysis, to rapidly produce a series of increasingly sophisticated and eventually modified models corresponding to the degree of design information available in the database. Relatively coarse load path analysis would be followed by more detailed models of partial sections of the ship leading to extensively detailed models incorporating typical geometrical imperfection patterns, stiffeners idealised as plates, or shells, brackets and intercostal details. Obviously linear elastic static, buckling or dynamic calculations of this class would rely on supercomputer power for processing and extensive development of expert postprocessors, implemented on local host driven high performance interactive graphic terminals, to fully utilise the potential of such models in terms of effectively improving structural designs before build and obviating, or at least minimising, expensive structural modifications during or after fabrication.

SUBMARINES

Recent finite element analyses of submarine structures has included several MSC/NASTRAN calculations relating to the development of forward end domes, hull bulkheads and GRP deck casings.

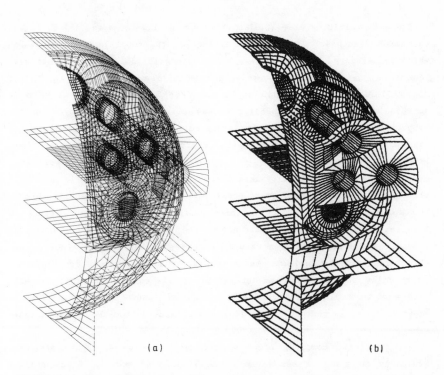

FIGURE 3a and b. (a) Symmetric Finite Element Idealisation with (b) Hidden Line Removal Plot of a Forward End Dome.

Figure 3a shows the superelement idealisation of a 1/5th scale forward end dome experimental model fabricated and tested under uniform external pressure at ARE (Dunfermline). The finite element model [35] utilised the centre line plane of transverse symmetry and consisted of seventeen first level superelements with an intermediate connector to the residual struc-ture. FEMGEN was used initially to generate the complete model as a series of suitably concatenated patches. Twenty noded curved isoparametric solid hexahedron elements were employed within and adjacent to the penetrated surface of the dome and along the torpedo tubes adjoining the dome inter-sections with the remainder of the dome, torpedo tubes, decks and support structure represented by eight noded curved isoparametric quadrilateral shell elements with stiffeners idealised as beams. Within this complex model the aim of keeping the mesh as coarse as possible while taking account of stiffener positioning, maintaining reasonable element aspect ratios and minimising element distortion controlled the size, and shape, of the FEMGEN patches. This in turn influenced the superelement subdivision which was achieved by developing a utility program [36] which automatically generated the relevant superelement definition data from the basic MSC/NASTRAN bulk data produced by the PRENAS interface to the FEMGEN database in which each superelement was originally defined by a unique property identification tag being assigned to all the elements within it. Care was taken to ensure that heavily distorted elements, generated where FEMGEN patches necessarily had two sides forming one boundary, were kept clear of the areas of primary interest. Transition between solid and shell elements was accomplished, where possible, by overlaying the shells through the solids and elsewhere by defining suitable multipoint constraints to transfer edge bending moments along the interface. The unmodelled cylindrical support ring was assumed to exert encastre constraints on the structure which was subjected to uniform external pressure loading applied, by manually editing the bulk data file, to all exterior element surfaces with equivalent longitudinal loads imposed corresponding to the pressure exerted on the torpedo tube ends which were omitted from the idealisation.

Significant computer cpu time and on-line disk storage space were necessary to generate and process the 75,569 dof model. High priority interactive and lower priority batch VAX-11/780 cpu time required for preprocessing was of the order of 150 hours spread over several months. Error free batch cpu time for FEMGEN model generation which extended the database from 0.1 Mbyte to 5 Mbyte, amounted to 3.5 hours and 1 hour 20 minutes of interactive cpu time was required to produce the hidden line removal plot shown in Figure 3b, on a Tektronix 4014 screen. Initial MSC/NASTRAN superelement model checkout using solution sequence (SOL) 60 enabled the bulk data to be stored in a disk database of suitable maximum size together with user transparent resequencing of first level interior node numbering in order to reduce superelement band widths prior to providing estimates for computation times and storage requirements required primarily for stiffness matrix generation, assembly, reduction and solution subject to the single given load vector. Further checking was performed by examining undeformed structure plots and load vectors obtained from a superelement SOL61 restart limited to the generation of element stiffness and load matrices. Since the predicted disk storage requirement was greater than available on-line disk space, the model was processed mostly during weekends as a series of staged SOL61 restarts using a database. This consisted of the union of a permanent on-line 500 Mbyte downstream database, which contained the bulk data, superelement map and eventually the reduced superelement stiffness and load matrices together with the solution for the residual structure and several removable upstream database subsets which stored the computed matrices required for reduction and retracking of one or more superelements on removable 167 Mbyte disks with the exception of the connector which, owing to its size, required a larger fixed on-line disk for storage with the reduction necessarily performed, by utilising the FIXEDB parameter, in two stages owing to a mid-week machine failure during the elapse time of 170 hours. The postprocessing files required as input to the POSTNAS interface to FEMVIEW were generated by the subsequent relatively undemanding residual structure solution and individual superelement retracks which, in spite of being very efficient, required the relevant database subsets to be on-line. Although the error free cpu time for the calculation was 320 hours 9 minutes with a nominal elapse time in a low priority background batch queue of 438 hours 54 minutes, the actual elapse time was two months. This was primarily due to competition for extended use of both removable and fixed disk space, necessary scheduling to avoid known hardware or software maintenance periods and on only two occasions machine memory errors. Even using database subsets the disk storage demands were crucial since in addition to the total database size of 1.3 Gbytes, scratch space of up to 100 Mbytes and 200 Mbytes was needed to process the first level superelements and the connector respectively. In addition the expedient necessity to carry out double 6250 bpi magnetic tape back-ups of the upstream and downstream database subsets after each stage of the calculation imposed a not insignificant housekeeping task limited to day shift operating conditions, as were the reloads when two of the disks containing upstream database subsets developed hard errors during retracking. Moreover if a 456 Mbyte RA81 disk rather than a 512 Mbyte RP07 disk had been used for the downstream database then disk binding to form a suitably sized multi-disk file with subsequent reload of the back-up file and a rerun amounting to an additional 50 cpu hours would have been necessary to complete the reduction of the connector.

Comparative cpu, I/O wait, database channel and elapse times for processing the datachecked model directly, without recourse to database

TABLE 1
Comparative Dedicated CRAY Processing Statistics for Dome Model.

CPU Type	COS Version	Database Disc Device	MSC/NASTRAN SOL61 Version	CPU Time (secs)	I/O Wait Time (secs)	Database Channel Time (secs)	Elapse Time
1S-1000	1.12BF2D	DD-29's	63	7803	5801	2778	3 hrs 51 mins
X-MP/12	1.13BF3	DD-49's	64	5318	3711	1435	2 hrs 36 mins
Ratio X/1S	-	-	-	0.68	0.64	0.52	0.68

subsets or restarts and with no binary output for FEMVIEW or NASTRAN plots on dedicted one megaword CRAY 1S/1000 and CRAY X-MP/12 supercomputers are given in Table 1 which shows the respective vector processor and disk configurations to be in this instance 146 and 215 times faster than the VAX 11/782 configuration with respect to cpu time and 114 and 168 times faster in elapse time. The most significant gain in cpu time, by factors of 233 and 364 respectively was achieved during the collector phase. Part of the enhanced CRAY performance was due to the directly available 6.32 Mbytes of core memory, which dramatically reduced spill to disk and the resulting size of the scratch files, compared to the VAX where the core store working set size and extent were fixed at .5 Mbyte and 1.25 Mbyte respectively. Owing to the 1.3 Gbyte database generated during the processing, the use of database subsets and a limited number of staged restarts with concurrent degradation in elapse time would still be necessary under presently typical CRAY data centre batch operating conditions and disk subsystem resources. It has however been demonstrated that CRAY processing of models of this size and complexity would be routine provided that rapid file transfer to and from the I/O subsystem and front end processor peripherals is possible and, in particular, binary output file translation in a form suitable for onward kilostream transmission to remotely networked locations is efficiently implemented.

As usual extensive results validation was carried out including checks of total and maximum static reactions, maximum displacements and grid point force balance in addition to careful examination of residual norms of computed nodal forces, strain energy density and stiffness matrix diagonal decomposition ratios. The POSTNAS interface was then used to create the FEMVIEW database from which a detailed examination of the computed stresses and displacements throughout the model was obtained, greatly aided by

79·0
55·9
32·9
9·89

FIGURE 3c. Dimensionless von-Mises Stress Distribution on Dome Surface in Superelement Adjacent to Torpedo Tube Penetration.

hidden line removal plots of displacements, element stress components and von-Mises stresses as illustrated in Figure 3c. In addition, the MSC/NASTRAN stress sorting utility was used to order stress components.

A full scale GRP submarine hull casing test section, Figure 4a, consisting of a shell stiffened by five internal frames with a centrally placed reinforced circular opening has been subjected to various design and proof load tests in the Large Test Frame at ARE (Dunfermline). Initial tests consisted of simulated symmetric and asymmetric design loading by applying constant pressure to the casing top alone and to the top and one side.

FIGURE 4a. Casing Test Structure and Detail of Tripping Bracket Failure.

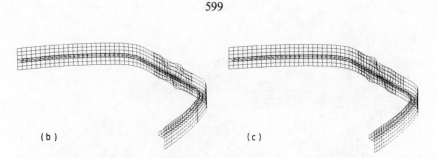

(b)   (c)

FIGURE 4b and c.   Predicted Buckling Mode Shape of (b) Symmetrically and
(c) Asymmetrically Loaded Unpenetrated Casing, of Infinite Length, with
Equally Spaced Identical Frames.

By imposing suitable boundary constraints simplified MSC/NASTRAN
models [37], built entirely from the well known lower order QUAD4 elements,
of one strip extending between two adjacent mid bay positions of a similar
simply supported unpenetrated casing of infinite length were generated via
FEMGEN using digitised profiles taken directly from the structural drawings
and processed using SOL5 to obtain pre-experimental estimates of the linear
displacements, stress distribution, buckling loads and corresponding
buckled shapes as shown in Figures 4b and 4c.   This simplified analysis,
which included transverse shear deflection, indicated that shell buckling
failure could be possible for loads slightly below the symmetric proof load
level at which none of the stress components exceeded ultimate strength
values but shear stresses in the frame web flange joints and the shell at
the casing top, although only 60% of the ultimate strength value, were more
than double the resin interlaminar shear strength.   Since this region was
unrepresentative in the original simplified model an idealisation more
closely resembling the tested structure was a necessary requirement for an
accurate prediction of proof load response.

Figure 5a shows a plot of such a FEMGEN generated MSC/NASTRAN model
which, in addition to incorporating the circular penetration, combing and
tripping brackets exactly represents the geometry of the frames including
the directions of the asymmetric flanges, the bottom flares and the line of
the frame web attachment to the shell which results in decreased stiffener
spacing in the casing top.   The casing attachment to the hull by mounting
plates bolted to each frame flare was idealised by constraining all nodal
freedoms throughout the areas covered by the mounting plates with the
exception of the rotations in the plane of each frame.   In addition to the

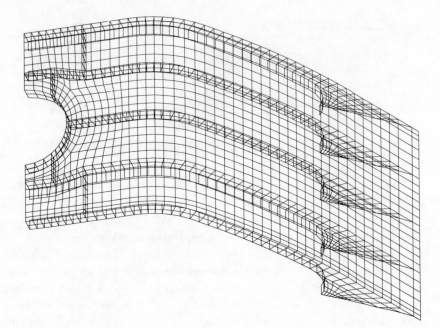

FIGURE 5a. Symmetric Finite Element Idealisation of Casing Test Section (viewed from underside).

pressure load applied to the casing top, point loads, equivalent to those exerted by pressure on the plate which spans the circular penetration in the experimental configuration, were applied to the casing nodes on the periphery of the hatch. MSC/NASTRAN processing of the resulting 10864 dof, 1962 element model with symmetric boundary conditions imposed along the centreline plane of symmetry for the elastic response and, in addition, antisymmetric conditions for the buckling response required 22.5 hours total cpu time.

Figure 5b shows the exaggerated shape of the elastically deformed casing model with maximum deflections, occurring at the transverse centre of the intermediate frames being identical to the experimental measurements. It also highlights the stiffening effects of the thicker casing material and the coaming surrounding the circular penetration both of which contribute to a marked dishing of the casing top to either side of the central frame in accordance with the experimental proof test which, as shown in Figure 4a, resulted in failure at the intersection of the outer

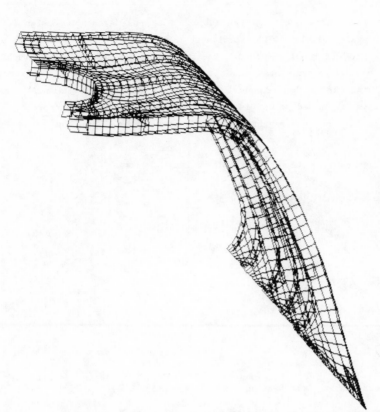

FIGURE 5b. Hidden Line Removal Plot of Exaggerated Deformed Casing Shape
Predicted by Symmetrically Loaded Finite Element Model.

tripping bracket and the intermediate frame where shear stresses marginally
greater than the ultimate shear stress of the GRP were predicted. Confirmation of the shear failure was obtained from the linear buckling analyses
which suggested a lowest positive eigenvalue corresponding to a load of
approximately twice the proof load and a mode shape indicating buckling of
the casing top between the centreline and the tripping bracket in the end
bay.

Figure 6a shows a model of the complete casing formed by mirroring and
merging the model of half the casing in a separate FEMGEN database. After
confirming the above results, the model was processed using the superelement solution sequences to calculate the elastic stresses and

deflections of the casing when subjected to the asymmetric design loads, which again correlate with experiment. Since the linear static solution of the 21710 dof model required 3 hours 40 minutes cpu time, SOL65 buckling analyses requiring 34.5 hours cpu time were carried out by restarts utilising the 73 Mbyte database generated by SOL61 to determine the lowest positive eigenload which is significantly higher than the proof load. Figure 6b shows the magnified displacements obtained from one of a series

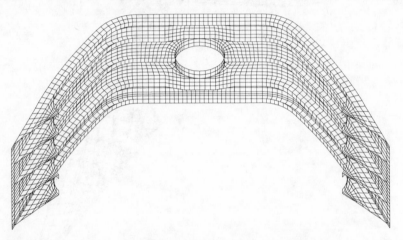

FIGURE 6a. Hidden Line Removal Plot of Finite Element Idealisation of Complete Casing Test Section (viewed from underside).

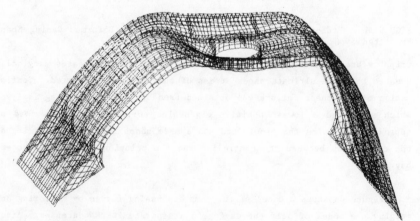

FIGURE 6b. Exaggerated Deformed Casing Shape Predicted by Finite Element Model subjected to Asymmetric Point Load.

of static analysis undertaken to identify the most critical regions of the casing in which to conduct dynamic drop tests simulating impacts from practice torpedoes. These calculations again utilised the SOL61 database to compute the solution for each new quasi-static load vector in a cpu time of 35 minutes.

A typical model used in an extensive study of submarine hull bulkhead integrity is shown in Figure 7. Various automatically generated out of circularities were assumed for the more coarsely modelled stiffened hull which was splined to the finer mesh grading used in the bulkhead. After rigorous examination of the SOL24 linear static response of the 4584 dof, 2030 element model which took 44 minutes cpu time, SOL5 linear buckling analyses, incorporating modifications to the longitudinal plane of symmetry constraints imposed on the bulkhead were carried out with cpu times of

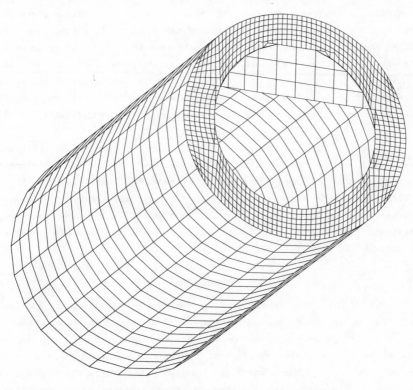

FIGURE 7. Hull Bulkhead Idealisation.

2 hours 10 minutes to extract the lowest eigenvalue and 19 hours 45 minutes to calculate the lowest ten eigenvalues. Further studies were carried out on more detailed models of the bulkhead using boundary conditions extracted from models incorporating the hull. Relevant techniques successfully applied in these analyses have been built into a specialised preprocessor [38] which automatically generates MSC/NASTRAN data to analyse hull bulkheads at cylinder/cone intersections.

MISCELLANEOUS DETAILED ANALYSES

In addition to major analyses, a selection of which have been described above, other smaller but more finely detailed linear analyses have recently included plane strain studies to determine the stress concentration factors in GRP interlaminar tensile strength specimens with U, V and saw-cut notch shapes [39], in various configurations of steel and carbon fibre reinforced plastic patches bonded to cracked aluminium plate [40] and in flexible resins used for bonding GRP frame-shell connections [41]. Other studies have been undertaken to calculate the effects of decks on the stress distribution in short submarine compartments [42], to determine equivalent membrane, bending and shear stiffness and accompanying stress fields for stiffened corrugated panels subject to unit displacements [43] and to parametrically evaluate GRP bulkhead stiffener configurations [44].

Accuracy studies involving the application of Robinson's well known tests [45, 46] to the SESAM-69C lower order membrane and bending elements and the SESAM'80 lower order membranes have been carried out [47] and MSC/NASTRAN QUAD4 linear buckling solutions for rectangular plates under either combined in-plane bending and compression or in-plane shear have been shown to provide accurate solutions compared to classical analytical solutions for moderately meshed models [47].

CONCLUSIONS

During the last five years the continuous evolution of relatively inexpensive in-house computer hardware with efficient implementations of major well proven proprietary finite element programs has enabled successful large scale applications of linear techniques to a range of naval structural problems which had previously been impracticable in terms of computing costs. In addition a host of smaller, often more finely detailed, but none the less valuable, detailed analysis have been carried out.

Experience with interactive preprocessors has shown them to be amenable to various submarine structural problems, particularly penetrated domes where the geometry of intersecting components can be readily defined in terms of analytic primitives contained in the generator with dramatic decreases in man time for model generation. Similarly interactive colour postprocessors have proved invaluable for the analysis and presentation of results of complex models.

Nevertheless, calculations for first of class designs, especially those concerning surface ships, with their proliferation of different stiffeners, plating thickness and limited repetitiveness, have a still too extensive timescale owing to the inevitable numerous changes in scantling details which occur as the design evolves. The need to create, if at all possible [48], suitable interfaces to efficiently extract the relevant data from commonly used and well developed CAD systems coupled with the development of specialised expert pre and postprocessors incorporating adaptive mesh refinement techniques [49, 50] and with interfaces to structural optimisation software [51, 52] has been identified.

The advantages of processing large models on suitably configured supercomputers has been demonstrated and will shortly be available for ARE (Dunfermline) use of MSC/NASTRAN, SESTRA and ASAS/NL [53]. This should enable the increasing capability and power of local host driven pre and postprocessors to be fully utilised and in order to maximise the investment in previously created large models convertors have been commissioned to translate SESAM-69C and MSC/NASTRAN data to forms suitable for input to SESTRA [54] and ASAS/NL [55] respectively.

REFERENCES

1. Yuille, I.M. and Wilson, L.B., Transverse strength of single hulled ships. Trans. R. Instn. Nav. Archit. 102 (1960) 579-611.

2. Clarkson, J. and Wallace, G., Transverse strength of a large steel frigate model. Trans. R. Instn. Nav. Archit. 109 (1967) 447-486.

3. Kendrick, S.B., The deformation of axisymmetric shells. Unpublished MOD(PE) Report.

4. Kendrick, S.B. and McKeeman, J.L., Pegasus computer specifications – axisymmetric stress analysis. Unpublished MOD(PE) Report.

5. Kendrick, S.B. and McKeeman, J.L., Pegasus computer specifications – axisymmetric stress analysis. Unpublished MOD(PE) Report.

6. Kendrick, S.B. and McKeeman, J.L., Pegasus computer specifications – plane frame analysis. Unpublished MOD(PE) Report.

7. Kendrick, S.B. and McKeeman, J.L., Pegasus computer specifications – plane grillage analysis. Unpublished MOD(PE) Report.

8. Hurwitz, M.M. and Cuthill, E., ASSSAI user's manual. NSRDC Rep. No. AML-69-69 (1969).

9. Pattison, D.R., Spencer, R.E. and W.G. Van Griethuysen, The computer aided ship design system GODDESS and its application to the structural design of Royal Navy warships.
In: Computer Applications in the Automation of Shipyard Operation and Ship Design – IV, Ed. by D.F. Rogers, B.C. Nehrling and C. Kuo, North Holland Publishing Co., IFIP (1982), 341-353.

10. Structural analysis reference manual, English Electric Leo Marconi Bureau Division, Publication BM/1004 (1967).

11. McVee, J.D. and Mitchell, G.C., A 3D structural analysis of Esso Northumbria. Unpublished MOD(PE) Report.

12. Kendrick, S.B., The structural design of supertankers. Trans R. Instn. Nav. Archit. 112 (1970) 391-407.

13. Wallace, G. and McVee, J.D., A structural analysis of a 400K tanker design. Unpublished MOD(PE) Report.

14. Smith, C.S. and Mitchell, G.C., Practical considerations in the application of finite element techniques to ship structures. Proc. I.S.S.C. Symp. Finite Element Techniques, Institut Fur Statik and Dynamik, Stuttgart (1969) 143-185.

15. Honnor, A.F. and Andrews, D.J., HMS INVINCIBLE the first of a new genus of aircraft carrying ships. The Nav. Archit. (1982) 1-13. Trans. R. Instn. Nav. Archit. 124 (1982)

16. Egeland, O. and Araldsen, P.O., SESAM-69 – A general purpose finite element method program. Comput. Struct. 4(1) (1974) 41-68.

17. Smith, C.S., Anderson, M. and Clark, M.A., Structural evaluation of GRP ship designs. Paper 22, Symp. on Fibre Reinforced Materials, Instn. Civ. Engns, London (1977) 221-239.

18. McVee, J.D., A finite element study of hull-deckhouse interaction. Comput. Struct. 12(4) (1980) 371-393.

19. Mitchell, G.C., Analysis of structural interaction between a ship's hull and deckhouse. Trans. R. Instn. Nav. Archit. 120 (1978) 121-134.

20. Gockel, M.A., Handbook for Linear Analysis – MSC/NASTRAN version 64, MacNeal-Schwendler Corp., Los Angeles (1985).

21. Smith, C.S., Application of fibre-reinforced plastic to ship structures.
In: Developments in Thin-Walled Structures – 2, Ed. by J. Rhodes and A.C. Walker, Elsevier Applied Science Publishers, London (1984) 1–48.

22. Shepherd, L. and Mitchell, G.C., Application of finite element methods to stiffened cylindrical shell structures. Unpublished MOD(PE) Report.

23. MacIntosh, A.M., An empirical examination of the performance of some elements in the finite element programs SESAM-69 and MSC/NASTRAN. Unpublished MOD(PE) Report.

24. Gockel, M.A., Handbook for Superelement Analysis – MSC/NASTRAN version 61, MacNeal-Schwendler Corp., Los Angeles (1981).

25. FEMGEN version 8.5 User Manual, FEGS Ltd., Cambridge (1985).

26. FEMVIEW version 3.5 User Manual, FEMVIEW Ltd., Leicester (1983).

27. SESAM'80 General Description, Veritec Sesam Systems A/S, Oslo (1985).

28. Caldwell, J.B., The effect of superstructures on the longitudinal strength of ships. Trans. R. Instn. Nav. Arch. 99(4) (1957) 664–681.

29. MacIntosh, A.M. and Mattin, R., Ship finite element mesh generation program. Unpublished MOD(PE) Report.

30. McVee, J.D. and McLachlan, L., Discretisation of loads for finite element analysis of surface ships. Unpublished MOD(PE) Report.

31. Foulger, K. and Chalmers, D.W., Cracking in R.N. surface ships. Jn. Nav. Engn. 28(2) (1984) 301–308.

32. Chang, P.Y., Effects of stress concentration and reinforcement on the fatigue strength of rectangular openings. Marine Technology 22(4) (1985) 339–350.

33. McLachlan, L., Automatic generation of SESAM-69C beam data including associated plate inertias. Unpublished MOD(PE) Report.

34. McVee, J.D. and Cross, R.L., Auxiliary postprocessors for SESAM-69C. Unpublished MOD(PE) Report.

35. Vinson, C.A., AMTE FE modelling report submarine fore end. Unpublished Scicon Ltd Report, (1983).

36. Whyte, D.A., Ancillary superelement preprocessor for PRENAS. Unpublished MOD(PE) Report.

37. Archibald, H.V., Finite element analysis of a GRP casing. MSc Dissertation, prepared at AMTE(S), Dept. of Mech. Engng., University College London (1983).

38. McKeeman, J.L., NASTRAN preprocessor for structural idealization in way of a submarine bulkhead. Unpublished MOD(PE) Report.

39. Bird, J. and Allan, R.C., The development of improved FRP laminates for ship hull construction.
In: Composite Structures, Ed. by I.H. Marshall, Applied Science Publishers Ltd, Barking (1981) 202-223.

40. Clarke, J.D., Stress analysis of warship hull patch repairs. Unpublished MOD(PE) Report.

41. AMTE glass reinforced plastic channel stress analysis. Unpublished Computas Ltd Report, (1984).

42. Robertson, K.A., Finite element analysis of a short submarine compartment with decks. MSc Dissertation, prepared at ARE Dunfermline. Dept. of Mech. Engng., University College London (1984).

43. King, S.M., MSC/NASTRAN finite element analysis of typical corrugated hull section. Unpublished SIA Ltd Report to ARE Dunfermline, (1984).

44. Unpublished Report, Atkins R and D Ltd, (1986).

45. Robinson, J. and Blackham, S.D., An evaluation of lower order membranes as contained in the MSC/NASTRAN, ASAS and PAFEC FEM systems. Report to RAE Rarnborough (MOD contract no. A93b/494) (1979).

46. Robinson, J. and Blackham, S.D., An evaluation of plate bending elements - MSC/NASTRAN, ASAS, PAFEC, ANSYS and SAP4. Robinson Ford Associates (1981).

47. McVee, J.D. and McLachlan, L., An accuracy study of some SESAM and MSC/NASTRAN membrane and plate elements.
In: Accuracy, Reliability and Training in FEM Technology, Ed. by J. Robinson, The Pitman Press, Bath (1984) 202-210.

48. Soerensen, M. and Boehmler, G., The missing link between CAD and FEM - does it exist?
In: Finite Elements in Computational Mechanics, Ed. by T Kant, Pergamon Press Ltd, Oxford (1985) 967-984.

49. Peano, A., General purpose systems based on adaptive finite elements- software design considerations.
In: Accuracy, Reliability and Training in FEM Technology, Ed. by J. Robinson, The Pitman Press, Bath (1984) 211-219.

50. Babuska, I. and Rheinbolat, W.C., Computational error estimates and adaptive processes for some nonlinear structural problems. Comput. Meths. Appl. Mech. Engng. 34 (1982) 895-937.

51. Balling, R.J., Parkinson, A.R. and Free, J.C., Methods for interfacing analysis software to optimization software. Comput. Struct. 22 (1) (1986) 87-98.

52. STARS - the RAE structural analysis and redesign system - revision 4 User Guide, Scicon Ltd, London (1985).

609

53. ASAS-NL User Manual, Version 12, Kins Development Ltd, Epsom (1984).

54. McCulloch, C.F. and Hall, A., Development and supply of software for conversion of data from SESAM-69C to SESAM'80 format. Unpublished Davy Computing Ltd Report, (1986).

55. Hale, A.B. and Ramsey, A.C., A program for conversion of NASTRAN bulk data to ASAS input format. Unpublished Scicon Ltd Report, (1986).

   N.B. MOD(PE) Reports quoted are not necessarily available to members of the public or to commercial organisations.

COMPUTER AIDED STRUCTURAL DESIGN
IN GODDESS

D.R Pattison and N. Moores, Ministry of Defence (PE),
Chief Naval Architect, Foxhill, Bath, England.
W. J. Van Griethuysen, University College, London.

ABSTRACT

The GODDESS computer aided ship design system is briefly described with particular emphasis on its application to the structural design of surface ships. The programs incorporated in the system provide a means for estimating the loading and structural response for both primary and secondary loads using a variety of methods acting on a fully integrated data structure. Basic finite element data can be created which can be further modified if required. Applications are discussed both in general terms and in relation to the specific problem of transverse strength analysis. The derivation of suitable idealisation techniques is briefly discussed. It is concluded that the system confers considerable benefits on the ship designer.

INTRODUCTION

The Ministry of Defence (PE) Computer Aided Ship Design system GODDESS (The Government Defence DEsign System for Ships) was conceived eighteen years ago to meet a predicted large naval design program in a climate of diminishing manpower, particularly professional naval architects and engineers. Early development was at the Admiralty Research Laboratory (now ARE) at Teddington by a team under Dr I Yuille in conjunction with the Forward Design Groups in the Ship Department, reference [1]. In 1978 the system was brought into general use and development was also transferred to the Ship Department, reference [2], and is now in the Chief Naval Architect's division. Since 1978 all major surface warship designs have used GODDESS and since 1982 all new submarine designs have also used the system. GODDESS is considered a most important tool for assisting the warship design, procurement, and through life support projects in the Warship Department.

SYSTEM DESCRIPTION

The aim in developing GODDESS is to support:

* concept and feasibility design of surface ships and submarines, leading to the technical aspects of contract definition.
* assessment of ship designs, including the analysis of tender submissions, to be an 'informed customer' at all stages of ship procurement, and for intelligence work.

* feasibility design for ship modernisation.
* safety endorsement throughout ship life.

The system does not support the later more detailed stages of ship design as these are invariably carried out under contract in the shipbuilding industry. Detailed layouts, the design of pipe and electrical systems, design for production, and the generation of drawings are more effectively carried out on a general purpose CAD system.

The system consists of a large number of computer programs, 120 for surface ships alone, linked through a common computer model of the ship, the 'Ship Description'. Wherever appropriate the programs are interactive, and make extensive use of high quality computer graphics to illustrate the models being worked on, to display results of analysis, and most important, to provide an interface with the user which encourages him to provide the correct data at each stage and helps to highlight errors before they can lead to wrong results.

Hardware

GODDESS has now been converted from PDP-11 to work on VAX computers using the VMS operating system. A typical installation using a VAX 11-730 to support two user terminals, one with and one without a Lundy Ultragraf refresh graphics display, is shown in figure 1. More powerful VAX computers support more user terminals, and there are now 6 full graphics terminals in use in the Warship Department. The more powerful central facility is based on VAX 11-785 and peripherals include a large Calcomp series 7000 Flat Bed Plotter.

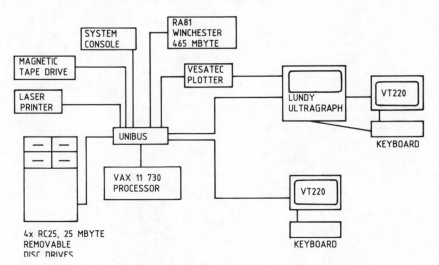

Figure 1. Typical GODDESS hardware.

Operation

The system users are naval architects, engineers and technical grades, rather than trained computer operators and training in the use of the system or individual programs is given on the job as required. The system is user friendly and most programs can be used after about 2 hours training. All GODDESS programs are permanently loaded on the RA81 fixed system disc. Users Ship Descriptions may be highly classified, as may the Ships Database, and these are inserted on the RC25 cartridges, there being an allowance for two user discs, one database, and a spare drive for copying. When not in use these discs are removed from the machine for security. The VMS directory structure is used to separate different Ship Descriptions and designers can also create personalised versions of data in the Ship Database. Simultaneous use of one Ship Description by more than one user is not allowed (except by making copies of the directory) but special arrangements have been made to allow the more lengthy analysis programs to run in background or batch mode while the Ship Description is being modified interactively. This is done by using an interactive program to validate the data being used and then to make a separate copy for use by the batch program which is automatically deleted on completion. Once the Ship Description is reasonably advanced the designer can use almost any of the programs at any time, to modify the design, audit what he has created, or carry out analysis.

Ship Description

This is the database describing a particular ship design or option and consists of two main parts:

(i) The numerical description contains the major dimensions and operating parameters of the ship, together with weight, space and cost information.

(ii) The geometric description contains the hull and superstructure shapes, together with the position of all decks and bulkheads, figure 2, and the topology needed to identify the breakdown of spaces, reference [3].

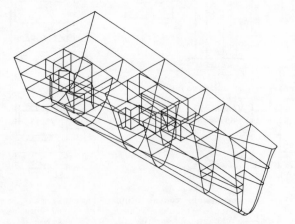

Figure 2. Layout of frigate bow

For flexibility in use these two elements of the Ship Description may be modified separately and a program is provided to check the consistency of the two databases, eg to compare the beam of the ship held in the numerical description with the beam of the ship defined in the geometry. There are also specialised databases associated with particular analysis programs such as structures, seakeeping etc.

Design Database

As well as the Ship Description the programs use much data which is not specific to the particular design being developed:

Form Ships – hull forms of past designs
Type Ships – numerical data on past designs
Weight and Space Scaling Laws and Formulae
Equipments – numerical and geometric data
Structural Design Data
Resistance and Propulsion Data
Sea Spectra
etc.

Designs which have been defined in detail on the system, and which also have the results of some analysis stored, are called Base Ships, and also form part of the Design Database.

Programs

The programs fall into four groups:

(i)   Design programs which primarily create or modify the ship description.

(ii)   Audit programs which provide information on the contents of the Ship Description at any desired level of detail.

(iii)   Analysis programs which perform the Naval Architectural calculation required by the Warship Department and some Marine Engineering tasks.

(iv)   Support programs.

The major programs in each group are shown in Table 1.

SURFACE SHIP STRUCTURAL DESIGN

The remainder of this paper will describe briefly the GODDESS programs for carrying out preliminary structural design of warships and also illustrate its validation and application to the analysis of the transverse strength of a frigate compartment. The programs divide into three groups:-

*   Calculation of loading.
*   Synthesis of structural configuration, analysis and weight estimation.
*   Finite element analysis.

There are two programs that calculate overall ship loading: BALANCE carries out the traditional quasi-static "balancing on a wave", while the sea-keeping programs RAOBLD and MOTION calculate extreme design loads for a given probability of exceedance through the life of the ship. The

longitudinal distribution of mass required for these calculations is
produced in the AUDIT program.

Using the program STRUCT the scantlings of longitudinally continuous
structure and of transverse bulkheads can be defined, and the strength
analysed, panel by panel, under the design load. Once scantlings are
decided, the structural weight data in the Ship Description can be updated.

To carry out more complex analyses of the structure, such as the
transverse strength of a compartment subjected to hydrostatic load, STRUCT
can create 3D finite element data automatically from the structural
definition. After detailed editing in a preprocessor if required, the data
is passed to a remote mainframe computer for analysis using MSC Nastran.
The inter-relation between the structural analysis programs and the Ship
Description is shown in figure 3.

TABLE 1

Major GODDESS Programs

Design	Audit	Analysis	Support
Design Definition	Weight	Hydrostatic Stability	File Editor
Control	Space	Stability Criteria	Curve Editor
System Grouping	Cost	Powering and Propellers	Geometry
Surface Design	Ship Systems	Endurance	Verifier
Hullform Distortion	Electrical Systems	Wave Balance	Data
Hull Layout	Tank Contents	Longitudinal Structure	Checking
Equipment Layout	Draughting	Bulkheads	Operating
S/M Control	S/M Weight	Finite Element Interface	System
	Comparison of	Seakeeping RAO's	Utilities
	numeric and	Motion Prediction	
	geometric data	Motion Criteria	
		Missile Arcs of Fire	
		S/M Pressure Hull	
		Structures	

Structural loading

The two programs that calculate overall hull girder loading take as
input a group of cross sectional curves to describe the hull shape and the
longitudinal weight distribution in the chosen ship condition, produced by
the AUDIT program. To improve the accuracy of the weight distribution,
individual weight items may be distributed along a length of the ship.

  i. BALANC uses the traditional quasi-static approach, and balances the
     ship on a wave of chosen shape, size and position. No dynamic or
     Smith correction is used. The output is histograms of shear force and
     bending moment along the length of the ship.

 ii. RAOBLD calculates Response Transfer Functions (RAO's) for overall ship
     girder bending moments and shear forces as well as ship motions, for
     various speeds and headings.

MOTION calculates long term design loads using statistical data on short
term sea spectra and their probability of occurrence, operational data on
ship speed and heading in various significant wave heights, and the number
of load reversals expected in the ship's life.

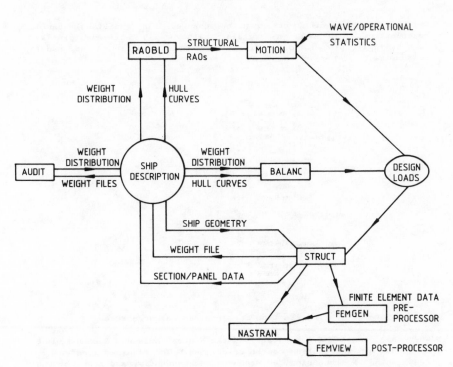

Figure 3. The relationships between the structures programs and the Ship Description.

Structural Synthesis and Design Analysis

To create a new section to define either longitudinal or transverse structure, STRUCT displays a profile of the ship and performs an intersection at any chosen position along the length. Up to twenty sections can be taken in this way and separate structural synthesis and analysis packages are then available for longitudinal or transverse bulkhead analysis of each section.

i. Longitudinal Structure. The designer indicates the length of the idealised prismatic compartment centered on the section and the number of transverse frames in the compartment for strength and weight analyses. At this stage, every curve created in the section by intersecting a plane or curved surface is defined as a panel. The designer can modify the panel arrangement by removing unwanted panels to reduce complexity, or by dividing panels into two or more panels to allow for different plating thickness, or to position deep longitudinal stiffeners on panel boundaries. The designer then defines the properties of each panel in turn as shown in figure 4. Bending and shear efficiencies allow for departure from simple beam theory due to shear lag in superstructure or short decks etc and are the ratio of actual stress to that found from simple beam theory. The plate and stiffener type numbers refer to tables in the database.

Grillage length and width can be changed for individual panel
calculations. As well as regular orthogonally stiffened panels,
longitudinal plates or stiffeners can be positioned at panel
boundaries.

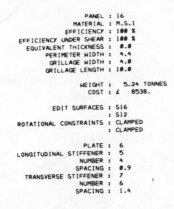

```
                   PANEL :  16
                MATERIAL :  M.S.1
              EFFICIENCY :  100 %
   EFFICIENCY UNDER SHEAR :  100 %
    EQUIVALENT THICKNESS :  0.0
         PERIMETER WIDTH :  4.4
          GRILLAGE WIDTH :  4.0
         GRILLAGE LENGTH :  10.0

                  WEIGHT :   5.24 TONNES
                    COST : £    8538.

          EDIT SURFACES :  S16
                        :  S12
   ROTATIONAL CONSTRAINTS :  CLAMPED
                        :  CLAMPED

                   PLATE :  6
   LONGITUDINAL STIFFENER :  5
                  NUMBER :  4
                 SPACING :  0.9
     TRANSVERSE STIFFENER :  7
                  NUMBER :  6
                 SPACING :  1.4
```

Figure 4. Panel definition for longitudinal structure

When all panels have been defined the Neutral Axis and Second Moment
of Area of the section can be calculated. The required load cases,
from BALANC, seakeeping, or produced independently, are input by the
designer who may then calculate the stresses in chosen panels, and use
these stresses to assess the compressive strength of any panel. For
compressive strength assessment the followed load cases are used:

* Longitudinal in-plane direct stress
* Shear stress
* Transverse in-plane direct stress
* Normal pressure loading

(the last two being input by hand). The computer then calculates a
matrix of load factors against collapse in the following failure
modes;

* Interframe stiffener collapse using column collapse curves derived
  from elasto-plastic theory allowing for the effects of imperfections
  and residual stresses.
* Longitudinal stiffener tripping using elastic solutions.
* Overall grillage failure based on orthotropic plate theory including
  both stability and stress criteria.
* Individual plate panel failure under normal pressure using classical
  elastic analysis.

Where relevant, combined load factors are also calculated as shown in
figure 5. Most of the analysis methods implemented are closely based
on those developed at ARE(Dunfermline).

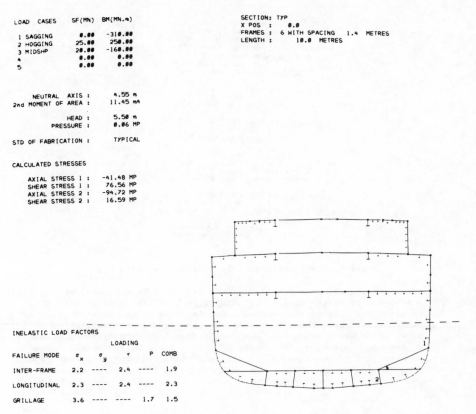

```
LOAD  CASES    SF(MN)  BM(MN.m)          SECTION: TYP
                                         X POS :    0.0
  1 SAGGING     0.00    -310.00          FRAMES :  6 WITH SPACING   1.4  METRES
  2 HOGGING    25.00     250.00          LENGTH :     10.0  METRES
  3 MIDSHP     20.00    -160.00
  4             0.00      0.00
  5             0.00      0.00



      NEUTRAL  AXIS :     4.55 m
2nd MOMENT OF AREA :    11.45 m4

            HEAD :       5.50 m
        PRESSURE :       0.06 MP

STD OF FABRICATION :    TYPICAL


CALCULATED STRESSES

    AXIAL STRESS 1 :    -41.48 MP
    SHEAR STRESS 1 :     76.56 MP
    AXIAL STRESS 2 :    -94.72 MP
    SHEAR STRESS 2 :     16.59 MP
```

INELASTIC LOAD FACTORS

	LOADING				
FAILURE MODE	σ_x	σ_y	τ	P	COMB
INTER-FRAME	2.2	----	2.4	----	1.9
LONGITUDINAL	2.3	----	2.4	----	2.3
GRILLAGE	3.6	----	----	1.7	1.5

ESCAPE

RESPONSE OPTION ? ▯

Figure 5. Panel strength assessment for longitudinal structure

ii. Bulkhead Structure.   For bulkhead structure every area enclosed by
    curves in a transverse section is defined as a panel. The designer
    can modify the panel arrangements by removing a bounding curve and
    combining panels or by dividing up an existing panel. He may then
    define the structural data for each panel independently as shown in
    figure 6.   On any panel the stiffening must be regular and vertical
    and/or horizontal.   For irregular stiffening, additional stiffeners
    may be added at panel boundaries.

618

```
                    PANEL ID:   6
                PANEL HEIGHT:   4.277 METRES
                 PANEL WIDTH:   4.441 METRES
                    PLATE ID:   5
              MATERIAL TYPE:   M.S.1
                   THICKNESS:   8.00 MM
        CORROSION ALLOWANCE:   NONE

         VERTICAL STIFFENER ID:   4
                      NUMBER:   9
                     SPACING:   0.500 METRES

       HORIZONTAL STIFFENER ID:   2
                      NUMBER:   2
                     SPACING:   1.392 METRES

             GRILLAGE HEIGHT:   4.175 METRES
              GRILLAGE WIDTH:   4.441 METRES
      VERTICAL STIFFENER EFF NO:   8
    HORIZONTAL STIFFENER EFF NO:   2

         ROTATIONAL CONSTRAINTS:  PINNED
                       AND  PINNED
     PLASTIC MOMENT CONSTANTS:  0.000 0.000

                      WEIGHT:   1.8322 TONNES
                        COST:   0. POUNDS
```

Figure 6. Panel definition for bulkhead structure

The structural idealisations used in STRUCT for the strength assessment of bulkheads are rectangular regular orthogonally stiffened panels or single stiffeners. Panels need not, of course, be rectangular, and the dimensions of the grillage idealisation are included in the panel data. A normal pressure loading is used, either a constant value or by reference to a free surface height. Load factors are determined for elastic and plastic design criteria. The modes of failure considered are shown in table 2.

TABLE 2

Bulkhead grillage failure criteria

Elastic Design	Plastic Design
Plate failure - small permanent set	Plate failure - large permanent set
Plate failure - no permanent set	Stiffener tripping
Stiffener tripping	
Stiffener web yielding	Stiffener web yield
Stiffener flange yielding	Plastic mechanism collapse

For the stiffener failure modes separate load factors are determined for horizontal and vertical stiffeners as shown in figure 7.

Vibration analysis of panels and stiffeners may also be performed, to find the five lowest modal frequencies. The complete grillage and individual plate panels are analysed separately and the added mass effect of fluid backing on one or both sides of a bulkhead can be included.

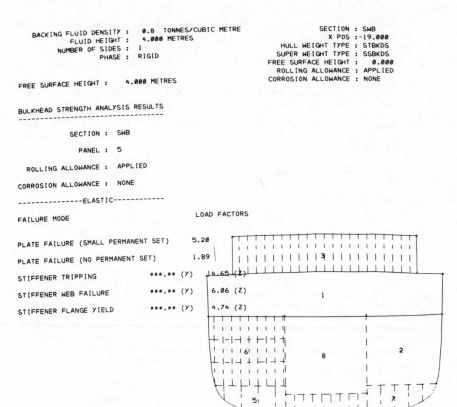

BACKING FLUID DENSITY :   0.8 TONNES/CUBIC METRE
        FLUID HEIGHT :   4.000 METRES
     NUMBER OF SIDES :   1
               PHASE :   RIGID

FREE SURFACE HEIGHT :   4.000 METRES

           SECTION : SWB
             X POS :-19.000
   HULL WEIGHT TYPE : STBKDS
  SUPER WEIGHT TYPE : SSBKDS
FREE SURFACE HEIGHT :   0.000
  ROLLING ALLOWANCE : APPLIED
CORROSION ALLOWANCE : NONE

BULKHEAD STRENGTH ANALYSIS RESULTS

           SECTION : SWB

             PANEL : 5

  ROLLING ALLOWANCE : APPLIED

CORROSION ALLOWANCE : NONE

--------------ELASTIC------------

FAILURE MODE   LOAD FACTORS

PLATE FAILURE (SMALL PERMANENT SET)   5.20

PLATE FAILURE (NO PERMANENT SET)   1.89

STIFFENER TRIPPING   ***.** (Y)   14.65 (Z)

STIFFENER WEB FAILURE   ***.** (Y)   6.06 (Z)

STIFFENER FLANGE YIELD   ***.** (Y)   4.74 (Z)

Figure 7. Bulkhead Panel Strength Assessment.

iii. Estimation of structural weight. One of the primary purposes of the
     STRUCT program is to estimate the total structural weight and its
     distribution along the ship. In setting up the ship geometry in
     HULLAY, each surface and plane may be allocated a particular
     structural type (hull structure, maindeck structure, etc). At each of
     the transverse sections defined in STRUCT the weight per unit area of
     the structure associated with each surface or plane may be calculated
     and a distribution for each structural type established at up to 20

sections along the ship. For the future it is planned that the weight and distribution for any structural type may be calculated by combining the weight per unit area distribution with an audit of the areas of each type of structure, which is carried out in the AUDIT program.

iv. Comparative cost estimates. To allow the designer to offset the gains due to reduced weight against the extra cost of more complex structure, STRUCT calculates the cost of each panel or member using empirical formulae. The costs include material labour and overhead elements which may be factored by current unit costs to give prices for:

* material preparation

* panel assembly

* erection at berth

Finite Element Analysis

The definition of longitudinal and bulkhead structure at any section may be used to generate Finite Element Card Image files for more detailed analysis using NASTRAN. Finite element data files are created by STRUCT independantly for longitudinal or bulkhead structure and the designer is first shown a 3-D display of the whole structure. By default, a prism is generated for longitudinal structure, figure 8. In line with the section definition, the data is made up of individual panels and the designer can delete panels that are not required for his analysis.

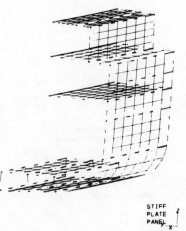

```
               SECTION : TYP
            X POSITION :    0.00
            Y SYMMETRY : YES
         FRAME SPACING :  1.43 METRES
         MIN FRAME NO :   0
         MAX FRAME NO :   7
TRANS. GRID LINE SPACING :  1.43 METRES
           LOAD FRAME :   2
   FREE SURFACE HEIGHT :  10.00
```

STIFF
PLATE
PANEL

ESCAPE

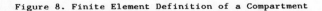

Figure 8. Finite Element Definition of a Compartment

Specification of finite element data, such as mesh spacing, element type, loading and constraints, is performed on a panel basis. On selecting a panel with the light pen, the display of the whole structure is replaced by the individual panel, figure 9. For longitudinal structure it is also possible to define panels to be of different lengths, to model discontinuous structure such as superstructures.

```
                          PANEL :  16
                 PLATE MATERIAL : M.S.1
                     PLATE TYPE :   6          THICKNESS :  10  MM
     TRANSVERSE STIFFENER TYPES :   7 AND   0
   LONGITUDINAL STIFFENER TYPE  :   5              NUMBER :   4
            START FRAME NUMBER  :   7
              END FRAME NUMBER  :   0
                  PANEL LENGTH  :  10.00     METRES
                   PANEL WIDTH  :   4.43     METRES
            PLATE ELEMENT TYPE  : CQDMEM1
  TRANSVERSE STIFFENER ELEMENT TYPE : CBAR
LONGITUDINAL STIFFENER ELEMENT TYPE : CROD
   LONGITUDINAL GRID LINES, NUMBER :   4          SPACING :  0.89 METRES
     SUPPRESSED DEGREES OF FREEDOM : 6
                      PRESSURE :   0.05 MP      HEAD :  5.00 METRES
```

LOADING ON TRANSVERSE GRID LINE   1

STRESSES-   LOCAL X : 6.00 MP
                 LOCAL Y : 0.52 MP

FORCES/LENGTH- LOCAL X : 0.00 MN/m
               LOCAL Y : 0.00 MN/m
               LOCAL Z : 0.00 MN/m
                     X : 7.64 MN/m
                     Y : 0.00 MN/m
                     Z : 2.30 MN/m

CONSTRAINTS-   1 :   1
                      2 :   1
                      3 :   1
                      4 :   0
                      5 :   0
                      6 :   0

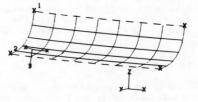

DISPLACEMENTS- LOCAL X : 0.0 mm   0.00 RADIANS
               LOCAL Y : 0.0 mm   0.00 RADIANS
               LOCAL Z : 0.0 mm   0.00 RADIANS
                     X : 0.0 mm   0.00 RADIANS
                     Y : 0.0 mm   0.00 RADIANS
                     Z : 0.0 mm   0.00 RADIANS
        STRAIN FORMULA :   0
     CURVATURE FORMULA :   0

Figure 9. Finite Element Panel Definition

When the finite element data for every panel has been defined a file of card images may be generated and stored on disc in NASTRAN format. In addition to the local loading applied to individual panels, it is possible to specify primary loading (bending moment plus shear force) at a given frame station, or pressure loading to a given free surface height. The program is not designed to generate "whole ship" finite element data, but restricted to prismatic or tapered idealisations suitable for analysis of:

* transverse strength of compartments

* superstructure efficiency

* local discontinuities eg end of double bottom

* bulkhead structure

* deck openings

The editing of finite element data in STRUCT is restricted to regular panels but includes powerful loading and constraint functions. The more general editing needed, eg for mesh refinement around a deck opening, is provided by a commercial finite element package purchased from FEGS Ltd. The package consists of two main parts; a preprocessor FEMGEN, and a post processor FEMVIEW. These programs use the Lundy Ultragraf display, and, like NASTRAN, run on the VAX computers.

Application Example:- Transverse Strength

The structural models resulting from the use of any tool such as GODDESS need some degree of validation by correlation with experimental results. Consistency with the relevant structural design code is also essential. The work described below was carried out within the ship design section responsible for the design of the first major warship to use the GODDESS system. The work was regarded as an important pre-requisite for using its powerful facilities in a design situation.

Previous Work

The case of transverse hydrostatic loading of a main compartment in a conventional frigate/destroyer form is discussed because it illustrates several of the issues involved and is a problem which was not amenable to accurate analysis before the advent of computer methods. For single bottomed hulls the form of the structure and the applied loading is such that the case of hydrostatic load can be uncoupled from that of primary longitudinal bending of the hull girder and the two treated as independent load cases for the purposes of strength analysis. Work at ARE(Dunfermline) established that the traditional approach of analysing an isolated two dimensional frame subjected to lateral pressure loading was subject to gross errors and capable of giving quite misleading results, Reference [4]. Pioneering work in the field of computer based structural analysis followed and matrix methods were validated against small scale model results, Reference [5]. A large scale steel model was tested in the large test frame at ARE and the results were compared with those from the theoretical approach previously developed, Reference [6]. Because of the limitations of computing facilities available at the time it was necessary to make several simplifying assumptions which nevertheless did not seriously affect the accuracy of the calculated results. The problems now facing the designer are rather different. What was previously a state of the art analysis, necessarily reserved for check calculations at a relatively late stage in the design is now seen as desirable in the context of feasibility studies when a range of alternative solutions are still available and the objective is to find the optimum solution (however defined). Thus economy of computational effort remains an overriding consideration albeit for different reasons. It should be pointed out that optimisation in this context remains a manually controlled operation, mainly because this is simpler and more effective than building a suitable constrained objective function into the computer program and allows the more satisfactory exercise of engineering judgement.

Finite Element Idealisations

In order to establish a satisfactory compromise between computational effort and the accuracy of the calculated stresses, it was decided to benchmark a NASTRAN finite element idealisation against the experimental results reported in Reference [6] for the case of hydrostatic loading. Full details of the scantlings and the experimental procedure are given in reference [6] and are not repeated herein. Much previous analysis of structures of this type had been based on idealisations in which the stiffening and associated plating were represented by beam bending elements (type BAR in NASTRAN) with either no representation of the shear stiffeness of the plating, or a simplified form such as direct modification of the relevant terms in the stiffness matrix or the addition of notional rod type elements acting as diagonal shear ties. Simplification was also often necessary in terms of the number of structural members represented. Thus for example the structural design manual used within MOD(PE) in the mid 1970's did not require that minor longitudinals should be included in the main finite element analysis but should be analysed independently as secondary elements. This results in necessarily conservative criteria.

The current study therefore started with framework idealisations composed of BAR elements. The properties of these elements were derived by assuming proportion of the plating to be effective in acting with the stiffener. In principle the plating contribution to the bending properties (effective breadth) and direct stress carrying properties (effective width) could be chosen independently but this was not pursued. The results from a framework model consisting entirely of BAR elements is shown in figure 10. The gross errors arise from the neglect of the shear stiffness of the plating and it must be concluded that such a simple representation is of little value even for a single bottom structure.

The logical development was to include a representation of the plating. In terms of NASTRAN elements this was achieved by adding a single QDMEM (now superseded by type QUAD4) plate membrane element between each stiffener of the same thickness as the actual plate. The bending properties (out of plane moment of inertia) of the BAR elements were those associated with the stiffener plus an effective breadth of plating but the direct load carrying properties (cross section area) of the bar element were those of the stiffener alone. The torsional stiffness of open section stiffeners in such a structure does not exercise any significant effect on the overall response and the polar second moment of area of the element was arbitrarily chosen as that of the stiffener alone about its toe. In-plane bending of the stiffeners is constrained by the plating and the second moment of area about an axis normal to the plating was generated with the effective breadth of

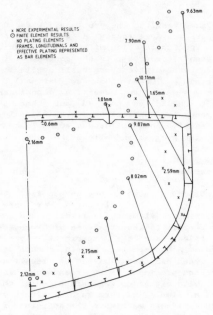

Figure 10. NCRE Frigate Section (Short Compartment) Deflections at Frame 8
with no Shear Elements

plating acting with the stiffener, but as with the torsional properties this
assumption is not, within reason, relevant to the response of the structure.
Two different assumptions regarding effective breadth were made ie. 30 and
40 times the plating thickness. An isometric view of the deflected finite
element mesh is shown in figure 11 for the case of 4.27m head of water above
the keel. Such post processing facilities are a valuable aid to the rapid
assessment of the quality of the results. The results for the stresses and
deflections in the frame flange are plotted in figure 12 for the case of a
hydrostatic load of 8.53m head of water above the keel. Similar good
correlation was obtained for the other experimental results reported. As is
evident from the results the differing assumptions regarding effective
breadth have only a small effect on the calculated deflections and even less
on the stresses. This is because, as is commonly the case with such
structures, the neutral axis of the combined section is relatively close to
the plating. The inclusion of the full thickness of the plate membrane
element might be expected to reduce the direct compressive stresses compared
to the experimental results since the effects of shear lag are not accounted
for. However, although this tends to make the analysis less
conservative,comparison with the experimental results indicates that the
effect is not important in this case. In any particular case the
significance of shear lag effects can be investigated by mesh refinement.
The facilities in GODDESS enable both transverse and longitudinal grid
spacings to be specified independently. Although a large number of plate
elements may be required for slender structures, the indications are that

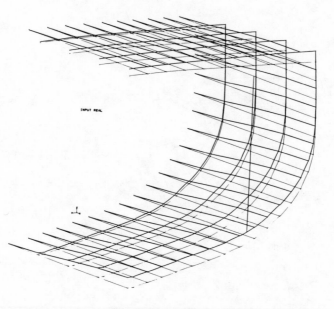

Figure 11:   Isometric View of Deflected Finite Element Mesh

for scantlings typical of ship structures, only a relatively small number is
required to obtain an acceptable accuracy. Alternatively the latest version
of the program permits the use of shear panel elements (type SHEAR). These
can be used in conjunction with BAR elements in which case the section
properties of the latter should be those appropriate to the stiffener plus
the effective breadth of plating   in respect of both bending and direct
loads.   The agreement with the experimental results is considered to be
acceptably good and certainly adequate as the basis for a design procedure.
The calculated deflections are slightly smaller than those actually measured
even in areas where the stresses are nearly identical, indicating that the
finite element model is less compliant than the actual structure.   This may
be due to the effect of residual stresses, which would lead to a lower
structural stiffness than that based on Young's Modulus of the material.

Further refinement of the finite element model was not pursued since the
results were deemed acceptably good and, as stated above, economy of
computational effort was of paramount importance. The aspect ratio of some
of the plate elements was about 3:1 but, partly because of the relatively
small stress gradients in the structure, no significant adverse effects were
noted.

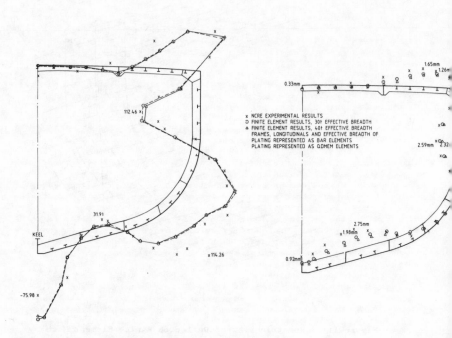

Figure 12. NCRE Frigate Section (Short Compartment) Stresses and Deflections
at Frame 8 with Plating Elements (units N and mm)

Double Bottom Structures

Double bottom structures are considerably more complex in their
behaviour. Out of plane shearing actions and torsional rigidity of the
closed cells cannot generally be ignored. Further complications arise as a
result of web openings which are invariably present in such structures.
Again finite element methods provide a means of analysing these structures
but the designers problem of producing a simplified idealisation which can
be modified to explore the range of possible options is even more acute than
is the case for single bottomed structures because of the greater inherent
complexity of the structural response.

Effect of Web Openings on Torsional & Shear Stiffness

A suitable means of accounting for the considerable reduction in shear stiffness resulting from web openings was reported in Reference [7]. This is achieved by including a factor K which represents the proportional reduction due to the presence of openings in the web and varies with the percentage of web area removed. Two values of K are discussed in Reference [7]: Ks to represent the loss of shear stiffness and Kt the loss of torsional rigidity. Values of K were deduced from a parametric survey using detailed finite element models and comparison with experimental data.

This work was aimed at producing a representative framework idealisation of cellular structures, and the values of Ks and Kt could be used directly to modify the section properties of the beam elements comprising the framework. However, when incorporated as a part of a larger analysis including the turn of bilge and secondary stiffening, it becomes advantageous to retain plate elements. One way of achieving this would be to use a model in which the thickness of the plate elements is reduced by the factor Kt and compensating rod elements are placed at the edges of the plate to restore the direct stress carrying capability. A disadvantage of this method is that different section areas for the rod elements are dictated by the bending and direct stress components. An alternative method is to specify values of Young's Modulus, Shear Modulus and Poisson's Ratio independently for the plate elements. This method has been used with some success but requires some care in use. The resulting material properties are anisotropic but the correct results are obtained in the directions of the elements basic co-ordinates.

Since, when plating elements are used only one value of K can be chosen independently, the question arises as to the value of the dependent K factor. In the study undertaken Ks was the taken directly from Reference [7]. Refering to figure 13, the torsional stiffness, J, of a single cell is given by:

$$J = \frac{2b^2 d^2}{\left(^b/t_f\right) + \left(^d/t_w\right)} \quad\quad\quad (1)$$

The shear modulus of the plate webs is reduced by the factor Ks:

$$Ge = KsG$$

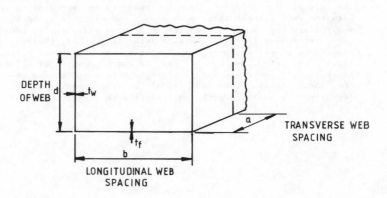

Figure 13. Nomenclature for Double Bottom Cell.

This is modelled by reducing the web thickness which leads to a proportional reduction in torsional stiffness given by

$$\frac{Je}{J} = \frac{Ks(\beta+\gamma)}{(Ks\beta+\gamma)} \hspace{2cm} (2)$$

where: Je = effective torsional stiffness allowing for web openings

J = torsional stiffness without openings

$$\beta = \frac{b}{d}$$

$$\gamma = \frac{t_f}{t_w}$$

Comparing values of Kt(=Je/J) calculated in this way with those obtained directly from Reference [7] shows acceptably good agreement for geometries of current interest. For example results for 25% web opening and $\gamma = 1$ are shown in table 3.

TABLE 3

Values of $^{Je}/J$ for γ=1 & 25% Web Opening

$\frac{a}{d}$	β	Je /J from (2)	Je /J from [7]
2	2	.458	.51
4	2	.309	.31
2	4	.585	.62
4	4	.427	.43

Effective Breadth of Plating

As with single bottom structures, shear lag reduces the effectiveness of the plating subjected to direct stress arising from bending and axial loads. Convergence studies have shown that in a typical case results within 10% of the asymptotic solution can be obtained by representing the web plating between each intersection by as few as two elements along the length of the web. Since typical double bottom structures will usually contain additional open section stiffeners between webs (figure 5), their inclusion and the requirements of achieving a suitable element aspect ratio will often in itself dictate the use of an adequate number of plating elements. Alternatively,as discussed for single bottom structures,use can be made of the shear panel elements. Final designs should always be checked by repeating the analysis with a different mesh density.

Validation

The above techniques have been the subject of limited validation against the sparse experimental data available for closed cell structures, notably that contained in Reference [8]. Further data, particularly relating to the effects of structural details and the boundary conditions relevant to actual structures, would be valuable.

Limitations

This work covers only the basic elastic response of the perfect structure as is consistent with the design codes in use. The determination of local stresses, especially around openings, will require further mesh refinement but the overall response can be estimated with sufficient accuracy for determination of the scantlings of the main structure using the methods described here. Ultimate strength will be affected by fabrication details which can be determined from standard approved practices. There is less scope for optimisation in this area since the effects on structural weight are only minimal although it might be argued that fabrication costs could be significantly affected.

For double bottom structures in particular, limit state criteria may be considered appropriate. Although this goes beyond the scope of the work described here, an elastic global analysis would usually be a pre-requisite for the practical application of ultimate strength criteria in design.

CONCLUSIONS

This paper has presented the views of both CASD system designer and ship designer of a large, complex, and specialised structural design package developed to assist in warship feasibility design.

The system has proved very successful, but there are benifits besides the obvious ones of speed and efficiency in carrying out particular calculations:

* Errors are reduced due to enforced standardisation of the idealisation and method of analysis, and due to better control of the data used.

* Improved analysis methods developed in the research establishments become routine tools for the designer.

* Tasks are brought forward in the ship design process, speeding up the convergence of the design, and improving accuracy.

* More ships design options can be generated, giving a route to more cost effective ship designs and giving more scope for innovation.

A drawback of such complex packages is the difficulty and cost of validating the system to an acceptable level. Systems of this type certainly cannot be proved to be correct.

There is no sign that user competence may be reduced by the use of these powerful tools, rather the reverse, but it is encouraging to find that as the speed and volume of design work increases the designers learn faster and become more competent.

The ship designer now has access to enormous analytical power, previously only appropriate to research environments, but this must not be allowed to diminish the importance of structural idealisation or of the interpretation of results. The ability to refer back to experiment to check new methods is vital and emphasises that analysis complements and does not replace experiment.

REFERENCES

1. Yuille, I.M. The Forward Design System for computer aided design of ships using a mini-computer. The Naval Architect, November 1978

2. Holmes, S.J. The application and development of a computer systems for warship design. The Naval Architect, July 1981.

3. Duncan, J.M., Yuille, I.M., Representation of compartmented spaces for computer aided ship design. CAD Journal 16 No 1 January 1984

4. Faulkner, D., Yuille, I.M., Accuracy of the ring frame calculation used to estimate the transverse strength of ships. Unpublished MOD(PE) Report.

5. Yuille, I.M., Wilson, L.B., Transverse strength of a single hulled ships. Trans. R.I.N.A. 102 [1960]

6. Clarkson, J, Wallace, G., Transverse strength of a large steel frigate model. Trans. R.I.N.A. 109 [1967]

7. Evans, H.R, Shanmugam, N.E, The elastic analysis of cellular structures containing web openings. Proc. Inst. Civ. Engrs. Part 2 67 [1979] 1035-1063.

8. Mitchell, G.C, Structural tests on a 1/4 scale ships double bottom model. Unpublished MOD(PE) Report.

WELDING: PRESENT DEVELOPMENT AND FUTURE TRENDS

J Bird
Admiralty Research Establishment
Dunfermline, Fife, Scotland

ABSTRACT

The paper describes the welding techniques used for submarine construction. It outlines current procedures and the steps being taken to improve weld quality and production rates. A number of new techniques have come about because of continued difficulties with respect to weld quality, such as hydrogen induced HAZ cold cracking, slag entrapment, porosity etc.

The use of the submerged arc and pulsed MIG processes are highlighted. The former is used to fabricate, with single or multiple arcs, both the stiffeners and the stiffened submarine cylinders. The latter process is more versatile in that vertical seam welds, circumferential butts can be made using automated equipment, whilst the process can also be used semi-automatically to weld the intricacies of the submarine units.

Finally the paper examines a number of other processes such as electron beam, laser and narrow gap welding and comments on the potential of the processes for the future, with the current level of technique development.

HISTORICAL

Wrought iron was first used by the Royal Navy in the construction of HMS WARRIOR in 1860 [1]. Gradually the use of iron in naval ships grew until, in 1901, HMS HOLLAND, the first submarine for the Royal Navy, was built from an early version of mild steel, using rivetted construction [2]. It was to be another 40 years before submarines with all welded hulls were to be built, the modified T class built under the 1940 war programme, although submarines with welded external tanks had previously been constructed. These vessels, together with the A class from 1943 onwards, the first submarines designed with an all welded hull, had distinguished service in the Second World War and were eventually superseded by the O & P classes before HMS DREADNOUGHT the first of the UK Nuclear submarines was commissioned in 1960.

The early welds were made using the manual metal arc process with rutile electrodes and a DC power source. Many of the early consumables were made by Murex Welding Ltd using mild steel wires with helically wound asbestos coverings. These electrodes eventually evolved into a rutile flux covered mild steel consumable, producing gaseous and liquid emissions to protect the molten weld metal.

Early mild steel structures were quite lowly stressed and the mild steel was tolerant to some of the welding problems currently observed with high strength steels. As the plate strength increased with a change in the material of construction from mild steel through UXW, QT28, QT35 and now QlN, the problem of weldability, particularly hydrogen induced HAZ cold cracking increased. This meant that a solution to the problem of HAZ cold cracking had to be developed. By using basic low hydrogen electrodes instead of electrodes with rutile coatings and either DC or AC power sources, the early problems have been largely overcome in current submarine constructions.

Manual metal arc welding is labour intensive, has an inherent low production rate and is subject to welding defects such as porosity, slag entrapment, lack of side wall fusion, and hydrogen induced HAZ cracking problems. Because of these difficulties other welding techniques have been adapted and developed to overcome many of these problems in the construction of submarines.

PRESENT DEVELOPMENTS

Manual Metal Arc Welds

The advent of high strength quenched and tempered steels QT35/HY80/QlN, with their inherent hard heat affected zones, up to 420 Hv, necessitated the development of low hydrogen electrodes. A number of these consumables, Table 1, are used in the UK and all give moisture levels of less than 0.5% and weld metal diffusible hydrogen levels of less than 5 ml/per 100 gm weld metal provided they are correctly baked, properly stored, the preheat is correctly applied, and the weld area is free of grease, paint, etc. If one or all of these requirements are not met, HAZ cracking can occur as in fillet welds for permanent and temporary attachments, Figure 1.

TABLE 1
Typical Properties of Some MMA Electrodes (10H Position)

Consumable	0.2% PS N/mm^2	UTS N/mm^2	El %	R of A %	C_v at -20°C Joules	Moisture %	H_2 ml/100 gm
A	642	731	25	67	65	0.21	6
B	675	848	28	67	64		
C	744	850	23	54	79	0.22	4
D	822	929	22	62	58		3
E	716	816	24	68	84	0.15	4
F	670	870	18	63	72		

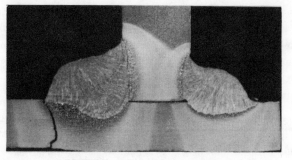

FIGURE 1.   HAZ Cold Cracking.

There are a number of relationships which are used to indicate the preheat required to prevent HAZ cold cracking [3, 4, 5, 6, 7, 8] but many have been developed for particular circumstances and so may not be generally applicable.   In the UK an early relationship is regarded as being sufficient for the requirement of Q1N [3].

$$CE = C + \frac{Si}{24} + \frac{Mn}{6} + \frac{Ni}{40} + \frac{Cr}{5} + \frac{Mo}{4} + \frac{V}{15}$$

$$PH = 213 \ CE - 26.5 \ ^{\circ}C$$

Unfortunately the application of the correct preheat in a shipyard is not always as efficient as one would like.   In particular when gas preheating is used, as an alternative to electrical strip heating, it is often difficult to ensure the effectual heating through the plate or the correct plate temperature existing when welding is commenced.   Supervision of preheat temperature is all-important.

In the latest US Mil Spec E-0022200/10A(SH) [9] the requirements for moisture levels have been tightened so that diffusible hydrogen content of the as-deposited weld metal can be reduced. This really is the most sensible solution in that control of preheat becomes of secondary importance if the potential diffusible hydrogen content can be reduced. This has been already achieved to some extent with the use of basic fluxes containing potassium and lithium compounds to replace the more hygroscopic sodium compounds.

With adequate control of welding conditions and the use of low hydrogen electrodes it has been possible to reduce the preheat requirements for the fill passes of MMA welds to 70°C, provided the root passes are completed with the minimum preheat specified, 120°C. Bulge explosion tests have indicated that adequate performance can be achieved with MMA electrodes provided the above conditions are closely adhered to.

Spray MIG Welds

This technique has only limited use. When employed it is used to weld the extruded T frames to the main hull to form a full penetration T butt weld. The main requirement is for a sound weld and an acceptable weld profile particularly at the weld toe, Figure 2. Although it is possible to make the welds without difficulty when the web is 25 mm thick, thinner webs are more difficult to weld with an acceptable profile. In these cases it has been necessary to raise the heat input requirements above 2.2 kJ/mm,

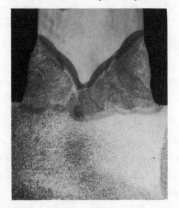

FIGURE 2. Typical Profile of T Butt Weld.

whilst maintaining adequate mechanical properties, in order to obtain an acceptable profile. The shielding gas for all Spray MIG welds is an Argon/2% oxygen mixture fed into the weld area at 30-40 litres per minute.

Pulsed MIG Welds

The first pulsed MIG welds used in the construction of UK submarines were the longitudinal seams. These were made in the vertical up position using a Hulftegger torch, weaving gear and tractor, running on KAT track. The power source was AWP constant current equipment of the 450 series. The weld profile was a double Vee preparation, with an 8 mm root gap and 3 mm root face. With this technique a MMA root run is first laid onto a glass rod to form a bridging weld, Figure 3. When the glass rod is removed the weld needs no backgouging and only slight grinding before welding can be continued. The weld on the inside of the profile is finished using the MMA process, but can alternatively be welded with semi automatic pulsed MIG.

FIGURE 3. Root Weld Using Glass Backing

The outer portion of the weld profile is filled using the pulsed MIG process. Welding is completed using a single run split weave technique, the weave width being dependent on the width of the profile which to a large extent depends on the thickness of the hull plating. As with the spray MIG technique an Argon 2% Oxygen shielding gas is used at a flow rate of 30-40 litres/minute, although an Argon Helium mixture gas is also being considered, and Argon 5% CO_2 could be used.

SUBMERGED ARC

The submerged arc technique is used in the downhand position with OES3 wire and OP41TT flux at a heat input of 2.2 kJ/mm. It is used when the individual hull units are joined in the shop by rotating the hull butt below the welding head. Because a double Vee profile is used only the outer section can be welded using the submerged arc technique at present, the inner position being finished using the MMA process. The MMA process is also used to weld the root run of the profile. The root run is subsequently backgouged before the inner weld is finished after the submerged arc weld has been completed. Trials have been made which show that with the use of OP41TT flux adequate properties can be developed using high current up to 700 amps and high heat input values, up to 4 kJ/mm.

In recent years the submerged arc process has been used to weld the T frames to the hull. This has been achieved with what is termed a squirt gun, where the welding wire and flux are forced together through a welding torch. The flux used is OP41TT with the same particle size as would be used for hull butts. It has been possible using the technique to recirculate the flux after filtering, with a 25% addition of new baked flux, the excess flux left over one day being rebaked before use on the following day. Problems do occasionally occur with the technique. This is mainly due to the presence of drawing lubricants on the wire which, unless effectively removed, can eventually stop the wire feeding properly. The use of recirculated flux has not led to serious problems of flux feeding, the filtering technique being effective.

FUTURE TRENDS

It has been the policy of the UK Navy to specify the overmatching of weld metal strength to that of the plate, ie the minimum strength 655 N/mm^2 of the weld metal shall be greater than the maximum strength of the plate, 650 N/mm^2. At the same time it was also specified that the toughness as specified in Charpy Cv tests carried out at -20°C should exceed 55 joules. In addition the whole weldment should pass the plain and the crack starter bulge explosion test as specified in the US Mil Spec [10].

The requirement to overmatch the plate strength has meant continuing difficulties in meeting the mechanical property requirements with other than a handful of consumables. This problem has been further exacerbated now welding of a higher strength steel, HY100, is being investigated.

These problems have been carefully considered over the past few years in the UK, and a new specification for weld metal acceptance devised based on a more clearly defined fitness for purpose basis.

The new specification requires that all consumables are tested by making welds in 50 mm thick plate using a standard profile or one which will be used in construction. This enables both consumable approval to be achieved and also procedural approval to be cleared, by testing the welds for specified mechanical property requirements concurrent with the new bulge explosion test requirement. In the new bulge explosion test a notch is machined along the weld (Figure 4) before extending with a fatigue crack to the required length and depth. This new test piece is subjected, under-water, to an explosive charge which produces a standard amount of plastic strain in the weld. The acceptance requirement is that the fatigue crack shall not extend more than a fixed amount at the temperature of testing, $-5^{\circ}C$.

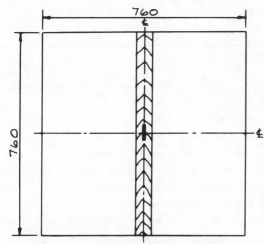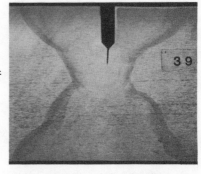

BULGE EXPLOSION PANEL
NOTCH DEPTH 4m.m. AT DEEPEST POINT.
NOTCH SURFACE LENGTH 50mm TO 60m.m.
NOTCH TO BE AT CENTRELINE OF WELD.

FIGURE 4. Bulge Explosion Test Criteria.

In addition to the above changes the requirement for overmatching of the 0.2% proof stress in the weld has been dropped, a 550 N/mm^2 minimum now being specified. This has enabled an increased number of consumables to be considered for possible submarine use. It has also meant that with lower strength a significant increase in toughness may accrue which is beneficial as regards passing the new bulge explosion test criteria. This increase in toughness is regarded as necessary for the performance of the weldments in service and is reflected in the new specification of 80 joules minimum at -20°C in the Charpy V notch test.

Manual Metal Arc Welds

The use of MMA consumables will diminish rapidly in the coming years as submerged arc and pulsed MIG welds gradually take over. This will result in an inherent improvement in weld quality with these more easily controlled processes. However MMA consumables will be required in the future, and they will still be subject to the present difficulties with MMA electrodes. But, with the lower 0.2% proof stress requirements, the problem of HAZ cold cracking should be diminished because of the lower level of strain induced in the weld on cooling.

It would be advantageous if preheat levels could be reduced for all MMA applications - thus enabling a decrease in the reliance of the fabricator, on the conscientiousness of the welder in applying the specified preheat and cleanness regulations. Work to this end is being pursued in the US and UK, so as to enable either electrodes to be used directly from the packet and/or have a moisture resistant coating to ensure a longer life is maintained after baking. The object must be to reduce the diffusible hydrogen level after welding. However, if moisture is to be reduced, a compromise must be met where mechanical properties are offset against usability. Consumables with high toughness and low moisture will of necessity be more difficult to use. Thus, although minimal hydrogen levels are possible, a recognised limit may have to be reached or the skill of the welder will have to increase.

Some work at ARE and at Renneslaer Polytechnic has shown that factors other than plate composition may affect the level of the required preheat. For example, where electro slag refined plate has been welded the required preheat temperature as defined by controlled thermal severity tests [11] has been significantly reduced. The work at Renneslaer [12] and ARE has indicated not only an improvement in lower sulphur contents, but sulphide shape may have a significant effect on crack susceptibility. With the addition of inclusion shape modifiers to the steel the reduced cracking susceptibility has been attributed to the rounding off of the sulphide inclusions. This observation is however at variance with some recent work with micro alloyed carbon-manganese steels where small round inclusions did not give steel increased resistance to hydrogen induced HAZ cold cracking [13].

Submerged Arc

In the development of submerged arc welding for future application in submarine production, the major advantage is in increased productivity by increasing production rate. This can be achieved either by increased heat input per pass or by using a multiple head technique, whilst at the same time maintaining the specified strength and toughness properties. The use of single or multiple wire high heat input welds [14, 15, 16] particularly in pipe welding is well known and widely used. The welding of a submarine hull is only a pipe technique in somewhat different circumstances.

When looking for improved productivity the use of OP121TT flux was found to be preferable to OP41TT with high heat input welds, as the specified weld metal strength was more easily met. The flux composition is less prone to breakdown at high heat input levels than OP41TT and the weld pool kinetics plus the flux deoxidants result in improved weld metal mechanical properties at the increased heat input levels. There is a problem however and it must be recognised. The flux OP121TT is more hygroscopic and must be properly stored and prepared. In general the flux, because of its low initial moisture content, produces welds with low hydrogen levels, less than 5 cc/100 gm weld metal. Thus for offshore structure it may be used direct from the drum as supplied by the manufacturer. However, with high strength materials such as HY80, which have hard HAZ's, 420 Hv, the level of moisture may be more critical and direct use without initial baking, to the manufacturer's specification, may not be prudent. Also, unless adequate baking is available, flux recirculation should not be attempted because of possible increased crack susceptibility with high strength steels and weld metal over mild steel structures.

Welds with increased productivity have been made using twin arcs and
OP121TT flux.   These have been   produced with 4 mm diameter wire and a
current level of 700 amps.   In these cases adequate strength and toughness
have been achieved, resulting in adequate bulge explosion test behaviour.

The use of twin arcs will obviously increase the productivity in butt
welds. The system, as with single arc welding processes, will be useful in
producing welded frames and welding these frames to the hull.   However,
because of the increased heat input, distortion of the frame will be
increased.   Although the distortion can, as with single arc welding of
frames, be overcome by welding the subsequent pass on the other side of the
frame it would be preferable if distortion could be kept to a minimum.   The
distortion would be minimised if the frames were welded on both sides
simultaneously.   This could be done with single arcs or twin arcs, the
latter being preferred due to the possible higher deposition rates.   The
use of twin arcs to weld either side of a frame web will undoubtedly reduce
distortion, but the profile as presented for welding must be balanced.
This is best achieved by using a machined profile or the extra weld metal
used to fill an unbalanced flame cut profile will almost certainly result
in distortion.   The use of multiple arcs in the twin tandem mode can be
achieved using a number of   configurations, Figure 5.   The properties of
welds made with these configurations are shown in Table 2.   It can be seen

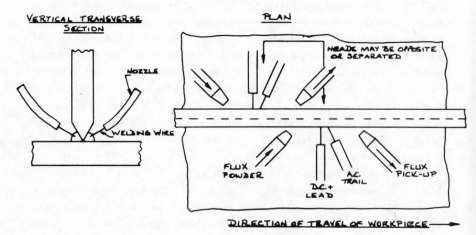

FIGURE 5.   Tandem Arc Configurations.

that the properties of the directly opposed arcs are poorer than the staggered arcs. This is most probably due to a slow cooling rate in the weld metal for the former configuration. The staggered arcs have been located so that when the first arcs have passed, the temperature of the weld drops to below $300^{\circ}C$, before the second arcs arrive, and raise the local temperature again. This ensures an initial cooling rate in the weld zone giving an initial weldment which is subsequently effectively tempered by the subsequent weld passes.

TABLE 2
Typical Properties of Tandem Submerged Arc Welds

Weld No	Weld Profile	Welding Configuration	0.2% PS N/mm^2	UTS N/mm^2	El %	R of A %	C_v at $-20^{\circ}C$ Joules	Remarks
A	T butt	Twin Tandem	642	724	18	72	70-136	Opposing Arcs
B	T butt	Twin Tandem	720	814	20	66	100-124	Staggered Arcs
C	T butt	Twin Tandem	705	770	20	66	157-175	Staggered Arcs
D	Single V	Tandem	681	810	27	68	68-142	----

It is proposed to fabricate frames vertically, as complete hoops, with twin tandem arcs welding downhand, using OP121TT flux which will be used as baked and recycled with a make-up rate of 25%, the flux being held in heated hoppers before use. All as-received flux will be baked in separate ovens before transfer to the welding station.

The weld profiles produced by this technique are shown in Figure 6 for two sizes of frame. It is clear that a good profile is achievable especially at the weld toe where crack initiation may occur by the imposition of cyclic stress.

The use of twin tandem arcs need not be restricted to frame fabrication as the technique can easily be applied to the attachment of frames to the hull envelope provided the individual hull unit can be rotated to enable the submerged arc welding to be carried out in the downhand position. In all cases of unit construction it is possible to rotate the hull whilst attaching the frames to the hull.

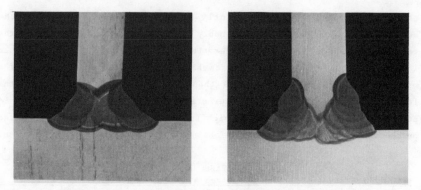

FIGURE 6. Typical Weld Profiles Using Twin Tandem Arcs.

Tandem arcs could be used in place of the single wire process for hull butts where the hull can be rotated. (The properties of Tandem arc welds made in this position can be seen in Table 2 and are similar to those for Twin Tandem arc welds). It may be preferable for welds in these areas to be made with a single Vee profile provided the distortion can be accepted. In practice single Vee welds have a backing run to give an acceptable profile and this may be a MMA or pulsed MIG weld. It is still thought necessary to make the root pass with a process other than submerged arc, to reduce the probability of root cracking. Rather than back gouge, which is an additional operation, the root pass could be made on glass backing which, with a minimum of grinding, gives a good surface for subsequent submerged arc passes. Because of the inherent toughness of the submerged arc welds, the use of MMA will not impair the crack resistant properties of the submerged arc weld.

Pulsed MIG

The pulsed MIG welding process has been used for many years. The first power sources used a constant voltage system, the upper and lower voltage levels being set for fixed perods of time, to give a pulse rate of 60-120 Hz, such that the current was stabilised at a level to give a controllable deposition of the weld metal, producing welds with acceptable mechanical properties.

The policy of the MOD for welding submarine hulls has been to investigate the use of constant current power sources. In using these power sources the upper and lower levels of current levels are set for specified periods of time within a range of pulse rates. Usually pulse MIG sets work on a sinusoidal waveform, but MOD developments have investigated the use of square waves, in order to give improved droplet detachment. This has involved the development of electronics to give a clean square rather than one with associated spikes, Figure 7.

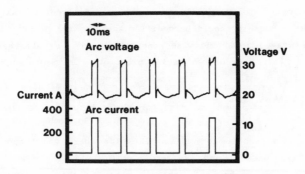

FIGURE 7. Preferred Waveform

When using the pulse MIG technique MOD has concentrated on the development of a synergic system. This means that for a fixed set of welding parameters, current and voltage, if the wire feed speed is varied, say with increased travel speed, the pulsing rate also varies automatically in order to compensate so as to maintain a consistent deposition rate and thus nugget size. In order to do this, it is necessary to monitor the wire feed speed. It is hoped by this means to maintain more consistent mechanical properties and improved weld integrity.

Pulsed MIG welds can be made using a stringer bead technique but it is more usual to use a weave pattern to fill a standard double V or single V weld profile. Weaving is achieved using an oscillatory motion with a dwell built in at the side walls to adequately burn in so as to reduce side wall lack of fusion. In all cases as the width of the weld profile increases a split weave technique is used to enable adequate mechanical properties to be developed. With the stringer bead technique the normal heat input relationship can be applied HI = $\dfrac{VA}{Travel\ Speed}$. However when weaving is used this may not fully describe the prevailing conditions. A number of suggestions have been made to accommodate this situation and another is now proposed for consideration, which is based on current, voltage and weave speed, ie HI = AV/W Speed. However this neglects the fact that a weave in one direction is almost immediately followed by a weave in the opposite direction whilst the initial bead is still hot. Thus the weld metal will cool more slowly than in normal circumstances. In order to take account of this, the relationship should be modified to take account of linear speeds, as well as weave speed, and wire consumption rate, as all these factors affect the fill rate of the weld profile. The proposed relationship could be written:

$$HI = \frac{AV}{\sqrt{WS^2 + S^2}} \quad x \quad time\ for\ 100\ gm\ wire\ to\ be\ consumed$$

Using this relationship for pulse MIG welds there would appear to be a relationship between HI and the resulting 0.2% PS of the weld. This has been examined for mechanical vertical welds, Figure 8, but needs to be substantiated for welds made in all welding positions.

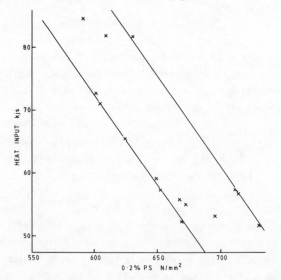

FIGURE 8. Relationship between HI and 0.2% PS for Vertical Pulse MIG Welds.

The use of the pulsed MIG technique has now been taken up by the UK shipbuilder, to make the vertical seams in the hull units. It is possible to use the process with single and double Vee profiles with a root run made on glass backing or ceramic. Often it is also preferable for a cosmetic pass to be made on the vertical seams with single Vee profiles.

The welding parameters have been developed to make pulsed MIG welds in the downhand, vertical and overhead positions, with adequate mechanical properties for welds made in these positions. Because the intention is to use the technique to weld the hull continuously around the circumference, some method must be devised to enable the welding parameters to be built into a computer so that the welding parameters can be changed automatically to suit the welding position. The work programme undertaken at ARE has indicated that this change can most probably be achieved by altering the welding speed.

Electron Beam Welding

It is probably not possible to develop conventional welding processes, MMA, Pulsed MIG and submerged arc further, other than to full automation. However, there could be advantages for the shipbuilder in the use of narrow gap, laser and electron beam welding. Narrow gap welding can be considered as a modification to one of the well known conventional processes, eg submerged arc, rather than a newly developed process. The main problem is the development of an adequate torch if positional welding is desired. Laser at present is restricted to thin material because of the power requirements. Thus the most promising new developments could be in the area of electron beam welding.

For some years it has been possible to use electron beam welding to weld thick aluminium and steel components [17]. Thus it should be fairly easy to transfer the technology to weld high strength steels such as HY80. Because of the severe fit-up requirements, it is probably not sensible to think of using EB for welding the main submarine hulls at present. However there may be advantages in welding small components using the process. For example, some simpler castings could even now be made from EB welded plate, Figure 9, so reducing the cost of production. This is particularly relevant when it is appreciated that weld repair of castings accounts for a considerable amount of the cost of production. Also where frames are fabricated, it could be beneficial to use EB welding rather than submerged arc as this will reduce the total weld area and reduce the susceptibility to defects such as root problems and HAZ cold cracking.

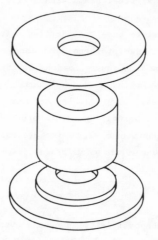

FIGURE 9.   EB Welded Valve Body.

ARE (Dunfermline) has been involved with EB welding of QlN steel plate and castings.   The results have shown that excellent properties are possible when the material is heat treated after welding.   Bulge explosion

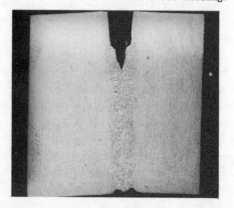

FIGURE 10.   Explosion Bulge Test on EB Weld.

tests carried out with fatigue cracks in the weld show no sign of crack propagation, Figure 10. However the toughness of EB welds, in the as-welded condition, is dependent on the composition of the parent material. The toughness problem appears to be associated with a raft-like micro-structure which forms with the impure materials. Elimination of this structure greatly increases crack propagation resistance and changes an intergranular type failure under impact loading to a ductile transgranular mode. For good as welded properties, the cost of providing high purity steels may outweigh the advantages of EB welding. Where necessary, the heat treating of EB welds, may be all that is required for strong tough welds in small components.

The reason for poor toughness, associated with laser welds in HY80 type steel, could be similar to that described above, for low toughness EB welds.

CONCLUDING REMARKS

Increasing production rates demands a move from MMA welding to processes which lend themselves more easily to automation. This has increased benefits of weld integrity, such as the elimination of slag entrapment, porosity, reduced lack of side wall fusion and a lower suscept-ibility to HAZ cold cracking. This is always provided the gas cover in MIG welding or the flux quality in submerged arc welds is adequately maintained. Both these processes are low hydrogen processes and thus weld metal or HAZ cold cracking should be at a minimum. However correct flux drying is also essential to prevent weld metal hydrogen cracking in submerged arc welds, especially when OP121TT flux is used with high heat input welds, because this flux is less resistant to moisture pick up.

The use of Pulsed MIG and submerged arc welding are obviously amenable to greater automation. This could be achieved by the use in the former case of equipment to run welds around a submarine hull, in a more remote and fully programmed manner or in the latter case, where applicable, the use of multiple arcs. The use of twin and twin tandem arc is a major step forward but multiple arcs could be considered for welding rotating circum-ferential butts, in the downhand position.

If it is thought beneficial to reduce the quantity of weld metal in a joint then techniques such as EB welding should be considered. Although the increased fit requirements may be expensive the reduction in residual and restraint stresses could make the technique attractive. The main problem in using EB welding is the requirement for large vacuum chambers but an effective locally applied vacuum system could be an adequate solution.

REFERENCES

1. Brown, D.K., The introduction of iron warships into the Royal Navy. Naval Architect, March 1977.

2. Brown, D.K., The corrosion of Holland No 1. Journal of Naval Science, May 1984.

3. Kihara, H., Suzuki, H. and Nukamura, H., Weld cracking tests of high strength steels and electrodes. Welding Journal 1962, Vol 41, p365-485.

4. Suzaki, H., Cold cracking and its prevention in steel welding. IIW Doc IX-1074-78.

5. Coe, F.R., Welding steels without hydrogen cracking. Welding Institute publication 1973.

6. Yurioka, N., Ohshita, S. and Tamehiro, H., Study on carbon equivalents to assess cold cracking tendency and hardness in steel welding. AWRA Symposium 'Pipeline Welding in the 80s' March 1981. JWS Weld Met Comm WM-784-80 1980.

7. Ito, Y. and Bessyo, K., Cracking parameter of high strength steels related to HAZ cracking. IIW Doc IX-576-68, 1968.

8. Suzuki, H., Carbon equivalent, maximum hardness and cracking in welding steel. Jour ISIJ 70 (1984) No 16.

9. Electrodes, welding, mineral covered, iron powder, low hydrogen medium, high tensile and higher strength low alloy steels. Mil-E-0022200/10A(SH).

10. Standard procedures for explosion testing ferrous and non ferrous metallic materials and weldments. MIL-STD-2149(SH) Nov 1983.

11. Winn, W.H., Weldability of low alloy steels. British Welding Journal, August 1964.

12. Savage, W.F., The effect of rare earth additions on hydrogen induced cracking in HY80 weldments. ASM International Conference 'Sulphide inclusions in steel. 7-8 Nov 1974.

13. Ito, Y., Nakanishi, M. and Komizo, Y. Carbon equivalent and hardness for cracking tendency of C-Mn microalloyed structural steel. IIW Doc IX-1349-85.

14. Fraser, R., McLean, A., Webster, D.J. and Taylor D.S., High deposition rate submerged arc welding for critical applications.

15. Bunher, T.A., Multi electrodes in SAW with square wave AC power. Welding Journal, July 1982.

16. Wolff, L., Getting the most out of SA welding. Welding and Metal Fabrication, March 1980.

17. Russell, J.D., Electron beam welding – A review. Metal Construction, July 1981.

STRUCTURAL DESIGN FOR MINIMUM COST

D W CHALMERS OBE C Eng FRINA RCNC
Ministry of Defence (PE), Chief Naval
Architect's Department, Foxhill, Bath BA1 5AB, UK

There is always pressure to reduce the cost of acquiring ships, and in recent years this has been emphasised for warships by comparisons between the apparently high cost of warship structures and low cost of merchant ship structures. The relative costs of labour and materials in merchant and warship structures is therefore examined to discover where the most scope for reducing cost lies. It is shown that much of the cost of a warship is implicit from its operational requirements, but there is some room for reducing structural cost at the expense of a little weight by simplifying the structure and reducing the number of stiffeners and stiffener connections.

INTRODUCTION

Ever since ships have been built there has been pressure to reduce the costs of construction and ownership whether the owner be a national government or a commercial enterprise. In recent years the pressures on financing of government owned vessels have become acute as governments resort to every possible means for cutting costs, while, for warships at least, prices have far outstripped inflation.

A large proportion of the cost of a ship is in its equipment and fittings, and this is particularly evident in warships when the cost of weapon systems is taken into account. In fact the cost of the hull structure of a warship is only of the order of 10% of the total unit production cost (UPC) of which the majority is labour and only a small proportion material. Consequently the potential for savings in reduction of hull structure costs as a proportion of UPC is small; nevertheless, if the cost of the structure could be reduced by, say, 10%, that would be a saving of about £1M on a £100M ship, which cannot be disregarded. However, to enable savings of this relative order of magnitude to be discussed seriously, it is necessary first to consider how costs are estimated, and to what likely accuracy.

COST ESTIMATING AND ACCURACY

For any useful decisions to be made on structural style and details intended to reduce costs it is essential that realistic cost estimates can be made at the design stage. Traditionally shipyard costs have been recorded on a unit weight basis (£/Tonne) of the finished structure. However, these records are not used by the Shipbuilder in estimating labour costs, which is usually done subjectively in terms of man hours, with some adjustment being made for the complexity of structure to be built. Unfortunately a consequence of recording total cost in £/Tonne is that the designer may perceive it to be a significant costing parameter and it is a factor leading to the traditional warship lightweight structure (Figs 1, 2).

FIGURE 1. General View of Lightweight Warship Structure

FIGURE 2. Complex Detail of Orthogonal Stiffening

Shipbuilders are aware of the problem of providing realistic labour cost estimates but records on which they can be based are generally lacking, although a few yards have begun to build up suitable data bases. To achieve an objective estimating approach to replace the current haphazard subjective one, it will be necessary to assemble more data which will need to be actively based[1]. That is costs of carrying out different types of activity under different conditions and using different processes. The costs are likely to be based on unit length, number or area, etc with weighting factors for the different controlling conditions. However, to enable a realistic estimate to be built up for a complete hull, there are very many different processes to be considered and an enormous quantity of data to be collected and analysed, which will take some years, and which incidentally is likely to be unique to each shipyard. An interesting example comes from IHI in Japan[2] where an approximate 25% reduction in man hours has been achieved by a careful study of the labour costs of different processes followed by redesign to limit the more costly ones.

A consequence of the uncertainty surrounding labour cost estimating is that many opinions are expressed concerning the relative costs of warship and merchant ship style hulls. Firm statements have been made, for example, that warship structures are five times as costly per unit weight as merchant ships based on graphs such as Fig 3.

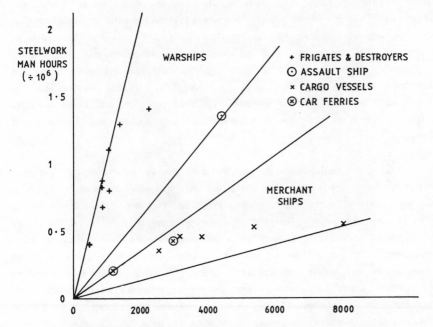

FIGURE 3. Steelwork man hours/Steelweight for Various Ships

In fact the recorded man hours per unit steel weight vary enormously from 800-900 man hours/tonne for the most complex frigate down to less than 100 for the simplest and largest merchant vessel. There is a strong size dependence in the figures, with smaller vessels taking proportionately many more man hours/tonne than larger ones. This can be demonstrated simply when considering handling plates; the man hours required to lift and position a heavy plate are little different from those for a light plate and the man hours/tonne will be almost inversely proportion to plate thickness. Generally, whatever aspect of structure is considered, it will be seen that man hours/tonne must be higher for small complex warships on account of their implicit small size and complexity of layout and systems[3]. What limited data there is on larger warships such as assault ships shows man hours/tonne to be much closer to the more complex "one-off" merchant ships (Fig 3).

This is not to say that warship structure is no more expensive than merchant structure; however, the difference lies principally in the use of lighter scantlings and more structurally efficient symmetrical stiffeners, continuous welding, etc. The lighter scantlings lead to difficulties of alignment and distortion and consequent rework, and the long stalk tee sections are inherently more expensive than offset bulb plates or angles. A further cost in warships is the level of quality required to be demonstrated by the shipbuilder. However, for a prescribed ship function and configuration the reduction in cost by moving from warship design rules to those of a classification society is unlikely to be more than 25%, certainly nowhere near the factors of 3 or more sometimes quoted, and the consequent additional structural weight and space and reduction in reliability will largely offset any structural cost savings.

A further complication is the fact that cost recorded by the shipyard and price paid by the owner are not the same thing; the price quoted to the potential owner is only partly related to the actual shipyard costs, and includes profit. The price will often be adjusted to improve the yard's chance of obtaining an order[4] and indeed may be subsidised to the extent that the price quoted is less than the actual cost. Nevertheless, for practical purposes it can be assumed that overheads are a direct percentage of total labour costs and profits are an independent variable and therefore both can be ignored in any arguments concerning optimisation or reduction of structural costs. This appears not to be always the case and authors[5, 6] have found that including overheads can have a significant effect on the results of the optimisation process. However, unless the designer has access to a specific shipyard's data he cannot allow for overheads, and any general discussion of structural cost minimisation can concentrate only on material and labour costs.

ELEMENTS OF STRUCTURE COSTS

The two main elements of cost, material and labour will be discussed in more detail below. However, material cost is mainly proportional to the weight of steel, modified by the cost of sections which may be up to twice the cost/unit weight of steel plate. Higher strength steels are also significantly more expensive than mild steel. Labour costs, measured in terms of man hours/unit weight of structure, are strongly dependent on style and arrangement of structure, in particular the relative extent of compartmentation and ease of access, the number of equipment seatings and small strucutral components, the number of service penetrations etc. The complexity and arrangement of stiffening and details also has a significant effect however, and it is on these aspects that the structural designer can have most influence. Availability of shipyard processes, such as automatic or semi-automatic welding, and jig built sub-assemblies can also influence the result of a cost minimisation exercise.

It follows that the most costly structures will be those which are complicated with many intricate connections between small parts on light plate, where, in addition to the difficulty of assembly, form and alignment are not easy to maintain (Fig 2). It is conceivable that cost could start to rise again in a very heavy structure due to the cost of materials begining to dominate, but such a structure is unlikely ever to be realistic for a ship. In a warship which has implicitly many components and compartments, and many services to fit through structure the designer has a most difficult task in striking a balance between acceptable strength (as well as all the non-structural attributes) and ease of production.

The above arguments have been applied to UPC but throughlife costs also merit a brief discussion. The cost of maintaining a structure will depend on the amount of preservation and painting necessary, or the amount of replacement of material due to wastage. Cost will also be incurred if the strength of the structure is such that damage, usually fatigue, occurs in service and requires repair. Maintenance and preservation will be simplified and so the likelihood of repair reduced by simplifying the structure, making it more open and easy of access, which is also likely to be in line with reducing UPC labour costs. The effect of damage in service is reduced by using heavier scantlings which may result in higher material costs but it is possible that the structure can at the same time be arranged for lower labour costs by taking advantage of the potential of heavier scantlings for a less intricate structure.

The numerical breakdown of structural cost has been discussed by a number of authors over the years[eg 5, 7, 8] but has mainly concentrated on labour costs over which it is deemed the designer has most control by simplifying the structure to be built. However, simplifying the structure will almost certainly increase its weight and material cost and it is first worth investigating the sensitivity of material cost to changes in structural style.

MATERIAL COSTS

For the purpose of this paper it will be assumed that the structure is entirely of steel, although the extension of the arguments to other materials would not be difficult. Beginning by taking the basic cost to be that of mild steel plate to

BS 4360[9] grade 43A (or MOD NES 791 Part 1[10]) then the information in Table 1 has been assembled from unpublished sources.

TABLE 1 - Plate Cost and Strength

| Plate Material | Relative | |
	Cost	Yield Strength
Mild Steel BS 4360 grade 43A	1.0	1.0
Mild Steel BS 4360 grade 43D	1.1	1.1
MT Steel BS 4360 grade 50D	1.2	1.35
'B' Quality (NES 791 Part 3)	1.25	1.35

All these materials have the same Young's Modulus and, for practical purposes, fatigue life, as this is dependent mainly on quality of assembly and welding. It may seem that by using B Quality steel the higher strength will lead to less material being required, and the consequent reduction in weight will more than offset the increased cost. However, as the critical modes of failure will be elasto-plastic buckling and fatigue, full advantage cannot be taken of increased yield stress and at best the reduction in weight achieved by using higher strength steels will no more than offset the increased cost. Nothing is therefore achieved in departing from mild steel unless there are other overriding requirements such as toughness (which is not guaranteed in grade 43A steel[9]) or weight reduction irrespective of cost.

Considering now the stiffening, the arguments above on steel type will apply again, but additionally there is the question of stiffener type. Table 2 has again be derived from unpublished data, the column on weight being taken from work undertaken by Smith et al at ARE Dunfermline.

TABLE 2 - Stiffener Cost and Weight - All Mild Steel

Stiffener Type	Cost/Unit Weight Relative to MS Plate	Relative Weight For Equal Strength Grillage
Long Stalk Tee	2.0	1.0
Offset Bulb Plate (OBP)	1.4	1.08
Flat Bar	1.20	1.20-1.23

From the product of the two columns in Table 2 it can be seen that there is an approximate 25% cost reduction in moving from Long Stalk Tees to either OBP or flat bar and this reduction may be even more if the full strength of the Tee cannot be utilised because of the limited number of sizes available. However, in a warship there is a distinct disadvantage in departing from Tees due to the space taken up by the less efficient sections and in particular in the examples analysed at ARE(D) the use of OBP's involved an approximate 45% increase in depth of structure, although for flat bars, due to their inherent symmetry, the increase was only about 5%.

The conclusions that can be drawn are that if space is no object, but cost and weight are to be minimised together, then OBP's are the best stiffener to use. This explains why they are used in merchant ships where such conditions apply. In warships, traditionally, weight and space have been the critical factors and Tees have been the obvious choice. However, there is a case for accepting a small increase in weight with little effect on space by judicious use of flat bar stiffening to replace Tees in some of the structure. These decisions also have implications on the design of details which will be discussed later.

LABOUR COSTS

There is clearly a trade-off between material and labour costs. Labour is expended mainly in welding and assembly, and the more of this there is, and the more complex it is, then the more the labour man hours expended will be. A number of authors have addressed this optimisation process both for specific cases[5, 8,11] and by writing general purpose computer programs[1, 6, 12, 13] but have only served to reinforce this general conclusion. Careyette[7] has analysed many shipyard records and concluded that total steelwork man-hours are proportional to:

$$\frac{W_s^{2/3} L^{1/3}}{C_b}$$

Where:

W_s = steel weight

L = length BP

C_b = block coefficient

The implication for warships is the inclusion of block coefficient showing the dependence of steelwork man-hours on shape, but the relationship still does not allow for simplification of structural style reducing man-hours at the expense of weight. As noted earlier the man hours/unit weight of warship structure is always likely to be more than that for a merchant ship structure, the main reasons for the differences being given as:

a.   the greater number and complexity of parts, and more curved surfaces.

b.   lighter scantlings of a warship being more difficult to assemble and frequently requiring more rework; closely stiffened orthogonal structure with continuous welding which cannot be readily automated.

c.   longer build time per unit weight.

d.   higher volumetric density for assembly and installation.

e.   higher standards of workmanship, quality control, inspection, documentation, etc.

Item c. is implicit in the construction of a warship and is outside the designers' control. Item d. is also implicit in a warship but can be partially alleviated by providing more space for access at the expense of a larger hull, but with consequent increases in many other costs and a potential reduction in performance for the same machinery. Usher and Dorey[14] draw attention to the improved productivity that can be achieved by providing adequate space, and suggest some limits of congestion beyond which productivity cannot be improved, but given warship requirements of sub-division and the quantity of equipment to be fitted, there are only very limited possibilities for improvement. Item e., workmanship and quality control should not intuitively vary significantly between warships and merchant ships. All owners should be equally keen to get value for money. Nevertheless, due to the emphasis placed on reliability under wartime conditions and the requirement for a longer hull life, navies have to pay more than civil owners for quality assurance, and because again of the complexity of warships a given level of assurance is more expensive to achieve. Item a. is only partly under the control of the structural designer but to the extent that he can reduce the number of stiffeners and connections he can make some cost reduction.

This leaves us with item b., the lighter scantlings of warships, which is directly under the designers control but which probably only accounts at most for 25% of the cost difference between merchant and warship structures. The use of merchant ship style materials such as offset bulb plates has been discussed earlier and shown to promise only limited savings as a material. OBP's and flat bars are easier to bend and fit and some savings should accrue in this way though there is no quantitative evidence available. The scope for varying plate thickness and stiffener spacing and size is limited in reality, and it can be shown that the variation between cost and weight as complexity is varied for a simple stiffened panel of constant in-plane strength is of the form of Fig 4 derived from an algorithm in the MOD GODDESS system[15]. Current designs are in the region of the minimum, and while there is a clear risk of increasing cost if complexity is increased, there is also a risk of a small increase by reducing complexity, and increasing weight.

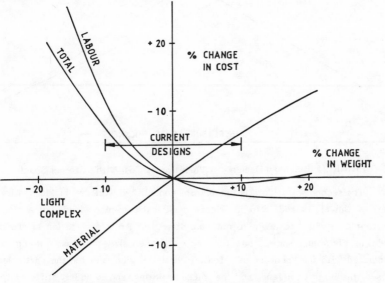

FIGURE 4. Effect on Cost of Varying Complexity of a Grillage

To investigate further the potential for reduced cost by simplifying structure, two other sets of data have been identified. The first, presented by Caldwell and Hewitt[5] is for a merchant ship bulkhead design and is for nearly constant bending strength; an interpretation of the data is given in Fig 5, showing that over the range in question stiffener weight and spacing, and total cost, vary nearly linearly and that the minimum cost is achieved for maximum stiffener spacing, minimum stiffener weight and maximum plate thickness.

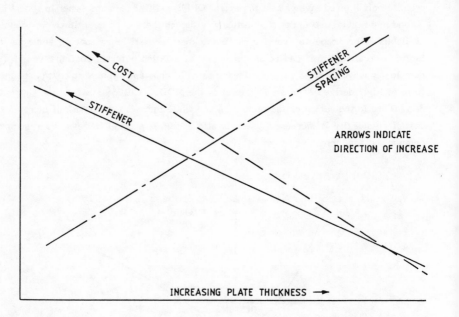

FIGURE 5 Bulkhead Design[5] - Variation of Cost with Stiffener Spacing

The second set of data is taken from unpublished work by Winkle and Irvine at Glasgow University and is for a frigate deck under in-plane load, but arranged for constant area while achieving a minimum strength. An interpretation of the data is given in Fig 6 and shows that for each stiffener size there is a minimum cost associated with the boundary of a feasible design region, and for the particular case chosen, the largest stiffener and the thickest plating (and so widest stiffener spacing) gives the cheapest option.

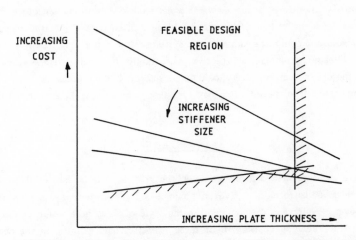

FIGURE 6. Frigate Deck - Design Lines for Different Stiffener Sizes

The three plots, Figs 4, 5 and 6, although derived from very different data, all lead to a similar conclusion, that the lowest cost is associated with a wide stiffener spacing and appropriately thick plate which then generally leads to larger stiffener sizes. However, for in-plane load at least, the minimum is very flat and there is a range of options of stiffener size and spacing for which total cost will vary very little.

Further quantitative corroboration of the insensitivity of cost to arrangement of structure is provided by Rains[16] who reports some reduction in displacement from the use of lightweight decks (although the method of reducing weight is not defined) but with little overall effect on ship cost.

The evidence therefore that structural cost is not very sensitive to arrangement of stiffening (within a reasonable range) is fairly conclusive, although in general heavier scantlings and fewer stiffeners will be cheaper. An extreme example is demonstrated by Nappi et al[17] who have investigated the design of a frigate structure with no transverse frames, but only transverse bulkheads and longitudinal stiffening. They concluded that such a design was feasible and an optimum arrangement would save about 14% of hull cost while adding about 7% to hull weight. However, at least half the estimated cost saving is due to the reduction in ship fitting man hours from the removal of transverse frames which otherwise provide obstacles to the running of systems.

There is, therefore, scope in warship design for simplifying structure and so reducing labour costs, although this scope will be limited by the inevitable requirements of layout and complex equipment and systems. Where the penalties in space and weight of cheaper "commercial" sections, especially flat bar stiffeners, can be accepted, the use of such sections should be considered, but the potential for material cost saving is small compared with that for labour cost saving in a cost optimised design.

COST OF DETAILS

There is no published information on the cost of details, indeed there is no quantitative unpublished data. However, a number of shipbuilders have been asked by MOD(PE) over recent years to comment on the style of structural design of warships with a view to reducing costs. All of these exercises have pointed to the need to simplify detail to make it easier to assemble. There are, however, a number of overriding constraints on the extent to which this simplification can go, in particular:

a.   Stress concentrations must be acceptable to minimise the risk of fatigue failure.

b.   Discontinuities should not lead to risk of failure under shock loading.

c.   Shape discontinuitities should not be introduced which would affect other design requirements, for example hull form, to an unacceptable extent.

The details which are structurally significant in this context are:

a.   Connections between stiffeners, both in plane on a grillage, and between grillages.

b.   Compensation around holes, that is coamings and insert plates.

c.   Supports to deckhouses and heavy masses on decks.

d.   Arrangement of stiffening around penetrations.

Taking these in turn, connections between stiffeners will always be expensive because of the need for accuracy of alignment and for short lengths of weld in awkward corners. It will never be possible to eliminate these, but unidirectional stiffening or at least the minimum number of stiffeners in one direction should be used when possible. Where stiffened structure is connected at an angle, for instance between decks and bulkheads or the ships side, there is usually the need to transfer a significant bending load between the parts. The apparent cheapest type of connection is to stop each part short and fit a bracket (Fig 7).

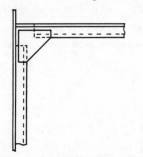

FIGURE 7. Simple Bracketed Connection

However, it is essential that the bending stiffness of the connection is nowhere less than the weakest of the two members connected which generally means a very large bracket or a rider plate which itself adds expense, indeed the SSC in its review of structural details[18] shows brackets to be by far the most labour intensive detail. In addition alignment must be maintained, or high out of plane bending stresses will be induced in the bracket, probably leading to premature fatigue failure.

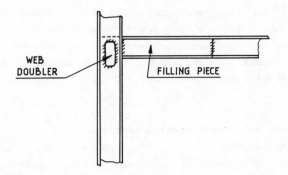

WEB DOUBLER

FILLING PIECE

FIGURE 8. Connection Allowing for Misalignment

There is no simple solution but a good compromise is shown in Fig 8 where one member is kept deliberately short and a filling piece inserted after assembly so minimising the effect of any misalignment while maintaining in plane bending stiffness. The web doubler on the main member may not be necessary, but where there is a need to prevent buckling of the web it is probably the cheapest solution.

The examples quoted have been for Tee stiffeners but would work equally well for flat bar or offset bulb plate for the secondary member as long as the main member has a table on which to land the filling piece. However combinations of flat bar and OBP cannot conveniently be connected in this way and a lapped joining piece is probably necessary, but consequently needing either heavy low stressed structure or very good alignment.

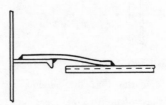

FIGURE 9. Misaligned Lapped Bracket

A misaligned lapped bracket (Fig 9) is probably the worst of all worlds as it is difficult to weld effectively as well as being highly stressed.

For compensation around holes the important aspect is to ensure stress concentrations are kept down to an acceptable level. In practice this will mean rounding the corners of the hole and fitting a thicker insert plate and possibly a coaming. Due to the extra welding involved a coaming should only be fitted if essential. It should also be noted that a higher stress concentration can be accepted if there are no welds in the highly stressed zone as discussed for steel bridges in BS 5400 Part 10[19].

In support to deckhouses and heavy masses there are really no short cuts and stiff efficient structure must be worked. Good alignment of structure, for example deckhouse ends and their supporting bulkheads, is essential, and there must be no discontinuities in joints between associated stiffeners if severe fatigue problems are to be avoided.

For the arrangement of stiffening around penetrations the only need is to keep it as simple as possible. To that end it is always easier if penetrations are lined up (Fig 10) so that a straight run of stiffening can surround the holes.

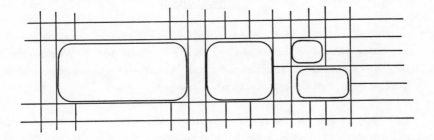

FIGURE 10. Aligned Deck Penetrations

If there are good reasons why the holes cannot be aligned then the designer must balance the requirement of strength and ease of assembly. Fig 11 shows good and bad examples.

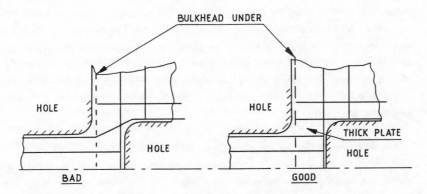

FIGURE 11. Examples of Good and Bad Stiffening Arrangements

666

The lesson for cheapness in all detailed arrangement is to keep it simple. However, the designer must remember the conditions under which ships are assembled, when frequently good alignment is difficult, especially on the slip where local distortion may be high. To avoid problems in later life, in particular fatigue cracking, it will often be better to work a slightly more costly connection but one which is tolerent of misalignment.

CONCLUSIONS

The conclusions that can be drawn from the foregoing discussion are mainly qualitative, but the important point to bring out first is that the potential for cost savings on a warship hull structure is limited. Nevertheless some saving is possible by reducing the complexity and sophistication of design.

Following on the idea of sophistication, it has been shown that the use of higher strength steels can give no reduction in cost, indeed, due to the inherent cost of the material itself the usual effect of including it in a structure will be a significant increase in cost. The use of high strength steels can only be justified where they are needed for their toughness or to withstand high stress concentrations. In such cases there is then merit in choosing the cheapest available acceptable steel, such as HSLA[20] in place of HY80 (Q1N).

There is potential for small cost savings by using merchant ship materials for warships and it is greater for larger ships where the penalty in space and weight can be accepted. It is unlikely that any significant savings can be made on frigate size ships as the structure cost is driven by the complexity of the subdivision and equipment and services fitted. There is scope however for limited use of flat bar stiffeners in place of Tee sections. The use of offset bulb plates involves a significant increase in space and weight at the same time as increasing complexity of stiffener connections or the risk of fatigue failure.

Whatever stiffening scheme is used, the principle should be to fit the minimum possible number of stiffeners consistent with maintenance of form, buckling require-ments and support to the edges of large holes. Plating should as far as possible be stiffened in the direction of the principal load (logitudinally in main structure) with the minimum number of crossing members. Nappi[17] has shown that it is possible to design a frigate without any frames at all, at the same time as saving significantly in labour cost. Incidentally, such a scheme also saves many man hours of outfit labour as it is much easier to fit pipes and cables between longitudinal stiffeners when there are no transverse obstacles. The plating in these designs will be heavier but the increase in material cost and ship displacement is small, and is easily offset by the savings resulting from less welding distortion, greater accuracy and less consequent rework.

Great care needs to be taken with the design of details, and as these are expensive in man hours, merit much more attention from designers. Schemes of details, as for example in [18], need to be devised and arranged in order of applicability allowing for the required accuracy of fit-up and associated risk of failure in service, while maintaining ease of assembly.

To reduce the cost of maintenance in service, structures should be as open and accessible as possible. This will ease preservation and reduce the likelihood of severe corrosion, at the same time as simplifying the task of surveying and repairing fatigue failures before they get too severe.

To enable the designer to make objective judgement on the cost effectiveness of different structural arrangements, more work needs to be done on obtaining cost data for different assemblies and activities. These can then be built into a design and costing model for parametric studies and ultimately cost optimisation studies to be undertaken. The Chief Naval Architect is sponsoring research in this field at Glasgow University.

For a final word on materials, this paper has assumed throughout that steel is the most cost effective material for all ships except those with very specialised requirements such as mine countermeasures vessels. This is probably true today, but there are many new materials, principally composites, coming on the market and it is likely to be sooner than later that one or more of these will compete with steel for some ship components. Ship structural designers will need to keep a close eye on developments if they are not to be taken by surprise.

ACKNOWLEDGEMENTS

The views expressed in this paper are those of the author and do not necessarily reflect Ministry of Defence policy.

The assistance of Mr I E Winkle of the Department of Naval Architecture and Ocean Engineering at Glasgow University in making available the results of his most recent investigations on cost modelling is gratefully acknowledged.

Yarrow Shipbuilders Ltd are the source of Figs 1 and 2.

REFERENCES

1. Baird D and Winkle I E, "Cost Optimisation of Buoyant Steel Structures", Seminar on Advances in Design for Production, Southampton University, April 1984.

2. Abe M, "Quantification of Production Factor", Seminar on Advances in Design for Production, Southampton University, April 1984.

3. Andrews D J and Brown D K, "Cheap Warships are not Simple", SNAME Combined Symposium on Ship Costs and Energy, New York, October 1982.

4. Summers L S, "The Prediction of Shipyard Costs", Marine Technology, Vol 10, No 1, 1973.

5. Caldwell J B and Hewitt A D, "Towards Cost-Effective Design of Ship Structures", Conference on Structural Design and Fabrication in Shipbuilding, Welding Institute, London, November 1975.

6. Shenoi R A, "An Effective Computer Approach for Design for Production", Computer Application in the Automation of Shipyard Operation and Ship Design IV, Ed Rogers D F et al, North Holland Pub Co, 1982.

7. Careyette J, "Preliminary Ship Cost Estimation", Trans RINA, Vol 120, 1978.

8. Kuo C, MacCallum K J and Shenoi R A, "An Effective Approach for Structural Design for Production", Trans RINA, Vol 126, 1984.

9. British Standard Specification 4360, "Weldable Structural Steels", 1979.

10. Naval Engineering Standard 791, "Requirements for Weldable Structural Steels - Part 1 - Mild Steel - Plate, Sections and Bars", May 1984.

11. Kuo C et al, "Design for Production of Ship and Offshore Structures", SNAME STAR Symposium, Washington DC, April 1983.

12. Hughes O F, Mistree F and Zanic V, "A Practical Method for the Rational Design of Ship Structures, J Ship Res, Vol 24, June 1980.

13. Hughes O F, Janava R J and Wood W A, "SHIPOPT - A CAD System for Rationally Based Ship Structural Design and Optimisation", Computer Applications in the Automation of Shipyard Operations and Ship Design IV, Ed. Rogers D F et al, North Holland Pub Co, 1982.

14. Usher P J and Dorey A L, "A Family of Warship", <u>Trans RINA</u>, Vol 124, 1982.

15. Pattison D R et al, "The Computer Aided Ship Design System GODDESS and its Application to the Structural Design of Royal Naval Warships", <u>Computer Applications in the Automation of Shipyard Operation and Ship Design IV</u>, Ed. Rogers D F et al, North Molland Pub Co, 1982.

16. Rains D A, "Design Trade-offs for Destroyers", <u>Naval Eng J</u>, Vol 95, May 1983.

17. Nappi N S, Walz R W and Wiernicki C J, "The No-Frame Concept - Its Impact on Shipyard Costs", <u>Naval Eng J</u>, Vol 96, May 1984.

18. Glasfield R et al, "Review of Ship Structural Details", <u>Ship Structures Committee</u> Report SSC266, April 1977.

19. <u>British Standard Specification</u> 5400, "Steel, Concrete and Composite Bridges", Part 10, "Code of Practice for Fatigue", 1980.

20. Johnson R A, "Innovation in Ship Design - Are We Willing to Risk?", <u>Naval Eng J</u>, Vol 97, January 1985.

RECENT PROGRESS IN PROBABILISTIC
STRUCTURE DESIGN

Jean-Michel Planeix, Consultant (1)

ABSTRACT

The title of this paper may be a misnomer: rather than presenting, in a formal fashion, probabilistic structural design procedures recently developed or under development, the author has elected to introduce some of the important facets of the application of reliability theory to structures. By means of simple examples relating to the reduction of a time-dependent problem to a time-independent one, failure surface linearization and safety index, probability-based design codes, the treatment of structures as systems, progressive collapse, component fatigue, and utility functions as aids to decision-making, the advantages and some of the problems associated with probabilistic structural design procedures are discussed.

FROM IMPLICIT TO EXPLICIT PROBABILISM

Before we attempt to present general ideas concerning recent developments in advanced procedures for the design of marine structures, it may be well to spend a few moments on the notion of probability, central and pervasive in these procedures.

A dictionary defines probability as: "The quality or state of being probable (probable: that can reasonably but not certainly be expected); likelihood; math: the number of times something will probably occur over the range of possible occurrences". One perceives the difficulty of defining probability, although, in an undefined sense, the notion is easily accepted. Probability is inherent in future events and, as far back as we go into the history of mankind, we find prophets, oracles, auspices, who divine the outcome of sundry human undertakings such as wars or politics. This they did

(1) *This paper was written while the author was scientific and technical adviser to Bureau Veritas and chairman of the "Design Philosophy" committee of ISSC 1985. An elementary presentation was deliberately adopted, with no references, but a bibliography of important papers on the subject, and no elaborated synopsis was judged necessary.*

by observing certain facts (the flight of birds, the aspect of the viscera of sacrificed animals, ...), to which given outcomes were thought, presumably by experience, to be attached.

From our ancestry we have inherited the concepts of auspice ("bird-seeing") and omens. Accumulated experience has taught us certain ways of estimating, from given omens, the chance that given outcomes of some events will take place, that is of obtaining a rough estimation of risk. But it is only in comparatively recent years that omens took the form of statistics, in particular - and perhaps first - to establish the premiums of insurance companies. It is interesting to note that, among insurers, those underwriting the risk presented by ships and the goods they carried were among the first who recognized the need to transform insurance from a gamble to a rational process. This is how, for example, Bureau Veritas was founded, very early (1827), as a "Bureau of information for marine underwriters".

Insurance companies today underwrite many risks, from minor to major accidents. As more and more importance is given to the welfare and safety of people, not only insurance companies, but also governmental agencies cover injuries to individuals. What is perhaps the most important is the factual - albeit generally not outspoken - acceptance of risk in human endeavours, professional or recreational. From statistics probabilities can be inferred for given types of injury to occur in given types of occupation. One might say that, in recent years, a marked - if often unnoted - transition from determinism to probabilism has taken place as a concept governing man's activities.

Classification societies have, for a great many years, accumulated experience on the behaviour of ships. However, important as their archives may be, they were of little avail when, in a few years' span, the size of tankers grew tenfold and new ship types, such as gas carriers and container ships, appeared on the scene. Direct calculations of ship behaviour at sea and related stresses had to replace "statistical" Rules formulae for the determination of the scantlings of such ships. Due to the stochastic character of sea waves, these calculations have a definite probabilistic connotation. More than in the domain of ships - with the possible exception of novel ship designs -, direct, probabilistic calculations are performed for offshore structures, for which the engineer does not have at his disposal statistics of behaviour covering such large number of platforms x years, relative to given types of units, as they exist for conventional ships.

Although probabilistic calculations are employed in the cases cited above, the procedure of structural analysis in which they are employed remains largely deterministic due to ignoring the randomness or uncertainty of a number of parameters, those relative to strength and modelling, in particular. New structural design procedures have been developed or are under development to compensate, on a rational probabilistic basis, the paucity of statistics concerning the design object.

It is an overview of these modern procedures that the following discussion attempts to give.

PROJECT ALTERNATIVES

An important feature of modern design procedures is that they give decision-makers the possibility of a choice between alternative solutions for a project. To introduce this aspect, let us consider the following imaginative simple example. Choice has to be made between two designs of an offshore unit, a more expensive one (E) and a more inexpensive one (I), their overall costs (initial outlay plus operating cost over the planned lifetime) being T_E and T_I. It is decided to base the choice on the susceptibility of each design to a certain damage costing C in lost production and repair. One estimates (through modern procedures of analysis) that, over the lifetime, the probabilities of occurrence of this damage are P_E and P_I, with $P_E < P_I$. The decision-maker will thus select the inexpensive solution only if:

$$T_E - T_I \ < \ (P_I - P_E)C$$

Since the designs have generally been worked out so that $P_E \ll P_I$, the selection criterion may be taken as $T_E - T_I < P_I C$. Without recourse to probabilistics, the decision would, reasonably, have had to be made between a design without damage and a design in which damage was accepted, so that the choice criterion would have been $T_E - T_I < C$, with much laxity in favour of the expensive design, for example: $T_E - T_I < C$ against $T_E - T_I < 0.1 \, C$, with $P_I = 0.1$.

Decision could also conceivably be made on the basis of damages occurring with the same probability P and costing C for design I and C/α for design E (α > 1). The choice criterion would then be:

$$T_E - T_I < \frac{\alpha-1}{\alpha} \, PC$$

If, to compare with the previous criterion, we set $P = P_I$, we see
that this one is more severe.

Not too much importance is to be attached to this elementary example,
but, to tell the truth, I intend to use it later, to illustrate the notion
of "utility function".

LIMIT STATE FUNCTION AND DESIGN SAFETY INDEX

In recent developments, the distinction between levels of design
procedures has been abandoned. Level I, or procedure with partial safety
factors, remains the level for codes or regulations - i.e., the one extensively used in practical design -, but the partial safety factors ought to
be estimated using advanced procedures. Level III, fully probabilistic, is
thought by researchers to be inaccessible for practical use. The procedures
of level II, in which the failure boundary is linearized around the design
point, have been shown capable of incorporating all the information on the
uncertainties of the design variables the engineer has at his disposal.
Therefore, advanced structural design procedures are now considered to form
a unique class, precisely named FORM, for "First-Order Reliability Methods".
Note that we consistently use the term "procedure" instead of "method",
which we reserve for the act of carrying out a practical calculation, e.g.
the finite element method, the boundary integral equation method. We thus
prefer the appellation of "Probabilistic structural design procedures".

The integrity or failure of a component of a structure can be expressed, for a given effect of the loads, by a "performance function":
$$Z \, [\, \underline{C} \, (t), \, \underline{D} \, (t)]$$
where, in all generality, $\underline{C}$ and $\underline{D}$ are random vector processes representing,
respectively, the strength (capability) and the loads (demand) and t desig-
nates time. $Z = 0$ defines the limit state, the component being safe if
$Z > 0$ and being in a failed state if the representative point of Z has
crossed the limit state surface or failure surface $Z = 0$, so that $Z < 0$.
The components of $\underline{C}$ and $\underline{D}$ are the various parameters of strength (yield
stress or ultimate resistance, modulus of elasticity, scantlings, attrition
situation, fatigue limit in the sense of a Miner sum or or a crack size,
...) and of loads (forces and moments exerted in the structural element by

adjoining ones, or by external action directly on the element or inertia and
damping forces proper to the element). To determine the state of the structural element, the scalar value c of the capacity is compared to the scalar
value d of the demand, both expressed in the same physical units, for
example both stresses, and the limit state function can take the forms
$Z = c - d$, $Z = \log (c/d), \ldots$

The problem of finding the probability P_f ($Z < 0$) in all generality,
with Z a random process, is sufficiently formidable to be judged unsolvable
but some simplifications, justifiable to varying degrees, make it tractable.
If the capacity were not time-dependent and if, for the demand, only one
load were time-dependent, the failure probability would be calculable as
$P_f [c - \max (d) < 0]$. Now, some of the components of $\underline{C}$ and $\underline{D}$ are, at
the worst, slowly varying functions of time, while those components of $\underline{D}$
resulting from the waves are rapidly changing with time (we do not consider
here the action of wind, which may qualify as comparatively rapidly changing, nor very rapidly changing impulse actions from slamming or ice; note
that currents are slowly time-varying). The reliability problem can therefore practically be solved taking a selected time t (for which the design
will be made) for the evaluation of the slowly varying components of $\underline{C}$ and
$\underline{D}$, which we now consider as forming random vectors $\underline{C}_o$ (r) and $\underline{D}_o$ (r), r
designating a (general) random variable, and taking the demand $\underline{D}_w$ (r,t)
due to wave action at its maximum value, as a random vector process
(stochastic), over the planned life of the structure (application of the
"Turkstra rule").

The performance function now becomes:

$$Z[\underline{C}_o \ (r), \ \underline{D}_o \ (r), \ \underline{D}_w \ (r,t)]$$

It is decomposed subtractively (to conform to the expression c - d)
into a time-independent part and a time-dependent part (2); thus:

$$Z = Z_1 \ [\underline{A}_o \ (r)] - Z_2 \ [\underline{A}_o \ (r), \ \underline{D}_w \ (r,t)]$$

---

(2) Such a decomposition may be done in an infinite number of ways:

$$f(x,y) = f_1(x) - [f_1(x) - f(x,y)]$$

where f_1 is arbitrary. Fortunately, there are, in the problem at
hand, obviously advantageous ways of making it, as will be shown on a
simple example.

where $\underline{A}_O$ is a random vector formed with the components of $\underline{C}_O$ and $\underline{D}_O$.

The problem of "finding the maximum of the wave effect" is solved by replacing Z_2 with a random variable x defined by its function of repartition (cumulative distribution):

$$Z_2 \rightleftharpoons x \mid F(x) = P_\ell (Z_2 < x)$$
$$x = F^{-1}(P_\ell)$$

where, for each value of x, P_ℓ is the corresponding probability, calculated over the design life of the structure. The problem is now time-independent and the probability of failure is given by:

$$P_f = P \left[Z_1(\underline{A}_O) - x < 0 \right]$$

Before pursuing, it may be worth applying the above steps to a simple example: a cylindrical structural element with sectional area S, section modulus m and yield stress σ_e subjected at its ends (action of neighbouring elements and lumped external forces) to axial forces and bending moments with time-independent and time-dependent (wave) components, N_1, N_w, M_1, M_w. Capacity and demand are represented by the vectors:

$$\underline{C} = \{ S(r,t), \, m(r,t), \, \sigma_e(r) \}$$
$$\underline{D} = \{ N_1(r), \, N_w(r,t), \, M_1(r), \, M_w(r,t) \}$$

The performance function for stress effects may be written as:

$$Z = \sigma_e(r) \, S(r,t) m(r,t) - \{ [N_1(r) + N_w(r,t)] m(r,t)$$
$$+ [M_1(r) + M_w(r,t)] S(r,t) \}$$

and, by application of the Turkstra rule, may be decomposed into:

$$Z = (\sigma_e S_o m_o - N_{1o} m_o - M_{1o} S_o) - [N_w(t) m_o + M_w(t) S_o]$$
$$= Z_1(\underline{A}_O) - Z_2 \left[\underline{A}_O, \, \underline{D}_w(t) \right]$$

with (3):

$$\underline{A}_O = \{ N_{1o}, \, m_o, \, M_{1o}, \, S_o, \, \sigma_e \}$$
$$\underline{D}_w(t) = \{ N_w(t), \, M_w(t) \}$$

---

(3) *This is a notation, but forms such as $N_{1o} \, m_o + M_{1o} \, S_o$ can be mathematically derived from $\underline{A}_O$. Consider the vector $\underline{A} = \{x, y, z, t, u, \ldots\}$ and look for an operation (corresponding to Z_1) which transforms it into $x\,y + z\,t$. The following one does the trick:*

$$\begin{bmatrix} 1 & 0 & 0 & - & 0 \\ 0 & 1 & 0 & - & 0 \\ 0 & & & & \end{bmatrix} \{ A \} \left(\begin{bmatrix} 0 & 0 & 1 & 0 & 0 & - \\ 0 & 0 & 0 & 1 & 0 & - \\ 0 & & & & & \end{bmatrix} \{ A \} \right)^T$$

The failure probability of the structural component under scrutiny is:

$$P_f = P(\sigma_e S_o m_o - N_{1o} m_o - M_{1o} S_o - x < 0)$$

with x defined by its function of repartition:

$$F(x) = P_\ell [N_w(t) m_o + M_w(t) S_o < x]$$

Having reduced the problem to a time-independent one, the task at hand is now to evaluate probability P_f. It would be nice if the new problem were simpler than those already tackled. It is not, or, rather, it would be if all the random variables appearing in the limit state function, i.e. the components of $\underline{A}_o$ and the variable x, were normally distributed and, to make the matter even easier, if they were standard-normal (zero means, unit variances). Mathematicians have theoretically solved this problem for engineers: the "Rosenblatt transformation" yields, from the set of ("abnormally") distributed random variables, which we now call x_i (i = 1, ... n), with conditional repartition functions F_i, a set of standard-normal variables a_i; thus:

$$a_1 = \phi^{-1} [F_1(x_1)]$$

$$a_2 = \phi^{-1} [F_2(x_2 \mid x_1)]$$

$$\cdots\cdots\cdots$$

$$a_n = \phi^{-1} [F_n(x_n \mid x_1, x_2 \cdots x_{n-1})]$$

where ϕ denotes the standard-normal function of repartition and the vertical bar means that the repartition F_i of x_i is conditioned on the x_{i-1} former variables.

We (finally) fall on the (easy?) problem of finding $P [S (\underline{A}) < 0]$, where S is the performance function in the standard-normal space and $\underline{A} = \{x_1,..,x_n = x\}$. It is so easy that to show it, it is best to consider the two-dimensional problem where $\underline{A} = \{x_1, x_2\}$. The limit state equation $S(\underline{A}) = S(x_1, x_2) = 0$ is represented by a curve (C), the failure boundary, in the (a_1, a_2) plane (fig. 1).

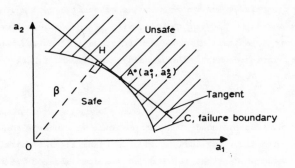

FIGURE 1. Linearization of the failure boundary.

We linearize S around point $A^O (a_1^O , a_2^O)$:

$$S(a_1,a_2) \simeq (\frac{\partial S}{\partial a_1})^O (a_1 - a_1^O) + (\frac{\partial S}{\partial a_2})^O (a_2 - a_2^O)$$

since $Z (a_1^O , a_2^O) = 0$. Letting $(\partial S/\partial a_1)^O = \alpha_1$ $(\partial S/\partial a_2)^O = \alpha_2$ and since a_1 and a_2 have zero mean and unit variance, $\alpha_1(a_1 - a_1^O)$ and $\alpha_2(a_2 - a_2^O)$ have $-\alpha_1 a_1^O$ and $-\alpha_2 a_2^O$ for means and α_1 and α_2 for standard deviation, respectively. They are normally distributed and so, also, their (approximated) sum S, which has for mean and standard deviation:

$$m_S = -(\alpha_1 a_1^O + \alpha_2 a_2^O) \; ; \; \sigma_S = (\alpha_1^2 + \alpha_2^2)^{1/2}$$

The probability we are looking for, if we design at point A^O, is therefore (4):
$$P_f = P(S < O) = \Phi(-m_S/\sigma_S)$$
$$= \Phi [\frac{\alpha_1 a_1^O + \alpha_2 a_2^O}{(\alpha_1^2 + \alpha_2^2)^{1/2}}]$$
where $\Phi (.)$ is the standard-normal repartition function.

We now look at the tangent to the failure boundary at A^O; its equation is:

$$\alpha_1 (a_1 - a_1^O) + \alpha_2 (a_2 - a_2^O) = 0$$

and the distance from the origin to the tangent, denoted by β, is:

$$OH = \frac{|\alpha_1 a_1^O + \alpha_2 a_2^O|}{(\alpha_1^2 + \alpha_2^2)^{1/2}} = \beta$$

Now, the origin, which represents the means of a_1 and a_2, should be the safe region, so that, with the concavity of the failure boundary as pictured in figure 1, a small displacement (da_1, da_2) along the tangent, around A^O, lets S go into the unsafe region, and thus, α_1 and α_2 are < 0. Hence $\beta = m_S/\sigma_S$ and:

$$P_f = \Phi(-\beta)$$

We have not yet finished with the problem: we rather wish to overestimate the failure probability than to underestimate it. We therefore look for the maximum value of P_f, that is, for the minimum value of β. An adequate search algorithm is needed to find the design point $A^*(a_1^*, a_2^*)$ at which the tangent of the failure boundary has the minimum distance β^*, which is the "design safety index". The design failure probability of the structural component studied is then:

$$P_f = \Phi(-\beta^*)$$

So, even the simplified problem, made easy in the two-dimensional illustration, is not so simple after all. Along with β^*, the values of the standard-normal design load effects are obtained, then, by inverse transformation, the values of the design parameters in the original space.

For an n-dimensional vector A, we would have:

$$\beta^* = \frac{|\alpha_1 a_1^* + \ldots + \alpha_n a_n^*|}{(\alpha_1^2 + \ldots + \alpha_n^2)^{1/2}}$$

... and the search for β^* would be (somewhat) more complicated than in the two-dimensional case.

The safety index may be considered as an n-dimensional vector $\underline{\beta}^*$, the components of which are:

$$\beta_i^* = -\frac{\alpha_i}{\alpha_1^2 + \ldots + \alpha_n^2}(\alpha_i a_i^* + \ldots + \alpha_n a_n^*)$$

---

(4) *The normal distribution of x, with mean m and standard deviation σ is:*
$$f(x) = \frac{1}{\sigma\sqrt{2\pi}} \exp[-\frac{(x-m)^2}{2\sigma^2}]$$
and its repartition function is therefore:
$$f(x) = \int_{-\infty}^{x} f(x)dx = \frac{1}{\sigma\sqrt{2\pi}} \int_{-\infty}^{x} \exp[-\frac{(x-m^2)}{2\sigma^2}]dx$$
We are looking for F(0) and we let $t = (x - m)/\sigma$, so that:

$$F(o) = \frac{1}{\sqrt{2\pi}} \int_{-\infty}^{-m/\sigma} \exp(-t^2)dt \equiv \Phi(-m/\sigma)$$

As a piece of bravery, I have pictured in three dimensions, in figure 2, the failure surface, its tangent plane at the design point (or a design point: there may be an infinity if the failure surface is made of a family of straight lines, but, in that case, the problem degenerates into a two-dimensional one, or if that surface is partly made of such families).

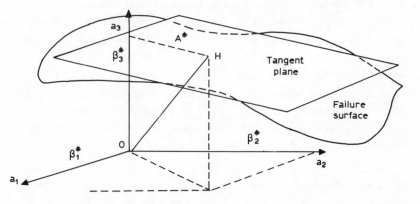

FIGURE 2. Failure surface, tangent plane at the design point and safety index vector in three dimensions (a piece of bravery?).

The above discussion of probabilistic design procedures is shaky, much to my grief, in that it presents some advanced ideas, backed-up by not-so-common mathematics, along with some elementary considerations and semi-proofs. This was at the same time willful and necessary. It would take more than a short paper to explain (and to discuss, which is most often not done) in a strict mathematical fashion, important steps of these procedures: the reduction, from several random vector processes in capacity and demand, to one at a time (in practice, one and that is all); the passage from a time-dependent problem to a time-independent one; the transformation of the time-independent problem from the original parameter space (or spaces) into a standard-normal space; the study of the geometry of the n-dimensional failure hypersurface and the search for the minimum distance from the origin to its tangent planes.

I have not either touched on the questions of modelling errors on the environment description (e.g. statistics of sea states), on the computation of loads (e.g. wave kinematics and mechanics of energy transfer between fluid and obstacle), and on response computation (calculational methods, e.g.

strip theory, 3-D methods, finite element method, frame analysis)... To
account for these errors, the engineer multiplies the corresponding design
parameters, e.g. the bending moments and axial forces of the above example,
by a random factor with an accepted mean value and coefficient of variation,
together with an assumed distribution (normal, log-normal, exponential).
Thus, the "practical" probabilistic structural design procedures are, really, a mixture of mathematically rational procedures and engineer-developed
level one procedures, with partial safety factors taken from "engineering
judgement".

There is nothing wrong in that and the problem of reliability of structures ought always be thought of in terms of a physical problem: mathematicians may devise ways and means to solve a physical problem posed by engineers; the solution, however, always belongs to engineers who may, here and
there (and everywhere), interject "common engineering sense".

This last remark, and some interjections spread out in the preceding
discourse, should not be taken as jocular comments or my part on probabilistic procedures. On the contrary, they are meant to show that, to fully
demonstrate the unique qualities which make them the design procedures of
the future, they need both to be confirmed by mathematicians on the validity
of some treatments accepted in the procedures (of utmost importance "inter
alia", the maximum, over a lifetime, of the combination of load effects,
with the problem of tail of distributions) and by engineers on the feasibility of their practical application.

The hodgepodge approach I have adopted to present probabilistic design
procedures precisely reflects the above comments and it clearly results that
I consider these procedures, today, as a domain for specialists. Tomorrow,
they will become usable by design offices, thanks to advances in hardware
(for the handling of the many point-in-time values of random variables) and
in software (for the routine use of these procedures). Concurrently with
the widespread use, in the future, of probabilistic design procedures, will
be the employment of probability-based design codes, well suited for designers.

PROBABILITY-BASED DESIGN CODES

Probabilistic design procedures are particularly adapted to make codes
evolve. They supply a rational basis for the determination of the partial
safety factors and a methodology for updating these values as experience on
the behaviour of given structures is gained.

A typical probability-based structural code is the "CEB-FIP Model Code
for Concrete Structures", proposed by the "Comité Euro-International du
Béton" (CEB) and the "Fédération Internationale de le Précontrainte" (FIP).
Its format for the evaluation of design load effects S_d is:

$$S_d = \text{result of application of } \{\gamma_g G + \gamma_p P + \gamma_q [Q_{1k} + \sum_{i>1} (\psi_{oi} Q_{ik}]\}$$

where G is the nominal dead load, P the prestressing force, Q_{1k} the characteristic value of the main variable load and the Q_{ik} (i>1) are the other,
less important, variable loads. The γ's are the corresponding partial
safety factors; they take account of the variability of load magnitudes from
the characteristic values and of the structural response to each load type,
as well as of the redistribution of load effects. The ψ_{oi}'s are load combination factors which must reflect the degree of correlation between the
variable loads. To the multiplicative partial safety factors for the demand
correspond dividing factors for the capacity, which account for variations
in the strength of materials. All partial safety factors are adjusted
according to the type of failure considered for the structural component and
the failure consequence.

The parallel with probabilistic procedures is clear, starting from the
combination of variable loads in the code format (refer to the application
of the "Turkstra rule" mentioned above) down to some partial safety factors
which, in effect, take into consideration the modelling of the environment.

The partial safety factors of the code should be developed, "whenever
possible", by the use of probabilistic design procedures. To do this,
several approaches may be adopted. We shall briefly present a possible
one.

In codes, the nominal values of the load effects considered for design
are usually what is considered as the means $\bar{x}_i$ of these parameters. If a
probabilistic procedure yields the value x_i^* for the design point of the

structure taken as example, the i-th partial safety factor is $x_i^*/\bar{x}_i$. If the variances of the design parameters are known, an explicit form may be found by a method such as the one sketchily presented here as an exercise.

The limit state function is expanded around the mean point (not the design point):

$$Z(x) \simeq Z(\bar{x}) + \sum_i \alpha_i (x_i - \bar{x}_i)$$

where the bar denotes a mean value and:

$$\alpha_i = (\frac{\partial Z}{\partial x_i})\bar{x}$$

If σ_Z is the standard deviation of Z and δ the safety index of the structure if designed at the mean point, we have:

$$\delta \, \sigma_Z = Z(\bar{x})$$

Defining, for each parameter x_i with standard deviation σ_i

$$a_i = - \frac{\alpha_i \sigma_i}{\sigma_Z}$$

the variance of Z, if all the x_i are uncorrelated (remember, we are doing an exercise) may be expressed as:

$$\sigma_Z^2 = \sum_i (\alpha_i \sigma_i)^2 = - \sigma_Z \sum_i a_i \alpha_i \sigma_i$$

Hence:

$$\sigma_Z = - \sum_i a_i \alpha_i \sigma_i \; ; \quad Z(\bar{x}) = - \delta \sum_i a_i \alpha_i \sigma_i \; ;$$

$$Z(x^*) = - \delta \sum_i a_i \alpha_i \sigma_i + \sum_i \alpha_i x_i^* - \sum_i \alpha_i \bar{x}_i$$

Writing $v_i = \sigma_i/\bar{x}_i$, coefficient of variation of x_i, and setting $Z(x^*) = 0$, we obtain:

$$\sum_i \alpha_i x_i^* = \sum_i (1 + \delta \, a_i v_i) \alpha_i \bar{x}_i)$$

By replacing the mean point with a design point conveniently selected to give the structure the target failure probability, the nominal values are multiplied by safety factors:

$$\gamma_i = 1 + \delta \, a_i v_i$$

These factors (> 1 for load effects; < 1 for strength parameters) are then the ones to use in the code.

For example, for the state parameters capacity C and demand D:

$$Z = C - D \; ; \; \alpha_C = 1 \; ; \; \alpha_D = -1$$

$$a_C = - \frac{\sigma_C}{\sigma_Z} \; ; \; a_D = \frac{\sigma_D}{\sigma_Z} \; ;$$

$$\gamma_C = 1 - \delta v_C \frac{\sigma_C}{\sigma_Z} \; ; \; \gamma_D = 1 + \delta v_D \frac{\sigma_D}{\sigma_Z}$$

The method is rational in that it distributes the "nominal" (central) safety factor δ between the parameters (partial safety factors) according to their sensitivity coefficients α_i and their variability v_i.

The American Petroleum Institute has sponsored work for the transition from a "working stress design" (WSD) philosophy to a "load and resistance factor design" (LRFD) philosophy in its "Recommended practice for planning, designing and constructing fixed offshore platforms" (APIRP2A). Partial safety factors have been calibrated against the present RP2A, for a number of components of existing designs. It has been remarked that the new procedure tends to give uniform component reliability over the structure. It has also been noted that LRFD seems more conservative for environmental effects and stability failure modes and less so for effects of operational loads and bending failure modes.

STRUCTURES AS SYSTEMS

The strict extension of the probabilistic design procedures from structural components to whole structures seems, at present at least, to be a task of unsurpassed difficulty. For one thing, the generalized (structural) failure surface is very difficult to define and, if it can be done, its shape (curvature) renders impractical the general procedure outlined for components.

However, using the failure probabilities estimated for components, the failure probability of the structure may be evaluated by considering the structure as a system. We have no space here to do justice to this domain of structural analysis, in full development and with a great future, were it not only for the accumulation of knowledge in development and application of system reliability theory in the electronic, electrical, mechanical, aeronautical and nuclear fields. The best I can do here (really, even more so than in other parts of this discussion) is to present ideas by means of an illustrative (again, simple) example. Consider (figure 3) a typical sub-structure, made of elements 3 (twice), 4, 5 and 7 (twice) of a jacket plat-form or of the leg of a jack-up platform.

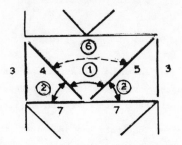

FIGURE 3. Substructure of a jacket platform or a jack-up platform leg.

The substructure and the whole structure are considered to fail if, for some "mode" (or effect: bending, punching shear, plasticization, above limit fatigue crack,...):

. either component 3 fails,
. or components 4 and 5 fail (indicated by ① on figure 3),
. or components 4 and 7 fail (②),
. or components 5 and 7 fail (②).

On the figure, the dashed line noted ⑥ indicates the failure of 4 or 5.

The structure function may be written:

$$S = 3 \cup (4 \cap 5) \cup (4 \cap 7) \cup (5 \cap 7)$$

meaning that, if one component is safe, its number must be replaced by 1, if it has failed, it must be replaced by 0; S = 1 means that the structure is safe, S = 0, that it has failed.

The fault tree of the system may be drawn as shown on figure 4. From this representation we can write the structure function:

$$s = ① \cup ② \cup 3$$

685

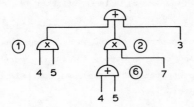

FIGURE 4. Fault tree of the (sub) structure.

With:

$$\text{①} = 4 \cap 5; \quad \text{②} = \text{⑥} \cap 7; \quad \text{⑥} = 4 \cup 5$$

That is:

$$S = (4 \cap 5) \cup \; [\,(4 \cup 5) \cap 7\,] \; \cup 3$$
$$= (4 \cap 5) \cup (4 \cap 7) \cup (5 \cap 7) \cup 3$$

as "prima facie".

This decomposition is as far as we can go in terms of unions: the intersections (or the lone component) are not contained in any other of the decomposition; they are the "minimal cut sets" of the structure's logical representation and the structure function is expressed as a "minimal cut set" representation.

The minimal cut sets form the links of a "series system", as depicted in figure 5, i.e. which fails if any of its components fail.

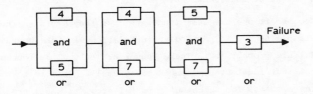

FIGURE 5. Minimal cut set representation.

A decomposition of S into intersections of unions is also possible. Starting from:

$$(5 \cap 7) \cup 3 = (5 \cup 3) \cap (7 \cup 3)$$

and proceeding in the same way, one arrives at:

$$S = (4 \cup 5 \cup 3) \cap (4 \cup 7 \cup 3) \cap (7 \cup 5 \cup 3) \cap (7 \cup 3)$$

The last union is contained in the last but one, so that:

$$S = (4 \cup 5 \cup 3) \cap (4 \cup 7 \cup 3) \cap (7 \cup 5 \cup 3)$$

This is as far as we can go in the decomposition of S into intersections of unions of components (or individual components): these unions are the "minimal ties" and this decomposition of the structure's logics is its "minimal tie set representation". These minimal ties form a "parallel system", pictured in figure 6.

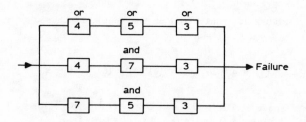

FIGURE 6. Minimal tie set representation.

In the minimal cut set representation, the failure probability of the structure is:

$$P_f = P \ (\cup \cap \ F_i = 0)$$

while, in the minimal tie set representation, it is:

$$P_f = P \ (\cap \cup \ F_j = 0)$$

where F_i and F_j are the structure functions of components (= 0 or 1) taken in the unions or intersections.

These decompositions are less innocuous than they may seem from the elementary example taken, in particular in relation with the bounds for the calculated failure probability. These bounds are only close bounds if the probability of individual events concerned is small. This is to the advantage of series systems, for which union of failures, of small probability each, is considered, while, for parallel systems, the union has to be taken over survivals of large probability (the structure survives if either ... or ... component survives). Hence an incitation to logically decompose a structure into minimal cuts.

Needless to say, the little set algebra into which we indulged is a school exercise, since efficient computer routines obtain minimal cut or tie sets in a record time.

When applying reliability theory to structures by considering them as systems, a very useful concept is that of the ranking of components, according to their "importance". Several "measures of importance" may be defined. One is "criticality importance" or the probability that, the system being in a failing state, the component considered is critical for failure and has failed. Another is "diagnostic importance", that is, the probability that, the system having failed, the component considered has contributed to it. Measures of importance may be applied to minimal cut sets. To improve the system reliability, it is most important to act on components of greatest importance.

PROGRESSIVE COLLAPSE

When a structure is treated as a system, its failure should be seen as progressive collapse, or as a mechanism of successive failures of some of its components. A proposed algorithm for the selection of failure paths (sometimes called "modes") is that of Murotsu, which is presented here in a simplified fashion.

The failure of component i at the i-th stage of the damage process is denoted by F_i, with the probability $P(F_i)$. From a pre-selected set of components, sub-sets S_i from which to choose the i-th failing component are formed according to:

$$s \in S_i \mid P(F_s) \geqslant 10^{-\alpha} P(F_1 \cap \ldots \cap F_{i-1}) \; ; \; i > 1$$

From this restriction on the components to be made to fail, results that only "dominant modes" of collapse are considered. The i-th candidate for failure is chosen so that:

$$P(F_1 \cap F_i) = \max P(F_1 \cap F_s)$$

Component i is removed from the set to consider at the (i+1)-th stage but its residual contribution to the strength of the structure is taken into account by imposing fictitious forces on its ends. The failure probabilities of the remaining components candidates for failure are re-calculated. If the structure becomes unstable for i=p, a collapse mode m has been found and its probability is:

$$P_m = P(F_1 \cap \ldots \cap F_p)$$

sometimes taken as: min $P(F_i \cap F_j)$; i=2, ...p.

If, after the mode has been found, the set S_p is not empty, other modes have to be looked for. When all n dominant modes have been found, one can obtain an upper and lower bound to the collapse probability of the structure (not the exact theoretical probability, due to the fact of life that all possible "modes" could not be investigated). Thus:

$$P_u = \sum_{m=1}^{n} P_m + R \quad ; \quad P_\ell = \max_{m=1}^{n} P_m$$

The residual R is estimated on the basis of an error probability each time components are discarded as candidates for failure (e.g. $P(F_1 \cap F_i)$).

Figures 7 and 8 show the diagram of a jacket platform the collapse of which was studied and the dominant collapse "modes" found.

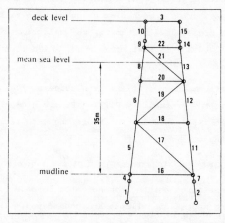

FIGURE 7. Diagram of a jacket platform studied for collapse. (After Crohas *et al*., 1984)

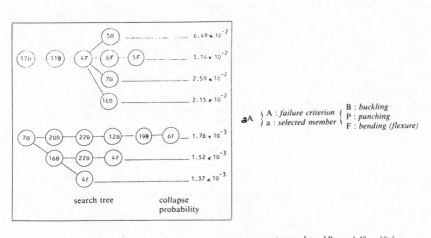

$$aA \begin{cases} A : \textit{failure criterion} \\ a : \textit{selected member} \end{cases} \begin{cases} B : \textit{buckling} \\ P : \textit{punching} \\ F : \textit{bending (flexure)} \end{cases}$$

$$\text{probability of failure} \begin{cases} \textit{upper bound } P_{FU} = 1.48 \times 10^{-1} \\ \textit{lower bound } P_{FL} = 6.49 \times 10^{-2} \end{cases}$$

FIGURE 8. Dominant collapse modes identified.

(After Crohas *et al.*, 1984)

FATIGUE OF STRUCTURAL COMPONENTS

Fatigue of structural components is (Should I say: has become?) a prominent consideration in the design of marine structures. It is thus appropriate that we touch on this important subject and the best I can do here is to extract a table, shown in figure 9, from the important work of Paul Wirsching, in connection with the American Petroleum Instutute's project of the probability-based fatigue design of offshore structures, and to briefly explain some of the formulae in the table. For this we take, as example, the "spectral analysis" approach and we adopt the notations of the table.

Fatigue damage at time τ

$$D = \tau B^m \Omega / K$$

where $\Omega = \begin{cases} \lambda(m)(2\sqrt{2})^m \Gamma\left(\frac{m}{2} + 1\right) \sum\limits_{j=1}^{k} \gamma_j f_j \sigma_j^m & \text{spectral analysis} \\[3mm] \lambda(m) f_o \delta^{m\phi} \psi \Gamma\left(\frac{m\phi}{\xi} + 1\right) & \text{analysis based on long term distribution of wave height} \\[3mm] \lambda(m) f_o S_m^m [\ln N_T]^{-m/\xi} \Gamma\left(\frac{m}{\xi} + 1\right) & \text{analysis based on long term distribution of stress range} \end{cases}$$

Definition of fatigue failure $D \geq \Delta$
($\Delta = 1$ for Miner's Rule)

Fatigue life (time to failure)
$$T = \Delta K / (B^m \Omega)$$

Reliability analysis

. Notional probability of failure, p_f

$$p_f = \Phi(-\beta)$$

. Safety index, β

$$\beta = \frac{\ln(\tilde{T}/T_S)}{\sigma_{\ln T}}$$

. Median life, $\tilde{T}$

$$\tilde{T} = \Delta K / (\tilde{B}^m \tilde{\Omega})$$

Note:

1. Median values indicated by tildes, e.g., Median (T) = $\tilde{T}$.

2. Coefficients of variation denoted by C's, e.g., the COV of B is C_B.

. Standard deviation of $\ln T$.

$$\sigma_{\ln T} = \sqrt{\ln[(1 + C_\Delta^2)(1 + C_K^2)(1 + C_B^2)^{m^2}]}$$

FIGURE 9. Summary of basic equations for fatigue analysis.
(After Wirsching, 1983)

691

On sea state j, where the distribution of maximal extensions (from zero to crest) s_a of stresses (in the component studied) is:

$$p(s_a) = \frac{2s_a}{\langle s_a^2 \rangle} \exp\left(-\frac{s_a^2}{\langle s_a^2 \rangle}\right)$$

where $\langle\ \rangle$ designates an ensemble average. If $\overline{s^2(t)}$ designates the temporal average of the point-in-time stresses, we have:

$$\langle s_a^2 \rangle = 2\ \overline{s^2(t)}$$

and the standard deviation of s(t) on sea state j is:

$$\sigma_j = [\overline{s^2(t)}]^{1/2} = (\tfrac{1}{2} \langle s_a^2 \rangle)^{1/2}$$

The Miner's law is expressed as, for total damage D:

$$D = \sum_j D_j = \sum_j \int \lambda\, \frac{dn_j(S)}{N(S)}$$

where λ is the "rainflow factor", to account for the fact that the stress process due to wave action is usually a wide band process, $dn_j(S)$ is the range of number of cycles, on sea state j, for which the stress range is S, with $S = 2\,s_a$, and N(S) is the number of cycles the component can suffer without developing (or developing and nurturing) cracks (there is, really, no difference between the law of crack propagation, in linear elasticity, and Miner's law, in what concerns fatigue limits: one can be deduced from the other).

With the fatigue curve: stress range S/ acceptable number N(S) of cycles at that range (Wöhler curve) defined by:

$$N(S)B^m S^m = 2^m N(S) B^m s_a^m = K$$

one has:

$$dD_j = \lambda\, \frac{dn_j(S)}{N(S)} = \lambda\, \frac{dn_j(s_a = S/2)}{N(S)}$$

$$= \lambda\, \frac{n_j}{N(S)}\, p(s_a)\, ds_a$$

where n_j is the number of stress or wave cycles in sea state j.

This results in:

$$dD_j = \lambda \, \frac{B^m 2^m}{K} \, n_j \, (2\sigma_j{}^2)^{m/2} \, u^{m/2} \, e^{-u} \, du$$

Hence:

$$D_j = \frac{\lambda B^m (2\sqrt{2})^m}{K} \, \Gamma(\frac{m}{2} + 1) n_j \sigma_j{}^m$$

where Γ is the Eulerian gamma function.

With γ_j the fractional amount of time the structure experiences sea state j in total time τ and f_j the "average" frequency of stress reversals (number of reversals per unit time) in sea state j, we have:

$$n_j = \tau \, \gamma_j \, f_j.$$

From this, the formula of the table results. The interest might reside in pointing to the "averages" accepted for the occurrence of individual sea states and the wave frequency on the sea states, but, mostly, it is, as I believe, the acceptance of a random variable Δ (we still follow the nomenclature of the table) as the Miner sum, so that the time to fatigue failure is:

$$T = \Delta \cdot K/(B^m \Omega)$$

In this expression, Δ, K, and B are considered stochastic, while Ω is taken at an assumed "average" value (if it were a maximum, we would see here an application of the Turkstra rule).

We could stop here on this interesting subject, but it is hard to resist demonstrating the appeal (not physical, but mathematical) for lognormal distributions.

Suppose $y = \ln x$ is normally distributed:

$$f_y(y) = \frac{1}{\sqrt{2\pi}\sigma_y} \exp\left[-\frac{(y - \mu_y)^2}{2\sigma_y{}^2}\right]$$

where μ_y is the average and σ_y the standard deviation of y. With the transformation $y = \mu_y + \sigma_y \, u$, the distribution comes to:

$$f_u(u) = \frac{1}{\sqrt{2\pi}} \exp\left(-\frac{u^2}{2}\right)$$

The median value $\tilde{x}$ of x is obtained from:

$$\int_{-\infty}^{(\ln \tilde{x} - \mu_y)/\sigma_y} f_u(u) \, du = 0.5$$

and we have:

$$\mu_y = \mu_{\ln x} = \ln \tilde{x}$$

The average value of x

$$\mu_x = \int_{-\infty}^{\infty} x\, f_u(u)\, du$$

is, with convenient changes of variables, transformed into:

$$\mu_x = \tilde{x}\, e^{\sigma_y^2/2}\; \frac{1}{\sqrt{2\pi}}\; \int_{-\infty}^{\infty} e^{-z^2/2}\, dz = \tilde{x}\, e^{\sigma_y^2/2}$$

Since:

$$\sigma_x^2 = \mu_{x2} - \mu_x^2$$

we have to calculate μ_{x2} to obtain σ_x^2 .

After adequate changes of variables, we have:

$$\mu_{x2} = \tilde{x}^2\, e^{2\sigma_y^2}\; \frac{1}{\sqrt{2\pi}}\; \int_{-\infty}^{\infty} e^{-z^2}\, dz$$

$$= \tilde{x}^2\, e^{2\sigma_y^2}$$

Hence:

$$\sigma_x^2 = \tilde{x}^2\, e^{\sigma_y^2}\, (e^{\sigma_y^2} - 1)$$

and, for the coefficient of variation:

$$v_x = \sigma_x/\mu_x :$$
$$v_x^2 = \frac{\sigma_{x2}}{(\mu_x)^2} = e^{\sigma_y^2} - 1$$

Hence:

$$\mu_x = \tilde{x}\, \sqrt{1 + v_x^2}$$

"Und so weiter" concerning the table in figure 9, particularly in what concerns the last formula for $\sigma_{\ell nT}$.

Again, I intended to show here, in the simplest fashion, the application of probabilistic procedures to a factual problem. The simple (but not trivial) calculus involved is incidental. What is most interesting is the inclusion, in the safety index, of the stochastic nature of the fatigue curve (K), modelling of stresses (B) and the Miner sum (Δ). This type of intervention of the engineer in the expression of the limit state function is a modern trend and should be pursued for the advancement of structural analysis, but controlled, both on the theoretical side (academics) and on the engineering side (those who have practical experience).

AID TO DECISION-MAKING: UTILITY FUNCTIONS

A particularly interesting use of probabilistic design procedures is
that of tools to help decision-making. Let us say that several alternatives
are envisaged for a given structural project, probabilistically designed.
To select one, some "attributes", characteristic of the project type, are
considered, such as cost, downtime, damage, injury to personnel,...
Numerical values, or "consequences" y_i of these attributes are modelled by
"utility functions" $u_i(y_i)$ the choice of which is made in concert with
decision-makers, according to their "preference", i.e. of their liking or
dislike for the consequences of the various attributes. To each set of
values $u_i(y_i^*)$, $i = 1, \ldots n$ of the utility functions, the design procedure
associates a joint probability (or a probability density)$P(y_1^*, \ldots y_n^*)$of occurr-
ence.To evaluate the "utility" of each alternative, one forms the "multi-
attribute utility function" from the individual utility functions of the
attributes. In the additive model (there is also a multiplicative model),
this is:

$$u(y_1, \ldots y_n) = \sum_{i=1}^{n} k_i u_i(y_i) \; ; \; \sum_{i=1}^{n} k_i = 1$$

where the k_i are scaling factors, again chosen by appropriate questioning
of decision-makers to show to what extent they are willing to favour some
attributes to the detriment of others (trade-off factors).

For each alternative, the expected value of the utility is calculated
thus:

$$E(u) = \sum_{\text{all } \underline{r}^*} u(\underline{r}^*) P(\underline{r}^*)$$

where $\underline{r}^*$ designates the vector $\{y_1^*, \ldots y_n^*\}$ and the sum extends over all
possible $\underline{r}^*$'s (all possible combinations of consequences).

Depending on the "units" adopted to "measure" the consequences (for
example, actual cost or a function being zero for a maximum cost and one for
a vanishing cost), the alternative decision-makers should select to be consistent with their preferences is the one which has the maximum or minimum
expected utility.

To illustrate in our fashion this procedure, let us look again at the
elementary problem used in the preamble to this discussion. It is decided
to gauge the two alternatives with two attributes: total cost (c) and damage

(d). First we take utility functions measured in terms of money. Figure 10 shows the corresponding utility functions u_c and u_d, with the probabilities attached to each of their values. The function u_c is scaled by factor k. The expected utility for each alternative is given by:

$$E(u) = (1-P)[kT + (1-k)x0] + P[k(T+C) + (1-k)C]$$

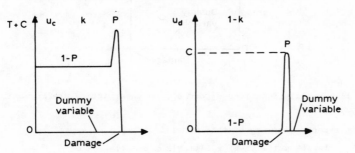

FIGURE 10. Utility functions u_c and u_d, on cost basis.

The expensive design (E) must logically be preferred to the inexpensive one (I) if:

$$(1-P_E)kT_E + P_E(kT_E + C) < (1-P_I)kT_I + P_I(kT_I + C)$$

or, taking $P_E \ll P_I$:

$$T_E < T_I + \frac{P_I C}{k}$$

With k = 1, this condition is the one found at the beginning of this paper. This is logical, since, taking k = 1, decision-makers, in addition to having selected money values to measure the consequences, finally show no aversion to damage "per se" ($k_c = 1$; $k_d = 0$), which is consistent with the philosophy adopted in treating the initial problem. If, on the contrary, they show to be sensitive to damage occurrence, they take k < 1, which means that design (E) should be selected even at a larger total cost.

Consider now utility functions u_c and u_d which show the preferences of decision-makers for total cost or damage in the following way: they are taken equal to one when there is no damage (reducing total cost or avoiding troublesome damage), and to zero when damage occurs. The graph of u_c and u_d then looks as pictured on figure 11.

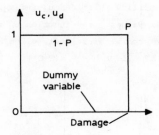

FIGURE 11. Utility functions u_c and u_d, on an arbitrary preferential basis.

The expected utility of this model is:

$$(1-P)[k \times 1 + (1-k) \times 1] + P[k \times 0 + (1-k) \times 0]$$

and design (E) should be selected, this time on the basis of maximum
utility, if:

$$1 - P_E > 1 - P_I \quad ; \quad P_E < P_I$$

that is, always, by definition of this design. This, again, is consistent
with the decision-makers' preference shown in the selection of the "unit"
to measure consequences, here not directly related to cost.

No need to say that this simple example has no pretension to actual-
ity. I believe, though, that it sufficiently demonstrates the consistency
of the decisions arrived at with the preferences shown by decision-makers.

SENSITIVITY TO PARAMETERS, CHOICE BETWEEN ALTERNATIVES
AND BAYESIAN UPDATING

This elementary discussion of probabilistic structural design procedures begets a simple conclusion concerning their advantages: they tend to
lead to a balanced design and they allow the engineer to check the design
(or the code) against the influence of the various parameters; they provide
a logical framework for the choice between alternative solutions; with a
subjective acceptation of the estimated probabilities as degree of belief in
the reliability of the structure and a Bayesian updating of these probabilities, they make possible improvements of the reliability estimate of a
structure and of the safety factors (and even the format) of a code, as
operational experience is gained.

SHORT BIBLIOGRAPHY

- Committee V.1 Report - Design Philosophy.
  ISCC 1985.

- Committee V.2 Report - Applied Design.
  ISCC 1985.

- Ferro, G. and Cervetto, D.,
  Hull girder reliability.
  Ship Struct. Sympos., Arlington, VA, Oct. 1983.

- Östergaard, C.,
  Zuverlässigkeit von Konstruktionen, Germ. Lloyd,
  Univ. Hannover, 1984.

- Crohas, H., Taï, A., Hachemi-Safai, V. and Barnouin, B.,
  Reliability of marine structures under external loading.
  Bull Tech. B.V., Engl. issue, Vol. 13, No. 4, Oct. 1984.

- Wirsching, P.H.,
  Probability-based fatigue design criteria for offshore structures,
  API-PRAC Project 81-15, Univ. of Arizona, 1983.

- Bea, R.G., Hong, S.T. and Mitchell, J.S.,
  Decision analysis approach to offshore platform design.
  J. Str. Eng., Vol. 110, No. 1, Jan. 1984.

Index of Contributors

Subject Index

ABAQUS finite element program,
220, 224
ABS/CONOCO shell buckling test
program, 264
ABS/CONOCO–CBI and UG tests,
264
ABS/CONOCO–MHI tests, 264, 266,
267, 272, 276
ABS/USAS computer program,
141
Acoustic pressure–density
relationship, 349
Added mass of water, 396
ADINA code, 359
Afterflow coefficient, 378
Aligned deck penetrations, 665
Alternating Current Potential Drop
(ACPD), 311
Analogue recordings, 5
Analytical methods, 510
ASME code case 263, 269, 276, 277

Bayesian updating, 696
Bending
maximum longitudinal, 509–10
transverse stress distribution
induced by, 523
Bending loads, buckling of cylindrical
shells under, 219–37
Bending moment
irregular waves, in, 34
still-water, 147–8, 159, 163
time history of, 31
wave, 147–8
see also Midship bending moment

Bending moment distribution
hull girders, 391, 587
ship length, 20
Bending moment–mean curvature
plots, 227, 233
Bending strength, hull program, 157–8
Bending tests, corrugated hull
construction, 552–3
BOSOR4 computer program, 416, 419
Bracketed connection costs, 663
Bryant formula, 418
Bubble geometry, 401
Bubble hydrodynamics, 396–8
Bubble pulsation characteristics,
393–4
Buckling, 141, 150
collapse pressure, 249
corrugated shell under longitudinal
compression, 524–8
cylindrical shells under bending
loads, 219–37
design pressures, 243
displacements in deck laminate, 191
externally pressurised dome ends,
238–61
fabricated ring-stiffened steel
cylinders under axial
compression, 262–80
intact and damaged offshore shell
structures, 201–18
interstiffener, 415
overall, 415
Buckling mode
corrugated panels, 527
shape prediction, 599
Buckling performance, 149